THE
PROFESSIONAL
SERVICES FIRM
BIBLE

THE
PROFESSIONAL SERVICES FIRM
BIBLE

JOHN BASCHAB

JON PIOT

160401

WILEY

John Wiley & Sons, Inc.

Published by John Wiley & Sons, Inc., Hoboken, New Jersey.
Published simultaneously in Canada.

For general information on our other products and services please contact our Customer
Care Department within the United States at (800) 762-2974, outside the United States at
(317) 572-3993 or fax (317) 572-4002.

Wiley also publishes its books in a variety of electronic formats. Some content that appears
in print may not be available in electronic books. For more information about Wiley
products, visit our web site at www.wiley.com.

Library of Congress Cataloging-in-Publication Data:

Baschab, John, 1968–
    The professional services firm bible / John Baschab, Jon Piot.
        p.   cm.
    Includes bibliographical references and index.
    ISBN 0-471-66048-5 (cloth/cd-rom)
    1. Service industries—Management.   2. Professions—Marketing.   I. Piot,
Jon, 1966–   II. Title.
    HD9980.5.B368   2005
    658—dc22

                                                        2004011607

Printed in the United States of America.

10   9   8   7   6   5   4   3   2   1

Contents

SECTION I
Managing and Governing the Professional Services Firm

SECTION II
The Front Office: Driving Sales and Growth

Section III
The Organization: Attracting and
Retaining the Best Professionals

Section IV
Services Delivery: Taking Care of Business

Section V
The Back Office: Efficient Firm Operations

Preface

If you assessed the available books on the topic of managing professional service firms, you probably arrived at the same conclusion we did about a year ago. You can find over a hundred books on the topic. Ninety-five percent of these books are written for the independent consultant who wants to learn how to incorporate, how to develop a proposal, how to sell themselves, and how to individually deliver a project to a client. The other 5 percent of the published books target the executives of large, national consultancies with thousands of consultants/employees. There were no books available to help the professional service firm with anywhere from 2 to 1,000 professionals. Yet, almost 75 percent of all professional services companies are in this group. In the books for independent consultants, you learn the basics (e.g., how to act on the client site, what the start-up costs are). In the books for large consultancies, you learn how to expand internationally or about developing philosophies. In this book, you learn how to grow an existing firm. You learn at what points you need to make decisions such as adding administrative support, opening another office, building another service line. You learn how to determine what is the best sales organization structure for your firm. You learn what information systems you need to build and when. This book is for the growing consulting company and its associates and management.

The bulk of our consulting experience has been in the technology consulting and management consulting fields. We have had interesting consulting problems involving 50,000-, 2,000-, and 500-person consulting organizations. Significant input in this book has come from lawyers, accountants, doctors, and many other professionals. The contributing authors have varied and successful professional services backgrounds. This book consolidates the best practices for the mid-size consulting company. We have observed consistent patterns of success and failure in consulting and have been fortunate enough to survive them. The main goal of any professional services company is to add enough value to your clients that they will pay you enough to cover your costs and make a decent profit. We have captured the lessons learned and the tools, techniques, and practices that can help a professional services firm as it grows to include more and more professionals.

Benefits for the Reader

From this book, you gain valuable skills, including:

- Identifying the main management areas of a successful professional services firm.
- Understanding of the scope and key success factors in each management area.
- Developing approaches for auditing current performance by area.
- Understanding the main sources of wasted resources.
- Identifying the industry average spending and investment commitments by area and professional services type.
- Distinguishing the business of managing the firm from the delivery of professional services.
- Understanding symptoms and sources of professional services firm inefficiencies.
- Learning the critical improvement steps in each of the main management areas.
- Learning how to make better decisions in firm strategy and direction setting, hiring practices, operations, technology, marketing, and overall management.
- Using specific cases and anecdotes from professional services firms to illuminate and further explain the material.
- Becoming familiar with specific advice from well-known practitioners in each of the service areas.
- Achieving higher utilization from their existing professional services assets/consultants.
- Achieving higher ROI from capital and operating expenses.

In addition, you develop a keen understanding of not only the building blocks of successful firm management, but also how to grow and leverage current assets.

Language Specific to Professional Services

There are terms we use repeatedly throughout the book. These terms are used throughout the field. They are:

- *Backlog:* The value of committed sales contracts that will be executed in the future.

- *Bill rate:* The average billing rate to the client achieved by a particular or group of professionals. In many cases, firms will "set" standard bill rates for classes of professionals.
- *Billability:* The total hours billed during a specified period (e.g., year) divided by the total hours available in during the same period. For example, a lawyer that bills 2,000 hours in a year where 2,000 hours are available for work would have 100 percent billability. Also called *Utilization rate.*
- *Billable:* The status of a professional when they are billing time to clients generally for a protracted amount of time.
- *Client:* The customers of a professional services firm.
- *Firm:* The professional services business or company.
- *Gross margin:* Calculated as *Bill rate* minus *loaded pay rate.*
- *Leverage ratio:* The ratio of junior staff to senior staff. If there are 10 professionals working under a partner, the leverage ratio would be 10 to 1.
- *Loaded pay rate:* Loaded pay rate includes the professionals base pay rate plus taxes and benefits.
- *Partner:* Term used to describe a senior member of a professional services firm. A partner typically has the same rights as an owner of the business.
- *Principal:* Term used to describe a senior member of a professional services firm that works just under the partner.
- *Professional staff:* Term for firm employees directly engaged in providing services to clients.
- *Service revenue:* Revenue associated with billable time.
- *Staff:* Term used to describe support personal (e.g., administrative assistants) also called administrative staff.
- *Utilization rate:* See *Billability.*

Acknowledgments

Clearly, an endeavor of this type is the end-result of countless investments by mentors, clients, friends, and teachers.

This book was a major collaborative effort on the part of many people. In addition to our contributing authors, we would like to thank the following people for their invaluable contributions:

- John Martin
- John Rosenbaum
- Manish Limaye
- Chris Loope
- Audrey Penrose
- Jay Espaillat

We would also like to thank our agent Neil Salkind and the team at Studio B, as well as Matt Holt and Tamara Hummel, at John Wiley & Sons. Their continued support and expert counsel is much appreciated.

We'd like to recognize the special people in our lives who lose us for weeks on end with an endeavor like this: Susan, Lauren, Allison, and Will Piot, and Mary, Emily, and Will Baschab.

About the Authors

This book was a major collaborative effort that involved untold hours on the part of many people. We were fortunate to have some of the best minds in professional services contribute to this book. All the professionals listed here contributed significantly to the entire process from design, content, to writing, editing, and publishing.

Primary Authors

JOHN BASCHAB began his career with a degree in MIS from the University of Alabama, where he was selected as the top student in his major by university faculty and was awarded the prestigious Seebeck Award for achievement in computer science. John continued his career in the IT department of Bell-South and at Intergraph Corp. After receiving his MBA with honors in behavioral science from the University of Chicago Graduate School of Business, John worked as a technology consultant to Fortune 500 companies in the Chicago office of management consultancy Booz Allen Hamilton. John is a cofounder of Impact Innovations Group, a privately held management and technology consulting firm. Impact Innovations employs over 400 consultants in offices in Dallas and Atlanta and manages Impact's IT optimization practice.

JON PIOT received his degree in computer science from Southern Methodist University and joined Andersen Consulting, developing computer applications and providing technology consulting services to Fortune 500 companies. Jon continued his career as vice-president of DMACS International, a software company whose international software rights of Fox Software products were later acquired by Microsoft. After receiving his MBA from the Harvard Business School, Jon joined the information technology strategy group of management consultancy Booz Allen Hamilton. Jon is a successful entrepreneur, cofounding Impact Innovations Group. Jon serves as Chief Executive Officer of Impact.

Contributing Authors

T. GREGORY BENDER is currently the president and CEO of Message Logix, Inc., a growing e-mail marketing, messaging, and consulting company. In August 2001, Gregory formed Message Logix, Inc. Its e-mail marketing software product, CampaignBuilder, helps corporations increase revenue, brand perception, customer loyalty, and e-commerce transactions over the Internet. In late 2003, Mr. Bender created K-12 Alerts, which is an emerency e-mail and text-based messaging to the cell phone management platform for school districts as part of CampaignBuilder. For the past two years, Mr. Bender also has acted as a managing partner in mediaSPA LLC developing interactive database driven applications for corporations.

Mr. Bender founded BDInter@ctive (BDI) in 1994, an award-winning interactive agency. In 1998, Bender cofounded YourGrocer.com (YG); as interim CEO and investor, he helped YG in 1998 to 1999 dramatically build the e-business and customer base through strategic relationships and online marketing strategies. In 1999, Bender sold a majority stake in YourGrocer.com to Brand Equity Ventures.

From 1996 to 1999, Mr. Bender worked with the Interactive Advertising Bureau and its board of directors to develop the first advertising and privacy standards for interactive advertising on the Internet. Bender has been a featured speaker at Internet and marketing industry conferences in New York and San Francisco and provided expert opinions and quotes to the *New York Times,* Forrester Research, Forbes.com, Internet.com, and Channelseven.com.

In 2000/2001, Bender served on the senior advisory board of CarePackages.com (CP), an e-commerce gifting and online greetings service. In September 2001, he helped CP engineer a merger with Student Advantage (NASDAQ: STAD).

Mr. Bender has over nine years of new media and marketing experience and has provided strategic Internet and Intranet direction to numerous well-known companies and organizations such as AOL, GE Capital, School Guide Publications, Gettysburg College, Motorola, Renaissance Capital (IPOhome .com), BarnesandNoble.com, and AMC (AMCtv.com).

Mr. Bender and CampaignBuilder consult with many Internet, education, finance, entertainment, and technology companies. Bender is a specialist in strategic direction and partnerships, marketing, web design/technology, and business development. He is a graduate of The New School/Parsons School of Design.

TIM BOURGEOIS is the CEO at Pixel Bridge Inc, a Boston-based Internet consulting firm that specializes in helping small and mid-size organizations use the Web for competitive advantage. He works with strategic clients to develop Internet strategies and ensure their online goals are aligned with underlying corporate goals. Tim also leads the firm's professional services industry practice. In addition to his role at Pixel Bridge, he is a partner at the Hocquet Group, a talent management and executive recruiting firm focused exclusively on the management consulting and IT services industry.

Previously, Tim was vice-president at Kennedy Information, a publishing company serving the consulting and executive recruiting businesses, where he managed market research and consulting activities. During his time there, the company increased revenues tenfold and subsequently was acquired for $48 million by the Bureau of National Affairs. Prior to his role at Kennedy, Tim was an analyst in the Services Group at International Data Corporation. He is a graduate of Bowdoin College in Brunswick, Maine.

JANA CARPENTER has over 25 years of experience in leadership and consulting roles with Fortune 500 corporations in the financial services industries, including FTI Consulting, Inc., Arthur Andersen, BaxterHealthcare, Hewlett-Packard, Bank of America, and Allegiance. Jana is currently the vice-president of sales and marketing for FTI, where she is responsible for managing the sales activity for all of its litigation businesses, as well as firmwide marketing initiatives. In this capacity, Jana supervises a team of 30 sales consultants and develops strategic and business development programs to sustain growth and strengthen FTI's market position. In addition to her sales and marketing achievements, Jana is an accomplished entrepreneur, and in 1995 she founded *Build Your Business,* a business education forum for entrepreneurs, and *Boss School,* a boot camp for business owners.

CRAIG E. COURTER is COO at Baker and McKenzie, one of the world's largest law firms with more than 3,000 lawyers serving in more than 68 offices across 38 countries. He is responsible for significant aspects of the firm's operations, including technology, knowledge management, professional development, marketing, business development, benefits, strategic planning, and firm meetings. Prior to becoming COO, he served as chief technology officer. Before joining Baker & McKenzie, Craig was technology partner and CIO of San Diego-based law firm Seltzer Caplan McMahon Vitek. He was previously a practicing lawyer for 13 years—practicing in the areas of high technology and intellectual property—and he lectured at the University of San Diego School of Law for 3 years. Formerly, he served as executive officer of the USS *Pluck* where he received two Navy commendation medals and the Navy Achievement Medal. He received his JD from the University of San Diego (magna cum laude) and completed his undergraduate work at Eastern Illinois University.

GINA GUTZEIT has over 20 years of experience in operational and financial restructuring, interim management, and bankruptcy proceedings. She is a senior managing director at FTI Consulting, Inc., a publicly traded corporate finance, restructuring, forensic accounting, and economic consulting firm.

Previously, Gina was a partner in PricewaterhouseCoopers' Financial Advisory Services Group, where she served as interim CFO for a mid-size global management consulting firm and as a financial advisor to numerous companies experiencing financial and operational changes. Her industry experience includes professional services firms, health care, transportation, financial services, telecommunications, retail, distributors, securities/commodities, and hospitality. Gina received a bachelor's degree in public accounting from Pace University. She is a CPA, a Certified Insolvency and Restructuring Advisor, and a Certified Fraud Examiner.

MICHAEL W. MALAKOFF is a managing member and cofounder of the Trisul Group, LLC, a management consultancy specializing in growth strategies. Michael has a proven track record of providing value-added consulting, developing new businesses, and improving operating effectiveness, both as a consultant and an executive. His experience covers a wide variety of industries, including professional services, financial services, and travel. Michael also has significant entrepreneurial experience, having previously cofounded a successful e-business consulting startup. He began his career as an attorney.

Michael earned a BA in economics from the University of Texas, a JD from Pepperdine University School of Law, and an MBA from the Southern Methodist University Cox School of Business.

THOMAS MARBACH has worked for two leading consulting and systems integration firms. As a part of his consulting and industry experience, he has served as project manager on large-scale implementations of accounting and finance, human resource, and other administrative systems. He has also worked in the service firm's functions of finance and accounting, recruiting, and new service development. His professional experience includes technology management consulting to clients in a variety of industries.

Tom received his doctorate in business administration with a major in information systems from the University of Texas at Arlington. He received his MS in accounting from North Texas State University and his BS in computer science from East Texas State University. He is a CPA in the state of Texas.

BRANT C. MARTIN is an attorney with Puls, Taylor & Woodson, LLP. He has an active national trial practice consisting of class actions, personal injury, professional malpractice, and commercial litigation disputes. Brant has prosecuted numerous complex lawsuits and class actions in federal and state courts involving securities fraud, defective products, and consumer protection. As a plaintiff's lawyer, Brant draws on his unique background as a former corporate and securities lawyer and as a former law clerk to the Honorable Richard A. Schell of the Eastern District of Texas.

Brant received his JD from the Southern Methodist University School of Law where he was valedictorian of his law school class, served as editor-in-chief of the *SMU Law Review,* and received a full scholarship as a Hatton

W. Sumners Scholar. Prior to attending SMU, Brant earned a master's in religion and literature from Yale University and a bachelor's degree in Spanish and English from Washington and Lee University. Currently, he serves on the board of directors of the Tarrant County Trial Lawyers Association and on the board of advocates of the Texas Trial Lawyers Association. Brant was also selected in 2004 as one of the "Best Lawyers Under 40" by *D Magazine*.

D. MICHAEL MCDOWELL is cofounding partner of McCrory & McDowell LLC and is currently managing partner of the firm and chairman of its executive committee. He and Ken McCrory formed McCrory & McDowell in 1983 and built it into one of the largest accounting and consulting firms in Pittsburgh.

Mike focuses his practice on strategic planning, which includes developing the strategic process for clients such as law and accounting firms, facilitating clients' strategic retreats, and assisting with the implementation of strategic initiatives. Mike provides consulting services to the health care industry and has served as COO for multispecialty physician networks that employ hundreds of physicians and generate more than $500 million in annual charges.

Before founding McCrory & McDowell, Mike worked in the international division of a large international accounting firm. He holds a BS from Indiana State University and is licensed as a CPA in Pennsylvania. Mike is a member of the National Association of Certified Valuation Analysts and has been qualified as a facilitator through the Institute of Cultural Affairs. He has published a number of articles on the strategic management of professional firms.

SCOTT M. MCELHANEY is a partner at Jackson Walker LLP, a Dallas, Texas, law firm, where he practices commercial litigation and employment law. He has handled a wide range of cases in state and federal trial and appellate courts. He has significant experience in employment discrimination, FLSA, and ERISA litigation; trade secret misappropriation claims; noncompetition agreement injunction proceedings; fraud and breach of fiduciary duty cases; defamation cases; and copyright infringement claims.

Scott is also an instructor at the Southern Methodist University Dedman School of Law, where he teaches employment law and has taught legal research and writing.

Scott received his bachelor's degree, summa cum laude, from Dartmouth College and his JD, cum laude, from Harvard Law School. Prior to entering private practice, he was a law clerk to Chief Judge Barefoot Sanders, U.S. District Court for the Northern District of Texas, and to Judge Irving Goldberg, U.S. Court of Appeals for the Fifth Circuit.

JEFFERY B. NEMY is a senior vice president at The Interpublic Group of Companies, one of the largest marketing communications companies in the world. Interpublic provides advertising, public relations, and other marketing services globally through its network of over 40,000 employees in approximately 130 countries. Prior to transferring within the company to his role in developing a new global IT shared services organization, he served as senior vice-president, regional finance director for the San Francisco office of Foote, Cone & Belding, one of the largest advertising agencies on the West Coast, with approximately $1 billion in billings and over 400 employees. Previously, he was director of financial services during the startup phase at Nextel Communications where he led the development of the company's financial planning and reporting systems. Prior to that, he was responsible for managing the financial planning and analysis functions for Chronicle Broadcasting Company. For the first decade of his career, he worked as a management consultant at both Arthur Young and Price Waterhouse and provided valuation analysis services while working for a boutique M&A advisory firm. He received his MBA from the University of Santa Clara and completed his undergraduate work in business administration and economics at California State University, Chico. He is a CPA in California.

K. TODD PHILLIPS is a founding partner of Wick Phillips, LLP, a Dallas-based law firm focused on providing its clients with innovative solutions to a wide variety of commercial disputes. From counseling clients on potential litigation issues, to aggressively and creatively litigating complex disputes, Wick Phillips, LLP is committed to providing the highest level of service throughout all phases of the dispute resolution process.

Todd was born in Anchorage, Alaska, and was raised in Laguna Niguel, California. Todd earned his BA degree with honors from Michigan State University and a law degree from Southern Methodist University School of Law.

After graduating from Southern Methodist University, Todd began his career as an associate in the business litigation section at Haynes and Boone, LLP. Thereafter, Todd was employed as an associate in the litigation department of Weil, Gotshal & Manges, LLP, which was recently recognized as one of the nation's top litigation departments by *The American Lawyer*. Todd is admitted to practice in the State of Texas.

JOHN J. REDDISH is founder and president of Advent Management International, Limited. John and his associates work with, and speak to, leaders who want to master growth, transition, and succession.

Prior to starting his own consulting practice in 1978, John served as vice president of the Presidents Association (PA) of the American Management Association. From 1971 to 1976, he was president and director of client services at RA Group, an advertising and public relations agency. John has also been associated with the New York State Nurses Association, IBM Corporation, Edison Electric Institute, and the Civil Service Employees Association.

John is a member of the National Speakers Association, the American Arbitration Association panel of arbitrators, and the Pennsylvania Business

Brokers Association. He has written and spoken widely and is the author of the audiocassette program, "New Techniques for Motivation and Discipline" (Dible, 1983). He holds a bachelor's degree in communications from Fordham University and a master's degree in administration from West Chester University. He has also taught management classes for several universities and training organizations, including Penn State University, Boston University, Texas Tech University, AMA International, INC Seminars, and others. John is a Certified Management Consultant.

LESLIE REISNER is a professional lecturer and clinical psychologist in private practice in Los Angeles and Newport Beach, California. Leslie received her BS degree in human development from Cornell University, her MS degree in experimental psychology from Villanova University, and both her MA degree and doctorate degree in clinical psychology from Hofstra University. She received her clinical training at the Institute for Rational-Emotive Behavior Therapy (REBT) in New York City, under the direct supervision of Dr. Albert Ellis, the founder of REBT.

Leslie is one of the West Coast's leading experts in REBT, a form of brief cognitive-behavioral psychotherapy that focuses on the present behaviors that can sabotage a fuller experience of life. Instead of focusing on what can't be changed (the past), Leslie teaches effective, present-day strategies to problem solving, relating to others, and personal self-enhancement. She has lectured and leads numerous workshops nationwide on stress management, increasing motivation, overcoming compulsive eating and addictive disorders, assertiveness training, improving relationships, and many other topics at law firms, hospitals, universities, professional conventions, and various professional groups.

FRANCISCO "FRANK" RIBEIRO is a principal in Booz Allen Hamilton's Organizational & Change Leadership practice focusing on the communications and technology industries. He specializes in business strategy and the transformation of technology-driven companies from product to customer-centric organizations. His expertise lies in the areas of strategic transformations, growth strategies, and high-performance organizational design to help global communications and technology companies sustain growth and profitability. Frank has coauthored articles focusing on new operating models and services/solutions-focused strategies for telecommunications and technology-driven companies.

Prior to joining Booz Allen Hamilton, Frank was an experienced executive in the telecommunications industry. He held leadership roles in the areas of engineering, product development and management, and strategic planning. He holds an MBA from the Stern School of Business at New York University and a BS degree in engineering from the New Jersey Institute of Technology.

JOE SANTANA is a director with Siemens Business Services. He is also coauthor of *Manage I.T.,* a book that taps into his technology and professional services management experience to provide IT managers with those competencies needed to succeed in the highly competitive twenty-first century. In addition to his years of experience designing and executing learning and development solutions, Joe has extensive personal experience as a manager and executive working for and servicing Fortune 1000 clients. For 15 years of his career, Joe served as an enterprise executive in the fast-paced, zero-tolerance for error, global financial services arena where he launched and managed highly profitable projects. In all of his roles, his key area of success has been in the transformation of nonprofitable service organizations or poorly organized in-house departments into business-aligned, revenue-driving operations that run like a well-managed professional services business. Joe is a highly sought-after media commentator and speaker whose views are well known to readers of various publications including *Fortune, Computerworld,* and the *Outsourcing Journal,* as well as other media channels including radio and television. For more about Joe, visit him on the web at www.joesantana.com.

ROBERT H. SCHWARTZ is the managing principal and chief executive officer of the firm of Raymond & Prokop, P.C., with offices in Southfield, Grand Rapids, and Sault Ste. Marie, Michigan. He has extensive experience in business planning, mergers, and acquisitions. He also has considerable experience assisting physicians, hospitals, and nursing homes in the health care regulatory areas, including reimbursement, fraud and abuse, and hospital-physician relations, among others. He is also involved with matters concerning international practice with a particular emphasis on Mexico, Latin America, and Canada.

He received his Bachelor of Arts and Juris Doctor from Wayne State University. He is a member of the Health Law Section of the American Bar Association and Michigan Bar Association, the American Health Lawyers Association, and the Business Law Section of the American Bar Association. Schwartz has also authored a number of articles for various publications, is a frequent lecturer on topics relating to health care, and has been interviewed on many occasions by Detroit area media agencies. Mr. Schwartz lives in Southeast Michigan with his wife and two daughters.

BRYAN J. WICK is a founding partner of Wick Phillips, LLP, a Dallas, Texas, based law firm focused on providing its clients with innovative solutions to a wide variety of commercial disputes. Bryan has a national practice and has prosecuted and defended numerous complex commercial disputes in federal and state courts throughout the United States and the United States Virgin Islands. Additionally, Bryan has significant experience representing debtors and creditors in bankruptcy proceedings.

Bryan graduated from the University of Pennsylvania with a BA in international relations and a minor in economics and then received a Juris Doctorate from Washington University School of Law in St. Louis, Missouri. Bryan has worked for two U.S. Magistrate Judges and one U.S. District Court Judge and is currently licensed to practice law in Texas, New York, and the U.S. Virgin Islands. Bryan was also selected as one of the "Best Lawyers Under 40" by *DMagazine*.

Managing and Governing the Professional Services Firm

Managing the Professional Services Firm

JOHN BASCHAB, JON PIOT, AND ROBERT H. SCHWARTZ

Some problems are so complex that you have to be highly intelligent and well informed just to be undecided about them.

—Laurence J. Peter

It was a cool and rainy day in Texas, drizzly weather odd for mid-June, when the cell phone began to ring. It was a friend of ours from Chicago who was running a consulting company. After a bit of small talk, she said, "Speaking of drizzle, we have been facing a constant drizzle of problems in our practice group."

She related a few of the problems that had been keeping her awake for weeks:

> The market hasn't changed, the demand for services seems to be strong, but our company sales are down and our pipeline is weak. I cannot figure out how to keep our pipeline building as we deliver more and more work. It always seems like we have a few large deals that we close, we execute those deals, and then our pipeline dries up. As our projects come to a close, we scramble to refill our pipeline. We just finished two of the largest projects in our company history, which was great while they lasted, but now I have 20 consultants sitting on the bench with no work to give them. I cannot keep them there indefinitely. Last year we had a similar situation, and I had to lay off 12 staff; believe me, that was not pleasant and really hurt our morale. Two months later, we closed a major bid, and our HR department hustled for weeks to hire back some of the people. We had to push the start date on those projects back by three weeks. On top of that, my controller is telling me we are behind on cash flow,

so I need to call the VP at my largest client and ask them to pay their outstanding invoices, so we don't run into any trouble covering payroll. I just hope all of this doesn't affect my buyout negotiations with Stan, my original partner. You know he and I have not been working well together, so I have decided to buy him out. His management skills are horrible, and he was really hurting the culture around here. Besides, he hasn't sold any new business in probably two years. I can't wait to get some closure; however, the bank may balk on the loan if business performance isn't stable. Anyway, I know you guys run a larger firm, and I'm sure you've had to face some of these issues. Can you help me?

We responded quickly and to the affirmative. It would be a long couple of weeks as we helped her sort through the many issues we have witnessed both through direct experience and through helping other professional services firms. Those experiences prompted our conversations with other professional services firm executives, who had all experienced similar management issues in their firms.

Professional Services History

People have been offering their expertise in exchange for compensation for centuries, probably dating back to trade route guides, mercenaries, and early forms of bookkeepers. In fact, traces of accounting as a professional service date back 5,000 to 7,000 years with the invention of clay tablets that were used to track property records.

Interestingly, there is little evidence of large professional services firms predating the nineteenth century. There seem to be a few turning points in history that led to larger firms. First, in the 1600s, England saw the emergence of the professional accounting firms. In England, feudal law was replaced by the law of royal courts. The royal courts developed common law in the early seventeenth century. This drove a surge in litigation and a growth in law firms. Then, 200 years later, in the 1800s and early 1900s, most of the large U.S. accounting, legal, and consulting firms were started.

Why this period and why not before then? There were major technological inventions during this period. The early 1800s saw the invention of the steam engine, which allowed easier transportation between major cities. The telephone allowed communication within and between major cities. Then, in the early 1900s, the invention of the automobile again provided another mechanism of transportation. These inventions allowed the emergence of multioffice firms that could now communicate and meet more frequently. Additionally, the inventions enabled big businesses in other industries. This period saw the emergence of the large industrial manufacturing companies, which would require more professional services. As companies built multicity offices, professional services firms had to follow suit. Higher demand, higher need for specialization, larger customers, and ability to communicate and travel across greater distances are all factors in the transformation of the one- to two-person proprietorship to the growth of the large professional services company. These factors are also relevant as we determine how to build a business from a handful of professionals to several hundred. In short, no reasonable person today contemplates life without professional services (hiring a lawyer, selecting an accountant, hiring an architect, retaining an advertising agency). Additionally, professional services firms can now scale to multithousand-employee firms while just a few hundred years ago, these firms were limited to fewer than a handful of professionals.

Another Book on Professional Services?

With the increase in professional services over the recent past, it might be expected that guidance for executives in those firms would be readily available. We scanned the virtual bookshelves of our favorite online bookseller and located about 50 books on professional services. The topics covered in these books range from how to get started, how to sell, how to incorporate, how to minimize risk, to how to market your services. Surely, another book on running professional services companies was not needed.

However, closer examination yielded a surprising result about most of these books. The vast majority are focused on the yet-to-be-created professional services company. The books are focused on professional staff who are part of a larger firm but wishing to branch out and start their own company as an independent provider. These books are geared to giving them the know-how and the courage to branch out. Topics range from where to purchase office supplies to creating letterhead. This set of books is also targeted at the one-person shop—how to network, how to send out marketing material, how to create a contract—hardly topics of interest to anyone who has been in business for any amount of time. Book after book targets this sole proprietor market. Lacking, however, is a book focused on the mid-size professional services group, employing 5 to 250 professional staff, with strong growth aspirations.

Another subset are the popular and widely known books about professional services, yet these tend to address the problems of multinational firms with enormous numbers of professional staff. The concepts included are both appropriate and valuable but geared toward steering a massive ocean liner and modifying its direction by a few degrees—again, hardly the tactical and pragmatic text reference for the small to mid-size firm trying to grow.

How Do We Define Professional Services?

While there are a large number of books on the subject, there doesn't appear to be a standard definition of *professional services*. A formal definition of professional services found in most dictionaries is similar to the following: Professional service is a service requiring specialized knowledge and skill usually of a mental or intellectual nature and usually requiring a license, certification, or registration. The definition posted on the web site of one state legislative agency is:

> PROFESSIONAL SERVICE means work rendered by an independent contractor who has a professed knowledge of some department of learning or science used by its practical application to the affairs of others or in the practice of an art founded on it, which independent contractor shall include but not be limited to lawyers, doctors, dentists, psychologists, certified registered nurse anesthetists, veterinarians, architects, engineers, land surveyors, landscape architects, accountants, and claims adjusters. A profession is a vocation founded upon prolonged and specialized intellectual training which enables a particular service to be rendered. The word "professional" implies professed attainments in special knowledge as distinguished from mere skill.

Governments, industries, businesses, and people use different definitions for *professional services* depending on the situation. They include or exclude different vocations in the definition. For the purposes of this book, professional services are businesses in which professionals are providing a *service* not based on a tangible product. In our definition, we include accountants, appraisers, attorneys, business consultants, technical consultants, political consultants, architects, engineers, physicians, advertising agents, real estate brokers, and insurance agents. These types of occupations must deal with similar issues in delivering specific and specialized services through people. While the types of services delivered to clients are diverse, many of the mechanisms and operations of all professional services firms are similar. For example, a medical practice and a commercial real estate brokerage firm are very different in the services they provide. However, for much of their operational decision making, they have similarities—for instance, both firms might analyze whether they should promote a professional staff member to be a full partner in the practice/firm. The thought process and the decision framework for analyzing this question are very similar for both. How much profit will the new partner add to the practice? How dilutive will the new partner be to existing partners? Will the new partner have voting rights? Many other operating aspects are similar for the firms as well (e.g., utilization, profit per employee, invoicing, record keeping).

Because of the comprehensive treatment of the business of managing a professional services firm, this book addresses major operational and business issues that affect almost every firm manager, partner, or owner on a daily basis.

The approximate number of U.S. firms in each professional service category is shown in the following table:

Segment	Approximate U.S. Firms (Thousands)
Health care	35
Business consulting	35
Insurance	30
Legal	25
Financial services	25
Real estate	20
Counseling	15
Architecture	5
Political advisory	5
Marketing	5
Staffing services	5
Education	5

The first six segments are covered in depth in this book. We underscore, however, that the concepts can be applied to most professional services firms.

What Is Covered in This Book?

The intent of *The Professional Services Firm Bible* is to help professional services firm executives turn their companies into highly productive organizations, help readers become better managers of their firms, and solve many of the problems alluded to earlier. The book provides sharply defined, specific policies, practices, and tools for each important aspect of managing the professional services firm, from sales and marketing, to human resources (HR), to operations, to risk management. The approaches facilitate the assessment of current operations and the development of a step-by-step improvement plan designed to improve current firm management and provide measurable productivity improvements. The book will help firm management improve the financial performance of their practice by managing costs, getting the most from external vendors, and improving revenues.

Each chapter in the book is devoted to a key operational area of managing the firm, such as marketing, finance, HR, and risk management. Topics and features include:

- Identifying the main management areas of a successful professional services firm

- Understanding the scope and key success factors in each management area
- Identifying approaches for auditing current performance by area
- Understanding the main sources of waste
- Identifying industry average spending and investment commitments by area and professional services type
- Distinguishing the "business" of managing the firm from the delivery of professional services
- Identifying symptoms and sources of professional services firm inefficiencies
- Finding critical improvement steps in each of the main management areas
- Making better decisions in firm strategy and direction setting, hiring practices, operations, technology, marketing, and overall management
- Achieving higher utilization from existing professional services assets/consultants
- Achieving higher return on investment (ROI) from capital and operating expenses

Specific cases and anecdotes from actual departments and consulting engagements illuminate and further explain the material. Quotes and advice from well-known practitioners in each of the service areas are included.

The book has five sections. Section I, Managing and Governing the Professional Services Firm, focuses on understanding the difference between the business aspects of operating a professional services firm and the actual delivery of the services. Additionally, the contrast between front office (sales and marketing) activities versus back office (operations) activities is drawn. The section presents benchmarking research by functional area (HR, information technology [IT], finance), by professional services firm type (law, medical, etc.), and by size for spending and focus on each area. The section explains why the topic is important for the professional services firm manager and discusses what key operations, sales, and marketing processes all professional services firms have in common. Case studies and cautionary tales about failures of professional services firm initiatives or businesses where the fundamental business pieces were not well executed emphasize the importance of the topic. The section also covers the effective senior level management and decision-making structure for the professional services firm and topics such as partnership management and legal governance structure.

Section II, The Front Office: Driving Sales and Growth, covers the topic of sales and marketing. While most professional services providers are highly proficient in delivering their actual services, a common shortcoming for many is the often uncomfortable subject of effective selling. This section addresses the key marketing and sales issues for service providers, with specific tips and approaches for ensuring that the front office efforts are consistent with the specific market and industry under consideration. Key topics in this section include: sales management and tracking, marketing, service-line creation, qualifications and reference management, proposals and bids, strategic partnering, and intellectual capital development and protection.

Section III, The Organization: Attracting and Retaining the Best Professionals, discusses human resources and related topics. One of the top drivers of client satisfaction and successful delivery in the services industry is the quality of the professionals within the practice; we devote an entire section of the book to achieving world-class recruiting and retention. This section covers the topic in depth, including organization structure, career paths for professional and internal staff, training and professional development programs, recruiting, and on-boarding new employees.

Section IV, Services Delivery: Taking Care of Business, focuses on delivery of service to clients. While the services delivered in professional providers differ widely, many of the core approaches to successful management apply. These approaches include service delivery (planning, building, and managing), project management, resource (bench) management, risk management, and project P&L management.

Section V, The Back Office: Efficient Firm Operations, covers all the activities that support the operations of the firm. The back office section outlines the specific back office operations that must operate smoothly to ensure that the professional services firm operates efficiently. Topics include finance, accounting, HR, purchasing and procurement, asset management, IT, vendor management, real estate/facilities, legal, and office management.

Unique Issues of Professional Services Firms

Professional services firms are different from other companies because there is no tangible product to sell. Regardless of how services are billed, the professional services firm gets paid for expending labor time on behalf of a client's problem or need. The input is time, and the output is thinking or documents in most cases. Since billings/revenues grow as the input grows (e.g., labor time), professional services firms are inherently labor, management, and HR intensive. This kind of firm may be contrasted with, for example, Ticketmaster, an online provider of tickets to sporting events, concerts, and theater. At midnight on the U.S. East Coast, while everyone in the firm can be expected to be away from the job, Ticketmaster is selling hundreds, if not thousands, of tickets online to people all over the world. One additional ticket sold does not equate to any labor input of one of its employees. Ticketmaster is a business that scales without a tremendous amount of incremental direct labor. Contrast this to a large law firm. If that law firm wins a new client with a large case, the law firm must provide enough attorneys to cover the case sufficiently. In most cases, the law firm will be paid for each hour that one of its attorney's bills. As the firm hires additional lawyers, it has to find space, manage their careers, provide training and tools, and so on. The professional services firm, more so than any other type of firm, requires the balancing of a large number of variables. Thus, the trick in scaling a firm is to develop simple processes, a successful hiring formula, and a recurring sales model, and strike a balance between customer loyalty and employee satisfaction.

The tendency in most firms is to concentrate on "delivering" the actual expertise to the client at the expense of all other things. Architects by training and experience enjoy designing structures. They are not necessarily proficient at (or even interested in) managing a business. Yet, as the firm grows, it requires more management time from the principals, causing stress on the organization. Do the principals continue to bring in revenue at top rates, or do they spend time on internal management issues?

Not only is more time required on internal management, but also the individuals need to be "good" at management. For example, we worked with a graphic design firm several years ago. A principal of the firm called to ask if we could assist him with a business strategy. He was one of the best graphic designers in the city, and his firm kept adding more and more clients. He had around a dozen employees, and while his revenue kept increasing, he was perplexed about how to manage the business going forward without jeopardizing the financial well-being of the firm. He was the primary designer and the lead sales generator. His firm's clients included a large airline and prominent sports team. Some near-term steps for improvement included carving off nonstrategic management items to an administrator, including all infrastructure, facilities, and operations issues; outsourcing nonstrategic areas where possible (e.g., payroll); and defining both sales and delivery processes and roles more clearly so that discrete activities could be delegated to junior staff more easily.

How balanced is your firm? Here are some questions we ask when trying to get a quick overview of the status of a firm:

- What is your revenue per professional?
- What is your attrition rate? Do you have any difficulty retaining staff?
- How long is your sales cycle?
- Who sells and who delivers the service? Are these the same duties or are they separated? Where is the leverage in the sales cycle?
- What is your annual marketing plan?

- What is your firm's value proposition?
- Why should a client hire you?
- How do you hire professionals? Have you had any difficulty bringing in experienced people?
- What is your training program?
- What does your organization chart look like?
- What are the levels in your organization?
- What are the career paths by level?
- How many direct reports do you have?
- What is your leverage model?
- How loyal are your customers?
- Do you have sufficient capital to grow?
- What is your growth rate? What is your sustainable growth rate?
- Are your invoices clear and accurate?
- What do your employees and customers have to say about your back office?
- How satisfied are your employees?
- Where do employees typically go after they leave your firm?

The answers to these questions are covered in subsequent chapters. However, sitting down and asking yourself these questions should be eye opening and self-revealing. Areas with ambiguous answers may drive you to a particular chapter of this book.

Although our complete prescription for fixing or scaling your professional services firm is covered in this book, we are often asked for the short version of our program. The following checklist of specific steps across the key areas will help you think through a growth plan for your company, scale and improve financial performance, and begin reaping the rewards of a productive company:

1. Make sure the senior management team is following the same plan.
   a. If anyone in senior management does not agree to the overall direction of the company, you can't be successful. You will need to develop a plan that all can agree to.
   b. Make sure everyone on the senior team deserves to be there.
   c. If there are any weak senior team members, replace them with stronger candidates.
2. Fix your organization structure to enable the firm to grow.
   a. Figure out the division of labor that allows you to spend the most time on things you do best.

b. At most, you probably have three or four levels in your organization. If you have only one or two, you need to be building and planning for three or four to allow your firm to gain leverage as it grows by moving more mundane and routine tasks to less experienced, less expensive resources.

c. A multilayer organization will help you develop career paths for employees as well, improving employee retention and attracting new candidates to the firm.

d. Make sure each direct report is strong and that you have good lieutenants, which will greatly free up more executive time for important activities.

e. Determine appropriate standard bill rates for each level of your organization. This step will help keep you profitable and make you more disciplined in negotiating with customers when they ask for pricing or price breaks.

f. Ensure that the variable incentive compensation is set at each level of the organization and that the incentives are aligned to the major goals of the organization.

g. Write down the principles and doctrine that define the firm's culture and communicate these regularly to employees.

3. Develop simple, straightforward processes for recurring activities.

a. Like any company, you will die the "death of a thousand cuts" if the professional staff is always reacting to the latest business issue.

b. The only way to avoid reacting is to develop standard processes and checklists for your top issues.

c. The typical processes that can be standardized include recruiting, HR, on-boarding employees, training, cash flow management, accounting, quality assurance, customer satisfaction surveys, weekly progress reports, and so on. Anything that is repetitious and managed by routine is a candidate for standard operating procedures.

d. Take the firm's top 20 standard activities and make sure there is a repeatable process written down with job responsibilities for each one.

e. Through this process, the next time the firm encounters the activity, it will be handled with an automatic response from an administrative employee versus a decision or activity that you or, worse, multiple professionals in your organization are reacting to.

f. Add rigor and objectivity into hiring plans such as cognitive or other testing and other non-interview data points.

g. Make sure the organization routinely counsels underperforming employees and eventually eliminates them from the firm if their performance does not improve.

    h. Set hiring triggers by quarter or annually based on revenue or incoming business. This schedule will help the firm proactively recruit instead of reacting to the next project on an ad-hoc basis.

4. Eliminate any non-core service lines and focus on what you do best.

    a. Ask the question: How many service lines do you have? *Service lines* are services that your firm performs for customers. Service lines generally include a concept, a set of offerings, a methodology, a process, standard pricing, standard work plans, and standard resources.

    b. If you have no service lines, you probably view your firm as generalists, and you may have too few differentiators.

    c. On the other hand, 10 service lines are likely too many for the mid-size professional services company. It is difficult to be expert at a wide range of activities with limited resources. A large number of service lines will hurt delivery quality and confuse your customers to the point where they won't know what your firm does well.

    d. Determine what you are good at; determine what you can be the best at. Develop that into a service line and focus on it. The marketplace rewards focus, particularly for small and mid-size services firms.

    e. The firm must develop intellectual capital, build qualifications, and train employees on how to sell and deliver if they are to provide differentiation in the marketplace.

5. Improve your relationship with customers.

    a. Each piece of business you have should be profitable and referenceable. If it is not, then it either needs to be cleaned up or the customer may need to be given up.

    b. Make sure you are staying in front of your customers. A quick litmus test for ensuring external focus is this question: Have you met with your top five customers in the past month?

    c. Ensure that the firm is engaged in "good business." Produce a spreadsheet with each customer listed in the left column and the profitability of the customer along the y-axis. Any customer that does not generate the gross margin that is your goal should be dealt with in one of two ways. First, attempt to set up a meeting to discuss rates. If rate discussions are not successful, try to reduce your cost to serve the customer. As a last resort, stop providing services to the customer.

    d. It is easier to have these discussions with customers when you know them well. Make an effort to visit your clients or take them out for nonbusiness lunches and dinners to solidify the relationship. Remember: Your services help them.

e. Additionally, while with customers, ask for feedback on your services. You will be surprised what you hear and the suggestions that they have for you. Often, important new services will emerge from direct customer feedback.

6. Ensure that your sales and marketing plan is leveraged.

   a. What are the sales steps from finding a prospect to completing a deal?

   b. Outline and define these steps clearly.

   c. Determine how much time is involved and by whom in the organization.

   d. Develop standardized proposals, qualifications, and reference sheets.

   e. Train professional staff on how to sell your services.

   f. Track metrics on each step outlined. You will begin to understand better how your marketing and business development efforts translate into work for the firm.

7. Improve fiscal management/budgeting.

   a. Based on your leverage model, there should be an assumed utilization rate for all staff. What is the actual utilization rate for your staff?

   b. Crack down on frivolous spending by tightening expense policies and holding up capital expenditure requests that are not important. This step will alleviate cash flow pressures and ensure that all employees are carefully monitoring expenditures.

   c. Plan major capital expenditures so they are spaced out appropriately and allow adequate preparation time.

   d. Watch cash daily. Develop a one-page scorecard that shows incoming and outgoing cash on a daily basis.

   e. Always have a plan B for handling firm expenses (e.g., payroll) in case cash does not materialize. Have you established a line of credit at the bank? Have you adequately planned for receivables and payables?

These steps should put you well on your way to building the scalable firm. Always think *strategy, system, process,* and *people*—if you're constantly thinking about the next client sales call or delivering another document to a customer, chances are no one is thinking about how to grow the firm.

With the right leadership in place and enthusiastic engagement from the senior management team, you can lead your company to the next level. As evidence that you can lead your entire firm toward growth and success, we share a note received from the CEO of a client for whom we had previously completed an extensive effectiveness engagement:

We are a totally different company today than when you started working with us. It all started with the assessment you completed. We eliminated a number of the services we were providing and focused on what we do best. We are now one of the largest providers of our services in the city, our consultants are fully utilized, and our bill rates have increased by 50 percent. Thanks to a number of other things you suggested, we have been able to grow and manage our firm effectively.

Note

1. Laurence J. Peter, Peter's Almanac, Sept. 24, 1982.

2

Professional Services Firm Benchmarking

GINA GUTZEIT

It is a funny thing about life; if you refuse to accept anything but the best, you very often get it.
—W. Somerset Maugham[1]

Professional services firm benchmarking is an often-overlooked process that is one of the most powerful management tools the firm has at its disposal. While firms can measure the most important financial benchmark, profitability, when it is underperforming (or doing well), does the firm have the ability to drill down further to understand why? And, even if the firm is profitable today, what do the leading indicators (such as turnover and pipeline) say about tomorrow? And, how is the firm doing relative to the industry and to its competition? Perhaps the firm is profitable, but not as profitable as it could be. In sum, benchmarking can help ensure both the present and future success of the professional services firm.

Profit is the number one unit of measure in any professional services firm. Profits are a factor of bill rates, billable hours, labor costs, sales, and general and administrative expenses (SG&A) taken into account as well.

$$Bill\ rate \times hours = revenue$$
$$Direct\ labor\ cost \times hours = direct\ costs$$
$$Revenue - direct\ costs = gross\ margin$$
$$Gross\ margin - SG\&A = profit$$

Leverage can significantly alter the number of billable hours. *Leverage* is the number of senior professionals (partners/vice presidents) in relation to other

16

professional staff. Key strategic decisions have a significant impact on profits (e.g., bill rates, staff ratios, billable hours). One of the best methods to determine whether the professional services firm is operating at an optimum profit is to benchmark these critical areas.

Why This Topic Is Important

Benchmarking is an analytical tool that measures and compares a company's key functions, systems, and performance to respective industry standards. Benchmarking is a straightforward concept for improving business practices and financial performance. Although it can seem daunting or complicated, particularly to firms who have not done any benchmarking, it is nothing more than taking a snapshot of other firms' practices, comparing them with your firm's current methods, and then implementing the best practices. Or, put another way, "Benchmarking allows a company to climb the learning curve quickly by benefiting from the experience of other companies."[2]

Used effectively, benchmarking is a practical means of spurring action or change within an organization that results in increased profits, reduced cycle time, higher client satisfaction, and a better understanding of the business and the underlying drivers of profit, staff retention, and client satisfaction. It allows executives to pinpoint areas for improvement, set more meaningful goals, and provide external criteria against which to measure progress and achievement. Whether benchmarking is focused on one particular area of operations or across a range of business functions, it provides a common basis for comparison and discussion between line and functional leaders.

Professional services firms must ensure the consistent, efficient, and optimal delivery of client services. Benchmarking is potentially more important for professional services firms than any other type of firm because client service is their product; thus they must always strive to ensure their service offerings and business practices are best in class. Unlike a manufacturing operation, where the tolerances and quality of a product can be measured directly, a services firm must measure as accurately as possible conceptual things like "satisfaction levels."

Benchmarking is a tremendously powerful tool for improving business performance, yet it is not as commonly employed as other well-known management techniques such as project management, budgeting, or demand management. According to one estimate, among businesses in the $1 million to $20 million annual revenue range, only 5 percent of all business owners understand and implement benchmarking.[3] Given the potential benefits, it is surprising that benchmarking is not more frequently used by business owners and executives. Are there invisible barriers to benchmarking? Does it seem too difficult an exercise to undertake or perhaps too expensive? Is the data on best practices not readily available?

There is surprisingly little written about the process of benchmarking for professional services firms beyond the occasional journal articles and even less practical information about the benchmarking performance measures themselves. In addition, much benchmarking data is proprietary or difficult to locate. However, benchmarking is a highly worthwhile endeavor and one of the most cost-effective and least disruptive ways to assess and improve a professional services business.

This chapter demystifies this important tool to make it more accessible and useful to professional services firms. We provide a primer on the basics of benchmarking, then focus on four areas that can be most valuable to professional services firms: revenue and expense, finance and accounting, information technology (IT), and human resources (HR). We then review the philosophy, objectives, and process. Although there are no formulas, hard-and-fast rules, or fixed schedules for conducting this analysis, guidelines can aid the professional services executive in planning and implementing benchmarking and related business improvement initiatives.

The Value of Benchmarking for Professional Services Firms

The busy professional services executive may think that benchmarking sounds sensible but that it will take time that isn't available to the firm or its staff. Days are already too full, and time is a scarce resource (and valuable commodity) in the service industry. However, the benefits of improving service and profitability can be significant, and the benchmarking initiative can be as simple or complex as the firm needs or can handle at a particular point in its business cycle. It is even possible to benchmark just one area of business—associate unbillable time, for example—and to reap tangible benefits from improvements made to that single business variable. Or, a firm may choose to analyze its billing rates: If the rates have not been changed in two years, it is likely that the firm could and should adjust the amount charged for its professionals' time. Susan Leandri, managing director of Global Best Practices, with PricewaterhouseCoopers says, "Benchmarking provides you with the tools to know where you are at, but once you know where you are at, where are you going? That's where best practices come in. They are the roadmap to process improvement."[4]

Another incentive for conducting benchmarking is to survey best practices among other service firms. Best practice learnings can yield important advantages for professional services firms, particularly since advisors tend to be better at client service than at practice management. In 2001, most advisory firms experienced growing revenue yet declining professional productivity and higher professional compensation along with increased overhead expenses. As a result, partner/owner income at advisory firms declined.

There is a cure: Focus on strategy, control operations and overhead costs, leverage the business, and build depth in the practice. Benchmarking best practices can help achieve many, if not all, of these goals and others as well. For example, a study that examined the financial and operational characteristics of 566 participating advisory firms demonstrated that strong management increases partners/owners' compensation, provides opportunities for the staff, and adds value to the business.[5]

Firm size is a key factor in achieving best practices, and larger firms may have a distinct advantage when it comes to realizing the benefits of best practice benchmarking. Larger firms are better able to achieve economies of scale in and across geographic markets where they have a large market share, and since many expenses are fixed, the operating costs can be leveraged over a larger revenue base to achieve higher profit. In addition, these firms have a larger employee base and thus an advantage in recruiting, training, and retaining employees. Size also enables large firms to invest more in technology, benefits, and marketing, which further increases the leverage of their resources.

Role of Professional Services Executives

As all successful executives know, to be "average" is never an acceptable standard for a growing business, particularly in professional services where client expectations are high and controlling costs are low. For the executive of a professional services firm, this is a critical business fact—the caliber of the enterprise, of its people, and of its operations has a direct impact on the firm's service offerings and client satisfaction. Benchmarking can play a key role in helping the firm achieve or maintain best in class standards and practices, but the execution of the findings and actions requires the commitment and quality of its senior leadership. This is the foundation for a successful benchmarking exercise. At the heart of every flourishing professional services firm are executives who demonstrate characteristics that drive their businesses to excel. These executives share similar characteristics of introspection, critical business analysis, assessment of operations, and benchmarking. They:

- Know their firm inside and out and continuously examine the organization closely and objectively. They are not micromanagers but they are aware of all critical policies and procedures and demand that they be followed and consistently applied to enable the firm to operate efficiently.
- Are involved, proactive executives who continuously seek improvement and desire to innovate and exceed industry best practices. Even when the business appears to be running smoothly, they compare individual areas against competitors with an eye toward improvement.

- Look for opportunities to drive for positive change, particularly when fact-based such as benchmarked versus competition.
- Know that execution is critical to realizing this change. If they do not execute, they will have missed an opportunity to make improvements and will have wasted time and money on an exercise that served no purpose.
- Understand that introspection can help identify unnecessary costs and dismantle levels of complexity that have built up over the years.
- Value the fresh thinking that benchmarking can generate because the process gives license to look at a situation or problem from a different perspective, one that encourages long-term solutions and not quick fixes.

For many firm managers, having an external perspective comes automatically—they are always focused on clients, the marketplace, and how they and their organization are perceived by critical audiences. But introspection is necessary for benchmarking. Executives need to spend time understanding their organization, its functions, and processes. No matter how beautiful the veneer or elaborate the carving, the inner workings of the grandfather clock are what keeps it running. How an organization functions internally is a clear indicator of its attention to details—and how well it serves its clients, both today and in the future. It may be a cliché, but the devil is in both the detail and in the execution of a well-thought-out plan or process.

An example of the types of key questions that can indicate whether it is time for a critical analysis of the professional services firm includes:

- "Do I know how many client invoices on average are prepared per month?"
- "What is the firm's average bill rate over the past 12 months?"
- "What is the profit margin for any specific client?"

As this example indicates, the typical executive may know the firm's revenue or expense dollars by category but be unaware of things at the next level of detail.

An appropriate starting point of any analysis of the firm is to begin by listing the questions for which you would like answers. Which activities might be accomplished by the staff more efficiently? Why has the staff utilization declined by 5 percent over the past year? The overall process starts by understanding the questions that need to be asked and the information needed to formulate answers.

Knowledge First, Benchmarking Later

An experienced HR director recently began running the HR function for a newly formed property management firm. The firm has 100 full-time and 75 part-time employees. Without any staff, she set up the HR department from scratch and handles all health care and COBRA benefits, 401(k) plans, and disability, immigration, and disciplinary issues—and those are just some of her responsibilities.

She knows she should conduct benchmarking in a number of areas but feels certain that now is not the right time. "I'm still establishing policies and procedures," she said. "I must go through one complete cycle of coverage enrollment and at least one full year of assessing the existing benefits offered before I have enough grounding in the company. Prior to benchmarking, I must understand the firm's needs, strengths, and weaknesses. That takes time."

A Primer on Benchmarking

This section outlines the key elements of implementing a benchmarking program and outlines the specific steps and analyses that should be part of the program.

Performance Measures

Benchmarks are performance measures. Benchmarking is an action that involves discovering the specific attributes that lead to higher firm performance, understanding how these practices work, and adapting and applying them to your organization. Benchmarks are facts that, when applied, enable real business improvement.

Performance measures are the "vital signs" of a business. They quantify a process or the results. There are many ways to measure a company, a department, or a person's performance, but all share a single trait: They are fact-based, not subjective. They are measurable and quantifiable. Performance measures focus on cost, quality, and time:

- Cost-based measures cover the financial aspects of performance (e.g., direct labor cost).
- Quality-based measures assess how well a company's products or services meet customer needs (e.g., client satisfaction).
- Time-based measures focus on the efficiency of the process (e.g., how long it takes to produce a proposal).

There are two different types of performance measures. *Outcome measures* identify the results of a process and allow firms to evaluate how well they are performing in a particular area. Typically, they are based on a company's overall goals and objectives and are intended to demonstrate the effect of a process on the company's finances and efficiency.

Activity measures focus on the incremental efforts that are necessary to enhance process improvement, specifically issues that concern the employees in charge of process-specific activities. Therefore, managers identify problems in a business process as soon as they occur, which allows for correction.

One example of an activity measure is full-time equivalents (FTEs) versus number of invoices, as compared to revenue. For the professional services firm, it is critical to invoice clients and collect cash. How accurate, fast, and efficient these processes operate has a significant impact on revenue and cash flow of the organization. A three-day reduction in the invoicing process can improve cash flow by 10 percent. Conversely, a three-day bottleneck in the invoicing process can reduce cash flow by 10 percent. No matter how great the client service delivery of a company, there is an bottom-line impact if the firm can't bill correctly or collect revenue in a timely manner. Billing rate and hours billed errors also erode client satisfaction and trust.

How Are Benchmarks Determined?

To conduct benchmarking, measurements are required—ones that can be performed consistently and reliably with a basis in fact. The specific benchmarks are typically determined through surveys, questionnaires, and interviews. Question sets are designed to establish qualitative as well as quantitative metrics for the following performance dimensions:

- Process
- Technology
- Leverage
- Organization
- Strategic alignment
- Partnering activity

Qualitative tools are used to gauge where a firm stands in relation to best practices for a particular business process. They are subjective, judgmental, and focused on activities behind a particular business practice.

Quantitative tools are used to see how an organization compares itself to others for a particular business process. They are objective and focused on the measurements of specific operating or financial performance metrics.

Best Practices

Best practices are a key focus of benchmarking. Simply stated, they are the best way to perform a business process or practice within specific parameters, as perfected by the leaders in a given industry. Best practices, documented by quantitative and qualitative data, serve as a framework for achieving or striving for excellence. Benchmarking is one of the fastest ways to determine where the firm stands with industry best practices and to identify areas where best practices may be of highest benefit to the firm.

The American Productivity and Quality Center (APQC) offers a definition of best practice:

> There is no single "best practice" because best is not best for everyone. Every organization is different in some way—different missions, cultures, environments, and technologies. What is meant by "best" are those practices that have been shown to produce superior results; selected by a systematic process; and judged as exemplary, good or successfully demonstrated. Best practices are then adapted to fit a particular organization.[6]

The best practices method is an integrated, comprehensive way of doing business more efficiently or with greater operational effectiveness. Best practices are determined by interviewing experts, sifting through company experiences, reviewing current business literature and academic research, and gathering information from employees, experts, consultants, and field specialists.

Potential Benchmarking Targets

What processes are typically benchmarked? A benchmark target can be any function within a firm that is important in enabling the organization to successfully deliver its products and services. Almost all professional services

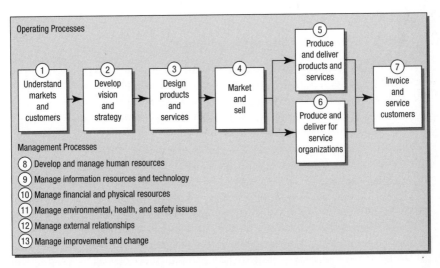

Exhibit 2.1   Operating and Management Processes

organizations perform similar business functions that are categorized as either operating or management oriented. Exhibit 2.1 shows a process classification framework codeveloped by PricewaterhouseCoopers' Global Best Practices® and APQC's International Benchmarking Clearinghouse with its founding members. The framework targets the objectives behind benchmarking the major operating or management processes.

"These categories create a common ground for business professionals in different industries to compare similar processes, ensuring an 'apples to apples' approach to benchmark processes against one another and against best practices,[7] as business processes are the lowest common denominator of companies," says Susan Leandri, managing director of Global Best Practices, for PricewaterhouseCoopers.

When Is It Time to Benchmark?

There are no predetermined points in a firm's life cycle when executives should initiate benchmarking. Still, there may be some clues or triggers. It could be the realization that the HR department isn't running as efficiently as possible. Or, it might be when the firm reaches the next plateau in size, such as when a law firm that had comfortably run with 15 employees suddenly expands to 50 employees following a merger. Or, it could arise in considering, "Are there ways to bring administrative costs per professional staff down?" Change is difficult, but the stress of change on staff can be mitigated by implementation of benchmarks that have a visible, positive impact. Furthermore, the objective nature of benchmarks can help highlight the need for change and reduce the impression that the firm is simply "rearranging the deck chairs."

When There Isn't Time to Benchmark

The chief financial officer of a medium-size consulting firm of 1,100 people, of whom 850 are billable professionals, has 70 people reporting to him in the areas of finance, HR, real estate, and IT. He believes in running a lean operation, with staffing for each function kept at exactly the headcount required to get the job done.

Still, he tries to stay ahead of the curve; since 1999 there have been six acquisitions, and as a result he maintains a staff that verges on overstaffing because he never wants to be caught at the next acquisition with inadequate back office support. His mission at the time of an acquisition is to physically integrate functions such as billing almost immediately after the transaction closes. When the company was launched five years ago, it had $35 million in revenue. It went though a public offering and today has revenue of approximately $500 million, with SG&A coming in at 20 percent of revenue.

"Should I benchmark to be more efficient?" he asks. "Of course I should. But I don't have the time. My one concession: I try to pay close attention to billing rates and how billable the professionals are, as well as establishing criteria for billing hours at each level that are market-based and cost-driven. And one day I'll do a formal benchmarking study. For now, this interim system works for us." This chief financial officer (CFO) has discovered that whether he likes it or not, triage is often the operative phrase in a professional services firm. The outlay of time for a benchmarking exercise won't equal the benefits—at this point in the firm's life.

Getting Started

An early decision in the benchmarking process is whether to handle the project internally or whether to hire an outside consultant. For a number of industries with large and organized professional associations, such as the American Bar Association (ABA), Society of Human Resource Managers (SHRM) or the American Medical Association (AMA), the data required for benchmarking can be easily and reasonably purchased. For example, the ABA can provide statistical data on the industry standards for billable hours for associates and partners and for hourly fees, broken down by firm size and geographical location. There are numerous other large industry organizations that offer dependable information and forums in which they discuss performance issues and other useful information resources.

If the internal benchmark targets are complex, if there are too many areas to benchmark, or if it is difficult to access data for your particular industry, the firm should consider hiring an outside consultant. To minimize the costs of consultants, a firm can do a great deal of preparation work itself and/or pare down the list of possible benchmarks to critical categories so that there are fewer areas to explore.

Whether conducting the benchmarking internally or using an outside consultant, the following multistep process will help achieve reliable benchmarking results:

1. Decide specifically which area(s) to benchmark.
2. Identify and communicate the objective of the benchmarking study.
3. Understand and communicate the processes involved.
4. Recognize and understand the best practices.
5. Compare performance data.
6. Import and adapt new standards.
7. Implement change.[8]

Other factors for success are less obvious or process-driven but are just as critical to the success of any benchmarking effort:

- Management commitment
- Clear objectives and plans
- Consistent and accurate data
- Openness/willingness for improvement (and change)
- Implementation[9]

It is essential that the firm identify the objective of the benchmarking process. All too often firms do not identify the objective of the project and find themselves losing sight of the targeted goal for the exercise, whether it is continuous improvement, understanding the process, or just for informational purposes.

Benchmarking a Professional Services Firm

We now take a closer look at the benchmarking process in four areas that are key functions in any professional services firm: revenue and expense, finance and accounting, IT, and HR. These benchmarks are best developed through collaboration with the professional and administrative staff in each area. They are in the best position to suggest changes and innovations—and they will know best which changes will work.

Benchmarking Revenue and Expense

Within the actual "business" of the services firm, there are five critical areas to examine: time management, revenue drivers, controllable costs, professional costs, and profitability.

TIME MANAGEMENT. Executives, partners, and vice presidents' time is usually oversubscribed between competing priorities and activities. These activities could include but are not be limited to:

- Client service
- Marketing and business development to sell and promote the firm and related tactics to build the business pipeline and generate future revenue for the organization
- Managing and developing people—the firm's principal asset

- Performing support/administrative services to ensure that the organization runs smoothly, efficiently, and in accordance with the firm's business requirements

Time allocation should reflect the tasks required to achieve the business plan and strategic goals set by the organization. However, even that may be difficult because professionals tend to focus on tasks they are comfortable doing (usually client service), as opposed to tasks at which they are not as proficient. We next examine time allocation of managing partners and regular partners.

Managing Partner Time Allocation. By definition, managing partners or chief executives must devote more of their time to managing the firm and less to client work. How much time allocation toward firm management is reasonable? The answer to this depends on the size of the firm. One study found that the larger the size of the law firm, the more time partners spend on firm management rather than practicing law. In fact, the study found that the managing partner typically spends 12 percent of his or her time on firm management if there are fewer than five employees but more than 60 percent once the employee count reaches 100 or more. This is a staggering adjustment and in one sense seems counterintuitive. Certainly, a 100-attorney law firm would have additional administrative support for a managing partner; however, this support is counterweighted with the complexities of the business thus requiring greater attention from the managing partner. The finding is congruent with the laws of leverage. If the managing partner can improve the efficiency and effectiveness of 100 or more attorneys, even a slight improvement in this efficiency would greatly outweigh the economic benefit of the managing partner billing a few more hours that month. Why wouldn't a managing partner drop all client service work altogether? The main reason is that they want to stay sharp and "practice" the business; otherwise, over time, their client skills, knowledge, and capabilities would dull to the point that they may not be a good representative of the firm, which would jeopardize their managing partner status. As the firm gets larger, it will take more and more time to manage, and this time usually comes from the managing partner.

Regardless of the size of the firm, managing partners spend approximately 10 percent of their time on business development to ensure a steady flow of new prospects and revenue stream (see Exhibit 2.2).[10]

Partner Billable/Nonbillable Hours. Regular partners/vice presidents have large time demands similar to the managing partner; however, the driver of these demands will be more client focus and staff development. Each firm will have its own economic model for partner target utilization. Time spent

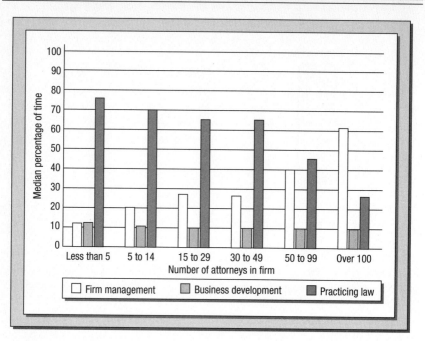

Exhibit 2.2   Managing Partner Time Allocation (average hours per week)

on other areas such as professional development, administrative tasks, and marketing will all depend on the partners' strengths and the needs of the firm. Typically, time spent is 50 percent on billable activity, 10 percent on client relationship development, 20 percent on sales activities, 10 percent on personnel development, and 10 percent on administration. As the firm grows and the administrative management time increases, the partner will typically work more hours to keep the same number of hours in the other activities. Exhibit 2.3 demonstrates this trend.[11]

Partners in smaller consulting organizations spend approximately 50 percent of their time on billable work and 50 percent of their time on nonbillable work. Partners at midsize management consulting firms spend the same number of hours as their small company counterparts, yet the percentage of billable time decreases to 36 percent. Hours have been added to manage the overhead of a larger company. The trend continues to a great degree for partners of larger size firms. Again, these partners spend the same number of hours billing, yet that billable time is now only 31 percent of their workweek.

REVENUE DRIVERS.   What differentiates professional services firms from other industries is that they bill clients for the time incurred by their

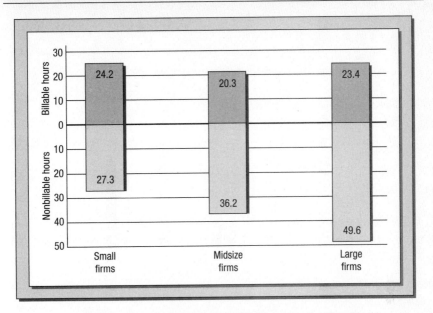

Exhibit 2.3   Partner Billable/Nonbillable Hours by Firm Size
(average hours per week)

professionals instead of charging for delivering a packaged product. The billing can be based on an hourly rate, a set fee for performance of a project, or a set fee for a recurring service. Revenue is a factor of the following:

1. Bill rates
2. Billable hours
3. Professional staff leverage

In addition, the following definitions of firm size are useful:

- *Small:* Less than $5 million in annual revenue
- *Midsize:* Between $5 million and $25 million in annual revenue
- *Large:* Greater than $25 million in revenue

Primary metrics besides these factors are used to understand revenue trends, including:

1. *Utilization:* Billable hours divided by hours available
2. *Realization:* Actual hours billed times actual bill rate divided by billable hours times standard bill rate.
3. *Sales pipeline:* Initial contacts through bids/proposal submitted

While it doesn't drive revenue, accounting efficiency can have a dramatic impact on it, notably:

- Are the proper billing rates being used?
- Has all time and expense incurred during a particular billing period been accurately captured?
- Was the project profitable (billed versus incurred)? If not, it is crucial to identify why and how the project could have been approached differently.
- Is the client paying its bills? If not, do we continue working on the account?

There are two methods to develop bill rates. Most firms develop billing rates by professional staff level (e.g., consultant, associate). In the first method, they start with the level's average direct labor cost (average salary); burden this cost with taxes, benefits, and overhead (i.e., occupancy, general administrative, technology); and add on a target profit margin. The billing rate for a particular professional staff is generally fully loaded with certain costs and a built-in profit margin.

The second method used by firms with better brand recognition or proprietary services (e.g., bankruptcy processing services) may set billing rates based on a tradition pricing curve or supply/demand approach—basically setting the bill rate as high as the market will bear. Law firms and financial consulting firms operate in a competitive marketplace with little regulation and thus may set bill rates at the level their clients will pay. However, in some professional service areas, rates may be regulated, such as the health care industry or services for the government, which dictates acceptable rates and guidelines for billing structures.

We next examine several recent studies on bill rates.

Standard Hourly Billing Rates by Staff Level. Standard hourly billing rates vary among different staff levels at law firms. As a general rule, equity partners/shareholders and of-counsel attorneys typically bill at the highest rates. The biggest jump in billing rates occurs between the associate and partner levels, as shown in Exhibit 2.4.[12]

Median Hourly Billing Rates by Firm Size. As the size of a law firm grows, the median hourly billing rates increase at all staff levels. However, as Exhibit 2.5 demonstrates, equity partners' rates increase at a greater rate than associates' rates as the firm size increases.[13]

Quartile Analysis of Billing Rates by Position for Management Consulting Firms. As Exhibit 2.6 illustrates, billing rates vary significantly: up to 25

Standard Hourly Billing Rates

STATUS	NUMBER OF OFFICES	NUMBER OF LAWYERS	AVERAGE ($)	RATE			
				LOWER QUARTILE ($)	MEDIAN ($)	UPPER QUARTILE ($)	NINTH DECILE ($)
Equity partner/shareholder	626	7,384	261	200	250	300	375
Non-equity partner	324	1,531	237	190	230	275	315
Associate lawyer	606	6,572	178	140	170	200	250
Staff lawyer	101	355	171	135	165	200	231
Of counsel	256	692	254	200	245	300	350

Annual Client (Billable) Hours Worked

STATUS	NUMBER OF OFFICES	NUMBER OF LAWYERS	AVERAGE	HOURS			
				LOWER QUARTILE	MEDIAN	UPPER QUARTILE	NINTH DECILE
Equity partner/shareholder	588	6,466	1,744	1,486	1,729	1,969	2,236
Non-equity partner	284	1,098	1,751	1,501	1,773	1,990	2,203
Associate lawyer	544	4,322	1,842	1,674	1,869	2,031	2,194
Staff lawyer	58	160	1,630	1,391	1,628	1,855	2,044
Of counsel	144	302	1,534	1,219	1,544	1,840	2,067

Exhibit 2.4   Standard Hourly Billing Rates and Billable Hours

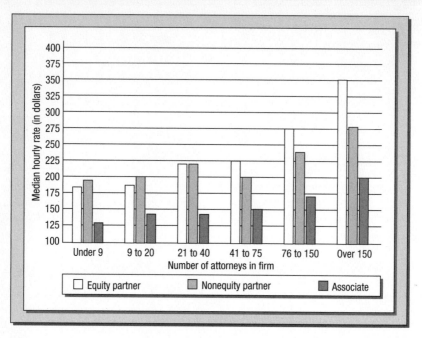

Exhibit 2.5   Median Hourly Billing Rates by Firm Size

percent between the 50th and 75th percentiles and up to 44 percent between the 50th and 25th percentiles. The distribution of rates around the median is fairly tight for partner and project manager positions, although consultant and associate rates fall across a wider range.[14]

CONTROLLABLE COSTS.   While labor consumes 50 percent to 70 percent of the firm's costs, managing other costs in SG&A can still provide dramatic improvements in profits. There are specific criteria and guidelines that will assist a prudent businessperson in keeping down costs, which have

QUARTILE	PARTNER ($)	PROJECT MANAGER ($)	CONSULTANT ($)	ASSOCIATE ($)
Twenty-fifth percentile	184	144	100	70
Fiftieth percentile (Median)	250	200	160	125
Seventy-fifth percentile	300	250	200	150
High value	750	500	350	250

Exhibit 2.6   Analysis of Billing Rates by Position

an impact on the bottom line. Critical areas of focus in cost management opportunities are:

- Internal meetings, seminars, and training
- Travel time and expenses
- Staff expense reimbursement

As a professional services firm, it is important to train, develop, and communicate with professional and administrative staff. Staff meetings—by practice group, office, department, or firmwide—are critical, but the methods and costs of these meetings can be managed. Some suggestions for cutting meeting costs include: holding internal meetings in the office rather than at hotels or resorts; if multiple locations are involved, holding the meetings in the city where the majority of the participants reside; consolidating multiple areas/topics to eliminate multiple trips; and using videoconferencing/web-based meetings for both internal and clients.

Although there are capital expenditure costs to videoconferencing, in the long run, it saves time and relieves employees of burdensome business travel. Companies with multiple locations or clients in remote or difficult-to-reach locations often find videoconferencing helpful and much more personal than conference calls.

A recent analysis of a multioffice management consulting firm with revenues of $200 million determined the optimal target for meeting expenses to be 1 percent of revenue. To maintain such a ratio, managers must make specific decisions about implementing policies that reduce expenses.

Professional staff training is a necessary part of the development and growth in any professional services firm. But it is important to evaluate the training need by level or department. For example, CPAs and attorneys need a certain number of hours of continuing professional education within a given year to maintain their licenses. The controller and others on the accounting staff may need to use outside training and courses to ensure the firm's CPAs adhere to Sarbanes-Oxley training requirements. As an executive seeking to control costs, your job is to ask about the necessity and reasonableness of such expenditures.

When nonclient travel is required, the same policies and procedures should be enforced as they would be in client travel. Consider bringing outside consultants into the office to conduct training for a group of employees, versus the cost of sending those employees outside to attend an accredited course. And, by all means, encourage the professional staff to present to one another to promote learning and continuing education. This can be a worthwhile, cost-effective, and enjoyable way to educate and train. Chapter 10 covers the topic of professional staff training, development, and career tracks in greater detail.

PROFESSIONAL COSTS. A major cost in a professional services firm is personnel cost for the professional staff whose primary responsibility is to serve clients and generate revenue. Determining appropriate compensation is a multifaceted process that includes analysis of the industry, a firm's rank within its sector (including industry/benchmarking studies), current market rates (what it would take to replace the level of experience and expertise that a certain professional has), and compensation ranges within your organization.

For law firms and financial consulting firms, compensation varies significantly based on the following factors:

- Size of the organization
- Industry specialty
- Geographic location
- Target utilization of staff

For example, a law firm may expect first-year associates to charge 1,800 billable hours in a typical 2,080-hour year (based on 80 hours of holidays and 120 hours of vacation time). Thus, an associate is expected to work 50 hours per week on average, which could vary from 40 to 100 hours, based on client needs.

In most professional services firms, billable hours play a significant role in the overall performance assessment of a professional, affecting promotions and compensation. While each organization has a required number of billable hours for each staff level, cultural expectations of the organization play an equally weighted role in measuring performance. For example, the dynamic of "face time" is a crucial measurement within law firms and other professional services organizations. Even if not engaged in billable work, legal associates are expected to stay in the office, seek additional work, and provide assistance to others in need. These parameters vary from firm to firm, so each organization should establish its own billable hour requirements and measurement standards.

The two most important measurements regarding professional staff in a services firm are the generation of revenue by billing time to clients (billable hours) and total compensation of the professionals generating that revenue. Chapter 10 covers compensation issues in more detail.

Billable/Nonbillable Hours by Employment Level (Average Hours per Week). As Exhibit 2.7 shows, billable hours vary between 45 percent and 75 percent for management consultants. Consultant-level professionals achieve the highest percentage, while project managers are billable roughly two-thirds of a workweek. Partners, who have additional selling and firm management responsibilities, average roughly 45 percent billable time per week. Associates are billable 56 percent of the workweek.[15]

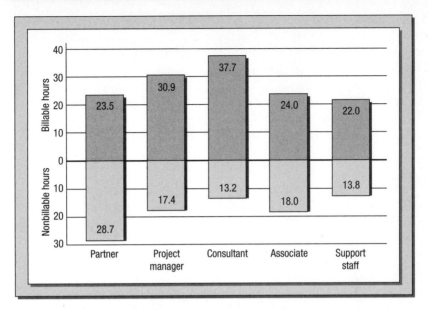

Exhibit 2.7 **Billable/Nonbillable Hours by Employment Level
(average hours per week)**

Total Compensation. Exhibit 2.8 summarizes total compensation for the various levels of employees at law firms. The average compensation across all levels is $172,000. Equity partners/shareholders' average total compensation is $299,391, which is significantly greater than that of other levels.[16]

Median Total Compensation by Firm Size. Similar to hourly billing rates, the median total compensation increases at all staff levels as the firm size increases, as shown in Exhibit 2.9. The higher partner levels are rewarded more significantly as the firm size increases in comparison to the average and lower partners.[17]

PROFITABILITY. The senior executives of professional services firms are responsible for the overall profitability of the organization. This can be measured in many ways, but one helpful statistical tool is the average income and expenses per professional.

Average Income and Expense per Lawyer as a Percentage of Receipts. The majority of expenses per lawyer as a percentage of receipts are allocated to employees' compensation—approximately 60 percent to lawyers, 15 percent to support staff, and 4 percent to paralegals (see Exhibit 2.10).[18]

STATUS	NUMBER OF OFFICES	NUMBER OF LAWYERS	TOTAL COMPENSATION				
			AVERAGE ($)	LOWER QUARTILE ($)	MEDIAN ($)	UPPER QUARTILE ($)	NINTH DECILE ($)
Equity partner/shareholder	615	6,986	299,391	181,692	246,799	342,125	474,580
Nonequity partner	290	1,133	175,447	134,116	159,051	191,997	265,000
Associate lawyer	540	4,203	116,585	91,635	109,4196	133,087	163,749
Staff lawyer	56	139	102,841	79,919	96,788	118,365	138,471
Of counsel	160	349	165,641	118,142	149,648	201,622	264,089

Exhibit 2.8   Total Compensation

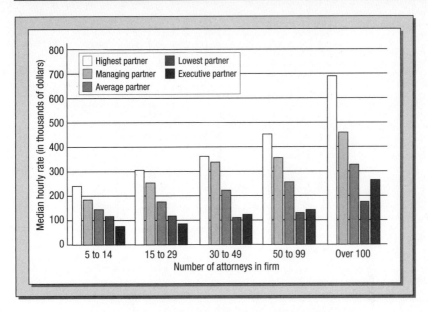

Exhibit 2.9   Median Total Compensation by Firm Size

Average Total Expenses per Lawyer.   Contrary to intuition, there appear to be no economies of scale in a private legal practice, as Exhibit 2.11 demonstrates. Larger firms almost always spend more per lawyer on staffing, occupancy, equipment, promotion, malpractice and other nonpersonnel insurance coverage, office supplies, and other expenses than do smaller firms.[19] This is

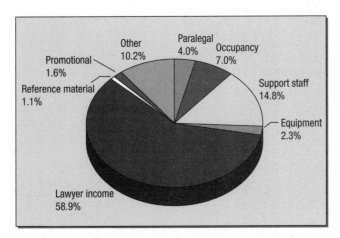

Exhibit 2.10   Average Income and Expenses per Lawyer
as a Percentage of Receipts

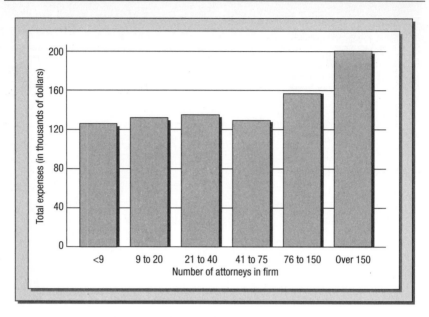

Exhibit 2.11 Average Total Expenses per Lawyer

likely due to firms spending more on such things as their size increases to improve productivity, firm perception, and so on. For example, a successful firm may move into a more upscale office space.

Benchmarking the Finance Department

The finance and accounting department in a professional services firm provides nearly the same functions as that of any other industry. In a professional services firm, a well-functioning department is critical to delivering outstanding client service. The primary business objective of a finance department is to provide accounting services and financial information in an efficient, accurate, and timely manner. A finance department includes the following processes:

- Accounts receivable
- Accounts payable
- Billing
- Payroll
- Travel and entertainment accounting
- Financial reporting (closing the books)

- Budgeting and analysis
- Fixed assets accounting
- Internal audit
- Tax

The objectives of a highly efficient and effective finance function are to provide users (senior management, board of directors/partners, operations, and outside constituencies) with the right information, at the right time, and in the right format. PricewaterhouseCoopers' Global Best Practices® created a benchmark report profiling companies in the $7 million to $486 million range with the average at $195 million. This report attempts to understand the multifaceted characteristics of a finance department through benchmarking. Their report includes the following critical best practices benchmarking data:

- Total finance department cost as a percentage of revenue
- Total finance head count as a percentage of total
- Finance department cost as a percentage of revenue by process

As reflected in Exhibit 2.12, if the percentage is above the benchmark group's median, it may indicate:[20]

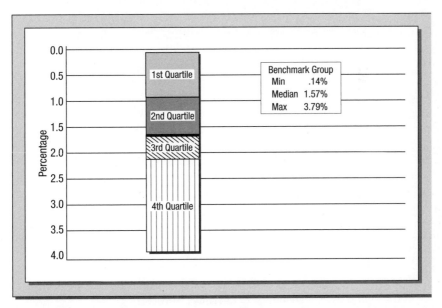

Exhibit 2.12   Total Finance Department Cost as a Percentage of Revenue

- Revenue is disproportionate to the cost.
- Compensation to the finance and accounting staff may be high.
- Excess staffing exists.
- Processes are highly decentralized.
- Technology is underutilized.

Exhibit 2.13 represents the most favorable percentage in the benchmark group.[21] Firms can improve performance on these measures by reducing costs to operate the departments. Strategies to accomplish this may include redesigning work processes to eliminate the causes of errors and wasted time, implementing technology that speeds the transactions, and addressing excess labor costs.

The measures in Exhibit 2.14 represent the number of finance employees relative to the organization as a whole and whether the finance departments are staffed to adequately address the firms' needs. This percentage can be used as an indicator of the departments' ability to design and plan work effectively.[22]

Leading companies improve performance on this measure by increasing the expertise and productivity of the finance professionals, while reducing the total number of finance employees. Strategies to accomplish this may include

PROCESS	BEST IN BENCHMARK (%)
Total finance	0.145%
Payroll	0.010%
Travel and entertainment accounting	0.002%
Accounts payable	0.030%
Billing	0.005%
Accounts receivable	0.001%
Close-the-books/financial reporting	0.027%
Financial budgeting and analysis	0.002%
Fixed-assets accounting	0.004%
Internal audit	0.002%
Tax	0.005%

**Exhibit 2.13   Finance Department Cost as a
Percentage of Revenue by Process**

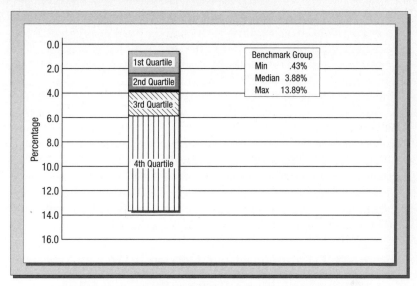

Exhibit 2.14   **Total Finance Head Count as a Percentage of Total Business Unit Head Count**

centralizing the finance functions; implementing technology that reduces routine, repetitive work; and employing fewer staff in total, while elevating the level of expertise for each position.[23]

Benchmarking Information Technology

Information technology is one area where there is nearly universal agreement: Costs are both mysterious and confusing. Executives generally do not know how to determine what their firm's IT costs should be. We provide some guidance to help answer the following questions:

- What are considered reasonable IT expenses?
- What are the key drivers of IT costs?
- What is a reasonable spending level for the IT function?

MEASURING INFORMATION TECHNOLOGY EXPENSES. IT expenses in a professional services firm should be considered as a percentage of revenue. For example, in a mid-size firm, IT costs should range from 1 percent to 3 percent of revenue. This is a key metric used in all organizations and is a helpful planning and benchmarking tool. Remember, though, that the range can be significant based on the nature of the users and the type of business. The higher end range would be applicable to financial consultants, who work long hours, often on the road at client locations. They are considered "intense users" requiring laptops, connectivity (the ability to dial in and have access to Internet and firm servers), and a 24/7 help desk. By comparison, a medical practice typically requires desktop computers for select staff, has set work schedules, and deals more with application-based requirements such as billing and Health Insurance Portability and Accountability Act (HIPAA) compliance.

One significant factor that increases a professional services firm's IT costs is multioffice locations, which typically need to communicate with both the front and back offices of an organization. The thinner the spread of the firm, the greater is the potential for diseconomies of scale. The topic of benchmarking and IT costs is discussed in detail in *The Executives Guide to Information Technology,* (Wiley, 2002) Chapters 3 and 13.

INFORMATION TECHNOLOGY COST DRIVERS. There are many potential IT cost drivers. Exhibit 2.15 outlines a number of factors to consider when analyzing a firm's IT spending.[24]

ECONOMIES OF SCALE IN INFORMATION TECHNOLOGY—ARE THEY ACHIEVABLE? Scale economies have an impact on spending levels and are an important consideration when looking at purchasing power and the ability of size to drive down costs. This makes perfect sense—but current trends and recent IT benchmarking show that, as companies grow, so do their IT requirements. When growing or expanding through acquisitions, firms want more technological capability. That means more service (e.g., they want to expand help desk hours from five days to seven days a week), more sophisticated software, or upgraded hardware. They perceive larger competitors as awash with IT perks or simply believe they have been sacrificing until now and that their growing organization should have all the bells and whistles.

As law firms expand, all costs expand as a percentage of revenue, not just IT costs. In addition, labor costs are a significant expense for firms' IT departments. Labor costs are 30 percent to 40 percent of the average IT budget.

Five key drivers determine IT staffing levels:

1. Number of end users supported
2. Number of systems supported
3. Number of sites supported and geographic dispersion
4. Support requirements
5. Complexity of the environment (number of different types of applications, systems, and networks)

IT COST DRIVER	COMMENTS	AREAS AFFECTED
Industry	Some industries dictate higher IT spending, e.g., Transportation-airline reservation systems	General spending
Company size (sales, profitability, number of end users, type of end users)	Company revenue Number of knowledge workers Number of professionals	General spending Support Capital items
Number of computers per knowledge worker	IT costs rise with the number of personal computers deployed	Purchase of PCs Support
Complexity of internal operations	Outsourcing functions should lower IT costs since no longer have to support Computational intensive environments will increase IT costs	Personnel Hardware Maintenance Integration
Historical capital spending	Historical CapEx spending does not drive increased cost, however increased depreciation expense will affect the IT budget, e.g. purchasing Mainframe will affect depreciation for 3 to 5 years of useful life of the equipment	Depreciation Capital expenditures
Current economic/marketplace condition	Economic pressures will increase need to cut IT spending Profitable companies tend to spend more on IT	Personnel Overhead
Competitive initiatives	Major business transformation projects such as supply chain reengineering will precipitate major IT expenses to support	Personnel Software Hardware
Demands from customers or suppliers	Pressure from customers or suppliers for electronic information flows and other types of computer-related messaging can drive up IT expenditures in the short term	Software
Merger and acquisition activity	Acquisitions and mergers acquisitions will drive IT integration costs Potential economies of scale in the long term	Personnel Integration

Exhibit 2.15   Key Drivers of IT Cost

(continued)

IT COST DRIVER	COMMENTS	AREAS AFFECTED
Age of infrastructure	As age of infrastructure increases, cost to support generally increases	Maintenance
Central vs. decentralized IT operations	Decentralized IT operations tend to increase IT spending due to lack of controls and volume discounts	Personnel Software Hardware
Number of platforms	Costs increase in relation to the number of supported platforms Standardization of environments lowers IT costs	Personnel Maintenance
Application complexity	Application complexity drives higher support costs	Maintenance
Application age	Application age drives higher support costs	Maintenance
Central v s. decentralized purchasing	Decentralized purchasing tends to increase IT spending due to lack of controls and inability to leverage purchasing volume	Personnel Software Hardware
Standardization	Standardization of environment, technical platform and tools reduces IT spending	Hardware Support/Maintenance
Chargeback mechanism employed	Chargeback mechanism can lower IT spending by driving more rationale behavior with business units, for example, market pricing	General spending

Exhibit 2.15   *Continued*

Creating an IT budget requires the analysis of a large number of variables and the weighing of multiple competing priorities, while devising the most cost-effective approach for delivering mission-critical services. Because of the impact the budget has on the IT department's ability to run effectively, budget creation is one of the most important jobs of an IT manager.

One area to consider for benchmarking is the breakout of spending for an IT budget. A professional services firm IT budget should have these spending ranges:

Labor (staff, professional services)	25 to 35 percent
Software/software maintenance	10 to 20 percent
Hardware/hardware maintenance/hardware depreciation	20 to 30 percent
Data communications	5 to 15 percent
Miscellaneous/supplies/travel expenses	5 to 10 percent

Determining IT spending decisions is a critical factor in enhancing firm profitability. Estimation and benchmarking of IT spending provides focus and validation of the firm's current spending and investment strategy. This process can also educate senior management and provide deeper insight into company-specific IT spending and its impact on profitability. Regardless of the outcome of the benchmarking exercise, firms should invest only in projects that meet the business or strategic criteria of their organization.

Benchmarking Human Resources

HR departments should be managed as strategic assets and that HR performance should be measured in terms of its strategic impact on the business of the firm. Such an initiative forces managers to regard HR as an entity that must be structured and managed to create value.

While viewing HR as a strategic asset is certainly a best practice, planning and implementation can be successfully undertaken only if staff understand how their jobs contribute to company success. Often, employees don't understand how their job fits into the big picture.

The people factor is a simple concept: Investing in human creativity delivers high returns in terms of job satisfaction and shareholder returns. Implementation requires sustained attention to a set of basic rules. In a poor economic climate, managers who are overly focused on achieving short-term returns through cost cutting often run against the grain of the people factor. People must understand where they fit into the overall strategy and believe they are valued. Evidence suggests that companies with the foresight to see beyond immediate business difficulties will emerge from a business or economic downturn with renewed strength.[25]

When developing, managing, or expanding the human resources department to meet a company's changing needs, it is important to focus on the services HR provides. A firm's approach to building and staffing its HR function should parallel its approach to client service and should be guided by some key qualitative and quantitative determinations. Service firms understand the need to not staff a client engagement or project with too many or too few professionals or too inexperienced or too senior professionals. Similarly, firms should seek the same balance of staff to handle the most important element in its own organization—its people, also known as "the inventory that goes home at night." Exhibits 2.16 and 2.17 illustrate target ratios of partner to professional staff for law firms and management consulting firms.[26, 27]

PARTNER LEVERAGE

For each partner in a typical management consulting firm, there are an additional five to six FTEs in other positions. This includes other professional positions, leveraged at 1:25 to 1:75, and a support staff position.

AVERAGE PERSONNEL RATIOS BY FIRM SIZE FOR LAW FIRMS

As the size of the firm increases, the ratio of associates to partners/shareholders increases. The most significant increase occurs when firms grow from 75 to 150 lawyers to greater than 150 lawyers. The ratio of associate to partner/shareholder jumps from 0.69 to nearly 1.

No organization achieves 100 percent satisfaction among employees; however, the firm must strive for high levels to ensure proper retention of professional staff and high-quality delivery of services. As a company grows, it is imperative to instill equality and to document the company's policies and

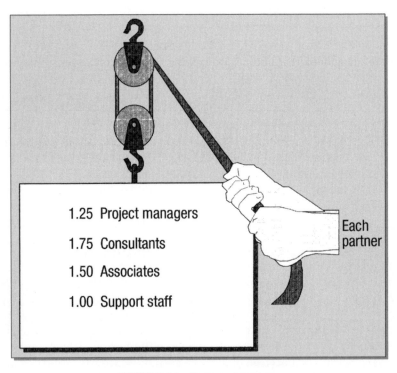

1.25 Project managers

1.75 Consultants

1.50 Associates

1.00 Support staff

Each partner

Exhibit 2.16   Partner Leverage

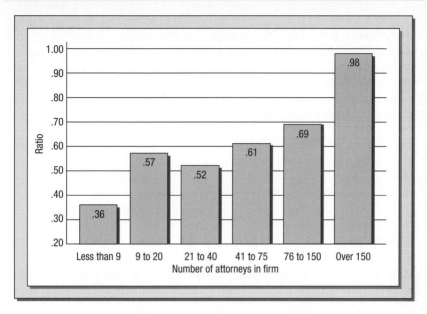

Exhibit 2.17   Average Personnel Ratios

procedures. Whether your firm has 20 or 1,000 employees, you must have an employee handbook that outlines everything that affects how employees are treated. Rules are helpful both in sports and professional arenas, and employees want to know what the rules are and what happens when they are not followed. In many ways, a firm's employee handbook mirrors its approach to business, where attention to detail and explanations of services are provided. Consequently, an employee handbook can serve as a good benchmarking tool. (The CD-ROM accompanying this book includes a sample listing of policies and procedures that should be considered for inclusion in standard employee handbooks.) Chapters 10 and 11 cover the topic of employee retention and satisfaction in more detail.

Applications and Limits of Benchmarking

Benchmarking can be an invaluable tool for the professional services firm executives. While it can provide insight for improvement in areas such as quality, costs, revenue, and time, benchmarking does not provide the definitive answer to *every* business problem. As with any analytical tool, benchmarking has a number of limitations and can even pose potential challenges. However, none of these need be insurmountable. In fact, attuned executives can use the following issues to their advantage during the early stages of the benchmarking process, when they can serve to clarify thinking and intent. We have demonstrated a few areas that the professional services firm may consider benchmarking. The senior executives within a given firm will undoubtedly identify a variety of additional areas that can be improved and monitored with benchmarks.

Benchmarkers Beware

Common pitfalls that can cause potential problems in benchmarking include:

- Objective of the benchmarking process is not clearly defined.
- Level in scope set is too detailed or not detailed enough to be used for implementation.
- Confusing benchmarking with participating in a survey. Benchmarking is the process of finding out what is behind the numbers, not just where you rank.
- Believes that pre-existing benchmarks can be found. These may not be applicable to your firm; therefore, you must identify your own benchmarking partners.
- The process is too large and complex to be manageable.
- Confusing benchmarking with research. Benchmarking presupposes that you are working on an existing process that has been in operation long enough to have some data about its effectiveness and its resource costs.
- Misalignment—choosing a benchmarking topic that is not aligned with the overall strategy and goals of the business.
- Selecting a topic that is too intangible and difficult to measure.
- Not establishing the baseline. Analyze your own processes thoroughly.
- Not researching benchmarking partners carefully. Do not ask questions that you should have been able to answer yourself.
- Not having a code of ethics and contract agreed with partners.[28]
- Not being open to change and seeking to understand benefits potentially outside the firm's industry, geographic location, or organizational size.

The number of potential pitfalls versus benefits may seem to be a disincentive for undertaking the benchmarking effort—is the potential gain worth the pain? It is helpful to view benchmarking as a holistic process that encompasses and ultimately benefits the entire firm; thus, the benchmarking remedy may be more palatable to the entire organization.[29]

After Benchmarking—What Next?

According to Michelle Porter, Global Best Practices—Benchmarking Services group manager:

Understanding the business, establishing clear objectives, customizing a benchmark group that is aligned with those objectives, managing the users' expectations, and being open to change are essential components for a successful benchmarking project. Benchmarking results are the beginning of a continuous process for an organization to further understand their business and identify their strengths and areas of opportunity. It is equally important for the users to be open to new ideas and consider best practices when evaluating the benchmarking results.[30]

A major rationale for benchmarking is to provide context from which measurements and recommendations can be made to senior management. While you can make the scope of the benchmarking as narrow or far-reaching as desired, it should always have objectives that mesh with a business strategy, a budget, and an expectation of return. It should elicit senior management approval and lead to senior management consensus about the reasons for conducting benchmarking.

Therefore, when presenting benchmarking data, executives should consider the business strategy of the firm and attempt to compare spending with the industry, taking into account the life cycle of your firm. Through identification of the right areas to tackle for benchmarking and hard work on the firm's benchmarking initiative, executives may be able to more easily implement the findings—or not, if findings do not support the firm's business strategy.

An assessment that indicates that the firm's spending is low compared to the industry may indicate that the firm's strategy is to increase profits. As a result, this does not necessarily indicate that spending should rise in response. A minimal spending approach may make the most sense for a company in a low growth mode, as opposed to an expansion and acquisition strategy that would indicate higher spending levels than the industry benchmarking.

Just Do It!

Benchmarking is not just about identification of best practices, but implementation as well—putting the data to use. Changing the way a firm or department performs a business process generally requires the involvement of both the human and financial resources dedicated to the task over a period of time. In addition, successful implementation needs a single point of accountability, realistic goals, and the ability to track the progress toward those goals.

Best practices implementation requires mastering the ability to work within your own firm once the benchmarking is complete. Successful implementation is possible only if diligence and focus are given utmost importance throughout the process, including:

- Establishing a project sponsor who is actively involved in key meetings
- Selecting a dedicated team with a defined role for the team leader

- Clearly defining the roles and responsibilities of team members and designating the team member in charge of communications
- Developing measures of progress and milestones for the implementation team
- Creating a budget for the project[31]

"You must have a clear, consistent vision and dedicated, full-time teams assigned to an implementation project," says Mark Krueger, managing director of Ohio-based AnswerThink Consulting Group. "Technology has to be viewed as an enabler, not the change agent. You also need to have open, honest communication and rely on leadership by example."[32]

Finally, it is important to remember that benchmarking is not just a tool, but also a process—not an end in itself, but a means to improving performance. Thus, it should not be viewed as a one-time event, but as an ongoing commitment to continuous improvement.

Summary

The lawyers, consultants, real estate brokers, and others who work for professional services firms may provide superior advice to their own clients, but sometimes forget to apply basic management tenets and techniques to their own firms. Yet, if professional services executives understand that benchmarking helps improve delivery of client service and is a practical, cost-effective tool that can help build consensus within the organization, they might be more willing to consider using it.

The ingredients for successful benchmarking can be found in best practices, committed management, and a well-run business. Effective management of a company or department is not achieved simply by reducing costs; it is also demonstrated by managing and controlling the business. Whatever pressure executives may be under to improve the bottom line quickly, they also face the danger of eliminating key resources that are essential to managing or growing the business or practice. It is smarter and safer to strike the right balance between functional cost and overall business value.

In a growing firm, it is easy to lose sight of the excessive costs, duplicate support services, and lack of consistent processes and procedures. But in today's competitive environment, these costs can't be ignored, even in the short term. The result of implementing best practices achieved by benchmarking is greater operational efficiency and effectiveness.

For those who believe they should benchmark but are hesitant because of time and resource constraints, some last words of advice: Do a quick mental inventory of your firm. It is a safe bet that there are certain elements of your operation that are not entirely satisfactory or could use improvement—

whether those areas manifest themselves through complaints from clients about billing errors, a competitor charging higher rates with no trouble attracting business, or a certain department in the firm isn't pulling its weight in billable hours. Pick just one of those bothersome areas and begin benchmarking.

You will find it easier than you could have imagined. Implement the changes that seem appropriate. Then tackle the next area. You'll wonder why you didn't use this cost-effective tool earlier.

RESOURCES

Practitioners and students who are interested in further reading and research surrounding the topic of benchmarking are encouraged to consult the following web sites:

www.abanet.org	American Bar Association
www.ama-assn.org	American Medical Association
www.metricnet.com	Metricnet
www.globalbestpractices.com	PricewaterhouseCoopers LLP—Global Best Practices
www.shrm.org	Society for Human Resource Management
www.hackettbenchmarking.com	The Hackett Group

NOTES

1. Norman Vincent Peale, *Words I Have Lived By* (Peggy Pinson, 1993).
2. Robert J. Kennedy, "Benchmarking and Its Myths," *Competitive Intelligence Magazine* (April 2000).
3. Jeff Stimpson, "The Benchmarking Engagement," *Practical Accountant* (February 2003), p. 26.
4. Susan Leandri, Managing Director, PricewaterhouseCoopers, LLP, "Global Best Practices," telephone interview by author, New York, March 8, 2004.
5 Mark Tibergien and Philip Palaveev, "Advisors Are Better at Client Service than at Practice Management," *Journal of Financial Planning* (October 2002), pp. 5052.
6. "National Interpretation Project: Definition of Project Terms," American Association of Museums [accessed July 2004]. Available from http://www.aam-us .org/initiatives/other NIPglossary.cfm.
7. PricewaterhouseCoopers LLP, http://www.globalbestpractices.com.
8. Catherine Lennon and Andrew Tank, eds., "Benchmarking in the Finance Function," The Conference Board (1994).

9. Charles B. Green, "Benchmarking the Information Technology Function," The Conference Board (1993).

10. Altman Weil Inc., *2001 Managing Partner & Executive Director Survey* (Newtown Square, PA: Altman Weil Publications, 2001).

11. Kennedy Information, Inc., *Partner Billable/Nonbillable Hours by Firm Size* (Peterbourough, NH: Kennedy Information, 2002).

12. Altman Weil Inc, *2003 Survey of Law Firm Economics* (Newtown Square, PA: Altman Weil Publications, 2003).

13. Altman Weil Inc, *2002 Survey of Law Firm Economics* (Newtown Square, PA: Altman Weil Publications, 2002).

14. Kennedy Information, Inc., *Quartile Analysis of Billing Rates by Position* (Peterbourough, NH: Kennedy Information, 2002).

15. Kennedy Information, Inc., *Billable/Nonbillable Hours by Employment Level* (Peterbourough, NH: Kennedy Information, 2002).

16. See note 12.

17. See note 10.

18. See note 12.

19. See note 13.

20. PricewaterhouseCoopers LLP, *Finance and Accounting Global Best Practices* (New York: PricewaterhouseCoopers, LLP, 2004).

21. See note 20.

22. See note 20.

23. See note 4.

24. Barbara Gomolski, *Mid-Size Company Summit* (Stanford, CT: Cartner Measurement Services, 2002).

25. James Pickford, ed., *Mastering People Management* (London: Prentice-Hall, 2003).

26. Kennedy Information, Inc., *Partner Leverage* (Peterbourough, NH: Kennedy Information Inc., 2002).

27. See note 12.

28. Anne Evans, *Avoid These 10 Benchmarking Mistakes* (Melbourne, Australia: Benchmarking PLUS, 1999).

29. The Hackett Group, http://www.thehackettgroup.com.

30. Michelle Porter, Group Manager, PricewaterhouseCoopers, LLP, Global Best Practices, telephone interview by the author, New York, March 8, 2004.

31. Christopher E. Bogan, "Benchmarking for Best Practices: Winning Through Innovation Adaptations" (New York: McGraw-Hill, 1994).

32. Ivy McLemore, "Just Do It! Part One of a Series," *Business Finance Magazine* (March 1999).

3

Partnership and Governance Structures

JOHN J. REDDISH

What do we live for; if it is not to make life less difficult to each other?

—George Eliot, *Middlemarch*, 1871

This chapter identifies and clarifies the key issues governing the leadership and governance structure of the firm: legal protections; allocation of equity, compensation, perks, and benefits; and procedures for making and communicating both policy and operational decisions. Each profession has its historical way of organizing, and within each profession, individual firms adopt unique forms, yet the basic tenets of good management apply. Like any other business, the professional services firm is engaged in two businesses—the business of the profession and the business of managing—and both present distinct challenges.

Traditional top-down management structures are the exception rather than the rule, because firm performance encompasses the sum total of the contributions of many peer professionals, professionals with other specialties, as well as other support personnel within its ranks. Most professional services firms operate in project-based environments where individuals with specialized knowledge come together in ad-hoc teams to handle an assortment of individual and multiple projects and/or complex cases on a more collegial basis.

Outside business development or rainmaking activities, firm performance is seldom attributable to a single individual's contributions. And, while individual performance is always important, a better understanding of overall performance is achieved when everyone's contributions are factored into assessing organizational success. More likely, several professionals cooperate to achieve the desired result. When cooperation is lacking and results are not forthcoming, key players (and the best move fastest) tend to vote with their feet, making new combinations with like-minded individuals or firms when differences become too severe or too prolonged.

Professional services firms range in size from the sole practitioner to the multinational megafirm. Resources on managing the business abound for entrepreneurs and for the largest firms in virtually every profession but not for the mid-size firm. Therefore, we have chosen to focus our attention on mid-size firms employing multiple professionals in, or with near-term expectations of, ownership and (potentially) a more junior group with ownership aspirations. We also address the issues associated with growth through acquisition and the need to create ownership structures flexible and scalable enough to facilitate growth.

Why This Topic Is Important

Structure is often a major contributing factor in how well staff perform and get along in the professional services firm. A structure that is not appropriate can:

1. Lead to stakeholder (owners, employees, suppliers, customers) disaffection
2. Impede corporate development and growth, including the raising of capital
3. Limit exit strategy options
4. Result in inordinate, and unnecessary, liability being assumed by the principals

After structure, equity must be allocated and compensation plans must be designed and aligned to reinforce the business objectives of the firm while recognizing the individual contributions of each principal and professional employee. Allocation of initial ownership interests is critical, and the ground should be laid to prepare the firm for future growth by setting scalable standards as early as possible in the firm's life. Equally important is to think of future ownership participation when the founder makes the first allocation of ownership interest to key professionals at a later date. Fairness and constancy are two elements of this process that will save the company from needless problems down the road. The decisions made must be documented to ensure orderly transitions. They include, but may not be limited to (depending on the structure chosen and various federal and state statutes and industry requirements for professional service licensure and ownership):

1. Equity agreements between the principals, providing for:
   a. A definition of the ownership interests of each principal
   b. Terms under which ownership can be transferred, including restrictions
2. A mutually agreed on valuation approach and an ongoing valuation schedule
3. Employment and noncompete agreements for all principals and key employees, including provisions for termination

Firms failing to adequately separate equity and performance issues run the risk of eventual failure. Falling prey to the notion that the owner gets his or her compensation through the profit of the firm is faulty. Firm profit is only one element of compensation. In addition, there is the need to provide fair pay, perks, and benefits to principals as well as employees. Particularly in the early days of an enterprise, failure to account for performance, whether money is actually paid or merely accrued (and the taxes paid), can lead to major problems at a later time.

Compensation issues include base salaries, incentives, leverage items (commissions or gain sharing fees), bonuses, "sweat equity," options/warrants, generally accepted employee benefits packages, and executive perks.

Once structure, equity, and compensation for performance are established, the decision management aspect of the firm needs to be established. Who makes decisions and how decisions are made can make the difference in whether a firm survives or fails. The decision-making and management process need not be complicated, but principals must strive for clarity and fairness or an exodus of the best people will soon begin. This chapter reviews several models, noting their strengths and weaknesses.

Ways to Organize: An Overview

There are many ways to structure the professional services firm. But before a structure is chosen, some strategic issues have to be considered:

1. The scope of the business (local, national, or international)
2. The nature of the business (type of practice/industry)
3. Risk and personal liability considerations
4. Tax treatment
5. Capital needs and availability
6. Succession
7. Attracting and retaining talent

While there are a wide variety of ways to structure a business, the most popular are: subchapter C corporations, subchapter S corporations, and limited liability company (LLC) models. Some smaller firms are sole pro-prietorships, and some firms, particularly in the legal arena, are still part-nerships but the unlimited liability issue and the potential challenges of equitable distribution work against these models. Moreover, professional li-censing or industry codes prohibit ownership in a firm by professionals from other disciplines; sole proprietorships and partnerships are not flexi-ble enough to accommodate growth with such restrictions. Exhibit 3.1 (pp. 63–64) summarizes the advantages and disadvantages of each form.

Sole Proprietorship

Sole proprietorships are generally unattractive for a professional services firm of any size. While easy and cheap to start, usually requiring only the fil-ing of a local business license, sole proprietorships provide little or no flexi-bility for growth.

Advantages
1. Start-up costs are inexpensive.
2. Income and expenses of the business flow through directly to the owner.
3. As an extension of the individual, there are no business income tax is-sues.
4. This form works best for smaller, low-risk personal service and some retail businesses.

Disadvantages
1. Personal liability is unlimited for all claims and judgments against the business.
2. It is difficult to bring in others to accommodate growth.
3. Loan capacity is limited to personal loans and personal net worth, plus the value of accumulated assets.
4. Income sheltering and favorable tax treatment options are not gener-ally available.
5. Exit strategies are limited.

Partnerships

Partnerships, whether limited or general, are legal entities in their own right. Partnerships can be formed by individuals, companies, or individuals and companies. A partnership can sign contracts, hold property, and file suit in its own name. Partnerships are dissolved on the death or insolvency of one of the partners, and all partners have unlimited liability for partnership actions irrespective of initiating partner. Most states have minimal requirements for the creation of general partnerships, while limited partnerships typically require only the filing of a one-page certificate of limited partnership.

Advantages

1. Start-up costs are inexpensive.
2. It is easy to establish with two or more entities.
3. Limited registration is required.
4. Partnerships are their own legal entities.
5. Tax treatment is favorable because income and expense flow through to partners.
6. Limited partners' liability is normally restricted to their investment (they can become liable if actively involved in the business).
7. Limited partner income is not subject to self-employment tax.

Disadvantages

1. General partners have unlimited liability.
2. Creditors of a general partner can pursue the partnership and force its liquidation.
3. The partnership normally ends when one partner dies or becomes bankrupt (other partners elect to continue under some circumstances).
4. Adding new partners generally requires consent of all existing partners.
5. Limited partnerships have been attractive to passive investors but pose problems for investors (angel investors, venture capitalists, equity funds) who wish to assume an active role in the company.
6. Valuing partnership interests can be complicated.

Limitations of a Partnership

A good example of organizational structure impeding growth is the case of a construction management firm. The firm, a partnership, employed 7 principals (senior and junior partners) plus about 15 others and was managing about $35 million in construction contracts.

Due to the nature of partnerships (unlimited liability of all named partners for any and all partnership liabilities) and bonding requirements (the need for hard assets to secure bonds), taking on larger projects was problematic. Many bonds required personal guarantees from the principals and were often secured by their homes. This led to variations in opinion among the partnership about acceptable levels of risk and pursuit parameters for new projects.

Within nine months, the firm, with the help of an outside adviser, became a corporation. Bank financing for projects was secured. A valuation formula for the company was established, and one partner was bought out. The remaining principals grew the firm to more than $100 million in sales, eventually selling it to a larger company.

Limited Liability Companies

The LLC is a relatively new organizational structure developed to overcome some of the shortcomings of the limited partnership. All members of an LLC are essentially treated as limited partners in relation to liability issues, but with a difference. Creditors of individual LLC members cannot pursue the entity; bankruptcy (bankruptcy and assignments for the benefits of creditors terminates membership) or the death of a member does not necessarily force its dissolution. A well-thought-out operating agreement explaining all rights and remedies is critical to the LLC's success.

Advantages
1. LLCs can be created by one or two members (individuals, corporations, other LLCs) depending on state law.
2. Most states require the filing of a single-page certificate of formation.
3. Members enjoy limited liability status but may be involved in the business.
4. Members have protection from creditors of individual members.
5. Members have interests, rather than shares, which are more scalable in accommodating internal growth.
6. LLCs may not offer options.
7. Flexible handling of ownership interests, distribution rights, voting rights, income distributions, losses, credits, and deductions can be allocated to members.
8. LLCs can be easily converted to the corporate form.

Disadvantages
1. Adding new members requires the agreement and consent of all existing members (unless provided for in the operating agreement).
2. LLCs are not true corporations and lack case law to support a full range of activities.
3. Interests do not provide for awarding of employee options or stock.
4. LLCs may restrict investment options if outside capital is sought, except in cases of foreign investment where the LLC is a familiar structure.

Subchapter S Corporation

A popular structure for many professional services firms is the subchapter S corporation (S-Corp). The S-Corp has been in existence for many years, and its corporate structure provides well-defined case law in support of the rights of officers, directors, and shareholders. In addition, it allows income and losses to pass through to the individual shareholders. The S-Corp follows the corporate form of the subchapter C corporation (C-Corp) in many ways but without the imposition of a second level of taxation. It has, however, some restrictions such as limitations on the number of shareholders and restrictions on who can own shares. Some of these restrictions have been eased by recent legislation.

For example, S-Corps are no longer limited to 35 shareholders. Under the new regulations, that number has been increased to 75. Stock ownership has also been relaxed. Currently, other corporations can own shares, as can pension plans, stock bonus plans, and profit sharing plans. The new regulations also allow S-Corps to provide stock incentives to employees.

Some restrictions still remain, including restrictions on employee benefits allowable to large shareholders. The S-Corp may still have only one class of stock. Foreign investors are not permitted. Only small business corporations are allowed to elect S-Corp status. While conversion to a C-Corp is possible, conversion to an LLC requires that the corporation be dissolved, leading to potentially adverse tax implications.

Advantages
1. S-Corps have a proven corporate structure.
2. S-Corps have a favorable tax treatment similar to partnerships.
3. Liability protection and regulations as in the corporate form apply.
4. Regulations were recently liberalized.
   a. S-Corps can now have up to 75 shareholders.
   b. Ownership is now open to other corporations and nonprofits.
   c. S-Corps can own subsidiaries.
   d. S-Corps can provide stock incentives to employees.

Disadvantages
1. Only one class of stock is allowed.
2. S-Corps are available only to qualified small business corporations.
3. Foreign investors are not permitted.
4. The form restricts investment options.
5. Employee benefits are limited for large shareholders.
6. Conversion options to LLC may trigger unwanted tax implications.

Scalability Is an Issue in S-Corp Succession Plans

The founding principal in an architectural firm had, over the years, sold a small percentage of ownership to his second-in-command, a person several years his junior, with the understanding that he might eventually purchase more shares. In time, the firm identified another potential owner. He was hired with the express understanding that he would be able to purchase shares pending a one-year trial period. As the year was coming to an end, many issues were left unresolved. No valuation formula had been agreed to by the founder and the candidate, nor had there been any discussion with the second-in-command relative to a new valuation and its impact on his shares. Moreover, the founder had made a decision as part of his personal succession plan to begin a process of divesting his shares to new shareholders as able candidates were identified and invited to join the practice. A scalable and equitable valuation and stock transfer procedure was needed, along with updates to all the corporate documentation. In addition, provisions needed to be made for nonarchitects (designers and specialty engineers) who could not, under American Institute of Architects (AIA) rules, participate in direct ownership of an architectural firm. Finally, options governing the sale of additional shares to current shareholders and potential dilution issues needed to be addressed. Within a year, these programs were in place just in time for the acquisition of a competing firm and the absorption of a new equity owner in the company.

Subchapter C Corporation

The C-Corp is the organizational structure most adaptable to growth. For principals wishing to give the firm maximum advantage in managing rapid growth, attracting investors, providing incentives to key employees, possibly forming an Employee Stock Ownership Plan (ESOP), or wanting to go public,[1] this is the structure to adopt. There are no limitations on the number of shareholders or subsidiaries, and there is ample case law to provide guidance in protecting both majority and minority shareholders.[2] Despite the normalization of corporate law across America, both Delaware and Nevada still enjoy reputations as corporate havens for maximum legal flexibility.

C-Corps provide maximum tax benefit for employee benefits with up to $50,000 in individual benefits deductible. Various classes of stock can be issued on terms favorable to even the pickiest institutional investor or venture capitalist, including provisions for preferred stock options and preferential liquidation rights. The form is also the best choice for owners considering ownership succession.

The biggest downside is the double taxation issue. Unlike other forms of organizational structure, the C-Corp is a taxable entity—which means owners pay taxes at both the corporate and personal level. Similarly, losses do not pass through to the individual investors. Many professional services firms address these challenges by "managing the bottom line," but this practice has limitations, and principals must be careful not to run afoul of IRS rules restricting, and possibly penalizing, this practice when taken to excess (using excessive compensation guidelines and personal holding company penalties as their tools).

An additional challenge also being seen more today has emerged as some attorneys have initiated novel (fraudulent conveyance) strategies to "pierce the corporate veil." Actions usually follow Racketeer Influenced and Corrupt Organizations (RICO) or Employee Retirement Income Security (ERISA) violations, charges of corporate fraud or malfeasance on the part of key shareholders or officers, are related to creditor disputes, and/or are the product of equitable distribution actions in marital dissolutions. Because fraud statutes are often very broad, some plaintiff attorneys use the statutes to "discover" hidden assets or challenge "valuation" approaches.

Advantages

1. The C-Corp has maximum flexibility for growth and expansion.
2. Liability protection and regulations as in the corporate form apply.
3. Companies can convert from S-Corp and LLC.
4. Number of shareholders or subsidiaries are not limited.
5. There are no limitations on who may own shares.
6. Multiple classes of stock and other securities are allowed, along with flexible rights and preferences.
7. This form is not restricted to small business companies.
8. Ample case law exists to defend rights of all involved parties.
9. This is the most attractive form for institutional investors.
10. Stock options are available for employees.
11. Maximum employee benefit deductibility is provided.
12. The C-Corp is the best structure for eventual IPO and/or succession strategy.

Disadvantages

1. There is a potential for double taxation (on corporate income and dividend income).
2. Corporate income and loss cannot be used on a personal level.
3. C-Corp structure requires more formality to be in conformance with legal requirements (failure to conform may become problematic if firm leaders are challenged by dissident shareholders, creditors, estranged spouses or disaffected employees). Conformance requires regular board and shareholder meetings, preparation and maintenance of formal corporate minutes, maintaining records of resolutions, and

some arm's length restraint regarding personal distributions to key shareholders.

4. There are limits on the amount of earnings that can be retained in closely held companies as well as limits on executive compensation levels (before unreasonable compensation and personal holding company penalties are pursued).

Equity and Compensation

It sometimes appears that there are nearly an infinite number of ways to divide equity and establish creative compensation plans. The most popular and accepted plans separate equity and return on equity from job performance. Firms that fail to make this separation and/or cloud compensation issues often experience high turnover and spotty overall firm performance.

Equity

Equity can be allocated in many ways. It can be gifted or awarded, purchased or sold, earned or inherited. Provided the firm has taken the time to establish an ongoing valuation procedure and engages in strategic planning, most processes proceed slowly and peacefully.

The most basic need when dealing with equity in the firm is to determine if those who currently own it want to retain it, give or gift it to a relative, use it to retain the best firm talent, sell it to an individual, or even dispose of it by initiating an ESOP.

With the largest shareholders' intent in mind and a valuation formula in place, serious consideration can be given to how best to use expanded equity participation as a strategic tool.

In increasing the pool of shareholders, the leadership should always be sure to restrict the shareholder's ability to freely resell firm shares. The firm should have the right of first refusal for all outstanding shares at the time of a shareholder's separation or death (shares are often repurchased over a period of time—often 5 years for a friendly parting and 7 to 10 years when asked to leave). This is usually accomplished by adding a legend to each stock certificate detailing the procedure for selling shares.

Stock can be gifted, earned, or awarded based on the operational performance or profitability of the firm and the roles played in achieving those results by those being gifted. So called *sweat equity* programs are defined within this scope and represent a way to acquire excellent talent at what amounts to discounted prices. All stock awards should be commensurate with results over and above a predetermined base level of performance. Shares to be allocated to new and prospective owners in such programs are

ENTITY	ADVANTAGES	DISADVANTAGES
Sole Proprietor	No formation formalities	Unlimited liability
		No structure for investors
		Not suitable if business has other employees
	Partnership-type tax treatment	All income subject to self-employment tax
General Partnership	Flexible management structure	Unlimited liability
	Recognized legal entity with right to contract	Difficult to add new partners
		Difficult to raise capital without bringing in new partners
		Requires 2 or more partners
		Any partner can commit the others
		Death of partner dissolves partnership
	Partnership tax treatment	
Limited Partnership	Limited liability for limited partners	Requires 2 or more partners
	Ability to attract passive investors by making new limited partners	Requires general partner responsible for all obligations
		Limited partners cannot actively participate in management
		Adding new partners may require consent
		Not attractive for institutional investors
		No stock to use for options
		Death of partner may affect continuity depending on partnership agreement
	Partnership tax treatment	
	Income to limited partners not subject to self-employment tax	
Limited Liability Companied	Flexible structure	Body of law not well developed
	Can have different classes of stock, different rights and allocations	No stock to use for options
		Not attractive structure for institutional investors
	Owners can be persons, corporations or other LLCs	Many states require 2 members (not DE or NY)
	Conversion to corporation easy	Death of member may affect continuity
	Familiar structure for foreign investors (GmbH, SARL)	

Exhibit 3.1   Selection of Entity—Summary

(continued)

ENTITY	ADVANTAGES	DISADVANTAGES
	Partnership tax treatment Can convert to C corporation without adverse tax affects	All income may be subject to self-employment tax
Subchapter S Corporation	Security of corporate structure Well defined law on corporations Death of shareholder does not affect continuity of company Qualified tax exempt entities can be shareholders Can have corporations and LLCs as subsidiaries	Can have only 75 shareholders Can have only 1 class of stock No foreign investors Only for qualified "small business corporations" Not suitable for institutional investors Limited employee benefits to large shareholders
	Partnership tax treatment Only salary (not profits) subject to self-employment tax	Conversion to LLC requires liquidation and adverse tax effects Issues on conversion to C corporation Limited flexibility on allocations of income, leases, credits, and deductions
Subchapter C Corporation	Limited liability for shareholders Maximum flexibility on classes of shares, liquidation preferences, voting rights Preferred investment choice for institutional investors Suitable for initial public offering Stocks options available No limit on number or type of shareholders Well-defined law on corporations	More formalities—Board meetings, shareholder meetings, voting issues, etc.
	Most favorable structure for employee benefit plans	Double taxation on dividends (but rate reduced to 15%) Limits on how much of earnings can be retained in closely held companies Limits on level of salary to avoid dividends of closely held companies No pass through of net operating losses to personal return

Exhibit 3.1 *Continued*

often limited to the value of not more than one-third (collectively) of all gains, but actual numbers can vary. The one-third share represents an equal distribution of increased profitability or sales with the other two-thirds being distributed equally—as profit to existing shareholders and as reinvestment in the firm. Shares to family members can also pass from one generation to the next in family firms, depending on stock restrictions. In family firms, before any shares are transferred, the impact of such distribution on nonfamily members should be assessed.

Stock purchased, whether from founder's stock, shares of other large shareholders, treasury stock, or stock from departed employees, is sold as it becomes available. Pricing is based on the share valuation in place at the time of sale. Stock purchases may be cash transactions, or they may be financed over a period of years.

The Succession Leader

In some instances, particularly during a succession process, an interim or bridge CEO or managing director may be engaged. This executive's contract will almost certainly involve either a share-based reward for overseeing a successful transition or some form of *shadow equity* (contractually promised sharing in either a change in control or in the establishment of a new ownership/leadership team) scheme. Most firms and CEOs favor some small stock holding coupled with shadow equity. The benefit of this preferred approach is that capital gains taxes are not due on shadow equity until received (at some future point when the change occurs), as opposed to an equity position that is taxed as received. Vesting in a shadow equity plan does not constitute constructive receipt for IRS purposes.

Whether to pay dividends is a C-Corp issue. Many owners consider that the appreciation in a C-Corp firm's shares, as demonstrated by the annual valuation update, constitutes fair consideration. Any "profits" that can't otherwise be legally expensed are typically given to shareholders as bonus dollars. In the S-Corp and LLC forms, profits pass through to the individual shareholder. For those who take the "appreciation" route, it should be remembered that the shareholders have invested in the company's success. Their shares are the representation of that investment. A fair return should be expected on that investment. The firm should also be careful not to adopt a practice of declaring bonuses that too closely coincide with the salary or shareholder equity percentages of the major shareholders. The IRS sometimes determines that bonus programs that track key executive salaries and stockholdings too closely are really undisclosed dividends. For a quick rule of thumb on industry averages, firm leaders should consider asking their banker for information on their type of firm from their industry research teams. Other benchmarking information can be found in the Annual Statements Study, published periodically by banking industry trade group Robert Morris Associates.[3]

Compensation

Compensation is not only about money. In a professional services firm, where the most valued assets of the business walk out the door every day, it's also about recognition and stability. The elements of compensation create a balance that affords the professional and his or her support staff the peace of mind to focus on the creative work of the firm, thereby enhancing performance (see Exhibit 3.2).

Because there are typically few hard assets, sufficient cash flow is critical in maintaining organizational dynamics. In firms where cash flow is a problem, productivity is adversely impacted almost immediately.

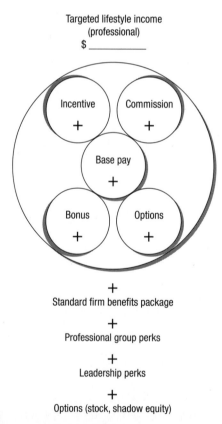

Targeted lifestyle income
(professional)
$ _____

Incentive +   Commission +

Base pay +

Bonus +   Options +

+
Standard firm benefits package

+
Professional group perks

+
Leadership perks

+
Options (stock, shadow equity)

Exhibit 3.2   Typical Compensation Options for Professional Services Firms

Firms should focus on a *targeted lifestyle* income range for all employees. This comprehensive look at compensation permits great flexibility in the allocation of benefits (typical cafeteria plans) and in the development of risk management initiatives, such as self-insurance, that the firm may wish to pursue.

Firms should also be aware that ongoing, uncritical offers of benefits could turn those benefits from a competitive tool into a potential liability. The subject of compensation, benefits, and staff retention are covered in detail in Chapters 9 and 10.

When a Benefit Becomes an Obligation

All compensation issues should be reviewed on a regular basis and modified periodically to prevent the potential risk of a benefit turning into a "condition of employment." Conditions of employment have been the grist of many court cases and can be construed to occur when companies award the same benefits consistently, and without review or alteration, for many years. When, in hard times, a company suddenly begins to cut back on such benefits, and employees have sued, the courts have often supported the employees' claim that the "benefit" had become "a condition of employment."

Compensation, or pay for performance, is typically composed of:

1. Base salary
2. Bonus
3. Incentive plan and gain sharing programs (Items that can be subjected to leverage)
4. Options
5. Commissions
6. Employee benefits
   a. Health, wellness, and lifestyle benefits
   b. Long-term benefits
7. Professional group perks
8. Leadership perks

Regardless of what elements are included in the compensation package, it is important to identify a targeted income level for each principal and employee. Base pay, depending on the nature of the professional's work (e.g., business development versus staff auditing) and the amount of, and leverage potential for, incentive pay usually ranges from 40 percent to 80 percent of total compensation and should be based on comparative wages within the firm's geographic region or industry. Numerous sources for comparative salaries exist, including the U.S. Department of Labor's Bureau of Labor Statistics,[4] various online sources,[5] and local development agencies[6] that track wages as part of their services in attracting companies to a locality. These sources can also provide extensive lifestyle cost information, including prevailing information concerning employee benefits programs.

Bonuses for senior level and other professionals and staff may be established by employment contract, by firm history, or by industry practice. Bonuses are usually discretionary and should be used only to reward extraordinary performance that has been identified and documented. Bonuses are typically paid from profits and represent a share of excess profits before taxes (if a C-Corp), shareholder dividends, reinvestment objectives, and any extraordinary reserves have been paid.

Incentive plans and gain-sharing programs are targeted programs designed to promote a limited objective or to spur short-term objectives. These programs will lose some of their potency if they become de facto awards. These plans are often funded as a percentage of gross income for specific lines of business, accounts, or overall revenue gains. Risk/reward calculations (or leverage) are key to developing and administering effective incentive and gain-sharing programs.

Options represent rewards given to promising professionals within the firm whom firm principals view as next generation leaders. Options usually offer equity participation at a fixed price to eligible participants. Participants can exercise their options with their own monies or, in some instances, can be underwritten by the firm as a form of sweat equity. The value of options floats with the fortunes of the firm, and participants should receive continuing updates on the value of the firm and their options. Shares associated with options programs are usually restricted and may have additional antidumping provisions.

Commissions are normally available only to firm members involved in corporate development and/or sales, although many firms have a finder's fee program that extends to all employees who refer new business to the firm. Commission plans proliferate, and plan terms vary by industry and by locality. Principals should consider a few things in establishing any commission program: Commissions should almost never be paid on gross billings (structure them on net income numbers), and commissions should be keyed to net collected revenues. While employees, including principals, want to be paid commissions in a timely manner, either reserving a portion of the commission or delaying the commission until funds are received is recommended. Charge-backs should never be handled as lump sum transactions. If it is necessary to charge back a commission, do it over a period of time.

Employee benefits programs usually have two parts: short-term benefits characterized as health, wellness, and lifestyle benefits; and long-term benefits characterized as sustenance benefits. The short-term benefits include health insurance; vacation, sick, and personal days; short-term disability;

child care; educational reimbursement; skills training; and so on. Many of these can be bundled into so-called cafeteria programs where, up to a certain dollar amount, employees can choose their own benefit "cocktail." Unemployment insurance and workers' compensation are also considered benefits and need to be considered. Long-term benefits include long-term disability insurance, 401(k) plans, Simplified Employment Pensions (SEPs), profit-sharing plans, and so on and often pick up when short-term benefits expire. Most benefit plans are offered to all employees, typically after a short waiting period.

Principals and professionals in most professional services firms are also accorded perks, which may include reimbursement for certain entertainment and business development expenses and participation in community activities and networking costs. For some, there are company cars or car allowances. For others, there are club dues. The list goes on. Who participates and to what extent is a decision for firm leaders. Perks represent out-of-pocket money. Each expenditure should be periodically reviewed and its value reassessed.

Leadership team members typically have additional perks associated with their roles in guiding the firm. Often these perks are associated with privilege, but if the funds are well spent, it is in the interest of the business to accord them.

All costs associated with compensation need to be viewed both comparatively to ensure marketplace competitiveness and discretely because they are a major component of the firm's pricing structure. How much to bill and how to support pricing decisions are covered in detail in Chapters 7, 9, and 10. The higher the labor content (total costs measured against individual performance) in any firm's capital structure, the more difficult it may be to compete. Costs should be justified by a value proposition that provides an attractive profit margin. In all, a professional services firm is trading hours for dollars. With a finite number of hours in the year and a variety of overhead and necessary investment commitments that eat into those hours, the firm (and individual professionals) must be cautious how billable hours are spent (Exhibit 3.3).

How the professional services firm makes its collective business and policy decisions is extremely varied from firm to firm. Because of the nature of professional services, rigid hierarchical models seldom work for long—professionals tend to want a collaborative environment. Some firms gravitate to a model featuring a moderate leader working collegially with a larger group of influential peers who, in turn, represent critical practice areas or profit centers. Others are attracted to a strong leader moderating the discourse among a larger leadership group. In some instances, professional services firms have reached out and hired professional managers for all, or most, operational functions while reserving practice issue decisions to internal peer groups.

The term *decision management* is appropriate because many professional services firms engage in a less formalized process of decision making. This

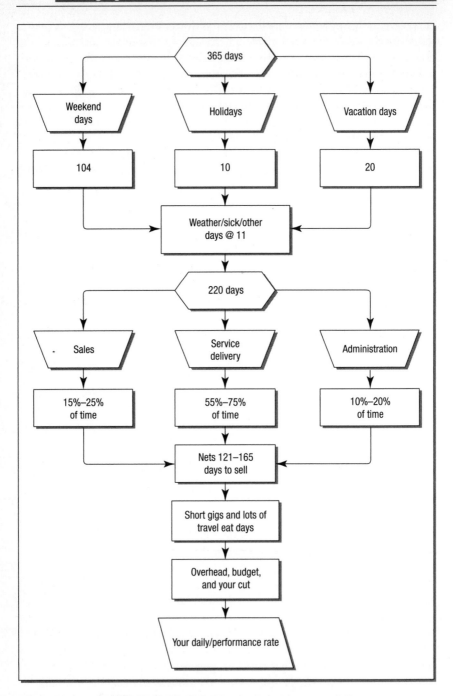

Exhibit 3.3 The Time Professionals Have to Sell

informality allows for a broad discussion of ideas and issues before decisions are made. Often a general consensus is reached through the attrition of options rather than in response to a targeted call to action. In this peer environment, such an approach helps promote a sense of participation, although it can tend to slow problem resolution. Those firms that have documented their processes and follow consistent procedures further enhance their decision flow while at the same time allowing concerned professionals to focus only on problems as they arise.

Many professional services firms that have attempted to adopt corporate, top-down models for decision making in a quest for efficiency have found that this approach is met by great uneasiness within the ranks and may, in fact, be vigorously resisted.

Home Office/Branch Office Model

In the first application of this two-part model, the firm's main office sets broad policy guidelines, including profitability and burden targets, then typically stands back and allows broad autonomy to the various branch office leaders. This approach can work well when branch offices and the home office are relatively independent and the branches depend on the home office only for items such as systems support, financial services, and research. Under this system, branches have maximum latitude and minimum regulation.

In the second application, the main office provides orthodoxy throughout the practice with all branches replicating main office policies, procedures, and processes. In this application, branches operate more like franchise units in a chain. The economies of scale generated by consistency are intended to make up in profit what they take away in creativity. This works well for narrowly focused and/or easily systematized professional services and less well for those with much discretion and a broad array of services.

Managing Partners and/or Chief Executive Officers

Some firms choose to keep as close to the traditional corporate profile as possible, by choosing a managing partner, president, or CEO to lead the firm. Typically, the leader takes on the additional role of chairman of the board. In this structure, a single leader manages policy and operational performance. The benefit of this approach is that the firm is led by one of its own. The disadvantage is that the leader often goes from being a key rainmaker and performer to a cost center, and an expensive one at that.

Some firms lessen the impact on the firm by selecting an able, but not stellar, performer for this role and support this leader with a strong executive committee (see later discussion). Still others rotate the position among the executive committee group.

Other firms choose to hire a professional manager, an administrator (not one of the firm's professionals), to oversee all administrative and marketing functions. Practice management is still usually controlled by the firm's professionals, either in the form of a broad-based committee or through the managing partner for the specific practice area.

Candidates for these positions, who often carry a chief operating officer (COO) title, come from all disciplines. Those with marketing and administrative experience, often having earned an MBA or similar degree, are typically the firm's best choice. Policy decisions typically remain with the firm's inner circle of professionals.

Rebellion in the Ranks

While professional services firms have traditionally sought ways to maximize profitability and demonstrate strong leadership, it can be a struggle. One early client, a professional services firm with several offices and more than 800 professionals, was being run by a chairman and an executive committee. Committee members were unhappy with the amount of time managing the firm took away from their billable time. The chairman was so busy with his management duties that his practice was declining. Consulting intervention pointed to some process improvements and recommended the hiring of a professional manager as CEO. The leadership group agreed with this strategy and a search was conducted. A candidate was found at a large financial institution and was hired. The chairman was delighted and very supportive. Committee members were initially pleased but were in open rebellion within eight months, forcing the ouster of the CEO and leading to the chairman's resignation from the firm. The partner who led the rebellion was soon serving as the new chairman, and the firm retained this model until several years later when they were acquired by a large financial institution. The reason cited for the rebellion was that the professional manager never absorbed the culture of the firm.

Executive Committees

Many professional services firms use an executive committee approach to firm governance. Firms large enough to have a professional administrator often use the executive committee as a mini-board of directors to interface with the administrator and moderate his or her decisions. In the smaller firm, this committee frequently serves as a virtual office of the president, making day-to-day decisions for the firm and submitting these decisions for ratification by the board of directors when they meet or by poll. Most often, executive committee members are also members of the board of directors of the firm, and operational and shareholder issues are handled simultaneously (though specific resolutions may be required to meet legal requirements). Firms that do not follow the bylaws they have established or fail to maintain complete and accurate records open the firm and themselves to potential risk. When in doubt, it is always better to draft a simple resolution and get it approved by the larger board than to take the risk of a future challenge to an oral decision.

Practice Management Teams

In this model, members typically rotate on and off a small team that may focus only on service quality or may involve itself in both service quality and business results. Decisions are often determined by consensus, and few substantive issues are decreed by the team's chair. The span of control for the team may entail only setting goals for their specialty and monitoring progress against plan, or the committee may oversee all issues related to specific performance of the practice specialty.

This model allows those closest to the work to manage the creative and work product unencumbered by the disparate concerns of other firm members, who often operate in different specialty areas that may not share the same operational or profit guidelines. In a consulting firm with a litigation support practice, for example, the work flows and processes differ sharply from those of an applications' engineering practice focusing on problem solving and code generation.

Representatives from each of the practice management teams within the firm usually constitute either the board or its executive committee.

Summary

Managing the professional services firm has never been easy. The analogy of herding cats comes to mind. Firms that adopt an effective structure for governance, wealth accumulation, and equity transfer give themselves the best chance for prosperity and growth. Whether the firm begins with one principal or a key group, creating a structure using one of the models identified will enable rather than constrain opportunity and is a first step in increasing the likelihood of long-term success.

Building on this structure, initial equity is allocated fairly, and the processes of the firm govern the flow of equity into new hands. This process is the lifeblood of the professional services firm. In the Four Stages of Business

Growth[7] (survival, liquidity, profit, and sustained growth), we see a cycle that many businesses in general, and professional services firms in particular, fail to master. Few survive into a second generation of leadership. But those few firms that do survive have mastered the flow, and their vitality is evident, both professionally and financially.

Principals and professionals in these firms have been nurtured both in terms of equity participation and performance recognition. Sound and progressive compensation programs provide a stable environment that nurtures and sustains high performance professionals. Such policies also facilitate retention and, coupled with a full array of competitive benefits, encourage both the best and the brightest to cast their long-tem lot with the firm.

Successful firms have also identified and documented their workflows and supported those workflows with decision management techniques designed to facilitate process. Mastery of workflows allows for leveraging the potential of each professional and support person within the firm.

Finally, successful firms typically acknowledge that there is no shortcut to improved performance, no magic pill. Success is earned on a day-by-day basis. Structure supports ownership and facilitates reward. Defined processes make the going easier and propel the firm into its future. In speaking to clients in professional services firms over the years, I have often asked what most facilitates growth, given a talented group of professionals. In hard times and prosperous times, the answer is the same: flexibility.

NOTES

1. John J. Reddish, CMC, IPO Decision Tree (included in the Resource CD).
2. Mark J. Gundersen, Esq., PSI 2004 Technology Conference, 2003, pp. 5, 6.
3. Robert Morris Associates, Annual Statement Studies (also known as the Ratio Book) includes comparative historical data and other sources of composite financial data categorized by SIC code, available from www.rmahq.com.
4. U.S. Department of Labor, Bureau of Labor Statistics, www.bls.gov.
5. Several online sources provide individual salary surveys, including www.salarysource.com.
6. One national source for site selection and local demographics is available from www.developmentalliance.com.
7. John J. Reddish, CMC, press release and article, © 1995, 2004 (included in the Resources CD).

The Front Office: Driving Sales and Growth

4

Sales Management

JANA CARPENTER

If there is no wind, row.
—Latin Proverb

This chapter introduces a totally unconventional concept: *The formation of a separate sales organization within your professional services firm.* While the direct salesforce model is a generally accepted practice in technology consulting, performance consulting, and product-driven companies, the formation of a separate sales organization does not have serious traction in the professional services industry. Buckle up. This chapter—through guiding philosophies, anecdotes, and case examples—demonstrates why going against the mainstream is good for your business. In fact, a professional salesforce is required for any professional services firm looking to grow with velocity. This chapter provides you with the steps, tools, and insight to build and manage an effective sales organization in your firm.

It is very easy for people to understand the need to hire salespeople to sell a product; however, professional services firms are typically not trained to put a structure around selling intellectual capital and the process of consulting, nor do they often want to. An *Economist* article notes that consultants' professional skepticism teaches them to "dig holes in constructive new ideas,"[1] and to many practice leaders, a dedicated salesforce is a new idea. Reasons for the reluctance to hire and work with sales professionals are many and include the stigma associated with sales; the belief that sales is personality driven, thus a formal organization and sales "professionals" are not necessary; and, most importantly, *sales conflicts with the rainmaker mentality of the "expert" industry.* Traditionally, partner status, esteem, and big money in the professional services industry are associated with strong sales ability.

The highest status for a consulting professional is to be identified as one who can make rain, and bringing in salespeople creates conflict.

To illustrate the pervasiveness of these challenges, I share a story that describes the process navigated as I introduced a sales organization into FTI Consulting, Inc.

Coming Out

Three years ago, FTI posted an online employment advertisement for a director of sales for the Chicago office. The Chicago office was looking at different ways to drive revenue. They built their business on a few major client engagements, did extremely well, and grew exponentially. In 2001, as litigations pushed and settled, the practice leaders found themselves with a good-size organization of outstanding professionals, but not enough clients. One creative and innovative practice leader understood the need for new revenue streams and decided to try an experiment. He hired one experienced sales professional and identified and dedicated two current employees with great client facing skills to outside sales. In 2000, I joined FTI as their supervisor and FTI's first director of sales (or so that was my impression coming in). However, as I began my career with FTI, I saw that I was identified as a senior consultant, even in the language contained in my offer letter, and not as a director of sales. As a new employee with a background in sales, this struck me as, "Yikes, what have I gotten myself into?" Here was a company in need of new revenue streams and not ready to "go public" about the hiring of a sales management professional.

I continued in the sales management role, with the support of my direct supervisor. Focused on generating new revenue, we dug in and did the hard work. After one year, the sales team was performing exceptionally well, and the division president asked my supervisor, "How did you get these budget busting months?" Even with demonstrated results, my supervisor was hesitant to "come out," but the time had come to disclose the truth—that a sales team, in concert with the consulting professionals, was responsible for the tremendous revenue growth. When I met the division president and shared our methods, he said to me, "But, I thought you were a senior consultant." While the division president was ecstatic with the new revenue stream and improved sales performance, he still found it hard to believe that a salesperson could sell professional services. In his disbelief, he put the sales team through rigorous tasks including recalculating our forecasts repeatedly and testing our ability to sustain the growth. Even after our group brought in $13 million in self-originated engagements that year, the division president still did not want to acknowledge the need for salespeople. Slowly and hesitantly, the firm leaders came to acknowledge the impact a dedicated sales organization within a professional services firm could have on the bottom line, and today FTI's sales organization is viewed as a tool for success.

The lesson I learned from this journey is: While there is still an enormous stigma attached to the word *salesperson* and a fear that sales professionals and professional consultants cannot mix, you *can* establish a sales organization in your firm, no matter how biased it is against such a measure, as long as you have the *support of at least one person* who is willing to sustain you until you prove yourself. Today, I am a respected leader in FTI and a vice president in charge of sales and marketing, where I lead an organization of 30 sales and marketing professionals.

If you're convinced of the value of forming a direct sales organization in your firm, this chapter will help you greatly. While the "Coming Out" scenario might convince your of the challenging nature of the task, the fact is that more and more professional services firms are experimenting with the direct sales model, with wider industry acceptance. In the context of maintaining an awareness of the challenges of instituting a sales organization within the professional services firm environment, this chapter gives you insight and actual tools to enable you to:

- Organize, build, manage, and coach your sales team.
- Understand your sales process and sell effectively.
- Track, measure, and promote your results.
- Choose the systems and technologies that will best benefit your firm.
- Generate revenue!

Whether yours is a firm of 10 or a firm of 10,000, a sales organization is an effective tool for revenue generation and enhanced client service.

Why This Topic Is Important

The professional services industry is marked with intense competition. In the 1990s alone, the United States added a net of 2,600 new accounting firms and 2,300 advertising firms.[2] Add to this competitive environment an increased pressure to perform. The partner ownership business model is shifting, and more professional services firms are now accountable to shareholders. Shareholders demand results in the form of increased profits, and this requires new business. On top of these two pressures, the professional services firm faces a unique challenge: Professional services firms traditionally look to their "product," the experts, as the salesforce. Because of increased pressure to generate new revenue, the professional consultant is faced with a critical question: *How do I give excellent client service and grow my practice at the same time?* Exhibit 4.1 shows the answer to this dilemma.

A separate sales organization addresses the "juggling plates" (juggling of client and sales responsibilities) dilemma faced by professional consultants and delivers great benefit at the same time:

1. A sales organization is an effective tool for revenue generation.
2. A sales organization is an extremely targeted, low cost solution to acquiring new business.
3. A sales organization sells the service and the consultants that best fit the client need.

Exhibit 4.1   The Formation of a Separate Sales Organization

A Sales Organization Is an Effective and Essential Tool for Revenue Generation

- A strong sales organization gives professionals increased sales opportunities—more *at-bats.*
- A strong sales organization enables professionals to focus on the delivery of your core product—*fanatical client service.*
- A strong sales organization helps your firm to reach its revenue potential. When integrated with the professionals, your firm, and your clients, you will get the benefit of all *playing at the top of their game.*

One Door Leads to Four Opportunities

Jeff Litvak, senior managing director at FTI Consulting, Inc., shares a revenue success story related to his willingness to work with the internal sales organization. Jeff's involvement on the lecture circuit put him in contact with many legal industry leaders, one of whom was the general counsel for a large retail corporation. A strong practice leader, Jeff was keen to new business opportunities and thus telephoned a particular attorney to request a background meeting. After securing the appointment, Jeff asked a sales professional to accompany him on the call. During the initial meeting, the general counsel referenced a large suit that the corporation was involved in and provided the names of the attorneys FTI would meet to pitch the business. As Jeff tells the story, the sales professional was organized and tenacious about his follow-up, contacted everyone named in the meeting, and secured meetings with the four key decision makers—translated, he got FTI the next "at-bat." On his own, Jeff would not have had the time to dedicate to this new business process; he already had too many client responsibilities. The sales professional organized an FTI team appropriate to the needs of the contacts, brought this team on the subsequent sales calls, and managed the process. The quality of the team presented to the client, the sales management, proposal development and follow-up skills of the sales professional, and Jeff's willingness to work with the sales organization, resulted in FTI's closing the deal, forming a new client relationship, and generating revenue.

A Sales Organization Is an Extremely Targeted, Low-Cost Solution for Acquiring New Business

Traditionally, professional services organizations acquire business via two methods—marketing programs and consultant sales efforts. Although marketing programs are essential, they can be costly and the return on investment can be difficult to measure; and while consultants possess deep knowledge of their service lines, they must juggle client service with sales responsibilities and are not always trained to sell outside their area of expertise. When integrated across your firm, the sales organization provides a high return on investment:

- A sales organization is *highly trackable*. Sales effectiveness can be accurately measured, tracked, and improved with the right tools and processes.
- If a sales organization *targets effectively*, it *minimizes wasted effort or expense*. An advertisement might reach 15,000 individuals, with only a small percentage of those targets being qualified. Sales professionals target only those individuals who buy your service.
- A sales organization is *flexible*. Sales professionals can be quickly redeployed to launch a new service, unlike consulting professionals who are trained to sell within one practice area.

A Sales Organization Sells the Service and Consultants That Best Fit the Client Need

A sales organization, composed of professionals who are conversationally competent across a full range of consulting services, can focus on delivering what is best for the client. An effective sales professional will sell the right service and the best consultants every time.

The rewards associated with establishing a sales organization are significant for both your firm and your clients' business. This chapter outlines the questions to consider and the steps to take to establish a strategic sales organization in your professional services firm. It is not enough to simply hire salespeople and to then expect results; an understanding of management and coaching, sales processes, and technological needs is essential.

Organizing Your Sales Team

If you can find a way to create a sales organization that belongs to the entire company, you will have unbelievable velocity in the marketplace.

The American Marketing Association defines salesforce organization as an arrangement of activities and job positions involving the salesforce.

The starting point in organizing a salesforce is determining the goals or objectives to be accomplished; these are specified in the firm's overall marketing plan. The selling activities necessary to accomplish the firm's marketing objectives can then be divided in such a way that the objectives can be achieved with as little duplication of effort as possible. The organizational structure provides for specialization of labor, stability, and continuity in selling efforts and coordination of the various activities assigned to different salespeople and departments within the firm.[3] Two key words to pull from this definition are *continuity* and *coordination*—these allude to *teamwork*.

Many professional services firms have experimented in creating a sales organization, and some have been successful in some places. In general, however, professional services firms that set out to establish a firmwide sales organization have not been very successful. Two common characteristics that plague these organizations are the inability to gain support at a high level, whether at the partner or executive management level, and the inability to figure out how to do it together or, in other words, how to get the professional consultants and sales professionals to partner. Jeff Litvak, who was previously a partner with KPMG, highlights integration between the consultants and the sales professionals as one of the top three critical items in ensuring your sales approach is successful. Litvak observed that while KPMG had a sales organization, the organization was not as integrated with the professionals like the salesforce at FTI; a level of independence still existed and this sales structure was not very successful. Where increased independence equates to less effectiveness, it is clear that *to succeed, consultants and sales professionals must "marry up."*[4]

In learning from this experience, we can confidently state that to establish a successful sales organization in a professional services firm, four critical success factors exist:

1. *You must have support for your sales organization at the highest level,* even if that support lies in only one individual who is willing to keep the objectors away until you have a chance to be successful.

2. *Your sales professionals must belong to the entire company.* Your sales professionals cannot work for one consultant or one service line. Organizing your sales organization by a particular service line will lead to competition, or "fiefdoms," and a lack of continuity and coordination in the sales effort.

3. *You must integrate your sales and marketing organizations.* Branding, creating high quality, relevant content, and reaching the customer via multiple channels is the value marketers bring; however, this can be leveraged only if efforts are closely aligned with sales objectives and an understanding of the buyer.

4. *Over time, your sales professionals and your consulting professionals must marry up.* Independence equates to a decrease in effectiveness. If sales professionals commit themselves to learning the business and professional consultants commit to respecting and understanding sales, a true partnership can form.

Assuming you are moving toward meeting the four critical success factors, then, what makes a good sales organization? Characteristics of any good sales organization include:[5]

- An organizational structure that reflects a market orientation
- An organization that is built around activities and not around the people performing these activities
- Responsibilities that are clearly spelled out and sufficient authority granted to meet the responsibility
- A reasonable span of executive control
- Stability combined with flexibility
- Balanced and coordinated activities both within the sales department and between sales and nonmarketing departments

The following sections provide insight into integrating sales and marketing, establishing territories, determining the size of your team, and creating a compensation plan.

Integrating Sales and Marketing

Sales and marketing are both engines of revenue generation; thus it is imperative that these organizations be aligned with the firm's overall business strategy and with each other. So, how does a firm align sales and marketing?

Before understanding how to move forward, it is important to understand from where we're starting. Let's take a step back and look at a fairly universal marketing and sales model:[6]

- Marketing's responsibility is build brand awareness, generate leads, and provide sales tools.
- Marketing generates leads through a number of vehicles.
- As leads come in, the leads are handed off to sales.
- At that point, marketing's role has been fulfilled and they disengage.
- Sales takes over by a field sales lead maturation process.

This approach toward lead generation and selling does work; however, this traditional model has some drawbacks, most noteworthy the lack of *continuous teamwork*. In the preceding process outline, sales and marketing do not operate as a unified, long-term client team, with a common goal of selling and servicing the client and the overall firm. There is a hands-off process once the lead shifts hands from marketing to sales. While this model is based on a product-centric company, it can be applied to professional services as well. An integrated sales and marketing organization and approach, focused on serving the whole company and the client will reduce, or even eliminate, the animosity and finger pointing that sometimes exist between sales and marketing. And, in the end, both the client and your revenue stream will benefit.

As you strategize the organization of your salesforce, remember to integrate sales and marketing. Three key areas to keep in mind are:

1. *Reporting structure:* Create an organizational reporting structure in which the heads of both organizations report to one individual. Ideally, this individual is a marketing generalist with a strong sales background. This reporting structure facilitates communication and cooperation.

2. *Sell the way your customers want to buy:* Your sales and marketing organizations should focus on the customer and facilitate the buying process. The goal of any sales organization is to sell the way your customers want to buy; in other words, assume an "outside looking in" view of your sales process. Regular communication between the sales and marketing organizations is thus essential in understanding the client and developing the right tools to touch the customer and facilitate the sales process.

3. *Understand each other's role:* To truly work as a team, both sales and marketing need to understand what each function does and then learn to balance and coordinate those activities. Marketing needs to understand the sales process, and sales needs to understand how marketing works and have knowledge of the resources available to help generate leads *and* close business.

A sales organization, integrated with marketing, will strengthen your firm's ability to generate revenue and build sustainable client and industry relationships.

Establishing Territories

The word *territories* suggests the division of a salesforce on some basis of specialization, whether geography, type of product or service sold, class of customer, or some combination of these or other meaningful categories. In the professional services environment, two key criteria must exist as you establish your sales territories:

1. *The salesforce must belong to the whole company.* To belong to the whole company, your salesforce must represent the firm's entire range

of services *and not a single professional.* Your salesforce must be trained to cross-sell. This approach contrasts with the standard consultant sales model, in which the professional sells only his or her particular service line to a wide range of clients. This model is inwardly focused because the selling mirrors the firm's internal structure. The consultant sales model often promotes an organization based on fiefdoms, as practice leaders are faced with a pressure that says, "I have to sell in order to feed the people in my pyramid." Establishing a sales organization, if done correctly, will help your firm operate as a consistent, consolidated team, selling and providing the full benefits of all service offerings to clients. The firm and the client will benefit as the sales professional will sell in a wider set of services and the right consultant team every time.

2. *The salesforce must be organized by the external marketplace.* Territories are collections of people who buy your firm's services; thus, organize your territories as your client groups are organized. For example, FTI's buyers are law firms and corporations, and sales professionals are assigned prospective accounts within these two markets. Training your sales professionals to sell the firm's complete line of services is also characteristic of organizing by the external marketplace, because a client's service need is often broad, encompassing much or all of what the firm offers.

In addition to the preceding key criteria, three tips to establishing sales territories are:

1. *Ensure that each sales professional has his or her own "patch," or territory.* You don't want a sales structure that leads to territory competition between peers.

2. *Make sure that each sales professional has the same number of buyers to call on.* Over time, be open to changing territories to match chemistry between the sales professionals and the prospects. Take a hard-to-crack account and give it to a new, enthusiastic sales representative.

3. *Divide territories along geographical lines where feasible.* Travel is extremely expensive, and this is the economically sound approach to sales organization.

While these tips are straightforward, it is important to note that the assignment of territories is a science. Managers have an inclination to assign large territories to generate increased market penetration. To the contrary, making territories smaller is often the right answer.

When Less = More

While I was a sales professional with a large data processing company, our territories were assigned by Dun & Bradstreet (D&B) breakdowns. During my first year, I was handed 1,000 D&B cards with all of the companies in my territory that might buy our services. Every year, sales management took away some of my territory and raised my quota, and every year, I sold more than the previous year. During my last year with this company, my territory had dwindled to only 200 D&B cards, 25 percent of what I had my first year, and yet I sold four times as much as when I had five times as many prospects!

The message in this story is that if a sales professional focuses on something, he or she gets results. The ability to go broad and deep within the target base is important to good selling. On average, you can get about 20 percent revenue growth by totally serving your current clients and selling more services; *however, you can't get 30 percent.* Your job, as a manager, is to coach your sales professionals on how to go broad and deep within their target market and add new accounts at the same time. You will likely find that your sales professionals will often ask for larger territories, especially when they are new. In response to this, give them as many targets as they ask for and tell them that, over time, together you will reduce the list. Let the sales professional feel some control of his or her territory.

Determining the Size of Your Team

The size of your sales organization will depend on many variables, including:

- *Budget:* How much is firm leadership willing to invest in the sales organization? An effective sales organization is not created by headcount alone; you must have the supporting budget for recruiting, commission schedules, training programs, and marketing activities.
- *Market potential:* What will the market bear? Is the market growing, or is demand for your services declining? How many potential buyers are there for your services?
- *Revenue potential:* What quota is attached to your organizations? How many sales professionals are required to generate that level of new business?

In the initial stages of salesforce development, I recommend that you start small and focus a handful of sales professionals on a number of key territories. This first phase of your organization development is aimed at gaining traction in the marketplace and demonstrating your worth to the firm's leadership. As the support for the sales organization grows, the budget, market, and revenue potential variables can then drive your decision on sales numbers. However, as you build your organization, over time, it *has to be of sufficient size to be effective*. Sales professionals juggle many responsibilities, from prospecting and closing to generating proposals. Make sure that there are enough sales professionals to be effective in a target region or industry marketplace.

Creating a Compensation Plan

According to research conducted by the Society of Human Resource Managers (SHRM), a solid sales compensation plan:[7]

- Creates a beneficial relationship for both the company and the employee.
- Can expand and contract, depending on economic conditions.
- Focuses on increasing profit, not just revenue. This is a slight difference that is sometimes difficult to measure but much more advantageous to the company.

A poor compensation plan may have the following problems:

- Inflexibility/inaccuracy in quota setting
- Quotas that are inconsistent with company goals
- The absence of a clause allowing the company to make changes or to respond to exceptional events

A poorly designed pay plan causes salespeople to focus on the wrong things or causes them to stop selling completely—either because they have surpassed their goals or have no realistic chance of attaining them.

The preceding research provides some guidelines for developing your total compensation plan. However, structuring a sales compensation plan within the professional services firm is more intricate. It is a uniquely challenging subject, primarily because the sales professional and the professional consultant, or service provider, are asked to *share* the account and the revenues generated by that client. *Who gets credit and who pays are the biggest challenges in securing practice leader buy-in.* Patrick Strong, managing director at FTI Consulting, Inc., termed compensating the salesforce as the single biggest problem[8] in securing practice leader buy-in. Sales is not free. On average, 7 percent of the client professional fees go to supporting the sales organization. While practice leaders will be fine with paying for *found revenue*, or new revenue that is brought in by a sales professional, it becomes more complicated when sales professionals begin working with veteran clients or when a consultant uncovers a lead and the salesperson accompanies that consulting professional on the sales call.

Understanding this delicate terrain is essential for the manager in a professional services firm. Before covering actual commission schedules and structured compensation plans, here are three management techniques to help in this challenging environment:

1. *Get buy-in from consulting practice leaders.* Demonstrate the value add of sales, and lead practice leaders to feel confident in their decision to "purchase" the sales service. In other words, sell-in sales before introducing your commission schedule.

2. *Clearly define the rules of the game.* Territories and commission schedules must be clearly detailed, simple enough to understand, and directionally correct. The schedule should be based on revenue and should fit your firm's culture and comfort level.

3. *Everyone should operate in his or her "sweet spot."* Let the sales professional create the "at-bats" and manage the sales process, and let the professional consultant close the deal. Let each player deliver his or her greatest value. Allowing consultants to close deals ensures that the client-consultant relationship can form at the early stages of the project and gives the consultant some ownership of the process. Then, while the consultants are providing outstanding client service, the sales professional can be looking for more "at-bats." This encourages a true partnership between sales and client service.

COMMISSION SCHEDULES.   The most important thing in setting commission schedules is to be directionally correct—the schedule should be simple and should fit your firm's culture and comfort level. In the end, the firm must arrive at a commission structure that the client services and sales professionals are comfortable with. If the salesforce is organized correctly and the firm has established a culture in which your sales professionals work for the entire company and are viewed by the client service professionals as partners, coming up with a commission schedule will be relatively simple. However, if a true partnering mentality has not been formed between the sales organization and the practice areas, agreeing on a commission schedule will likely be marked by conflict. In a true partnership, your client service professionals will respect the sales professionals and will be comfortable with their earning the same amount of money or perhaps even more. If the client service professionals think of the salespeople as less valuable to the firm or capable at their specialty, a true partnership does not exist. In this situation, the professionals will want to control the salespeople through elaborate commission schedules. This is the wrong place for client service professionals to place their control, and legislating behavior through commission schedules will not benefit your firm or your clients.

As you strategize your commission schedule, know that there are many ways to structure a total compensation plan. Your guiding objective should be to develop a plan that provides the fewest obstacles for professionals to partner with salespeople. At FTI, first-year sales professionals are compensated with an annual salary, plus a management-by-objectives (MBO) bonus. After the first year, sales professionals are on a straight commission plan. A straight commission compensation plan makes using a sales professional relatively risk-free for the practice leaders; the sales professionals pay for themselves. FTI's commission plan includes three elements:

1. *Highly reward self-originated business.* If the sales professional does the heavy lifting and finds business the organization would not have found easily on its own, this is worth a lot and is rewarded the highest. The commission schedule is up to 7 percent of any professional fees realized.

2. *Reward for value added.* If a client service professional brings a sales professional into a meeting, the sales professional is rewarded for his or her value added, specifically in helping to develop the client team, managing the sales process, and so on. The commission schedule is 2 percent of any professional fees realized.

3. *Account growth incentive.* Each year, FTI identifies client targets that are key to the firm's growth strategy. These targets are accounts in which the firm is already engaged and wants to grow. Each year, one to three accounts within each salesperson's territory are targeted as VIP accounts. Sales professionals are paid a bonus, usually a 2 percent incentive on the aggregate revenue growth over the prior year, for growth in those accounts.

Remember, the compensation/commission plan is not simply a question of whom you pay for what. Compensation plans are designed to motivate people toward the right behavior, in this case, to sell more. Your goal is to organize your sales compensation/commission plan within the parameters of what your firm is comfortable spending in order to drive the most revenue into your organization.

Building and Managing Your Sales Team

Success is not the result of spontaneous combustion. You must set yourself on fire. To be a successful sales manager, you have to believe that everyone comes to work wanting to be successful, wanting to play at the top of his or her game.

Your job as a sales manager is to remove the obstacles that stand in the way of your sales professionals and enable them to be their best. Once this is accomplished, then look out; the sales team will deliver for you. This section, dedicated to building and managing the sales team, focuses on providing the insights and tools to recruit and staff the sales organization and to train and coach them to do their very best. It also provides insight into the nature of the sales professional to help you understand how to motivate your team and thus succeed in the marketplace.

Recruiting

Recruiting the best talent for your sales organization is one of the three pillars of your role: recruit, train, and coach. It is too common for managers to be drawn into desperation and time constraints when filling a sales role—they react to the fear of an open territory with the philosophy that any warm body will do. While this might offer a stopgap solution and at times might even result in a successful hire, it is not a good approach to recruiting. The "Coming Out" story at the beginning of the chapter depicted a firm that, in a desperate need for new revenue streams, selected current employees who were outgoing and friendly and assigned them to a sales role. Without professional sales management, those friendly folks were destined for failure because the sales profession is not solely personality driven; there are specific qualities and characteristics that are common to successful sales professionals.

To help establish your recruiting processes, this section reviews a standard sales job description and details the core skills and competencies that are common to successful sales professionals. This will help you to understand *whom* to hire. Next, this section details *where* you can look for these candidates and, finally, *how* to evaluate them through the interview process. Although there is a data-driven approach to recruiting a sales organization, don't get buried in mechanics and forget to use your "gut." Even more important than evaluating your candidates along set competency lines, the most critical thing to ask when recruiting a sales professional is whether he or she is ready to "bust a move." Try to find people who are at a point in their career where they have enough experience but are blocked by something, for example, an income cap or no prospects for advancement. *Hire people who will take responsibility for their own success.* If you follow this philosophy, you can't go wrong.

JOB DESCRIPTION. The first step in recruiting professionals to join your team is the development of an employee job description. The job description documents a job's major functions or duties, responsibilities, and/or other critical features, such as skills and attributes required, education requirement, and position classification. Based on your organization's needs, the job description may be specific and detailed or generic and general. The job description is an important recruiting tool, because it ensures that the candidate clearly understands the duties and expectations associated with the

Position Title
Employee Status
Employee Name
Office Location
Department
Supervisor
Effective Date

Primary duties:	Develop and implement sales plans for assigned accounts, create prospecting campaigns, maintain sales activity in CRM tool, negotiate and close deals
Additional duties:	Act as client advocate, communicate client needs effectively to staff, perform client satisfaction audits, other duties as assigned
Skills required:	Proven consultative selling skills, excellent verbal and written communication skills, superior organizational skills, deep computer proficiency
Attributes required:	Flexibility and ability to work under tight deadlines; ability to multitask; comfortable with change; able to command respect; high degree of integrity; creative, innovative, and brave
Education/experience:	College degree or commensurate work experience
Position classification:	Exempt or nonexempt

Exhibit 4.2   Standard Categories for Sales Job Description

specific sales job. This helps you to achieve a win-win hire, in which the new hire understands his or her role clearly, and you have a clear road map as to how this sales professional will fit into your organization.

Standard categories to include in your job description, with sample detail included in the duties, skills, and attributes categories, are shown in Exhibit 4.2.

While the job description provides you with great insight into the skills and attributes you are looking for, it is important that you stay connected to the recruitment philosophy of looking for *sales professionals*. Do not try too hard to make somebody into a sales professional. Key skills and attributes to look for include:

- Discipline
- Competitiveness

- Proven sales success
- High activity in past roles
- Fearless on the phone
- Hungry to learn
- Willing to be responsible for their own success
- Sturdy and relentless—not deterred by "no"

SOURCING CANDIDATES. Now that you know what you are looking for in candidates, where do you find them? Depending on the size of your firm, you might have a human resources or staffing team available to help you locate sales professionals, and help from these internal partners can be extremely valuable. In addition, ways to source candidates for your sales organization include:

- *Partner with recruiters.* Don't hesitate to employ corporate recruiters and outside recruiting firms; they form long-term relationships with leading sales professionals and have the lead on when certain high-performing individuals might be ready for a career move.
- *Answer the phone.* Sales professionals who are at the point in their career at which they know what they want and where they want to go will often target you. Respond to those who cold call you—a new superstar might be on the other end of the line.
- *Institute a referral system.* Referral programs teach employees to be internal headhunters and result in prescreened candidates for you. Cash is the most popular award given to employees who refer individuals, with awards varying based on the role being filled. For example, FTI offers a bonus of $5,000 for any sales referral hire. In addition to being an excellent recruiting tool, the referral system also results in improved retention rates.
- *Remember who has called on you in the past and impressed you.* Go through your Rolodex and call those sales professionals you have met in the course of doing business. Seek out those who have sold you, those whom you wanted to buy from. Call them.
- *Ask your clients.* Reach out to your clients for names of sales professionals with whom they have been impressed over the years.

INTERVIEWING TACTICS. The next step in hiring sales professionals is the actual interview process. Possible interviewing questions include:

- Tell me about a time you identified a problem and came up with the solution? What did you do? Why did you follow that course of action? Were there other alternatives you could have pursued?

- What's been the most difficult obstacle you have ever overcome? Why was it difficult? What plan did you execute to get past it? Why do you believe you were successful? Based on your experience today, what might you have done differently?

Are you familiar with these questions? All of these questions focus on specific past behavior, and they come out of the structured behavioral interviewing technique, which I recommend for interviewing your sales candidates. Structured behavioral interviewing is a standardized way of getting information from candidates about their past behavior and performance. The premise of this interview technique is that *past behavior is the best indicator of future behavior.* According to Kathryn Neiner, principal with The Chrisa Group and an expert on employment interviewing, two reasons for using behavioral interviewing are:[9]

1. *It's more valid* than traditional interviews. Questions are designed to evaluate only competencies that have been shown through job analysis to be required for successful job performance. This prevents you from assessing irrelevant knowledge or skills.
2. When used properly, behavioral interviews *reduce legal risks* because all candidates are treated the same. Regardless of who conducts the interview, all candidates are asked the same questions, assessed against the same set of job-related competencies, and rated using the same method.

An effective structured behavioral interviewing program requires you to develop job-related competencies (which you developed in your job description), write behavioral questions about those competencies, and train interviewers to use the system. To institute this technique in your sales organization, don't hesitate to bring in outside consultants who will help you to identify the key behaviors of sales professionals in your organization. These consultants will rigorously detail the nature of the sales process and the behaviors that make an individual successful. For leads, ask your peers who they use and search for vendors via the Internet. Find 5 to 10 people who conduct interviewing workshops and talk with them on the phone, take a look at their materials and approach, and meet with them. If after meeting with the various vendors you find that you don't have the budget to work with an outside consultant, through conversing with the various salespeople and consultants, you will have already learned a great deal. You can use this insight to inform and guide your interviewing process.

Training

Professional services staff come to work every day wanting to play at the top of their game. Salespeople are no different, and the aggressive ones are going to be demanding about what they need to deliver consistent, outstanding performance. It is your job to deliver on resources and training. *Don't hesitate to give your people everything they need to succeed, if you believe they have the potential—and the heart and attitude—to be successful.* Training is core to your job as a sales manager; and to a willing heart and mind, you can teach all the skills a person needs to succeed at selling. Although you can't make someone a superstar—you can help all of your professionals develop along the lines of skills, knowledge, and process.

SKILLS, KNOWLEDGE, AND PROCESS. Sales training needs to be focused on three core areas—*skills, knowledge,* and *process.* The skills component is behavioral; for example, the ability to communicate, listen, present, and negotiate are skills. The best training techniques for skills development are role-playing exercises, video training, and group work. Regardless of industry or company, sales-specific skills are universal and include:

- Prospecting
- Qualifying
- Precall planning/strategy
- Engaging/probing
- Closing

Knowledge is information and understanding, and the specific knowledge areas on which you train will be unique to your particular firm. The best training techniques for knowledge development are studying and reading, video training, e-learning, and experiential learning, for example, accompanying client service professionals to client meetings or client engagements. In the professional services industry, knowledge includes an understanding of:

- The firm—its history, mission, and key strengths
- The key service lines, or practice areas, that you are selling
- The consultants, or intellectual property and capabilities, that you are selling

Sales professionals at FTI, for example, are trained on the core knowledge areas of litigation process, forensic/litigation, complex data, web hosting, and trial services; they are also trained to "mine" consultants or know who their key consultants are and what they've delivered. In this way, when an existing or potential client has a specific area of inquiry, the sales professional can immediately identify the proper expertise.

In addition to skills and knowledge, process training is another core area for sales training. Process includes all of the structures, systems, or sales processes unique to your firm, for example, account management, running conflict checks, or using customer relationship management (CRM) systems.

The best training techniques for process training are case study review and experiential and workshop-based learning, in which you apply the processes you are supposed to be learning to your own scenarios.

The following sections detail FTI's training programs, which are designed to develop the sales organization along the skills, knowledge, and process lines detailed previously. The FTI training program begins with new hire Boot Camp and extends through the ongoing quarterly review process.

BOOT CAMP. Boot Camp is an organized training for new sales professionals. In keeping with its military meaning, Boot Camp is *hard work;* and to complete Boot Camp, new sales recruits must take responsibility for their own success. The duration of the training program is typically one week, and the goals of Boot Camp are threefold:

1. *Training:* Boot Camp delivers extensive training across skills, knowledge, and process areas. It provides new sales recruits with tips and tools to succeed.
2. *Testing:* Boot Camp identifies the best. Because of the intense nature of the training and the set standards that new recruits must meet, only those who are "hungry" will complete the training.
3. *Team building:* Boot Camp training brings new sales professionals together, forging a team bond.

The steps to establish a new Boot Camp training practice in your firm are:

1. *Set the dates:* Dependent on the hiring frequency of new sales professionals, determine set times each year when Boot Camp will be held, for example, quarterly or two times per year. Work to hire new sales professionals in groups, or waves, so that Boot Camp is their first introduction to the company.
2. *Confirm a budget:* Boot Camp training requires resources, but it can be done inexpensively. Expenses include travel and accommodations, facilities, trainers, curriculum development, and entertainment. To reduce your expense, before looking outside your firm for training resources, look into your salesforce to identify a professional who is an excellent mentor, is well-organized, and has demonstrated an interest in developing people. Reach out to this individual to see whether he or she would like to take a leadership role in running your Boot Camp; offer a flat quarterly fee for running the program. If you do not have an internal resource, ask your peers for trainer recommendations.
3. *Locate a site:* FTI's Boot Camp is conducted on-site. Some firms prefer to conduct this training off-site. The location is up to you and will be influenced by your training budget. In addition to the training facilities and technology capabilities of the site, consider the entertainment

facilities. While Boot Camp is hard work, to meet the team-building goal, outside networking opportunities should be included.

4. *Design your training:* Structure your Boot Camp as an intense graduate course in selling for your firm. Breaking down your firm's sales process is a good first step. Once you determine the key categories of your training, you can then determine specific content and identify the right trainers.

5. *Determine passing criteria:* To retain only the best sales recruits, it is important that you incorporate a testing and evaluation process into your Boot Camp. For example, at FTI it is mandatory that new sales recruits be able to deliver a strong demo and sales presentation in support of one of their core service lines, TrialMax®. If a sales candidate does not meet this expectation, he or she is deselected.

Exhibit 4.3 outlines the core sections that comprise FTI's Boot Camp training. Note that each section addresses skills, knowledge, or process, or some combination of the three core training areas.

As you develop your new recruit Boot Camp, seek out insight from your firm's consultants and current sales professionals regarding content. You can also research the best practices employed at leading firms.

90- TO 100-DAY MARK: SALES PREFERENCE QUESTIONNAIRE™ EVALUATION. Each new business win begins with the sales call; without the phone call there can be no connect and no win. Thus, for a sales professional, ability to call and prospect is critical. After a sales professional is on board for approximately one quarter, or between 90 and 100 days, the next step in training is to conduct an assessment that will analyze and predict the success potential of the individual professional. The assessment tool that I recommend is the Sales Preference Questionnaire™ (SPQ°GOLD®), The Call Reluctance® Scale. This tool detects and measures all 12 types of sales call reluctance. It is a 110-question computer-scored assessment that was developed by behavioral scientists George W. Dudley and Shannon L. Goodson. It is internationally recognized and considered one of the most rigorously validated instruments of its kind. The tool can be used to streamline selection procedures, maximize training, and improve sales productivity. As both a training and a coaching tool, it is invaluable. It provides on-target insight into individuals and, if used correctly, can help your sales professionals overcome potentially career-limiting emotions and have a better chance at great success.

No More Cups

We jokingly refer to Elisabeth as having been "born in the lobby" of FTI; she had been with the firm since its beginning and had performed well in many different roles before moving into sales. As a manager, I considered Elisabeth to be a high-potential salesperson—she had both deep

BOOT CAMP TRAINING SECTION	CORE AREA	DESCRIPTION
Firm Research	Knowledge and process	Firm Research gives steps and tips associated with researching your sales prospect. Topics covered include locating firm overviews and bios, locating a list of prior engagements by client and recent news coverage, and tips on managing a binder on each prospect.
Conflict Check/New Matter Form	Process	Conflict Check details how to run a conflict check and includes samples of all forms and processes required to run a comprehensive check.
Starting a New Case (Engagement)	Process	Starting a new case outlines all of the steps the sales professional must take to officially begin a new engagement. For FTI, this process details the letters of engagement (LOE), standard terms and conditions, and sample budget letter.
Selling Product X	Skills, knowledge, and process	Selling Product X trains your new recruits on selling one or more service lines. Ideally, you will train your new recruits on one core or starter service line during Boot Camp. Training in this section includes presenting or demonstrating the service line/technology, reviewing the supporting marketing collateral, and preparing a proposal customized fo this service line/technology.
SalesPlus (or CRM tool)	Process	SalesPlus is a contract management system. This section trains on the systems and processes your sales professionals must use to enter contracts, track calls, schedule meetings, and detail opportunities.
Sales Phone Calls	Skills	Sales Phone Calls covers a core skill requirement of the sales professional—cold calling. It reviews the goals the firm has set about call volume per professional and provides sample call scripts and suggestions for developing your script.

Exhibit 4.3   Boot Camp Training Topics for Sales Professionals

(continued)

BOOT CAMP TRAINING SECTION	CORE AREA	DESCRIPTION
Send Me Something First	Skills and process	Send Me Something First trains on writing cover letters and determining to include a mailed sales kit.
Proposals	Skills and process	Proposals provides the key steps that the sales professional should take when entering the proposal stage and details tips for developing a winning proposal. Case studies detailing winning proposals are presented and discussed.
La Firm (specific industry) Presentations	Skills and knowledge	Law Firm Presentations trains your sales professionals to present to their key industry audience. this section provides tips to understanding the differences in presenting to, for example, a law firm versus a corporate account
Reports	Process	Reports details the processes unique to the sales organization, for example, the call log form, weekly call report, and pipeline report. The expectations of the sales manager are presented in this section.

Exhibit 4.3   *Continued*

knowledge of the firm and the capability to succeed. However, Elisabeth could not pick up the phone. It was so painful for Elisabeth to pick up the phone that, as an incentive to phone canvass, she created the "cup" system. On her desk were two cups and a stack of dollar bills. If she dialed the number, she moved one dollar to the first cup. If she booked an appointment, she moved the dollar to the second cup. At the end of the week, she allowed herself to spend the dollars that were in the second cup.

Now, here was a sales professional with immense potential who could not pick up the phone. As a manager, I chose to invest in Elisabeth and reached out to an outside consultant, Rose Venditto, principal, Sales-Essentials Group, Inc., to employ the SPQ°GOLD® tool. Rose worked one-on-one with Elisabeth for a full week to help her overcome her phone canvassing challenges. She helped understand her reluctance, create a discussion script, and better understand the kind of sales conversation that will get a positive result from clients and prospects. Now there are no cups! The insight gathered via the assessment tool, combined with intensive coaching and the willingness of the sales professional, resulted in great success. Today, Elisabeth is FTI's number one salesperson, with $10 million in sales this year.

This one-time assessment tool will give you the insight you need to help your professionals meet their mark. A number of qualified consultants distribute the SPQ tool, and I encourage you to bring one in. After the initial assessment, don't hesitate to give your people personal coaches if you believe they have the potential—and the heart and attitude—to be successful.

QUARTERLY REVIEW. The quarterly review is essential to developing your people and ensuring that they are properly supported and given the tools to perform at the top of their game. At FTI, we use an MBO performance development tool. This quarterly review based on revenue and skills and examines two critical areas: (1) actual revenue and sales activity versus quota and (2) progress in achieving set development objectives or an evaluation of competencies in relation to identified skill and knowledge areas. Within the performance evaluation, manager and peer feedback is included.

Like any performance-based evaluation tool, the quarterly review is used as a coaching tool not only to assess areas that need improvement and potentially further training, but also to determine when a sales professional is ready to achieve more and take on more responsibility. Remember, superstar sales professionals are aggressive; if they are not continually challenged and provided with growth opportunities, they will seek out a more challenging position with another firm. The quarterly review should not be viewed as simply a report. It is a powerful interaction between you and your team. It provides insight into where each salesperson is performing in the key categories for success and enables you to remove obstacles, provide resources, make mid-course corrections, and *celebrate success.*

Tracking

Two definitions of *tracking* are: (1) to search by following evidence until found and (2) to observe or plot the moving path of something. These definitions apply to sales tracking, as sales tracking does provide "evidence" of what is happening in the sales process and helps a manager to forecast and "plot." However, too often, tracking becomes synonymous with *monitoring.* If you institute activity-measuring tools because "I'm tracking you," it's useless. *Tracking should be used to improve performance—to leave people better than you found them.* It is this philosophy that leads me to include tracking in this Building and Managing section.

Tracking serves many purposes:

- *Enforces accountability:* Encourages ownership and responsibility.
- *Helps professionals "analyze the game":* Provides insight into the sales process. Just like a baseball pitcher analyzes his game and the game of his batter, tracking gives sales professionals stats to measure their progress objectively and relative to others.

- *Motivates:* Brings another level of competition to the sales organization and the entire firm.
- *Forecasts and provides utilization data:* Helps practice leaders to manage staff and provides insight into the sales organization's performance. Justifies existence of sales organization.
- *Coaches:* Enables managers to identify key areas for growth so they can help sales professionals get to the next level.

There are two types of tracking:

1. *Coaching:* Sales activity presented in weekly, monthly, and quarterly meetings between the sales professional and the sales manager; it focuses on improvement.
2. *Public tracking:* Sales activity presented in a weekly and monthly report card format to the entire firm and sales organization; it informs, motivates, and inspires competition.

Tracking, if set up and managed appropriately, can help sales professionals to *analyze their game.* If you've developed a sales organization with a culture in which tracking and coaching are intertwined, your sales professionals will want to use a tracking tool and will be hungry for their weekly, monthly, and quarterly reviews. Remember, tracking is about improving performance, and your job, as a manager, is to repeatedly ask, "How can I help you improve?" Three key tracking tools are instrumental to successful coaching and are useful to any firm.

TRACKING TOOL 1: ACTIVITY-BASED SALES MODEL. The activity-based sales model helps the sales professional and the manager track the sales process and, more importantly, identify what things in this process are within the sales professional's control, and thus are able to be improved, and what things are outside their direct control. Exhibit 4.4 is an example of the activity-based modeling tool used at FTI, Inc.

This activity-based sales modeling tool enables sales professionals and managers to evaluate their performance metrics on a regular basis. Examine this model, looking at each metric, the detail surrounding this metric, and, most importantly, whether this metric is within the span of human control; that is, can the sales professional impact this metric significantly?

To gain the full benefit of this activity-based sales model, it is essential that you incorporate this analysis into regular progress meetings with sales professionals. Using the model as an analytical tool, a manager can act as a coach and help sales professionals to analyze their individual game. Two example cases illustrate the combined coaching power of the activity-based sales model and the sales manager.

DIALS	CONNECTS	APPOINTMENT CLOSING RATIO	TM BOOKED APPOINTMENTS	NO SHOW/ APPOINTMENTS CANCEL (%)	APPOINTMENTS ATTENDED	LOES PER YEARR	LOES PER YEAR	MINUS 30 PERCENT	MINUS PUSH 10 PERCENT	TRANSACTIONS PER YEAR	REVENUE ($)
100	25	30	7.50	20	6	0.90	45.0	13.5	4.50	27.0	1,350,000
100	25	25	6.25	20	5	0.75	37.5	11.25	3.75	22.5	1,125,000
100	25	20	5.00	20	4	0.60	30.0	9.00	3.0	18.0	900,000
100	25	15	3.75	20	3	0.45	22.5	6.75	2.25	13.5	675,000

Note: This activity-based sales model was created in Microsoft Excel, and the data is populated by a CRM tool. If you don't have a CRM system, a simple Excel spreadsheet will work fine. If you do have a CRM or contact management system, work with your IT department to synchronize the two databases.

Exhibit 4.4   Tracking Tool for Activity-Based Sales Model

Example Case Number One: Joan, a new sales professional, doesn't have enough appointments. Why? During her quarterly review, you and Joan analyze her numbers. Does her lack of appointments come from an inability to articulate the company's value? Fear of the phone? Not asking for the appointment? Calling the wrong people? Through this dialogue and analysis, you can put together a coaching plan for Joan. In the meantime, as Joan is acquiring new skills, you can help her to positively influence the metrics she does have control over—in this case, the number of dials. Using the modeling tool, you can determine how many additional dials Joan must make to book enough appointments to reach her revenue goals. After suggesting this short-term solution, you can then implement a coaching plan that will help her to reach the standard rep appointment close ratio of 30 percent.

Example Case Number Two: Gary, a veteran sales professional, does not particularly like call canvassing—who really does? When you sit down to your quarterly review, you see that Gary's dials number is very low—well below the standard rep minimum of 100 per week. While at first glance you see a need to discuss (in negative terms) this number with Gary, the modeling tool shows that Gary's appointment closing ratio is at 40 percent, exceeding expectations, and his closing ratio is also high. Gary will clearly meet his quarterly sales quota. As a manager, you can use the sales modeling tool to show Gary how much more money he would be making if he increased his dials by just 10 or 20 calls, motivating him to achieve more. You can also pinpoint Gary as an effective closer and turn to him when there is another professional who needs coaching in that particular area.

The activity-based sales model is an essential tool; it has value for both the sales manager and the sales professional. It helps managers see how they are going to grow the business and develop a strong sales team, and it helps sales professionals get to the next level.

TRACKING TOOL 2: WEEKLY REPORT. The weekly report follows a report card format and lists a subset of the categories included on the activity-based sales model. The weekly report focuses on letters of engagement (LOEs) and provides highlights of prospect accounts. Sales call reports, which are entered into the contact management or CRM system, are automatically aggregated into the weekly report (see Exhibit 4.5).

TRACKING TOOL 3: MONTHLY PIPELINE. This detailed and high level tool forecasts revenue by sales professional and details the prospect company, stage of sales cycle, date contact initiated, forecasted revenue and probability of close, factored revenue, and a quarterly revenue pipeline.

The weekly report and monthly pipeline tracking tools provide the sales manager with traditional pipeline information. When used as coaching tools,

Jane Smith: Chicago	CALLS	CONNECTS	MEETINGS SCHEDULED	ATTENDED	CONFLICTS	LOES	LEADS	HIGHLIGHTS
1/4/2004	16	7	3	3	1	1	1	Conflict check/LOE: *Plymouth v. Matson* (Strauss); Lead: Turner Industries
1/11/2004	43	17	3	2	3	2	0	LOE: *Schmidt v. Cosmos* (Johnson Bell); LOE *Gallagher v. Tabb, et al.* (Becker Strong); Conflict check: *Smith v. Craig* (Jones Davis)
1/18/2004	33	16	8	6	1	0	0	Conflict check: *Paxo v. Lyons Corporation* (Johnson Bell)
1/25/2004	26	15	5	6	0	0	2	Corporate Securities Presentation (Straus)

Exhibit 4.5 Weekly Report

103

the manager, together with the sales professional, can examine the leads on a case-by-case basis. The manager might ask pointed questions, such as, "Is this a real opportunity?" and depending on the sales professional's response, the lead might be removed from the pipeline. Alternatively, the manager might ask, "How can I help you close this lead?" and can then contribute his or her industry or intuitive knowledge to help the sales professional win the business.

TRACKING THAT IS PUBLIC. Complementing tracking that is coaching is tracking that is public. Public tracking is primarily informational and *motivational*. In addition to reviewing tracking tools numbers 2 and 3, the weekly report and monthly pipeline, with the individual sales professionals, these reports should be distributed to a larger audience: the *firm leadership* and the *entire sales organization*.

We know that sales professionals and professional consultants are competitive; this public disclosure of pipeline information *encourages friendly competition*. Sales professionals do not want to look bad in the eyes of their peers or their leaders, thus they work competitively to bring up their numbers. From the consultant's perspective, if Joe in the trial services practice sees that a sales professional is working on a number of hot leads in conjunction with a competitive associate, Joe might think, "Hey, I want to work with one of those salespeople."

Finally, in addition to serving as a motivational and forecasting tool, tracking that is public helps you, the sales manager, to promote the contributions of your organization and to justify the existence of the sales organization. Exhibit 4.6 provides a detailed key to the metrics and concepts for the activity-based sales model discussed in this section.

Sales Meetings

Communication within the sales organization and within the larger firm community is essential. Through effective communication, professionals share general knowledge, best practices, and intuitive insights. The agenda and schedule of sales meetings will be unique to a specific firm because the agenda is dependent on what the sales professionals want to cover, and the schedule will vary based on the size and development stage of your sales organization. New sales teams might require more frequent meetings, while seasoned teams might move to biweekly or monthly meetings. *Learning, sharing, getting better, and practicing—this is the purpose of sales meetings.* An overview of three meeting formats that will improve the communication, knowledge sharing, and productivity of your sales organization follows:

1. *Weekly sales meeting:* Weekly sales meetings form the core of team communication. These meetings should follow a standard format, focus

METRIC	METRIC DESCRIPTION	IN CONTROL/NOT IN CONTROL
Dials	The number of outbound calls a sales professional makes per week. Early in the development of a patch or territory a sales professional is expected to make a minimum of 100 calls per week. Some might have to make 200 to hit their numbers.	*In control:* The sales professional can make more or fewer calls.
Connects	The number of calls that actually connect to a live prospect. On average, the number of connects will represent 30 percent of the dials. this statistical average can be applied across sales environments	*No control:* The sales professional can try to connect by calling early in the morning, bypassing the administrative assistant, but really doesn't have much control over this metric.
Appointment closing ration and booked appointments	The appointment closing ratio details the percentage of connects that should result in meetings. A new sales person will be expected to hit an appointment close ration of 20 percent. A more senior professional is expected to hit 30 percent. Booked appointments details the actual number of connects that resulted in scheduled meetings.	*Control:* Skill and knowledge influence the sales professionals's appointment closing ratio and number of booked appointments.
No show /cancel.	The number of appointments that did not show or cancelled.	*No control:* On average, 20 percent of booked appointments will no show or cancel. The sales person can try to influence this by reconfirming, but these tactics will not likely improve this ratio.
Appointments attended	The number of appointments that were actually conducted.	*No control:* The sales professional might show up to attend, but the prospect might not. Thus, the only control the sales professional has in his or her ability to show up.
Matter closing ratio	The number of deals that the sales professional closes. A new sales professional would be expected to close 10 percent of the actual appointments attended. A more senior sales professional is expected to close 30 percent.	*Control:* Skill and knowledge influence the sales professional's close ratio.

Exhibit 4.6   Activity-Based Sales Modeling Tool

(continued)

METRIC	METRIC DESCRIPTION	IN CONTROL/NOT IN CONTROL
LOEs per week and LOEs per year	The number of letters of engagement (LOEs) or contracts that the sales professional generates. This metric self-generates based on the closing ratio and includes both conflict checks and LOEs to calculate a blended number.	*Control:* Skill, the ability to close business, influences this metric with the caveat that if the business doesn't clear conflict, the sales professional has no chance of closing.
Minus the 30 percent settle and minus push 10 percent	These columns are unique to litigation consulting.	*No control.*
Matters per year	Based on the statistics, the number of matters or contracts that are sighed and proposals that are implemented per year.	*NA:* This metric is a reflection of the previous metrics.
Revenue per average matter	The average dollar amount of the deals closed.	*In control:* Skill influences the sales professional's ability to ask for more money. Over time, sales professionals become more comfortable with closing bigger deals.

Exhibit 4.6   *Continued*

on education and sharing, and last no longer than 60 minutes. Reach out to the sales team to identify special topics that they would like covered at each meeting and rotate leadership of this meeting so that all sales reps have an opportunity to lead, teach, and learn.

2. *National sales meeting:* The national sales meeting is held once or twice a year at an off-site location. This is an opportunity to celebrate success, share best practices, sharpen everyone's sales skills, and introduce new service lines and professionals.

3. *Phone blitz:* The phone blitz is a highly targeted competitive call canvassing exercise that brings the salesforce together in a friendly competition to see who can secure the most sales appointments on a given day within a set time. To encourage participation, prizes are awarded to the sales professionals who book the most qualified meetings. This competitive exercise works well as a team-building exercise and can be a training exercise if you build in pre-blitz brainstorming and debriefs at the completion of the contest. It is also a great way to launch a new service.

Selling Your Services

Sell the way people want to buy—not the way you want to sell. "Selling is a science, not an art," notes Wendy Lea, managing partner with Chatham Group, LLC.[10] According to Lea, the art aspect of selling comes in only as it relates to personal dynamics and politics, which are important, but sometimes overplayed. The science aspect of sales is that selling is a systematic, professional *process*. This section walks you through the process of understanding your customer and *selling the way people want to buy, not the way you want to sell.*

A typical sales cycle includes the phases or components shown in Exhibit 4.7.

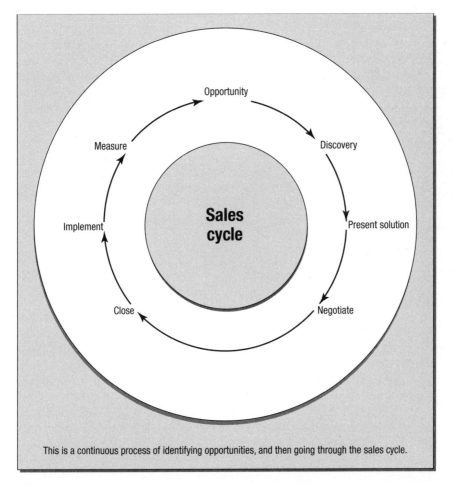

This is a continuous process of identifying opportunities, and then going through the sales cycle.

Exhibit 4.7   Phases of the Sales Cycle

While these phases are universal to most sales cycles, your sales process is going to be unique depending on your firm, the services that you sell, and the industries that you target. The first step in successful selling is to understand your sales process.

Exercise: Mapping Your Unique Sales Process

This exercise asks and answers the question: How do we get to "closing" on a new engagement? Bring together a group of veteran sales and consulting professionals for a brainstorm session. During this session, select two or three successful new business wins, and backtrack through the sales process. Be painstaking during this dialogue, and examine all of the detail involved in targeting and closing a new business deal. This exercise will help your organization to see all of the steps involved in your sales process, and, over time, a pattern will emerge. This pattern is your unique sales process.

Once you have insight into your unique sales process, you can then map it against the typical sales cycle as outlined in Exhibit 4.7 to create an informational flow chart that depicts your firm's process.

Selling the Way People Want to Buy

As stated earlier, successful sales professionals sell the way people want to buy, not the way they want to sell. There is a contagious energy that results from this approach to selling.

Before going on a sales call, it is necessary to understand the nuances of selling professional services. Selling professional services is unique in that you are positioning *capabilities;* this is different from positioning a solution or a product. In the early stages of selling, finding the right amount of positioning (positioning the firm in addition to the practice), without having done a lot of discovery about the client need, is difficult. However, in the professional services sales environment, it is critical that you position the capabilities of both the firm and the practice to gain the legitimacy that is required to gain access and the confidence of the prospect's decision makers.

In selling professional services, *the most important part of the selling process is the beginning.* This beginning, or discovery stage, is the second step in Exhibit 4.7. In a typical selling environment, consultants often walk into a new client meeting feeling pressured to present a solution before having a clear understanding of the problem. Or, out of confidence (or arrogance), a consultant will walk into an initial sales meeting claiming to already know the solution that the client needs. In both of these situations, the consultant immediately starts selling; there is no time to assess and re-flect on the situation and position the value of the solution in the context of the client need. This approach to selling results in a decrease in selling power.

Selling power directly correlates with contextual power. Contextual power results from placing your solution in the context of the client need. It is at the beginning of the sales cycle that the sales professional and consultant have an opportunity to clearly understand the client challenge, to identify the right solution for the client, and to then position and sell that solution in the context of the client's need. This is why the beginning of the sales cycle is so impor-tant. To establish selling power and sell your capabilities through the eyes of your client, sales professionals must continually challenge themselves with three key questions, as listed in Exhibit 4.8.

According to Wendy Lea, within the professional services sales environ-ment, there are five stages that make up the ideal discovery phase of the sales process. These five stages guide the initial dialogue between the sales professional and the client service consultant, and the prospect:[11]

1. *What is the client trying to accomplish?* This is the first question to raise in any discussion with an enterprise. Typically, a consulting orga-nization is brought in when something has gone wrong and the client needs assistance or the client does not have the in-house capabilities to deliver on a particular project. A team of professionals on the client side is responsible and accountable for meeting a commitment.

2. *What is keeping the client from accomplishing what they've committed to?* Or, what is your challenge? It is critical that the sales professional and consultant understand what challenges and obstacles the func-tional group has encountered in its attempt to accomplish the project.

QUESTIONS TO CONTINUALLY ASK

1. What is your (client) challenge?

2. What decisions do you (client) have to make?

3. How do I lay my value on top of that?

And most importantly:

Does this (solution) make sense for my client?

Exhibit 4.8   Key Selling Questions

Remember, typically, an internal group at the client site has made a commitment that they are accountable for achieving and have encountered bumps along the way.

3. *How can the prospective client solve the problem?* At this stage of the discussion, there are three options the client can choose to pursue:

—*Do nothing.* The prospective client makes a determination that there is a problem, but perhaps the problem does not have enough weight or is not understood well enough to proceed with a solution.

—*Solve internally.* The prospective client more clearly understands the problem and determines that the best route is to use an internal team to manage the project.

—*Go outside.* The prospective client more clearly understands the problem and determines that the best route is to bring in a team of external professionals to manage the project.

4. *Research the solution.* If the prospective client decides to pursue a structured solution or to "do something," the client will either assign an internal team to research a solution or retain an external firm to research the solution. Ideally, your professional services firm will be engaged at the solution research, or proposal development, stage.

5. *Evaluate the proposed solution:* Once proposals have been developed, the prospective client will then look at the proposal through a set of evaluation criteria and determine whether they have the budget to proceed.

The challenge for many professional services firms is that the consultants get brought in at the middle of the buying process; thus, they walk in and start selling a solution. Or, some professional services firms are so confident in what they think they know that they either go through the five stages in a surface fashion or don't go through them at all. However, if your sales professionals are trained to sell as your clients buy and to continually ask the right questions, you will create context for the dialogue with the client, which will result in greater selling power and, ideally, greater client satisfaction.

Targeting and Lead Generation

The terms *targeting* and *lead generation* both equate to identifying and touching potential customers. As a salesforce, it is important to focus on *generating a steady hum of revenue.* In a professional services firm, if you don't have new business, your consultants are on the beach. While this steady revenue might not be the most interesting business, it will keep your firm's consultants active. At the same time, however, your sales organization needs to be available for and attuned to the big deals. During the exercise in which you defined your unique sales process, you likely uncovered some marketing and lead generation tactics that resulted in qualified prospects for your firm. In addition to this insight, tips to effective lead generation include:

- *Identify the buyers of your service on a regular basis.* The buyers of your service depend on the nature of your consulting services and might be broken down by industry, size, or geography. Know them intimately: What do they read, what organizations do they belong to, what authority impresses them or regulates them? Invest in market research to understand their buying behavior and preferences.

- *Frequent "touches" with your buyers.* By using an activity-based sales model combined with specific targets, you increase the number of times that you are in conversation with the buyers of your services. In conversation with your targets, continually ask yourself what information you can share with them that creates the perception of the value you provide and gets you in front of them. You want to get your prospects excited, whether through opportunity or pain. Storytelling is a proven way to touch your buyers. People listen and remember through stories, and whether you are phone canvassing or selling in front of a client, leveraging your great case studies, dressing them up, and sharing them is a home run tactic. And, above all, brand your touches. If you want to be memorable, you have to be branded.

- *Be opportunistic.* While you are paying regular attention to your steady buyers, pay attention to what's happening in the marketplace. If you see a need that your services can meet, go after that business. Your professional consultants, the experts, will be attuned to marketplace shifts, and it is important that sales professionals stay close to this pulse of knowledge. Intranets and knowledge portals can be helpful with this level of knowledge sharing. In addition, the daily business papers and weekly trade journals are excellent sources of knowledge, as well as industry-specific databases. For example, FTI sales professionals regularly access Lexis Nexis, CourtLink, and CourtEXPRESS to check the dockets for significant upcoming cases where the firm's services might be useful to a law firm or corporation.

In relation to targeting, John Salomon, forensic advisory practice leader at FTI Consulting, Inc., stresses the critical role that the sales professionals play in being in front of a prospective buyer *at the time they have a need.* Salomon notes that while he might meet an attorney (prospective buyer) at a function and talk with that prospect extensively at that time, if there is no immediate need for FTI's services, that prospect is most likely not going to remember Salomon and FTI when a need arises three months or one year down the line. The sales professional, on the other hand, is trained to identify prospective buyers on a regular basis and, in an ideal situation, can get in front of prospects when the need is hot.[12]

Mining Your Firm's Consultants

Mining your firm's consultants equates to knowing who and what you are selling. John Salomon notes that a key role of the sales professional is to "assemble the best client service delivery team."[13] To do this, the sales organization must have intimate knowledge not only of the key practice and service areas, but of the practice leaders and consultants within those practice areas.

There are a number of processes, all communication based, that you can institute to help your sales professional mine your firm's consultants:

- *Regular meetings:* When your firm is small, hold regular meetings where client service and sales professionals get together and discuss what they've done. As your firm grows, regular networking opportunities and attendance at national sales meetings provide good discussion and networking forums. In addition to information exchange, meetings provide opportunities for the client service professionals to get to know, respect, and trust the sales professionals.

- *Relationships with client service leaders:* One of the most direct routes to locating the best consultant for the client need is to ask the senior practitioner in a practice area: Where do I find this skill set? For relationships to form, meetings and networking are essential.

- *E-mail:* A simple use of technology is the firmwide e-mail distribution. When searching for the ideal consultant for a new business meeting, the sales professional can quickly send out an e-mail to the firm or a particular practice area, providing some background on the potential deal and indicating what skills he or she is looking for (e.g., a senior practitioner who has experience in intellectual property damages in the auto aftermarket industry).

- *Intranet knowledge database:* A more sophisticated use of technology is the creation of an intranet (internal) knowledge database that maintains updated information on the firm's consultants. Ideally, the sales professionals can search this database on key criteria such as region, service experience, industry experience, and other more qualitative information, such as average client engagement size. This information will help the sales professional put together the best team for a particular client.

- *Decision matrix:* At FTI, the sales professionals found that the practitioners were able to speak clearly in relation to what they did, but they could not talk about themselves in relation to the client or in a way that was helpful or appropriate for sales professionals. To meet this communication gap, the FTI sales organization developed a matrix that asks key questions and helps sales professionals to "mine" their client service professionals:

—Who is your ideal prospect (client)?

—What are the client's decision triggers?

—What are the typical questions you get asked on a sales call?

—What is the marketplace competition for your service area?

—What is the structure/process associated with a typical sales call?

—What are the steps in your typical sales cycle?

—How do we price your services?

—Includes frequently asked questions the practitioner receives from client prospects.

Communication is the cornerstone of effective mining. It is important that sales professionals and client service teams get to know each other and build relationships on mutual respect and trust. It is this integration that will help sales professionals to identify and pull together the best team based not only on skill and expertise but also on working style.

Measurement

When thinking about measurement, there are two distinct questions: How much does it cost the firm, on average, to win a significant piece of new business? How do I measure the success of my sales organization?

The costs associated with closing a new business deal in the professional services environment are complex. One approach is to measure your sales success in terms of efficiency. Your sales professionals, in this environment, touch many people; and you can assess how many calls were initiated, presentations delivered, and deals closed. Another approach measures effectiveness. In measuring effectiveness, understanding your sales cycle and how much resource investment, in terms of time and money, it costs to get to the end of the deal is the overarching issue. Measuring effectiveness is difficult, and it can be even more difficult in an environment in which professionals and salespeople are often in reactive mode and responding to requests for proposal (RFPs) and other reactive sales efforts. In this environment, the professional services firm is spinning its resources to respond to a client prospect in a relatively short time and invest a significant number of hours and money into winning new business. In this selling environment, it is difficult to step back and honestly assess how much it costs to bring in a deal and then measure the cost of sales in relation to that figure. The challenge for your particular firm is to assign some costs to time and touches. How much time does it usually take for us to close a deal, and how many times do we need to touch the prospect within this time period? Then, the question becomes: How do we economically touch and educate a reasonable number of prospects to reach our revenue goals?

Once you determine the costs associated with selling, you can more accurately predict the investment the firm will need to make in sales to achieve set revenue goals. Two metrics you can use to measure the success of your sales organization are *cost of sales* and *revenue.* Your sales managers should be compensated based on these two metrics; this ensures that the managers work both to control the costs associated with selling and to drive revenue.

Support Systems, Processes, and Technologies

Technology is central to good selling and good sales management; this chapter has touched on many sales and management processes, most enabled by technology. As you begin to form your sales organization, a crucial question will be: What technology do I need? The software that you choose will be distinct based on your firm's current technology, the structure and size of your sales and marketing organizations, your unique sales process, and, most importantly, how your sales and client service professionals actually work. Choosing the right technology is important and at times difficult. Kevin Hoffberg, of Decision-Quality, LLC, states, "For the most part, technology for sales organizations is a miserable failure."[14] This failure primarily results from a lack of understanding about how people work. Organizations often purchase and implement technology solutions to improve productivity or streamline processes without understanding what sales and client services professionals do on a day-to-day basis. If you have done the work suggested in previous chapters, you have a good understanding of your sales process; you have worked to integrate your sales, marketing, and consulting professionals; and you know a bit about how your people work. This is the first step in ensuring a successful technology implementation. To help you further along the technology journey, this section marks a path through the layered world of technology to help you evaluate your options.

Layer 1: Create access. Of prime importance is your professionals' ability to communicate and to communicate remotely. Thus, the first technology layer enables access—access to clients and colleagues. To facilitate communication, every firm should have e-mail. After this rudimentary step, the communications challenges mount. Sales professionals, who spend much of their time out of the office, need the ability to remotely access, send, and receive e-mail; do text messaging; and make telephone calls. For any size firm, remote access technology, such as the Blackberry, is rapidly becoming a cost of entry. Your firm must invest in this technology if you want your sales professionals to be available and responsive to clients and prospects. Over time, you might consider providing your sales professionals with laptops or PDAs that enable remote access to documents or hardware with Wi-Fi access. It is important that sales managers investigate the latest technologies. Sales professionals will be hungry for communication technology that improves their access to clients, colleagues, and their work, and they will actively use it.

Layer 2: Find ways to share. This layer is collaboration. Every professional services firm needs to share information in a way that allows sales and client service professionals to access collective wisdom and knowledge. This collaboration helps professionals to mine data, build client service teams, and create more compelling sales presentations. But, how do I collaborate? Before you can answer these questions, you need to examine how people work.

How do they work? Most likely, both your professionals and salespeople spend most of their time using office automation/desktop tools such as MS-Outlook, MS-Word, MS-Excel, and MS-PowerPoint. After all, these professionals are in the business of communicating and building documents. Now, management decides that the firm needs to share information and monitor customer and pipeline data and asks sales and client service professionals to jump to another console to input numbers. This approach will not work—there will be resistance. In a call center environment, you can configure a CRM tool, such as Siebel, so that the call center sales professionals can do all of their work within that system. But, if you work for FTI, an advertising firm, a law firm, or any other professional services firm, you will be hard pressed to get your professionals to jump from Outlook or PowerPoint to another console. They just won't go there.

So, what is the solution? There is no simple answer; however, there are some guidelines and tips that you can follow. The decision about what technology you need is driven by complexity. Access is the first and most critical layer, and after that comes sharing. Dependent on the size of your sales organization, your sales process, and your go-to-market touchpoints, your technology needs will be different. When your firm is small, collaborating will be relatively easy. You can simply share information via meetings and simple e-mails saying, "Has anybody got . . . ?" or "Does anybody know . . . ?" As your firm grows and you have multiple client access points, you will want to evaluate an Application Service Provider (ASP) hosted solution, such as Microsoft CRM or Salesforce.com. These solutions interface with MS-Outlook, so your sales professionals can continue to work primarily within the e-mail system. However, as your firm grows even bigger, you will want to consider working with an outside consultant to implement a CRM tool. Implementing a complex technology solution often sparks a firmwide culture war—after all, technology changes the way people work and impacts the very nature of the way you conduct business. To navigate this tension and this process, it is helpful to have a customer relationship expert at your side.

Exhibit 4.9 summarizes software solutions designed to facilitate the sales and customer relationship management process and provides information to guide your initial software evaluation.

	OUTLOOK 2003 WITH BUSINESS CONTACT MANAGER	ACT!	GOLDMINE FRONT OFFICE	SALESFORCE	MICROSOFT CRM	SIEBEL	SAP	PEOPLESOFT
Target market	Individuals, small- to medium-sized business	SOHO businesses and individuals	Small- to medium-sized businesses with up to 100 users	Companies who do not wish to hire additional IT staff or purchase new hardware	Companies of any size with at least 5 to 10 professionals	Large enterprises with CRM budgets	Large enterprises running SAP R/3 ERP on the back-end	CRM 8 for large businesses and accelerated CRM for small to mid-sized businesses
Average cost	Included in MS-Office Professional and Business editions	$200/seat or license	Approximately $500/seat depending on volume	$65 to $125/user per month	$5,000 to $50,000	$$$	$$$	$$$
Key benefits	Included in MS Office. Easily managed contacts, sales opportunities, and accounts, all in one place	Basic contact management, degree of sales and pipeline analysis	Business partner network, add-ons focused on vertical industries, industry award winner	Low overhead CRM No additional IT staff needed; lower total cost of ownership; scalable; sales, marketing, and service functionality	Low overhead CRM Provides fully integrated customer relationship management; includes sales and customer service modules	E-sales, partner relationship management, employee relationship management, marketing and support. 200 application modules, support for over 20 industries	Products span entire customer interaction cycle	Covers sales, marketing and service processes Integrates with non-PeopleSoft back-ends
Contact information	www.microsoft.com	www.interact.com	www.frontrange.com	www.salesforce.com	www.microsoft.com	www.siebel.com	www.sap.com	www.peoplesoft.com

Exhibit 4.9 Software Solutions for Customer Relationship Management

As you move across the technology terrain, remember that technology alone does not equate to an increase in productivity. In a paper published in 2003 titled, "The Measurement of Firm-Specific Organizational Capital,"[15] researchers found that investments in organizational capital accounted, on average, for 71 percent of sales growth across the 250 companies they researched. The report found that organizational capital is driven by how information is communicated and coordinated and that technology can enhance this process. For technology to show results, it must be integrated into your firm and its work processes. The company has to value it, and the professionals must be willing to use it.

The decision as to what technology to implement is specific to your firm. At FTI, we are implementing a CRM tool that will integrate with our accounting system. As long as your system is maintaining your data, is simple to use, and can be accessed and mined to meet your reporting, management, coaching, and prospecting needs, it is sufficient. The various process documents, activity modeling, and pipeline tools discussed in this chapter were developed using Microsoft Excel in conjunction with contact management software. As your firm grows, you will likely find that your technology needs will grow as well. The key point to remember, however, is that you must have a defined sales process before you implement a contact management or CRM technology solution.

Our philosophy of integrating technology within your organization is similar to the philosophy associated with sales tracking. If your technology is used for tracking time or as a control tool, it won't work. For a technology implementation to succeed, it must:

- Have value for its users, the sales and client service professionals.
- Be integrated with the firm's unique sales process.
- Achieve buy-in. Those who are expected to use it must be both willing to use it and be held accountable for using it.

Summary

Right now, you are contemplating something new, a sales organization in a professional services firm, and you might be tempted to go with the more orthodox, traditional approaches in professional services sales. As you read this chapter, perhaps something intrigued you or resonated with you. Now the "something new" feels possible, and perhaps achievable. But, as with all new challenges, peering over the edge is likely to bring you a feeling of anxiety. You might be thinking about turning back. For inspiration, I suggest this excerpt from the book *True Success*, by Tom Morris:[16]

> Have you ever watched bungee jumping? You know people screaming like maniacs, or praying like crazy, leap off high bridges over rivers attached by a long elastic

cord tied around their ankles. They fly through the air like acrobatic suicides, and then at the last second before contact with earth or water, are snatched back to security by the cord. Since not everyone lives near a tall bridge over a deep gorge, the bungee jumping companies began bringing large cranes into parking lots to lift adventurous souls on metal platforms high above asphalt for the daring dive. For $60 or so you can line up and get on the platform. It is very interesting to watch, especially the first timers. You can see on their faces the transition from bold to tentative to terrified. Hoisted up into the air peering over the edge of their little perch, these folks confronted something the likes of which they had never done before. Most froze. But the bungee pros, the operators, were ready. A companion on the platform spoke reassuring words of encouragement, a little pep talk. A guy with a mike blasted, "three, two, one, bungee."

And on the count most people jumped. But some stood there with jelly legs, shaking and trembling and thinking this might not be such a good idea after all, willing now to offer twice the admission to get back to solid ground the slow, safe way. But their platform coach said, "hey, you can do this, you'll be fine, it will feel great, just do it." And the crowd is yelling, "jump, jump, jump." And the announcer, "three, two, one, bungee," and with a roar from the crowd below, the novice dives. Some took three countdowns, nonstop pep talks, and lots of cheering. *But they all jump.*

Take a lesson from the bungee crowd. We all need support when we confront something new, particularly in some of the more staid professional services enterprises. It can be difficult to leap into something different. It can take a lot of reassurance. It can take pep talks. It can take a great deal of cheerleading. But with enough support, with enough confidence, and with the momentum that comes just by starting, you can do it. When you set yourself the high goal of creating a world-class firm, you gave yourself a challenge. Now, use this chapter and the resources as your mentor and your cheerleader. Each section provides you with insight and actual tools to enable you to:

- Organize, build, manage, and coach your sales team.
- Understand your sales process and sell effectively.
- Track, measure, and promote your results.
- Choose the systems and technologies that will best benefit your firm.
- Generate revenue!

Remember, whether yours is a firm of 10 or 10,000, a sales organization is an effective tool for revenue generation and enhanced client service.

RESOURCES

The following online and printed resources will help you as you establish a sales organization within your professional services firm:

Selling, Marketing, and Management

American Marketing Association: www.marketingpower.com

Robert B. Cialdini, PhD, *Influence: The Psychology of Persuasion* (New York: William Morrow & Co., 1993).

Kevin Hoffberg, www.decision-quality.com and www.kevinhoffberg.com

Al Reis and Jack Trout, *Positioning: The Battle for Your Mind* (New York: McGraw-Hill, 2000).

Recruiting, Training, Hiring

Achieve Global, www.achieveglobal.com

Sales Essentials Group (SPQ Distributor), Rose Venditto, rose@salesessentials-group.com

Society for Human Resource Management, www.shrm.org

Customer Relationship Management

CRM Research: www.crmguru.com

Kevin Hoffberg, www.decision-quality.com and www.kevinhoffberg.com

NOTES

1. "Like herding cats," *Economist* (April 18, 2002).
2. See note 1.
3. Available from http://www.marketingpower.com/live/mg-dictionary-view2714.php (February 19, 2004).
4.
5. Rosann Spiro, William J. Stanton, Gregory A. Rich, William E. Prentice, *Management of a Sales Force* (New York: McGraw-Hill, 2002).
6. Lisa Burris Arthur, "Guided Selling: Merging Marketing and Sales," available from http://www.marketingpower.com/live/content15696.php (February 19, 2004).
7. "Should You Adjust Your Sales Compensation," available from http://www.shrm.org/hrmagazine/articles/0202/0202agn-compensationa.asp (February 19, 2004).
8. Telephone interview with Patrick Strong, managing director, FTI Consulting, Inc. (February 8, 2004).
9. "Structured Behavioral Interviewing: Oldie But Goodie," available from http://www.shrm.org/ema/library_published/nonIC/CMS_006200.asp (February 2004).
10. Telephone interview with Wendy Lea, Managing Partner, Chatham Group, LLC (February 6, 2004).
11. See note 10.
12. Telephone interview with John Salomon, managing director, FTI Consulting, Inc. (February 16, 2004).

13. See note 12.

14. Telephone interview with Kevin Hoffberg, Decision Quality, Incorporated, LLC (February 19th, 2004).

15. "The Measurement of Firm-Specific Organization Capital" (Baruch Lev and Suresh Radhakrishnan National Bureau of Economic Research, April 2003).

16. Tom Morris, *True Success: A New Philosophy of Excellence* (Berkley Publishing Group, April 1995).

5

Marketing and Business Development

BRYAN J. WICK

Don't be fooled by the calendar. There are only as many days in the year as you make use of. One man gets only a week's value out of a year while another man gets a full year's value out of a week.

—Charles Richards[1]

This chapter identifies and outlines successful marketing techniques and models used by professional services firms to develop business. While most professionals would rather practice their profession, developing business is perhaps the most crucial function of a professional services firm. The success of any venture is dependent on its ability to develop a client base and drive revenue. Without a strong client base, no firm can survive. In this chapter, we discuss various models and techniques used by a variety of professional services firms to market themselves, develop business, and, consequently, drive revenue. Additionally, because it is also important to know what not to do, we discuss the effectiveness of the various strategies.

There are three prevalent models that professional services firms use to market themselves and develop business:

1. Most common is the partner model wherein firms use their owners, shareholders, and partners.
2. Firms use internal human capital in the form of professional sales staff and marketers (as discussed in the previous chapter).

3. Firms use external sources such as marketing, advertising, and public relations firms.

Each of these models can be productive. Chapter 4 outlines the dedicated salesforce option in detail. Because the partner model is the most prevalent in professional services firms, it is the focus of this chapter. The sales and outsourcing models are touched on briefly.

This chapter focuses on a number of business development topics, including:

1. Defining yourself and the target or ideal client;
2. Using human capital and financial resources efficiently and effectively;
3. Developing business by demonstrating your expertise and competency by writing, speaking, organizing seminars, publishing newsletters, and facilitating business between and among the firm's clients;
4. Developing business through relationships by (a) developing a network for the referral of business, (b) forming strategic alliances, (c) participating in charitable and community organizations, (d) maintaining and cultivating relationships, (e) presenting yourself with confidence, (f) practicing diligence and perseverance, (g) focusing, and (h) offering assistance to existing and potential clients;
5. Successfully managing clients and their expectations; and
6. Advertising as a means of driving business.

The ideas and strategies discussed in this chapter use techniques that have been proven over time. However, the list of techniques discussed is not exhaustive, and the professional will quickly realize that there is no right or wrong way to market firm services or develop business. Professionals in a cross-section of the market experience varying degrees of success depending on their personalities and the strategies implemented. Depending on the firms personnel, lines of business, target market, and target clients, you may opt to use some of these techniques and variations of others.

Why This Topic Is Important

The first step toward successfully marketing your firm and developing business is to define yourself and your target market. You cannot efficiently allocate your resources and effectively market your firm unless you have done this. Professionals are often tasked with the dual role of servicing their clients and developing business by securing new clients or expanding the scope of existing relationships. Because there are limited hours in the day, you must work efficiently as a professional and as a marketer. The first step in the path to success is to develop a detailed game plan. In doing so, you must define yourself, your firm, and your target market or ideal client.

Defining Yourself and the Firm

Firms differentiate themselves from the competition by carefully defining their attributes and characteristics. This step is critical to success. Firms that have focused service offerings generally have better performance than firms that try to "do it all." To attract new clients and retain existing clients, you must define yourself and the firm in such a way as to differentiate yourself and the firm from the competition. It is imperative that you convince existing and prospective clients that you offer something unique that the competition does not. Failing the ability to offer a unique service, you become a commodity product. Additionally, differentiating yourself and thus taking the firm out of the realm of the fungible product enables the firm to charge more for its services.

Defining and differentiating yourself may seem like a daunting task. However, a highly productive team-building exercise begins by gathering partners and principals in a room to discuss the basic tenets and unique capabilities of the firm. Each of the participants should spend a few minutes identifying the attributes that make the firm a better option than the competition. Write this list on a board or flipchart. After the list is complete, the group should identify the competition and list their attributes. Finally the group compares the lists by crossing off every characteristic that you identified as also being a characteristic of the competition. What remains are the attributes that make the firm different. These differences could lie in the culture of your firm or a unique service that you offer. Regardless, these differentiating factors must be the focal point of any marketing discussion with potential or existing clients.

As part of this exercise, you may engage the strengths, weaknesses, opportunities, and threats (SWOT) analysis that focuses on key marketing issues and should be a technique incorporated into the exercise of defining the firm and the ideal client. When conducting the SWOT analysis, the participants should be realistic and extremely critical of the firm's weaknesses and external threats. The analysis will not be effective unless the group avoids the natural tendency to ignore weaknesses and threats. Specificity in identifying the firm's strengths and weaknesses and the market's opportunities and threats will make it more valuable and effective.

Strengths and weaknesses are internal factors. Strengths might include such things as the firm's focus or expertise, the quality of the firm's work product, the firm's recent successes, the firm's ability to think outside the box, the quality of the firm's process and procedures, and any other aspects of the firm's business that add value for the firm's clients.

Weaknesses may include undifferentiated services that the firm offers in relation to its competitors, previous damage to the firm's reputation, a historic inability to successfully manage the expectations of the firm's clients, and lack of experience in particular areas of the firm's practice.

Opportunities and threats are external factors. Opportunities might include developing markets that represent potential new clients, strategic alliances, new services that offer additional ways for the firm to drive revenue, and areas of the market currently being serviced by a competitor that offers an ineffective or inferior product.

Threats can include new competition within the firm's market, new and innovative services offered by the firm's competition, successes of the firm's competition, and superior expertise and experience being offered by the firm's competition.

Defining the Firm's Target Market and Ideal Client

In addition to defining the firm and its capabilities, you can most effectively utilize resources by identifying a specific target market or type of client. The shotgun approach is an inefficient way to develop business and usually results in bad business for both the firm and the client. Defining a focused market and identifying specific clients or industries allows you to focus marketing efforts and better understand prospective clients and their concerns. After identifying the ideal market or clients, the firm will be positioned to efficiently market its services and ensure the efficient use and allocation of your financial and human resources. A common mistake, made particularly by smaller firms, is to attempt to be all things to all clients. Not only does this lead to disappointed clients but also to burned out delivery staff as they move from project to project with very little carryover of knowledge, skills, and intellectual property to help them. A tight focus on a specific, narrow service offering is important for small to mid-sized firms.

When defining the target market, the firm should evaluate the following characteristics:

- Whether the client is an individual or business entity,
- The industry in which the ideal client does business,
- The annual revenue (or other measure of size) of the ideal client,
- The geographic location of the ideal client,
- The number of employees, and
- Whether the ideal client is publicly or privately held.

After determining a target market, the firm should focus its efforts on the ideal client based on the analysis. For example, if the best client for the firm is a mid-size manufacturing company, then all marketing efforts should be targeted toward acquiring business from new clients in that industry or market. Putting the firm in front of the target market and developing a reputation within that market will ensure success.

A few years ago, a New York-based law firm specializing in securities compliance found itself assisting several privately held companies with general corporate issues. After engaging in this exercise, the firm discovered because of specific expertise that it had developed, that its ideal clients were actually publicly held companies and organizations involved in the securities markets. The firm then refocused its efforts and was able to increase its client base significantly. Additionally, by focusing on larger companies and well-established securities firms, the firm was able to achieve higher billing rates. Finally, by developing a niche and becoming an expert in its field, the firm soon found itself turning away business to manage its rapid growth. Although this firm's experience may be exceptional, it is not unique and is a useful example of the value of focus in service offering and target market.

Using Human Resources Efficiently and Effectively

An important challenge facing professional services firms is the efficient allocation and utilization of its human and financial resources in the pursuit of new business. While the firm may offer an excellent product and exceptional service, if you are unable to market those services and develop a reputation within your target market, your firm will fail to satisfy its potential and may even fail to survive.

As discussed in Chapters 3 and 10, most professional services firms are structured as partnerships or corporate entities with members who serve as decision makers. Therefore, in the spirit of maximizing the return on human and financial capital, it is not surprising that most professional services firms use their partners/members and employees to market the firm and develop business.

The Partner Model

There are numerous techniques and models used by professional services firms to market themselves and develop business. However, using the firm's personnel—the partner model—is by far the most common method employed by small and mid-sized firms.

ADVANTAGES AND DISADVANTAGES OF THE PARTNER MODEL. There are numerous advantages of the partner model. Some of them include:

- Professionals are often motivated by monetary gains and personal gratification to successfully market the firm. Using the firm's personnel ensures that financial and personal interests are aligned. The synergy of aligning financial and personal interests is a powerful motivating factor. This is important because developing business is difficult and requires a great deal of hard work, dedication, and comfort with rejection. Aligning firm and personal interests increases the chances of success.

- The professionals within the firm are well positioned to understand the product and speak knowledgably about it. While it is possible to educate a professional salesforce or marketing firm about the firm's services and attributes, it is expensive and, if not managed appropriately, can be less productive than the partner model. Further, it is a powerful message for clients to realize that the firm's personnel are personally dedicated to the firm and its success.

- By utilizing the firm's partners and members, the firm preserves its financial resources. While the firm potentially loses revenue through the loss of billable time, it is able to preserve its financial resources that would otherwise be spent on outside services or a dedicated sales team.

- The relationships developed during the marketing process are the same relationships that continue during the firm's work with its clients. An important determinant of professional services firms' success is their client relationships; this is an important characteristic of the partner model. The sales approach is grounded in the concept of establishing relationships rather than selling services. It is important to establish a strong bond with your clients from the start.

The partner model, while relatively efficient and appropriate for small- and some mid-sized firms, is not without its disadvantages:

- When using firm partners or professional staff to drive business, ensuring the efficient allocation of resources is critical. Typically, as firms grow and the number of clients increase, management is faced with the decision of offering additional services to leverage existing clients while continuing to develop new business. It is difficult to quantify but it is much easier to expand on an existing relationship than to develop new ones. Exhibit 5.1 illustrates the issues surrounding allocation of resources as the firm continues to grow and increase its client base.

    The most efficient use of human and financial resources is traditionally found along the slope of the line. As a firm grows at some point management will be faced with the opportunity to develop additional services through leveraging its existing client relationships. As a general rule, professional services firms should, as they increase in size and client base, begin to offer additional services (as opposed to adding new clients) as a means of securing efficient growth.

    The small firm, including the traditional litigation boutique, is represented by Firm X. Exhibit 5.1 shows that Firm X has relatively few professionals as compared to its larger competitors and that it is offering only one or two primary services. However, within its target

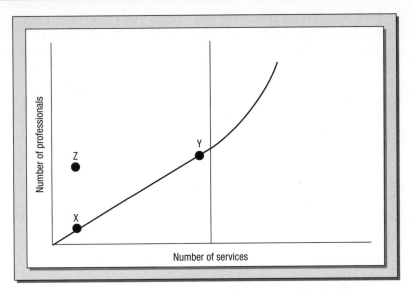

Exhibit 5.1   Firm Resource Allocation over Time

market, Firm X is specifically focused and proficiently services its clients. In fact, by specializing in the services it offers, Firm X, even with its limited human resources, can experience great success. Firm X is also uniquely situated so that it can, as discussed earlier, preserve resources by specifically focusing its marketing and business development efforts.

The mid-size firm, represented by Firm Y, is at a fork in the road. Firm Y must determine whether to offer new services to existing clients as a means of increasing its revenue or focus its resources on developing new clients. Firm Y may be able to expand on its existing relationships by offering additional services more efficiently than developing new client relationships. If Firm Y offers additional services to existing clients, it can increase revenue without being forced to expend the human and financial resources to develop new clients. Financial modeling, which is discussed in Chapter 15, is critical when determining whether to expand your human capital and increase your financial obligations.

There are, however, always exceptions to the rule. For example, a specialized commercial litigation firm, which is represented by point Z on the exhibit. As a general rule, Firm Z should offer additional services to its existing clients to maximize its efficiencies and capitalize on its human resources. However, this is where pragmatism and theory diverge because Firm Z is, with its numerous attorneys, focused solely on high-stakes commercial litigation. Despite its extensive supply of human capital and singular focus, Firm Z is profitable and successful. Firm Z's success originates and is in large part attributable to its ability to differentiate itself from its competition and focus on a specific segment of the marketplace.

- Marketing and developing business are not easy tasks, and in fact, are one of the most difficult tasks faced by the professional services firm. As a result, a great deal of diligence, perseverance, and discipline is required to do both well. The firm should set specific expectations and well-defined goals to ensure the diligent pursuit of developing business for the firm and furthering its reputation. An effective tool to ensure the appropriate level of effort in the pursuit of business is to require professional staff to attend regular marketing meetings. Each meeting should focus on the firm's goals and the means by which those goals can most efficiently be obtained. In addition to defining the firm's target market, the participants should discuss their network and marketing ideas. The meeting should begin with a brainstorming session and end with the allocation of specific business development or sales-oriented assignments. The assignments can range from entertaining an existing or potential client to speaking at a forum or symposium attended by existing or potential clients. It is imperative to provide direction and make each person accountable for his or her actions or, as the case may be, failure to act. Peer pressure as a form of accountability is a powerful tool that should be incorporated into the firms approach.

    A large Houston-based law firm focuses a great deal of its marketing efforts on its partners. The firms sales volume is, therefore, reliant on the diligence of its partners. Every month, each practice area holds a marketing session. After the partners discuss their ideas and identify their current network, each partner is given an assignment. There are no quantifiable penalties for failing to complete your assignment. However, the desire to succeed and the fear of letting down partners and peers significantly outweigh the inertia that professionals must overcome to market the firm and develop business.

    Conversely, a mid-size accounting firm in Seattle uses the "carrot" as opposed to the stick. This firm has instituted a series of incentives to encourage its professionals to market the firm and develop business. For example, the firm awards two round-trip tickets to the professional who brings in the most new business in a given quarter. Further, the firm shares fees with the professional(s) responsible for originating every client. Significant accomplishments can result from ensuring that the incentives of the firm and its human capital are aligned.

- Managers or the management committee of a firm must understand the boundaries of the firm's human capital. Certain members of the team will not be well suited nor have the desire or aptitude to market the firm or develop business. For example, an accountant may be able to perform his or her work functions proficiently but have no desire and little ability to market the firm or develop business. However, so long as the decision makers understand that every team has its utility players and that certain professional staff are not well suited for developing business, this obstacle can be overcome.

The inherent inefficiencies of the partner model, while oftentimes outweighed by the benefits, should be evaluated by the firm. Many professional services firms adhering to this model are concerned that their human capital will, at the expense of servicing their clients and driving revenue, spend too much time marketing the firm and developing business. While you can never lose sight of the fact that the firm drives revenue and succeeds as a result of the work effort put forth by its personnel, you have to complement those efforts with a diligent marketing and business development strategy. If the firm does not continuously build on its existing relationships and work to develop new relationships, it will eventually collapse. Successful professional services firms are able to maintain a constant flow of new business.

TECHNIQUES ASSOCIATED WITH THE PARTNER MODEL. Two central techniques are used to develop business and drive revenue with the partner model. The first technique focuses on the firms ability to demonstrate expertise in specific practice areas. This technique concentrates on the exhibition of substantive, relevant proficiencies of interest to clients.

The second technique focuses on your ability to develop relationships as a means of driving business. The relationship approach is controversial in that some believe it the most efficient way to develop business while others question its effectiveness. However, most professionals would agree that clients typically hire firms or specific professionals that they like and trust. The techniques are complementary and not mutually exclusive, and in fact, work best together.

Developing Business by Demonstrating Your Expertise and Competency

As with any marketing effort, it is critical to define the target market before implementing any strategy. After defining the target market, there are several ways to ensure that potential clients understand the focus of the firms expertise and services, including:

- It is important to write well and often. People believe what they read and recognize authors as authorities on a given topic. Further, writing is an effective means by which you can display your analytical skills. Publishing an article on a specific area or focus of your practice allows you to build your reputation as an expert in that field. Additionally, writing an article and publishing it in a reputable venue, such as an academic journal or industry publication, provides instant credibility with the audience.

  It is important, as we have discussed, to focus business development efforts on the target market. It is most efficient, and a better use of resources, to publish in the trade journals or periodicals most often read and relied on by existing and potential clients in the target market. Establishing expertise within the target market builds reputation and leads to more business. However, many professionals argue that there is an additional tangible benefit to publishing in journals and periodicals within the profession. By establishing the firm as an expert or an authority on a given topic, the firm is in a position to receive referrals from peers when issues arise within the specific area of expertise.

- In addition to writing, members of the firm can enhance the reputation of the firm by speaking on issues central to the firm's expertise. Most people are uncomfortable speaking in public, and therefore such opportunities are well suited to separate the firm from the competition. However, as with every technique discussed in this chapter, the firm should focus its efforts on the target market. It is more productive to speak to a room full of potential clients than to a room of existing and potential competitors. Being in front of the target market and speaking on issues important to the audience, makes the firm a reliable and respected authority on the topic. Secondarily, it helps establish expertise in a unique area of practice, and puts the firm in position to receive referrals from others in the profession.

- Market your proficiencies and assist your clients and prospective clients by offering periodic seminars or discussion groups wherein recent developments or important areas of the profession are discussed. Rather than arranging to speak at a function organized by another (possibly competitive) group, you may consider hosting round-table discussions or seminars at your offices. A large accounting firm in the Southwest believes in this marketing strategy. In fact, this particular firm invites all of its clients as well as many prospective clients to monthly luncheons where its members discuss recent developments in the accounting profession. By providing a forum for the free exchange of ideas and the presentation of recent developments affecting its clients, the firm is able to assist the community while developing its reputation, securing its existing client base, and developing new clients who become aware of the firm's competency based on their participation in the discussion groups. It is important to stay in front of existing and potential clients and to continually remind them of your services, reputation, competency, and abilities.

- Publishing periodic newsletters is another way to provide clients and prospective clients with valuable information while displaying the firm's competency and focus. Remember, it is critical to continually develop the firm's reputation within the target market. Further, and more specifically, it is important to keep the firm's reputation in the forefront of clients' and prospective clients' minds.

- An additional technique is to help clients and prospective clients by assisting them with their business. By sponsoring an activity that brings together clients and prospective clients who can work with or assist one another, you become known as a facilitator. If you can help your clients and prospective clients accomplish deals and drive business, they will likely want to help by giving you their business. A large consulting firm in the Southeast exemplifies this strategy by sponsoring an annual retreat attended by bankers and business owners. The synergies of this connection are obvious, and the firm has experienced a great deal of success in pairing up its clients and prospective clients. By assisting the members of its target market with their respective businesses, the firm ensures its place at the forefront of their thoughts and has driven extensive business from these outings.

Developing Business through Relationships

Developing business for a professional services firm is not a function of merely selling the firm and the skills of its human capital. Rather, business is driven by developing relationships of trust and confidence with existing and potential clients. Several years ago, professionals experienced substantial success by merely befriending clients and potential clients. However, competition today mandates that you do much more than just be a good friend. In today's competitive market, it is critical that you instill in your clients and potential clients a sense of trust and confidence in your abilities. The combination of a strong, competitive service offering and a personal trusted relationship is a powerful driver of successful professional services business development.

When considering the strategies outlined here, keep in mind a few basic rules:

- Make sure you have sufficiently defined the firm, the services, and the target markets.

- Develop relationships within the target market. For example, if the firm is targeting money managers, then the most helpful relationships will be with professionals in that area, or in related areas.

- Before beginning a relationship, do your homework. Business development professionals should become acquainted and proficient with research tools and learn as much as possible about a potential client before even meeting him or her.

After defining the firm and its service offerings, defining the target market and ideal client, and doing your homework, there are several techniques that, if utilized, can effectively drive business through the development of relationships. Those techniques include the following: (1) developing a network for business referrals; (2) forming strategic alliances; (3) participating in charitable and community organizations; (4) maintaining and cultivating relationships; (5) presenting yourself with confidence; (6) practicing diligence and perseverance; (7) focusing; and (8) offering assistance to everyone, even those who may not be able to help you as much as you can help them. More specifically:

1. Many smaller and even some larger firms receive a great deal of new business through referrals. Firms are often conflicted from representing new or existing clients based on actual conflicts of interest due to existing clients and staffing issues. By establishing relationships with your peers, which may also be competitors, you can position yourself to benefit from referrals. However, it is important exercise diligence in following up on referrals and delivering for them. "Dropped" referrals and poorly executed delivery will end all further referrals from that source.

2. Firms offering specialized services often form strategic relationships with firms that offer other and complementary services. For example, if you operate a law firm that exclusively focuses on serving the litigation needs of its clients, you can benefit by forming a relationship with firms that specialize in other areas of law such as securities compliance. By doing this, you can establish mutually beneficial relationships. For example, the litigation firm can refer its corporate work to a firm specializing in corporate law and vice versa. However, be careful to select your strategic partners wisely—they may become an important source of revenue. Strategic partnerships are the focus of Chapter 6.

3. Giving back to the community by participating in charitable organizations is beneficial on a personal level for professional staff and often provides the additional benefit of improving networks and driving business. When selecting a charitable organization, pick one that

focuses on a cause you believe in. Although participating in charitable organizations is hard work, it is very rewarding. You can enhance your reputation within the community by giving your time to help others. Further, you will be surprised how many potential clients you will meet during your involvement. It is human nature to want to help those who are helping others. For example, many professionals have found that joining their local Rotary Club has positively impacted their practice while providing them with a rich sense of community.

4. Take advantage of your past. Keeping in touch with childhood, college, and postgraduate friends is helpful on several levels. For purposes of developing business, those long-term relationships can prove invaluable. You can either maintain these relationships on your own or through the assistance of organized alumni associations. Every major university, fraternity, and sorority organizes reunions around the country. The easiest way to locate these groups is to search the Internet for organizational information. By being involved, you are assured of meeting people with interests similar to yours. This is a great way to begin new relationships and further develop existing ones. When searching out clients, you will be pleasantly surprised at the difference a common bond will make.

5. While it is important to always present yourself as confident and engaging, professionals must be aware of the fine line between confidence and arrogance. While confidence is contagious, arrogance is not.

6. Be diligent and persevere. Networking is time consuming and difficult to do well. After every encounter, you should follow up with an e-mail, a handwritten note, or a telephone call. The personal touch of a note or call is always appreciated and memorable, but if time does not permit then an e-mail will suffice. The most important reason, however, to be diligent is that most people are not. Diligence and perseverance in your personal relationships is an easy way to differentiate yourself. Remember, if you decide to use relationships as a means of driving business, keep your focus, remain diligent, and you will see results.

7. Maintaining focus, while difficult, is essential to successfully developing business and operating a professional services firm. Without focus, your ability to develop business is greatly compromised. For example, it is important to address administrative issues. However, if you spend too much time worrying about administrative issues, you may lose sight of your primary goals and the firm will suffer. Often internal, administrative, and delivery issues are more attractive to professional staff than developing new business. Addressing such issues does not carry the risk of rejection and still feels like "work"

to firm management. Guarding against this tendency and staying focused on new opportunities is critical for the firm, particularly with the partner-based sales model.

8. It is important to always be willing to offer assistance to others before asking for assistance yourself. If you are truly willing to help someone and ask for nothing in return, it is almost certain that he or she will return the favor at some point. Ask what you can do to help and make sure to follow through. When those whom you have assisted, or even offered to assist, return the favor and offer to help you, be ready with a response. Be specific. Always let people know exactly what they can do to help. By being specific in your request for assistance, you increase the chances that assistance will be provided. For example, if people ask you how they can help, it is not constructive to merely ask them to refer business to you or keep your firm in mind if they are ever in need of assistance. Rather, be specific. Ask to be introduced to someone in particular. If you are an accountant, you may ask to be introduced to a high net-worth client. By being specific, you can more easily follow up. If you ask people to refer business to you, it is difficult to follow up by asking why they have failed to do so. However, if you ask for a specific introduction, you can follow up if the introduction is not made in a timely manner.

In summary, the main characteristics of a successful marketer are (1) diligence and perseverance, (2) focus, (3) confidence, (4) a willingness to assist others, and (5) an ability to maintain and cultivate relationships.

When deciding which marketing and business development techniques work best for a given situation, remember that you can mix and match. There is no wrong technique, provided it assists in developing business. Although the subject matter and relationship approaches are discussed separately, firms should not focus exclusively on one at the expense of the other. The most successful rainmakers blend multiple techniques. Demonstrating your competency while developing relationships is a powerful marketing combination. You never know where your next big client will come from. Therefore, always make sure you are positioned to capitalize on every opportunity.

Successfully Managing Clients and Their Expectations

The challenge of maximizing the potential of a new client immediately follows the development of the new relationship. Earlier we discussed the fact that it is many times more expensive to develop a new client than cultivate and nurture an existing one—commonly referred to as "farming versus hunting." While client management may not initially appear to be an appropriate discussion in the context of marketing and developing business, a closer look reveals that it is a crucial component of developing business. Properly managed client relationships allow the firm to reap a windfall with repeat business. Further, the firm should strive to expand on the relationship so that they eventually service all of the appropriate client needs. Managing clients and their expectations is not, however, an easy task. To the contrary, there are several things to keep in mind when managing your client relationships.

First, and perhaps most importantly, you must always remember to manage expectations concerning service and results. Successful professionals face the difficult challenge of maintaining their relationships while being careful not to overextend themselves. There are only so many hours in the day, and the professional can be in only one place at a time. Therefore, it is important that each client understand from the beginning which member of the firm will be primarily responsible for servicing its needs. The firm must be careful to match compatible personalities and provide the client with proficient and competent service. If the client expects the firm's lead rainmaker to process its matter, the client will likely be disappointed if someone else is assigned the job. However, if the firm manages the client's expectations, it can avoid this unpleasant scenario.

In addition, it is important to manage expectations concerning results. Nothing is guaranteed and there are very few certainties in the professional services business. Therefore, be careful when guaranteeing results. If you come up short, the client relationship may be permanently damaged. However, if you explain to the client that there are numerous contingencies, many of which are beyond your control, the client will be prepared for the bumps along the way. Further, if you discuss with your clients the obstacles to overcome in servicing their needs, your clients will be more appreciative when you fulfill their needs and provide a successful result.

Second, if you take care of your clients, they will take care of you through repeat business and referrals. Exhibit 5.2 illustrates this point.

There are many professional services firms that can provide acceptable solutions or results. The differentiating factor, however, is to ensure that each client enjoys the process while receiving good results. The X on Exhibit 5.2 denotes a poor client experience. Client X did not receive very good results and did not enjoy the process. It is not likely that this client will provide you with repeat business or referrals. More troubling, however, is the fact that you are now in danger of a former client talking negatively about your firm and its service.

The inverse of Client X is Client Z. Where Client X received a poor result, Client Z received a very good result. Perhaps just as important, however, is the fact that Client Z enjoyed the process. Client Z may have

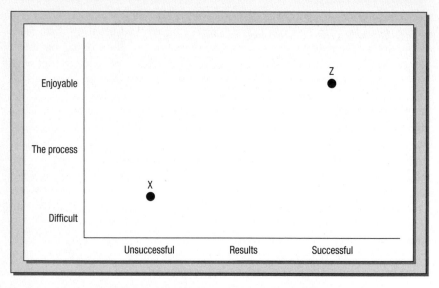

Exhibit 5.2   Professional Services Firm Delivery Outcome versus Client Satisfaction

enjoyed the process for a wide array of reasons, including the attention provided, the speed with which the result was obtained, and/or the cost associated with the result. Regardless, Client Z not only will be a repeat client and refer business to the firm but also will be likely to praise the firm's performance to all who will listen. Client Z just became the firm's most effective and cost-efficient source of marketing.

Chart your clients on a graph like this to see where the majority of your clients fall.

When considering how to make the process more enjoyable, remember these basic tenets:

- The client should always feel that he or she has your full and undivided attention when you are discussing his or her goals and concerns.
- Never tell a client that you are too busy to talk.
- Always return your client's telephone calls and e-mail messages as soon as possible, but at a minimum within the same day.
- Treat everyone the same—from the most senior officer to the newest staff member—because you never know who will be making the decisions next year or even next month.

Chapter 12 covers the topic of effective client service delivery in more detail.

Advertising as a Means of Driving Business

Initially, the consensus among professional services firms is that mass marketing and advertisements are not an effective way to drive business. Part of the reason for this negative attitude toward advertising stems from the fact that the results are difficult to quantify, and it is difficult to find a sufficiently targeted venue for the specific service and client base. Like every rule, however, there are exceptions.

Plaintiffs' attorneys have experienced a great deal of success advertising to the public at large. However, the success of these sometimes-massive campaigns depends on their focus. For example, many plaintiffs' attorneys arrange to have their advertisements aired during the day, relying on the fact that those suffering from injuries are at home and watching television. Based on the success of many personal injury attorneys, it is clear that advertising can work with certain professional services models.

While advertising can directly drive business, it is more often useful in increasing brand awareness. If the firm provides a service targeted to a mass market, such as personal injury, brand awareness among the public, which can be achieved through advertising, is beneficial. However, if the firm elects to advertise, make sure that the advertisement is focused toward the target market.

Additionally, when advertising, make sure to highlight the firm's recent and most significant accomplishments. It can be effective to advertise that you were able to save a client significant resources through your efforts or that you procured a significant win for a client. The key is to focus on your successes, particularly those that the target market will view as significant.

Finally, always advertise with a call to action. Passive advertisements are not very effective. It is not very effective to tell everyone how great the firm is without a specific directive to act. It is, however, compelling to command your target market to pick up the phone and give you a call.

Using Internal Sales and Marketing Personnel to Drive Business

In addition to using its partners or members, some professional services firms take advantage of internal sales personnel as a means of marketing and driving business. This approach was the focus of Chapter 4.

Using Professional Marketing and Public Relations Firms

Professional services firms also use marketing and public relations firms to assist them in developing business. Marketing and public relations firms specialize in developing name and brand recognition across selected segments of the population. Some of the many tools at their disposal include media such as television, newspapers, and periodicals. Additionally, these firms can assist in securing public speaking engagements, which, as we have discussed, are valuable tools for developing business. However, this technique is not widely used by professional services firms for several reasons:

- Outsourcing your marketing efforts is widely viewed as a passive method of developing business and, therefore, is not a common technique among professional services firms. More specifically, the outsourcing model does not require or even allow for much, if any, interaction between professionals and their clients or prospective clients. Rather, because this model focuses on developing the recognition of brands, this model has primarily been adopted by companies selling their products to the public at large, not professional services firms.

- As with advertising, many firms have chosen to steer away from the outsourcing model because it is can be difficult to quantify the return on your investment. Human and financial resources are limited. Therefore, most firms are more comfortable with techniques that either don't require a large capital investment or those for which they can quantify a return on investment.

- The outsourcing model can be costly and a severe strain on the financial resources of a smaller professional services firm.

- This model should only be considered if the firm is willing to expend significant resources (time and money) on the efforts of your external marketing team. There are enough large companies to keep the marketing and public relations firms busy so that the smaller professional services firms are often not attractive targets for them. As a result, the smaller firm will receive little, if any, attention.

The Pitch

The focus of this chapter has been on developing business. However, most of the techniques and models discussed herein will not, in and of themselves, result in paying clients. There is usually an additional step. Techniques such as relationship building and public speaking will open the door to opportunities, but before those opportunities develop into paying clients, you will need to close the deal. At this point, the pitch becomes the most important area of focus. Developing a strong pitch is multidimensional. Rob Levinson, a columnist for *Startup Journal,* wrote an article titled, "Help! I Got the Meeting, Now What Should I Do?" In that article, Levinson discussed the three stages for pitching business to prospective clients: (1) the prepresentation, (2) the presentation itself, and (3) the postpresentation. Many of the techniques involved in these stages have been discussed and are used on a daily basis to develop business.[2] While the topic of proposals and qualification management is covered in detail in Chapter 7, we briefly address a few points here.

Prepresentation

ALWAYS APPEAR PROFESSIONAL AND PREPARED. It is often the little things that separate the firm from the competition. Therefore, always look professional (e.g., wear a suit or appropriately formal attire) when meeting a prospective client. Even if the prospective client is not dressed in a suit, he or she will appreciate your professionalism. Further, whenever you travel to a meeting, always park far away from the entrance to the building to allow an opportunity to assemble yourself without appearing disheveled or disorganized to the potential client, who may be looking out the window or awaiting your arrival at the entrance.

WALK IN SMART. Before your meeting, call the prospective client to introduce yourself and thank him or her for agreeing to meet with you. During this conversation, ask pointed questions that will help you discover information about the prospective client's situation and allow you to tailor your presentation accordingly. Further, during this call you will be able to assess the prospect's sincerity and confirm that the prospect has the resources, decision-making authority, and mind-set to hire you.

Your success depends on how well you understand your potential client's business. The SWOT analysis will assist you in pinpointing the company's strengths, weaknesses, opportunities, and threats. Weaknesses and threats are "pain points"—areas where the organization is vulnerable and needs attention. This, combined with the specific client feedback garnered in the previous step, will be the basis for the solution you offer in the presentation.

CREATE A STORYLINE. Based on the information uncovered through the SWOT analysis, build a presentation that communicates your understanding of the prospective client's industry, illustrates your related experiences, and convinces the prospect that you can solve their problems. While your industry experience may make for interesting chatter, all a prospect really wants to know is: "What can you do for me today?" Therefore, it is important to include only information that is directly relevant to the prospective client in your presentation.

ANTICIPATE YOUR AUDIENCE. Your presentation should fit the audience and the environment. Presenting to an entrepreneur at a local coffee shop is far different from meeting with a CEO and his or her management team in a conference room. Assess your audience so you can make educated decisions about format, for example, a slide show versus a printed presentation versus a conversation, equipment and audiovisual requirements, and even dress code. Presenters should always bring a few more copies of material than they believe they will need, to provide for unanticipated participants.

If the meeting includes multiple people in a conference room, plan on a more businesslike format. However, if you are meeting one person in a home office, you will likely just talk. Regardless, make sure your audience knows what to expect before you arrive.

REHEARSE . . . A LOT. You have the meeting. You are smart and know your business. You offer a quality service that your competitors do not. You want this client. Remember to rehearse at least once, preferably several times. This is particularly important when you are presenting with a colleague to ensure that you interact proficiently.

While the basic presentation may be universal, you will likely change anecdotes or success stories for different prospects. However, it is important to make sure you are comfortable and conversant with the storyline. You will likely have only one chance to secure the business. Further, it is certain that you will have only one chance to make a first impression. Do not blow it.

Presentation

The presentation is where the "rubber meets the road" in the business development process.

OWN THE ROOM AND THE MEETING. Always arrive at least 20 minutes early to allow time to check your appearance, set up and test your equipment, and decide where you and your team should sit or stand in the room.

Sometimes, a prospective client may have requested presentations from several firms. If you arrive early, it is surprising how often you will find a competitor's materials left on a conference room table. This allows you an opportunity to glance at your competition and to make sure you differentiate yourself.

Once your prospect arrives and you have made all of the appropriate introductions, recheck to determine how long you have to state your case. You have rehearsed and have your presentation down to the minute. However, you always must be prepared to truncate your presentation and adapt to changes in circumstances. It is better to know at the beginning than to have your prospect interrupt you on his or her way out the door to another meeting.

CLOSE THE LOOP.   Be sure to restate your understanding of the prospective client's issues, the budget, timing, when results can be expected, and the manner in which the working relationship will be structured. Your goal should be for you and your prospect to be clear on these issues when the meeting ends. Mention again how much you want the business.

Postpresentation

Follow-up and pursuit after the presentation will help close the deal or, at a minimum, glean learnings from the client to provide improvement in future performances.

MANNERS MATTER.   At this point, the firm must plan on waiting for the client's response. Send a thank-you e-mail and any requested materials in a prompt manner. Also, make sure to answer any questions that may arise. If you do not hear back from the prospect within an agreed period of time, the firm should not give up. Stay in touch with the prospect, alternating between leaving a friendly telephone message and sending e-mails.

Never act annoyed or impatient because of the lack of response. Seeming curious is an appropriate approach. Remember, while closing the business may be your top priority, hiring you may be at the bottom of the prospect's list. At some point, sooner or later, the target client will need the services of the firm, and ruining a long-term relationship because of short-term impatience is a bad choice.

LEARN FROM FEEDBACK.   Requesting feedback is another technique. Regardless of whether you land the business, ask what the prospective client thought of your presentation, what was learned, what was missing, and how you can improve. We all like to be asked for our opinion. This discussion allows you to show your respect for the prospective client—and the process—while gaining vital insight for your next presentation.

Summary

There are numerous models and techniques that successful professionals use to market themselves and their firms in an effort to develop business. However, there are a few essential points, including organization, diligence, and focus. Given the cost of human capital to the professional services firm, it is imperative to take an organized and diligent approach to ensure that you maximize the firm's resources. Further, remember to have patience. Developing business can be a long and arduous process. Do not expect immediate results, and be prepared for the long haul. Additionally, perseverance is a non-negotiable quality of any successful rainmaker. It is one of the ways you can separate yourself from your competition. Finally, preparation and focus in pitching new business is critical and lack of preparation can rapidly undo many weeks of business development effort.

NOTES

1. Charles Richards,

2. Rob Levinson, "Help! I Got the Meeting, Now What Should I Do?" *Wall Street Journal—Startup Journal,* accessed March 2004. Available from http://www .startupjournal.com/columnists/marketing/20031203-marketing.html.

6

Service Line and Intellectual Property Creation

Thomas Marbach

They are all people who are in trouble about something and want a little enlightenment. I listen to their story, they listen to my comments, and then I pocket my fee.

—Sherlock Holmes[1]

The business world is splitting into two types of companies: those that have intellectual property and those who do not.

—Gordon V. Smith and Russell L. Parr[2]

This chapter presents two major elements of the professional services firm's creative process, the ideation and maturation of services that are offered to prospective clients as products or firm proprietary knowledge, and the subsequent protection of intellectual property that often comprises the essence of these services. Exhibit 6.1 depicts an overview of this creative process.

Why This Topic Is Important

In Sir Arthur Conan Doyle's first tale of his infamous consulting detective, Holmes informs Watson that it does not matter to him whether the earth orbits the sun or the moon. Watson sees Holmes as a paradox. Holmes's ignorance of topics such as the earth's orbit is beyond comprehension while his knowledge of seemingly minor and unrelated topics is extraordinary. As Holmes reasons, he is merely being practical, and in his eminently practical

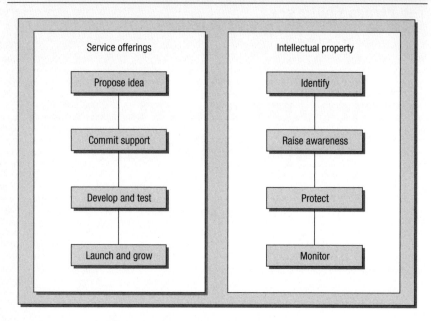

Exhibit 6.1   The Service Firm's Creative Process

view, he believes it is the skillful worker who focuses solely on relevant knowledge. Similarly, Albert Einstein was reputed, when asked for his phone number, to have looked it up in the phone book. When asked why he did not know his own phone number, Einstein allegedly replied "Why should I memorize something, when I know where to find it?"

In deciding where to focus the firm's service development efforts, the skillful professional services firm will attempt to determine its relevant knowledge, how to offer this knowledge so that the marketplace deems it of value, and thus where to focus the firm's new service development effort. Further, the firm will make efforts to ensure that the knowledge is instutionalized so that the firm professionals "know where to find it." To this end, the firm should endeavor to understand key dynamics that represent the firm's challenge, the client's challenge, and the firm's response to these challenges. Three related questions arise:

1. What forces are impacting the firm's development of new services?
2. What are client organizations experiencing and how are they responding?
3. How will the firm respond as it relates to developing new services and products for its clients?

The Firm's Challenge

Professional services firms face multiple forces that drive the need for innovation in the services they offer to the marketplace. These forces include competition, market trends, regulatory changes, and rapid improvements in technology. In addition, the services firm's clients continue to adjust their buying tendencies over time, as well as respond to their own marketplace pressures. These adjustments include: (1) the capability/desire to provide their own solutions, (2) changes in discretionary spending levels due to market economics, and (3) the extent of client deal-making or shopping around, especially as choices in services are deemed to be more widely available. Combined, these forces lead to difficulties in retaining long-term customers that consistently buy predictable levels of professional services and pressures to create new and enhance existing services that will lead to steady streams of revenue.

The Client's Challenge

Change is as inevitable for client organizations as it is for the professional services firm. As the new millennium dawned, noted marketing expert and the S.C. Johnson & Son Distinguished Professor of International Marketing at the Kellogg School of Management at Northwestern University, Philip Kotler[3] identified general trends in the way companies are responding to their customers' increasing demands. Kotler's analysis is shown in Exhibit 6.2.

The Firm's Response

Professional services firms are in the sometimes unenviable and yet potentially profitable position of responding simultaneously to their own as well as their clients' challenges. In developing a response, a firm may elect to develop its new service offerings using a mixture of reactionary, opportunistic, and forward-looking strategic approaches. These can be a function of work the firm is performing for current clients as well as work it hopes to do for clients in the future. Although described as three separate approaches, many firms find it desirable to blend the following approaches, as there are certainly valid reasons to adopt a portion of each approach.

CLIENT-BASED OPPORTUNITY. This approach views the development of new services as a *reactionary* response to existing client work. Existing engagements serve as a model for new service offering development. One example is the use of existing client projects to codify best practices to support the delivery of future engagements. A second example is the use of multiple similar engagements to justify the establishment of a new service line, practice,

TREND	FROM	TO
Reengineering	Functional departments	Process teams
Outsourcing	Internal services and goods	External if it can be done cheaper or better
e-commerce	Brick and mortar store-fronts and face-to-face	Internet for products, specs, terms, prices
Benchmarking	World-class	Best practices
Alliances	Winning alone	Networks of partner firms
Partner-suppliers	Many suppliers	Fewer but more reliable
Market-centered	Product emphasis	Industry segment
Global and local	Local only	Both global and local
Decentralized	Managed from top	Local level control

Exhibit 6.2 Organizational Responses and Adjustments

or business unit. This approach has the advantage of being relatively low cost and highly successful because the service offering is field-proven and clear empirical demand exists for the service. Disadvantages include the risk that this approach is unlikely to lead the firm into innovative service areas, and there also may be issues with scalability due to firm constraints and tendencies. Furthermore, it is likely that other competing services firms will have identified the same need and will be moving to create similar service offerings, resulting in rapid competitive parity in the area.

COMPLIANCE-BASED OPPORTUNITY.   This approach views the development of new services as an *opportunistic* response to client needs as these organizations strive to respond to changing regulatory, statutory, and compliance demands. Examples of these demands include financial reporting requirements and state and federal legislation (e.g. Sarbanes-Oxley compliance, or the Year 2000 system compliance problem). This approach has the advantage that nearly all client organizations face some need for outside help especially as the compliance burden continues to grow. The disadvantage is that it can take years to get individual employees up to speed on the intricacies of a given industry and its associated nuances. Furthermore, there has been a proven "gold-rush" mentality for some of the larger compliance-based service initiatives, making it difficult for a firm to have its services stand out from the crowd. While this pursuit can be very profitable, it can be highly competitive as well.

Market-Based Opportunity. This approach views service development as a *forward-looking* response to anticipated market changes. In the vein of a venture capital model, the firm chooses among competing ideas and supports those ideas that are deemed most advantageous. Competing ideas, for example, may include modifying existing services to enter new industries or introducing completely new services. The advantage of this approach is that it can be growth-oriented especially if existing capabilities are included in the new service offering. The primary disadvantage is that it may become inordinately expensive especially if the firm chooses the wrong services to invest its resources. Building new service lines without market validation can be risky. Firms considering pursuit of market-based opportunities should explore ways to validate demand for the service line with potential customers prior to investing significant capital in the new offering.

The remainder of this chapter is organized into two sections. The first section provides rationale, context, and suggested processes and roles for supporting the creation of service offerings. The second section discusses the various types of intellectual property and its protection once it has been created.

Service Line/Service Offering Creation and Development

Each firm has differing needs both for the outcomes and associated processes for new service creation. The level of process formalization is largely dependent on the intended outcomes. In keeping with general management principles, large intended outcomes tend to require more formal processes. Process formalization has two primary benefits. First, it is useful for helping ensure successful outcomes. Second, formalization may be used as evidence to assert the firm's ownership rights over its intellectual property.

This section provides a discussion of several interrelated topics—benefits, definitions, expectations, processes, and roles. Benefits associated with formality in the service offering creation are presented followed by a distinction among three terms (service lines, service offerings, and capabilities). Setting expectations for the firm's service offering creation effort is then discussed. Finally, a proposed process to support the creation of new service offerings and the associated roles needed to support the creation process are discussed.

Benefits

Focusing the firm's attention and resources on the underlying development process for the creation of new service offerings may provide some of the following benefits:

- Improves the likelihood of successfully launching new ideas
- Formalizes and rewards the generation of and competition between new ideas
- Reduces wasteful spending on unprofitable ideas
- Improves time-to-market response for new ideas
- Integrates new idea generation with the firm's financial targets
- Provides a differentiating advantage as a given services market becomes more crowded and thus more competitive

The Cost of Ignoring Service Offering Development

In addition to potentially foregoing the preceding benefits, the firm that elects to underemphasize its service creation process may incur negative consequences. The application of investment dollars toward new service offerings, like all firm assets, can be an indication of a firm's priorities, values, and outlook for the future. Even those firms that do make significant investments toward new service offerings take a risk if a structured process is not utilized. Without a consistently understood and applied process, the firm's investment-allocation practices may be internally viewed as a form of selective favoritism between competing business units.

Defining the Terms

One of the first issues with adopting any process is the difficulty in reaching agreement on terminology. Though reaching this agreement may seem tedious and somewhat unfulfilling, it is recommended that a firm endeavoring to formalize its new service creation process make the effort to agree on the meaning of key terms. For purposes of this discussion, three terms are defined:

- *Service line:* A combination of multiple offerings to improve organizational efficiency in sales and delivery and demonstrate comprehensiveness of services to the marketplace.
- *Service offering:* The specific service that is marketed by the firm. Generally, clients buy the firm's services at this level.
- *Capability:* A skill possessed by individual members of the firm. Clients may elect to engage the firm for individual capabilities, but these resources tend to be viewed as staff augmentation.

In the context of these definitions, capabilities are combined with software, knowledge repositories, and other elements to create service offerings, and these service offerings are combined to create service lines.

Setting Expectations

Before adopting a service creation process, the firm should endeavor to identify its goals for new service creation. Goal setting in the following areas will increase shared perspectives among interested parties and help ensure agreement on the desired end state:

- Level of desired (optimal) formalization such as investment performance hurdles and management reviews
- Financial strategy (growth versus maintaining market share)
- Market positioning strategy (boutique/niche services versus all purpose)
- Organizational strategy (trendsetting versus following, first-in versus reactive approach to service development)

In addition to goal setting, design considerations should be evaluated, for example: (1) the preferred use of a dedicated lab for research and development versus a field-based client-engagement approach, (2) the need for evolution versus innovation of new services, (3) the firm's ability to build versus buy its position, (4) the balancing of the firm's delivery structure with its service creation process, and (5) whether local business unit discretionary funding of a given idea is encouraged/permitted.

The Service Creation Process

Regardless of the level of formality introduced into the creative process, four basic steps are involved: propose an idea, commit support, develop and test the market, and launch and grow. Each of these steps is described here followed by Key Deliverables and Key Questions for each step. In addition, an itemized list of suggested work steps is provided on the accompanying CD-ROM.

Propose Idea. The objective of this step is to encourage the firm to seek market-oriented information to support its idea generation, surface the largest number of ideas from across as many areas of the firm as possible, and then identify and focus on those ideas with the most perceived potential. An essential ingredient for choosing between two or more ideas is gathering information that supports a comparison. Emphasis should be placed on three elements of this step:

1. Using a standardized format to capture proposed ideas
2. Making the idea submission process as straightforward as possible

3. Adjusting the idea selection criteria (including financial aspects and strategic value) as the firm's need for new service offerings changes

Key Deliverables

- Market information
- Ideas documented in a standardized and comparable format
- Work plan for commit support step

Key Questions

- What client need does the proposed service offering address?
- How does this offering meet the client need?
- What is the current status of the service offering? (Existing intellectual property and client(s) versus green field)
- How well does this service offering idea match the firm's current capabilities?
- Does the firm need to acquire internally unavailable capabilities using an alliance or through other means?

COMMIT SUPPORT.   The objective of this step is to commit resources to those ideas that are most likely to succeed. This step begins the conversion of an idea to service offering and will likely be the most difficult to complete adequately. Competing demands between (1) profit-seeking motives to show immediate results and (2) the analyst's tendency to remain in the research stage indefinitely must be balanced. This is a challenge in professional services firms that tend to emphasize current billability above investment. A real commitment by the firm partnership or management, as well as a culture shift toward investment in future services, will be required in such firms.

Although it often will prove difficult, it is essential that each proposed service offering be detailed with a sufficient level of specification. This includes elements such as individual skills and capabilities, knowledge repositories, and support from software and hardware. Ideas that are elusive to sufficient specification may entail risk that the firm is not willing to accept. Along with each service offering's proposed contents, a full understanding of the financial aspects (anticipated revenue, cost of service) and strategic benefit of the envisioned service offering is needed to ensure that a comparative analysis is possible.

Key Deliverables

- Service offering specifications
- Initial version of business plan with financial and strategic objectives
- Initial market research to support investment case
- Work plan for develop and test market step

Key Questions

- How will competing offerings be evaluated and compared?
  - —Client value proposition
  - —Fit with existing—firm's direction, offerings, sales, and delivery channels
  - —Prospective market value (required investment)
  - —Perceived sustainability and expandability
- At what level in the firm should development of a given offering be funded?
- How much of the service offering can be developed internally? What elements of the service offering need to be acquired from outside resources?

DEVELOP AND TEST MARKET. The objectives of this step are to develop the service offering, perform trial engagements with receptive clients, and determine whether rollout of the service offering is desirable. A development team is organized and is tasked with building the service offering based on the specifications created during the previous step. Depending on the complexity of and cost associated with developing the envisioned service offering, it may be desirable to create a prototype. The completed service offering is then test-delivered to a trial client under the auspices of a trial engagement. Trial clients should be chosen carefully. Selection criteria should include the client's willingness to participate in and provide support for the firm's efforts. Trial clients should also be willing to provide feedback and ideally possess size, industry, and other attributes that are reflective of the intended market. Client feedback serves two purposes. First, it provides input about weaknesses in the proposed service offering that can be corrected. Second, feedback provides the basis for documenting prospective clients' business benefits. Multiple trial engagements may be used to provide useful input such as the realized benefits and associated monetary value of the service offering, sales and marketing requirements for the next step of rollout, and the amount of training and type of support needed to deliver the service offering.

Key Deliverables

- Service offering solution or reasonable facsimile via prototype
- Completed trial engagements
- Client feedback
- Financial and other considerations for rollout
- Sales and marketing materials
- Work plan for launch and grow step

Key Questions
- What level of completion is required for the proposed service offering so that a target client can effectively evaluate it?
- What criteria should be used for target client selection? How will prospective clients be approached?
- What is this service offering's value proposition for prospective clients? Why should a client buy this service? Who in the client's organization will likely make the buying decision?
- How will the firm ensure that the client's expectations are met?
- How much and what type of sales and marketing material and support will this service offering require?
- What will be the attributes of a typical client engagement (duration, staffing, revenue)?

LAUNCH AND GROW. The objective of this step is to begin sales and delivery of the service offering to the market. Early client engagements should be viewed as extensions of the trials conducted in the previous step with client feedback actively pursued and acted on. As sales and delivery are optimized, engagement profitability receives added emphasis and attention. Long-term plans, including enhancement objectives, sales and marketing approaches, and ongoing management structure and responsibility, are developed for service offerings that attain projected growth and profitability targets.

Key Deliverables
- Service offering refinement
- Various plans and deliverables to support marketing, sales, delivery, and training
- Transition of service delivery responsibilities to designated unit

Key Questions
- What steps are needed to ensure adequate deployment of the service offering?
- Are elements of the service offering suitable for intellectual property protection?

Roles to Support the Process

As the firm defines and adjusts its process for new service creation, it is essential to clearly delineate roles. Regardless of the level of formality introduced, accommodation for sponsor and director roles is recommended. The sponsor role is tasked with establishing the firm's strategy for developing new service offerings, laying a foundation with clearly defined responsibilities, providing oversight, and allocating resources. The director role assumes responsibility for the effective execution of the service creation process and oversees financial accountability. In addition to these roles, depending on the formality of the process, provision should be made for mentoring, coaching, and marketing support for those individuals tasked with new service development along with resources to enable the associated development effort.

Intellectual Capital/Property Development and Protection

As service lines and offerings are created, it is inevitable that intellectual property will be developed. Once developed, each firm should evaluate whether this property needs to be protected by addressing one key question: Does this property warrant the effort required to protect it, or does change occur so rapidly that the need to protect is ameliorated? This section provides a synopsis of other authors' insights into the fundamental elements of this important topic.

A brief visit to any well-supplied library or Internet book site shows that the topic of *intellectual property* continues to receive considerable attention. This comes as no surprise, as innovative protected intellectual property can be a real source of competitive advantage in a services firm. Reading options include a variety of practice-oriented and socioeconomic perspectives including local, state, and federal legislation with its current interpretation as well as accounting for and the use of economic valuation for intellectual property. Chapter 19 touches on this subject as well and has links to associated resources for additional study.

Understanding Intellectual Property[4]

The origins of U.S. intellectual property law are traceable to the constitutional convention of 1787 and the first draft of the constitution. The rationale for this constitutional emphasis is the notion that the formation of a prosperous society is, to a large extent, dependent on the ability of individuals to protect their rights in intellectual discoveries.

Four classifications of a firm's intangible assets include rights that arise from: (1) contractual agreements; (2) relationships with its workforce, customers, and distributors; (3) undefined intangibles such as goodwill; and (4) intellectual property. Smith and Parr state that intangible assets ". . . typically appear last in the development of a business and disappear first in its demise."[5]

The types of intellectual property are: patents, trademarks, copyright, and know-how. Each of these types is briefly outlined next. Readers in need of a more comprehensive treatment are referred to texts similar to those listed in the notes section at the end of this chapter.

Patent

- Right to exclude others from making, using, or selling
- Types (utility, plant, design, animal)
- Granted by the federal government

Trademark

- Types (trademark, service mark, collective marks, certification marks)
- Valid as long as the mark is actively used and protected
- May be registered (federal-interstate, state-intrastate)

Copyright

- Idea-expression dichotomy. Copyright law is based on the notion that the expression of ideas is subject to protection, but the underlying idea cannot be protected.
- Establishing ownership—employees. A "work made for hire" is owned by the employer. Best to use written agreements for both employees and independent contractors to reduce likelihood of ownership disputes.
- Federal protection only.
- Benefits of registration—provides public notice. It establishes a validity of claim that is a prerequisite to bringing an infringement action. Creates a record with the customs service.

Know-How

- Types (trade secrets, proprietary technology, and other information used in the course of business such as customer lists, sales information, business methods, and financial forecasts).
- Primarily subject to state jurisdiction.
- No statutory time limits on protection. Information that has not been protected by patent, trademark, or copyright, but its protection is still vital to the firm's success and, if known to competitors, would provide them with an advantage.
- Protection is through physical measures and written agreements.
- Computer software can be protected with patents or copyrights or may be retained as part of a firm's know-how.

Though some authors recognize a difference and distinguish between intellectual capital and intellectual property, the names are often used interchangeably. Smith and Parr[8] define *intellectual capital* as a combination of human capital, intangible assets, and intellectual property. Within the context of this definition, the remainder of this discussion focuses exclusively on intellectual property.

Protecting Intellectual Property

Protecting intellectual property should be seen as a bidirectional process that involves not only the protection of a person's own property but also ensures that the person is not infringing on the rights of others.[6]

As shown in Exhibit 6.1, the protection of intellectual property is summarized in four key activities: identify, raise awareness, protect, and monitor. For each of these activities, a list of suggested strategies and steps follows.

IDENTIFY INTELLECTUAL PROPERTY. The emphasis of this activity is defining what constitutes the firm's intellectual property. Proactive identification can help reduce the time and effort needed to later assert the firm's rights. Periodic audits can be used to inventory intellectual property with special emphasis placed on computer data security. Consideration should be given to obtaining outside assistance such as legal counsel. Chapter 19 covers this topic as well.

RAISE AWARENESS. A key concern is the adequate demonstration of the firm's intent to protect its intellectual property.[7] Intent can be a forceful indication of the firm's desire to assert its rights and may be demonstrated with organizational attention in the form of oversight, policies, procedures, and education. Periodic reviews and legal counsel are recommended, as statutory changes can be frequent. Oversight is optimally provided by a committee of senior members from all areas of the firm including operations, human resources, accounting, legal, sales, and marketing. Established firm policies and procedures help to define and codify firm stances on information confidentiality, Internet usage, ownership rights, and employee/contractor agreements such as nonsolicitation, nondisclosure, and noncompetition. Employees should be educated on the proper use and protection of intellectual assets. Also, Walsh recommends the firm validate that employee/contractor agreements are appropriate for the work assignment, governing jurisdiction and effects on existing agreements after business reorganizations such as mergers and acquisitions. The firm should consider adopting employee exit processes that collect confidential and proprietary information and use this opportunity to remind the individual of ongoing obligations.[10]

PROTECT AGAINST INFRINGEMENT. Once intellectual property has been identified, it should be assessed for the optimal method of protection (patent, trademark, copyright, and know-how). For property that is deemed suitable for know-how protection, one option is to control access. Trade secrets may be marked as confidential. The firm should consider obtaining insurance coverage for possible infringement claims made against the firm.

MONITOR.   The final and perhaps most essential activity is to monitor the behavior of your own staff as well as the actions of others. The firm's staff should be encouraged to review periodicals, marketing literature, web sites, and other sources to check for infringement. Retaining legal counsel may be required when infringement is perceived. The firm's goal is to maintain diligence in its practices and meet its secrecy objectives by demonstrating an intention to protect its intellectual property and then backing its intent with action.

Other Aids to Understanding Intellectual Property

In addition to intellectual property texts such as those discussed earlier, numerous journals and texts address intellectual property issues. Topics recently addressed by the *Intellectual Property and Technology Law Journal*[8] include:

- International developments such as foreign recognition of and cooperation in protecting property rights and the links between international property piracy and terrorism
- Effects of mergers on intellectual property rights
- Noteworthy court rulings that impact both the defense and assertion of property rights
- Economic valuation of intellectual property
- Practice aid such as a sample agreement designed to help organizations protect their intellectual property when working with contractors

Along with topical advice and guidance, various sources[9] discuss contemporary as well as competing views on the current state and future direction of intellectual property. Opinions range from the all-for-free knowledge advocates to those who argue for market rules to dictate ownership rights. The interested reader is encouraged to explore the diversity of intellectual property readings.

Summary

The professional services firm's ability to increase and protect its knowledge should be considered of paramount importance to its continued existence. In a tangible way, its clients are paying the firm for the skilled use of knowledge. As such, effort that is expended to create service lines, develop intellectual property, and subsequently protect it is inevitable. As Sherlock Holmes points out, the skillful worker focuses on relevant knowledge, listens to others' troubles, provides enlightenment, and then pockets a fee. As Einstein notes, the best firms will be sure that they have effective ways of "finding" the information that they need when they need it.

RESOURCES

A list of suggested work steps for new service offering creation is provided on the accompanying CD-ROM.

The US Patent and Trademark office provides a variety of on-line resources, including search capabilities at http://www.uspto.gov.

The copyright office of the Library of Congress provides information, frequently asked questions regarding registration for copyrighted works and is found at http://www.copyright.gov.

NOTES

1. Sir Arthur Conan Doyle, *The Original Illustrated "Strand" Sherlock Homes* (Great Britain: Wordsworth Editions, 1989), p. 15.

2. Gordon V. Smith and Russell L. Parr, *Valuation of Intellectual Property and Intangible Assets* (New York: John Wiley & Sons, 2000), p. 10.

3. Philip Kotler, *Marketing Management.* (Upper Saddle River: NJ: Prentice-Hall, 2000), p. 27.

4. Except where noted, material for this section has been adapted from Smith and Parr. See note 2.

5. See note 2, p. 15.

6. Deborah E. Bouchoux, *Protecting Your Company's Intellectual Property: A Practical Guide to Trademarks, Copyrights, Patents & Trade Secrets* (New York: AMACOM, 2001), p. 14.

7. Marguerite S. Walsh, "The Ten Top Reasons Employers Lose Trade Secret Cases—And How To Prevent Them," in *Intellectual Property & Technology Law Journal* (New York: Aspen Law & Business, 2003), pp. 1–4.

8. Technology and Proprietary Rights Group of Weil, Gotshal & Manges LLP, ed., *Intellectual Property & Technology Law Journal* (New York: Aspen Law & Business, 2000).

9. Jennifer Peloso, ed., *Intellectual Property* (New York: H.W. Wilson, 2003).

7

Proposal and Reference Management

TIM BOURGEOIS

Services are invisible. Services are just promises that somebody will do something. How do you sell that?

—Harry Beckwith, *Selling the Invisible*[1]

This chapter addresses the role of proposals in the professional services firm business development cycle and how to manage the proposal development process most effectively. When viewed as a stand-alone document, the proposal is a straightforward item that can be 50 percent to 80 percent standardized across most prospects, depending on the specific nature of the services being pitched. However, when viewed as a component of a business development process, the proposal and all of the steps that lead to it and follow its submission are a complex system of interdependent actions that, when successfully applied, lead to regular and predictable new business generation.

To that end, this chapter addresses:

- *The role of the proposal:* How proposals are used in the business development process.
- *Presenting proposals:* Many sales processes begin with an opportunity to provide an overview of your firm, which is essentially a phase one proposal.
- *Written proposals:* The basics and nuances of developing a formal, written proposal.
- *Pricing and negotiating:* How to price projects and negotiate effectively once the proposal has been submitted.

- *Follow-up and closing:* How to manage the follow-up process and close new business.
- *Managing the proposal process:* If not managed properly, firms can waste hundreds or thousands of valuable hours on futile business development activities.
- *Complementary documents:* Many related documents are used before, during, and after the proposal submission.
- *Keys to success:* How to optimize your firm's proposal development process.

This chapter is organized similarly to the professional services business development process outlined in Chapter 5: prospect identification, generating genuine prospect interest, identifying a specific need and solution, delivering a proposal, and managing the postsubmission process. This chapter also consistently advocates a systems-based approach to managing the proposal development process. Too often, professional services firms suffocate and squander their precious resources because of ineffective business development practices that involve virtually meaningless proposal submissions in situations where the likelihood of success is remote. This chapter provides a foundation for avoiding that pitfall and creating a sound business development system for your organization.

Why This Topic Is Important

Depending on the source you use, 50 percent to 90 percent of the $7 trillion U.S. economy is service based. Manufacturing jobs continue to transition offshore, and the United States has evolved into a mostly knowledge-based economy. For example, IBM overhauled itself over the past 10 years and now derives more than half of its $89 billion in sales directly through services activities. Name a well-respected large company—GE, Citigroup, Wal-Mart, and so on—and you can bet the organization has integrated an aggressive services-based strategy into its plan over the past decade.

The service sector is booming, and that's great news for anyone with a knowledge-based offering. The bad news is that it's very competitive. Harris InfoSource estimates there are more than four million services firms in the United States with 25 or more employees or 10 or more professional services staff. That means there's one established services firm for every 72 people in the United States. These numbers don't even take into account the hundreds of thousands of "mom-and-pop" shops out there.

At the high end of the market, the largest services companies are beginning to creep into the small and mid-size marketplace due to increasingly competitive conditions for services contracts among the *Fortune* 1000.

Leading professional services firms have gotten savvier in their pursuit of new business over the past decade, employing time-tested techniques of their product-based brethren, such as aggressive advertising and highly formalized customer acquisition efforts.

So, it's a competitive market out there. However, small and mid-size professional services companies continue to do a poor job in their new business development efforts, which translates into enormous opportunity for organizations that take business development and proposal management seriously. Emerging services companies that develop formal marketing and sales plans and diligently pursue them can enjoy tremendous competitive advantage that leads to rapid growth.

In the sales and marketing process, a good proposal serves as the final confirmation before landing a new client—it's the powerful closer that is summoned in the ninth inning to strike out the side. But a good closer is rendered effectively useless if the team can't establish and hold a lead into the late innings of the game.

The Role of the Proposal

According to the *American Heritage Dictionary*, a proposal is defined as:

1. That which is proposed, or propounded for consideration or acceptance; a scheme or design; terms or conditions proposed; offer; as, to make proposals for a treaty of peace; to offer proposals for erecting a building; to make proposals of marriage.
2. The offer by a party of what he has in view as to an intended business transaction, which, with acceptance, constitutes a contract.

In the business world, a proposal is generally presented to one of two audiences—new business with a new client or new business with an existing client—but can take many forms, including:

- A conversation with the prospect
- A conversation with an influencer (an employee, colleague, investor, partner, etc.)
- An e-mail
- A letter by postal mail
- An in-person presentation
- A public speaking engagement
- A formal proposal
- A response to a request for proposal (RFP)

It's important to avoid getting too caught up in the technicalities of what a proposal looks like. Nearly all selling situations require some kind of formal, documented confirmation of the work to be done to be executed. But that doesn't minimize the importance of other proposal interactions. A good business developer is always on the lookout to help individuals in his or her sphere of influence solve problems. And that's at the heart of a proposal: providing solutions and ideas for problem solving, whether the problem is declining market share, impending litigation, or an atrophying technology platform.

What's more, a proposal plays vastly different roles in the selling process depending on the service being provided. Architects and insurance and real estate professionals rely more on the actual proposal than do management consultants or advertising agencies. Exhibit 7.1 illustrates one insurance executive's view of the role of the proposal in the selling process; while many of the points are applicable to all professional services, others are industry specific.

The Selling Process

At the highest level, selling professional services follows a generic sales process as illustrated in Exhibit 7.1, which highlights where the proposal fits into the cycle. Once a lead is acquired—a monumental task in itself and addressed in Chapters 4 and 5—the work, in many ways, has just begun.

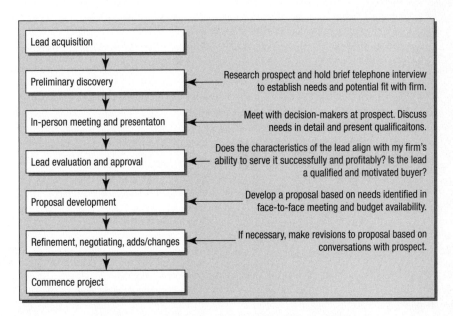

Exhibit 7.1   The Professional Services Sales Process

Each stage along the process should reinforce your firm's value proposition to the client and involve a go/no-go decision. "Selling services is a process of seduction, not brute force," says Jim Jonassen, partner at Riviera Partners, an executive search and placement firm. "Desperate moves are quickly identified by prospects, and no one wants to do business with a desperate firm," he notes.

PRELIMINARY DISCOVERY. Preliminary discovery determines whether the prospect has the potential to be a good client for your firm. There is a definite, though sometimes difficult to identify, differentiation between good business and bad business, also known as the *qualifying* or *prescreening* phase. This phase includes examining:

- High-level needs
- Industry specialty
- Availability of buyer/decision maker
- Credit history

Most of the areas can be understood through secondary research and a brief telephone conversation with the prospect. Though it depends on your pipeline and sales structure, securing an in-person meeting with a prospective buyer—assuming a financial decision maker or senior staffer who influences spending decisions will be present—is almost always a good idea. Regardless of whether the potential to serve that organization is a perfect fit, you'll be giving your firm the opportunity to display its capabilities and make a favorable first impression, which often leads to related opportunities. "The high-net worth financial community that I'm involved with is small and tight-knit," says Antony Abiatti, a director at SCS Financial, "so any time I can get in front of a member of that community and leave them with a positive impression of my firm, it's time well-spent."

However, at the same time, you want to make sure scarce sales resources are deployed effectively. To do that, your organization should already have in place a target client profile to use as a guide during the screening process. A prospect's size, industry specialty, geography, and buyer description (CEO, CIO, general manager, etc.) should be established based on the organization's success and failures serving diverse customers.

IN-PERSON MEETING AND PRESENTATION. You never get a second chance to make a first impression. There's no better opportunity to showcase your firm than during an uninterrupted, in-person 45 minutes with a prospective buyer. Making the most of that meeting—that is, taking the necessary steps to successfully secure a second meeting—requires staying focused on two initiatives:

1. Mining the prospect for detailed information about his or her specific needs
2. Demonstrating deep competence and some form of differentiation

"Good services salespeople have a knack for being able to identify good prospects and then extracting an incredible amount of information from them during the buying process, especially during the first in-person meeting," says Alan Osetek, senior vice president at Carat Interactive.

First meetings can be casual and informal or highly structured. Firms need to be prepared for either scenario, which can most times be ascertained before the meeting. To make the most of the initial meeting and get the organization in a position to craft an effective proposal, business developers need to be prepared to be active listeners and effective presenters.

A good business developer will have the following questions answered after the first in-person meeting:

- What is the driving force behind the issue being discussed (e.g., reduce operating costs, prepare for acquisition, improve profitability)?
- Who is most affected by the suggested improvement (e.g., CEO, shareholders, VP of HR)?
- What is an ideal outcome of what is being discussed?
- What, if any, budget has been made available, and how will the success or failure of this project be measured?

Depending on the nature of the project, there are endless additional questions to be addressed, many of them arcane and specific to the services being provided. But by making sure you also address high-level issues and, therefore, appeal to the fundamental needs of the buyer, who likely has to justify expenditures in some economic fashion, you ensure that the proposal will be aligned with the buyer's needs.

Firms also need to be prepared to address the core questions that every prospect is interested in getting answered:

- What does your firm do (services)?
- Who have you worked for (clients)?
- How do you do it (process/methodology)?
- How much does it cost (pricing)?
- When can you do it (timing)?

Though they won't ask for it explicitly, prospects are also interested in how you differentiate from the competition. Firms need to walk a fine line here. You need to differentiate to stand apart in a crowd, and one way to do that is to address the preceding questions completely. Present irrefutable examples of your work, and be prepared to talk about them in great detail. Tailor the examples to the expected needs of the prospect. Discuss the unique philosophical approach your organization employs when delivering services and how it benefits clients. Remember that prospects use the vendor evaluation process to attempt to mitigate risk while also maximizing return on investment and look good in the process.

LEAD EVALUATION AND APPROVAL. After the in-person meeting, you should have enough information about the prospect and his or her needs to determine whether there is a potentially good fit between your organizations. Can your organization serve the prospect successfully and profitably? Is there an opportunity for a mutually beneficial, long-term relationship?

Depending on the nature of your business, this decision could have huge implications. When talking about large-scale information technology projects, for example, the upfront investment can be significant. Sarah Casalan, vice president of IT at Ecko Unlimited and former Accenture consultant, comments, "Sometimes we want to see a free proof-of-concept, on a small scale, before we're willing to move forward on a project." In these scenarios, firms need to have a solid understanding of the opportunity before making such an upfront investment. The following questions help determine an answer:

- Does the prospect fit in the firm's "sweet spot"? If not, how far on the periphery is it?
- What is the history of the relationship between the firm and the buyer?
- What is the prospect's history in dealing with service vendors? Is the prospect a veteran, successful user of services or notorious for squeezing vendors?
- What are the prospect's future plans? Is the prospect on a growth trajectory or simply protecting market share?

Ultimately, the decision to move forward or not with the prospect relies on a variety of internal and external factors. The wise firm will walk away from a project for an attractive, strong brand name company that will bring a significant dose of favorable publicity along with it when there are too many warning signs—price sensitivity, low perceived value of outside vendors, no decision maker, and zero growth plans. The presence of several negative factors will turn an otherwise attractive prospect unattractive. Alternatively, firms also make the decision to take on projects as loss leaders because the prospect has the characteristics of a profitable long-term client, yet needs tangible evidence in the way of a small project to understand the value of the firm.

PROPOSAL DEVELOPMENT. It's usually time to develop a proposal after:

- A lead has been sufficiently qualified.
- A detailed needs assessment meeting has taken place.

- A company has selected your organization to be one of a few on a short list to submit a proposal.

The core requirements of a good proposal are covered in the following section of this chapter, but there are two considerations to heed at this juncture in the sales process:

1. *Understand the competition.* Just as there's such a difference between bad business and good business, there are times to submit proposals and times to abstain. If you're one of 10 firms submitting proposals and lack a strong relationship with the buyer, chances are you've been invited simply for comparative purposes and are wasting your time. Knowing the competitive environment will help to differentiate.
2. *When it makes sense, do your homework.* "I see some proposals and it was as if the vendor had read my mind," says Marc DeCourcey, a Washington, DC-based political consultant who helps clients evaluate and select vendors for government contracts. "And I know from having been on the other side of the fence selling services that it's because they did their research, talked to everyone in the community who might be helpful, and got as much information as they could from the buyer."

In an ideal situation, fee negotiations and other alterations to the proposal will be completed before the final submission of the document. But ideal situations require that many disparate factors come together neatly and cleanly, and they can be tough to come by. Thus, once the proposal is formally submitted, there is often the need to haggle and make changes. However, even when this situation arises, if business developers work to diligently follow a system—applying judgment when appropriate—each step in the selling process should build on the previous one and result in a firm's being in a favorable position to win new business.

Written Proposals

Regardless of specialty, proposals from professional services firms should address five to eight main areas. Proposals typically range from 3 pages to 50 or more, depending on the nature of the work and the size of the proposed engagement. Proposals should be easy to read and error-free, but because this is not always the case, the result is a differentiation opportunity for firms that pay attention to the details.

Executives are partial to delivering hard copy versions of proposals to prospects (and other documents as well). Each interaction with a prospect or client is a marketing event in itself, and delivering hard copies allows firms to demonstrate their professionalism, among other things. But prospects

SECTION	PURPOSE
Introduction	Provide a backgrounder that establishes and/or reinforces the premise of the project, especially if it involves an emerging technique. Example: "According to research by the Pew Internet & American Life Project, the importance of the Internet continues to . . ."
Situation Analysis	Demonstrate your understanding of the client's situation and be as specific as possible. I had one prospect tell me, after reading a proposal, "Well at least you were listening to what we were saying," which established instant credibility.
Recommendations	Based on what you present in the Situation Analysis, deliver broad recommendations for improving the client's situation. Provide any new ideas that the client may not have expected here to add value and differentiate.
About the Firm	While not always necessary, it may be helpful to include information about your organization depending on the proposal requirements. This could include history, service philosophy, processes, case studies, client lists, and references.
Project Summary	Describe the project in discussion at some level of detail, how you are going to accomplish the project, what the success criteria area, and assign respective responsibilities.
Staffing	Depending on your organization's service delivery model, be as specific or vague as necessary. Smaller firms can differentiate here by incorporating exactly who will be working on the project, especially when it involves experienced staff.
Costs and Payment Terms	Specify project/engagement costs and payment terms, billing information (purchase orders, ID codes), billing contact.
Conditions	Specify unique arrangements such as bonus terms, guarantees, stock grants, confidentiality, termination rights, and so on.
Engagement Agreement	Provide a separate page to accept and execute the proposal, by signing and mailing and/or faxing to your firm.

Exhibit 7.2   The Professional Services Sales Process

often request e-mailed versions of proposals, and though their requests should be honored, that doesn't preclude firms from sending hard copies along as well. Remember that every step along the way to successfully landing a new client is meaningful, and none should be minimized.

Exhibit 7.2 illustrates the key components of a professional services proposal and their respective roles, taking into consideration that the target audience is both individuals closely involved in the vendor selection process, as well as peripheral executives with a vested interest in its outcome, who may not be familiar with your firm. Also, keep in mind that some components illustrated may be extraneous if the sales process has been lengthy and the information has been presented thoroughly in other forums.

To promote user friendliness, longer proposals should contain a table of contents. Almost without fail, prospects immediately flip to the costs section and then make their way through the entire document. It's human nature and unavoidable. As we've discussed, once the proposal has been submitted, there should be no surprises because discussions have occurred along the way, so sticker shock should not be a problem.

Qualifications and References

In the services business, qualifications (including the firm's brand, which should play a significant role in the selling process) and references go a long way. They address risk management and can support premium pricing if used effectively. "When I was at Goldman Sachs, I was never asked even once by a prospect for a reference. Now that I'm out on my own, I've never landed a new client without being asked to provide references," says one money manager with an Ivy League education.

If you're a graduate of a top-20 law school working at a big firm, that means you'll be billing out at $300 per hour during your fifth or sixth year; that's the price the market is willing to pay as it's willing to pay $250 per hour for an established art director who consistently generates good advertisements that sell products. The same goes for the hot architect who has designed the latest-and-greatest building in town—premium pricing is justified if the services are presented and sold effectively.

As a professional services business developer, using qualifications and references in the selling process is a fundamental technique. These aspects of the firm should be promoted throughout the entire selling process and incorporated into proposals as necessary.

PRESENTING QUALIFICATIONS AND CLIENTS. Qualifications include anything about your organization and its staff that is relevant to the buyer(s), may persuade the buyer's decision to hire your organization, and/or establish common ground with him or her for future discussions (e.g., alma maters), including:

Company-Specific Information
- History
- Services
- Processes and/or methodologies
- Clients and specific client work
- Research, articles

Staff-Specific Information
- Background
- Project work
- Previous employers
- Education
- Nonprofit work
- Research, articles

For professional services with more than a handful of people, the most important qualification presented usually has to do with clients—a comprehensive list and what you did for them. The premise is obvious: If some other respected company thought enough of your organization to hire you, then we should be okay with it, too. Or, if you've completed a task successfully somewhere else, then it's likely you can do it for us, too.

The role of qualifications in proposals depends on what the prospect is looking for in the document and where you are in the sales process. In an ideal selling situation, the proposal will be a straightforward document that simply summarizes and documents what has already been agreed on verbally. Because this is not always possible, qualifications may play an active role in many of your proposals and should be well-crafted and compelling; professional services firms don't have clear features and benefits as products do, so they always need to reinforce their expertise and experience. Regardless of the role of qualifications in the proposal itself, this information should be presented and reinforced in all of the firm's collateral as appropriate: web sites, newsletters, postal mail correspondence, and so on.

MANAGING REFERENCES.   Referencing clients can be tricky business. However, most clients that are being served well are happy to serve as references. There are legal issues to consider, though, and you want to make sure that formal permission is obtained. There are three ways to acquire permission:

1. Using a separate, stand-alone request document (see Exhibit 7.3 for an example)
2. Requesting permission as part of a broader document that governs the terms of the relationship, such as a master services agreement

March 28, 2002

John Smith
Chief Operating Officer
Acme Manufacturing
72 Main Street
Boston, MA 02210

RE: Reference Permission

Dear John:

Thank you very much for allowing Pixel Bridge Inc to include your organization on our website client list, along with your testimonial. I would like to take this opportunity to confirm your quotation and the ways in which they may be used in the future.

You have offered the following quotation to be used in Pixel Bridge marketing collateral:

- "Pixel Bridge Inc has been a reliable Web development partner and I'm looking forward to a long and successful relationship with the organization."

We may use this quotation, fully attributed with your name, title, and company name and logo, in our current and future marketing activities, including but not limited to:

- In a case study appearing on the Pixel Bridge website

Your assistance will be invaluable to our own marketing efforts and will also reflect highly on the professionalism of your organization. Allowing us to review your organizations' use of the Internet should enhance Acme Manufacturing's image as an innovative, cutting-edge company that embraces leading Web technology to achieve its customer and business goals.

If you are in agreement with your quotation as reiterated here, as well as its uses outlined, please sign the attached authorization and return the signed original to my attention at the address below. If you have any questions regarding this matter, do not hesitate to give me a call.

Thanks again for your help.

Sincerely,

Tim Bourgeois
CEO

Exhibit 7.3   Example of a Request Document

3. Using less formal means, such as e-mail correspondence, to document the authorization

Pixel Bridge, a firm that provides marketing advisory services, includes the request in the following extract as a clause in its master services agreement, the document it executes with new clients after the proposal has been authorized:

PERMISSION FOR USE

Acme Manufacturing, by its duly authorized representative hereby irrevocably grants to Pixel Bridge Inc, its subsidiaries and affiliates, permission to use the Acme Manufacturing logo, name, and other promotional materials including testimonials as supplied by Acme Manufacturing, in whole or in part, in the Pixel Bridge Inc marketing programs and other programs described in the attached letter dated March 25, 2002. Use shall include but not be limited to reproduction, transmission, broadcast, publication and distribution in all present and future human or machine readable forms and media, provided that Pixel Bridge Inc shall not have the right to alter, edit or modify the Acme Manufacturing logo, name or other materials including testimonials without the prior written consent of Acme Manufacturing, except to size them for inclusion in the programs. Acme Manufacturing releases Pixel Bridge Inc from any liability in connection with these matters.

Acme Manufacturing

Signed: _____

Printed Name: _____

Title: _____

Date: _____

While obtaining the necessary client reference authorization is a straightforward task, managing the soft side of client references is a delicate process, especially for newly founded firms that heavily depend on a handful of clients to repeatedly act as references. Therefore, unless the individual is a good personal friend, the firm should be judicious about going back to the well. The best way to thank clients or partners for their help is by sending a referral their way, and that should be given the proper amount of consideration as well. "Whenever we have the opportunity to refer a client to one of our partners like a tax attorney or estate planner, we think long and hard about it," says a senior partner at a boutique money management firm, "because we know the value of the reciprocation can be potentially enormous."

Lawyers

Getting attorneys involved in the proposal management and/or development process is a necessary step for most firms, but one that must be managed. A few individual practitioners we know are comfortable doing business based on a handshake and short corresponding document and have never been burned, but we don't recommend it. Though attorneys are paid to have a particularly apocalyptic view of the world, doing business with a sound agreement in place that clearly establishes expectations for each party involved and addresses contingencies is simply good business. For firms that specialize in big government, health care, architectural, and IT projects, attorney involvement can be increasingly significant and necessary.

Legal expertise is most efficiently used during the development of boilerplate—or reusable—sections of the proposal. Attorneys should review a "typical" proposal to ensure that its terms and wording are appropriate and that it meets generally acceptable industry standards. Chapter 19 covers the retention of legal counsel extensively.

DEVELOPING BOILERPLATE DOCUMENTS. Developing customized proposals for attractive prospective new clients is a no-brainer; it gives your firm the best chance to win. But developing each new proposal from scratch is wasteful and unnecessary. Many components of the document can be preprepared and sitting on a shelf, waiting to be customized, especially since most firms are competing for similar types of business (e.g., corporate law, Internet marketing, disability insurance). These components include:

- Firm background
- Service offerings/project description
- Terms and conditions
- Staffing

For each new proposal, the Introduction, Situation Analysis, and Costs sections will differ significantly from opportunity to opportunity, as will the Project Summary, but even those areas will lend themselves to replication frequently.

Most professional services business developers are capable of doing a significant amount of proposal development and will benefit by leaning on marketers and attorneys when crafting boilerplate documents, but shouldn't need to rely on others much once the process is established, except in unusual circumstances.

Pricing and Negotiating

Once a proposal has been submitted, 90 percent or more of business development activities should be completed with the prospect, including cost discussions. However, negotiating, and more specifically, negotiating about price, often ensues.

Don't dread these discussions; embrace them. If it makes you uncomfortable, get over it or hire someone who is good at it. But remember that this is the most opportune time to address these issues and get them taken care of so you can move forward and build your relationship with the client, according to terms that are agreeable to both parties.

"I DIDN'T EXPECT IT TO COST THIS MUCH." If you get this response, you did a poor job communicating with the prospect during the needs assessment and proposal development process. Chalk it up as a lesson learned and vow to get better in the future.

When dealing with the issue at hand, walk the prospect through the process of how you arrived at the fee. Sticker shock is not unusual (though the proposal is not an ideal medium for delivering that shock), but further understanding will help the situation. Discuss the competitive conditions of your industry and provide third-party, objective confirmation of those discussions, such as cost ranges for similar services. Do not simply introduce cost-savings measures; discuss the proposal in the prospect's hands.

"THIS SEEMS EXPENSIVE." This response is similar to "I didn't expect it to cost this much," but with unique nuances. Expensive means relative to the competition, as opposed to a statement about the absolute cost of the project. The prospect is asking you to justify your premium, so now it's time to talk about your organization's pedigree and why the prospect will be getting the most for his or her money by deciding on your firm.

Alternatively, you can discuss the fee in relation to the value of the project. For example, "Our fee is $200,000 for the project, but the outcome will save your company $2 million in excess inventory over three years, so it seems fair to me." This is a desired approach, but not always possible, such as with large IT projects that are billed on a time-and-materials basis. In these instances, companies may be looking for a target blended hourly rate. "You'd better be affordable today," says Sarah Casalan, vice president of IT at Ecko Limited.

"WE NEED TO ADDRESS A FEW ITEMS." This is good news. This response implies general agreement on the proposal's terms, with the caveat of having to address a few items and iron them out before moving forward. These could be delivery dates, terms and conditions, staff assignments, and so on. Rarely will you lose a prospect at this stage if you act in good faith and negotiate reasonably.

When to Bend and How to Do It

Some organizations are smart users of professional services firms, others rarely use external vendors, and still others squeeze services companies at every opportunity. The type of organization you are dealing with will dictate your strategy to some extent.

Regardless, maintaining a focus on the long view is imperative. "No matter what sector your firm competes in, it's a small world and people have long memories," says Jim Jonassen of Riviera Partners. "If you give away the farm today, people will remember and expect the same treatment the next time around, which could be a month, a year, or five years later. It's a tough position to retreat from."

That's not to say you can't reposition or make smart concessions, though, and the firm should consider a variety of factors in pricing engagements or work including:

- *Establishing a relationship:* If you're looking to establish a relationship with a new client who is in your firm's sweet spot and has considerable potential, get creative. You can deliver on the project at a fixed rate that you know will fall short of desired profit margins, but you've inserted your firm at the hourly rate you are seeking. Or adjust the fee to weigh it more heavily on success criteria, such as project milestones, which will make the client feel better about the deal. Other options are virtually limitless: taking equity in lieu of cash, providing guarantees, reconfiguring payment terms, bartering, and so on.
- *Reducing scope:* Most proposals include at least a couple of "nice to have" deliverables. And most client organizations can offer some level of assistance with a project. These two approaches can be used to reduce the scope of the services delivered and, oftentimes, reduce the cost of the project. Never reduce fees without some kind of commensurate concession by the prospect; it's bad business and will negatively affect your reputation.

When you've pursued all of your options and still can't arrive at agreeable terms, the writing is on the wall and you need to demonstrate the courage to walk away. It's not easy, but if done professionally, you can maintain the relationship and continue to mine it for future opportunities. After all, different tools are appropriate for different jobs. Firms are often hired by companies that passed them by during a previous vendor selection process because of rate sensitivity or another reason.

Follow-Up and Closing

It's been said that consumers love to buy but hate to be sold. Even under the most vendor-friendly situation, that's not the case in the business-to-business world. It's not that personal of a transaction and rarely provides instant gratification. Even once the decision has been made to hire a firm, documents often take weeks to get through the system and authorized before the project can formally commence.

Professional services business developers need to be patient, yet diligent enough to keep the momentum going. Lance Armstrong, six-time winner of the Tour De France, once said, "I'm a big believer in momentum," and this principle holds true during the proposal process. Even though you've delivered a highly polished proposal on time or even in advance of the deadline, it's typical for prospects to inform you that they'll "be back to you with a decision in a week," but that decision gets tabled for a month. After all, one of the main reasons they are hiring an outside firm is that they are unable to handle the project themselves, so it should come as no surprise when they get overburdened by keeping the business running day to day.

In the meantime, staying in regular contact with the prospect is critical, while not being perceived as overzealous or even annoying. E-mail serves as an effective tool here, sending notes indicating that you are "just checking in and available for any questions," and sending along relevant articles and research when appropriate in an effort to differentiate and continue to add value. At this point, there is little you can do to hasten the process except remind the prospect of the time line or next steps they agreed to in the previous meeting/correspondence.

Managing the Proposal Development Process

The key to managing a successful services firm is staying focused on two initiatives: delivering superior client services and maintaining a steady new business pipeline. Working in concert with lead generation activities, the proposal development process is a service firm's gateway to new clients and opportunities. As such, it commands a firm's resources in the form of executive commitment, investment, and continuous improvement.

Services firms are generally organized in one of two ways: as a partnership or corporation. New business development responsibilities at partnerships fall on the shoulders of the partners; corporate entities operate more traditionally, employing a salesforce.

An effective proposal development process flows as follows:

1. Management and sales evaluate the opportunity to gauge its worthiness.
2. Assign a point person to manage the process once a "go" is determined.

3. Conduct preliminary meeting with prospect to present qualifications and gather detailed requirements.

4. Assemble the necessary experts inside the firm to discuss the project and determine the specific resource requirements.

5. The point person develops the proposal and distributes for review and feedback.

6. The proposal is delivered.

7. Negotiation and follow-up questions may ensue, and the point person accesses necessary experts and/or executives to address the issues.

Though the process management is fairly straightforward, a variety of factors contribute to regular and predictable new business acquisition:

- *Effective lead generation techniques:* At-bats are important.
- *Strong frontline people:* The quality of your business developers is paramount, since they are perceived as being directly representative of the quality of your firm (unlike product salespeople, whose wares can stand on their own). Partners selling services they deliver on personally is ideal but costly, especially when the sales cycle for big projects can last months and run hundreds of hours in investments. Nevertheless, smart account managers are what prospects are looking for, not shallow salespeople.
- *Team involvement:* When service delivery professionals are included in business development efforts and have a say in the process, they are much more likely to provide positive support to the ongoing servicing of that new client. They can also offer valuable insights, though they admittedly can sometimes hinder the process as well if not managed properly.
- *Establish the process and get out of the way:* Senior management, if not directly involved in new business development on a daily basis, will often be enticed to become overinvolved with these activities given their high stakes. But this can become counterproductive and hurt morale. Work hard to implement a solid process and then oversee it regularly, but keep a distance.

Related Documents

The main purpose of proposals is to secure new business with a new client. But a variety of documents are involved with either the new business development process or with the working relationship with a new client. These documents are described here:

- *Request for information (RFI):* An RFI is a document issued by larger or governmental organizations that are seeking to establish their short list of vendors for evaluation. RFIs are sent to 8 to 15 or more firms for completion, requesting general information about the vendors, with information organized in such a way that facilitates comparisons.

  The first time a firm completes an RFI, it is a time-consuming process. But future RFIs take less and less time because they are often similar in structure.

- *Request for proposal (RFP):* An RFP can follow an RFI process or be issued standalone. An RFP usually provides a fair amount of information about a project—the premise is to provide enough details so that firms are able to develop a proposal in response. However, there are usually holes in the RFP that must be discussed with the prospect.

  RFPs are widely used in public work—federal, state, and municipal—where formal processes are in place to try to guarantee objectivity. They are also used in the commercial sector. Because of the nature of RFPs, responding blindly—without establishing a relationship with the buyer—results in low conversion rates. Make every effort to make contact with the buyer and assess the opportunity before walking down this path, which can be costly and rarely yields new business.

- *Master services agreement (MSA):* An MSA is used by many service companies that do business with clients regularly over the long term—consulting firms, IT services companies, marketing companies, and so on. The document governs the overall terms of the relationship between the client and a vendor—issues such as ownership rights, fees, payment terms, termination, confidentiality, and so on.

  The MSA is effective because it allows clients to call vendors and request support quickly and easily without having to issue formal paperwork. Many of my firm's MSAs specify that any piece of work that requires fewer than 30 hours can be completed based on a telephone call or e-mail, whereas projects that require 30 or more hours require a statement of work.

- *Statement of work (SOW):* An SOW describes a specific project being completed, along with its details. For example, when Pixel Bridge contracts with a new client to build a new web site, it executes two documents: an MSA, which governs the general terms and conditions of the relationship, and an SOW, which describes the specific web site development project.

  An SOW provides a blueprint for the project, describes how a project will be completed, and assigns responsibilities. In the web site development example, if the proposal requires 1.5 pages to describe the project and how it would be completed, the SOW requires 6 to 10 pages because of the additional detail.

- *Change order:* A change order is issued when something changes during the project that falls outside the SOW. This generally happens when a new requirement is added to the project, such as a new system feature, or the project is expanded to include an additional assignment outside the original scope (e.g., instead of recruiting one sales executive for the client company, why don't we recruit two while we're at it?).

    Change orders have enormous importance in the professional services industry given the prevalence of scope creep. When clients are managed properly, scope creep is readily apparent and easily accounted for through the use of change orders; when projects aren't documented properly from start to finish, getting clients to pay additional fees for additional services can be a nightmare.

Keys to Success

Professional services firm executives are ambivalent about the exact role the proposal plays in the new client acquisition process. "In a best-case scenario, proposals aren't delivered until the very end of the sales process and aren't very important at all," says Alan Osetek of Carat Interactive. However, anyone who's been around awhile knows that best-case scenarios are the exception, not the rule, and that many cautious, risk-averse buyers use the proposal as an important tool for selecting service vendors. And its role differs depending on the service being provided, the prospect's industry, and a thousand other possible criteria. Nevertheless, there are four keys to successful proposal development, regardless of the service specialty or industry being served.

Hunt Wisely

Determine where your firm has a meaningful competitive advantage—making sure you can serve that market segment successfully and profitably—and focus new business acquisition efforts squarely on that sector. Establish and maintain a high profile in that sector so prospective buyers can find you. If you have an elephant gun, go elephant hunting and stay away from the small game, no matter how attractive it may seem. This approach will provide a solid foundation for the proposal development process and improve conversion rates. "My firm is three years old and growing. In the early days we took on a few clients that were out of our focus area because we felt we needed to be aggressive. In every case the situation failed and put excessive pressure on the firm that comprised our health and distracted us from much more important business development initiatives," says Antony Abiatti of SCS Financial Group.

Allocate Resources Intelligently

New client acquisition opportunities never materialize as often as we'd like, so it's important to make the most of them. Put your best resources on the job and be diligent in follow-up and nurturing a new relationship. Get a system in place and follow it; be process oriented. The first meeting with a prospect is critical. The firm must do whatever it takes to make a positive first impression—that means bringing in senior resources if the prospect has been qualified—and walk prospects down a proven path to convert them to clients. Too many services firms flounder not because their service offering is weak or market demand is soft, but because they presumptuously assume that prospects should be able to easily recognize their value, and if they cannot, tough. That approach may work for a lifestyle firm whose staff is content earning a comfortable living serving a handful of clients, but growth-oriented firms need to get serious about business development to prosper.

Give Prospects a Reason to Buy

Sales prospects are generally risk averse and constantly on the lookout for opportunities to maximize rate on return (ROI) with minimal investment, but buyers are also human beings, and they can recognize a well-managed and competent organization when they see one. And they're often willing to pay a premium for its services.

So think about how a new prospect interacts with your firm—from initial contact to signing up for services—and consider whether you'd do business with your firm if you were he or she. Would you be able to readily identify your organization's value proposition or how you are different from the competition? Does every interaction reinforce the firm's key attributes, or do prospects leave a meeting confused or unconvinced? Don't rely on the personality of the firm's point person to get the job done. Establish a formidable marketing strategy and nurture it. You'll realize dividends in client acquisition.

Take the Long View

The barriers to entry in the services industry are practically negligible—in some cases only a computer is required—which is why there are so many of us competing for business. Young firms hungry for business will always be around, providing seemingly comparable services for dramatically reduced fees. While that's a strategy for breaking into a sector, it's not a sustainable one. And we know that four of every five new businesses launched are out of business within 36 months.

While it can be difficult, taking the long view is what successful firms do, and they are disciplined enough to walk away from situations with undesirable characteristics. This philosophy includes losing gracefully. Top firms that employ a refined new business acquisition strategy win about two of every three proposals they submit, which means they lose 33 percent of the time. The good news is that they demonstrated competency along the way, and even though the prospect didn't choose them, they've developed a relationship that can be nurtured over the long haul. And it's amazing the number of "lost" clients who pop up somewhere down the road—either in the middle of a failing project or in a similar position at another company.

Summary

Best-in-class professional services firms view proposal development as a piece of an integrated new client acquisition process. The most effective business development efforts involve structured, in-person meetings with prospective buyers to present qualifications and accurately assess needs. The outcome is a highly specific proposal that exactly meets the needs of the prospect organization and ultimately gives the firm the best opportunity to acquire new business. Professional services firms that struggle with the proposal development process likely haven't allocated the necessary resources to developing a new client acquisition strategy and an accompanying marketing strategy that supports the effort.

RESOURCES

Alan Weiss, *How to Write a Proposal That's Accepted Every Time* (Fitzwilliam, NH: Kennedy Information LLC, 1999).

Harry Beckwith, *Selling the Invisible* (New York: Warner Books, 1997).

NOTES

1. Harry Beckwith, *Selling the Invisible* (New York: Warner Books, 1997).

2. Jim Jonassen, Partner, Riviera Partners, phone interview with the author (February 20, 2004).

3. Antony Abiatti, Director, SCS Financial, phone interview with the author (February 18, 2004).

4. Alan Osetek, Sr. VP, Carat Interactive, interview with the author (February 19, 2004).

5. Sarah Casalan, VP of IT, Ecko Unlimited, e-mail correspondence with the author (February 17, 2004).

6. Marc DeCourcey, Consultant, phone interview with the author (February 18, 2004).

8

Strategic Partnering

T. GREGORY BENDER

If there is a way to do it better . . . find it.
—Thomas Edison[1]

This chapter highlights the importance of strategic partnerships for professional services firms, and the critical success factors involved with building, maintaining, and growing those partnerships. Professional services companies face tremendous challenges in training their employees to keep up with the pace of innovation, new products, and services. Strategic partnerships help these service providers create new business opportunities, enhance their professional services offerings, leverage partner workforces, identify new revenue opportunities, and grow an organization on a faster track than otherwise possible. Partnerships also enable companies of all sizes to successfully compete in the marketplace with larger competitors through combined service offerings. In the 1990s, most successful startups embraced partnering to grow their organizations and provide better services to their clients. Big firms as well as small firms have learned that smart partnering is smart business. Partnering creates the fundamental building blocks for company success.

Think of strategic partnerships as similar to new business units that fill specific needs and services within the organization. Strategic partnerships can be a wide variety of things depending on organizational goals and the business plan. Partnerships can be service driven, product driven, sales driven, cost driven, competition driven, survival driven, or a combination of all these directions. Once a partnership is formed, it must be nurtured: neglect can kill the goose that laid the golden egg. Working to maintain partnerships can make the difference between success and failure. During economic

180

downturns, partnering makes even more sense because partners help bring each other business as well as leverage their employee skills and expertise. Partnerships can be high impact, medium impact, or low impact depending on what you want from them and the energy and time that you are willing to invest in them.

There are a variety of benefits available to companies who succeed at strategic partnering. According to Dr. Judith Kautz of Small Business Notes (www.smallbusinessnotes.com), companies participating in alliances report that as much as 18 percent of their revenues come from their alliances. Some of the benefits firms can achieve through partnering include:[2]

- Achieve advantages of scale, scope and speed
- Increase market penetration
- Enhance competitiveness in domestic and/or global markets
- Enhance product development
- Develop new business opportunities through new products and services
- Expand market development
- Increase exports
- Diversify
- Create new businesses
- Reduce costs

Why This Topic Is Important

Throughout the 1990s, strong strategic partnerships and alliances were the successful building blocks and winning strategies for companies such as IBM, Sun, Amazon, and many successful e-commerce startups. Many later turn-around strategies embraced the concept of creating and growing strategic partnerships to create and build new revenue areas for a company. Today a professional services firm can offer a broader range of services to its existing customers, increasing the value of each customer through strong partnering.

During the mid- to late-1990s, most traditional advertising agencies created strategic partnerships with newly established interactive agencies and/or web development companies that specialized in online branding, marketing, and web application development. This is a strong example of how these professional services organizations involved in branding and marketing could partner with companies that had other areas of specialization. The agencies focused on traditional branding and marketing while the interactive agencies and web development companies focused on digital marketing and interactive technologies.

During the 1990s, ad agencies could not keep up with the growth of technology, and their clients were demanding web-based services incorporating interactive technologies. It was too costly to build these new media in in-house departments overnight and train staff appropriately for these agencies. Many large agency conglomerates such as Omnicom Group, Inc. and WPP Group invested in interactive technology shops that specialized in web-based technologies (e.g., Agency.com). Ad agencies wanted these interactive shops at their disposal for their demanding clients. By investing in these shops and partnering with them, agencies created the ultimate partnerships and strategic alliances.

Traditional agencies turned to these growing upstart web shops that excelled in new media technologies and web marketing. During client pitches, the ad agencies came in as traditional marketers while their new media counterparts came in as web hotshots that understood the medium and could implement the technology required. Both were professional services organizations that shared revenue opportunities and brought deals to the table. This created win-win relationships and strengthened their ties.

In 1980, Microsoft was a fledgling, small company. IBM needed an operating system for the IBM PC. Microsoft, against all odds, was able to convince IBM to partner with it because Microsoft had a unique technology solution, even better than the one IBM was developing in its own labs. Microsoft's partnering deal with IBM set the foundation for Microsoft and catapulted them to unparalleled financial success. Microsoft would not be the success it is today without the IBM deal. In this brilliant partnering example, Microsoft (the startup) established its market by partnering with IBM, a huge company at the time.

In the 1990s, IBM focused its turnaround strategy on professional services and strong partnering relationships with IT software and service providers nationwide. This winning strategy helped IBM fuel new growth, sell more hardware, and drive up its stock price. IBM diversified the company and its offerings from hardware sales to professional services. For the foreseeable future, IBM is intent on aggressively growing its professional services divisions and weaning itself from hardware sales as a major source of revenue growth.

What Drives Strategic Service Partnering?

The trend to develop partnerships in the service industry is mostly driven by globalization and customer demands. In the new economy, customers require that their service providers supply a broad range of services; however, rarely is any one vendor equipped to furnish the complete range of specialized services that its clients require. This is particularly true of information technology companies. IT service firms such as Accenture and smaller IT firms spend time, energy, and dollars to create powerful strategic partnering opportunities to become the one-stop shop that their customers require. In recent years, downsizing has been a major focus as large corporations try to maintain competitiveness and solvency. Today, partnering makes more sense for large companies so that they can maximize their labor pools and capitalize on their partner's talent to fill specialized client needs.

For service firms to sustain and grow their businesses, strategic partners are crucial to their success and viability with their customers. If a solution provider cannot meet the total needs of the client in this highly competitive market, it runs the risk of losing that client over time to competitors that can provide expanded services through better strategic partners. With every new deal that is completed between strategic partners, the relationship builds, evolves, and leads to new business with a heightened sense of trust and reliability among the team members. Trust among the team players is paramount to creating a successful partnership.

Strategic Service Partnering Mind-Set

A service firm must truly embrace partnering as a core way of doing business if that firm wants to reap the benefits, rewards, and revenue of such an opportunity. The service firm must promote a win-win attitude and choose its partners wisely with growth in mind and strategic advantages in place. Otherwise, strategic partnering will not lead to the desired goal that management is expecting.

If the service provider embraces partnering, it will earn a large share of its revenues through a variety of partnering channels and arrangements. Well-planned strategic partnerships create sales opportunities through the identification of complementary service offerings and add-on services. Chapter 6 covers the topic of service line and service offering creation in detail, and should be considered a complement to this chapter.

Strategic partners can develop highly successful programs incorporating each company's services into a larger service offering for new or existing customers. Partners can exploit particular area(s) of expertise in each organization and leverage those skills for new business. In general, strategic partners find new opportunities through the salesforces that they share. New revenue opportunities are created in a symbiotic way where each partner benefits from the other partner's expertise and customer base. These benefits include the following:

- Increased market share with combined services
- Decreased capital expenditures for R&D and employee training (reduced need to build internal service skills and support infrastructures for some services)
- Increased value to clients through additional services

- Better economies of scale
- Expanded geographic areas of client coverage
- Decreased costs of sales lead generation
- Increased use of low/no cost external salesforces

Geographic Types of Strategic Partnerships

Strategic partnerships can be formed with local, regional, national, or off-shore companies based on the service offering needs of the partnering company. When selecting a geographic partner, key considerations include security, communication, speed, quality, and price. For example, it may make better sense to partner with a company in close proximity if the amount of face-to-face communication for the particular service is significant. However, pricing concerns and the size of the job may prohibit use of a local partner. Also, the intention of most geographic partnerships is to expand service offerings into new territories with less investment. Make sure you understand the objectives you are trying to accomplish, and then select partners who best enable those objectives on a variety of levels, including geographic location and servicing capabilities.

Supply Side Partnering

In today's professional services marketplace, rarely is any one provider equipped to furnish the complete range of specialized services that its clients require. Ad agencies went through merger mania in the 1980s and 1990s because their clients required them to provide every service imaginable. This was due in part to globalization of corporations and their desire to reduce the number of vendors they managed because of administrative costs and perceived ability to achieve volume discounts. Supply side partnering makes sense for professional services firms that do not want to carry the financial burden of funding employees for specialized or low demand services. These professional services firms can tap a partner when needed for specialized services and still make a profit via a referral fee or other similar arrangement.

Large companies demanding a broad array of services geographic coverage from the professional services firm pose challenges to the growing firm. Strategic partnering enables the growing firm to focus on its core services and conserve its capital while at the same time creating powerful alliances and opportunities to expand and build the firm. If a solution provider cannot meet the total needs of its client in this highly competitive global economy, clients will look elsewhere to have their needs met. More than ever, supply side partnering makes sense and helps partners leverage their combined skills when necessary.

Globalization and Service Partnering

The Internet and its digital convergence of information and communication technologies, such as e-mail, instant messaging, video conferencing, and voice-over Internet protocol (VOIP), have enabled companies to extend their reach for strategic partners beyond their borders. At technology trade shows in the United States, it is not uncommon for "offshore" companies to send their top professionals to develop strategic partnerships with U.S. technology companies. Over the past 10 years, the rapid expansion of technologies mentioned earlier has enabled companies to transmit work to distant locations instantaneously and receive completed work without delay from transportation. With a growing demand for complex and specialized services, U.S. companies need an ever-growing pool of talent and manpower. Certain areas of the world such as India, Russia, and China offer a wide range of high-quality talent where significant numbers of engineers are churned out every year from top schools comparable to MIT and Stanford. This global workforce is highly trained and well educated and has strong work ethics. Many global technology companies such as Microsoft and Cisco have developed corporate partners and technology campuses in India to augment their U.S. operations. Microsoft and Cisco have established these technology campuses to create a technology beachhead for future growth. IT workers in the United States cannot fill the increasing demand over the next 10 years. Exhibit 8.1 shows the approximate rates and workforce sizes in a variety of offshore markets.[3]

In the 1960s and 1970s, the communication infrastructure and technology were not adequate to enable service-based partnerships to work. U.S. corporations moved manufacturing offshore to cut costs in the 1970s and 1980s. Real-time, close, collaborative communications between U.S. offices and their foreign manufacturing counterparts were not necessary for the manufacturing process to be successful. Service-based industries require constant communication between partners. The convergence of Internet-related communication tools has enabled companies to manage offshore professional resources in a way that was not conceivable in the 1960s, 1970s, and 1980s. The emerging era of *digital globalization* has transformed the way that large global project teams collaborate. Global project teams collaborate over the Internet with digital white boards and conferencing tools in real-time, making it feasible to grow new workforces in dispersed locations. Large service-based projects can now be handled by multiple teams in more than one country or geographic area through global partnering and using Internet-related communication tools that did not exist 10 years ago.

PARAMETER	INDIA	CHINA	BRAZIL	MEXICO	ARGENTINA	UKRAINE	RUSSIA	CZECH REPUBLIC	POLAND	PAKISTAN	MALAYSIA	SINGAPORE
IT export industry size (US$ million)	9,500	1,040	200	NA	100 (200)	71	165	65–90**	65–80[a]	90–100[b]	NA	NA
Active export focused IT professionals	195,000	26,000	NA	NA	3,000	8,000–10,000	5,500	NA	NA	3,500[c]	NA	NA
IT employee cost (US$/year)	5,000–12,000	9,600	9,500	NA	10,550	9,000	7,000	7,500		4,000–6,000	7,200	27,000
Number of CMM Level 5 certified companies	60	2	0	0	0	0	3	0	NA	0	NA	NA
IT labor force	Low cost, high quality	Low cost, low quality	Moderate cost, low quality	Moderate cost, moderate quality	High cost, moderate quality	Low cost, high quality	Low cost, high quality	Low cost, high quality	Low cost, moderate quality	Low cost, moderate quality	Low cost, moderate quality	High cost, high quality

Infrastructure	Average	Poor	Good	Average	Poor	Poor	Good	Good	Poor	Good	Good
Main positives	Large number of IT professionals	IT centers of large MNCs, government support	Near shore, familiarity with U.S. culture	Large educated population	High quality engineers	High quality engineers	Solid infrastructure	Good intellectual capital	Focus on software quality and processes	High government support, investments of $10 billion in high-tech parks	Business-friendly governance offers high tax incentives for IT exports
Main negatives	Lack of project management	Language	Scalability may be an issue, limited skilled workforce	High salaries, political instability	Poor infrastructure	Unstable economy	Talent retention issues	Talent retention issues	Geopolitical risk	Political instability	Limited availability of skilled labor pool

a Offshore outsource software exports.

b Software development.

c Evalueserve estimates. (Average revenue per IT employee in Pakistan in $14 per hour. Average working hours per year assumed to be 1,850 hours. This gives a per-employee annual revenue of $25,900. Dividing total IT export revenues by the per-employee annual revenue gives the number of export focused IT professionals to be 3,474, which has been rounded off to 3,500.)

Exibit 8.1   Upcoming and Potential Destinations for Offshoring IT Services (Until March 2003)

Servicing the Client: Call Centers Move Global

Because of changes in communication technologies and voice-over IP, many large and mid-size U.S. corporations have partnered with companies in India and the Philippines to augment or replace their U.S. call centers. Communication technology changes have enabled call centers to be built all over the world. Countries such as India and the Philippines have highly educated workforces. Labor in these countries is less expensive than the United States, thus offering significant cost savings to companies while maintaining quality support services. Call center operations are significant and expensive but not a core competency for most companies, so it makes tremendous sense as a partnering opportunity. Partnering is limited only by the creativeness of those involved. Tips for creating strategic partnerships follow:

Creating Strategic Partnerships
- Keep an open mind; do not fear partnerships.
- Compete with larger organizations by filling service voids with partners.
- Discover that highly skilled teams are at your disposal.
- Partner selection is paramount to success.

Keep an Open Mind

Partnering may seem threatening at times, especially if your partner offers some of the same services that you do. Be open-minded and do not let fear stand in your way of developing partnerships that will help you grow your organization and its service offerings. No one company can be all things to all people and offer all the services that clients may need or want. Selecting a trusted partner, and clearly outlining the "rules of engagement" for operations, communication, lead sharing, and revenue sharing can help mitigate these concerns.

Compete with Larger Organizations

Any company, no matter how small, can compete with large companies by creating quality strategic partnerships. Small to mid-size service providers can compete against Goliath-size competitors through smart strategic partnerships and best-of-breed talent pools.

A small to mid-size company has two options for competing with larger organizations. First, focus on smaller clients that are not attractive to larger competitors, thereby eliminating the competition. Second, partner with firms that can help the firm service larger clients effectively. As long as the client receives good service at a competitive price and does not experience any "transaction costs" or disruption due to a partnership, the partner should enable most smaller firms to compete with their larger brethren.

Highly Skilled Teams at Your Disposal

Strategic partnerships enable the partners to create a combined group of highly skilled resources with diverse areas of expertise. Imagine creating the perfect team without having to increase infrastructure costs, training time, and time to market for any given project. Smart partnerships allow any company, regardless of size, to compete and grow its talent base quickly with the finest experts that it shares with its strategic partner.

Partner Selection Is Paramount

The selection of a good partner is paramount to the partnership's success. Service providers need to select their strategic partners carefully keeping many factors in mind. Critical elements in the selection include services provided, overlap of services, service demand, and the time horizon. For example, partnerships can have a finite life and should be dissolved if they no longer benefit both organizations.

Choosing partners wisely in areas where there is little overlap or competition will create a complementary team of professionals that can service large projects for any size client. Sometimes partners may offer some of the same services. This does not mean that those organizations should avoid partnering. The intended partnership may be narrow enough so that each company benefits from the other's highly trained workers in one specific area of expertise, while the other competitive services of the firms are excluded from the partnership. The goal is to create the best and brightest team possible to provide outstanding service to the client. Selecting the right partner will enable the professional services firm to field the best team to successfully complete the client's projects.

Guidelines to Developing Successful Strategic Partnerships

Here are six helpful steps in developing, implementing, and executing strategic partnerships:

1. Develop a system and implement a plan.
2. Quantify potential cost savings for new services.
3. Prioritize opportunities.

4. Mitigate risk factors.

5. Measure and monitor performance.

6. Reevaluate and deploy short- and long-term goals and continuously improve processes.

1. Develop a System and Implement a Plan

Develop a business planning process for strategic partnering that is a collaborative approach with decision makers in your group. Identify your strengths and weaknesses and where partnering makes the most sense. Find a partner who provides those services gaps that you cannot presently offer to your clients. Develop a management system to define how you will work with your new strategic partners and manage clients and their expectations. Get a contract in writing to help limit misunderstandings and establish upfront commitments between you and your partner early on.

Implement a plan that meets your company's strategic goals and is executed with precision. Prioritize client needs and quantify and identify strategic resources that fill service gaps in your organization that will offer more services to your clients. Establish internal milestones of what you expect from your strategic partner and your organization. Are your goals in line with your overall business plan and company direction? Plan your strategic partnerships with customer growth in mind. Develop clear revenue targets and goals for the partnership to reach.

2. Quantify Potential Cost Savings for New Services

Quantify potential cost savings where a strategic partner can round out client service offerings and increase revenue opportunities in a cost-effective way. There are many ways that you can work with your strategic partners. You will find new ways to leverage the relationship and skill sets that they have to offer. You may be able to cut your operating costs by letting your partner take over areas of service that cost you too much time and money and do not contribute to the balance sheet. Lock down significant discounts from your partner for the products and services that you will be reselling and get them in writing. Negotiate 30-day payment terms upon job completion and suspension of pay if your partner is not performing to your satisfaction. If you have special contractual payment terms with your client, get your partner to agree to similar payment terms based on your cash flow.

3. Prioritize Opportunities

Prioritize service and revenue opportunities, and develop new service offerings or intellectual property that you both can sell. Implement plans with your strategic partners that are executable and measurable over time. You may go through some planning sessions with your partner where there are seemingly too many opportunities and directions to go in. Narrow down your prospects with razor-sharp focus on executable and marketable services. Prioritize your opportunities with a shorter horizon in mind and test the waters. Do not be an opportunity junkie and spread yourself too thin. Develop core opportunities and then execute them with precision. One of the most fruitful opportunity areas are with clients with common issues with which only one of the partners is currently engaged.

4. Mitigate Risk Factors

Conduct appropriate due diligence and get client testimonials and references from your new strategic partner. Make sure that they can deliver what they are promising. Start off slowly with new strategic partners, and the trust will build with each successful project you complete together. Other ways to mitigate risk factors are:

- Have clear and ongoing project communications.
- Properly evaluate and manage client expectations.
- Establish timelines that work to your client's benefit.
- Set performance expectations for your partner.
- Manage your customer relationships.
- Project manage the process.
- Manage your strategic partner's progress and service offerings.
- Always communicate directly with your client.

5. Measure and Monitor Performance

Always be in close communication with your client and partner project teams, and manage the project and the new services to the best of your abilities. Do not take your eye off the ball. Choosing a great strategic partner does not mean that you should not monitor their performance. A key challenge to managing partners is the ability to properly project manage the process and your customer's expectations. Your strategic partner offers services that your client needs, but the firm should not assume that they will be delivered in a timely manner or at the level of excellence that is expected.

Set performance expectations for your strategic partners and evaluate their performance over time. Always make sure your client's needs are met to your clients satisfaction, as well as your own. Make adjustments when necessary. Set service level expectations for your partners, and evaluate those services in light of your partner's performance on projects.

6. Reevaluate and Deploy Short- and Long-Term Goals and Continuously Improve Processes

Develop short- and long-term goals and routinely reevaluate your progress. Are your goals being met, and is this the right partner for you? Do not be afraid to speak up. If things are not working to your expectations, communicate your concerns clearly with your partner and make appropriate changes as soon as possible. Good communication between partners will help to nurture a win-win relationship and lead to service offerings of which you both will be proud.

Continuously improve how you work with your strategic partners through planning sessions after each project is completed successfully. Find new ways to improve services that will successfully meet or exceed client expectations.

Success will be determined by both parties putting in time, energy, and resources. In evaluating short- and long-term goals, a strong commitment to your partner will result in great services and satisfied clients.

Summary

Select strategic partners carefully and decide where they provide the most value and where they will fill voids in your firm's current service offerings. Think of partners as specialized business units that provide select services. Involve your management team in developing a plan, and then implement that plan with energy, time, and capital. Look for partners with customers, culture and services that are congruent with your own.

Develop solid contracts with your partners so that there will be minimal opportunities for misunderstandings and common knowledge of the partnership's goals. Develop a business plan with the partner so that both parties understand the revenue milestones and expectations and are vested in executing the plan. Find areas where you and your partner complement each other and create broader service lines to offer to clients. Set performance expectations for your strategic partners and evaluate their performance over time.

Good partnerships will provide a clear and measurable financial return to both parties. Make sure the partnership meets rate and cash flow needs. If the marriage between you and your partner is not working, cut your losses and look for new partners. Trust, complementary services, and team players are the foundation of a successful partnership. Like Microsoft and IBM, a great partnership can build a company overnight. Determining areas for partnerships, selecting partners, and actively managing them is critical for today's professional services firm.

RESOURCES

Strategic-alliances.orgAlliancedworld.com

John R. Harbison and Peter Pekar, *Smart Alliances: A Practical Guide to Repeatable Success* (San Francisco, CA: Jossey-Bass, 1998).

Mitchell Lee Marks and Philip H. Marvis, *Joining Forces: Making One Plus One Equals Three in Mergers, Acquisitions and Alliances* (San Francisco, CA: Jossey-Bass, 1999).

Patricia Ward Biederman and Warren G. Bennis, *Organizing Genius: The Secrets of Creative Collaboration* (Oxford England: Perseus Press, 1998).

James E. Austin and Frances Hesselbein, *Collaboration Challenge* (San Francisco, CA: Jossey-Bass, 2000).

James F. Moore, *The Death of Competition: Leadership and Strategy in the Age of Business Ecosystems* (New York: Harperbusiness, 1997).

Harvard Business Review on Strategic Alliances (Harvard Business School Press, 2002).

Larraine D. Segil, *Intelligent Business Alliances: How to Profit Using Today's Most Important Strategic Tool* (New York: Times Books, 1996).

Stephen M. Dent, *Partnering Intelligence: Creating Value for Your Business by Building Strong Alliances* (Palo Alto, CA: Davies-Black Publishing, 1999).

Juli Betwee, William Berquist, and David Meuel, *Building Strategic Relationships: How to Extend Your Organization's Reach Through Partnerships, Alliances, and Joint Ventures* (San Francisco, CA: Jossey-Bass, 1995).

John K. Conlon and Melissa Giovagnoli, *The Power of Two: How Companies of All Sizes Can Build Alliance Networks That Generate Business Opportunities* (San Francisco, CA: Jossey-Bass, 1998).

Smart Alliance Partners website, a top destination for information on strategic alliances found at http://www.smartalliancepartners.com.

The Association of Strategic Alliance Professionals—a membership organization dedicated to the topic of strategic alliances—online at http://www.strategic-alliances.org.

NOTES

1. Widely attributed to Thomas A. Edison from a variety of sources including www.brainyquote.com/quotes/ quotes/t/thomasaed131432.html.

2. Dr. Judith Kautz, Small Business Notes at http://www.smallbusinessnotes.com /operating/leadership/strategicalliances.html.

3. Todd Jatras, *Forbes Magazine,* "Can India Retain Its Reign as Outsourcing King?" (February 28, 2001).

The Organization: Attracting and Retaining the Best Professionals

9

Organization Structure

FRANK RIBEIRO

Quality is the result of a carefully constructed cultural environment. It has to be the fabric of the organization, not part of the fabric.

—Philip Crosby[1]

The quality of an organization can never exceed the quality of the minds that make it up.

—Harold R. McAlindon[2]

This chapter identifies and defines the primary ways in which professional services firms are organized and discusses how different types of organizational models can enhance or impede the success of the firm. Because the most important asset of any professional services firm is its employees, it is critical that its organizational design allow people the freedom to operate effectively while supplying needed structure as well as checks and balances to keep the firm on track. This balance can be difficult to achieve.

Most professional services firms are made up of talented and intelligent people who are eager to develop new ideas and methodologies and have little patience for complex organizational structures that hamper their creativity. Yet, for a firm to be successful as a business, it must have a mechanism that forges the talent and intelligence of its professional staff into a cohesive whole. The organizational model must create and reinforce the alignment between the company's external and internal strategies, support the firm's chosen image and branding strategy, and be flexible enough to respond quickly to changes in the business environment.

Why This Topic Is Important

Employees are a professional firm's most important asset. The firm's product is intangible. When clients buy professional services, they are, in essence, buying a firm's people. Thus, a firm's reputation and success depend exclusively on the talent and intelligence of the people delivering it. To prosper, firms must hire the best people, develop them, motivate them, and build in career paths that keep them committed to the firm. Yet, the very people who make a professional services firm stand out can be those who are most difficult to manage. Regardless of specific industry, employees at successful professional services firms have the same general set of personality characteristics. They are energetic, strong-willed, opinionated, confident, and always in pursuit of new challenges. They work best in a dynamic environment that allows them the freedom to do what they do best.

Like any other business, however, a professional services firm needs to have adequate structure to coordinate everyone's efforts and offer one face to clients. The question top management must constantly grapple with is how to put in place an organizational structure that gives employees the freedom to operate creatively *within* the context of a stable, functional firm. How can the firm rein in employees appropriately without establishing so much bureaucracy that they no longer feel they have any choices? For an organizational structure to work under these conditions, it must balance the need for clear definition and explicit coordination of roles and responsibilities with the need to preserve enough autonomy to engender creative, cross-functional decision making and problem solving.

There are several different models for professional services firm organization, but they all have the same key success factors:

- They align systems, structure, and governance to forge strong links among employees, the firm, and clients.
- They manage and measure performance to establish firm priorities, articulate firm culture and values, and ensure employee buy-in.
- Systems and processes are stable enough to facilitate effective management, yet flexible enough to ensure responsiveness to changes.

The overall purpose of the chapter is to examine how to build these key success factors into the organization model for the professional services firm. It does so by discussing:

- Common organizational components of professional services firms
- How to determine organizational goals in order to choose the best organization model

- The three organizational models most professional services firms adopt, including the strengths and challenges of each
- Why ownership and governance issues have special significance for professional services firm organizations
- How an effective organization can support creativity while simultaneously facilitating the firm's business success
- Key responsibilities and typical promotion paths
- The role of support staff within the organizational model
- The importance of building training and career development support into the firm's culture to strengthen and reinforce the organizational structure
- How to create mechanisms that encourage knowledge sharing and eliminate as many boundaries and fiefdoms as possible, regardless of which organization model is used

Professional Services Organization Overview

Professional services firms are first and foremost service businesses. By their nature, they, and the professional staffs they employ, are customer facing. The responsibility of any professional services organization is to identify the specific nature of the customer's problem, define it in meaningful terms by focusing on the business impact to the customer, and offer meaningful solutions. As valuable as this is, the "product" being sold is intangible, the result of processes that flow through the organization, from customer inquiries to project delivery. Thus, the selling of professional services and the rendering of those services can seldom be separated. The firm must present a consistent face to clients throughout the entire sales/service cycle. All professional and administrative staff, though they may not have direct customer interaction, are a part of these processes, and, regardless of which specific model is used, organizational structure must reflect, support and sustain this. Firms must develop integrative systems that aid in this process. This is true regardless of which organization model a firm chooses.

There are other key components of all effective firm organization models. Because they, in essence, sell knowledge and expertise, firms must be learning organizations. Because they must be able to balance increasing client demand for specialized knowledge with need to develop generalists and maintain high levels of employee utilization and productivity, firms must create structured processes and methodologies to transfer knowledge and expertise throughout the enterprise. Because by their nature, they need creative, intelligent, individualistic people. They must create structures that attract and retain talent. Because the most successful professional services employees tend to be people who may not respond well to rigid bureaucratic structures, firms must systematically use other methods, such as compensation tactics, to change cultural attitudes and motivate behavior.

Organization Structure

The choice of organizational governance and structure has critical implications for professional services firms. In a typical corporate enterprise, roles and responsibilities are highly defined. But that model will not work in professional services firms where the key constituencies—owners, managers, and employees—are often overlapping groups of people. Senior people, generally partners, are not only the owners of the business and the leaders of the business but also the salesforce and the administrative leaders. Even employees with less seniority must be flexible and able to take on multiple roles. Generally, only the most junior staff members are focused exclusively on specific job content and delivery. Almost immediately, job responsibilities begin to expand to include managing client projects, identifying and developing important client relationships and opportunities, and taking on more and more responsibility for internal firm management. From an early point in their career, staff must begin to learn how to coordinate marketing efforts, as well, to present a unified face to clients. These topics are also addressed in Chapters 3 and 11, which should be read in conjunction with this chapter.

The organization model must provide the freedom to allow people to take on more and more responsibilities. While guidelines and standards are needed to keep the firm on track, it's important not to constrain professional staff with artificial boundaries. They must understand their roles and responsibilities, but they also need the freedom to explore and push their boundaries a little bit. This is best done by broadly defining roles and responsibilities, rather than narrowly defining specific jobs. Because it is counterproductive to limit individual potential, promotion of staff from one level to the next must focus around core competencies or skills that, once mastered, indicate readiness for the next level. That requires the firm to develop a clear path with explicit requirements and competencies for each level of promotion. Booz Allen, for example, has defined a set of core competencies and behaviors that professional staff are expected to master at each specific level. This gives them a benchmark for their current place within the firm, based on their capabilities, as well as clearly defining what will be expected of them at the next level and beyond.

The clear definition of roles and responsibilities is a business imperative as well. Process responsibility, or the explicit definition of roles, is critical to ensuring that all firm resources are harnessed and efficiently coordinated to best respond to the requirements of the enterprise and its clients.

Because professional services are knowledge businesses, training is a criti-cal piece of the organizational structure that requires ongoing commitment and investment. Most firms give inadequate attention to staff training, and training can easily be viewed as an expense rather than a necessary organiza-tional investment. This is a mistake because good training across the firm and from new level employees through senior partners reinforces and supports the firm's organization. It introduces the corporate culture and customer-facing approach to new employees. It develops intellectual capital among senior pro-fessionals. And it keeps the firm competitive by helping members keep cur-rent with new technologies, industry trends, and client issues. Chapter 11 discusses both career tracks and professional development in detail.

Another consideration when determining a firm's organization is that ownership and governance decisions, which determine the incentive struc-ture and set the organization's "cultural tone," have a significant impact on the firm's ability to recruit and retain talent. Chapter 3 discusses the con-cepts of partnership structures and governance in detail.

There are four main organization models common to professional services firms: practice, functional, hybrid, and geographic. Each has its strengths and weaknesses, and choosing between them requires trade-offs primarily be-tween economies of scale and degree of delivery staff involvement in cus-tomer relationships. On top of those four models, there are two types of ownership structure. Partnerships are the most common, although some pro-fessional services firms are publicly owned.

Ownership and Governance

Partnership, where firm management is the responsibility of senior partners and practice leaders, is the dominant ownership model in the professional services arena. This model has numerous benefits. For one, potential part-nership is a big incentive for junior employees. This ensures employee buy-in regarding firm development, as they will reap the rewards of a strong, suc-cessful firm when they earn a partnership stake. In addition, in partnerships, managerial decisions are made by customer-facing staff, which facilitates more rapid decision making and engenders less bureaucracy. These are all good reasons for the dominance of the partnership model.

However, partnerships have some significant challenges. Whenever own-ers are also managers, whether in a family-owned business, a start-up, or a professional services firm, there is the risk that leadership won't have the skill set or knowledge to maximize the firm's potential. In partnerships, each new partner generally moves up through the ranks and has their own ideas about how things have been done and should be done. It can be difficult to step outside preconceived notions about the firm to remain flexible. Another challenge for partnerships is that partners feel they have a proprietary stake in the firm, which can hamper their ability to be efficient and equitable managers. In addition, partners report to, and are appraised by, other partners, which clashes with the underlying concept of equal ownership by peers.

To overcome these risks requires a conscious effort to incorporate effective checks and balances into the organization model. One place to start is to look at some of the good lessons learned from corporations about governance. For example, partnerships often have outside boards that can help by playing the role that shareholders would play in a publicly owned company. A good outside board can help keep a firm on track, keep it from becoming too insular and provide objective, third-party advice that is in the best interests of the entity. It is a good idea to include members of the firm's leadership team on the board. Booz Allen has an outside board that includes internal members from across the company. The internal leadership team, which meets regularly on operational matters, also has membership on the board. The external board helps to keep individuals or small groups from wielding disproportionate power over critical firm decisions, and provides invaluable outside guidance and direction setting.

In most partnerships, it is also the case that there are differing levels of partner "rank." For example, Booz Allen has established three levels of partnership: entry level, lead partners, and senior partners. Partners progress based on how they perform against a set of pre-defined, agreed-upon partnership characteristics, as well as how much business they develop or facilitate for the firm. Senior-level partners have a higher equity stake than junior partners. That provides a further series of checks and balances and provides an increasing level of reward for seniority and performance, even within the partnership.

If a partnership has concerns about having equal partners appraising each other, it can overcome those concerns by making sure that the appraisals are based on wide input. The best kind of feedback for such evaluations is 360-degree feedback, with seniors, peers, and juniors who have interacted with the subject over time. Chapter 11 discusses the topic of appraisals as part of an overall professional development program.

Another challenge is that partners must devote intensive, nonbillable hours to management activities including mentoring, training, and business development, as well as leading client engagements. At the most junior staff levels, the goal is for each person to be 100 percent billable. At the senior partner level, however, a partner's billable time may represent 50 percent or less of total hours because the need to focus on business activities—including marketing and sales—becomes more imperative than delivering on specific engagements. Some partnerships put excessive pressure on their uppermost levels of management for billable hours. That quickly becomes an issue for that firm, leading to a vicious cycle of engagements followed by troughs between projects while partners try to generate new work for their firm. It is critical to put metrics in place that do not penalize partners for spending time on business development and sales activities. Rather, senior staff needs to be free to be only partially billable on assignments, using other time to feed the engagement pipeline. At Booz Allen, this is accomplished by assigning the lowest billability targets to the most senior people. While clients demand that senior people be involved with their projects, it is generally not a full-time requirement and has a fair amount of flexibility in arrangement. They understand very well that there is a team structure, with the most senior (and most expensive in terms of hourly rate) leveraged as counselors around specific issues, while actual delivery of services is performed by an expert working team that is thinking about the clients issues full time. Generally, clients demand a senior person on the case full time only if they are not comfortable with the underlying team. If that is the case, the firm has already damaged its relationship with the client, possibly irreparably and there are a variety of other issues that must be addressed.

While most professional services firms are structured as partnerships, some are publicly owned, and may be organized like a typical corporation. The benefits of this model include having a CEO and a COO to oversee operations, strategy, and other corporate functions so senior staff can focus exclusively on delivery and business development. In addition, a publicly owned firm can leverage capital markets to finance growth. Also, because the employees are not necessarily owners (except through stock purchases), systems and processes may be more efficiently managed, and there can be a perception that they are more objective. With public ownership, there is also a ready-made mechanism for checks and balances because of the more rigid structure, the reporting requirements, legal mandates for certain disclosures and shareholder pressure.

All of the benefits of public ownership can also be drawbacks. Public ownership can lead to increased bureaucracy, which hampers a firm's ability to respond with agility to changes in the market or business environment. Lack of partnership as an incentive can make it more difficult to attract and retain top employees. Employees may even feel less committed to developing the firm because they cannot aspire to ownership. Given that people are its most valuable resource and that a professional services firm grows by adding people, publicly owned firms need to be very careful that their ownership model doesn't hamper necessary staff growth because shareholders are too focused on revenues and profits. During the late 1990s dot-com craze, for example, Sapient and Scient Corp. could drive growth by adding people—an expensive but necessary proposition—but their shareholders were applying increasing pressure for profits. It put them in a difficult dilemma. A privately owned company can be more insulated from the roller coaster of public markets and the accompanying outside pressures. Partners tend to be much more tolerant and understanding of business cycles than distant shareholders, who are focused primarily on financial returns.

Organizational Model Options

Professional services firms typically follow one of three generic business models: the practice model, the functional model, or the hybrid model. Exhibit 9.1 outlines the characteristics of the three models for organizing the professional services firm. Figure 9.2 summarizes the pros and cons of these models. A fourth model, the geographic model, which can take the form of any of the previous models but on a regional basis, is also appropriate for larger firms with multiple geographies, particularly international offices. Within each model, most organizations employ matrix structures, which are aligned against various dimensions, including industry, geography, and service line.

Regardless of model used, successful firms create mechanisms that avoid silos and eliminate as many boundaries and walls as possible. Intellectual capital is developed and made available to the whole firm, and avenues of information exchange exist across the entire firm structure. Leadership encourages transparency by creating mechanisms to ensure that everyone is aware of what projects the firm is working on and what large deals are due to start in the near term. There must also be mechanism for tracking professional staff assigned to projects and overall professional staff availability. This encourages professional staff to work together on projects and opportunities regardless of their spot in the overall organization and provides a tracking mechanism to indicate when somebody is involved either too much or not enough. Many firms use an interlocking series of meetings to ensure effective information exchange. For example, there might be weekly practice meetings, biweekly cross-practice meetings, and monthly leadership meetings. Cross-practice announcements of new projects that include discussions of engagements, details of how the firm made the win, and suggestions for cross-selling opportunities can aid in achieving firmwide transparency. Because it can be all too easy for staff to become so involved in specific projects that the overall needs and goals of the firm are ignored, these key concepts must be built into any professional services firm organization structure. Resource and "bench management" are concepts covered in more detail in Chapter 13.

Transparency and organizational knowledge-sharing ensure lessons from previous experience are leveraged and inculcated to improve future performance. They also allow firms to create standard toolkits, methods and procedures to create scalable, lower cost solutions. They facilitate sharing of best practices for revenue growth and cost improvement. Finally, they help the firm leverage knowledge management platforms to enable broader cross-staffing, reduce rework, and maintain its knowledge base despite turnover. The organization model adopted by a firm will have one of the largest single impacts on how well the firm will share information and be able to take full advantages of the firms internal capabilities, knowledge and expertise.

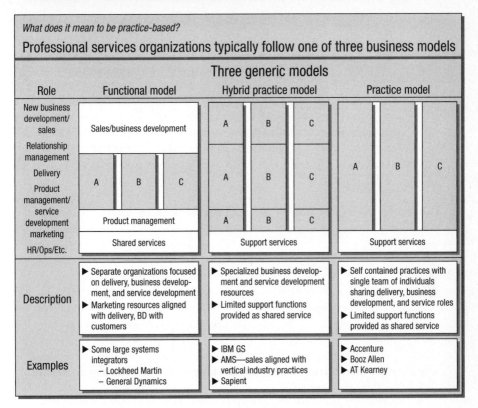

What does it mean to be practice-based?

Professional services organizations typically follow one of three business models

Role	Three generic models		
	Functional model	Hybrid practice model	Practice model
New business development/ sales	Sales/business development	A B C	A B C
Relationship management			
Delivery	A B C	A B C	
Product management/ service development marketing	Product management	A B C	
HR/Ops/Etc.	Shared services	Support services	Support services
Description	▶ Separate organizations focused on delivery, business development, and service development ▶ Marketing resources aligned with delivery, BD with customers	▶ Specialized business development and service development resources ▶ Limited support functions provided as shared service	▶ Self contained practices with single team of individuals sharing delivery, business development, and service roles ▶ Limited support functions provided as shared service
Examples	▶ Some large systems integrators – Lockheed Martin – General Dynamics	▶ IBM GS ▶ AMS—sales aligned with vertical industry practices ▶ Sapient	▶ Accenture ▶ Booz Allen ▶ AT Kearney

Exhibit 9.1   Three Professional Services Organization Models

Each organization model has its strengths and weaknesses. Which is best for a particular firm depends on the type of firm, what kind of services it provides, and how it chooses to leverage its staff. Choosing between them requires trade-offs primarily between economies of scale and degree of delivery staff involvement in customer relationship. Making the wrong choice can have dire consequences, the worst of which is that the firm becomes non-competitive. A firm cannot deliver what its clients need at the right cost point if it chooses the wrong organization structure. The organization model defines staffing structure, numbers of staff skill sets, and the cost and leverage model of staff, and drives hiring and promotion practices. If a firm's business involves large-scale technology implementation, for example, or requires large numbers of staff to work at the client's site for an extended time period, it is illogical for the majority of employees to be senior staff with billable rates. Instead, it is more practical and cost effective to have a smaller number of senior staff to strategize, design, and oversee projects supported by a large pool of staff with lower level people with commensurately lower billable rates who can perform the implementations—an example of a high-leverage firm. Chapter 2, professional services firm benchmarking addresses this issue in detail.

A firm that focuses on strategy requires a senior team that has the brain-power to perform analyses, think through strategy, and design customized, innovative business solutions for clients. For that firm, a smaller number of recent undergraduates to assist with research and delivery is more cost effective. Choosing the right staffing model allows a firm to be more competitive and dictates the arena in which the staff can play successfully.

Practice Model

The practice model, a group of self-contained practices, each with a single team of individuals sharing delivery, business development, and service development roles, is most commonly seen in management or technology consulting firms, or professional services firms that provide services across a broad set of industries and, in some cases, focus on more strategic issues. Within each practice, a pyramid of people, senior and junior, have a specific understanding of an industry or function. This makes it easier to create effective specialist teams, while offering the option of going outside the practice to other practices for specialists in other functions or industries when needed. Essentially, practices are smaller speciality firms within the larger company while still being governed by overall firm guidelines that are imposed across the organization.

Specific definitions of practice groups vary across firms and industries. They might be divided by substantive area, service line, or function. In consulting, for example, functions might include operations, strategy, IT, HR, change management, and business process management. In law firms, they might include labor and employment, corporate, tax, securities, and mergers and acquisitions. Other firms divide their practices by industry or client group, such as technology, financial services, media, telecommunications, and health care. Limited support functions such as finance, staffing, marketing, report production, research, and so on may be provided as shared services across practices. Chapter 20 on office management discusses categories of shared services that should be considered by the professional services firm in more detail.

Firms choose a practice group structure because it has the potential to attract a higher value of work and higher volumes of work from better clients. Practice groups can most easily achieve superior market recognition of expertise in particular industries or functions, and more easily create innovative intellectual capital and service lines. They also create cohesive units across offices to better target and develop existing and prospective clients. In addition, they can encourage and support the creation of cutting-edge products and services that differentiate a firm from its competitors and improve its margins.

Practice groups can also make it easier for firms to:

- Improve client-service orientation and enhance performance due to pooling of knowledge and resources and continuity through sale and delivery.
- Better leverage junior professionals through improved mentoring, training, development, and retention.

Organizing a firm by practice does have its drawbacks. It is common to find that partners who function as practice group heads possess deep functional or industry expertise but may lack requisite management or sales skills needed to grow or expand the business. This is exacerbated by the way most firms focus on developing employees' hard industry or functional skills while neglecting training in management and selling skills. Another drawback is that enterprisewide goals can be superceded by practice priorities.

To overcome these drawbacks, firms need should ensure that the organization supports and rewards development of management skills in addition to industry or functional expertise. This requires the senior delivery team for each practice to have strong business development competency. In addition, senior delivery team members must play multiple roles along the service/function and customer matrix. Regular cross-practice meetings putting together both junior and senior staff can also help facilitate communication, idea sharing and common business development tactics.

Functional Model

Firms that use the functional model have, in essence, created separate organizations focused on (1) delivery, business development, and sales and (2) service development and marketing. Traditionally, marketing resources are aligned with delivery while business development is aligned with customers. Small firms or those specializing in supporting cross-departmental or industry-independent functions such as operations or information technology might have a tendency to be more functionally focused.

An important benefit of the functional model is that a staff specializing in sales and business development can be very efficient in identifying and quantifying new business opportunities. In addition, a single point of contact with the customer allows for maximum control of customer activity.

At the same time, a generalist sales staff has less depth of expertise in its customer's business needs and, it follows, brings less specific insight to the table and is less able to provide the widest range of differentiated, custom solutions.

For firms operating under a functional model, it is important to build in a structure that encourages delivery team involvement throughout the sales and business development process, particularly in scoping. This is where the importance of transparency and knowledge sharing comes in. Unless sales and business development teams work with and share information with delivery teams, potential clients will not be able to understand the full possibilities and benefits of working with the firm. In addition, without clear channels of communication between the sales and business development team and the delivery team, it is impossible to present a united face to the client or to ensure smooth handoff of new clients to those who will deliver services.

Hybrid Practice Model

As the name indicates, hybrid practice models integrate practice and functional models to take advantage of the strengths of both types. They are divided into practices, but unlike strictly practice-based models, they include specialized business development and service development resources dedicated to each practice. Limited support functions are provided as a shared service. The hybrid model provides several benefits. With a staff dedicated to sales and business development, there is less chance of having troughs between engagements the practice models sometimes face. Because sales staff is dedicated to each practice, the staff members are more closely linked to the delivery team, therefore overcoming one of the drawbacks of the strictly functional model. With sales and business development staff linked so closely to the delivery team, the firm can gain increased credibility with customers and an increased ability to offer differentiated services. It can also offer better pricing and performance management.

This is not to say that the hybrid model is without challenges. One drawback of this model is that it comes with a higher cost structure due to staff redundancies and duplication of efforts across practices. Firms employing this model can also run into problems if their practices do not align well with customers and customer segments. The firm must, as with other models, see that the organization structure is frequently audited against the marketplace to be certain that it is of relevance to customers and is effective at developing new business and sharing knowledge internally. It is also a model that is most applicable to larger professional services firms—the matrix structure of the hybrid model may not make sense for smaller firms with a limited number of service lines, industry expertise areas and geographies.

Geographic Model

Some firms choose to use a geographic model. In this model, the firm is organized by region or country around vertical industry segments covering all functions. This can enable better focus on local and/or regional customer needs and market requirements. In addition, it supports better business development opportunities by facilitating stronger local relationships. It also allows for greater staff cohesion and promotes the development of office cultures. Staff lifestyles are improved because travel is minimized. Finally, cutting down on travel reduces overall costs to the firm.

As with all models, this one has some very real drawbacks. With a geographic model, if a firm is not careful it can wind up with what is essentially a portfolio of companies based on geography with a silo mentality organization that does not leverage the scale, knowledge, and expertise of the enterprise. Further, a strictly geographic organization can have difficulty in adequately serving the complex needs of multinational clients or successfully competing against more integrated rivals.

Firms can mitigate this challenge by developing and implementing firmwide knowledge management and information sharing mechanisms across office and geographic boarders. It is important to clearly articulate enterprisewide core values and to develop processes, including common training and professional staff development, that apply equally to all regions and offices. It can also be very effective to overlay a practice model on top of a geographic one so that the firm looks at not only the profitability of geographic regions but also the revenues of specific practices. This creates an incentive for people to share knowledge and expertise across regions, as well as to support sales and business development efforts on a firmwide rather than strictly geographic basis.

Role of Support Staff

No matter how good professional staff is, no firm can operate without a strong support staff to assist various engagement teams and practice groups. Support staff also perform necessary corporate functions such as finance, human resources, information technology, systems, and facilities management. Although support staff are not client-facing in the precise sense of the term, they are a vital part of the process that delivers value to clients. Chapter 20 discusses the role of administrative professionals as well.

Specific roles and titles may vary from firm to firm and from industry to industry, but all firms have some form of senior support staff that perform the role of firm administrators. These staff members run the day-to-day operations of the firm, in tandem and accordance with the wishes and preferences of the partners or managers. One of their key roles is to manage the remaining support staff. They play an important role in helping manage and mitigate the perception of second-class citizen status that many support staff feel.

	FUNCTIONAL MODEL	HYBRID MODEL	PRACTICE MODEL
Advantages	• Staff specialized in sales/business development more efficient in identifying and qualifying new business opportunities • Single point of contact with customer account for sale across all practices—allows for maximum control of customer activity	• Staff specialized in sales/ business development • Sales staff focused on particular practice facilitates closer linkage to delivery • Increased credibility with customer/ differentiation • Better pricing and performance management	• "True experts" involved in selling makes most compelling value statement—best positioned model for growth • Better pricing and performance management due to continuity through sale and delivery
Disadvantages	• Generalist sales people have less depth of expertise in customer's business needs or potential solutions • Sales bring less insight needed to identify need and provide differentiated custom solution	• Need to support higher cost structure of dedicated business development and product management • More complex customer interface, if practices do not align with customers/ segments	• Senior team needs to carefully balance use of time; can lead to higher cost structure • More complex customer interface, if practices do not align with customers/ segments
Key Success Factors	• Sales and B&P process needs to ensure delivery team involvement throughout—particularly in scoping • Clear interface and smooth hand-off between sales/ BD teams and delivery teams	• Senior delivery team members paired with customer-aligned business development • Tools to track allocation of time and resources among delivery, business development and capability development	• Senior delivery staff team members must have strong business development competency • Senior delivery team members play multiple roles along service/function and customer matrix • Tools to track allocation of resources among delivery, business development and capability development

Exhibit 9.2   Pros and Cons of Each Organization Model

Firm administrators are also heavily involved in recruiting, training, and career development mechanisms for support staff. They should play a critical role in the career development of employees and should have the ability to ensure that support staff is exposed to much-needed project variation.

Because they make contributions to deliverables across a range of functions and roles, it is critical to ensure that compensation and performance metrics for support staff are accurately set and defined.

Setting Responsibility for Pricing, Marketing, New Service Development, and the Budgeting Process

Professional services firms tend to place significant decision-making authority for pricing, marketing, new service development, and the budgeting process on their practice teams.

Firms most often set pricing policy globally, including target margins or billing rates, allowing local variations depending on organization structure (particularly the geographic model). Ultimately, pricing authority lies with the delivery team, although partner or higher authorization is most often required for discounts. It is important to include mechanisms for timely and accurate view of revenues, gross margins, average billing rates, utilization, investments, accounts receivable, and overhead costs; to be able to track margin realization versus target; and to ensure compliance with discounting and pricing policies.

Most organizations have a specialized marketing function providing support to individual practices. The role of the marketing function typically includes marketing communications, market research, sales support, and branding. Customer-facing staff is central to the marketing process, however, both through adherence to the firm's overall marketing and branding strategies and through activities such as writing white papers and articles and presenting at conferences.

Although firms may place responsibility for new service development with delivery teams, the marketing function, or a separate development group, initial development of new services usually comes about when services that are already done on an ad-hoc basis for one or some clients are turned into products or service offerings for use across multiple clients. Regardless of where responsibility for development lies, the marketing support function is generally involved throughout the process.

Generally, "hard" investment decisions are made through a centralized budgeting process with practice leaders accountable for their targets. However, firms often fund new service development and capability-building activities through allocation of delivery staff time. Chapter 6 discusses the process for determining investment priorities for new service lines.

Career Progression

At most firms, progression occurs along an established continuum from entry-level (associate) to stakeholder (partner); some models also support a nonpartner track. As in other aspects of firm organization, the expectations and responsibilities for progression within the firm need to be clear, explicit, and well defined.

As an individual ascends the firm hierarchy, responsibilities shift from a tight focus on delivery toward business development and other institution-building activities. A recent study[3] found the division of labor at typical consulting firms is as follows:

Division of Labor between Partners and Project Managers at Consulting Firms

	Percentage of Time Spent on Responsibility	
	Partners	*Project Managers*
Client engagements	45	64
Business development and marketing	25	12
Administration	8	7
Thought leadership	7	4
Recruiting/training	4	4

The apprentice model, with fixed leverage ratios for junior to senior staff, is dominant. It is important to make it clear to all new candidates in an "up or out" policy that only a select few will travel the entire path to partner. Other firms have a nonpartner track that provides long-term career options for individuals with specialized knowledge or training. Regardless of which model a firm chooses, training mentoring, work allocation, and feedback and evaluation are critical to ensure the professional development and preparation of junior staff. Firm training and development, both formal and on the job, are critical parts of preparing individuals to assume the increased business development and administrative responsibilities that accrue over time.

Typically, professional services firms use specific competency models as a part of their organization model, with those moving on a partner track needing the following:

- *Project delivery:* This competency follows an hourglass model where entry-level generalists develop specialized functional or industry knowledge and then build expertise that can bridge many industries and functions across projects.

- *Project management:* The lowest level staff begins as a team member, developing the skills necessary to manage increasingly complex projects and eventually evolving from a supervisory to advisory role.
- *Account management:* Over time, staff increase both their frequency and quality (in terms of seniority) of client contact. Senior staff "own" client relationships and are responsible for developing and maintaining new relationships for the firm.
- *Business development and implementation of marketing plans:* Eighty-six percent of consulting firms have no salesforce, relying instead on the partners and other staff for business development. New staff initially contribute to client proposals, but over time their role evolves into responsibility for revenue generation and the management of a portfolio of clients.

In addition, over time, employees are expected to increase their competency at firm administration and staff development, as well as to contribute to the firm's marketing efforts, initially by supporting the development of new ideas through directed research but eventually as visible and internationally recognized thought leaders (see Exhibit 9.3).

Organization Model Example

The general principles of career progression are similar across professional services firms regardless of specialty.

Firms are generally organized by practice model, with practices identified according to industry and/or functional specialization. The leverage of junior to senior staff is usually fixed. In a typical consulting firm, for example for each partner, the firm has an average of five to six full-time equivalent (FTE) professional staff as follows:

- 1.25 project managers (senior associates/principals at Booz Allen)
- 1.75 consultants (associates)
- 1.5 associates (consultants)
- 1 support staff

The organization structure usually includes an explicit career development path with well-defined standards for promotion in relation to performance, behavior, and client development. For a consulting firm, titles of levels might be:

LEVEL	DELIVERY	PROJECT MANAGEMENT	ADMINISTRATIVE/ STAFF DEVELOPMENT	ACCOUNT MANAGEMENT	SALES/NEW BUSINESS DEVELOPMENT	MARKETING & THOUGHT LEADERSHIP	EXPERIENCE
L5	Highly skilled individual contributor, "guru"	Responsible for multiple large projects; provides technical expertise and direction	May share in practice management and staff development	May manage overall relationship with some clients	May have responsibility for revenue generation and building client base; support BD in writing proposals	Internationally recognized thought leader—publishes articles, speaks at conferences	>12 years
L4		Multiple projects or single complex project	Share practice management and staff development	Manages relationship with clients; identifies and pursues opportunities with new and existing clients	May have responsibility for revenue generation and building client base; writes and presents proposals	Emerging position as thought leader; gaining recognition in select industries and regions	7 to 12 years
L3	Expertise or comprehensive knowledge in particular technical area	Smaller projects/ segments of projects	Supports	Moderate to heavy contact with min-senior clients	Participates and identified issues/ opportunities; writes and presents proposals	Assist in development of new ideas; making major content-driven contributions	4 to 7 years since advanced degree
L2	Beginning to develop expertise	Member of team	None	Daily contact with lower/middle level clients	None	Support development of new ideas through directed research	1 to 4 years since advanced degree
L1	Entry level	Member of team	none	Limited with lower level	None	None	

Exhibit 9.3 Professional Services Firm Competency Models. *Source:* Mercer Compensation Survey, Booz Allen Analysis.

- Consultants, senior consultants (entry level to between one and four years postadvanced degree)
- Associates, senior associates (four to seven years postadvanced degree)
- Principals (7 to 12 years)
- Partners, senior partners, and managing partners with ownership stakes (greater than 12 years)

Some models also have a nonpartner track and provide long-term career options for individuals with specialized knowledge or training.

Because only a select few progress to partnership, hiring and promotion model plans for natural attrition. If the workflow demand varies or changes occur in the business environment, lateral hiring is used to replace associates lost to attrition, or "up or out" policies are increased to diminish supply.

Under this career progression model, formal and informal training and mentoring on every level are perceived as "investment" in the assets of the firm and are expected to be core competencies of senior level staff.

In professional services firms, the management of complex interactions among client staff and support staff is critical to ensuring overall quality of work. Because under this model partners are the leaders and leading administrators of the firm, the ability to manage these complex interactions well is another core competency expected of senior client staff.

Summary

A firm's reputation and success depend exclusively on the talent and intelligence of the people delivering it. The optimal organization model for professional services firms is the one that allows the firm to best leverage its resources and intellectual capital for optimal competitiveness. Regardless of which model the firm chooses, it must allow people the freedom to operate effectively while supplying needed structure as well as checks and balances to keep the firm on track. It must incorporate transparency throughout the organization, clearly define roles and responsibilities, and make knowledge sharing a part of the corporate fabric.

RESOURCES

FIDIC (International Federation of Consulting Engineers): The Professional Services Firm: A Training Manual and Guide to Practice—see http://www1.fidic.org /resources/capacity/wb_flier_final.pdf for details on this publication.

Maister, David H., *Managing the Professional Services Firm* (New York: Free Press, January 1993).

Maister, David H., *True Professionalism* (New York: Free Press, January 1997).

NOTE

1. Philip Crosby, *Philip Crosby's Reflections on Quality: 295 Inspirations from the World's Foremost Quality Guru* (New York: McGraw-Hill, 1995).

2. Harold R. McAlindon and Michael Michalko, *The Little Book of Big Ideas: Inspiration, Encouragement & Tips to Stimulate Creativity and Improve Your Life* (Nashville, TN: Cumberland House Publishing, 1999).

3. Kennedy Information, Inc., *Benchmarks in Management Consulting: Operational Metrics for Sound Firm Management* (Peterborough, NH: Kennedy Information, 2002).

10

Career Tracks, Compensation, and Professional Development

JOHN BASCHAB AND JON PIOT

I haven't the strength of mind not to need a career.
—Ruth Benedict (1887–1948), U.S. anthropologist[1]

Show me the money!
—Cuba Gooding Jr. as Rod Tidwell in *Jerry Maguire*[2]

Of the internal operations issues affecting the performance and delivery of services to clients, staff satisfaction and performance has an enormous impact. The biggest predictor of that satisfaction and performance is happiness with firm career path, compensation, training, and professional development. However, the rewards of a well-articulated and deliberate career track, compensation, and professional development plan to the firm are indirect and often neglected.

Why This Topic Is Important

Professional services firms must have a systematic way to promote, train, and compensate those who are best at executing and selling the business of the firm. Effective measures will attract and retain the best professionals, as well as ensure the future of the firm itself.

Top professionals in any field generally have their pick of which opportunities they pursue and are attracted to positions with well-defined paths that will reward them consistently and objectively. They want to perform and to be recognized for their achievement by their firm. They also know that firms that have taken the trouble to provide clear career tracks to their professionals will attract other "A" players and are likely to be well managed in other critical areas, such as sales and operations.

Because planning in these areas is of indirect (and often delayed) benefit to the firm, it is an often-neglected area of focus for professional services providers. As firms grow from small and mid-size to encompass dozens or hundreds of professionals, the management of the staff becomes exponentially more difficult. Defined career tracks, compensation, and development plans can reduce the overall human resources effort required to be effective. Instead of every case being handled as a "one-off" proposition, with the attendant spaghetti-tangle of disparate compensation, bonus, and promotion decisions, decisions can be made according to predetermined policies and practices within the firm. These policies and practices remove the immense burden of case-by-case decision making from firm management and send a reassuring message of consistency, predictability, and reliability to the staff.

Additionally, properly constructed training programs can enhance the productivity, expertise, and capability of the professional staff. Well-executed professional development programs can reduce costs for services firms by allowing lower cost staff to perform higher level functions sooner in their career.

A company that has thoroughly thought through its compensation, career track, and professional development approach will attract and retain the best professionals and find itself executing most efficiently in a difficult-to-manage internal area.

Determinants of Staff Satisfaction

A variety of studies has highlighted key drivers of staff satisfaction. Based on our analysis of these studies, as well as first-hand experience, we list the following key drivers of staff job satisfaction, in priority order:

- *Satisfaction with immediate manager:* Because of day-to-day contact, professional staff identify with the company through their immediate manager. If an employee does not have a good relationship with his or her manager, that employee is at risk of leaving. Conversely, if that employee has a productive working relationship with the supervisor, risk of the employee's departure decreases significantly. To reduce the likelihood of uncontrolled attrition, firm executives must ensure that their managers are top performers and are respected and liked by the staff. The human resources group can help the firm track attrition by manager to determine whether there are any problems with a particular manager, principal, or partner.

- *Opportunities for training:* Investment in training is a major driver of employee satisfaction.
- *Satisfaction with team and coworkers:* Dysfunctional teams and coworkers drive out employees quickly. High-performing, cohesive teams can be a source of immense job satisfaction and are an important source of employee and client satisfaction.
- *Opportunities for career growth:* The firm must provide the professional staff members with challenges to satisfy their demand for learning.
- *Compensation:* Compensation, while the most obvious (and often cited) variable, is not the number one factor in the career decisions of professional services professionals, as long as the compensation is within 10 percent of the market rate. If an employee's compensation is far below market, he or she will, however, seek alternative employment (or possibly reduce his or her efforts).
- *Opportunities for promotion:* Most professional staff have ambitious interest in career advancement. The firm must ensure that there is a clear promotion ladder to satisfy these goals. The firm should also ask individuals to perform at the level of skills the promotion requires before receiving the promotion. This procedure ensures that staff who are promoted do not fail because they could not handle the rise in skill level required.

While compensation often receives the most attention as a determinant of staff satisfaction, simply increasing salaries is rarely the right answer. The preceding inventory of satisfaction determinants indicates that a well-planned career track for professional staff, as well as other noncompensation-related factors, is equally important. This chapter, along with Chapters 9 and 11, addresses these issues.

Career Tracks

A critical tool for managing professional and administrative staff in a services firm is a well-defined career path. A given firm will have a variety of titles and roles assigned to various professionals. An important distinction should be made between two major categories of employees in a professional services firm. First, professional staff are those who are directly responsible for the delivery of the services and overall management of the firm (attorneys in a law firm, doctors in a medical practice, agents in a real estate firm, consultants in a consultancy, and so on). The second category, administrative staff, is composed of those who are charged with supporting roles within the professional services firm. These employees are usually working on administrative duties (secretaries, assistants, receptionists, paralegals, or coordinators) or functional areas (human resources, finance, marketing, or information technology).

This distinction is made because there are usually important differences in firm compensation, career path, recruiting, roles, and responsibilities between the two types. Professional staff members are expected to focus their attention on building and executing the business of the firm, with an eventual path to management and perhaps equity participation. Because the majority of the employees in a given professional services firm are professional staff, this chapter focuses on career tracks and policies for those employees. The promotion path of administrative staff is usually determined by the firm on a case-by-case basis and follows the traditional patterns for these professionals.

The legal profession characterizes three key roles played by individuals in professional services firms as "finders, minders, and grinders." This assessment is a fairly accurate description, particularly for consulting and legal services. Finders are charged with identifying new clients, identifying needs at existing clients, and selling new engagements based on existing or new service offerings. Minders, usually mid-level managers, are charged with ensuring that the execution of the projects or assignments is proceeding smoothly. Grinders, usually analysts, consultants, or entry-level professional staff, execute the work and perform much of the analysis or heavy lifting during a project.

The specific titles for these roles varies from firm to firm and industry to industry. A list of the typical titles for each role follows:

- *Finders:* Partner, director, managing director or managing partner, vice-president, senior vice-president
- *Minders:* Senior associate, principal, director, manager, senior manager
- *Grinders:* Analyst, associate, senior associate, consultant, senior consultant

As would be expected, the ratio of finders to minders and grinders is a critical component of firm profitability and varies depending on the type of firm, specific services offered by the firm (type of work), and profit goals of the firm. David H. Maister, a leading thinker in the field of management consulting and author of numerous books on the topic of professional services firm management, provides an excellent overview of leverage approach in Chapter 1 of his book *Managing the Professional Services Firm* (see Resources section). An overview of leverage ratio benchmarks can be found in the benchmarking chapter of this book as well.

The leveraged professional services model creates a pyramid organization structure, as shown in Exhibit 10.1. Chapter 9 covers the potential ways in which a professional services firm may structure itself in more detail.

Elements of a Career Track

The critical components of a career track include well-defined levels, roles and responsibilities at each level, promotion criteria, and compensation plans for each level.

LEVELS. Each level within the firm (associate, senior associate, principal, partner) should carry a specific and clear title. As a firm grows, particularly across multiple geographies, it is helpful when a manager has the same set of expectations and responsibilities across offices and practices. Many firms, particularly those that grow through acquisition, have a wide range of titles assigned for a given role. A manager in one area group may be a senior associate in another and a technical lead in yet another. Setting the titles clearly and consistently is a critical element in bringing order to career tracks.

ROLES AND RESPONSIBILITIES. For each level, the typical roles and responsibilities should be clearly documented, including client delivery work, as well as internal firm administrative duties, operations work, and business development efforts. This means inventorying the skills, experience, education

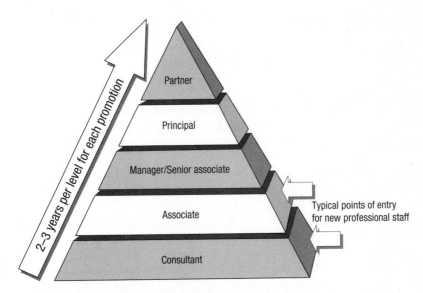

Exhibit 10.1   Representative Professional Services Firm Structure

profile, and detailed job duties for each staff position in the firm. Ill-defined roles and responsibilities leave ambiguity about what is expected of professionals at each level, as well as conflicting titles and compensation structures. Having defined roles and responsibilities properly sets expectations as to the appropriate skills required at each level.

The roles and responsibilities should be clearly linked to the organization structure (practice, firm, specialty group) as outlined in Chapter 9, as well as the levels mentioned earlier. Inconsistencies will make staff management, promotions, and appraisals unnecessarily difficult, case-by-case challenges for firm management.

The following attributes should be part of each level definition:

- Position title
- Role within the organization (position on the organization chart)
- Reporting relationships (direct reports supervised by this position and where this position reports)
- Job requirements: professional skills, educational background, work experience, company tenure
- Documentation of day-to-day, ongoing responsibilities, organized by area (e.g., client work, firm operations work, marketing/business development, firm direction setting, staff management)
- Priorities for responsibilities, how time should be allocated
- Objective and subjective measurements of success in the role
- Promotion criteria
- Success criteria or objectives

This information can also be used by internal or external recruiters as a hiring specification, as well as provide the evaluation criteria during the annual employee review process. The information also serves to emphasize skills required for advancement at each level and expectations for professional staff as they progress through their career with the firm. Exhibit 10.2 outlines the typical career responsibility progression in a professional services firm.

PROMOTION CRITERIA.   For each level in the firm, the criteria for promotion to that level should be outlined. These criteria are most often related to knowledge, capabilities, and experience of the staff, as well as other factors such as project types or tenure. The specific requirements will vary according to firm type, size, service offering, and existing customs and practices. In every case, the firm will benefit by the perception (and reality) that an objective standard exists for promotion. This sends the message that promotions are based on merit and establishes a level playing field for staff competing for

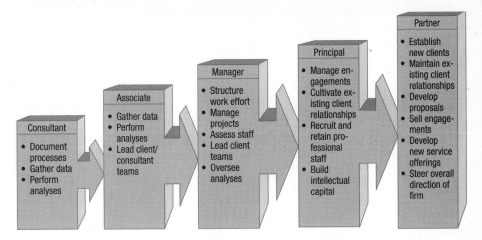

Exhibit 10.2   Typical Career Responsibility Progression for Professional Staff

advancement. The promotion and appraisal process (discussed later in this chapter) should also establish what levels in the firm are responsible for determining when promotions are handed out (e.g., principals are responsible for determining consultants promoted to senior consultant).

COMPENSATION. A range of compensation (base salary, bonus, other perquisites, and benefits) should be established for each level. Inevitably, compensation information is shared within the firm as well as outside. Compensation equity within a role will help minimize any dissatisfaction in the ranks of the professional staff. A set of policies regarding compensation will also reduce the amount of human resources effort that goes into setting compensation for each individual staff member.

It is critical for the firm to define the preceding four parameters. Having a well-defined career track will send a message that objective criteria are used to evaluate, promote, and compensate professional staff. The work of defining these elements will be recovered many times over in reduced human resources effort for appraisal, promotion, compensation, and hiring decisions. Firm recruiting efforts will be more competitive. The best professionals are attracted to firms that have clearly established tracks for advancement, and firms with fair, objective promotion and compensation systems retain those professionals.

A number of other considerations must be accounted for in designing the professional services firm organization structure and career tracks. These considerations are outlined next.

Parallel Career Tracks for Nonpartners

The first area is differentiating partner track staff and nonpartner-track staff. The skill sets required of staff in a professional services firm change significantly over the course of their progression from consultant to partner. Consultants are rewarded for data gathering, analysis, and individual effort. Partners are expected to perform in very different endeavors: direction setting, client relationships, sales, and business development.

Because of this disparity in requirements and expected skills, often firms find that high-performing consultants and individual contributors are ill suited for (or uninterested in) performing the duties and expectations of a firm partner. This phenomenon can be driven by personality, work style, interest, and capability of the individual staff member and means that firms are forced to make a choice: Should high-performing professional staff who show little affinity for the skills required of a partner be provided with a different professional track for advancement?

There are a variety of benefits to providing a parallel track. Depending on the type of work being sold by the firm, the existence of subject matter experts who can be used for specific engagements can be a very powerful tool in the firm's business development arsenal. Furthermore, an individual with proven project execution skills can be parachuted into difficult projects or can be counted on to manage projects and minimize overall delivery risk, freeing business-development-oriented partners to move on to more leveraged activities. A proven, high-quality senior level resource can be of immense help to the firm.

On the other hand, a specialized and rare skill can quickly fall out of favor with clients, leaving the firm with an expensive, difficult-to-retrain, and unbillable resource to manage. Such individuals can also become disgruntled with their career progress within the firm. If the parallel career track and advancement for their role is ambiguous, they may feel that they have been relegated to a backwater within the firm. This situation may eventually affect their job performance, and they may leave on their own.

The decision for parallel career tracks for individual producers or subject matter experts depends greatly on firm size, structure, type of work being sold, and client needs. While there is no general methodology for determining what is best for a specific firm, what is certain is that firms should make a clear-cut decision on whether they plan to support alternate (nonpartner-track) career paths. Firms that find this issue difficult are usually the ones that allow nonpartner-track individuals to stay with the firm but do not provide clear roles, responsibilities, and advancement paths for them. This puts the firm and the individual in the worst of both worlds.

While recruiting and retention for firms are covered in Chapter 11, recruiting is mentioned here because there are strong linkages between career track development and recruiting. One of the most important factors in selecting a firm for professionals is the potential for learning and advancement. Therefore, it is important that firm recruiting efforts and collateral reflect the defined career paths to set clear performance and promotion expectations with potential candidates as early as possible. Convey the message that the firm is well organized, and you will attract the best candidates.

Review and Update of Career Tracks

Like most firm governance structures, career tracks and promotion criteria should be reviewed periodically to ensure that they remain relevant and continue to reflect reality. Typically, firms review these criteria annually and make minor changes to the overall model. Complete overhauls of the career track system are usually driven by major industry changes, large-scale firm growth, mergers or acquisitions, large changes in the firm's service offering that occur over time, or changes in strategic direction. These major adjustments are rarely executed and may happen only once every 5 to 10 years. Large changes to the career track and promotion plan affect every professional in the firm and entail a resetting of career expectations by nearly all.

Compensation and Benefits

As outlined earlier in this chapter, compensation is an important element of overall employee satisfaction. Research has shown that as long as compensation is within reasonable (plus or minus 10 percent) range of employees' marketplace expectations, other factors are more important determinants of overall career and job satisfaction. However, when compensation strays outside those ranges, it becomes the number one predictor. Inattention to compensation can quickly ruin a firm through mass exodus of key staff.

Compensation setting can be challenging for professional services firms. Salaries and benefits are usually the largest direct cost by far in a professional services firm; therefore, controlling compensation expenses has the largest impact on overall firm profitability. On the other hand, the firm's effort to recruit the "best and brightest" and deliver the highest level of service for clients can be severely hindered by an uncompetitive overall compensation package.

Best practices for firms in the area of compensation include:

- *Clearly defined compensation programs:* Base salary, bonus, and other compensation expectations for each level should be clearly set. While firms may not elect to have an exact salary for each level, ranges of compensation are appropriate as outlined earlier in the chapter.

- *Total compensation concept:* Employee base salary and other cash compensation are only a portion of the total employee expense for professional services firms. Benefits, training, and other forms of compensation can range from 10 percent to 30 percent of the total cost of an employee. Because employees often consider only direct cash compensation when benchmarking themselves against peers in other organizations, the firm should establish the concept of total compensation for employees and highlight for staff the total package of compensation and benefits costs incurred by the firm. One major consulting firm sends employees a total compensation report annually and includes all of the compensation components for professional staff valued appropriately in dollars.

- *Periodic staff compensation reviews:* Annual review of compensation for each staff member. These reviews should usually be tied to the staff annual appraisal. Periodically, the firm may perform market-adjustment compensation reviews that are not linked to the appraisal cycle.

- *Periodic compensation benchmarking:* To avoid undercompensating staff, the firm should benchmark professional and administrative salaries against the market every three to six months. An annual schedule for compensation reviews, usually tied to performance appraisals, is sufficient. For certain high-demand skills, a six-month incremental check is necessary to make sure the market has not changed significantly. Salary adjustments can work both ways (i.e., down as well as up). If the market has come down significantly, downward salary adjustments may be in order. Downward salary adjustments can be incredibly demotivating and should be avoided if possible.

- *Publication of salary and benefit benchmarking data:* Because professional staff will inevitably conduct their own benchmarking research, the firm can mitigate any negative impacts by proactively researching total compensation appropriate for the firm employees. Benchmarks will vary by level, firm type, geography, and macroeconomic conditions. This benchmarking should be used to set total compensation levels competitively, as well as ensure that staff members are satisfied that objective criteria are used in assessing market levels.

- *Linkage of compensation and billing:* If salaries for a given level within the firm are confined to a certain band, the firm can more easily set bill rates with the expectation that staffing will produce a certain amount of gross margin. For example, the firm may set a policy of billing associates' time at three times cost. The bill rate for an associate making $75 per hour, thus, would be $225 per hour. The use of multiples of salary standards to establish bill rates makes project estimating and budgeting an easier process and can be facilitated through the establishment of clearly defined compensation for staff levels.

- *Adherence to external constraints:* Compensation packages should comply with any applicable federal, state, or local laws, as well as any other guidelines or regulations that may apply to the firm, voluntarily or mandated.

Compensation Disclosure

A difficult decision is whether compensation information should be publicized internally by the firm. Knowing the compensation ranges at each level can serve as an incentive to junior staff, creates a culture of openness, and eliminates time-consuming gossip and backbiting over salaries. However, there are some drawbacks to this approach. Competitors can easily benchmark themselves against firm pay rates. Furthermore, if salaries are perceived by the staff to be noncompetitive, attrition rates will be higher. If the salary ranges are too wide or regarded by the staff as inequitable, public salary information will be counterproductive as well.

Internal disclosure of salaries tends to work best in firms that have the preceding compensation best practices implemented: levels and roles clearly defined, easy-to-understand promotion criteria, and market-based benchmarked salary and compensation packages that are relatively competitive. Additionally, firms that disclose compensation information internally may elect to avoid partner compensation disclosure or may intentionally obfuscate the information for the higher levels of the firm.

Timing of Compensation Events

A retention technique related to compensation that can be employed by firms is to structure the timing of significant compensation events so that there is always a personnel event on the near horizon. For instance, the firm can have appraisals delivered in Q1, compensation adjustments in Q2, stock option vesting in Q3, and bonus payouts in Q4. With a real event taking place every two to three months, employees have something to look forward to and tend to do less looking for new opportunities.

Benefit Selection

Establishing a benefit package that fits all employees can be tricky. Staff members at different points in their careers and personal lives care about different things. For example, junior staff are usually focused on cash compensation and training opportunities, whereas mid-career staff with families may want more flexible hours, lower travel expectations, and comprehensive health coverage.

If possible, the firm should accommodate the wants and needs of different constituencies by providing a menu of benefits that employees may purchase to suit their specific needs. For smaller firms, this may be difficult; as a firm grows, such programs can improve retention, recruiting, and overall staff satisfaction.

Perquisites

In addition to benefits, the firm may elect to establish specific perquisites due for staff promoted to each level. These perquisites may range from the simple, such as a dedicated executive assistant for all principal levels and above, to more elaborate, such as paid country club memberships. Perquisites serve as incentives for promotion, and they are helpful in improving the productivity of the most senior staff of the firm.

Professional Development

As outlined earlier in this chapter, good professional development programs are a critical contributor to overall staff satisfaction and retention in the services firm. The three main components of professional development for staff are the appraisals, training, and management feedback.

Appraisals: The Keys to Career Tracks

Appraisals are the mile markers along the career track laid out by the firm. They serve as a forum for helping staff improve by providing a formal feedback mechanism, and a formal venue for promoting staff. A rigorous appraisal process is also a good discipline for the firm as a whole, sending the message that staff performance is important and that there is accountability for performance at all levels.

To get the most value out of the appraisal process, it must be taken seriously by the firm, the appraisers, and the appraisees. The very best firms have well-defined processes for executing staff appraisals and invest immense internal effort at all levels to complete comprehensive reviews every year.

While appraisals within a given firm may take many different forms, in general, they are working to accomplish several things:

- Determine whether professionals being evaluated have the skills, capabilities, and knowledge to do their current job well.
- Determine whether professionals have the skills, capabilities, and knowledge to advance to the next level.
- Identify, inventory, and plan around any gaps that need to be addressed.
- Provide a formal process for documenting and revisiting these issues.
- Celebrate achievement and recognition through a formal process (promotions are usually, but not necessarily, linked to appraisals).

While each firm should develop its own specific set of appraisals for each level, which emphasize the skills required at that level, issues to consider include:

- Does the individual have the core skills needed to execute the work?
- Has the individual demonstrated the necessary skills, capabilities, and knowledge to advance to the next level?
- Does the individual put forth the appropriate effort (work ethic)?
- Does the individual work to build new knowledge (client-specific, industry, or technical skills)?
- Does the individual contribute to firm intellectual property or help develop new service lines?
- Does the individual develop meaningful, effective relationships with client counterparts?
- Does the individual work to sell new business or expand business with existing clients?
- Is the individual capable of appropriately structuring and managing work independently or working in teams?
- Does the individual manage subordinates and teams well?
- Does the individual establish effective working relationships with peers and managers?

The CD-ROM that accompanies this book provides a sample appraisal form for a consulting-oriented professional services organization.

Because of the effort for appraisals and most firms' planning cycles, an annual appraisal cycle is generally most appropriate. Many firms also perform a quarterly or half-year appraisal for new hires to ensure that they get off to a good start. Staff with performance issues may need to have intracycle appraisals completed as well to ensure that they are raising the level of their production appropriately.

The firm must also make a choice about how many appraisals it wants to complete simultaneously. Some firms work on rolling appraisal schedules, which coincide with the anniversary of the individual's hire date. Other firms complete all staff appraisals during the period of a few weeks, once per year. This schedule is particularly appropriate for firms with seasonal business patterns. A drop-off in billable activity at the end of the year can make the ideal time to complete the appraisal cycle. Usually an annual appraisal cycle is most productive; rolling appraisals can be disruptive and are more difficult to organize.

The appraisal process should also define which professionals should be interviewed for the appraisal. Some firms limit interviews and input to managers or partners for whom the appraisee has worked, and other firms employ a "360-degree feedback" process, which interviews peers and subordinates as well. While the 360-degree approach is more time consuming, it often unearths additional useful information for appraiser and appraisee. Another consideration is whether client feedback should be incorporated. While this can be a tricky area, often clients appreciate being made part of the evaluation process and will have insights not found inside the firm. Clients of long-standing relationship to the firm and with direct experience with the appraisee's work product are the best targets for such data gathering.

To facilitate the appraisal process, professional staff may be asked to complete a self-appraisal as the first step of the overall appraisal. This is a useful practice because it forces appraisees to take a candid look at their performance and improvement needs. It can also reveal any self-awareness issues if there are large gaps between the appraisees' evaluations and the feedback from the organization. Generally, appraisees fill out the same forms that the appraiser completes.

Administrative staff should be included in the appraisal process as well. The appraisal areas for administrative staff are, however, different from those of professional staff.

Because of the large amount of effort that goes into each individual appraisal, the workload should be shared across the firm professionals. Thus, the appraiser for a given individual may be someone only one to two levels above that individual (e.g., a principal evaluating a manager or a manager evaluating a consultant). This approach has the added benefit of providing training for the appraiser and provides an additional perspective on the process because most firm professionals will be both appraisers and appraisees in a given cycle.

Creating Performance Plans

While a host of management books with advice and guidance on effectively managing your workforce are available, the effective management of employees can often be overcomplicated by the pundits. The firm managers should pick a management philosophy that matches their personality and capabilities. However, in most cases, creating a high-performance team boils down to four things:

1. Setting (and documenting) clear objectives and expectations of superior performance.
2. Developing a joint plan that lays out execution of those objectives and expectations over a period (usually quarterly or annually).
3. Measuring progress against those objectives and expectations on a monthly or quarterly basis and at annual review time.
4. Providing feedback to employees after analyzing the measures in step 3.

Feedback can occur in one of four ways, depending on the situation:

1. *Good feedback:* Give positive reinforcing feedback to the individual.
2. *Bad feedback, but employee has potential:* The firm manager must assist the individual who has potential to get back on track. This may entail weekly meetings to help mentor the individual.
3. *Repeated bad feedback:* After repeated attempts to help the person or after concluding the person is not capable, make the employee take responsibility by putting him or her on a performance improvement plan where he or she is accountable to achieve some short-term objectives in a short time (e.g., 45 days) or risk being terminated.
4. *Bad feedback and employee has failed his or her performance improvement plan:* It is the firm's responsibility to terminate the employee or move him or her into a position that requires fewer skills.

The 10 Percent Attrition Model

The 10 percent attrition model is focused on improving the average performance of the firm professionals by creating attrition in the poorest performing 10 percent of staff every year. In this model, the firm releases the bottom 10 percent of the workforce annually. This process ensures that the firm is constantly upgrading the team. It also helps the workers falling in the bottom 10 percent. This model is applicable to mid-size and large professional services firms. After a few cycles, the firm professionals will be a stable, high-quality group, and the attrition model may no longer apply; however, we have found this situation to be the exception. Although there are costs to any type of employee turnover, the costs of an ineffective, poorly performing team far outweigh the impact of turning out the poor performers.

To accomplish this attrition, during each review cycle, the firm management team should rank professional staff according to their relative performance. One method is to adopt the A, B, C, D model, which equates A to the top 10 percent of performers, B to the middle 60 percent, C to the next 20 percent, and D to the bottom 10 percent. Adhering to a 10 percent attrition model, particularly for the struggling firm, is effective because the cost of D staffers is significant.

The obvious costs include compensating employees who are not producing value for the organization. However, this is only a small portion of the cost to the department. D players traditionally command a disproportionate amount of management attention because of either personal issues or performance problems. The management attention could be used for driving projects forward and otherwise ensuring the firm's success.

Further, management or teammates have to cover for the nonperformance of the D-ranked staff members. Finally, and most corrosive, D performers tend to drive away the A and B players, who ask, "Why am I getting paid the same amount for producing twice as much work?" Management attention should be spent on caring for and developing A and B players and on reducing their attrition to zero. The forced attrition model and an employee swap analysis are powerful tools for managing a world-class professional services firm.

Training Programs for Professional Development

Training programs for professional staff can be a powerful tool for improving both staff performance and for staff satisfaction.

The hallmarks of a good training program are:

- *Relevance:* The training should provide skills directly useful to the professional in the execution of the major portion of their responsibilities, for example, legal research training for entry-level attorneys or project management training for managers.
- *Timeliness:* The best training is timely as well, and is delivered to staff at the point in their career where they have enough experience for the training to be relevant but early enough that they can reap the benefits of it.
- *Linkage to promotion objectives:* Training often takes a back seat to billability objectives, client work, and other unavoidable business emergencies. However, because training is an effective and important way of improving staff performance, the firm must find ways to promote and enforce objectives. One way to ensure that this happens is by tying standard training classes to promotion objectives.

Professional staff value training because they enjoy the challenge of learning new skills, and they recognize that keeping skills current (particularly for professionals in areas with rapidly changing skills required, such as technology) ensures interesting future assignments and helps guarantee job security.

To facilitate the delivery of this benefit, each position identified for the organization (as outlined previously in this chapter) should have a specific training regimen. This regimen should include both recommended and required training for each level. Promotion should be made contingent, in part, on completing the required training. Firm management can work to establish a training program and can help with conducting training, tracking completion and certification, as well as identifying outside providers for delivery of the training. This should be done in conjunction with the professional staff, who can be helpful in identifying the training that would be both interesting and useful for their role.

Because training, particularly training conducted by outside providers, invariably involves significant time and expense for the company, firm management may want to consider asking employees to make a reciprocal commitment to the organization. In exchange for the training, staff may sign a training certificate. This certificate outlines the training program and the cost for each piece. Employees should sign an agreement stating that they will reimburse the company for training costs if they leave the company voluntarily within 12 months after they complete the course. This acknowledgment accomplishes two things. First, it demonstrates to employees the actual dollar amounts invested by the department in their training. Second, it reduces the risk of investing in employees who depart the company as soon as they receive the training, lowering attrition in the firm.

As employees receive training, their market value increases, and they will likely graduate from one job to the next. To keep the staff interested and engaged, they must be provided opportunities to move ahead, use the new skills they have learned, and continue to learn new professional skills. If the company does not provide its team with these opportunities, the best employees will find an employer who will. Providing training, development, and a chance to use new skills generates a tremendous amount of loyalty and goodwill.

In some cases, the team member may be trained out of the company. After employees complete a training regimen and improve their skills, their value increases. At some point, the organization may not be able to provide them with the on-the-job responsibility that they would command in the open market and they may elect to move on. This is a natural outcome of having qualified employees and, while employee retention is critical, should not be cause for alarm.

We have heard good managers characterize it thus: "The department should be more like a college than a prison. We miss our best team members when they elect to move on, but if we cannot provide them opportunities to grow, then they must seek them on the open market." Allowing employees to leave on good terms also means that they may return eventually.

Providing rigorous training and development opportunities will entail some short-term expense for the firm, but it will be a crucial factor in the department's ability to retain the "A" players. Firms that fail to train, develop, and challenge their staff will retain only those who cannot find employment elsewhere.

For smaller firms with limited training budgets, creative approaches may be required to achieve professional development goals. Self-study, training provided by outside firms, or teaming with other small firms are some ways that this can be accomplished.

For firms of all types, voluntary training can be helpful, particularly for skills that are useful but fall outside the normal on-the-job experiences of the professional staff. One technology services company, seeking to improve the decision-making capabilities of its management employees, embarked on a "book club." The manager group signed up for readings and group discussions of a selection of landmark books on the topic of decision science. This was a low-effort, low-cost, high-impact way of accomplishing training that could not be accomplished as part of the day-to-day execution of the business.

Another often-overlooked source of training is simple networking and involvement in outside industry groups. Professionals can get significant advice and new viewpoints from discussing issues they are facing in the management of their firm or delivery of their service with others in the same or similar businesses. Professional networking groups that facilitate such meetings are easy to locate for a given geography and profession and can generate a large return on the time invested in them.

Certain professions or roles may have specific certifications that are helpful (or essential). The technology services business is rife with certifications; the fields of law, accounting, real estate, and architecture have a variety of professional certifications that are required or are helpful. As with training, the firm may elect to link the achievement or retention of certain certifications to promotion and advancement.

Finally, firms of a certain size may elect to create a department or group dedicated to professional training. Firms with more than 100 professionals may consider having at least one resource dedicated to internal training. Other factors determining the need for dedicated internal training resources include highly specific skills or knowledge needed to deliver firm services and high attrition rates resulting in large numbers of new staff over a long period of time.

Management Coaching

Much of the day-to-day professional development in a services firm comes from direct manager feedback to staff, delivered on an ongoing basis. This informal, real-time feedback is an important kind of training for staff; therefore, managers should be aware of the best ways to work with their teams in providing feedback.

Robert S. Bailey of the Center for Creative Leadership has developed a framework for guiding manager feedback styles for employees based on their current performance. The framework highlights that the management style most appropriate for underperforming employees is different for moderate-performing employees and again different for high-performing employees.[3]

The matrix, adapted here from *The Architect's Handbook of Professional Practice,* is shown in Exhibit 10.3. The distribution of employee performance falls roughly on a normal curve, placing employees in one of four quadrants. The most appropriate management style for each employee type is outlined in each quadrant.

A final management coaching issue for professional staff to be aware of is the challenges created for staff as they transition from individual producer

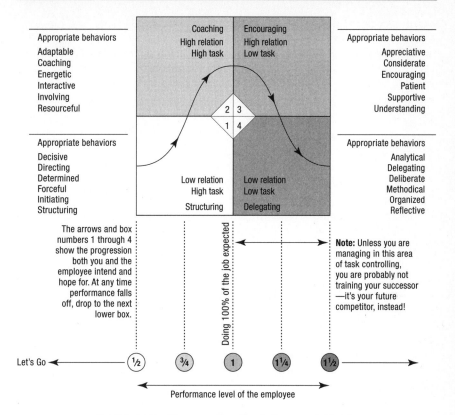

Exhibit 10.3 **Manager Feedback Approach Matrix**

roles to roles that incorporate management responsibilities. This can be a difficult transition, particularly in professional services firms, which tend to value high levels of output for entry-level and early-career professionals. These staff tend to fall back on individual producer habits, even after promotion to manager. Eventually, the amount of work required cannot be completed by an individual, making leverage and management expertise critical. Training and monitoring new managers to learn how to effectively achieve results from their teams is a critical part of helping the new manager to succeed and avoid burnout.

Summary

The professional development mechanism, compensation structure, and career plan for professional and administrative staff are one of the most important predictors of overall staff satisfaction and retention. These areas, however, often get overlooked in the daily focus on sales, delivery, and firm operations experienced by the growing professional services practice. It requires dedication and long-term planning on the part of the senior management team of the firm to ensure that these areas are properly addressed.

The elements of an effective career plan should include clearly defined levels, responsibilities at each level, and promotion criteria for achieving the next level. Compensation ranges (and components) at each level should be delineated as well. Compensation should be benchmarked periodically against market rates and adjusted accordingly.

The skills required for each level as well as promotion criteria should be consistently reflected in the appraisal process. The appraisal process itself should take place annually for all professional and administrative staff. New staff should be reviewed at the three- or six-month point as well.

While compensation, benefits, career planning, and professional development are a challenge to manage in the face of urgently competing sales and delivery priorities, the near and long-term benefits of increased staff satisfaction, performance, and retention will reward the attention paid to these topics by the professional services firm.

RESOURCES

David H. Maister, *Managing the Professional Services Firm* (New York, New York: Free Press, 1993).

NOTES

1. Ruth Benedict, as quoted by Margaret Meade in *An Anthropologist at Work,* part 1 (1959).
2. Cuba Gooding Jr. as Rod Tidwell in *Jerry Maguire,* written and directed by Cameron Crowe (1996).
3. Joseph A. Demkin and The American Institute of Architects, *The Architect's Handbook of Professional Practice* (Hoboken, NJ: John Wiley & Sons, 2001).

11

Professional Staff Recruiting and Retention

Brant C. Martin

Professionals, by their very nature, tend to be horrible businesspeople.
—Unknown

Numerous exceptions exist, and you need only to look at the hundreds of firms in all professional industries to see examples of well-run, multijurisdictional practices that generate significant profit for their partners and shareholders and staff to see that the old adage does not always hold. But as with many stereotypes, there is perhaps a grain of truth. Attorneys want to practice law, whether in the trial courts or the boardrooms. Accountants want to crunch numbers. Investment bankers want to "do deals." What they often do *not* want to do, however, is involve themselves in the messy logistics of hiring employees, leasing office space, buying computers, and the various and sundry other tasks that are necessary to make the *business,* not just the *practice,* perform.

Why This Topic Is Important

One of the most time-consuming nonpractice areas for any professional services firm is the hiring and retention of qualified and appropriate professionals. You have to find professionals to practice in the firm for there to be any practice at all. And, for there to be a practice, the professional employed in the firm must deliver. Therefore, the identification, hiring, and maintenance of a qualified staff of professionals is critical to any firm's success.[1]

No professional services firm can maintain its reputation merely on the backs of its founders or first generation of employees and partners. First, such a strategy necessitates a small operation, and is difficult if not impossible to scale and grow over time. There is only so much that two, three, or four people can do. Thus, any firm that rests its future only on a "cult of personality" around its founders can be assured of two things: very few clients and a shelf life that expires with the retirement, or simply the aging, of its founders. Speaking strictly from the idea of the future prospects of the firm, there can be no more important function for a firm than recruiting and retention. Simply put, the human capital of a firm must be constantly fed and maintained. Otherwise, the family tree of a firm will wither and die. The professional staff candidate today is the partner of the future.

Furthermore, recruiting and retention are critical not only for the future of a firm but also for its present. Most often, client-switching costs between professional services firms are low. If the firm cannot deliver qualified and professional service, clients will "vote with their feet" and find another service provider that can deliver what their needs entail. If the firm is not constantly delivering (and improving on) the quality of its work product and services, planning for a second generation becomes a moot point. Further, the nature of a professional services firm is that the clients need you because of a specialized body of knowledge that either cannot be performed within the corporation or is not economical to perform in-house. For example, the Securities and Exchange Commission (SEC) does not allow a company to present its own audited numbers. An outside accounting firm must sign off on the company's financials for a stock to be publicly traded. In the same manner, a corporation may have its own in-house legal team to oversee the various issues that the company faces on day-to-day basis. But any corporation also will be presented with legal issues that it simply does not have the expertise to handle. In that case, outside legal counsel is necessary. And in both of these situations and others, the trust of the client is critical to the success of the project. Whether public issuance of stock or "bet-the-company" litigation, the client must trust its outside vendors with a major project—and law firms, accountants, investment bankers, and others certainly fall into this category. Because of these issues, work product and trust, the professionals delivering the services are the baseline by which the firm will be evaluated. Therefore, every firm must have in place a process by which professionals are identified, recruited, retained, and advanced. And a significant portion of the nonpractice time and effort of any firm must be dedicated to this process. This chapter addresses the recruiting and onboarding of professional staff; Chapter 10 addresses career tracks, compensation, and advancement issues.

Most readers of this book will be familiar with the following categories of professionals in any service organization:

1. Rainmakers
2. Specialists
3. Worker bees
4. Misfits[2]

Each of these categories is absolutely necessary for the professional services firm (even the "misfits" category—you cannot know what works without knowing what *does not* work). If the successful firm is to maintain itself, each professional who is brought into employment must already know, or quickly find, his or her proper place in the proper category, which is discussed more thoroughly later.

How does this happen? First, the members of the firm have to be obtained—the process of recruiting. Second, the members of the firm have to be kept where they are, which means that one way or another, they must be kept happy—the process of retention.

In both recruiting and retention, institutional controls are critical. The process must be uniform in all respects, even if the results of the process are not. For example, it is likely that not every professional in a firm will be paid the same rate of compensation. However, it is critical that the process by which a compensation package is arrived at be uniform. Thus, the result can vary from individual to individual. But the process itself, to be perceived as fair by both incoming employees and ongoing employees, must be consistent. Any other path is a recipe for employee dissatisfaction, defections, and, at the end, disaster. The topic of compensation is covered in detail in Chapter 10.

Recruiting for Professional Services Firms versus Other Businesses

Recruiting for a professional services firm is by its very nature distinct from other businesses for several reasons. The primary differences between recruiting for professional services and other companies are a lack of fungibility, compensation, personality issues, and work product liability.

Lack of Fungibility

Professional services firms exist to provide specialized knowledge that companies do not have internally. Therefore, any professional who provides services to the client, from the most senior partner to the most junior associate, is in one sense the "face" of the firm. Also, each professional will gain some knowledge of the client and the client's business that another person will not have upon being assigned to the client. For these reasons, a professional staff employee providing services for a firm is not an inherently fungible commodity.

Compensation

This issue is somewhat self-evident: Because of a greater degree of education, licensing or certification, and specialization, professionals are paid a great deal more than other vendors of a corporation. They have paid a price to obtain their degrees, licenses, credentials, and knowledge, often in the form of school loans, missed business opportunities, and a heavy investment of time in their career. Professionals expect to earn significant compensation not only for their expertise but also for the price of being on call at the client's behest.

At some point in time, almost every client will question not only the fees that it is paying to the firm, but also the value that the client receives in exchange for the fees. This presents almost an inherent conflict of interest for the managing partner of a firm. He or she must pay market compensation rates to keep the firm's professionals happy. But at the same time, the decision makers at the client will often wonder at the level of compensation that the professionals receive and are likely to shop the competition if prices are too high.

Personality Issues

By definition, professionals are specialists who have a level of education and expertise in areas that others do not. Some aspect of their personality caused them to achieve a level of success, be it academic or otherwise. The corollary is that professionals also often have an attendant part of their personality that makes them difficult to manage. For the sake of clarity, let us simplify this issue by avoiding euphemism—professionals often have outsized egos that many other industries simply do not have or do not have in the abundance that a professional services firm does.

Suppose, for example, that Company XYZ is in the business of making widgets. The widgets are mechanical devices that are manufactured by piecing together a series of five separate components. Without all five components, there is no widget, but the process itself of assembling the components requires no specialized skill or knowledge. Company XYZ has a team of 10 persons that assembles widgets, two persons for each component. All of these people know the process by which they handle their own particular component, but none of the others. Therefore, it takes at least five of the persons on the team to manufacture a finished widget. Now, assume as well that Company XYZ has a CEO who started the company making widgets in his garage and has built the business into a multimillion-dollar enterprise. He knows everything there is to know not only about assembling the components but also about sales, marketing, accounting, shipping, and everything else necessary to run the business. None of the 10 people who assemble the widgets have the same level of expertise as the CEO, but the CEO has the knowledge and skill of all 10 people on the component team because he started out doing it all by himself. In Company XYZ, therefore, there is one person who is indispensable. Also, there are 10 people who are in some form or fashion dispensable because there is always someone who can do their job if they decide to leave, and they also know that they do not have the knowledge that the CEO has.

In a professional services firm, most often all the professional staff have the same basic education, the same basic licenses or permits to work, and have undergone the same basic life experiences to gain those assets. Therefore, they may not have started the firm and may never have managed a firm in their life, but they still have the same baseline starting point as the managing partner, who would otherwise be the CEO. Furthermore, they may also have a specialty that the managing partner does not have (e.g., ERISA law) that is necessary for the provision of services to the client. Therefore, that professional thinks that he or she is indispensable and should be accorded the same compensation or other perquisites as the managing partner. Add to this the unique structure of many professional services firms, and the problem deepens. Many firms, unlike corporations, are partnerships. In some way, each partner has input, if not a full vote, in how things are run. The end result is that the managing of such egos can be difficult, and it takes a unique leader to effectively run a business among "equals." Chapters 9 and 3 deal with partnership structures and organization issues in more detail.

The partner must evaluate any person being recruited with the idea that that person would eventually take his or her place as a partner with the other professionals. Therefore, if there are ego or team-player issues with a recruit, they need to be immediately identified and may justifiably form the basis for a negative hiring decision.

Liability

This issue cannot be overemphasized, especially if the firm is recruiting younger staff direct from professional schools. Most professional services firms have some type of fiduciary duty or quasi-fiduciary duty that informs every decision they make concerning the client. Therefore, there is a fiduciary or quasi-fiduciary liability that attends each person's work for the firm. If a "bad hire" is made in the world of commerce, productivity might go down or a bad product might get shipped. If a bad hire is made in a professional services firm, the firm could easily be exposed to liability that could threaten its existence.

Further, apart from legal liability, there is the issue of institutional reputation. The clients of a professional services firm provide its lifeblood, and without new clients the firm ceases to exist. But apart from selling the firm to new clients, the existing clients must be serviced in a way that conforms to all applicable standards of care and conduct. Professional services firms rely solely on their human capital to generate revenue. If the human capital is flawed, the client relationship is damaged and the institutional reputation of the firm is at risk.

Retention for Professional Services Firm versus Other Businesses

The concept of retention is viewed with disdain by many professionals. It is seen as a New Age or "touchy-feely" addition into the firm, an unfortunate consequence of the "me-first" mentality of the modern world. In almost every firm, there is at least one partner who the associates refer to as "old school" and who can always be counted on to regale new employees with stories of "how it used to be." This person invariably thinks that the junior employees are paid too much, are asked to do too little, and have no idea what it was like just to be happy to have a job, any job. This is the professional equivalent of your father or grandfather telling you about having to walk to school through five feet of snow, uphill both ways.

The truth of the matter is that this curmudgeon is 100 percent absolutely right. Never before in the history of our country have new graduates from school been paid so much in comparison to their (practically nonexistent) level of experience. Graduates of the top business schools and law schools often earn more money in their first year out of school than the top level of salary that their parents' *supervisors* made at any point in their entire career.

What the curmudgeon fails to take into account, however, is the immutable law of market forces. Simply put, barring a nationwide financial crisis, the salary level of new graduates from business, law, architecture, and other professional schools is dictated by the market, and is not likely to decrease by any significant margin. Therefore, the concept of retention, while unseemly to many veterans, is here to stay. Firms ignore it at their own peril, because for the most part, young professionals always have a continuous market for their services.

Because professional staff salaries are high and competition for professionals is so intense, firms have had to institute retention policies to keep professionals in the firm once they are hired. This is distinct from many businesses for several reasons.

First, the "revolving door" that characterizes much of American business is even more pronounced in the services business. Thirty or 40 years ago, the expected career path of young professionals was to get a job with the best firm that they could find and, once hired, pay their dues with the ultimate goal of making partner, managing director, principal, or other appropriate level within their industry. Once you made partner, in the former reality, you had made it. And firms had a significant advantage over their associates in keeping them—firms by gentlemen's agreements did not "raid" other firms for talent, and the stigma of being a "job hopper" was, for a young professional, potentially career-threatening.

Today, however, that world simply no longer exists. Professional recruiting firms are so widespread that many of them focus on a single industry: accounting, law, architecture, advertising, real-estate and so on. It is not uncommon for a lawyer in his or her first 10 years of practice to jump to as many as three or four firms before settling down for a longer period of time. Also, the cache of being made partner is not the Holy Grail that it once was. Issues of quality of life, family time, double-income families, and entrepreneurship are now much more likely to dictate individuals' employment decisions than the prospect of multi-decade employment with a single firm.

With the revolving door now a reality, firms must realize that their own business needs must take into account the damage that it can pose. Professional services firms, as stated earlier, rely on their work product and the institutional memory of their professionals to deliver their services. If a firm becomes too much of a revolving door for associates and partners, the consistency and quality of the work product suffers and the institutional memory of a client's needs or eccentricities is almost nonexistent. Many managing partners often hear the following refrain from clients: "Who is this John Smith? What happened to Mary Jones? She handled all of our matters before and she knew what she was doing. Now I have to teach this guy everything all over again." The resulting extra billable hours (from loss of institutional memory) and inconsistency of work product can irrevocably damage the client relationship. In fact, the change-out of a critical professional can often cause a client to reexamine his or her entire relationship with the professional services firm and possibly result in the loss of that client.

The Four Types of Professionals in a Professional Services Firm

Having discussed the importance of recruiting and the differences in recruiting for professional services firms versus other businesses, we now turn to the nitty-gritty—the processes of recruiting and retention. This forces us to break the inquiry into three parts. First, we identify whom the firm is looking for and who it is that works for the firm. Then, we identify how the target will be hired. Finally, we identify how that person will be retained once he or she is hired.

Each of the individual phases of recruiting and retention is examined more closely later. At the outset, however, we tackle a preliminary subject— the identities of the recruits and employees.

Although we have listed four types of professionals that exist in any professional services organization, there are many more variations of the overall archetypes. Each reader of this chapter will doubtless recognize some of the persons listed. This list is a learning device for the professional to realize two concepts: (1) Many professionals, even within the same firm, can be very different, and the way in which they are to be recruited has to be congruent with their own specific personalities, and (2) the manner in which each person views himself or herself within the firm can go a very long way to determining a successful retention policy. For you to successfully recruit and retain the different categories, it is critical ahead of time to establish which type of personality you are seeking. As can be seen, these levels are also consistent with the "finders, minders, and grinders" described in Chapter 10.

The Rainmaker

This individual is often a grizzled veteran with an established book of business in the beginning of the last third of his or her career or an ambitious midcareer networker who is viewed as the future of the firm. The job of the rainmaker is self-explanatory—it is to make the rain by which the grass grows, that is, go get business on which the firm can execute. This person must have social and communication skills to impress clients but also a base of knowledge to convince clients to use his or her firm.

Many professionals like to think of themselves in this category, but in reality, the number is far fewer than most people realize. You can test this theory for yourself, even without access to the financial records of a firm. Simply go ask a random number of partners in any professional services firm the identity of the firm's top rainmakers. Then ask the same question of the associates or managers. The partners' answers will most often vary widely, but the associates and managers will nearly always name the same three or four persons (in addition to their own direct supervisor, who can be discounted from the survey). Three times out of four, the persons named by the vast majority of associates will be the rainmakers who are responsible for a significant percentage of the firm's revenues.[3]

The Specialist

Often one of the most intelligent professionals in a firm, this person has a profoundly deep understanding of one specific area of the firm's services. Often the area is one that is so complex that no other professional can approach the level of expertise required: tax, employee benefits, financial derivatives, and so on. If the rainmaker is a jack-of-all-trades but a master of none, then the specialist is "a mile deep and an inch wide."

Specialists can be rainmakers and often are, particularly if their specialty is arcane or their experience cannot be easily matched by other firms. For example, a securities trial lawyer who is a former SEC director of enforcement will bring in a significant amount of business no matter which firm has the benefit of his services. At the same time, specialists also have the advantage that at some point in time, all of the firm's clients will eventually need their services. For example, in a larger firm, the tax partner always will have business regardless of his or her original orientation.

The Worker Bee

Ask any managing partner, and he or she will tell you that the worker bee is absolutely critical to the success of the organization. But a careful distinction needs to be made between the junior-level work that all professionals must perform early in their career and the organization and execution of all the moving parts of an operation that another professional, more senior, must perform to make sure the project gets executed. Both tasks encompass aspects of the worker bee, but the latter is far more important.

All professionals, at some point in their career, must play the role of the worker bee, whether they have any aptitude for it or not. This is known, in professional services and other industries, as "paying your dues." For accountants, there must always be the manager who is willing and able to spend months on a used-car lot, counting the number of green sedans. For the lawyer, someone has to pour through thousands or even millions of documents in the arduous process of discovery, especially in a complex case. For investment bankers, someone has to run the numbers backwards and forwards, sideways and upside down, and pass that information up the food chain that informs the structure of a deal. The war stories that every attorney, accountant, or investment banker inevitably passes on to younger colleagues will more often than not have their basis in the "dues-paying" portion of that person's career.

But these low-level dues-paying tasks are simply part of the learning process for any young professional. Everyone performs them, and, at some point, the young professional must make a choice to either continue performing them or move into the areas of rainmaker, specialist, misfit, or others. The larger issue is identifying the worker bee who loves the role, who does not necessarily want the spotlight, and has an incredible ability to perform the role. This is the partner or managing director who has the ability to execute on projects but not necessarily the skills or desire to perform the role of rainmaker or specialist. And these persons, perhaps above all others, are critical. They are the offensive linemen of a professional services firm, blocking and tackling even if they never see the end zone with the ball in their hands.

Unfortunately, worker bees may also not have many clients. They are by definition profit centers because of the quality and quantity of their work— as long as they are generating billable hours, they are producing a profit for the firm. Worker bees also must perform the tasks that rainmakers have no patience for or that specialists do not have the breadth of knowledge to perform. What worker bees are not, however, are revenue *generators,* and this is where they present particularly vexing problems in terms of retention. Rainmakers and specialists will always be paid more than worker bees, just as the star running back always gets paid more than the right tackle. But the running back cannot score and cannot even begin to achieve success without the tackle. It is the worker bee who performs the mundane tasks on which the client relationship depends. So keeping the worker bee happy is critical to the overall success of the firm.

The Misfit

The persons in this category are the source for many of the firm's stories that become part of the apocrypha of the firm culture. Any firm cannot know whom they really want, who will "fit" into the firm, without knowing who does *not* "fit." The reasons for being a misfit vary as widely as the firms themselves. A person who does not like to work long hours will never fit into a "sweatshop," and at the same time, a workaholic will never fit into a firm that emphasizes quality of life over quantity of billable hours. Neither the misfit nor the firm is necessarily right or wrong in either situation—it's simply a matter of one person not fitting within the culture of a particular firm.

The issue when dealing with a firm misfit is to identify such a person as rapidly as possible. The ideal, of course, would be to identify that person in the recruiting process. In that perfect world, neither the firm nor the person will waste any time in attempting to make a situation work that, by definition, cannot happen. But in the real world, this is not the case more often than not. Every year, in every firm, someone gets through the process who is a "bad fit" (referred to ironically as a PURE—"previously undetected recruiting error" by staff of at least one firm). When this happens, it is incumbent on both the firm and the person in question to rectify the situation in such a way that does no lasting damage to *either* the firm or the individual. For example, if the workaholic is thrown into the culture of a firm that prides itself on quality of life issues, it is likely that the problem will be identified by both the firm and the employee within a matter of six months.

Intuition would indicate that the best scenario would be to sever the ties between the professional and the firm immediately, but this is not necessarily the case. The firm, if it jettisons professionals too quickly, can quickly obtain the reputation of being too "clubby" and a difficult place to work. Further, the individual can obtain the difficult-to-overcome reputation of being a job hopper or one with whom it is difficult to work. Neither the firm nor the professional is well served, then, by an immediate severance. The challenge is either to find a manner in which the misfit can carve his or her own niche within the firm or to find a series of tasks and projects through which the firm can obtain a reasonable return on its investment and the professional can obtain a reasonable amount of professional development before leaving for greener pastures.

Having now identified some of the personalities (and attendant quirks) of the recruits and employees in a firm, the question now turns to how to recruit them. Recruiting focuses on the importance of putting in institutional benchmarks and cost controls for the following phases of the process:

- Initial screening/criteria for the candidate pool
- Initial identification and contact of potential employees
- Advanced screening
- Interviewing
- Strict decision-making process for offers
- Compensation negotiation
- After the offer: selling the firm and the opportunity

Retention involves the following phases:

- Periodic individual review and feedback (individual review)
- Employee satisfaction programs on a classwide or levelwide basis (group review and feedback)
- Mentorship programs
- Compensation programs on an individual and group basis
- Quality of life concerns

The Phases of Recruiting

Every firm has its own needs and resources for recruiting. Many of the attendant factors depend on the size of the firm. A CPA firm with four accountants may need just one more professional to grow its business to the size that it has identified in its business plan. Conversely, a huge consulting or law firm may need a constant influx of talent to service its clients and groom the next generation (taking into account planned-for attrition) to take over the firm in 20 years. But regardless of the needs of the firm, the recruiting process itself should be institutionalized. That is, it should be agreed on by all necessary decision makers. This serves several purposes. First, it prevents one partner or other decision maker from subverting the process or playing favorites. Second, it allows for the time spent on recruiting to be efficient. Throughout the recruiting process, the firm should always be concentrating the majority of its resources on its revenue-generating activities, not on the non-revenue-generating process of recruiting.

The ideal structure is to have a single person in the firm whose primary focus is recruiting. In larger firms, this role is almost always fulfilled by a professional recruiting coordinator. This is an industry unto itself that is discussed in more detail later and is a luxury well worth the investment for a firm that has large, continuous human capital needs. But even if this role is a luxury that a firm cannot afford with a full-time person, it is well worth it for any firm to have a person who is not a profit center in his or her own right (such as the business manager, accountant, or operations manager) to own the logistics of the recruiting process: identifying recruits, arranging interviews, researching compensation packages, and so on. This allows the professionals in the firm to do what they do best, which is generate revenue through the servicing of clients.

Initial Screening/Criteria for the Candidate Pool

At the beginning of the search process, there should be in place an initial screening that is completely dependent on what the candidate looks like on paper. Whether for new hires or laterals, the persons ultimately making the decision should set forth specific, detailed criteria. This is *not,* however, a mandate to create the ideal candidate—very rarely will such an animal be found, and the potential pool of candidates would be noticeably brief. Instead, this criteria should set forth the *minimum* criteria by which a firm will interview a prospective candidate. The idea behind this is to increase the applicant pool, not decrease it. With the criteria in hand, one of the search methods set forth in the next step can be used to establish the initial candidate pool.

Initial Identification and Contact of Potential Employees

There are a variety of sources for potential employees for the professional services firm. I will discuss the most important sources.

NEW EMPLOYEES IN THE WORKPLACE.   At some point in their lifetime, most professional services firms require some quantity of employees who are entering the professional workforce for the first time. In larger firms, the need can be quite large, with hundreds of new recruits being hired straight out of school. The target recruits in this situation are usually the easiest for the firms to identify: They must fit a certain predetermined profile, they must have a certain GPA, they must come from a school that the firm believes will have provided its graduates with a certain minimum level of knowledge, and they must have a level of maturity or other life experience that the firm considers valuable. The initial resume vetting is done by the person who is in charge of the recruiting process, and a potential candidate either fits the criteria or does not.

The talent pool for fitting the firm's criteria is also readily available, because it comes from the schools themselves. Almost every professional school has some form of career counseling, and most of the top schools have professional placement administrators, whose entire job consists of selling the schools and its graduates to potential employers. These schools most often have interviewing programs, whereby firms send a certain number of representatives for a day or multiple days, during which the firms interview a series of preselected candidates in 20- or 30-minute interviews. Once these initial on-campus interviews are concluded, the firm then informs the schools or the candidates directly whether they are interested in pursuing further action.

To access this talent pool, the recruiting coordinator (whether a professional or part time, as discussed earlier) need only contact the schools in which the firm is interested and ask to be a part of the process. The schools themselves have a vested interest in making sure *all* of their students obtain employment, regardless of GPA or other qualifications, and thus there is rarely a selective criteria for the firm to be able to participate.

Apart from the on-campus interviewing process, many firms accept resumes over the Internet or through the mail from potential employees looking for work. This is often the favored method for students whose grades are not as high as they would like or for students who are searching for job opportunities in less-traditional environments (e.g., public service or political arenas).

LATERAL HIRES.   The process of identifying lateral hires (professionals already in the workplace working for other firms or in other capacities) is trickier. First, there is no common pool such as universities where the candidates are readily ascertainable. Therefore, the initial identification of lateral recruits takes much more legwork. Second, the process of identifying lateral recruits by necessity means that you must find people who are unhappy at their current job or, at the very least, would consider moving to another firm. For example, you could obtain the names, professional schools, background, and even basic qualifications of every third-year associate in a given firm easily over the Internet, simply by mining through the web site of that firm. Finding which associates would contemplate a move, however, requires a level of information that is not publicly available. To compound the problem, cold calling each such associate is both time consuming and can reflect negatively on the firm doing the recruiting. Professional services firm within a given industry are a close-knit group, and if you begin calling every employee of a rival that fits your criteria, someone is likely to find out about it.

The most reliable method of identifying lateral hires is simply word-of-mouth. Professionals form lifelong bonds with other persons with whom they attended school. They socialize together (often to complain about their bosses with someone who will understand), they marry each other, and they live in the same neighborhoods. Therefore, an open-ended "bounty" for new hires can be offered by firms to their current employees. The logistics are simple: If Anne works for your firm and convinces her friend Robert (who she knows is unhappy at his job) to interview with your firm and Robert subsequently accepts an offer of employment, Anne is paid a recruiting bonus for her identification of a quality candidate.[4]

The other alternative, and one far more common than it was 20 years ago, is to hire a search firm to identify potential candidates. This completely outsources the process of identifying laterals and thus has the advantage of freeing up firm resources to deliver services to the clients while someone else goes through the arduous task of cold calling potential recruits. This also has the advantage, at least theoretically, of keeping the contacting firm's identity a secret. The outside recruiting firm can cold call and vet likely candidates, according to their qualifications and interest level, without revealing to a rival firm that you are raiding its employees. The potential lateral is not informed of the raiding employer's identity until the interview process is underway. The downside to using an outside firm is the cost. Many firms charge a flat fee, plus expenses, to conduct the search and insist on a contingent completion fee that is equal to a significant percentage of the new employee's salary (from 10 percent to as much as 50 percent, depending on the level of the search).

Advance Screening

Once the criteria are set in place and the potential candidates that meet the criteria are identified, the next step is the advance screening. This can be combined with one of the preceding steps. For example, if a school conducts on-campus interviews (OCI) for new hires, the OCI program itself is the advance screening. It consists of a 20- or 30-minute interview, and if either the firm or the recruit does not wish to pursue the opportunity, both sides can walk away with very little time or effort wasted. The same theory applies to lateral hires. If during the search process a potential recruit is identified and contacted but the person expresses no interest or does not, at second glance, fit the firm's needs, the process is terminated as to that candidate.

Interviewing

The beginning of the interview process is the turning point for the recruiting process. This is where a significant portion of firm time and resources begins to be spent, and thus the opportunity cost in lost business or lost opportunities for other candidates increases. Thus, firms should be careful as to how many persons are considered for interviews and how much time is allotted for them. If a firm interviews 100 people for five job openings, someone has invited far too many candidates to interview, and the firm should reassess its "advance screening" phase to rule out more candidates.

Because this chapter is focused on the recruiting and retention process overall, an analysis of interviewing itself is far too extensive for this space. Hundreds of books and articles are available on the subject.[5] Nonetheless, firms should always remember certain truths to the interviewing process that make the world of professional services unique:

- *Keep the interviews manageable.* Your employees are taking time out of their busy schedules to interview a potential employee and have other tasks that need to be done that presumably will generate revenue for the firm. At the same time, there needs to be sufficient time for the interviewer to get a feel for the candidate and for the candidate to feel comfortable and to obtain the information he or she needs to possibly make a decision. An hour is too long; 15 minutes is too short.

- *Keep the interviews friendly.* One source indicates that the "friendliness" of an interview was the single most frequently cited "best interviewing practice" for law firms and a major factor in the decision of recruits as to whether to continue the application process.[6] This can be more a function of *who* interviews potential candidates and can be a political football for the person in charge of the recruiting logistics. The office curmudgeon who is more likely to turn the interview into a pop quiz of the recruit is an almost sure-fire turnoff. However, if that person is also the managing partner who wants a hand in every decision the firm makes, some type of compromise will be necessary. A social situation, be it happy hour or lunch, where that person can be managed by another partner, is often a viable alternative. Firms should be cognizant of the fact that while they are possibly offering a job to someone, they are also selling the firm to that person. Ultimate recipients of these offers will accept only if they feel that this firm is the place they want to work.

- *Keep the interviews professional.* This is the other side of the coin from keeping the interviews friendly—they should by no means be *too* friendly. Inappropriate (and sometimes illegal) questions such as family or marital status or personal history other than past employment should be avoided. Candidates are often uncomfortable answering questions that they do not view as job-related.

- *Be sure the candidate has the opportunity to ask questions and that the questions are answered.* Members of many well-respected firms often fall into the trap of believing that their firms are the best possible place to practice their profession. As such, in interviews, they rattle on for the majority of the time about themselves and/or the firm, and the only information being imparted is nothing that the candidate could not glean from reading the firm's web site. Interviewers should be encouraged to allot a mandatory amount of time (and more than

30 seconds as the candidate walks out the door) to answer any questions the candidate has.

- *Have more than one person conduct the interviews.* If possible, have at least two, but no more than three, persons interview the candidate. A one-on-one interview tends to produce more awkward silences, which can leave a bad taste in the mouth of both the interviewer and the candidate. Having two people in the interview can minimize this risk. Also, the perspective of two persons witnessing the same conversation reduces the chance that bias and/or favoritism will unfairly prejudice the interviewing process.

- *Provide for some social interaction.* It is a fact of life that not all work is done in the office and that employment decisions are made on criteria beyond compensation and job titles. For good or for ill, candidates want to know what the professionals in a firm are like outside the office. And, a firm certainly should have an idea of candidates' ability to conduct themselves outside the interview process. For both firm and candidate, then, it is a good idea to have some type of social interaction, whether a lunch, dinner, happy hour, or any activity where both the members of the firm and the candidate can obtain an idea of what it would be like to work with each other and interact on a daily basis. However, the social setting should not be forced. Do not put candidates in the situation where they feel forced to drink alcohol or engage in other activities that make them feel uncomfortable—not everyone wants to play on the firm's softball team.

- *Require written evaluations from the interviewer.* These evaluations should be completed immediately after the interview and should provide for some type of numbered scoring system by which candidates can be compared with one another. It is not likely that every candidate will be interviewed by the same persons, and it is also certain that different interviews will contain different conversations and foci. By requiring written evaluations and scoring, the decision makers can have points of comparison from several different people to review when hiring decisions are made.

Checking References

As the candidate is being interviewed, or shortly thereafter, the recruiting coordinator should check the references provided by the candidate. This is ideally done by a single person for all of the candidates or by a specific team of persons. This procedure also ensures that bias and favoritism are taken out of the process as much as possible. Special care should be taken, however, with checking references for lateral hires. The firm and the candidate should be very clear on which references are going to be called and when the calls are going to take place. For obvious reasons, it is a bad practice for professionals in the interviewing firm to place calls on their own to friends or acquaintances about the candidate. Jobs are often lost, and firm reputations ruined, by the surreptitious investigation of a candidate. A side note: Potential conflicts of interest should also be thoroughly analyzed and cleared at this point, if not sooner.

Strict Decision-Making Process for Offers

This is the critical juncture in the recruiting process. The candidates have been interviewed, favorites have no doubt been selected, and the firm must decide who will receive an offer and who will not. A word of warning—speed is essential in this phase. Presumably, the candidate is interviewing with more than one firm, and many otherwise amenable professionals end up with other employers because their first choice simply did not move fast enough.

For the sake of speed and other considerations, this part of the process must be tightly controlled. Before the initial criteria for a candidate is established and well before any interviews take place, the decision makers in the firm should have a process in place that determines *who* will make the hiring decisions. It does not have to be, and probably should not be, a single person who makes the decision. A recruiting committee or hiring committee is a much better alternative. But it is important that once the committee is empowered to make hiring decisions, such power be unfettered by politics or other considerations. This allows the committee to move quickly (an attractive feature for almost all candidates), and it prevents political meltdowns within the firm.

Using a recruiting committee has several benefits. First, no one person shares the blame if a candidate turns out to be a bad hire. Second, a committee allows for a consensus dialogue, which avoids favoritism and bias. All too often in the recruiting process in law firms, for example, a powerful partner with a large book of business can subvert the process by "demanding" that a certain candidate be hired (or shown the door, in some cases). A recruiting committee allows for each person on the committee to have a vote and thus forestall any dictatorial moves. Third, the committee itself has the advantage of uniformity. The committee can view all of the candidates, both on paper and in person, through their resumes, interview evaluations, and their own personal interaction with candidates. If a large number of hires are to be made, the committee can pick and choose candidates, even across different sections of the firm, who are likely to provide a good fit.

After all interviews have been conducted, the hiring committee should meet and determine whether there is sufficient information to make a hiring decision. It is quite possible, especially with a lateral hire, that more information will be needed. If that is the case, the partner with whom the employee will be working can conduct further interviews or have lunch with the candidate to flesh out any concerns that he or she may have. Also, greater weight should obviously be given to the opinions of those with whom the employee will be working—everyone should have one vote, but there will always be votes that count more than others. Once the committee decides that it has enough information to make the decision, the appropriate compensation has to be decided *before* the offer is made.

Negotiation of Compensation

The issue of compensation is one of the most hotly contested and is one where much depends on the individual culture of the firm. Many firms, especially larger ones, subscribe to the theory of *lockstep* or banding compensation for nonequity employees. This ensures that every employee at a certain level gets paid the same amount or at least range of compensation, regardless of merit or other considerations. In most large law firms and accounting firms, the calculation is relatively simple: Each associate or manager gets paid a certain amount of salary in the first year out of school, a certain amount for the second year out of school, and so on. The only difference in compensation between employees of the same experience level comes in the form of periodic bonuses, which is outside the recruiting process and comes well after the employee has been hired and evaluated.

If the firm in question is hiring new workforce professionals, lockstep compensation is by far the preferred and most widely used method. The package will be the same for all new hires, and there is little, if any, negotiation. Candidates are simply told what the firm pays first-year associates and perhaps are apprised of the potential bonus range for first-year associates and what criteria determine the bonus. From the candidates' perspective, this system is beneficial because evaluating the compensation packages at different firms is easy and transparent.[7] From the firm's perspective, it is able to make hiring decisions based solely on the merits of the individual, without having to worry about price and a blind-bidding scenario. The firm is also able to include in its yearly budget the appropriate allocations.

There can be a more difficult scenario for lateral hires, however. If a firm is approaching a lateral hire for a nonequity position, the lockstep method is still viable, provided that the lateral candidate is satisfied with the compensation.[8] However, if a lateral hire is viewed as a potential superstar or has a practice in a sought-after specialty, the candidate may attempt to negotiate for a more lucrative pay package than others of his or her same experience. This situation must be handled cautiously. The candidate is attempting to gain the leverage in the negotiations, which is a situation most firms prefer to avoid. Also, if the firm allows this to occur, it is almost certainly inviting its existing associates to renegotiate their pay packages. Therefore, a firm can start out with every intention of maintaining a lockstep compensation package, only to have it fall apart with the first exception. Most firms faced with this scenario compensate such an employee through the year-end bonus structure, rather than change the base rate of pay. This allows for some (but certainly not complete) secrecy from other employees and takes the compensation negotiation out of the recruiting process. It does require, however, a leap of faith from the incoming employee that the promises being made will be fulfilled, and this is likely to become an issue before acceptance of the offer. The candidate may ask for some comfort from a decision maker that the expected "extra" compensation will in fact occur.

After the Offer: Selling the Firm

Once the candidate has been selected and the offer has been transmitted (preferably through a personal meeting or phone call, not by a letter), it will come as no surprise that more often than not, there is not an immediate acceptance. As stated earlier, the firm should probably not assume that it is the only suitor for the services of the candidate. Therefore, the members of the firm may be put into the situation where they will have to sell the candidate on the firm and themselves. For the most part, this varies by candidate: It is usually obvious whom the firm is competing with for the candidate and what the candidate believes are the sticking points for accepting the offer. The critical guidance here is that the members of the firm should not *oversell* and should be careful not to pressure the candidate into making a decision. Candidates appreciate the time and hassle-free period in which to make this important decision, and constant phone calls or lunches serve only to muddy the waters for many candidates, and to introduce undue pressure into the process. Suggested best practices in this time period are periodic personal letters from individual partners in the firm, offering to answer any questions that the candidate may have. A "hard sell" may also have the unintended consequence of making the candidate believe the firm is desperate or that it is trying to force an acceptance before the candidate finds out something the firm would prefer to keep hidden.

However, another possible scenario is that the candidate will have an offer from one firm, but is actually waiting on an offer from his or her first choice. Thus, the firm that has made the offer is the candidate's backup. There are a variety of ways to tell if this is the situation with a particular candidate. Members of the firm should be advised that by the third time you take the offered candidate out to lunch, his or her questions should already be answered. Either the candidate is having trouble making up his or her mind, in which situation no amount of cajoling is likely to do any good, or the firm is being played for a better offer from someone else. In either situation, it is critical that the firm handle the issue professionally. Once it is determined that sufficient resources have been expended on a candidate, the firm should make it clear that it will await the candidate's decision within a reasonable time frame, but that the offer does have an expiration date.

The Phases of Retention

Postrecruiting, professional staff retention becomes important. This section covers the issues related to retention. Chapter 10 discusses compensation, career tracks, and professional development in more detail.

Periodic Individual Review and Feedback (Individual Review)

Feedback, feedback, feedback. Regardless of a professional's view of *retention* in general, it is axiomatic that individual reviews are a staple of firm life. Questions remain, however, around how formal the review process is (or should be), the extent to which reviews affect compensation through bonuses and merit salary increases, and the time periods appropriate for review. Above all, the review process should be honest—do not allow the professional to hold views of his or her abilities or opportunities for advancement that the firm does not hold.

Formal reviews are the most widely accepted manner of providing feedback within the firm. The formal reviews should take place on a periodic basis, but no less than annually, and should take place at the same time of year for all professional employees. Six-month reviews can be beneficial, but this will depend entirely on the business of the firm. If the employee has been working on only one project, for one supervisor, for six months, it is likely that the employee and the supervisor both know exactly where the employee stands with regard to his or her work, and a formal review would be nothing more than window-dressing and a waste of everyone's time.

The reviews should have both a scoring system under certain categories and a section for the evaluating professional to add personal comments or expand on answers in the numerical section.

The written evaluation allows for the supervisors or evaluators to clearly document the professional's progress, strengths, and weaknesses. Farther down the road, when the professional is being considered for promotion or partnership, these evaluations can present a strong road map and argument either for or against the promotion. For this reason, firms should be encouraged to be honest on the evaluations. Nothing engenders bad will and inter-firm gossip more quickly than a firm that "strings along" its associates, only to tell them after seven years that they are not partner material. It is far better to keep professionals apprised on a yearly basis of their prospects for advancement and how such prospects, if bleak, can be improved. Also, once it becomes obvious that a person (such as a misfit, as described earlier) needs to find another home, that should be dealt with at the next yearly evaluation at least, and it can be done by a trusted advisor informally prior to that. Both the employee and the firm will be much better off if everyone is honest about the future direction of each party. Chapter 10 outlines the process of appraising employee performance in detail.

Employee Satisfaction Programs on a Class-Wide or Level-Wide Basis (Group Review and Feedback)

The concept of group feedback in a professional services firm can take many forms: associate committee, non-equity steering committee, associate compensation review, and so on. The basic premise behind each is the same: to serve as a conduit through which nonequity professionals provide input to the firm. The meetings are usually held at least yearly and in some firms, as often as quarterly. There is normally no voting power, and equity holders have no obligation to heed the committee's advice. However, it allows the associates to feel as if their concerns are being heard, and it provides for a source of information that many partners would never know.

For example, many partners speak only of "office matters" and would rather leave all other matters (including quality of life) to the hours when employees are "off the clock." However, if there is a competing firm that continually addresses quality of life matters, the associate committee at Firm 1 is likely to bring that to the attention of the equity partners. If the matter is a continual refrain, perhaps some partners will engage before their own associates decide to test the waters at Firm 2.

Mentorship Programs

The concept of a formal *mentoring program* in a professional services firm has gained far more credence in the past 10 years than at any time prior. However, it is a mistake to believe that the concept of mentors in the professions is anything new. In decades past, the only way to enter into a profession was to attach yourself to a mentor, and "read the law" within a law office by serving as a clerk for a number of years until you were ready to take the bar exam. Ask any lawyer about his or her formative professional years, and you will hear the stories of the mentor, whether it was a friendly one or not.

Professional services firms have taken the concept of mentoring and formalized it, thereby somewhat manufacturing what was previously an organic relationship. In years past, a mentor and a protégé found each other through a natural process—the younger professionals would work on a project here and a project there and eventually find a senior person whom they enjoyed working for, and vice versa. However, it did not always work out that way. Even today, there are younger professionals who bounce from partner to partner, simply because no one can determine the best fit for them.

Currently, many firms assign the mentor and protégé to each other, often on the protégé's first day of work. And while this is not as organic as the former system, it does have its advantages. First, it requires that some form of relationship exist, and it prevents wallflower partners or wallflower associates from hiding in their offices. Second, it forces protégés to work with someone to identify their goals and a plan for getting there. This is beneficial even if the goal is not necessarily a partnership or if the goal is unknown. It is one more way in which expectations can be managed. It also forces the younger professional to develop one or more career plans and to plan with contingencies. For the younger professional, this may be one of the greatest advantages to a mentoring program.

The expectations of mentoring need to be established at the beginning. Most professionals are extremely busy and cannot afford to waste time on what they perceive to be nonbillables. However, if mentors and protégés are educated on the positive aspects of mentoring and what it brings to the firm, they can slowly be convinced to spend their resources in this very important role and function. Written guidelines should include the following, taken from Ida O. Abbott's excellent book, *The Lawyer's Guide to Mentoring*:[9]

- Program purpose and objectives
- How the program objectives should be met
- How program objectives will be monitored
- How the program will be evaluated
- Responsibilities of the mentor
- Responsibilities of the associate
- How the mentoring relationship works
- Role of the program coordinator
- What to do if problems arise in the mentoring relationship
- How mentors and associates will be matched
- Duration of the mentoring relationship
- Time commitment
- How mentoring activities should be recorded on time sheets
- Confidentiality
- Budget

The advantages of an administered mentoring program are numerous, for the firm as well as the protégé. The firm can immediately begin instructing the professional on how it "prefers things to be done." This indoctrination (for lack of a better term) happens at most firms, whether it is overtly admitted or not. Formalizing it through the mentoring program raises it to an institutional truth that encourages communication about what firm culture can or should be. The mentoring program also builds a tremendous amount of loyalty from the protégé to the mentor, and thereby to the firm. This above all gives retention its worth in time and resources.

To make the process more efficient, many firms assign more than one mentor to each junior professional. This allows the junior professional to spread the questions around to more than one person, thus preventing the mentoring program from taking up too much time from one individual. It also prevents problems with bad mentors, bad advice, or simply a breakdown in what is a very personal relationship.

Mentoring is not, primarily, about the teaching of skills. The mentor is meant to provide guidance and advice, not necessarily strict training. It is assumed in firms today that the training will be provided by a number of professionals, mentors, and others, from project to project. In fact, one of the greatest benefits to a larger firm is that often the associates are exposed to a number of professional staff from all levels on different projects. Since each supervisor will perform tasks and projects in different ways, the training itself is varied and associates will eventually develop their own style. But supervision is not mentoring. Mentoring involves guidance, "showing the way of the world" to the younger professional. The mentor should provide experience and encouragement and should work to develop the interpersonal skills of the protégé.[10] The mentor is above all intended to be a background or a voice to which the professional can turn to on a variety of issues, not just a single question on a particular project.

Quality of Life Issues

It is no secret that professional services firms expect a great deal of sacrifice from their employees. In turn, those employees are compensated extremely well with pay packages, perks, and benefits. However, quality of life issues often are raised within firm surveys as a top five issue with which professionals have problems. The long hours and the travel time are difficult on young families and often lead to defections from professionals looking to have a life, not just earn a living. The strongest weapon that a firm has concerning quality of life issues is the group input panels discussed earlier.

When the non-equity professionals are listened to through these groups, it provides a cross-section of opinion on whether the quality of life at the firm is suffering. This validates that a problem is real and not the product of one or two malcontents. At the same time, it also ensures that the problem, once identified, is dealt with on an ongoing basis between the group input committee and the leadership of the firm.

Debriefing the Recruiting and Retention Processes

At some point on an annual basis, it is important that the recruiting process as a whole be reviewed separately by the hiring committee and by the management committee of the firm. This is a step in the recruiting and retention process most often overlooked, to the detriment of many firms.

The hiring committee should undergo a detailed analysis, concentrating on certain, quantifiable metrics: how many candidates were considered, how many were interviewed, what was the acceptance rate, and how much money was spent per candidate on a pro-rata basis. These and other metrics help the committee determine where the money and time should be spent in the next year's recruiting, and eventually the goal is to have most of the inefficiencies of the process eliminated. Keeping a running total of five years of rolling budgets is particularly helpful, as these can be charted against firm growth and the professional services economy to spot trends that can be anticipated for the next year. The data collected by the hiring committee should then be passed on to the management committee, along with any recommendations that the hiring committee has for changes to the program.

The management committee's review should be more in line with this second, five-year review of the hiring committee. The management committee should be able to take the 10,000-foot view of the recruiting process in general to determine:

- Are we getting the people that we need?
- Why are certain people accepting, and why are certain people rejecting?
- Once we recruit a new employee, what is the average length of tenure?
- What do exit interviews indicate are the top five reasons people give for leaving?
- Are there trends that we, as a firm, have not yet identified?

Summary

Professionals by their very nature can have difficulty in actually "running their business." Professionals would often rather be providing client services than be involved in the day-to-day details of operations. However, there are numerous opportunities for the firm to obtain objective data that affects not only its present, but also its future. The key is to institutionalize the processes and put the effort in on the front end to make sure the processes are correct and that each step gathers data that can be used to analyze what the firm does correctly and what the firm does incorrectly.

If the recruiting and retention process concentrates on obtaining objective criteria at every level, the management committee should be able to aggregate and report on all of the information and determine whether there are underlying problems in the firm's culture, compensation structure, or workload that indicate a wrong path.

Resources

"An Insider's Guide To Interviewing: Insights from the Employer's Perspective" (National Association for Law Placement, 1666 Connecticut Avenue, NW, Suite 325, Washington, DC 20009; 1996).

"Attorney Recruitment and Retention: A Showcase of Best Practices" (National Association for Law Placement, 1666 Connecticut Avenue, NW, Suite 325, Washington, DC 20009; 1996).

Ida O. Abbot, Esq., *The Lawyer's Guide to Mentoring* (National Association for Law Placement, 1666 Connecticut Avenue, NW, Suite 325, Washington, DC 20009; 2000).

Arnold B. Kanter, *The Essential Book of Interviewing: Everything You Need to Know from Both Sides of the Table* (Times Books/Random House, 1995).

H. Anthony Medley, *Sweaty Palms: The Neglected Art of Being Interviewed* (Ten Speed Press, 1978, revised 1984, 1992).

Notes

1. The scope of this chapter is limited to the recruitment and retention of professional employees, that is, individuals with the education and attendant licenses to deliver the core services of the firm, whether the practice of law, accountancy, investment banking, or others. Excluded from this chapter is the recruitment or retention of support staff and back-office functions. Those processes, equally, and in many cases more, important to the operations of a firm, are reserved for other chapters.

2. The names of these categories were chosen by the author, and certainly each category has numerous synonyms. None of the categories are intended as slights to any particular classification—in fact, each is wholly necessary to the successful functioning of a professional firm. And, contrary to the beliefs of many professionals, it is very difficult, if not impossible, for any one individual to perform adequately in more than two of these categories.

3. Terms used in this article that denote industry-specific terms, such as *associate* or *partner*, reflect the author's background as a lawyer but are not meant exclusively to reflect law firms, either big or small. The concepts can be equally

applied to accounting firms, investment banks, and other professional services firms. The reader is encouraged to substitute his or her own industry terms (such as *principal, manager, managing director,* or others) where appropriate.

4. These bonuses can be substantial. A bounty of $5,000 or $10,000 (and sometimes more) for recruiting a lateral hire is not uncommon.

5. One excellent resource is *An Insider's Guide to Interviewing: Insights from the Employer's Perspective* (National Association for Law Placement, 1666 Connecticut Avenue, NW, Suite 325, Washington, DC 20009; 1996).

6. *Attorney Recruitment and Retention: A Showcase of Best Practices* (National Association for Law Placement, 1666 Connecticut Avenue, NW, Suite 325, Washington, DC 20009; 1996).

7. Nor is it a secret. In larger cities, the vast majority of new hires at professional services firms can tell you almost to the penny what each of their friends and associates is earning at a firm across town.

8. Not all lateral moves are related solely to an *increase* in compensation. In fact, numerous firms hire lateral employees from high-paying, but difficult, firms, for a lower salary. The lateral often makes the move for quality-of-life reasons or for the opportunity for advancement.

9. Ida O. Abbott, Esq., *The Lawyer's Guide to Mentoring* (National Association for Law Placement, 1666 Connecticut Avenue, NW, Suite 325, Washington, DC 20009; 2000).

10. See note 9.

Services Delivery: Taking Care of Business

12

Service Delivery

D. MICHAEL MCDOWELL

To live through an impossible situation, you don't need the reflexes of a Grand Prix driver, the muscles of Hercules, the mind of Einstein. You simply need to know what to do (next).

—Anthony Greenback, *The Book of Survival*[1]

Successfully developing and delivering professional services present a unique combination of challenges and opportunities. Meeting these challenges and seizing these opportunities depend on the personal abilities of the professionals involved and the relationships they maintain with their clients. Experience, expertise, and reputation all play a part in the professional services firm's ability to build and sustain a successful practice.

If success were solely a function of personal and professional capabilities, all highly skilled professionals in practice would thrive. Clients would flock to them. Unfortunately, it's not that simple. There are countless examples of well-qualified law firms, medical practices, advertising agencies, public relations specialists, and accounting firms of every size that have failed to sustain success.

This chapter focuses on important issues affecting the successful development and delivery of professional services from a strategic management perspective. It offers a systematic approach to success that can be applied and sustained across a broad spectrum of professional services businesses—large and small, for-profit, and not-for-profit.

This chapter describes how a professional services firm can move from simply thinking strategically to *becoming* strategic in the manner in which the firm develops and delivers professional services and why becoming strategically managed is more critical than ever before as the marketplace becomes increasingly competitive. This chapter looks at developing a culture that embraces strategic management, which in turn ties together the business continuum of the firm, including the administrative, operational, and service and business development activities.

Overall, the chapter addresses these questions:

- What are the characteristics of a strategically managed practice?
- How does strategic management drive process improvement?
- How does process improvement lead to the successful delivery of services or, in other words, the sustainable success of the professional practice?

Why This Topic Is Important

The United States continues to move toward an economy based on professional services. Manufacturing jobs are being replaced by service jobs at a very high rate. This growth in the service industries is fueled by a number of important factors:

- The barriers to competitive entry are minimal.
- Initial capital commitments are less than in manufacturing-based industries.
- Advancements in technology have enhanced the professional's ability to access information.
- Experience is no longer the dominant characteristic of a successful professional that it once was.
- The growing senior segment of our population has increased the demand for professional services.

But with growth in the professional services industries comes a remarkable increase in the risk of failure. Professional services firms are under greater pressure than ever before and have no choice but to:

- Differentiate themselves from their competition.
- Understand the expectations of their target market and adapt to meet these expectations.
- Deliver clearly demonstrated value.
- Increase the quality of their services while not increasing the price.
- Shorten their service delivery time.

- Accept less client loyalty, greater client turnover, and unprecedented scrutiny of the underlying profitability of the firm.

Therefore, the case is made in the sections that follow that the successful delivery of services and development of your client base is a continuous process—a never-ending cycle of embracing change that is an innate characteristic of a strategically managed culture.

Improvement Is Not Possible without Change

Strategic management systems are about process improvement that drives change within the business environment. Creating a strategically managed environment depends on it. Success today does not guarantee success tomorrow. In extraordinary businesses—those that succeed and sustain their success for years—new beginning points instantly replace end points and the process starts anew.

To understand this concept, ask this question, "What is the firm's value objective as a professional services practice?" Is it net income? Earnings per partner? Market share? Number of constituents served? This isn't a restatement of the mission of the organization. It's a definition of what drives success (for the firm, and for the clients) and how it is to be measured. Once defined, the value objective can be measured over time. Exhibit 12.1 demonstrates this concept.

Components of the current state include:

- Management style/culture
- Professional resources
- Range of services
- Market share
- Strategic planning/budgeting
- Compensation structure
- Quality of client relationships
- Information systems

Exhibit 12.1 demonstrates that today this organization has delivered $150,000 of net earnings per partner, in a firm where net earnings per partner is the professional practice's value objective.

Once the value objective has been defined and measured in today's terms, the critical question is not, "Where are we?" Rather, it is, "Where do we want to be?" In value objective terms, "What is the targeted, desired future state?"

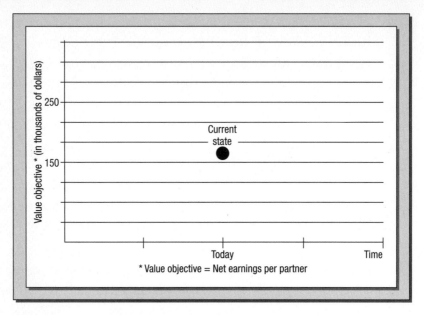

Exhibit 12.1   Value Objectives in a Professional Services Environment

Exhibit 12.2 shows that this practice has a future value objective ($250,000 of net earnings per partner) that exceeds its current condition. The difference between where the firm is and where it wants to be is the direction and goal of change.

Most professionals are inherently reluctant to change their approach to managing their practices. But progressive and successful professionals realize that they must embrace the argument for change because it:

- Creates a strategic management environment
- Solidifies the organization's commitment and focus
- Delivers incremental future value

The following section looks at the firm's internal strategic management. Without a strategically managed environment, the strategic delivery of professional services, and the strategic building of a firm's client base cannot be successfully accomplished.

Strategic Internal Management

Strategic management systems work when they become the way business is conducted, the way decisions are made, and the way new services are

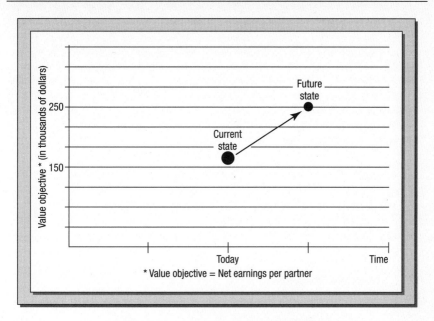

Exhibit 12.2   Value Objectives in Transition

developed and delivered to the market. In this manner, future value objectives can be realized.

Engaging the Management Team in the Strategic Process

Everyone on the management team in a professional services firm must learn how to use the strategic process firsthand. There is great power in understanding how a strategically managed business functions. As so well put by Eliyahu M. Goldratt, author of *The Goal:*

> So, what are we asking for? For the ability to answer three simple questions: *What to change? What to change to? How do we cause the change?* Basically what we are asking for is the most fundamental abilities one would ask from a manager. Think about it. If a manager doesn't know how to answer these questions, is he or she entitled to be called "Manager?"[2]

Equally important to strategic internal management is dedication to the process. It has to be backed by the leadership of the organization. This takes building a consensus among the leadership. Says Edi Osborne, principal of MentorPlus in Monterey, California:

Professional service firms, by definition, are made up of individual professionals, each with their own agenda, their own vision for the future. Professional service firms tend to focus more on the individual and their personal production. As a result, most firms lose sight of the big picture or collective outcome. For a firm to survive beyond particular individuals and their production, it has to adopt a sustainable business model, one that is team- and goal-oriented. Herding cats toward the same bowl of milk is much easier than trying to motivate collective behavior when each has its own bowl to go to. This assumes that the collective bowl yields more and better milk.[3]

Moving forward is not possible unless everyone is on the same page and has come to terms with previous disagreement or dissension. Once this occurs, the firm must define and understand its constituencies, which is discussed in detail in the following section.

Every business, whether professional firm or client, has at least four main constituencies:

1. Owners/investors/founders
2. Employees/volunteers/human capital
3. Clients/customers/consumers
4. Vendors/suppliers

A strategic internal management system focuses on the key elements of its relationship with each of these constituencies.

Owners/Investors/Founders

The focus on this group should be maximizing the return on investment (ROI), creating better, greater outcomes from the capital available, setting reinvestment parameters, and meeting the needs of all owners over the short or long term. A professional services firm's owners, that is, its partners, shareholders, or investors, must understand what their end game is. Why are they in this business? What is their value objective? If the value objective is to maximize personal net earnings on an annual basis, the firm must confront that objective in the way it manages its vendors, customers, and employees. It cannot be the sole driving force in the organization, but as the expectation of the owners, it will govern the way the firm spends money; provides incentives for its employees; and plans, prices, and delivers its professional services.

Firm owners can, however, have other value objectives besides maximizing their personal income, for example:

- Creating a legacy
- Growing the business
- Attracting new owners

Owners must decide whether they are willing to reinvest their capital today in their business and let it appreciate for the future. If they are, that willingness should govern the way the firm hires people, manages its vendors, and delivers services to clients. If they are not, important management decisions will be very different.

A firm's ownership structure can include one or many owners and is typically governed by the size of the firm and its history. The partnership structure, for example, is common in law firms, accounting firms, advertising agencies, and others. Most professional services firms have owners who, whether classified as partners or not, are typically highly compensated and share directly in the income of the firm. However, professional services firms should not be afraid to share revenue and income. Associates and the other professionals who participate in the delivery of services can have performance standards that offer the potential to earn additional income on the basis of performance. Performance-based incentives are a must for any professional practice in order to encourage the professionals in the organization to maximize their efforts. They may not be owners, but they should be paid fair market value for the services they help the firm provide. Organization and partnership structures are discussed in detail in Chapters 3 and 10.

Employees/Volunteers/Human Capital

The focus here is on fair compensation for performance, creating opportunities for advancement, participation in decision making, adequate resources, and support to successfully meet responsibilities.

A strategic internal management system addresses each of these concerns fairly giving due consideration to each side. Success is not possible without the commitment of the management team.

A firm must also create rewarding professional experiences for its employees and provide growth opportunities that help them maximize their career potential, yet match the organization's goal of being successful from business, operational, and economic viewpoints. The firm is sharing resources with its employees, even though they are not owners, by compensating them.

The employees are often a good place to start when deciding how to improve the management of a professional services firm, for example:

- Who is on staff, and what are their capabilities and qualities?
- How do the employees match up with the services the firm has designed and wants to deliver?
- Are there realistic career opportunities for the employees at the firm?

Assuming that all professional credentialing requirements have been met, selecting the appropriate staff members to deliver services to a client depends on knowing what the firm's marketplace says it needs from the firm (see next section, Clients/Customers/Consumers) and then determining the skill sets necessary to deliver services that meet those needs. Once the firm has established what those skill sets are, it should be uncompromising in recruiting, employing, and partnering with professionals who can supply the necessary inventory of skills. As Jim Collins, author of the bestseller *Good to Great,* emphasizes, "The main point is first to get the right people on the bus."[4] A firm that compromises by, for example, looking to spend less on people with fewer credentials ultimately will sabotage itself.

The goal is that a professional firm should adhere to a service delivery policy that is similar to the McDonald's hamburger concept. All over the world, from Singapore to London to New York, McDonald's objective is for its hamburgers to be prepared, and taste, exactly the same. In a professional services practice, the idea is that whether it is partner A or partner B or partner C delivering the services, the client should encounter a consistent level of quality service. Every patient who comes into a clinic with a complaint should leave the clinic having experienced the same high-quality encounter with the physician or the physician's staff. That's the objective. A firm that compromises on the skill sets, attitude, capabilities, or knowledge of the professional staff behind the delivery mechanism will not accomplish its objectives. This is a critical element to sustaining professional success.

It is acceptable to have less experienced, less qualified individuals within the professional practice performing certain defined tasks in the firm's service delivery model. What is critical is that they are doing the right things at the right time. Associates also need to recognize their potential for growth within the organization and for career advancement opportunities. The firm must constantly examine these issues and ensure that the way they are being handled meshes with the firm's organizational goals. Chapter 10 covers the topic of professional staff development.

Mismatches occur when overqualified people are delivering a low-quality task or service. This disrupts the firm's pricing model, which cannot be at fair market value in such cases. There is no economic value to having a racehorse pull a plow. An even worse mismatch occurs when a less experienced person tries to do something that requires a higher level of skill than he or she possesses. The firm might temporarily make a greater margin on those services because the cost to the firm is less than expected. However, the ultimate cost can be high if the firm did not deliver the highest quality services, thereby jeopardizing its very existence.

There is a fundamental difference between an accumulation of individual professionals in practice and a professional services firm. Every staff member in a firm should understand that everyone in the organization is working toward the same goal, which is to accomplish the firm's value objectives. If the firm has failed to establish a clear value objective, all of the professionals in the firm will be possessive about clients because they will not understand how they will benefit from pursuing the good of the organization. Individualistic attitudes—"This is my client" as opposed to "This is the firm's client"—are still too prevalent in professional services firms. That attitude undermines the long-term health of the organization. It reduces the firm to a mere collection of professionals who have rented space together and are sharing common overhead. In a highly competitive, professional services-based economy, sole practitioners or small, loosely organized firms are at a distinct disadvantage. Every professional in a firm must learn to think, "Our firm is our best and most important client."

Clients/Customers/Consumers

The key question for this group is: "Can we provide a better service at a lower cost?" An absolutely critical element of a strategically managed practice is the focus on the customer. It is essential that we understand what the customer needs and expects to develop successful services that add real value.

The key issue that a firm must address with its customers is whether they are in a position to demand higher quality services at a lower cost from the firm. If they are, the firm must respond both internally and externally.

This evaluation should start with every professional services firm asking this question: "What do our clients really want from us?" If a firm has not had focused discussions with potential clients, if it has not conducted surveys of the marketplace, if it has not taken a look at what its competition is doing and how they are packaging their services, or if it does not know the key indicators of what the marketplace is ultimately saying it desires, then the firm will not be able to design services around the expectations of the constituency it wants to serve. The firm is going to be disappointed by the market share that it gets. It will be disappointed by the value the marketplace is willing to pay for the services that it provides, and it will be distressed that its competition is far more successful. Success with clients depends on how well the firm satisfies their needs.

Dale Cordial, CEO of the PT Group, is a highly successful physical therapist who has developed a franchise of rehabilitation centers throughout western Pennsylvania. He has implemented a management system similar to the one discussed here. Mr. Cordial notes:[5]

> Success in any business starts with a philosophy. In our case it is a philosophy of patient care that we provide for our patients a very high intensity, high quality level of care to help them reach their maximum functional level in the shortest period of time, cost-effectively. With this philosophy in mind, we have developed clinical pathways to address patient compliance, number of treatment visits per diagnosis, and aggressiveness of care. Our measurement parameters are then defined around those goals. This process has made a difference in our business in two ways: First, the patient receives a very high level of care at a

very cost-effective price. Second, it has made our practice efficient so that we are able to maintain profitability in this very challenging health care environment, despite continual pressure on reimbursement rates and treatment visit limitations.

Our philosophy of care also matches most third party payer agendas in that they are continually attempting to decrease their overall case cost and control the number of physical therapy visits patients are permitted. Large third party payers actually track our performance and give us a report card. By meeting or being more cost-effective than their network averages, we become one of their preferred providers.

Edi Osborne observes:[6]

Obviously, having a client-centered focus is a given. Although firms know this, they tend to focus on how they serve the client and not what the client needs. Delivering a more timely and accurate tax return is important, but understanding what their client really needs is far more meaningful. That includes knowing what goals the client has and making sure that everything done for the client, even if it is just a tax return, moves the client closer to its desired outcome. Beyond that, helping clients articulate their goals, and develop strategy to achieve them, is a much better application of a client-centered focus.

Vendors/Suppliers

The key issue with vendors is: Are they in a position to give the firm lower quality products and services at a higher price? If the firm is vulnerable to its vendors, it must address the problem decisively. Vendor relationships affect everything the firm does. If the firm is able to maximize its margins or reduce its costs, it gains economic power to reinvest in its business and in the needs of its clients. But if vendors consume the firm's resources, the firm cannot reinvest them. Chapter 16 covers the topic of vendor selection and management in detail; it is addressed in brief here.

The relationship a firm has with its vendors should be the reverse of the relationship the firm has with its own clients. The firm should think of itself as the customer of the vendor, then be proactive in making sure the vendor knows exactly what it wants. But be aware of vendors that overpromise and underdeliver. That can be just as expensive as paying too much for a product or service.

Match purchases with the needs of the firm. For instance, if expensive office space in a tony financial district is critical to the profile of the firm's practice, it has to be there. If such a location is not critical, then do not consume resources on something that will not advance the profile of the firm. Look instead for less expensive space in more modest locations, and apply the resources saved to enhance the benefits provided to one of the firm's other three constituency segments. For example, if a firm saves money with a vendor, it could create performance incentives for its employees, upgrade its technological capabilities to impact the way it serves its clients, or simply provide a higher return to the owners.

The owners' challenge is maximizing the return to their business and ultimately to themselves. They must decide how much capital to reinvest in the future of the organization and how much capital to take out as a result of successful operations.

Management Structure

A firm can be strategically managed regardless of whether it has a single managing partner, an executive committee, or a decentralized management structure that may assign certain management tasks to people who are not owners. However, key decision makers must be involved. The manner in which the firm establishes its value objective is the responsibility of the management team. The team sets the goals and evaluates progress toward them. Timely management reports should provide feedback to the team—tell them how they are performing against the established value objective—and the management must be committed to keeping the teams involved in the key decisions that are being made. The more information provided, the better, as long as it is relevant to the pursuit of the value objective and is not just for the purpose of filling the office with paper.

It is a common misconception that to be part of the management team in a professional services firm, you must be an owner. In fact, with today's access to information, people at all levels of the organization can be capable of making informed decisions for the firm. Nonowner managers, however, must be educated about how the organization thinks strategically and manages strategically, as well as taught effective decision-making skills. The result should be a broader definition of "management team" that includes all individuals who have significant responsibility for ensuring that the firm reaches its goals.

Managers are the people who make decisions and supervise other employees. They are the ones who handle relationships and deal with vendors. All of their interactions have an impact on the firm's ability to achieve its value objective. They are the management team and they work in various layers. The firm can have a multitiered management structure that incorporates the contributions of employees from the top to the bottom of the organization, and all of them can have a strategic impact on the way the business is run. There is no reason that a firm cannot look at all of those individuals as being part of its management team.

Today, it is more important for a firm to be interactive than hierarchical. Exhibit 12.3, which depicts an organization that is ostensibly hierarchical, shows that successful organizations include all staff levels in running their business—from the owners who set the vision, to the management team

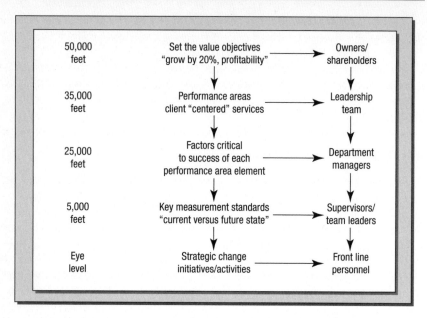

Exhibit 12.3   Top-Down Strategic Management Objectives

responsible for establishing the value objectives, to the front line people who are responsible for carrying out instructions, all the way down to the support group whose job it is to help the firm determine how to work more effectively and efficiently with clients. There is more integration and more top-to-bottom involvement in management today than there has ever been before, even in hierarchical firms.

Strategic Delivery of Professional Services

The strategic delivery of professional services is of paramount concern to the successful firm. It includes competitive response, results measurement, pricing, staffing, and managing the work. This section covers the topic of strategic delivery in detail.

Confront the Competition

In a professional services economy, there are few barriers to entry. Competitors do not need huge amounts of capital to buy manufacturing equipment or build large facilities. Practically anyone can enter the professional services marketplace tomorrow.

When Arthur Andersen, one of the world's largest accounting and tax practices, went out of business, its partners did not disappear. They simply moved to other firms where they again are providing accounting and tax services. Their former firm has been broken down into new competitors in the mid-level marketplace. Accounting firms that did not compete directly with Andersen now find themselves competing with many of its offspring.

That kind of change in market dynamics can happen rapidly in virtually any profession. In the health care industry, for example, the evolution of HMOs has dramatically reshaped the traditional medical practice market, such that most sole practitioners were forced to join corporate medical groups to survive.

Ask the Clients

The number of clients a firm has and the revenues they generate are obviously critical to the firm's success or failure. Logically, therefore, the most important source of information for shaping the service objectives and behavior of the firm should be its clients. Professional services firms need constant client feedback because their services are based on human interaction. Companies that build widgets in a factory and sell them to consumers through distribution channels do not have the same intimacy with the ultimate users of widgets. A professional services firm cannot be successful without having intense contact with its clients. Everything the firm does must be focused on satisfying the clients at the point of encounter. But the firm will not understand what clients need, what they value, what they are looking for, and what their highest priorities are unless it asks them.

Professionals are often out of touch with their clients' real concerns. For example, if asked what their clients need from them or value most, most CPAs would say that clients want more services at a lower cost. But surveys of accounting clients reveal that what they expect and demand most from their accounting firms is concrete business advice that delivers value. If a firm provides value, price is not a problem. A firm that does not understand this simple fact is not going to be successful at satisfying its clients.

One option for gathering client input is to put together a focus group of clients and take them through a process of understanding what the firm does, what it thinks it is there to do for its clients, how it has designed its services, and how it delivers those services. Tell the focus group members what the firm's philosophy is about quality and standards; explain how it deals with vendors, customers, and employees; and explain its philosophy on investing in its business.

Then ask the focus group for its feedback. It is amazing how much the firm will learn about itself using this process. A firm that does not do this will not understand the critical factors affecting its marketplace. But the process is never ending. Strategic management is a system that supports constant improvement, introspection, evaluation, analysis, change, and then analysis, introspection, and change—over and over again.

There are many other ways of measuring your customers' satisfaction, expectations, and demands. Mail surveys and face-to-face interviews are just two examples. However the firm decides to gather data about client satisfaction, the important point is to work from the viewpoint of the client. Firm personnel need to be gathering information about a client's experience with the firm every time they encounter the client. A strategically managed firm must be willing to accept criticism, input, and suggestions from the marketplace it serves.

Measure, Measure, Measure

A constant process of measurement and evaluation is critical for meeting the challenges that can break or make a firm.

As Edi Osborne says:[7]

Strategic measurement is: The identification of activities (and their associated measures) that are most critical to the implementation of strategies designed to help companies achieve their goals.

Strategic Management is: The difference between *doing things right* and *doing the right things.*

For example, a strategically oriented employee would handle a customer complaint very differently than one who is not. The strategically focused employee would have the information and insight to respond:

- Is this customer in our target market? If not, what is the minimum I can do to appease the customer? If yes, what is the best thing I can do to ensure the customer's loyalty?
- Depending on the gravity of the error and importance to target customers, they would also take the opportunity to "kaizen" (process of continuous improvement) the product or delivery system to ensure the error does not repeat.

A not-so-savvy employee would do the minimum in both cases (assuming they even know who the target customer is) and leave it at that, guaranteeing that the error would likely repeat itself sometime in the future.

Measurement is critical because it objectifies the behavior. It helps to identify the specific behaviors that need to be focused. The well-known 80/20 rule applies here. Rather than chasing every issue, measures help us zero in on the 20 percent that are causing 80 percent of problems.

Additionally, without measurement, managers are left to manage from a subjective perspective (what they think is going on—rather than really knowing). This is problematic because both the manager and employee are subject to inconsistencies.

Pricing Strategies

In a strategic environment, the first things a firm needs to decide are: "Why are we in this business? What do we want out of this? What are our economic expectations from this business?" After answering these questions, the firm can establish a pricing model based on expected volume. Then it must talk to its clients or prospective clients, research how its competition is pricing its services, and determine whether it is possible to deliver the desired economic outcome in its particular marketplace at the price established. Strategically, the firm has to be willing to go back and reanalyze, gather more data, make new projections, change its expectations, and so on. Pricing, no less than any other aspect of firm management, is an evolutionary process.

Ideally, the firm should desire an economic outcome that creates a fair market value for the services it wants to provide. This may mean that people who need low-level services cannot get them from the firm's partners within the pricing model established. For example, every year nurse practitioners see a larger volume of patients. Why? Because the patients' fundamental needs often can be served by a nurse practitioner at the nurse practitioner's price. They do not need to see the physician simply to have their throat swabbed for a strep test. The strategically managed medical practice will realize that it can still deliver its desired economic outcome, but it must bring in staff who can serve the "lower-impact" needs of clients at lower prices. As always, the right starting point when making this determination is the clients' own needs and expectations when they visit the medical practice.

The same is true for law practices. Staffing a project with a paraprofessional rather than an attorney alters the law firm's economic model according to the fair market value of the services the firm provides and the price clients are willing to pay. Clients who are going to court are normally willing to pay a much higher price to have their attorney with them than if they just have a simple question about a trust document that does not require a high level of expertise. In the latter case, the client may not want to pay a partner billing rate for a partner's answer to a question that could be satisfactorily answered at a lower level.

When a firm understands its economic objectives and the choices it can present to its owners and employees, it can set prices. But it remains essential to reach out to the clients and ask, "Is that fair market value?" If the client does not agree that the pricing for a given service is set at fair market value, that does not necessarily mean that the firm has overpriced the service; it simply means that the firm must create a more sophisticated delivery mechanism, with different layers of pricing, to satisfy its clients' needs, and that the firm must improve the perceived value for the service in the minds of their clients.

It is generally an easy task for a professional services firm to find out what the competition is charging. Most professional industries have support organizations that provide survey results on pricing. Take a close look at these studies. The respondents are usually fairly honest about the information they provide. A firm can also ask clients, prospects, former clients, or friends what they pay for the services provided by the firm's competitors. The answers will be enlightening.

This again highlights the fact that firms have greater access to information than ever before. Twenty years ago it was challenging for a professional firm to find valid data on what its competition was charging. Now, a great deal of price information is available on the Internet. Benchmarking services, such as Integra.com or First Financial, also offer incredible amounts of readily available and well-organized information.

It is less important whether a firm uses hourly rates, fixed fees, or some other arrangement to price its services. What really matters is whether its clients pay fair market value for the services the firm provides. The client's reaction to the bottom line on the invoice, however it was established, compared to the services received determines whether fair market value was provided. As noted earlier, many professional firms do not spend enough time learning what their clients expect from their services, so they are generally unable to determine whether their pricing standards are at fair market value. It is vital to invest time with clients, unambiguously defining the scope of the services to be provided, setting the expected outcomes, and establishing the value-added benefit that the client will receive. Spending this time upfront will greatly reduce problems with prices or fee collection.

Fee agreements with clients should *always* be set forth in writing. The profession's canons of ethics may already require this, but even if they do not, the firm must have a written understanding of what it is going to do, why it is going to do it, how it will satisfy specific needs of the client, and what the full cost of its services will be. The firm should not begin work without the fee agreement.

Collection Strategies

In any business, having a customer that never pays is the same as not having a customer. In a professional services business, when the firm bills its client for services rendered, the firm should, quite reasonably, expect to get paid. It is when the firm determines how much it is going to bill that it should make the decision about fair market value for services rendered. A firm cannot afford to have clients that do not respect the agreement they have made with the firm to pay for services consumed. If the firm has met expectations, understood the client's needs, and satisfied those needs, it has every right to expect to be paid.

A zero-tolerance policy does not mean that a firm cannot have empathy for a client's difficult economic condition or that it should not work out payment terms with a client. But it does mean that a firm should not write off billings because a client is exhibiting reluctance to pay in full. It is generally better to press for payment and then consider "writing off" the client. Slow-pay and short-pay clients are not the kind that the firm should build its practice around. Having a strategic management plan for the firm can provide the foundation for dealing with a nonpaying client when problems arise. It is not difficult to review the firm's internal objectives as set forth in the plan and conclude, "This client is not satisfying our internal objectives. We seem to be satisfying the client's objectives, but it is not satisfying ours. This is an unworkable situation." Adhering to this idea can be particularly difficult in a sales-oriented professional services culture. In such a culture, the firm should ask "when was the last time we walked away from a bad deal" or "when was the last time we culled a bad client from our list." If the answer is never, then either the firm has no bad deals or clients, or it is not being aggressive enough in managing its risk. The answer is most often the latter.

Quality Control

A constant program of self-analysis is essential to ensure the quality of professional services delivered. Client complaints should be channeled through someone who is not directly involved in providing services to the client. If the professional who is serving the client takes the complaint, the firm may not get an honest and immediate reaction to the complaint. Client satisfaction surveys and regular, focused discussions between clients and firm management should be used to create an independent channel through which clients can give the firm their complaints or suggestions for improvement, without the filtering bias of the service team that failed to meet expectations. Having an independent channel through which clients can contact the firm's management is critical.

Training, continuing education, and appropriate credentialing are also essential for quality control. Weak or unsuccessful professional practices usually do not have a dedication to the highest standards of training and supervision. Such firms do not survive for long. No professional services firm in any industry can enjoy sustainable success without a plan to ensure the constant improvement of its professional staff through training and education. The topic of training and professional development is addressed in Chapter 10.

Tracking the turnover of the firm's professional staff is another important part of quality control. If a firm has high turnover, it is clearly not meeting the needs of its professionals. Unhappy professionals can, unfortunately, often be translated into unhappy clients. The firm needs to understand how internal staff issues affect its client relationships. Consistently successful professional services firms do not have high turnover of professional staff. Professional staff retention is discussed in Chapter 9.

Summary

In a professional services firm that understands the needs of its clients, business development strategies are really just techniques for broadening the scope of the firm's market base. In other words, business development is a natural by-product of understanding the needs of the firm's clients. If the professionals in the firm understand how they are or are not satisfying the needs and expectations of their clients, then as the firm adjusts its service delivery model, it also affects its ability to compete and differentiate itself in the marketplace. The more proficient the firm is at meeting the specific needs of the markets it serves, the greater its ability to expand its business base.

That is what is so revolutionary about the process of strategic firm management. A firm that understands how to manage itself first, and do so strategically, gives every professional in the organization a strategic mind-set. When they are making contact with the firm's constituencies, they are automatically asking the right questions, inquiring about the strategic needs of their clients or prospects, and developing new business naturally. It's typically the same people developing new business who are delivering services because the two processes are integrated.

When professionals and administrative staff are managed in this way, the strategic perspective on professional services becomes a natural part of the way they think. When they are at lunch with a potential referral source or prospective client or they are speaking at a conference or seminar, they will adopt the strategic perspective: "How do I attack that problem with that client? How do I attack that need of the marketplace? How do I think about that issue? How should *they* think about it?" Staff who understand how to convey the message of the strategic approach of the firm ensure that the professional services delivered will be of consistently higher quality than those provided by competitors.

A firm, however, needs traditional marketing support to help grow its client base and sustain the clients it currently serves, but the firm must act strategically in the way it markets. It should also take some risks—redesign professional services and reach out to the marketplace that the firm currently does not serve.

NOTES

1. Anthony Greenback, *The Book of Survival: Everyman's Guide to Staying Alive and Handling Emergencies in the City, the Suburbs, and the Wild Lands Beyond* (New York: Harper & Row, 1968), p. xi.

2. Eliyahu M. Goldratt and Jeff Cox, *The Goal: A Process of Ongoing Improvement* (Aldershot, Hampshire, England: Gower, 1993), p. 337.

3. Edi Osborne, CEO, Mentor Plus, phone interview by the author, Pasadena, California (March 15, 2004).

4. Jim Collins, *Good to Great: Why Some Companies Make the Leap—And Others Don't* (New York: HarperBusiness, 2001), p 44.

5. Dale Cordial, CEO, PT Group, phone interview by the author, Greensburg, Pennsylvania (March 20, 2004).

6. See note 3.

7. See note 3.

13

Resource Management

JOE SANTANA

Nothing is denied to well-directed labor, and nothing is ever to be attained without it.
—Joshua Reynolds (1723–1792)[1]

In this chapter, we focus on the key ingredient behind the success of any professional services firm: the effective and appropriate utilization of its people. According to analyst firm Aberdeen Group, service-centric organizations make up approximately 75 percent of the economy in developed nations. In their report, Aberdeen states that "these organizations are now realizing that success hinges upon their ability to efficiently leverage their intellectual capital."[2] Clearly, nowhere is Joshua Reynolds's statement about well-directed labor truer than it is in the professional services industry.

Why This Topic Is Important

Professional services firms are classic knowledge-based service-industry enterprises that have few physical assets and are built on a widely distributed intellectual capital base. As noted by many in these consulting businesses, all you really have as the engine behind your offerings in a professional services business are people and their experience. If these people are utilized improperly, profitability will suffer, or at best it will be substantially lower than it could be for a similar organization that is more mature in its people practices. To build their profitability and competitive advantage, professional services firms, therefore, must (1) hire the best talent on the market in their space, and (2) make the best use of the talent they have in-house. This chapter focuses on the latter: how we make optimal use of the people already inside the organization.

To be successful and to gain and sustain a competitive advantage, professional services firms must specifically do four things very well with the people they have in their organization:

1. Maximize productivity through optimal utilization and engagement.
2. Reduce the hard cost of turnover (e.g., cost of replacement) as well as the associated soft cost (e.g., talent and experience drain).
3. Increase customer satisfaction through effective deployment and coordination of talent.
4. Maintain a high level of quality control through an appraisal process that ensures that only the best talent is kept in the organization.

In the balance of this chapter, we address how you can achieve these goals by focusing on the following key areas:

- Identify your requirement profile.
- Assess the talents, skills, capabilities, and passions in your resource pool.
- Determine the optimal level of individual sustainable capacity and potential resource utilization.
- Install an employee pool performance ranking and management system.
- Manage your aggregate billable resources.
- Automate the administration of your resources.
- Develop engaging management skills.

Identify Your Requirement Profile

For people-centric professional services organizations, having top performers is clearly a critical part of gaining a competitive advantage. In some instances, you may decide that for a small assignment with limited revenue potential, it will suit you to hire someone at a lower salary level with less talent, experience, or knowledge in order to get the job done and make a reasonable profit. Or perhaps part of your unique selling proposition to your market is lower prices for a finite medium-level set of skills that can get the job done. For example, the skills sought by a legal practice that specializes in tax preparation and advisory for corporate clients versus the skills sought by a tax preparation service for general consumers will be quite different in terms of the level of tax-knowledge depth and sophistication they seek in their employees. Unless you are pursuing the lower price end of the value chain or resourcing for a low-margin, short-term project, you should, for the most part, pursue the top talent in your field.

Many organizations, unfortunately, have a difficult time finding the top performers they need because of a common misconception. This misconception is often voiced when managers and executives speak of people as being either top performers or low performers as if some people were naturally born to excel at everything and others were doomed to plod through life. Numerous studies, however, show that being a superstar performer versus a poor performer is situational. More specifically, people generally perform as superstars when their work engages their best talent, skill, capability, and passion mix.

Talent is the natural endowments of a person, including special aptitudes sometimes referred to as the person's *gifts*. The Gallup organization, which has performed one of the most extensive studies in this area, has specifically identified 34 talent themes that explain the differences between how people relate to one another and why different people will excel or fall short based on various settings. These key themes grouped under talent types as presented by Gallup are shown in Exhibit 13.1.[3]

According to Gallup, it is the presence of some of these themes, that automatically guides and triggers both learning and emotional response as well as the absence of other themes that result in the differences in how people relate, impact, strive, and think. When we observe someone who seems to be able to perform exceptionally well and continues to learn and grow in a particular field or endeavor at a pace beyond the ordinary, we are witnessing these talent themes at work.

Capability is the potential for the future development of a person's talents into skills and competencies. Whereas talent focuses on an inherent gift or aptitude, capability focuses on the overall size or potential for development of gifts into skills and competencies that produce results. *Skill,* on the other hand, refers to the ability to perform work that results from acquired knowledge that

THEMES			
RELATING	**IMPACTING**	**STRIVING**	**THINKING**
1. Communication	8. Command	14. Achiever	23. Analytical
2. Empathy	9. Competition	15. Activator	24. Arranger
3. Harmony	10. Developer	16. Adaptability	25. Connectedness
4. Includer	11. Maximizer	17. Belief	26. Consistency
5. Individualization	12. Positivity	18. Discipline	27. Context
6. Relator	13. Woo	19. Focus	28. Deliberative
7. Responsibility		20. Restorative	29. Futuristic
		21. Self-Assurance	30. Ideation
		22. Significance	31. Input
			32. Intellection
			33. Learner
			34. Strategic

Exhibit 13.1   Talent Themes

enables the person to do something competently. Finally, the *passion* dimension refers to the intense set of emotions that compels a person to action. It usually appears as a strong liking or desire for or devotion to some activity.

A professional could have a talent that through knowledge has resulted in skills that he or she uses indifferently because of a lack a passion for the actual work. This person may also be performing at the top of his or her capability for using that talent and, therefore, may promise little in terms of future development. Another person could have a great reserve of untapped talent, some of which has been converted to skills through education and a huge passion for the work that drives him or her to reach for greater heights of performance. This person may also have huge capabilities and offer a great deal of future potential. Either of these people could be the right person for a role in your company. Either can be a superstar, depending on the role and your company. The important thing is that you first give the term *top performer* a more concrete definition relative to these four dimensions of talent, capability, skill, and passion, and then use the resulting criteria template as your basis for understanding the needs of your company.

The best question for business owners and executives who are seeking top performers to ask is, "Who can be a superstar in my business environment in the particular jobs I have in mind?" What are the key requirements for success in your company? The answer is . . . all of the talents, skills, capabilities, and passions that are needed to reach your company's business objectives.

Zeroing in on Your Requirements

One tool extremely useful in identifying the key success requirements for a company or specific team function is the alignment chart. An alignment chart enables you to clearly link company goals to the specific talents, skills, capabilities, and passions that are needed to reach them. To put together an alignment chart, simply:

- Create a form with your word processor.
- Across the top row, label the first three columns from left to right:.
  —Company objectives
  —Team goals
  —TSCP needed (talents, skills, capabilities, and passions)
- In the first column under "Company Objectives," list your main three to five key company objectives.
- Next, make one copy of the one-page document for each team in your organization, for example, copies for accounting, marketing, sales, and so on.
- On each of the copies for one of the teams, fill in under "Team Goals" the answer to the question: How will this team contribute to the company objectives?

- Finally, to fill in the TSCP column, ask yourself: What talents, skills, capabilities, and passions will the team need to have to be able to accomplish these goals?

The resulting chart should look like Exhibit 13.2. One way to test the strength of the logic of your charts is to check for the linkage in the opposite direction. In building the chart, you began with company goals and worked your way to the right by asking questions designed to help you operationalize your high-level strategy. Your questions were basically focused on, "How am I going to do this, or what do I need to do to accomplish that?" To test for solid linkage in the opposite direction, start from the TSCP column and ask yourself, "Why do I need these talents, skills, capabilities, and passions in my team?" If the responses logically flow well into a sentence that starts with, "In order to be able to . . ." followed by the list in the column to the immediate left, you have a strong linkage between your "TCSP" and "Team Goals" sections. Next, you can test the linkage between the "Team goals" section and the "Company Objectives" by similarly asking, "Why must these team goals be accomplished?" Make sure that there is a natural flow and connection in the response "In order to be able to . . ." followed by the list in the "Company Objectives" column. Columns to the right tell us how we will contribute to or support the success of an item to the left. Conversely, the answer to why we are doing something in any column should be to accomplish something listed in the column to the left of the column we are testing.

The two charts for our fictitious XYZ Company in Exhibits 13.2 and 13.3 show that the one thing the two charts share is the Company Objectives.

COMPANY OBJECTIVES	TEAM GOALS	TCSP NEEDED
5 percent increase in market share	Increase new business 5 percent	Prospecting
30 percent gross margin (up 3 percent)	Close only high margin business	Accounting/financial acumen
10 percent increase in overall revenue	Go deeper into clients (combined with new clients results in 10 percent revenue increase)	Relationship building
Establish niche brand value		Articulate
		Outgoing
		Energetic
	Gain trusted advisor status	A high level of knowledge about our services and best practices

Exhibit 13.2   Alignment Chart for a Sales Professional

COMPANY OBJECTIVES	TEAM GOALS	TCSP NEEDED
5 percent increase in market share	Complete work on time, on scope and on budget	Project management
30 percent gross margin (up 3 percent)	Identify other opportunities to add value	Subject matter content expertise
10 percent increase in overall revenue	Improve value driving skills	Business savvy
Establish niche brand value		Self-motivated learner
		Customer focused

Exhibit 13.3   Alignment Chart for a Project Manager

How the two teams contribute to the attainment of these objectives is clearly different. As a result, the skills they need to succeed are also different. If we were to continue this process with other teams in XYZ Company, we would find that the marketing team would own, for example, the responsibility for establishing the niche branding value. On the other hand, the accounting team's contribution to the Company Objectives might be faster billing and timely management reports to sales and delivery. Other teams would provide other contributions that would require other talents, skills, capabilities, and passions.

In the end, by summing up all of the TSCP listings on each of the charts, you would have a general picture of the talents, skills, capabilities, and passions specifically needed for superstardom in your company.

Assess the Talents, Skills, Capabilities, and Passions in Your Resource Pool

If knowing what you require is the first step, knowing what you have is without a doubt the next immediate step. Many small, as well as large, companies, unfortunately, do not have a clear idea of the vital talents that exist within their own organizations. As many knowledge management experts will point out, the biggest challenge in knowledge management is knowing what you have and then using it. Jason Averbook, a director in Global Product Marketing for PeopleSoft Human Capital Management (HCM), who is currently responsible for the delivery and development of PeopleSoft's entire HCM division, states, "Most organizations hire a bunch of people before looking for the needed talent in-house. They do this primarily because they don't really know what they have in-house nor do they possess the tools to effectively keep track."[4]

Problems That Result from Not Knowing Your Talent Pool

I vividly recall an incident many years ago when my team and I had a great opportunity for landing a new piece of business with a financial service client. The only catch was that we had to come up with three people who could work at the code level with three major applications and prepare them for integration into a new trading environment recently launched by the client. For the next few weeks, we struggled to find the right candidates. By the third week, after much effort, we had only one candidate and the client was breathing down our necks. Two more weeks later, we had a candidate for the second slot. Within the next few days after securing the second candidate, we found the third, not a minute too soon, because the client was threatening to go to a competitor if we did not get the project started by the beginning of the following week.

A few days later, I attended a meeting in another part of the organization within reasonable traveling distance of my client's office. While I was sharing my harrowing experience with my colleagues, one of the people in the meeting said, "Too bad I did not know about this assignment. I've got one guy on the bench and another severely underutilized that meet all of your client's requirements." Sure enough, when I explored his claim a bit more, I found that the company indeed did have two qualified resources. Had I been aware of the talent pool we had, I could have filled my client's request in three weeks (the time it took me to find the first external candidate) and saved the time, trouble, expense, and potential business loss risk. (I still wonder whether there was a third qualified and underutilized resource in another part of the company that would have enabled me to respond to the client's need in less than a week.)

The bottom line is that not knowing the talents and skills you have in your company can, among other things:

- Cost you business
- Needlessly increase your cost of doing business (e.g., time and expense of hiring for skills you already have)
- Demoralize your people who feel underutilized and valued
- Demoralize your people who feel overworked because they carry an uneven amount of the workload (since you recognize their talents, but fail to see those of others who could carry part of the workload)

In the final analysis, not knowing your talent pool is simply not a viable option for a professional services organization.

Assessing Your Resources

To secure an immediate snapshot of your in-house resources and gaps, I recommend you expand on the alignment chart model by adding two additional columns and proceeding as follows:

- Label the column to the immediate right of the "TCSP Needed" column: "Have."
- Label the column to the immediate right of the "Have" column: "Gap."
- In the "Have" column, list all the talents, capabilities, skills, and passions possessed by the members of that team, whether they are relevant to the team's goals or not.
- In the "Gap" column, list all of the talents, capabilities, skills, and passions the team needs but lacks.

Exhibit 13.4 shows you an example of what the outcome might look like for the sales organization first introduced in Exhibit 13.2. According to this, their weaknesses are in the areas of accounting and financial acumen. It also reveals that some of the sales people have niche branding skills. Perhaps the company can train the sales team in accounting and financial skills

COMPANY OBJECTIVES	TEAM GOALS	TCSP NEEDED	HAVE	GAP
5 percent increase in market share	Increase new business 5 percent	Prospecting Accounting/ financial acumen Relationship building Articulate Outgoing Energetic A high level of knowledge about our services and best practices	Prospecting Relationship building Articulate Outgoing Energetic A high level of knowledge about our services and best practices Niche branding skills	Accounting/ financial acumen
30 percent gross margin (up 3 percent) 10 percent increase in overall revenue Establish niche brand value	Close only high margin business Go deeper into clients (combined with new clients results in 10 percent revenue increase) Gain trusted advisor status			

Exhibit 13.4 Expanded Alignment Chart for a Sales Professional

and engage the team members with niche branding skills in the development of marketing plans (assuming they have the bandwidth for this work).

Knowing what you need to meet your objectives and who in your organization has the talents, capabilities, skills, and passion components are two of the three basic ingredients needed to effectively manage your workforce. The third is effective utilization, which refers to the degree that you are consuming the available talents, capabilities, skills, and passion of the resources in your organization, specifically the billable resources. Before we begin to explore the most effective ways for you to manage your aggregate billable resources, however, it is important that we first examine the area of individual sustainable workloads.

Determine the Optimal Level of Individual Resource Utilization

Two of the most common utilization mistakes are under- and overutilizing individuals. In the former, your company operates at suboptimal capacity because your resources are not being used as fully as possible. In the latter, you are also, surprisingly enough, still operating at suboptimal capacity because some of your people are at, or close to, burnout and they are performing at less then peak levels. Let's examine these two challenges more closely and then discuss what we can do to create a balance in utilization that ensures you will draw the best sustainable level of optimal output from your employees.

Underutilization

Individual underutilization occurs when you are unaware of what it takes to perform the steps in various processes and end up providing people with roles that contain a great deal of slack. With the exception of a few hardy and self-motivated souls, this slack time is often filled with other low-value activities. Some underutilized individuals also feel unappreciated as a result of being underchallenged.

Several years ago, I interviewed a number of people in a financial services company as part of an outsourcing program transition. The company had just outsourced much of their IT organization, and the outsourcing company wanted to know what these people did for the client in order to determine how to fill these needs. To my surprise, a number of them worked in shifts babysitting a data communication console. Their sole job was to call a technician if the third light from the right on the second row of the console turned red. This happened perhaps once or twice per month. (For the balance of the time, they sat there and read paperback novels, according to the local gossip.)

Overutilization

The flip side of the individual underutilization coin is overutilization. Overutilization occurs when a person in your organization, usually one who is highly talented and able to engage in various revenue-generating projects, is overextended. The results of being overextended for a prolonged period of time are disengagement, where the person starts caring less and less about the quality of his or her work and, in time, outright burnout.

Sometimes companies take the position that disengagement and burnout are personal problems that suffering employees need to handle. According to noted experts, however, such as Dr. Michael Leiter, coauthor of the book *The Truth About Burnout,* lack of a balanced resource utilization practice in today's workplace is the chief cause of burnout, which, in turn, costs these companies billions in lost revenue opportunities. "In today's workplace," states Dr. Leiter, "organizations are responding to the challenges of global competition, tightening budgets and downsizing by making people work harder instead of smarter resulting in the exhaustion, cynicism and ineffectiveness characteristic of burnout."[5] The fact is that overextending people or overutilizing does not increase real productivity as measured in results over the long run.

When it comes to dealing with burnout and stress, much of the advice we hear or read focuses on how managers can help people cope with the "stressors." These techniques are useful and come in handy as temporary symptom relievers, but, unfortunately, they do not position or fortify people to reach real higher levels of performance nor do they address the larger company problems. Simply treating the symptoms of burnout is like giving someone a medicine that provides temporary relief from the external signs of a cold. After the relief medication wears off, the person is still sick and operating at less than optimal levels. Likewise, after these temporary relief solutions, people are still "disengaged" and performing at less than peak levels. "The real solution," states Leiter, "to enabling people to effectively respond to the increase in demands will come from organizations and individuals significantly re-thinking the way people work and effectively managing work."[6] By taking this advice seriously, we create environments that support true peak performance as measured by business results instead of the "frenzied busy work" and late nights that mask the diminishing returns of people who are not producing at optimal levels of performance.

Given that we now have a good picture of the impact and causes of under- and overutilization, the question is: "What can you do to strike a balance and achieve optimal individual utilization?"

Optimizing Utilization of Firm Resources

The key to successfully driving individual optimal results is to secure a clear understanding of the work requirements and to set standard expectations and determine the level of sustainable performance. Specifically, you need to answer the following questions:

- What should be your reasonable expectations relative to revenue produced by billable resources?
- In connection with your nonbillable resources, what is a sustainable individual workload in your space? How many hours can you reasonably expect to draw from various resources based on the type of work they do? How do you objectively determine the answer to this question?
- What are the core activities that you want your resources in particular roles to focus on in order to contribute to key company goals?

Ronald A. Gunn, a managing director of Strategic Futures and a specialist in strategic management and human resource development issues, provides a very simple formula that helps us to answer the first question.[7] According to Gunn, the optimal goal of a professional services organization relative to billable resources should be to realize a return equal to somewhere between 2.5 and 3.0 times the employee's fully burdened salary. For example, let's assume you have a billable employee who earns $4,200 per month and your average burden rate is 30 percent. Based on Gunn's formula, you should be securing a monthly revenue yield ranging between $13,650 per month ($4,200 × 1.3 × 2.5) and $16,380 per month ($4,200 × 1.3 × 3).

"If you have an employee who on a monthly basis is producing three times his or her burdened salary, you may have a disaster in the making," states Gunn. "I think of this metric as being the indicator of engine performance on a tachometer. If I see someone remaining at the top of performance for an extended period of time without throttling back a bit, I know I am ready to burn oil."[8] Gunn advises managers to aim for the sustainable middle ground of 2.7 and 2.8 as an annual average. (These metrics, according to Gunn, are applicable to any professional services organization.)

If you consider the preceding rule together with the concept of billable hours, it will give you a basic idea of how to set adequate billing rates for your resources, so you can meet financial targets without burning out your billable team. For example, assuming a 40-hour workweek, two weeks' vacation, one week for training, 10 personal days, and 10 holidays, an organization would have 1,800 potential billable hours (2,080 − 80 vacation hours − 40 training hours − 80 holiday hours − 80 personal hours = 1,800). Using the $4,200 a month salary example, which translates into $50,400 per year, to attain a goal of, for example, 2.8 times salary as a revenue figure within the confines of your projected utilization availability, you would need to set a rate of $101.92 per hour (50,400 × 1.30 × 2.8 divided by 1,800 = $101.92). In actual practice, you would set your rates for a pool of resources, with some individual billing higher and others lower. You would also round out the rate to a whole dollar figure (e.g., $102). Essentially, your goal would be to achieve a billing rate of

2.7 to 2.8 across the entire pool. Competition and other business factors beyond available work hours and yield targets will influence your rates. The key message here is to make sure you keep all of these factors in mind when setting rates and expectations.

As for individuals who are in nonbillable positions, one tool I've developed specifically for the IT space, but which has global application and can be used by any professional services organization, is the Sustainable Workload Tool chart. To create this chart:

- Create a four-column, two-row table with your word processor.
- Across the top row, label the columns from left to right:
  —Company Objectives
  —Team Goals
  —Weekly Activity
  —Time Required
- Populate the "Company Objectives" and "Team Goals" columns with your alignment chart company objectives and team goals.
- In the next column to the right, list the person's weekly or monthly activities.
- Finally, in the rightmost column, list the amount of time spent on each activity.
- At the bottom of your one-page chart, outside the table grid, note how many hours a week you can reasonably expect a resource to operate optimally based on the intensity of the type of work.
- Beneath the targeted weekly time allotment, note the actual time utilized resulting from the tabulation of the results in the rightmost column of your chart.

Exhibits 13.5 and 13.6 contain examples of this tool and examples of how you can use it to assess an individual's current workload and determine whether it is business-focused and sustainable.

A careful look at these two exhibits reveals that sales rep 1 is overutilized. Perhaps, he or she:

- Has too many accounts.
- Needs help to reduce the amount of time it takes to prepare the weekly pipeline presentations, or maybe this meeting should be made biweekly.
- Perhaps, if the sales manager has more bandwidth, the salesperson should not be helping the manager with the regional presentation. (This may be something the manager can do alone.)

COMPANY OBJECTIVES	TEAM GOALS	WEEKLY ACTIVITY	TIME REQUIRED
5 percent increase in market share	Increase new business 5 percent	Prospecting	15 hours
		New customer meetings	10 hours
30 percent gross margin (up 3 percent)	Close only high margin business	Presentation preparation for weekly internal sales pipeline meeting	5 hours
			10 hours
10 percent increase in overall revenue	Go deeper into clients (combined with new clients results in 10 percent revenue increase)		15 hours
		Reviewing account financials	2 hours
Establish niche brand value		Relationship building meetings with existing clients	
	Gain trusted advisor status	Helping sales manager prepare for her monthly call with the regional management	

Notes: Target utilization = 45 hours per week; Actual utilization = 57 hours per week.

Exhibit 13.5   Workload Chart for Sales Professional—Rep 1

Sales rep number 2, on the other hand, appears to be:

- On the surface, balanced in terms of total work time, but
- Spending more time on internal work than sales rep number 1.
- Perhaps able to handle more accounts, but might need more training.
- Taking longer to perform back office account work as compared to sales rep number 1.

Surfacing the type of data displayed on the Sustainable Workload Tool will help you get a clear picture of what firm resources are individually capable of doing within various roles on a sustainable level. The next step is to set up the means by which you can effectively manage the aggregate activity and workload balances among your various teams to ensure that resources are collectively maintained at optimum levels of operation. For example, in the case of XYZ Company, assuming they have 20 salespeople, the goal would be to keep them each working no more and no less than 45 hours per week on a steady basis.

In summary, by tracking and managing the revenue generation of your billable resources within the established levels of expectation as well as the amount of time both billable and nonbillable resources invest in the organization using the Sustainable Workload Tool, you can maintain a high-performance, well-tuned operation.

COMPANY OBJECTIVES	TEAM GOALS	WEEKLY ACTIVITY	TIME REQUIRED
5 percent increase in market share	Increase new business 5 percent	Prospecting	5 hours
		New customer meetings	5 hours
30 percent gross margin (up 3 percent)	Close only high margin business	Presentation preparation for weekly internal sales pipeline meeting	10 hours
			15 hours
10 percent increase in overall revenue	Go deeper into clients (combined with new clients results in 10 percent revenue increase)		10 hours
		Reviewing account financials	5 Hours
Establish niche brand value		Relationship building meetings with existing clients	
	Gain trusted advisor status	Helping sales manager prepare for her monthly call with the regional management	

Notes: Target utilization = 45 hours per week; Actual utilization = 45 hours per week.

Exhibit 13.6   Workload Chart for Sales Professional—Rep 2

Of all the resources you have in your professional services organization, the effective aggregate management of your billable resources will have the biggest impact on your profitability. Appropriately, our next step focuses primarily on how you manage this special group of resources.

Manage Your Aggregate Billable Resources

Your billable resources are the revenue generators in your professional services organization. When these resources are working for your client, they are generating positive cash flow into your organization. Your goal in this area is simple. Have the right number of people engaged in billable assignments at the maximum sustainable level of utilization for the longest period of time. The more people you have performing billable work for your clients, the more revenue you generate and, based on absorption of your overhead expenses, the more profitable you are as an organization.

Benched billable resources, on the other hand, have the opposite impact on your profitability. Many industries use the term *benched* or *on the bench* to refer to a potentially billable resource (professional staff) who is not engaged in doing work for a client for which the professional services firm is billing. Also referred to as *downtime,* this is a state dreaded by managers and consulting resources alike. When resources move out of a billable project and onto the bench, they cease to be revenue generating and become overhead cost to the company. A short time on the bench can quickly erode a significant amount of gross margin. If, for instance, you pay a resource $75/hour, and when billable they generate a margin of $25/hour, then one hour on the bench will negate the effect of three hours of billability.

On the plus side, resources on the bench also represent an opportunity for the company to quickly fill a client's demand for service. Challenges often faced by professional services organization are:

- Estimating the end of billable engagements properly to be able to anticipate when people might be coming to the bench
- Determining the appropriate size for the bench resource pool to facilitate response to demand from new and existing clients
- Finding optimal strategies for properly funding and maintaining the needed bench strength

To illustrate the challenges of managing the flow of billable resources to the bench as well as the need for some bench strength, we'll look at a few phases of a year in the life of a fictitious professional services organization. For this example, we focus on an IT software consulting organization residing within an IT consulting company that generates approximately $50 million dollars in revenue per year:

- *January:* A large project run by 20 of your organization's billable resources comes to an abrupt and unexpected end and instantly increases your company's overhead costs. After carrying these resources on the bench for three months in hopes of closing another deal, you find partially billable work for two of them and decide to release the other 18 and pay them the appropriate severance based on industry practice.
- *May:* A prospect who represents potentially the biggest client your company will ever have for the next decade calls to tell you that they've decided to engage your company. The catch is that you must be up and running in 45 days. You currently have no one on the bench, and recruiters are telling you that it will take more than six weeks to find, secure, and orient the 50 people you need (the 18 people whom you released have moved on to other organizations). Four weeks into the process, the client becomes impatient because they don't see the progress they expected. (After all, they feel you are in this business and should be able to produce the people they need immediately and they did give you a generous 45 days.) They decide to give you only half the business and the other half to your competitor.
- *September:* You start the new program with only 20 of the 25 people you hired for the program because your new client decided to downscale a bit more, and five of your new hires went to the bench. You've

also started the project later than planned, so you've lost some of the projected revenue.

- *October:* Not being able to find billable work for the five extra people you hired, you release them.
- *November:* The client where you placed the two partially billable people tells you they want to increase to seven full time but gives you only two weeks to fill all the spots.

All of these activities represent the typical ebb and flow of resources faced by project-based professional services firms.

What Is the Cost to the Firm?

Cost factors impacting the firm in this example include:

- The cost of the period during which the company carried the people on the bench from the project that ended in January
- The cost of severance as well as the administrative costs associated with preparing and executing the release of employees
- The opportunity loss from failing to land the entire assignment with the new client
- The cost of hiring people for the new client assignment
- The revenue loss due to not being able to start the assignment on time
- The cost of having five newly hired resources land on the bench

Taking just this example and multiplying it by the countless projects being managed by a professional services organization, you will see the necessity and huge potential for fine-tuning this process to achieve more profitability and competitive advantages.

Steps to Take to Fine-Tune Your Organization

There are four basic areas that must be closely monitored to manage aggregate billable resources more effectively:

1. Business pipeline
2. Work backlog
3. Current business portfolio of contracts
4. Bench strength requirements

In the reminder of this section, we examine each of these in more detail and offer suggestions and models for managing these key components more effectively. Chapters 4 and 5 address the issues surrounding business development in more detail and are dedicated to the sales process.

BUSINESS PIPELINE. A *business pipeline* is the collection of future opportunities that are in various stages of the sales process. In many cases, these can be tracked with nothing more sophisticated than a simple spreadsheet that lists:

- Prospective client name
- Opportunity type (e.g., network security implementation)
- Expected revenue
- Probability of closing, based on current status of the sales process (more on this follows)
- Estimated engagement start date
- The name of the person leading the pursuit team (may be the sales rep or partner, depending on how the sales area is organized within the firm).

In assigning a "probability of closing," set up a standard set of metrics that is clearly defined. For example, you may wish to use the following:

Percentage	Status
0	A placeholder for a suspect.
10	A new referral.
20	An unqualified opportunity.
30	A qualified opportunity.
40	Prospect has requested a proposal.
50	Initial meeting has successfully occurred.
60	Proposal has been received and favorably reviewed by the prospect.
70	Firm has been selected as a finalist.
80	Client has given a verbal "yes."
90	Initial assessment team is now billing their time.
100	Contract has been signed and engagement has started.

By closely monitoring the progress of business through this pipeline on a regular basis, you can anticipate the need to ramp up or hold your position on resources (Exhibit 13.7).

If the firm is in a business where the flow through the pipeline is relatively slow and predictable, it is easier to schedule the ramping up of resources to coincide with when they are needed. Such a pattern allows the firm to achieve very high utilization rates and to manage toward a "just-in-time"

PROSPECT	OPPORTUNITY	ESTIMATED REVENUE ($K)	PROBABILITY (%)	START	PURSUIT LEAD
Akron Alum	Network	250	90	Jan XX	L. Doe
Beta Biz	Supply Chain	750	90	Jan XX	J. Smith
Capricorn LLC	Web Services	500	80	Mar XX	M. Cooper
Delta LLC	Security	800	70	May XX	J. Smith
Europa Ltd	Supply Chain	750	70	May XX	J. Smith
Finch & Co	Refresh	1,000	0	Aug XX	M. Cooper
Gregorian Inc	Web Services	500	60	Jun XX	L. Doe

Exhibit 13.7   Pipeline Management Chart

ramp-up process. Some business models, however, do not allow for this. There are instances where businesses may operate in an environment where opportunities may suddenly appear with a "short potential shelf life" requiring rapid sales and delivery execution. If this is the case, the firm may need to finance the cost of maintaining a bench of resources. Here the best course of action is to analyze the cost/benefit of running a "reserve resources" model by estimating the probability of these opportunities presenting themselves (note whether there are any seasonal or other key influencing factors) and the cost of maintaining the "reserve resources" bench.

WORK BACKLOG.   The firm's work backlog is composed of those projects where the client has signed the contract but the assignment has not begun due to the client's preference (they've picked a future start date) or your inability to start (e.g., the firm does not have the appropriate resources available). Having a well-managed backlog for the right reasons can be a good thing. On the other hand, having a backlog for the wrong reasons and one that is poorly managed can be detrimental to a professional services organization.

To effectively manage the backlog, regularly review delivery progress relative to commitments to clients. An effective way to do this is another simple spreadsheet that lists:

- Client name
- Assignment type
- Expected revenue
- Assignment start date
- Status/action
- The name of the person leading the engagement

Make sure that your actions and status are where they should be as you progress through the engagement from the signed contract to the start of execution. This analysis, coupled with your pipeline data, will help you decide how to manage your resource pool. Exhibit 13.8 is an example of a work backlog management tool.

CURRENT BUSINESS PORTFOLIO OF CONTRACTS. You need to anticipate growth as well as potential erosion in your current book of business so that you can effectively manage your resource pool. By maintaining and documenting valuable communication with your existing clients and reviewing this information periodically, you can minimize, if not altogether avoid, devastating surprises.

Again, an effective way to do this is a simple spreadsheet that lists:

- Client name
- Assignment type
- Annual revenue
- Assignment end date (more on this follows)
- Status/action firm is taking to obtain work extension, more business, or prepare to disengage
- The name of the person handling the client relationship

(Note: Some professional services firms may have engagements that are per diem and therefore do not have a stated end of contract date. While these projects do not have a specific end-date, clearly they should be carefully managed as well.)

Exhibit 13.9 is an example of a current business portfolio management tool.

PROSPECT	ASSIGNMENT	REVENUE ($K)	START	STATUS	ENGAGEMENT LEAD
Akron Alum	Network	250	Jan XX	Staffed/ready	L. Doe
Beta Biz	Supply Chain	750	Jan XX	Staffed/ready	J. Smith
Capricorn LLC	Web Services	500	Mar XX	Recruiting/sourcing	M. Cooper
Delta LLC	Security	800	May XX	Planning	J. Smith
Europa Ltd	Supply Chain	750	May XX	Planning	J. Smith
Gregorian Inc	Web Services	500	Jun XX	Planning	L. Doe

Note: Future start date of December of the year before the dates listed.

Exhibit 13.8 Work Backlog Management Chart

CLIENT	ENGAGEMENT	REVENUE ($K)	END DATE	STATUS	RELATIONSHIP LEAD
Akron Alum	Network	250	Jan XX	Disengaging in 90 days	L. Doe
Beta Biz	Supply Chain	750	Jan XX	Renewal with a few changes to the contract	J. Smith
Capricorn LLC	Web Services	500	Mar XX	Discussing renewal	M. Cooper
Delta LLC	Security	800	May XX	Discussing renewal	J. Smith
Europa Ltd	Supply Chain	750	May XX	Discussing renewal	J. Smith
Gregorian Inc	Web Services	500	Jun XX	Planning renewal discussion	L. Doe

Exhibit 13.9   Current Business Portfolio Chart

BENCH STRENGTH REQUIREMENTS.   Some firms have a fairly predictable progression of business through their pipelines as mentioned earlier, which makes it possible for them to operate with anything between a small- and zero-size bench, achieving high utilization rates. Others operate on a virtual "skeet-shooting" range where business appears quickly and goes to the competitor who can respond the fastest with the right resources. These companies must continuously invest in a bench and in processes for identifying and recruiting appropriate talent to be able to seize the moment.

In organizations where there is a need to respond quickly to fleeting customer demands, use an enterprise scorecard to track performance indicators on how staff resources are being consumed and what the firm need is for various skill sets. (More information on the automation tools that enable you to effectively track this are covered in the next section of this chapter.) "By setting up a dashboard of key indicators, you will be able to effectively use historical activity to project your future skill needs and determine how much of a bench you should be financing," states Averbook.[9]

It is tempting for the firm to load benched staff up with work. In many organizations, it is not unusual to find bench resources buzzing about busily as if they were on a client engagement. Gunn warns against this because it creates a false sense of productivity. He advises that organizations avoid using benched billable resources for nonbillable work. "Hire them for a specific piece of business with a specific time-table in mind. Let them work on other things that will provide some value to the firm while they are waiting for the billable assignment, but don't load them up on this stuff or let them stay beyond the time-table in these non-billable roles," states Gunn.[10]

One way to get value out of billable resources while they are on the bench is to have them work on unsolicited business proposals and responses to request for proposals (RFPs). This is especially valuable if the proposal they are working on is for the client where they will be assigned to work, since this also provides them with information that can serve as an orientation to the client and the details of the engagement. Furthermore, such an approach begins to train junior staff in sales, a skill that becomes more valuable to them as they progress in their career with the firm.

Another useful way to employ bench time is to use it to train and develop resources. If possible, use bench time to either provide formal training or give the benched resource an opportunity to shadow (follow and observe) others as a means of learning new skills and techniques. (Chapter 10 covers the topic of training and professional development in detail.) Sustaining overall firm utilization rates should always be the primary consideration, and resources should not be allowed to "hide" on the bench for lengthy periods. Benched staff should be assigned to their intended billable engagement as soon as possible.

In summary, the bench size must be established based on the needs of your business. The firm must then manage using activity indicators, and adjust as needed. Engage billable resources in productive work or development opportunities when they are on the bench, but don't lose sight of the original reason for which you hired them.

Having gone through the effort of a staff need assessment, resource inventory determination, productivity goal setting, and bench sizing, firm management should now turn their attention to planning how they will maintain and improve this resource pool. An important factor here is installing an effective resource pool performance ranking and management system. Chapter 10 covers the topic of employee appraisals and performance management in detail; an abbreviated example of this topic is offered here.

Implement Employee Pool Performance Ranking and Management System

Installing an employee pool ranking system is one of the most critical things that must be accomplished to effectively grow the quality of your resource pool. One possible process for establishing a resource pool ranking system is as follows:

1. Develop an individual performance appraisal system that provides each individual employee and you at a minimum with the following:

—Performance feedback against indicators/metrics that are relevant to the quality and timeliness of work performance in the industry and for the level of professional staff.

—Identification of performance inhibitors.

—Clarification of job result expectations for the coming period before the next review.

—Training and development needs.

Make assessment of performance and needs as objective as possible.

2. Develop a ranking system that enables comparison of the performance and potential of all the resources in each pool. For example, the firm might use a spreadsheet, listing each employee with columns that enable you to display how they are evaluated across a number of dimensions.

3. Once individual performance appraisals are completed for each member of a resource pool, performance relative to other members of their pool should be compared across several key dimensions using the resource pool-ranking tool.

4. Reward and further invest in the development of the top 20 percent performers.

5. Take action to drive the 70 percent in the middle toward a higher level of performance.

6. Take corrective action on the bottom 10 percent. Place them on a time-limited performance plan if appropriate and/or dismiss them and replace them with higher caliber people with the potential to be in the top 10 percent.

7. Based on the organization and the state of the resource pool, go through this individual performance appraisal and ranking process no more than quarterly and no less than annually.

Exhibit 13.10 is an example of a possible resource pool ranking chart. Successful resource management is a key to firm profitability. However, to do so requires immense amounts of data and (nonbillable) time. As firms grow, the level of effort and complexity required to accomplish these tasks increases exponentially. To handle the increased demand on time, firms must at some point in their growth automate portions of the administrative effort.

Resource Administration Automation

As a professional services firm grows in size and complexity, executives and managers face the daunting task of managing to the optimal levels of utilization across multiple projects and multiple skill sets. The complexity of a

REVIEW EMPLOYEE	QUALITY RATING	PRODUCTIVE RATING[a]	OUTPUT[b]	POOL ATTENDANCE[c]	RANKING RANKING[d]	RESULTS
F. Clementi	5	4	5	4	4.5	Top 20 percent performers
P. Chan	5	5	4	4	4.5	
M. Doe	4	4	4	4	4	Middle 70 percent performers
L. Sanchez	4	3	4	4	3.75	
M. Ried	4	4	3	4	3.75	
B. Miller	4	4	4	3	3.75	
T. Perry	4	4	3	4	3.75	
P. Rogers	4	3	4	4	3.75	
C. Dowd	3	3	4	3	3.25	
J. Smith	3	2	3	2	2.5	Bottom 10 percent performer

Rankings

1 to 5 = Poor to Excellent

Top 20 percent

[a] Based on individual customer satisfaction ratings.
[b] Based on timely project completion records.
[c] Based on HR attendance records where 5 or excellent means never absent during the period, 4 equals 2 absences or less, 3 equals between 3 and 4 absences, 2 equals 5 absences and 5 equals in excess of five absences.
[d] The product of the review rating, quality rating, productive output and attendance column divided by the number of columns (4)
Note: You may set up your pool ranking system in any way that suits your business as long as the results are as objective as possible, free of subjective bias and legally defensible. Consult your HR advisor and attorney before instituting this type of practice.

Exhibit 13.10   Resource Pool Ranking Chart

professional services organization is affected by a number of factors, making it difficult to estimate precisely at what size automation will become an appropriate option. Therefore, the firm must judge for itself whether the current administration justifies an investment of capital for labor. Here are just three of the many factors that can create complexity:[11]

1. Number of skill types needed and provided. (A technology company with 50 people that offers help desk, desk-side support, network support, application development, and acquisition management is more complex than a technology company of 75 people that offers only one of the preceding services.)
2. Variety of project contract length.
3. Variety of client types (e.g., financial services, pharmaceuticals, telecommunications).

To get an idea of how these factors might impact an organization, consider the example of a small IT consulting company specializing in help desk support for small financial services companies has a one-year renewable contract relationship. Now the firm adds two more client verticals, two more types of contract terms, and two more service offerings. They have progressed from offering one type of service to one client for a specific period of time to a model where they are selling more than nine possible offering combinations. Add to this a little growth in staff, and the situation can quickly spiral out of manageable control.

Not staying on top of all resource management and business activities can spell doom for the professional services firm. In one instance, a money-losing consulting division was further wrecked by increasing complexity. The firm found that 50 percent of the billable consultants were engaged in nonbillable and under-the-radar back office projects.

An inventory of activities in which underutilized, otherwise billable resources generally engage when they are off a billable project and below any radar follows:

- Monitoring processes that could be cheaply automated, thus removing the need for monitoring
- Doing research for other team members who are not fully utilized themselves
- Running reports of questionable value that few, if any, ever read (this one is a favorite)
- Conducting internally focused surveys and queries that do not lead anywhere
- Working on low-return/questionable return in-house projects

In many cases, these resources feel vulnerable and will not come to managers asking for more billable work. In other cases, they lack only one or two vital skills that would make them suitable for any of the current billable projects. Again, however, feeling vulnerable, they are unlikely to bring this to the attention of their manager voluntarily. The solution to this situation is for managers to maintain and manage according to a global view of the various activities within their organizations.

To help managers address this challenge, many organizations turn to software solutions, which substitute systems and capital for labor and are appropriate for mid-to-large sized firms. Enterprise service automation (ESA) solutions, as this family of application software is called, brings to service organizations benefits similar to those that enterprise resource planning (ERP) tools give to the manufacturing and distribution industries. Software tools can help professional services organizations to better manage things such as planning, scheduling, managing billable resource utilization across multiple projects, salesforce coordination, customer relationship management, performance management, and communications. In addition, some software tools can automate the processes of collecting professional staff billing information and carry it all the way through the generation of billing and invoicing clients.

ESA Options

Because the professional service firm market is so large, it is not surprising that more than 30 software vendors, including major players such as Icarian, PeopleSoft, and SAP, as well as a number of newcomers, including Augeo Software, ChangePoint Corp., Opus360 Corp., and PlanView, now offer software tools to the professional services industry. These tools vary in their capabilities. Some are able to handle end-to-end operations, while others focus on specific segments such as resource management across projects.

A number of professional services organizations will, from time to time, opt to build their own software tools. A number of these custom application are used by firms to automate timecard information collection, billing and utilization, and other important processes. While these tools tend to have a good fit to the business because they have been specifically built for the firm, they can often have a less than stellar performance over the long-haul because they are expensive to maintain, and lack the scalability to effectively evolve with the needs of a growing business. The bottom line is that companies that opt to build tools for themselves often end up paying many hidden and unforeseen costs in the form of operational expenses, maintenance expenses, and, ultimately, the expense of rebuilding to keep up with the growth and evolving requirements of their business.

Averbook is quick to point out that, on the other hand, companies that buy from vendors such as his firm, PeopleSoft, are avoiding these hassles and getting more than just task automation. "In addition to automation, buyers are getting the benefit of the best practices captured in the software solution," states Averbook.[12] He also points out that due to their ability to leverage their cost across multiple clients, operations and maintenance expenses passed on to the client through the pricing models are lower than they would be if directly managed and paid by the client.

In summary, if the firm has reached a level of complexity that benefits from automation, the firm should strongly consider a purchased package application instead of a custom-built, internally created solution. When evaluating the cost, the firm should also consider the immediate counter-balancing benefits of effective automation, which include, but are not limited to, the following:

- Days-sales-outstanding (DSO) reduction
- Administrative and overhead cost reduction
- Speed-to-respond to new business improvement

Naturally, the more appropriate the software solution is to the firms needs, the bigger and better the investment will pay off.

Buying the Right Software Solution

Such a broad array of choices with rich features, can make the task of selecting the right solution difficult. The vendor selection process is beyond the scope of this chapter. Chapter 10 of *The Executives Guide to Information Technology* has a thorough, detailed treatment of the process and should be considered mandatory reading for any firm considering the purchase of packaged software.[13]

Develop Engaging Management Skills

Up to this point, the focus of our discussion has been on:

- Being clear on the type of talents, skills, capabilities, and passions the firm needs to succeed
- Determining what needed talents, skills, capabilities, and passions are in the resource pool
- Determining the right level of utilization to expect from each individual resource
- Managing the billable pool of resources for optimal levels of revenue and profitability
- Determining when and how to automate some or all of these processes so that you can focus less on collecting, categorizing, and collating and more time making decisions, leading your business, and driving results.

All of these add up to the techniques and skills used to maximize billable resources. Another important dimension, however, is the topic of engagement. *Engagement* is the maximization of personal dedication and energy that each of your people puts into the hours worked as he or she applies talents, skills, and capabilities, toward meeting the needs of clients and the development of the firm and their professional careers.

In addition to bench management, the firm can achieve significant benefits by focusing on the practices that lead to engaging professional staff in their work as fully as possible. Without engagement, your resources may be physically present, and utilized in the proper quantities of time, but their output and the value delivered to clients will not reflect the fullest capacity of their talents, skills and capabilities.

According to a *Gallup* study, every year in America, companies lose $350 billion due to having disengaged employees. The primary reason is the lack of management and leadership capability among the ranks of their direct managers.[14]

New managers recently promoted to their positions from the ranks of high-performing contributors are especially likely to contribute to disengagement. These newly minted managers often lack the skills needed to engage team members. The skills, capabilities, and motivations that make for a top contributor are usually not the same ones that result in a top manager. These high-performing contributors can become excellent managers, but often they need to be given guidance and development in order to succeed. The firm's professional development program should train and monitor new managers carefully to help them make the transition from performer to manager without risking discouragement to these managers or disengagement for their teams.

How Does Professional Staff Disengagement Impact the Firm?

From a business perspective, the results of poor manager practices often manifest in the following ways:

- Increased turnover and the associated replacement costs
- Poor professional staff performance
- Missed deadlines
- Low quality work product
- Decreased morale and motivation
- Increased employee complaints

Without decisive action by the firm, the problems associated with this can quickly mount.

Compounding the issue, recent studies indicate the bad habits developed by new managers, if left unchecked, are unlikely to improve on their own. For example, a study performed by Towers Perrin,[15] one of the world's leading management and human resources consulting firms, found that managers of all tenures, across a number of companies surveyed, received low marks from employees on the behaviors that have the most significant impact on employee engagement, including:

- Recognizing and rewarding good performance
- Empowering employees
- Encouraging innovation and new thinking
- Exercising good decision making
- Team building
- Providing goals and directions
- Communicating effectively
- Global thinking and understanding the big picture
- Coaching and developing the skills of employees
- Displaying integrity

To maximize staff engagement, the firm must develop engaging managers and promote the fair and equitable treatment of all employees. "It has been my experience from observation and from looking at the data that an employee's perception of being unfairly treated by the organization is a major push towards cynicism or other distancing from work," states Leiter.[16] Being considered fair is often one of the most important and often overlooked elements of an engaging work environment. Employees will lose faith in management's good intentions and passion for a company when they perceive that company decision making is arbitrary and capricious.

Improving Manager and Staff Engagement

The firm can take early preventive action to help orient new managers (as well as "not so new" managers who've missed the basics) and avoid the issues discussed earlier. A condition of promotion within the firm should be the completion of manager training to help managers gain the skills they need to handle their new responsibilities. In their *2004 Workforce and Workplace Forecasts December 31, 2003,* Roger Herman and Joyce Gioia, strategic business futurists and certified management consultants, state that as employers discover the impact of serious inadequacies in management and leadership, "up and coming managers will be expected to learn and practice leadership skills before assuming new positions."[17] Stressing the importance of continuing to give new managers extra attention during their first few months in their new role, Leiter adds, "The transition to managerial status is itself a stressful time of identity shift for many new managers. The extra attention may be warranted just to assure that the new managers' own engagement is maintained throughout the evolution from the individual contributor role to the new manager role."[18] Some firms also provide follow-up training for new managers six months after promotion to reinforce their skills after they have additional context for understanding.

The initial manager ramp-up period should include the following steps:

1. *Start with a solid new role orientation.* Orientation must be the starting point for any role change, especially one resulting from a promotion into a totally different job. Orientation provides new managers with an overall direction and structure that enables them to see and understand the big picture of their new role. When newly promoted managers receive orientation, they are trained in the basic rules and objectives of the new role as well as information on tools and resources they can use to succeed. A few specific items include:

- Expectations the company has of them in their new role
- Where and how to gain access to reports, people, and information needed to do the new job
- A clear understanding of the incentives and disincentives impacting this new role

2. *Training.* When professionals in a "doer" role are promoted to a management role, many of their former core skills, knowledge, and experience become context that helps them to understand what their team is doing but are not necessarily helpful to them in their new role. To effectively execute their management role, they need a new set of skills (e.g., leadership, communication, negotiation, hiring). Once new managers are oriented into their new role, training can inculcate the new skills needed. Effective training will give new managers tools and strategies that they need to get their new job done. Orientation should take place before they assume their new role; management training is most effective after new managers have been in their role five to six months. By this time, they have developed a better sense of the management role and challenges, which gives them the ability to more fully appreciate the skills taught in the training program.

3. *Coaching.* By now, it is a well-known fact that most of what is learned through training programs, if not reinforced, is almost immediately forgotten. Coaching is recognized as the best way to increase retention and application of what people learn in training. I, therefore, recommend that you engage either an internal or external (professional) coach to support the retention, internalization, and application of the skills taught in your manager training programs. The type of *coaching* I refer to is the process outlined by W. Timothy Gallwey, author of the *Inner Game* series. Gallwey has referred to his

coaching approach as a "better way to [effect] change [in people]."[19] Gallwey's interpretation of coaching can be referred to as removing internal obstacles to performance.

4. *Testing for engagement.* The best way to determine how well your efforts in creating engaging managers are paying off is to conduct blind surveys of professional staff. In conducting these surveys, the firm asks employees to anonymously rank their managers as leaders who communicate clearly and produce a sense of personal connection with work and company objectives as well as a sense of belonging to a high-performance team. The Gallup Q12 questions[20] are an excellent example of this type of survey. Another in-depth example of an engagement feedback tool is the "Preventing Burnout and Building Engagement" program run by Leiter in conjunction with his university-based research center. Leiter consults with organizations far and wide in planning, conducting, analyzing, and using the information from these surveys to create more engaging work environments.[21]

5. *Give managers feedback.* Incorporate the results of the engagement survey into manager performance feedback. Recommend corrective actions where needed, and turn engaging practices into institutionalized best management practices in the firm.

By incorporating a program that promotes fully engaged managers, the firm can avoid the costs outlined earlier and ensure that newly promoted managers are best positioned to succeed in their roles as engaging leaders.

Summary

Managing people in a professional services organization for peak results and growth requires that you:

- Be very clear on the skill, passion, and talents required.
- Know the size and composition of the resource pool.
- Set and balance individual utilization targets to achieve the highest sustainable level of quality output the professional staff.
- Develop a comprehensive global view of billable staff and the drivers that impact the need to increase and decrease the resources.
- Understand the ideal for a bench resource pool if your firms business pattern requires one.
- Automate resource management administrative processes when the labor / capital trade-off is favorable.
- Develop management practices that fully engage professional and administrative staff.

"The strength of an organization is not I, but we," stated the German poet, novelist, playwright, and natural philosopher Johann Von Goethe.[22] In a professional services organization, "we" represents the company's most important asset. If, therefore, the firm is to enjoy the competitive advantages that result from organizational excellence in professional services, it will not come solely from the efforts of the senior management team, or those of a few company heroes. It will come only from the mass efforts of a well-managed, well-directed workforce where all individuals embodied in the collective "we" pursue excellence with all of their talents, capabilities, skills, and passions.

RESOURCES

Curt Coffman and Gabriel Gonzales-Molina, *Follow This Path: How the World's Greatest Organizations Drive Growth by Unleashing Human Potential* (New York: Warner Books, 2002, pp. 40–41).

Joe Santana and Jim Donovan, *Manage I.T.: A Step by Step Guide to Help New and Aspiring Managers Make the Right Career Choices and Gain the Skills Necessary for Peak Performance* (Austin Bay Publishing, 2002), pp. xii, 124–138.

W. Timothy Gallwey, *The Inner Game of Work* (New York: Random House Trade Paperbacks, 2001), pp. 4–14.

Christina Maslach and Michael P. Leiter, *The Truth about Burnout* (San Francisco: Jossey-Bass, 1997), pp. 14–16.

RESOURCES

Talent Assessment and Management

http://www.gallup.com/management/path.asp
http://www.hermangroup.com/alert/archive_12-31-2003.html

Managing the Business

http://www.osborne.com/products/0072226250/0072226250_ch01.pdf
http://www.strategicfutures.com

Sales Automation/Pipeline Management

http://www.aceleragroup.com/articles/Effective_pipeline_management.htm
http://dir.yahoo.com/Business_and_Economy/Business_to_Business/Computers/Software/Business_Applications/Sales_Force_Automation_SFA_/Makers/

Software Tools

http://www.cio.com/archive/031502/roboboss.html
http://www.aberdeen.com/ab_company/hottopics/reporttocs/PSA2001-TOC.pdf
http://www.aberdeen.com/2001/research/11030013.asp
http://www.peoplesoft.com

NOTES

1. Quotable online
   http://quotableonline.com/quotedisplay.php?lastName=Reynolds&firstName
   =Joshua
2. Aberdeen Group, available from http://www.aberdeen.com/ab_company/hottopics
   /sec/default.htm.
3. Curt Coffman and Gabriel Gonzalez-Molina, *Follow This Path* (New York:
   Warner Bools, 2002), pp. 40–41.
4. Jason Averbook, telephone interview by the author, Thursday, January 22, 2004.
5. Michael P. Leiter, telephone interview by author where Leiter quoted excerpts
   from the book he coauthored with Dr. Maslach, *The Truth about Burnout: How
   Organizations Cause Personal Stress and What to Do about It* (San Francisco:
   Jossey-Bass, 1997), Thursday, January 8, 2004.
6. See note 5.
7. Ronald A. Gunn, telephone interview, Tuesday, January 20, 2004.
8. See note 7.
9. See note 4.
10. See note 7.
11. See note 4.
12. See note 4.
13. Jon C. Piot and John Baschab, *The Executive's Guide to Information Technology*
    (New Jersey: John Wiley & Sons, 2003).
14. Gallup Organization, *Gallup Management Journal* (March 19, 2001), available
    from http://gmj.gallup.com/content/default.asp?ci=466.
15. Towers Perrin, *Towers Perrin Talent Report 2001* (New York:Tower Perrin,
    2004), p. 16.
16. See note 5.
17. Roger Herman and Joyce Gioia, *The Herman Trend Alert* (Greensboro, NC:
    Strategic Business Futurists, 2003), available from http://www.hermangroup
    .com/alert/archive_12-31-2003.html.
18. See note 5.
19. W. Timothy Gallwey, *Inner Game of Work* (New York: Random House, 2000),
    pp. 3–18.
20. Gallup Organization, *Gallup Management Journal* (March 19, 2001), available
    from http://gmj.gallup.com/content/default.asp?ci=466.
21. See note 5.
22. Johann Von Goethe, *Intrapreneurship Is the Corporate Solution* (March 22,
    2004), available from http://www.pfpweb.com/handouts.intrapreneurship.html.

14

Risk Management and Quality Assurance

JOHN BASCHAB AND JON PIOT

*When investors buy stocks, surgeons perform operations, engineers design bridges,
entrepreneurs launch new businesses, astronauts explore the heavens, and politicians run for
office, risk is their inescapable partner. Yet their actions reveal that risk . . . need not be feared:
managing risk has become synonymous with challenge and opportunity.*

—Peter L. Bernstein, *Against the Gods: The Remarkable Story of Risk*[1]

*You want a valve that doesn't leak and you try everything possible to develop one. But the real
world provides you with a leaky valve. You have to determine how much leaking you can tolerate.*

—Obituary of Arthur Rudolph, manager of the Marshall Space Flight
Center Saturn V program office[2]

For a senior executive operating a professional services firm, you might
think the work day consists of a parade of golf outings and client lunches.
But it does not. In fact, in many firms, time is spent running from one fire-
fight to the next. Your most important client just called to tell you that the
project you have been working on is being cancelled because the sponsor is
leaving to take another job. Human resources calls next—there is a sexual
harassment claim. Finance calling: The euro-to-dollar conversion rate has
changed, and the client wants to pay their invoice now, so our receivables
will be adjusted. The delivery manager for a key project called: The project
is over budget and behind schedule, and the client is demanding answers. IT
just called, and they have lost critical client data and billing records, and the
backups have failed. What to do?

What all these scenarios have in common is that they can either be avoided or mitigated through a proper risk management and quality assurance regimen. While it is impossible to entirely eliminate risk from any endeavor, even small efforts to identify, quantify, and manage risk and quality can pay large dividends to the professional services firm. Woe and ruin can rapidly strike the professional services firm that fails to address risk and quality issues.

Why This Topic Is Important

The risk and quality issues encountered by a professional services firm are generally "fixable" through enough scrambling and apologizing, but with a good risk management and quality assurance program, the time, expense, and effort required to fix a problem can be saved for more productive activities. Further, occasionally a professional services firm can receive a knockout punch in the form of a major disaster. In many of these cases, a good risk management or quality assurance program can be the difference between continuing as a going concern and failing.

Risk management is a topic that receives relatively little attention in professional services firms, in part because firms most often focus their attention on sales and delivery activities. This is appropriate, given that those activities are the ones that drive revenue and deliver value to clients. However, a little effort spent on thinking through the attendant risks and quality requirements, and taking preemptive actions where possible to avoid them, can pay large dividends later. During our interviews for this book, a senior manager from a consulting firm observed, "You can lose more business in one bad transaction with a client than you can sell in a year."

Quality assurance is an equally important topic. Switching costs for clients of professional services firms are generally fairly low, and clients are only as satisfied as the result of the most recent engagement. It is common knowledge that selling business to existing clients is an order of magnitude easier than acquiring new ones and that dissatisfied clients can quickly ruin a service firm's reputation. Good quality assurance measures can significantly reduce the likelihood of service delivery problems, or in the worst case, provide enough advance warning that the firm can quickly move to remediate the issues at the client and fix the problems.

Risk management and quality assurance are clearly important, even critical areas that the professional services firm must master. Unfortunately, effective execution requires a careful balancing act. Overmanagement of risk is paralyzing to an organization. Overly risk-averse managers will quickly be accused of being in the "sales prevention" department. On the other hand, partners who constantly sell risky, hard-to-deliver, difficult-to-scope business will quickly find themselves abandoned by terrified professional staff and dubbed a "cowboy" by their peers. Clearly, this is a topic of critical importance to professional services firms, as well as a skill that is difficult to perfect.

Risk Management and Quality Assurance Defined

Risk management is the process of identifying the various undesirable outcomes for the firm, estimating their cost and likelihood, and determining an approach for mitigating or eliminating the risks. It is focused on the full suite of potential problems that a firm may encounter, regardless of whether the firm controls them and regardless of their probability.

Quality assurance is a related, but different, discipline. Quality assurance is focused on ensuring, through process, policy, and training, the proper delivery of the end service to the client. It also addresses, secondarily, firm components related to delivery such as internal staff execution and sales. Because quality is delivery-oriented, and, therefore, easy to scope, estimate, and understand, it is usually better defined within a professional services firm and is embedded throughout the firm's delivery process. Professional services firms without a reasonable quality assurance program are generally rapidly extinguished by the market, after creating a trail of bad work and unhappy clients. In fact, it is firms of this type that create the bad reputation that can, unfortunately, affect the reputation of firms of good standing. Failure to adhere to a reasonable set of quality controls is bad for the firm, the staff, clients, and the industry.

Risk Management: A Balancing Act

Risk management is challenging because it requires judgment in the face of uncertainty. A simplified model of risk management (see Exhibit 14.1) shows the effect of too little or too much risk in a professional services firm.

Too little risk results in the cessation of all economic activity. In the world of complete risk elimination, contracts and projects become too cumbersome, and decision making and client pursuits take too long. Too much risk can be equally debilitating; the firm is in constant firefighting mode and is torn apart by bad reputation and even litigation that ensues post poorly sold and executed work. Each firm must find the appropriate balance of risk and return, which will vary from decision to decision and project to project. This balancing act is challenging, and the decisions made ultimately depend on a host of variables.

Because each firm situation and each individual decision is unique, it is useful to develop the general skills needed to effectively balance risk and

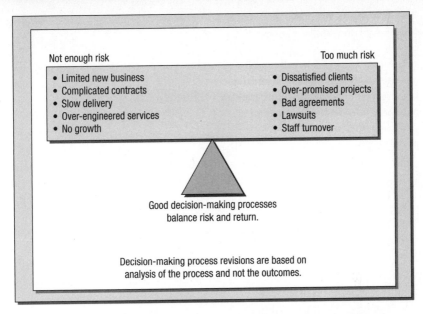

Not enough risk

- Limited new business
- Complicated contracts
- Slow delivery
- Over-engineered services
- No growth

Too much risk

- Dissatisfied clients
- Over-promised projects
- Bad agreements
- Lawsuits
- Staff turnover

Good decision-making processes
balance risk and return.

Decision-making process revisions are based on
analysis of the process and not the outcomes.

Exhibit 14.1   The Role of Good Decision Making in Risk Management

return in each case. The principle skill needed is high-quality decision making.

The Critical Role of Decision Making in Risk Management

Good risk management ultimately depends on good decision making. Good decision making, in turn, is based on the rapid acquisition of the proper amount and kind of data, building a framework for deciding, moving forward, and incorporating feedback from past decisions as the feedback becomes available.

The field of decision science has been well researched, particularly in the past two decades, and a considerable amount of information on how to improve organizational decisions is available in the related academic and popular literature. The University of Chicago and the Wharton School at the University of Pennsylvania in particular have strong decision science specialties.

Some of our recommended books and papers on the subject are referred to throughout the chapter, as well as in the resources section at the end of the chapter. One in particular is *Winning Decisions,* by J. Edward Russo and Paul J. H. Schoemaker.

In *Winning Decisions,* Russo and Schoemaker outline the fundamentals to a good decision-making process:

- *Framing:* Framing determines the viewpoint from which decision makers look at the issue and set parameters for which aspects of the situation they consider important and which they do not. It determines in a preliminary way what criteria would cause them to prefer one option to the other.

- *Gathering intelligence:* Intelligence gatherers must seek the knowable facts and options and produce reasonable evaluations of "unknowables" to enable decision making in the face of uncertainty. It's important that they avoid pitfalls such as overconfidence in what they currently believe and the tendency to seek only information that confirms their beliefs.

- *Coming to conclusions:* Sound framing and good intelligence do not guarantee a wise decision. People cannot consistently make good decisions using seat-of-the-pants judgment alone, even with excellent data in front of them. A systematic approach will lead to more accurate choices—and it usually does far more efficiently than hours spent in unorganized thinking, particularly in group settings.

- *Learning from experience:* Only by systematically learning from results of past decisions can decision makers continually improve their skills. Further, if learning begins when a decision is first implemented, early refinements to the decision or implementation plan can be made that could mean the difference between success and failure.[3]

Russo and Schoemaker point out that one of the biggest faults of the decision-making process is that the quality of decisions is often judged on *outcome* rather than the *process* that was used to generate the decision. "Many people believe that good outcomes necessarily imply that a good process was used. And they assume the converse to be true as well: that a poor outcome necessarily signals a poor or incompetent process."[4] Clearly, this is not true, particularly for decisions that are close (55 percent chance of a good decision and 45 percent chance of a bad decision) or in situations involving a significant amount of outside chance or luck. In fact, a good decision-making process often produces a failure but, on average, succeeds more often than it fails. Russo and Schoemaker illustrate their point with the chart shown in Exhibit 14.2.[5]

According to Russo and Schoemaker, the way decisions are evaluated will affect the way decisions are made in the future. Thus, in addition to a good decision-making process, the evaluation of decisions is a critical skill. This has serious implications for improving decision making in organizations, particularly for difficult-to-make decisions, such as those related to risk management.

A good conceptual model for the risk management-decision making balancing act is depicted in Exhibit 14.3.

Outcome

		Good	Bad
Process used to make the decision	Good	Deserved success	Bad break
	Bad	Dumb luck	Poetic justice

Exhibit 14.2   Relationship between Decision Making and Decision Outcomes

While there are myriad risks encountered by the professional services firm, most of them can be generally categorized into four key areas:

1. *Internal risks:* Risks of undesirable outcomes that emanate from activities taking place inside the firm, including financial risks, employee risks, hiring risks, and systems risks.
2. *Delivery risks:* Risks related to the delivery of services to clients, whether on-site or off.
3. *Client risks:* Risks associated with the specific client but not a particular project.

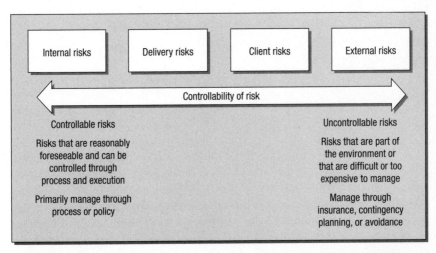

Exhibit 14.3   Professional Service Firm Risk Categories and Controllability

4. *External risks:* General risks such as natural disasters arising from being in business but not associated with a specific client, project, or internal operation.

These risks can be placed on a rough continuum of controllability, as depicted in Exhibit 14.3. Internal risks tend to be the easiest to manage because they are related to the firm's own operations and staff. Moving from left to right, delivery, client, and, finally, external risks become less and less easily controlled.

In general, controllable risks can be addressed via the usual methods—to mitigate these problems, senior management can simply dictate process, policies, and terms geared to providing the appropriate amount of flexibility and risk reduction. As the risk areas move down the controllability continuum, the less effective process and policy become, and the more important insurance, contingency planning, and avoidance become. The best written processes and policies have little effect on an earthquake in progress.

The following section details some sample risks that we have identified in each category, followed by a model for assessing risk and probability and evaluating options for mitigating risks.

Sample Risks by Category

The large number of risks faced by a specific professional services firm is difficult to inventory. The risks may vary by firm type (law versus medicine versus business consulting versus other), specific type of work, firm geography, client geography, staff type, project size, and even the personalities of the senior management team. We identify some of the possible risks in each category that may be faced by a professional services provider. While this list is clearly not comprehensive, it can serve as a good starter set or the foundation of brainstorming activities for firms to generate their own inventory of specific risks in each category.

Internal Risks

- *Fraud/embezzlement:* Internal theft by employees through fraud, embezzlement, or other intentional deceit
- *Accounting error:* Unintentional errors made by accounting staff that impact firm income statement, balance sheet, cash flows, general ledger, or other financial information
- *Billing accuracy:* Generation of bills that accurately reflect the proper fixed fees, time and material, and expense charges to clients
- *Hiring:* Hiring practices that ensure individuals of the highest ethics
- *Records:* Retention of accurate client records, working papers, financial statements, and other firm operating documents for appropriate length of time

- *Corporate espionage:* Loss of firm intellectual property, client information, or other proprietary information to competitors
- *Systems and data security:* Access to computing information systems and data restricted to authorized firm professionals and staff
- *Systems backup and recovery:* Reliable backups of data and rapid recovery from system crashes, errors, or inadvertently deleted information
- *Physical security:* Physical access to firm and client project sites and security of working papers and firm property
- *Staff malfeasance:* Theft of property, disparagement, or other deliberate misconduct by staff members that damages the firm
- *Intellectual capital:* Loss or theft of critical intellectual capital that distinguishes the firm or gives it competitive advantage or advanced capabilities
- *Staff departures:* Resignation of key internal staff due to retirement, dissatisfaction, outside recruiting, moves, or other reasons
- *Succession:* Firm senior and junior leadership succession plans
- *Resource management:* Pipeline of resources to be available for new business as well as proper management of resources during downtimes

Delivery Risks
- *Skills:* Availability of the specific skills or knowledge on the team to successfully complete the project or service
- *Scope:* Well-defined parameters for project or service activities; clearly delineated goals and milestones and an unambiguous understanding of what will be regarded as successful completion in advance of commencement of the project or service
- *Underbidding:* Underestimate of level of effort, skill set required, or other resources required to complete the project
- *Execution:* "Do-ability" of the project (Do resources or skills exist within the firm, or any firm, for successfully delivering the project or service—also known as the "bridge-to-the-moon" problem?)
- *Dependencies:* Project or service tasks that depend on client initiatives, staff, timelines, dates, or other events not controlled by the firm
- *Third-party reliance:* Reliance on outside individuals or entities for completion of critical tasks in delivery of the project or service (e.g., third-party contract labor)
- *Confidentiality:* Inadvertent or purposeful release of critical client information not for public consumption causing embarrassment or damage to the client, particularly sensitive for public companies
- *Travel/geography:* Risks associated with the specific point of delivery of the product or service, including difficulty of getting to client site;

specific dangers based on geography of the project (environment, political stability, neighborhood safety, etc.)

- *Staff knowledge:* Specific knowledge found in limited number of staff that is critical to the project or service; exposure to unplanned staff departure risk that will adversely affect the client
- *Resource availability:* Availability when needed of the proper internal delivery resources and professional staff

Client Risks

- *Personnel changes:* Critical client project sponsors leaving, being demoted, promoted, or having their responsibilities change
- *Financial trouble:* Client running into financial difficulties or bankruptcy, resulting in project or service contract cancellation and exposure on existing sunk costs and receivables
- *Gaming:* Dishonest clients attempting to procure additional services for free or dispute service quality or delivery in order to receive unwarranted fee reductions
- *Scope changes:* Changes in scope of project, affecting ability to complete the project, project budget, or client interest in completing project
- *Mergers and acquisitions:* Client acquisition or merger with another company, resulting in project or service contract cancellation, renegotiation, or elimination
- *Project or service cancellation:* Change in client priorities or budget, resulting in elimination of the project or service contract
- *Receivable prioritization:* Client in financial difficulties prioritizing receivables, resulting in nonessential service providers' exposure to bad debt
- *Client concentration:* High reliance on a single client or small number of clients for revenues, margin, and staff billability
- *Industry concentration:* High reliance on clients in a specific industry or related industries for revenues, margin, and staff billability

External Risks

- *Natural disasters:* Hurricanes, floods, earthquake, fire, tornadoes, volcanic eruptions, and other natural catastrophic events
- *Political unrest:* Political demonstrations, unrest, or instability resulting in danger to physical safety, client, or project viability
- *Terrorism/war:* War or terrorist acts that threaten staff physical safety, client, or project viability
- *Currency conversion:* Changes in currency exchange rates that adversely affect receivables

- *Legislation:* Legislative changes that adversely affect the project by eliminating its rationale or changing client priorities

Risk Management Methodology

Exhibit 14.4 shows a methodology for the risk management process in a professional services firm. The first step in generating a risk management program is to (within reason) identify the possible undesirable outcomes. The categories and risks mentioned in the previous section form a good starter set, but each type of firm must determine its specific needs. Doctors and lawyers must be concerned with malpractice, real estate agents with interest rates, and technology consultants with IT budgets.

After the possible risks have been identified and inventoried, the firm must determine the expected value of each risk—simply the likelihood of occurrence (probability) and the cost of a bad outcome. This is the most difficult step and the step most open to interpretation.

Probabilities of events are notoriously difficult to estimate, as are costs of outcomes. In fact, research shows that low-probability events are even more difficult to estimate. Studies conducted by researchers at the Wharton Schools Risk Management and Decision Process Center at the University of Pennsylvania demonstrated that individuals have the best chance of estimating expected value when a variety of low-probability events are aggregated to generate a probability (e.g., "estimate the probability that there will be

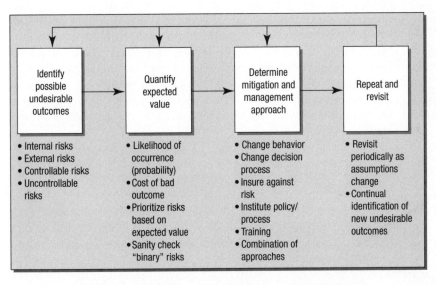

Exhibit 14.4   Risk Management Process Methodology

either an earthquake, flood, or hurricane" versus estimating the likelihood of each event individually).[6]

Studies by Kunreuther, Novemsky, and Kahneman also indicate that individuals are more effective when assessing possible outcomes relative to low-probability events they are familiar with (e.g. "estimate the risk of a chemical plant accident versus the risk of having a traffic accident").[7] Making matters worse, similar studies found that decision makers regarding low-probability, high impact events tended to either over-insure, assuming that recurrence of a low-probability event was inevitable, or ignore the event entirely, thinking "that can't happen to me."[8]

Once the expected value has been determined, the risks can be prioritized for management. In some cases, the probability will be very low, but the cost very high (e.g., "Pascal's Wager"). In these cases, a common-sense approach to prioritization and mitigation should prevail.

The mitigation for a given risk will likely be a combination of actions, policies, or decisions as opposed to a single approach. Some of the typical options are changing behavior ("no more sodas in the server room"), changing decision processes ("let's implement better screening for new employee hires"), instituting policies or processes ("two signatures required on every check over $10,000"), training ("all staff will attend client management skills seminars"), or other business changes.

Improving Risk Management

As mentioned previously in the chapter, the importance of good decision making in the risk management process cannot be overstated. A step that professional services firms can take to improve decision making is training and decision audits. Sales teams should focus training and development on mitigating client and project risk. Delivery teams should focus on project risk, internal resources on project and internal risk, and senior management on client, project, internal, and external risk. Good decision-making habits should be made part of the firm culture, and reading the basic literature in the field of decision science should be part of the basic training for all firm professionals.

Good decision making can be enhanced by implementing postmortem reviews for key business events: the conclusion of a large project, the acquisition (or loss) of a key client, the completion of a good (or bad) quarter. Significant events represent a chance to review what went well and what should change going forward, as well as understand better what went right (and determining if it was "dumb luck" or "deserved success"). In our own business consulting practice, after each major client engagement is completed, a full post-mortem analysis is required of the delivery team. The learnings from that postmortem are used to drive changes in all parts of the business: sales, delivery, training, intellectual property, hiring, and support. While this practice has entailed extra effort, the business improvement benefits have paid a more than adequate return to the investment.

A crucial part of good decision making for professional services firms is the pursuit decision for new business. Many successful service providers have an aggressive, sales-oriented culture. While this is effective for driving revenue, oftentimes the firm will overreach when selling the next deal and wind up too far to the right-hand side of the risk continuum. A successful senior executive from a professional services firm put it succinctly: "Good business in. Good business out."

This phenomenon has been dubbed "The Winner's Curse" and is a topic of study by Richard Thaler, a prominent behavioral economics researcher at the University of Chicago. In his book *The Winner's Curse: Paradoxes and Anomalies of Economic Life,* Thaler outlines the dilemma:

> Suppose that each participant in the auction is willing to bid just a little bit less than the amount he or she thinks the land is worth (leaving some room for profits). Of course, no one knows exactly how much [the project] is worth: some bidders will guess too high, others too low. Suppose, for the sake of argument, that the bidders have accurate estimates on average. Then, who will be the person who wins the auction? The winner will be the person who was the most optimistic about the [value of the project], and that person may well have bid more than the [project] was worth. This is the dreaded winner's curse. In an auction with many bidders, the winning bidder is often a loser. A key factor in avoiding the winner's curse is bidding more conservatively when there are more bidders. While this may seem counter-intuitive, it is the rational thing to do.[9]

Finally, one of the most effective risk-mitigation approaches employed by firms is simple, but rigorously enforced, policy and procedure. The larger the firm, the more important it is to put risk mitigation on "auto-pilot" through these methods. The importance (and positive effect) of this was recently highlighted for us. A senior manager of a service company we are acquainted with had his company acquired by a *Fortune* 50 entity. Immediately, all manner of new policies was implemented, which was both startling and amazing to a small company. Armed guards, sign-in protocols for guests, document disposal guidelines, new systems security requirements, and other changes both large and small were the order of the day.

While the majority of the changes made sense, others seemed to be overkill (e.g., the window blinds had to be closed in a certain way to avoid any incidence of espionage by occupants of errant helicopters flying near the 12th story of the building). The larger story, however, is that an enormous company manages to avoid any new risks through the blanket application of security protocols that had been designed over time and found to work. While not all of them made perfect sense in their specific application, it was easier to mandate them en masse and get back to work than sort through them individually. Thus, a large company with billions of dollars can still manage to control the day-to-day minutiae required for effective risk management.

Specific Actions to Reduce or Avoid Risks

There are a variety of specific actions that the professional services firm can take to avoid some of the risks outlined previously in the chapter. While by no means a comprehensive treatment, we have addressed a few.

INTERNAL RISK. The best prevention for internal risks is good hiring. Motivated and honest professionals provide mitigation against both expected and unexpected risks. Going beyond hiring practices, professional services firms should ensure that proper firm governance codes are established and followed, as well as codes of conduct and policies as outlined elsewhere in this chapter. Finally, appropriate finance and accounting checks and balances should be implemented. These common accounting practices are well-explored territory, with dozens of available books and guides available.

DELIVERY RISK. The best prevention for delivery risk is clear communication with the client. Eventually a project will suffer from scope creep, a key staff member will leave, or some other issue will be encountered. Clear, rapid, and open communication with the client that drives to solutions for both parties is the best cure for unanticipated delivery problems.

Other delivery risk mitigation tools include contracts (also covered in Chapter 19, "Legal Considerations," in this book) as well as errors and omissions (E&O) insurance (covered in Chapter 16, "Purchasing, procurement, vendor and asset management"). In short, the contract terms should limit the firm's liability to a reasonable amount (fees received or no more than the limit of the firm's insurance coverage). The contracts should also specify methods for managing disputes that fall short of litigation, such as arbitration.

CLIENT RISK. The best way to avoid the risks associated with clients is to avoid clients of questionable financial standing. Because services are generally impossible to repossess in the event of bad debt, a few bad receivables can erase firm profits. Firms can determine client viability through credit checks and other research inquiries (Dun & Bradstreet Small Business Solutions, smallbusiness.dnb.com, as well as other information on business research web sites such as Hoovers, www.hoovers.com).

While work is underway with a client, senior firm managers should ensure that they keep up with the clients financial health, as well as internal client politics, all of which can affect the firm contracts. Good managers will develop multiple sources of information inside a client and have more than one or two "sponsors" within a given client at different levels, providing additional insulation from personnel changes or client political battles. Going on-site with clients is one of the best ways to accomplish this, and senior managers should visit with their major clients on-site not less than once every two weeks.

Firms providing services to specific industry segments should also keep up with overall industry trends to avoid any surprises and stay ahead of surges or cutbacks in spending, changes in legislation, merger activity, or other industry news.

The level of acceptable risk may also vary according to the current level of the business climate. Firms with large demands on their time may be able to take on fewer, less risky clients, whereas firms hungrier for business will take on larger risks.

EXTERNAL RISK. External risks are the most difficult to estimate and control. Most mitigation against these types of risk come from either avoidance or the purchase of insurance. Firms must work diligently to ensure the safety of their internal and professional staff. For companies engaged in work in at-risk areas, firms such as Kroll Worldwide (www.krollworldwide.com) provide related risk consulting services.

Finally, for hard-to-estimate external risks, professional services firms should work with their insurance provider to determine proper policy types and coverages.

Quality Assurance

Many of the key elements of quality control are the same as those for risk management: leadership and expertise, quality professional staff, client-tested methodology, process, standard operating procedures, and policies. A firm that is good at risk management is generally good at quality assurance.

In the late 1980s and early 1990s, the "quality movement" produced endless literature on quality in manufacturing. Many of the same concepts from quality manufacturing apply to the professional services firm as well. The resources section of this chapter contains references to some of these. A personal favorite of ours is *Quality Is Personal* by Harry Roberts and Bernard Sergesketter. This book takes the concepts from quality management and applies them to the individual in daily business activities. Training programs or reading from this book will provide benefits to professional staff within the firm.

Another important factor in ensuring quality delivery is culture. Firms that celebrate whistle-blowing and institute a culture of senior management approachability will have a chance to solve problems before they become too difficult to handle. Unfortunately, the culture in many firms is one of "shoot the messenger." Senior management must work to instead glorify the messenger who delivers the bad news of a struggling project or a dissatisfied client. Client staff who work with a client on a daily basis are the best form of quality control. Aloof, unapproachable senior managers may not learn about problems until they have reached a true crisis point.

Finally, the senior managers in charge of the client relationship should establish the proper "early warning" mechanisms that will help identify delivery areas requiring adjustment or course corrections while underway. The focus of these reports should be on providing an overview of status, while directing the partners' attention to critical areas. Typical reports of interest include:

- Weekly status reports for each project or client
- Project scorecards (red/yellow/green status)
- Periodic project reviews
- Budget-consumed versus project-progress information

Senior managers should also solicit new ideas from professional and internal staff to help create new status reports that are helpful to both groups, usable for clients as well as not too onerous to prepare on a regular basis.

Crisis Management: The Best Laid Plans . . .

What actions should the professional services firm take if, in spite of all planning and risk management, a crisis occurs? The crisis response will take form based on the nature of the crisis. A good text on this topic is *Crisis Management: Planning for the Inevitable;* see the resources section of this chapter for details. For major events, the firm should consider retaining a crisis management and/or public relations firm. Naturally, the right time to establish a good relationship with firms of this type is prior to the crisis.

However, the day-to-day "crises" that professional service firms encounter are related to the delivery of services and client satisfaction. Because client delivery problems are inevitable for any firm, the best way that firm leadership can distinguish itself is through excellence in remediation. How well firms recognize, control and resolve their mistakes can make an enormous difference in client satisfaction.

Each salvage operation will be different and, therefore, requires the involvement and judgment of firm senior management. For example, our own company had a client for whom we had completed a very successful engagement. An unrelated, follow-on project had gone astray, with a brutal combination of scope creep, personnel problems, underbidding, and geography conspiring to create poor performance. By moving rapidly to remediate the situation and ultimately discounting the fees and recasting the project, we were able to get our services back on track and find a way to please the client. Over the long haul, we were able to continue working with the client, thus keeping an important relationship and a good reference for our services.

Litigation

Firms should avoid lawsuits related to the delivery of their services whenever possible. The distraction, expense, reputation damage, and opportunity costs emanating from even a successful lawsuit are immense. A failed lawsuit can be devastating. Firms that achieve a reputation for suing their clients will find their sales process an uphill battle.

"I learned long ago never to wrestle with a pig. You get dirty, and besides, the pig likes it," an unknown author wrote. Occasionally, a client will take an unreasonable position on an issue and will be intractable during remediation efforts. Even when the end client is on the wrong side of the issue, the firm can wind up a loser from the energy, effort, and attention required to resolve the issue. Internally, we often call this "pig wrestling" and attempt to avoid it if possible. There are a variety of other ways to resolve disputes with clients, from appeasement to arbitration. A good cost-benefit analysis will usually point the way to the most appropriate approach for resolution.

Responsibility for Risk Management and Quality Assurance in the Organization

Ultimately, responsibility for quality assurance and risk management falls on the shoulders of the senior managers of the firm. These are the individuals with the experience, background, and judgment to determine the best course of action in most cases. However, the information most needed to make the right decisions, as well as new ideas, can come from the professional and internal staff. Firms with effective risk management and quality assurance programs establish a culture that holds the entire team responsible for ensuring quality delivery and mitigating risks. Success depends on the involvement of all—the risks and trouble that assail the firm daily are too numerous and varied to be mitigated by anything less than total involvement.

Some firms may choose to elect or appoint an officer in charge of these areas. The research on decision making shows that certain personality types may be more effective than others in this role. In a 2001 paper titled "Worry and Mental Accounting with Protective Measures," Schade and Kunreuther[10] hypothesize that "a greater tendency to worry would intuitively be expected to lead to a higher level of [willingness to pay] for any protection." In fact, their research demonstrated that the reverse may be true—that worriers may make more cost-effective decisions than nonworriers. The researchers contrast anxiety ("an emotion") with worry ("a cognitive phenomenon"). Worry leads to thinking, analysis, data gathering, and effective decision framing. Prior research by Tallis, Davey, and Capuzzo[11] found that worrying:

- Acts as a stimulant
- Clarifies thoughts and concentration
- Gives the opportunity to analyze situations and work out the pros and cons
- Adds to the problems and, as such, leads to exploration of different possibilities

The research concludes that "low-worriers are likely not to care much about the risk, and hence may not calculate values of objects, losses and prices for protection."[12] The implications of this for firms attempting to improve decision making, quality assurance, and risk management are clear: Contrary to intuition, an effective worrier, not prone to anxiety—the emotional component of worry—may be their best asset.

RESOURCES

Norman Augustine et. al., *Harvard Business Review on Crisis Management* [HBR-Crisis Management] (Boston: Harvard Business School Press, 2000).

Thomas L. Barton, William G. Shenkir, and Paul L. Walker, *Making Enterprise Risk Management Pay Off: How Leading Companies Implement Risk Management*

Max H. Bazerman, *Judgement in Managerial Decision Making* (New York: John Wiley & Sons, 1994).

Steven Fink, *Crisis Management: Planning for the Inevitable* (Backinprint.com, 2001).

Matthew J., Hassett and Donald Stewart, *Probability for Risk Management* (ACTEX Publications, 1999).

Paul R. Kleindorfer and Howard Kunreuther, co-chairs. The Risk Management and Decision Processes Center at the Wharton School of the University of Pennsylvania, Available from http://opim.wharton.upenn.edu/risk.

James Lam, *Enterprise Risk Management: From Incentives to Controls* (Hoboken NJ: John Wiley & Sons, 2003).

Peter G. Neumann, moderator and chair, Risks Forum newsgroup, sponsored by the ACM Committee on Computers and Public Policy. Available from http://www.csl.sri.com/~risko/risks.txt.

Harry V. Roberts and Bernard F. Sergesketter, *Quality Is Personal* (New York: Free Press, 1993).

J. Edward Russo and Paul J. H. Schoemaker, *Decision Traps* (New York: Fireside Books, 1989).

J. Edward Russo, Paul J. H. Schoemaker, and Margo Hittleman, *Winning Decisions: Getting It Right the First Time* (New York: Currency, 2001).

Richard H. Thaler, *The Winner's Curse: Paradoxes and Anomalies of Economic Life* (Princeton, NJ: Princeton University Press, 1992).

R. Max Wideman, ed., *Project and Program Risk Management: A Guide to Managing Project Risks and Opportunities* (Project Management Institute, 1998).

Christopher Marrison, *The Fundamentals of Risk Measurement* (New York: McGraw-Hill, 2002).

NOTES

1. Peter L. Bernstein, *Against the Gods: The Remarkable Story of Risk* (New York: John Wiley & Sons, 1996, ISBN 0471121045).
2. Obituary of Arthur Rudolph, *New York Times* (January 3, 1996).
3. J. Edward Russo and Paul J. H. Schoemaker, *Winning Decisions: Getting It Right the First Time* (New York: Doubleday, 2002), p. 6.
4. See note 3, p. 3.
5. See note 3, p. 5.
6. Howard Kunreuther and Mark Pauly, "Ignoring Disaster: Don't Sweat the Big Stuff," working paper collection from the Risk Management and Decision Processes Center at the Wharton School of the University of Pennsylvania (October 11, 2001).
7. Howard Kunreuther, Nathan Novemsky, and Daniel Kahneman, "Making Low Probabilities Useful," working paper collection from the Risk Management and Decision Processes Center at the Wharton School of the University of Pennsylvania (December 2000).
8. Howard Kunreuther, "Wharton on Making Decisions," Chapter 15, "Protective Decisions: Fear or Prudence?" (New York: John Wiley & Sons, 2001).
9. Richard Thaler, *The Winner's Curse: Paradoxes and Anomalies of Economic Life,* Chapter 5, pp. 50–62.
10. Christian Schade and Howard Kunreuther, "Worry and Mental Accounting with Protective Measures," working paper collection from the Risk Management and Decision Processes Center at the Wharton School of the University of Pennsylvania (February 20, 2001).
11. Tallis, F., G. C. L. Davey, and N. Capuzzo, "The Phenomenology of Non-Pathlogical Worry: A Preliminary Investigation," in *Worrying: Perspectives on Theory, Assessment and Treatment,* ed. G. C. L. Davey and F. Tallis (New York: John Wiley & Sons, 1994), p. 77.
12. See note 9, p. 6.

The Back Office:
Efficient Firm Operations

15

Finance, Accounting, and Human Resources

JEFFERY B. NEMY

If you can't measure it, you can't manage it!
—Peter Drucker

Financial management of a professional services firm requires a delicate balance between shareholders' needs to control costs and grow the business profitably and management's responsibility to recruit, train, motivate, and retain talented employees. This delicate balance is an art, not a science, and requires a close interrelationship between finance and human resource (HR) functions. This chapter focuses on both departments because a clear delineation between them is difficult to draw, especially in small- to mid-size firms.

It is often said that a professional services firm's most valuable assets walk out the door every night. Management's challenge is to properly motivate those assets to return in the morning and deliver high-quality professional results. Importantly, such motivation encompasses far more than a healthy salary, as training, evaluation, mentoring, and bonus programs contribute significantly toward an employee's attitude of the firm and his or her individual performance. Successful firms balance these needs well, although seldom to everyone's satisfaction. In this chapter, we address key issues in managing both human and financial resources.

Why This Topic Is Important

Millions of dollars pass through even the smallest professional services firms. In many cases, the firm may act as an intermediary agent of the client, procuring goods and services on its behalf, and accordingly has a significant fiduciary responsibility to safeguard its assets. Executive management of the professional services firm must be reasonably well versed in essential financial concepts and related HR issues to provide effective leadership.

Without such knowledge, it is relatively easy to make decisions that, even though they appear to be the "right thing to do," may conflict significantly with fundamental financial planning and accounting principles and in the most serious situations could be deemed illegal. Further, by understanding where potential liabilities may be hidden, executives can take appropriate action a priori to ensure that proper procedures are employed. Clearly, a firm must also be well managed financially to exist as a going-concern. Finally, solid HR management is vital to a firm's ultimate success because it has only the knowledge, skills, and abilities of its employees to sell.

Human Resources

Management of the professional services firm requires a unique focus on the firm's most critical asset, its people. The interrelationship among HR, accounting, and finance is so close that a clear delineation of responsibilities often is difficult to find, particularly in smaller organizations. Smaller firms will oftentimes aggregate the responsibilities of overhead departments such as HR and finance together. Compensation management, payroll processing, vacation tracking, management of legal issues, and timesheet management are among the traditional HR areas that often may be managed to greater or lesser extent by the finance department. Because of the critical integration between these two functions in the professional services firm, financial managers and HR managers often must be well versed in each other's craft.

Typically, smaller professional services firms do not have the wherewithal to recruit and retain seasoned HR professionals. Instead, mid-level financial professionals with industry experience are routinely tapped for the senior financial and HR leadership roles in small firms. These employees are often well qualified to meet the needs of a small firm. But as the firm grows, the need for specialized leadership becomes more critical. Systems, processes, and procedures that work well on an informal basis in a small firm are quickly rendered ineffective once the organization has more than a few dozen employees. Senior leadership of the firm must augment those resources themselves when the firm is small and then be prepared to recognize when it is time to recruit professional HR talent to the team as the firm grows.

The Role of Human Resources in a Professional Services Environment

The HR department plays a key role in every organization, although in a professional services firm, effective execution of that role can be a major factor in success. With nearly all the firm's current and future human assets as part of their purview, HR professionals need to provide critical insights and leverage to balance management and employee needs. As such, their role is multifaceted and, in addition to their significant role as an advisor to senior management, includes the following:

- *Recruiter:* The search for top talent is never ending. As such, an HR manager's role is to stay connected with key players in the industry and constantly seek out the best and brightest. By maintaining relationships with a pool of highly qualified candidates year-round, even when market conditions are poor and layoffs are prevalent, successful firms can improve their bench strength by hiring top talent at reasonable rates.

- *Counselor and intermediary:* From time to time, certain situations may require some form of counseling to resolve. Whether it is simply the employee's need to discuss a minor issue with a neutral party or the need to find an intermediary to resolve a major conflict, the HR manager must be prepared to manage and resolve such issues in a confidential and professional manner.

- *Legal interface:* Many of the issues facing HR managers often involve significant legal questions relating to employment, discrimination, and work rules among a myriad of other topics. Well-trained HR professionals know how to recognize these issues and subsequently seek advice from qualified legal counsel. The ability to recognize and articulate such issues, as well as effectively debate their resolution with counsel, distinguishes the HR professional from the HR administrator. The HR professional needn't be an attorney, but the need to be well aware of legal issues is a must.

- *Record keeper:* Maintaining current, accurate, and complete personnel records is a fundamental HR function. Ensuring that management prepares timely performance reviews, documents performance and personnel issues, as well as maintains all government-mandated forms in an orderly manner, is the most basic, yet rarely well-executed, HR function.

- *Enforcer:* When it comes to resolution of the myriad issues facing management of a professional services firm, HR is often designated as the "bad guy" to convey unwelcome news. HR professionals must convey a sense of fairness yet remain firm in support of legal and managerial issues. The ability to do so effectively is rare, but further distinguishes valuable professionals from mere administrators.

- *Cheerleader:* Developing and administering programs to boost morale is a key HR function. Ensuring that company events are well planned to promote teamwork and consider the tastes and preferences of both the majority and minority of the employee population is a key aspect of the HR role.

As described earlier, the role of the HR team is broad and can be technical, particularly from an employment law standpoint. Small firms, in many cases those with fewer than 100 employees, often cannot afford to invest in a qualified HR management team. Many firms settle for less expensive HR managers in the mistaken belief that such positions are merely the "personnel department" that ensures all forms are filled out properly.

As outlined in earlier chapters, HR management is far more than form management, and the failure to properly staff that function can result not only in lawsuits but also in weak staff morale and employee performance. Outsourcing of this function has grown popular in recent years and can provide smaller firms with access to highly qualified HR management at cost-effective rates.

The Importance of Competent Legal Counsel

The HR function, by its very nature, involves a significant level of legal interpretation. Although some rules and regulations are clear and can be executed by trained administrators on a routine basis, many issues require legal interpretation. The failure to identify such situations can lead to the imposition of significant fines, penalties, or judgments being levied against the firm. HR professionals know how to identify such situations and will seek competent legal counsel before taking action to resolve a situation. Some of the more common issues for which legal counsel should be sought include:

- Terminating a single employee for performance or behavior issues
- Mass layoffs
- Independent contractor versus temporary employee status
- Immigration and related visas
- Sexual harassment
- Age discrimination
- Benefit eligibility
- Vacation pay compensation upon separation
- Performance evaluation form development
- Writing employee handbooks/manuals

In these instances, legal counsel normally is necessary to review specific facts and circumstances of the matter at hand from which a legal opinion can be formed. One of the best investments the professional services firm executive can make is to ensure proper funding to secure highly qualified legal counsel to augment internal resources. Encouraging HR professionals to utilize these external resources can help the firm avoid costly litigation and, most importantly, maintain a positive and productive work environment free of the distractions caused by weak HR management.

To ensure compliance with all federal, state, and local laws as well as best practices, many law firms that specialize in HR issues can conduct an audit of the HR department for a relatively modest fee. Such audits typically include a random review of personnel and related files as well as a thorough review of all policies and procedures. Completion of such an audit every five years or so, with a follow-up review the subsequent year, will contribute significantly toward full compliance with all relevant rules and regulations as well as help to ensure a solid legal foundation in the event legal action is taken against the firm. Chapter 19 covers this topic in more detail.

Recruiting

As the firm grows, management of the recruiting process matures as well. In a small firm, recruiting typically occurs through word of mouth and networking. But as multiple positions become available, the HR team must use a basic set of procedures to coordinate its efforts and maximize its effectiveness. Typically, some of those procedures include:

- *Open position tracking:* Formalize the process by using an "open position" list to track the status of all open positions, including the date the position was officially authorized and by whom, department, position title, target compensation level, list of qualified candidates under consideration, and the overall status of the search effort. This report should be distributed to senior management weekly to keep them aware of the status and ensure that all open positions have been properly authorized.

- *Offers:* Ensure all employment offers are made in writing. By authorizing only the HR department to make an offer to a candidate, the firm can ensure consistency in the communications that are made to confirm the offer of employment. Legal counsel should review and approve a standard offer letter template for use by HR administrators. If circumstances require that an offer letter be tailored to the needs of a particular situation, legal counsel should be consulted to validate any significant changes as the offer letter forms the foundation from which future legal action may be taken.

- *Negotiations:* Bifurcate the employment negotiation process. Implementation of a policy that only an authorized HR department employee may make an employment offer to a candidate will help the firm avoid many mistakes that untrained line managers can make. By insisting that only the HR department can negotiate an offer, management will have a clear line to follow to determine responsibility in the event something should go wrong. Further, by taking the line manager out of the negotiations after he or she has decided to hire the individual, HR can execute its role as the intermediary and help ensure that any difficulties experienced during the negotiations are not translated into ill will between the line manager and the new employee.

- *Temps and freelancers:* Ensure that all employment procedures are managed through HR, particularly including the utilization of temporary employees, freelancers, and independent contractors. When line employees are allowed to retain the services of a freelancer, significant liability can be at risk, including:

  —*Rates:* The opportunity to hire an individual's friend or past acquaintance can diminish the motivation to negotiate a fair market rate for the services to be rendered. By having HR negotiate the rate, management can be better assured that a reasonable rate was negotiated through this segregation of duties.

  —*Employment status:* Very few managers are familiar with the tests to determine if a person can qualify as an independent contractor. Through its training, the HR department is best qualified to determine whether a person who wants to be treated as an independent contractor meets sufficient criteria to qualify for such status. Failure to properly classify such personnel may result in significant claims for overtime, benefits, taxes, and other perquisites to which employees may be entitled long after their temporary assignment has ended. If not accounted for properly, significant penalties may be assessed.

  —*Purchase order control:* To ensure firm control over the use of independent contractors and consultants, it is best to use a purchase order that clearly spells out the terms and conditions of the assignment including the commencement date, due date, deliverables, rate of compensation, and the maximum amount of money authorized under the agreement. The topic of recruiting is covered in depth in Chapter 11.

Performance Evaluations

One of the most important managerial tools used in the professional services firm is the performance evaluation process. Legal review and approval of forms used in the process can significantly improve the firm's position in a legal action, but only if the forms are used on a regularly scheduled basis. In general, it is the HR department's responsibility to distribute such forms and follow up with managers/supervisors to ensure the form is completed in a timely manner and reviewed for content before being discussed with the employee. That review should ensure that all statements made, particularly those that may not be well received, are supportable and written in such a manner that would not create a potential legal liability.

Employee performance should be evaluated formally at least once a year, with at least one or two feedback points made during the year. Some firms stagger their evaluation process to coincide with the employee's anniversary while others conduct them in batches once or twice per year. Either way may be used based on management's personal preference; however, the critical factor is to ensure that at least one written evaluation is given to every employee at least once per year, with a signed copy placed in the employee's personnel file. Done properly, this is one of the simplest ways to improve performance and morale. Employee appraisals and career tracks are covered in depth in Chapter 9.

Layoffs/Reduction in Force

The decision to lay off a significant number of workers is always a difficult task. Invariably, such decisions become muddled with personal conflicts, performance issues, and, simply, who likes whom. Life-altering decisions made by managers who are under a tremendous amount of stress subject the firm to increased risk of liability. Before "the list" of names of employees to be terminated is assembled, the firm should fully evaluate its revenue and expense forecasts and ensure that it has identified not only its most likely projection, but also its best and worst cases. Layoff plans should be developed around all three of these scenarios so that management can build as much of a holistic plan as possible. It is important that staff remaining after the action is taken be confident that the worst is over, and are enthusiastic about pulling together and moving forward.

Key points in the layoff process include:

- *Keep the list confidential.* Only those who absolutely need to know should be involved, and great care should be taken to shield irrelevant information (e.g., a manager may see only a layoff list of people he or she selected within his or her team/department). The only people who should see the entire list are the CEO, COO, CFO, and HR director. Department heads should be concerned with only their own lists. For every person who has a copy of the list, there is an exponential increase in the probability that a leak will occur. Often these lists evolve over time and change right up until the last minute before an employee is notified that his or her position is being eliminated. If people found out that they were supposed to be laid off but ended up being taken off the list, their attitude toward the firm and management may be forever tainted. Key points to safeguard the list's security include:
  —Never label it with titles or headings that may suggest its true meaning.
  —Never let someone else copy it.
  —Never let it leave your possession.
  —Never allow more than the absolute minimum number of trusted staff members in finance and HR to have access to it.
  —Never print it out on a network printer—memory problems are not uncommon, and it is possible that the report could print out long after anyone responsible for it leaves the printer unattended, leaving it available for the first set of curious eyes.

Unplanned Communication

The administrative assistant to the CFO of a professional services firm was assisting in the late night preparation for a major presentation of the local office's plan to reduce staff in light of a wave of significant client losses over a short period of time. The multipage presentation was prepared in a very short amount of time and required that several charts be printed out in color. The only color printer was located in another part of the building, far removed from the assistant's desk. For some reason, initial network print commands failed to work, so the assistant printed the pages a second time. That night the presentation was completed; however, the next morning, a single copy of the page that failed to print the night before was found sitting on top of the printer by another employee. Within minutes, copies of management's layoff plans were photocopied and posted throughout the building. Needless to say, morale plummeted over the following days and weeks leading up to the layoff action as a result of this very innocent error in the printer system network.

- *Set financial targets for each department to achieve rather than target a specific number of people to lay off.* Let the department head prioritize his or her needs and then challenge that team's ability to perform its function in the post-layoff environment. Don't nitpick or micromanage the decisions of the department head.

- *Have a legal review of the list.* Include searches for discrimination based on age, sex, and other protected classes. Further, counsel should review documentation supporting the action being taken and the specific reason(s) each person was selected to be included in the RIF.

- *Do it only once whenever possible.* Often, employees are aware that the firm is facing financial difficulties before a layoff action. Their anticipation of the date can be distracting and lead to morale problems and productivity declines. If all cuts are made at once, management is in a much better position to make an affirmative statement to the remaining staff that acknowledges the action taken and assures them that "there is no other shoe to drop, so let's get back to business as soon as possible." Without such a statement, nagging concerns can continue to drag down the firm and become a self-fulfilling prophecy. In many situations, it is not possible to complete all layoffs at once and actions must be taken in stages; but minimizing the time that elapses between those stages is very important.

- *Reorganize workflows and improve processes before taking action.* Simply cutting the number of personnel is an exercise almost anyone can execute. However, great managers will anticipate potential business downturns and prepare for that day by working to constantly improve internal processes. By developing process improvements before a layoff, staff remaining after the action will be prepared and equipped to complete all required work without undue burden. Unless the firm has allowed nonproductive employees to remain on the payroll, simply cutting the number of workers without a plan in place to achieve each department's workload objectives will result in chaos and confusion, and key work may not be completed properly, if at all.

Recognizing Job Function

Management of a large professional services organization ordered that accounting operations personnel be reduced by an arbitrary amount because of consolidation with another division. Almost immediately, a third of the combined staff was laid off under the belief that the team would be more productive even though new procedures had not been developed and the workload remained the same as before the consolidation. Once the staff left, their work was attended to by remaining staff on a "when they could get to it" basis. One of the tasks performed by the departing staff was the reconciliation of the travel advance account, including airline tickets. Over the next two years, the firm lost more than a half million dollars in airline ticket fares because unused tickets were not reconciled with the airlines in a timely manner, a function that had been performed for less than $30,000 per year by staff that had been laid off without the benefit of improved procedures.

Records Management

The HR department is responsible for maintaining all government required forms and other prudent information on each employee. Depending on local legal requirements and firm policy, this information should be maintained in separate files for each employee with current data on a regular basis (e.g., daily, weekly, or monthly). Rules as to specific data requirements vary from state to state, but, in general, these records should be maintained in separate file folders: (1) personnel file, which is available for the employee's inspection, (2) employee's benefits file, (3) medical or disability files, and (4) an "investigation" file, which may be used to temporarily house confidential meeting notes and other forms of documentation related to the employee. Contents of these files may include:

Personnel File
- Resume and employment application
- Employment offer letter
- Immigration paperwork (e.g., I-9) and tax verification forms (e.g., W4)
- Copy of Social Security cards and driver's license

- Personnel action forms
- Temporary employee authorization forms (if applicable)
- Written acknowledgment of the firm's key policies
- Leave of absence approval
- Final reports related to investigations made of employee's conduct
- Disciplinary documents
- Performance and bonus evaluation forms

Employee Benefit File
- Benefit forms supporting the employee's selection of specific benefits
- Vacation earnings and usage details
- Benefit tracking documents including requests for reimbursement

Medical or Disability File
- Workers' compensation claim data
- Relevant medical and/or disability-related documentation

Investigation File (Confidential)
- Interview notes
- Complaints against employee
- Preliminary results of background investigation
- Manager's documentation of performance incidents

As a matter of policy, report drafts and notes should not be included in files and should routinely be destroyed after their immediate usefulness has expired in order to maintain only relevant information in each employee's files. Further, no information about any other employee should be included in an employee's files to maintain each employee's privacy rights. The investigation file is a confidential temporary file used to collect relevant information related to an investigation of the employee. After a summary level report about the incident(s) has been written and included in the personnel file, preliminary information should be destroyed in accordance with local legal counsel guidance.

Benefits Administration

In general, HR personnel are responsible for designing and administering benefits offered by the firm. This is a critical element in remaining competitive in the "employment" market. Well-managed firms ensure that at least one person in the HR group is fully versed on all aspects of every benefit offering and has been trained to know where the line is drawn among offering a full explanation, including some interpretation based on the individual's situation, and advice (which should not be offered). Discussions about benefits typically are one of a new employee's first impressions of the firm and, if well executed, can help the new employee form a long-lasting, favorable opinion of the firm. Getting this one right is a no-brainer that many firms often miss.

Compensation Administration and Forecasting

Responsibility for salary administration and forecasting is both a finance and HR function. Which group takes the lead on these critical processes is generally a function of the relative strength of the personnel involved as well as the personal preference of the executive team. Either way, both teams must work together to ensure that forecasts coordinate all changes in compensation known by both HR and finance. In particular, HR should review compensation plans to identify potential equity issues that may present legal liabilities. Compensation plans are discussed further in Chapter 10.

SALARY ADJUSTMENTS. The art of determining actual salaries paid to employees and all adjustments made thereto relies heavily on being competitive in the local, regional, and national marketplace, depending on the nature of each position. Salary surveys often are the best measure of determining the relative worth of a position. National or regional salary surveys for many industries and positions are available for free or a nominal cost from various professional organizations including placement firms, trade organizations, and consulting firms. In certain situations, competitors within a city or region work together to retain an independent consultant or CPA to conduct an industry-specific salary survey tailored to local economic conditions and position descriptions. Such data, when updated annually before initiation of the annual planning process, can be used very effectively to ensure that employees are compensated fairly for their efforts.

A general rule of thumb to guide the use of survey data is that employees should be paid within a 20 percent band (i.e., ±20 percent) around the median compensation level for any given position. When an employee first begins taking responsibility for a position, he or she is paid at a rate that is 20 percent below the median for the position. Over time, and as the employee becomes more competent at the position, the employee would receive raises within that band until such time that he or she reaches the top of the band at 20 percent above the median. After that point, raises generally would reflect only cost of living adjustments (i.e., to the median salary) as reported for each position in the annual salary survey. To receive a larger pay adjustment, an employee would have to be promoted into a higher paying position. Maintenance of such a salary administration program generally results in an equitable pay scale that balances the internal payroll with realities of the relevant local market.

BONUS PROGRAMS.   When properly administered, bonus programs can be tremendous motivational tools that help propel a firm to be a leader in its field. If not well conceived and executed, bonus programs simply increase costs with very little in return. Three types of bonus programs are found frequently in well-managed professional services firms:

- *Profit-related "executive" bonuses:* Generally reserved for only the most senior executives or partners of the firm, payment of profit-related bonuses can either be discretionary or tied to a formula. In general, these bonuses are tied to the firm's overall financial success and are designed to motivate the senior leadership team to make decisions that are best for the growth and profitability of the firm. Long-term deferred bonus plans are designed to reward performance over several years while incenting the most senior executives to remain with and build the firm. The less discretionary these programs are, the closer the link may be between decision making and results.

- *Management by objective (MBO)-related bonuses and deferred salaries:* Unlike profit-related bonuses, MBO-related bonuses may be considered more like part of a salary that has been deferred for a period of time (e.g., quarterly, semiannually, or annually) and are paid only after successful performance of a set of predetermined tasks or responsibilities. Effective MBO programs begin with a written statement of quantifiable objectives that the employee is to perform. In general, it is best to focus the program on three or four of the employee's most important responsibilities that can be quantified. Once those objectives are discussed and agreed to with the employee, they should be documented in writing, with a copy given to the employee and another filed with his or her personnel records. The advantage of this technique is that it minimizes the amount of time required to perform the evaluation at the end of the year and record new objectives for the following year. Finally, the costs of such incentive programs, if properly established and managed, may be accrued ratably as a salary expense each month instead of being charged to bonus expense at the end of the year when paid. In some client compensation agreements, this may properly increase the allowable amount of expense the firm may recover from its client, thus improving the firm's profitability.

- *Spot bonuses:* Spot bonuses are, as the name implies, paid on the spot with short notice in recognition of a job well done, generally to lower level staff. Imagine the euphoric feeling of having your supervisor walk up to you, tell you that you did a fantastic job on a particular assignment, and then hand you a check for $1,000. Although not a material amount, the fact that the firm's management recognized your performance and rewarded it with something tangible can be a powerful tool that builds loyalty and improves overall productivity.

MONTHLY SALARY FORECAST BY PERSON. To provide both a control point over the payroll process and the foundation for what is normally the largest cost element of the financial forecast, a detailed salary forecast should be prepared/updated each month. A salary forecast is a detailed spreadsheet (or database) that lists every employee, basic statistics about the person such as hire date, annual salary rate, date and amount of the last few salary adjustments, as well as a monthly spread of each individual's compensation, including all bonuses and other salary adjustments. Employees are listed within their respective departments, with a copy of the worksheet given to the department head so that he or she can plan compensation adjustments for the year and the resulting numbers can then be used to develop departmental budgets to the extent used within the firm.

Each month, as new professional staff are hired, employees leave, salaries are adjusted, bonus amounts are refined, and new positions are approved and removed, the salary plan is updated to reflect as many of these changes as possible. Many of these updates are recorded in some form of personnel action request form that the HR department uses to manage and control changes to the employee population. The salary forecast is one of the professional services firm's most important management tools and must always be maintained in a current state and reconciled against actual payroll each month by someone other than the one who administers payroll. This simple control is vital in a well-managed firm.

Steps management can take to safeguard its payroll include:

- *Reconcile actual payroll against the payroll forecast every month and, if possible, as part of the monthly close process.* Ensure all variances to plan, however small, are investigated fully and resolved to the satisfaction of at least one senior financial supervisor.
- *Segregatee duties.* Segregation of the payroll process itself from the person responsible for developing and reconciling the forecast can help to ensure that internal controls are properly balanced to safeguard the payroll account.
- *Ensure that staff responsible for payroll-related issues take vacations.* No single employee should have control over the payroll process. When a backup person periodically takes charge of the payroll process, anomalies are more likely to be uncovered than if the same person always takes responsibility for the process.

All Jobs Need Oversight

A large Midwestern professional services firm discovered that its trusted payroll clerk had been diverting payroll funds to his own account while he took a vacation after more than five years without doing so. During that five-plus-year span, the employee managed to divert over a quarter million dollars to his personal account. The employee was prosecuted and sentenced to jail for his actions.

Timesheets

The foundation for all cost accounting (and billing) in a professional services organization rests with the integrity of its time accounting system. Every employee in a professional services firm is responsible for completing his or her own timesheet, including the CEO and all other executives, even if their time is not charged directly to a client.

The actual amount of time worked on each client or project is recorded on some form of timesheet, whether it is a sheet of paper or direct input into an electronic system. General and administrative time is recorded in a separate account (or in detailed subaccounts) set up for that purpose, with all other client-related time charged to a specific client or project. For administrative personnel who otherwise would not need to complete a timesheet because their time is not charged directly to a client, use of the time accounting system to track vacation/paid time off (PTO) days used is generally the most efficient procedure because it avoids having to create a separate process/procedure to track such time.

Best practices call for all time reports to be reviewed and approved by the employee's immediate supervisor. Any modification to the original time reported should be made only by the employee himself or herself, with a supervisor's written approval, and documenting the reason for the adjustment. Time records may be used as evidence in legal proceedings, and the procedures surrounding their formation must be above reproach.

Vacation/Paid Time Off Tracking

Laws about PTO and vacation time vary from state to state, and local rules may supersede anything written here. However, as a general rule, employees earn vacation or PTO time ratably through the year and, in some cases, any unused time may be carried over into future years. To the extent that an employee leaves the firm with unused vacation/PTO time remaining, the firm is liable for payment of the value of that time based on a pro rata amount of the employee's base salary. In states that mandate unused time be carried over or paid to employees (as opposed to other so-called "use it or lose it" arrangements), the collective value of that time is a liability to the firm and is recorded in its financial statements at its gross value. Some firms elect to pay out the value of unused vacation time in cash at the end of the year to minimize risks from these regulations and to reduce its balance sheet liabilities. If not managed properly, vacation or PTO time can become a significant liability to the firm.

In general, a firm can best protect itself by having a written policy that clearly spells out the firm's vacation/PTO program and maintaining the records to support the program in strict conformance with that written policy.

Importance of Records

In California, a professional services firm was sued by its former controller for unused vacation time not paid by the firm on his last day of employment. The firm maintained a written policy that stated clearly that nobody could accrue more than 25 days of vacation time. While finalizing his separation paperwork, the controller claimed that he was owed 35 days of vacation pay. Neither the HR department nor the finance department maintained a current record of each employee's unused vacation time balance that should have been capped at the 25-day level in support of the policy.

Instead, when an employee left the firm, the HR department manually counted the number of vacation days the employee reported on a special vacation authorization form and subtracted that from the total number of days the person had earned during his or her employment period; if employees ended up being owed more than 25 days when they left the firm, they were paid 25 days in conformance with the written policy. On the surface, management believed this policy and practice to be prudent. However, in this case, the former controller maintained his own records, which showed that he was owed 35 days.

The Labor Commission ruled against the firm and ordered it to pay not only the additional 10 days of vacation but also an additional month's salary plus interest because the full payment was not made on the employee's last day of employment even though the ruling was issued a year after he left the firm. The Commission ruled against the firm primarily because the firm did not maintain a vacation tracking system that clearly computed the actual vacation balance at any point in time and mechanically capped that accrual amount once the limit was reached. In this case, the person who arguably should have been responsible for ensuring that proper records were kept by the firm was able to legally profit from his own mismanagement.

Accounting

Accounting in a professional services firm should be among the least complicated in our economy. The firm bills its clients for services rendered, the client pays the invoice, and the firm pays its employees, landlord, and other overhead suppliers. That's about as simple as can be expected in a business. However, once the firm begins to enter into complicated client compensation agreements, complex vendor contracts, and spend its client's money with the understanding it will be reimbursed for its outlays, the accounting issues and risks to the firm's financial statements begin to multiply.

Management of the financial records is the responsibility of not only the CFO but also the board, CEO, COO, department heads, managers, and supervisors. Each of those managers is responsible for ensuring the integrity of his or her respective area's revenues, expenses, assets, and liabilities. This section reviews key accounting issues of which the senior executive should be aware. Our discussion generally centers on corporate structures, but also are, for the most part, applicable to partnerships and Subchapter S corporations that may rely on the cash basis of accounting.

Fundamental Accounting Concepts

The most basic checkbook accounting system tracks total deposits and total withdrawals. If your deposits are greater than your withdrawals during a specific period of time, you made money, but were you profitable? Maybe yes and maybe no.

The answer to that question lies in the definition of the word *profit*. For hundreds of years, accountants have worked to develop a standard set of rules to follow to determine whether a firm was in fact profitable during a specific period of time. Those rules, which are continuously being refined over time, are referred to in the United States as *generally accepted accounting principles* (GAAP). These principles are a collection of theories, rules, pronouncements, and writings that have evolved over time to meet not only the general needs of investors and managers but also specific issues faced by each industry. Although most accounting principles have been published in any of a number of authoritative publications, no single list of all GAAP exists. Rather, they reflect the cumulative consensus of industry conventions, current writings, and pronouncements on any particular accounting issue.

GAAP, in their simplest form, adhere to a set of about a dozen foundational principles that guide the formation of all other rules. Today these principles are even more rigorously applied in the audit process in response to Sarbanes-Oxley and other related legislative and regulatory actions. Key principles that professional services firm executives should understand include:

- *Revenue realization:* Revenue should be recognized when it is *earned*, not necessarily when an agreement is made or cash is received.
- *Cost:* Assets and liabilities generally should be recorded at their historical cost and expensed during the period to which they pertain.
- *Matching:* The matching principle guides timing of the recognition of revenues and expenses and seeks to ensure that revenues are recognized in the same time period costs related thereto are expensed. For example,

if salaries are paid to work on consulting projects during a year, the net realizable value of those services should be, in general, recognized as revenue during that same period even though cash for those services may not be received until the subsequent year.

- *Objectivity:* Revenues, expenses, assets, and liabilities should be booked at values that can be established through objective evidence. Documentation supporting any value used in the accounting records should be maintained and made available to authorized third parties to verify (e.g., tax authorities, auditors, investors).

- *Consistency:* Financial statements should be prepared on a consistent basis from period to period using similar methodologies in order to yield meaningful comparisons among time periods.

- *Disclosure:* Financial statements should be complete in disclosing to investors and managers all pertinent information to ensure that the statements by themselves are not misleading. Explanatory notes normally are included with financial statements and are intended to supplement the numbers presented to ensure that the complete package presents fairly critical information to prevent the statements from being misleading. Such disclosures include: changes of accounting methods, summary of significant accounting policies, descriptions of lease and other long-term debt obligations, stock option plans, and significant subsequent events.

- *Materiality:* Accounting principles recognize that it may be impractical to account for all transactions in the same theoretically correct manner; thus, immaterial transactions do not necessarily need to be accounted for in a manner consistent with larger transactions. This is particularly true if the cost of doing so exceeds the value of reflecting the transaction in the theoretically correct manner. For example, a $500 chair may have a useful life of 10 years or more, but the cost of capitalizing that asset and depreciating it over 10 years would far outweigh the cost of expensing it in the period it was purchased.

- *Conservatism:* In preparing financial statements, many assumptions and estimates are made in order to present fairly the full financial position of the firm. When a reasonable basis exists for two or more different estimates or values to be used for a particular item in the financials, the one that shows the *least* favorable effect on the firm in the current period should be selected. By selecting the least favorable method, management enhances the quality of the earnings reported, which, over time, can strengthen both the firm's credibility and its relative financial position.

In summary, GAAP are the set of rules to be followed in the preparation of all financial statements, and these general principles form the basis of all other accounting concepts and practices. Other key concepts and issues of which professional firm executives should be aware include:

- *Cash versus accrual basis of accounting:* GAAP call for the financial records of an organization to be maintained using the accrual basis of accounting. Accrual accounting requires revenues to be recognized when earned and costs to be expensed when incurred, without regard to the time period in which cash is received or payment is made. Cash basis accounting, which does not follow the matching principle described earlier, recognizes revenue when cash is collected and expenses when they are paid in cash. Because the cash basis does not follow the matching principle, it is not GAAP; however, some form of it may be used in specific cases for income tax purposes, particularly in partnerships.

- *Book versus tax:* Financial statements prepared for management and investors normally are referred to as the official "books" of the firm. Although large firms should always follow GAAP and prepare financials using the accrual method, smaller firms that are not publicly traded may employ either the cash or accrual basis of accounting or a hybrid thereof that best suits its business purpose relative to the cost of adhering to a full accrual system. Use of the cash method frequently defers income taxes because revenue is not recognized until collected, and expenses, particularly personnel costs, are deducted when paid. However, when preparing tax returns, a specific set of rules set forth by federal, state, and local taxing authorities must be followed. When tax methods are used for "book" purposes in the preparation of financial statements, the firm will invariably report results different from those prepared using GAAP. Such differences include depreciation and amortization methods, limits on executive compensation, allowable meal expenses, pension expenses, and the tax calculation itself.

- *Revenue recognition:* As stated earlier, under GAAP, revenue should be recognized when it is earned, not when an agreement is made or cash is collected. Many of the accounting scandals that have occurred over time have involved material problems with the timing of revenue recognition. When in doubt, a good general rule of thumb to follow is to determine whether it would be likely that a judge would order your client to pay you solely based on the work performed through the closing date of the financials—without any further work being completed. To answer that question affirmatively, client compensation agreements need to be written carefully to ensure that revenue can be recognized in tandem with costs incurred (i.e., the matching principle).

The Matching Principle

A mid-size Western professional services firm that used the calendar year for its financial statements performed a variety of services for its client, normally using separate written agreements to summarize the scope of work and compensation terms. The client's fiscal year began on December 1 each year, and the annual letter agreements were written with that December 1 start date. For many years, the firm recognized the full 12-month value of the contract in December, in effect taking 12 months of revenue for only one month's work (payment was made quarterly over the year). During the remaining 11 months, the firm did not recognize any revenue even though it continued to employ staff to serve its client. This situation clearly conflicted with two accounting principles—revenue recognition and matching.

- *Expense recognition:* Expenses should be recognized in the financial statements during the period to which they pertain. In general, this means that costs should be expensed in the month in which an irrevocable commitment was made to secure the goods or services, unless it qualifies for special capitalization treatment. *Capital* items are generally assets that are material in value (e.g., over $1,000) and have a useful life in excess of one year. Unless a purchase meets both those criteria, in general, it should be expensed in the month incurred (not necessarily the month paid).

Value of Labor

The same professional services firm capitalized the significant cost of temporary help used to help prepare a proposal to a client during the fourth quarter. Financial managers in the firm based that decision on the argument that the cost was material and, under the matching principle, the value of that labor would benefit the firm for many years to come if it won the proposal. This treatment, which did not conform to GAAP because such costs should always be treated as period costs and expensed immediately, resulted in an overstatement of profit during the year the costs were incurred.

- *Audits versus reviews versus compilation services:* CPAs offer three types of accounting services: audits, reviews, and compilations. Audits are comprehensive reviews of a firm's financial statements and are required of publicly held companies. Other organizations may secure audits of their financials if they are in a position of public trust, have multiple investors, or if required by other creditors. Because of the amount of time involved in testing the firm's internal controls and a sufficient percentage of its transactions, audits are the most expensive of the three types of services, but yield the highest level of assurance that the financials conform to GAAP and that the system of internal controls is satisfactory to protect the assets of the organization.

  Reviews of financial statements are just that; the CPA conducts a relatively high-level review of the financial statements and reports his or her findings in a letter report but does not opine that the statements present fairly the financial position of the firm in accordance with GAAP as he or she would in an audit. Reviews, which in general are more appropriate for small closely held firms, consist of an analysis of the statements, noting the reason for significant variances and an overall test for reasonableness. In general, a review would not include a detailed study of internal controls nor would it involve extensive testing of account balances, but it does provide owners with a basic level of assurance that the financials generally conform to GAAP.

Compilations, as the name suggests, involve the CPA acting in the client role of assisting in the preparation, or compilation, of the financial statements themselves. Because the CPA essentially prepares the statements based on the balances presented in the books and does not perform testing of the underlying data, the CPA does not opine as to the fairness of the statements themselves because it would be a conflict in his or her attestation duties. In general, this is the least expensive service but also provides investors with the lowest level of assurance that the financials conform to GAAP. However, in a small, closely held firm, a compilation may be more than adequate to meet the needs of the owners.

In summary, executive management that supports the broad accounting principles and issues outlined earlier should, over time, build a credible financial foundation as well as strong fiscal footing that will add value to the firm.

Accounting Systems

Accounting systems for professional services firms come in all shapes and sizes. Industry-specific systems, tailored to the nuances of the general requirements of the industry, offer enhancements to facilitate management of financial and operational needs beyond that offered by relatively generic accounting packages such as QuickBooks, Turning Point, Peachtree, Everest, and Microsoft CRM. Although in recent years these programs have been tailored to specific industries such as professional services, in general, they are not scalable beyond a dozen or so accounting employees and may not meet the specific needs of your clients or business. However, these packages can, for a relatively modest investment, meet the basic needs of many professional services organizations until they reach a point where the accounting department exceeds a dozen employees.

After that point, more robust financial packages may be in order, such as Solomon IV, MAS90, MAS 200, Lawson, and Microsoft Great Plains, among many others. Before any system is selected, the firm should prepare a detailed list of its financial accounting, reporting, and budgeting needs, and then use that list to ensure that whatever package is selected will meet all essential and important requirements. Because the total cost to convert to a new system can be more significant than the upfront cost of the software itself, time and money is well spent at the outset in ensuring that a package is selected that best fits the firm's needs within the current budget.

Managing the Balance Sheet

Every executive maintains a certain style and set of managerial tools close at hand with which he or she governs. Because most people can relate to the concept of making a profit, they are reasonably comfortable with it and rely first and foremost on the profit and loss statement (P&L) as their guide to the firm's financial performance. However, a strong P&L may not necessarily mean that the firm is in a strong financial position because many potential liabilities may be hung up within certain balance sheet accounts. Concepts inherent in the balance sheet require a slightly more technical understanding of accounting, and many executives fail to review it in detail, or at all, and miss many of the key economic indicators of the firm's relative financial health.

When a balance sheet is well managed, the integrity of the P&L is maintained. Depending on the size of the organization, millions of dollars can be hung up or never recorded on the balance sheet that, if not addressed in a timely manner, can overwhelm otherwise well-managed firms. In this subsection, we address some of those key balance sheet components that should be watched carefully by every professional services firm executive.

ACCOUNTS RECEIVABLE (A/R).   A/R represents amounts billed/invoiced to clients or customers that have yet to be paid as of the closing date of the financial statements. At a minimum, executive review of three key items is critical: (1) the absolute change in balance from prior periods, (2) the change in balance relative to changes in revenue or other client billings, and (3) the aging of billings to specific clients. The objective of this review is to ensure that all accounts are collectible and that adequate reserves have been established to cover all potential bad debts. Further, and equally important, by conducting regular executive reviews of the aging, staff responsible for collecting invoices are more likely to be proactive in taking effective collection actions sooner if they know management is focused on this key metric. When comparing against prior periods, management should evaluate the change in balance from the prior month, beginning of year, and same period a year earlier to better understand the macrolevel elements responsible for the majority of the change. When reviewing the detailed aging report by client, all extraordinarily large balances should be evaluated as well as any balance over 30 days past due. Many companies today unilaterally extend payment to 45 days knowing that little, if any, adverse consequence is likely to occur by being two weeks past due. However, once a receivable extends beyond the 30-day past due column, some sort of problem most likely exists, such as:

- Invoice is sitting on the desk of someone who may have forgotten about it.

- Invoice was never received or is lost.
- Invoice was sent to wrong person and recipient fails to forward it to the responsible person.
- Invoice was sent to the right person, but that person is either on an extended leave or no longer works for the company.
- Invoice contains a billing error or questionable item on it, and client refuses to pay until the item in question is removed from the bill. Even though the majority of a bill is correct, some clients refuse to short pay the undisputed portion under the belief that it will give them more leverage in correcting the error or questionable item.
- Work was never authorized in writing, and a valid purchase order was never issued even though the client's representative verbally authorized the work.
- Client is maximizing their cash position.
- Client is in financial difficulty and may not be able to pay.

All of these items, arguably with the exception of the last issue that relates to a client's creditworthiness, can be managed effectively with phone calls, meetings, and constant follow-up. The longer an invoice remains unpaid, the higher the probability it may never be paid, thus it is critical to the firm's cash flow to constantly monitor its receivables position. Many of the actions a firm can take to collect amounts owed to it in a timely manner may be intuitive to seasoned professionals, but lower level staff responsible for those collection efforts may benefit from a list of clearly stated objectives and strategies, including many of those listed below. It is important to recognize that each firm is different with respect to the composition of its client base and the volume of invoices issued to each. Accordingly, the following list of collection efforts should be tailored to the appropriateness of each firm's situation:

- Maintain a consistent billing schedule so that clients know when to expect their invoices and, whenever appropriate, tailor that schedule to dovetail with a client's accounts payable process. Time the release of your invoices to best coincide with the client's internal accounts payable payment schedule, thus minimizing the amount of time your invoice is held within the client's payment process/system.
- When the promptness of payment has been a problem in the past for a particular client due to routing/approval issues, call the client a few days after mailing to ensure that invoices have been received.
- For larger clients, ensure that your billing and collection personnel know the client's internal payment procedures, who to contact, and the person(s) responsible for mechanically paying the bills. Development of a close relationship between these individuals can significantly improve the timing and collection of cash, thereby increasing interest income

and decreasing interest expense. If the client is not located nearby, schedule an economical flight for your billing and collection staff to make a trip to the client's offices at the outset of the relationship to establish a bond that will yield significant dividends (particularly if the client is large enough and an ongoing relationship is expected).

- Your CFO, controller or top financial executive should know senior financial executives at the client well enough to pick up the phone and discuss any payment delays.

- When practicable, hand deliver invoices that may have unusual items on them, and take a few minutes to sit down with the payment contact to ensure that they understand the issues surrounding the anomaly.

- When appropriate, call the client within 10 days of an invoice due date or before it will roll into another aging category to prompt payment, particularly before an invoice rolls into its first overdue category (e.g., 50 days from invoicing).

- When requested to send invoices directly to the main client, send a list of invoices to the finance contact so that he or she has a summary of invoices sent in order to help track the invoices internally. When requested to send invoices directly to the financial contact, send the summary to the main client to keep him or her aware as well.

- Understand the client's payment process, and ensure that if POs are required, all invoices are properly matched with their respective POs before mailing the invoices to avoid delays in processing.

- Set the pace of communication by returning all calls within an hour of a client's returning your call. By setting such a pace, you communicate to the client the importance of your efforts, that you will manage that process in a professional manner, and you inherently appreciate the same treatment from them.

- Correct billing errors quickly and err on the side of making immaterial concessions to clients when payment liability is less than crystal clear.

- Ensure that your staff has a clear understanding as to who holds primary responsibility for invoice collection (e.g., finance or another client-facing firm employee). Measure their performance and graph it. Review those graphs monthly and acknowledge and reward good collection results (as opposed to efforts), for example, less than 1 percent of all billings being past due.

Many unpaid invoices never should have been issued in the first place, and professional firm executives should investigate and understand fully the chain of events that resulted in an invoice being rejected for payment. In most cases, that investigation will uncover internal operational issues within the firm that executive management needs to address outside a financial context.

WORK IN PROGRESS. Work in Progress (WIP), sometimes referred to as unbilled expenses or work in process, reflects accumulated out-of-pocket expenses made on behalf of a client that have yet to be billed/invoiced. Some firms also may include the value of staff time at standard billing rates that include profit in WIP accounts. For expenses to be booked in these accounts, the firm should have a written agreement with the client that specifically states that such costs will be reimbursed. Without such an agreement, costs incurred on behalf of a client should be expensed during the period in which they were incurred, just like any other operating expense. Once WIP balances are billed, the balance of the WIP account is reduced by the amount of the invoice, which in turn increases the A/R balance.

The objective in managing WIP is to maintain the balance at or below zero. Successful firms are able to do this by entering into prebilling arrangements based on an estimate of expenses to be incurred where the client has agreed to pay the firm based on that signed estimate and then the firm uses that money to cover expenses it incurs on the client's behalf. In those cases, the firm would credit WIP for the amount billed and as expenses are incurred, debit the balance as it would under an arrears-based system. Until accumulated expenses exceed the amount prebilled, the balance in the account will be a net credit (negative). Individual arrangements may be negotiated based on the facts and circumstances with each client and project, but often the balance is reconciled at the end of the project and the difference is either billed to the client (if a debit) or paid back to the client (if a credit). The logic behind these types of prebilling arrangements is that the firm is not a bank, and it should not be responsible for borrowing material amounts of money to finance client initiatives. However, insignificant sums such as nominal travel-related expenses normally are financed through the firm's working capital.

Separate WIP accounts should be established for each client and, if the firm has undertaken more than one project for the client, separate accounts for each of the client's projects/jobs. As the number of open jobs increases, so does the risk that amounts included therein may not eventually be collectible from the client. Because these accounts are not part of the P&L, they traditionally receive little attention from senior management. When little attention is paid to these accounts, it is very easy for unbillable amounts to be charged to them instead of to operating expenses within the period incurred. Thus, the opportunity exists for expenses to be hidden and the firm's profits to be overstated. Executive management can take action to prevent this from occurring by:

- Reviewing an aging report for all jobs comprising WIP and investigating any unusual amount that has not been billed within 30 to 60 days of being booked. Obviously, the exact number of days and the amount of investigation required will vary by type of firm, but the point here is that any unusual amount should be resolved as soon as possible.

- Ensuring a signed client agreement is on file that specifically authorizes the firm to bill the client for the expenses being incurred *before* opening the job in the accounting system. However, it may not always be possible to do this as certain clients may need the firm to move more quickly than their own internal approval process will allow. In those cases, a second senior firm manager should authorize the opening of all such jobs in the accounting system to ensure proper visibility of the client approval issue.
- Conducting monthly reviews of a report of all open jobs that are not yet authorized in writing by the client and follow up on those that have been opened more than a month without the client's written approval.
- Having the CFO conduct a quarterly review of all aged WIP accounts, with appropriate follow-up on all unusual amounts.

FIXED ASSETS AND DEPRECIATION. Fixed assets in a professional services firm generally consist of leasehold improvements, furniture and fixtures, and information technology equipment. To qualify for capitalization treatment as a fixed asset, an item must be substantial in nature and have a useful life in excess of one year. Although there is no rule as to the specific dollar level that must be used, many firms today set a policy that the cutoff level for capitalization is $1,000 per item purchased since costs to account for items of lesser value most often outweigh the benefit of capitalization. Any item that is short-lived (less than one year) or has a unit cost less than $1,000 should be expensed, unless it is an inseparable part of a project costing more than $1,000 in total.

The capitalization dollar limit should be applied on a per unit basis and not the total invoice amount. For example, if two component parts are purchased for $700 each within the same order, they should be expensed even though the invoice total is above the $1,000 threshold for capital treatment. Similarly, this same general rule applies to software. If a perpetual license of a software program was purchased and the cost was under the $1,000 threshold, the purchase should be expensed. However, if multiple copies are purchased as part of a major project initiative (e.g., rollout of Windows 2000), the cost should be bundled and capitalized even though the per unit cost is below the threshold. Annual licenses should be expensed in the year purchased because their useful life does not extend beyond one year. Training costs normally are expensed unless bundled within the cost of the base asset. Purchases under these thresholds should be expensed in the month the cost is incurred.

Depreciation and amortization of these costs are based on estimated useful lives. With respect to leasehold improvements, their useful lives should never be longer than the base period remaining on the lease, excluding any option period. Computer-related equipment normally is depreciated over a three-year period as technological advances, coupled with wear and tear, particularly on portable units, leave any longer period misleading. Once useful lives of assets are established, that schedule should be followed consistently for all similar items until such time that it is proven that materially shorter or longer periods are appropriate to ensure consistency in applying the matching principle. All of the rules that a company decides to follow for capital should be thoroughly reviewed against IRS regulations by a qualified tax expert.

ACCRUED LIABILITIES. Accrued liabilities are obligations that the firm owes at the end of an accounting period that have yet to be paid. Under GAAP, the value of those obligations must be reflected in the financial statements of the firm even though they have not been paid. When closing the books each month, well-managed firms employ procedures to ensure that all material liabilities are properly included in the financial statements in conformance with GAAP. When firms are relatively small, owners and bookkeepers are able to track most every liability in their head and easily estimate them in the financials. But as the firm grows, processes and procedures must be utilized to formalize the tracking and expense estimation process.

For example, in a firm of 10 to 20 people, the bookkeeper can easily track the number of business trips made each month and estimate the cost of each based on the destination and duration of the trip. However, in a firm of 500 professionals, organized within multiple departments and perhaps offices, it is difficult enough to know all of the names of the staff much less track their whereabouts and travel expenses throughout the month.

In this example, one process that could be employed to track travel expenses is to compare reports from the travel agency against expense reports processed to determine the value of trips yet to be accounted for before closing the books each month. However, if the firm does not require employees to use a single travel service that can deliver such a report in a timely manner each month, alternative approval and tracking procedures must be established if travel is a material expense for the firm. As firms grow, the probability increases significantly that material liabilities will not be included in the financial statements, thereby overstating profits and balance sheet strength. To help ensure that the financials include all material liabilities, the firm can employ a variety of tracking and estimating procedures, including:

- *Purchase orders:* A firm that successfully implements a purchase order (PO) system to ensure all purchases are properly approved also creates an excellent tool to track its liabilities that remain unpaid at the end of the month. A simple compilation of outstanding POs, organized by expense type, can provide most of the information necessary to accrue unrecorded liabilities during the close process.

- *Account review by vendor:* A very useful procedure to employ during the close process is to review a spreadsheet for each account, which shows a line for each vendor and the amount of money that the firm paid that vendor each month during the year (and the prior year if possible), with a separate column for each month and some basic statistics such as the average monthly activity for each vendor. By arraying all this data on a single page for each account, it is very easy to track anomalies, which often lead to the discovery of unrecorded liabilities.

   For example, assume a firm's monthly telecommunication expenses were between $50,000 and $60,000, depending on usage patterns. In the current month, the trial balance for the firm showed that it incurred only $25,000. Under these circumstances, the financial staff should begin a search for unrecorded liabilities because the variance is material to the firm's financial statements. If their financial systems were designed to deliver a report by vendor and month for each account, the analyst can search for trends in spending to see which vendor was showing an abnormally low balance for the month. In this case, the analyst might have discovered that the long distance bill, which normally runs between $30,000 and $40,000 of the total, had been booked at only $15,000. A quick investigation might reveal that the invoice was still on the IT director's desk because the director had been on vacation since it arrived in the mail and thus it had not yet been processed. The accounting staff can then quickly accrue an amount approximately equal to the bill (if found) or the historical average spending level (if not found) until the bill is paid, thereby ensuring that the P&L reflects a full month's expenses and the balance sheet includes the value of unpaid liabilities.

   Even if a PO system is in place, it rarely is used to cover all expenses, particularly those that are recurring in nature such as utilities, so the method described earlier represents a parallel process that can be employed to help ensure that accurate financials are prepared.

- *Special valuation estimates:* Certain accounts, such as accrued vacation pay and pension expense, must be valued periodically based on specific assumptions and the resulting calculated liability. Executive management review of the assumptions underlying the calculations is important to ensure visibility as to the reasonableness of the resulting balances included in the financials. For example, in the case of accrued vacation pay in a state that mandates an employee cannot "lose it," the liability should reflect the total amount that would have to be paid to all employees as of the end of the accounting period if the firm were shut down on that day. Accordingly, the number should be based on the actual unused vacation balance for every employee as of that date multiplied by his or her respective salary. To do this, the firm must employ a vacation tracking system that computes the vacation days earned each period, the number of days taken, and the resulting balance as of the end of the period. Further, the system must adhere to any limits as to the total number of days an employee can accrue in accordance with local law and firm policy.

Revenue and Expense Recognition: The Games People Play

In spite of the wide application of GAAP and diligent efforts of the firm's auditors, many financial statements still are not presented fairly in accordance with GAAP. Often, this happens because managers who are paid based on achieving certain revenue or profit levels are motivated to deliver those results, often without a full understanding of GAAP, relying instead on their own understanding of the way it should be. Professional firm executives should be aware of the areas in which financial statements have been misstated in the past and keep alert for warnings that their statements may include anomalies that include:

- *Booking revenue based on a verbal agreement:* It is not unusual for sales/business development professionals to come to a verbal agreement with a client. When those agreements come at the end of a reporting period, they may consider that agreement to be worthy of booking as revenue since they "closed the deal" in their mind. Rarely could revenue be booked under GAAP if the agreement had not been reduced to writing and the firm had yet to do the work.

- *Booking revenue before it is earned:* On contracts that span multiple accounting periods, revenue may be recognized either at the end of the project or on a rational percentage of completion method. If the firm estimates its percentage of completion in an arbitrary manner, revenues may be manipulated to suit certain managers' desires but may not reflect accurately the actual amount of revenue earned.

- *Double booking intercompany revenues:* In some cases, different groups within a firm will work on a client project. In those cases, care must be taken to ensure that each group records only the revenue to which it is entitled. For example, if Team A has an annual contract to provide services to a client and the client needs work from Team B from within the firm and that work is to be paid from the annual fee paid to Team A, then Team A must be sure to reduce its normal contractual revenue by an amount agreed on with Team B so that the total revenue recognized by the firm is not overstated by the amount to be transferred to Team B. Once a firm has several hundred employees, it is very easy to misunderstand the billing arrangement and have Team B recognize revenue to which it is entitled while Team A continues to book its monthly fee in the same manner as it always has, thereby overstating revenues.

- *Failing to book intercompany expenses:* In some firms, particularly those with multiple offices and separate accounting teams for each, managing the intercompany chargeback process can be especially challenging. If one office invoices another office for goods or services rendered and the receiving office disagrees with the charge, it is unlikely that that office will record the expense. In the meantime, the office issuing the invoice will most likely have booked either revenue in the amount of the bill or an offset to expense in the same amount; either way, the consolidated financial statements of the firm will be overstated by the amount of the invoice until the receiving office books the expense. This exact situation resulted in a major, multinatinal advertising agency, having to restate its earnings in 2002 when it was discovered that numerous offices failed to record intercompany charges they disagreed with. The total effect of these transactions was to overstate the firms profits by more than $130 million over several years.

Monthly Close and Financial Statement Review

The monthly close is the process by which transactions booked during the month are summarized, accruals are made for items not yet booked, and financial statements are prepared for management review and analysis. This process is iterative and is intended to result in a summary of the firm's financial performance that presents fairly its financial position as of the close date. This doesn't necessarily mean that the numbers are precise, but rather fair, in that financial statements, by their very nature, include estimates as well as actual amounts. Accordingly, a well-managed close process includes:

- Preparation of the trial balance—first cut
- Search for unrecorded revenues
- Search for unrecorded liabilities/expenses
- Preparation of the second draft of the trial balance now reflecting accruals for revenues and expenses
- Analysis of the second draft trial balance, which includes a comparison of all variances from budget, last forecast, and prior year
- Ratio analysis of certain key metrics including gross margin and salary/compensation expenses as a percent of revenue
- Final adjustments resulting from those analyses and preparation of the final draft of the financial statements as well as processing of all journal entries necessary to close the books for the period

The key deliverable from this process is a comprehensive set of financial statements and graphs that provides senior management with a solid understanding of its past financial performance as well as a view of its pacing to achieve current and, to a certain extent, longer term financial projections. Many executives prefer to receive a bound package each month in which the following statements are included:

EXECUTIVE SUMMARY. Often referred to as a "dashboard," this one- to two-page narrative summarizes key results and variances, pointing out the important issues an executive should know in case he or she were not able to study any other report in this briefing package.

PROFIT AND LOSS STATEMENT. P&L should reflect performance for the month and year to date and be compared against budget, the last forecast (and any other quarterly forecast that the firm chooses to measure itself against), and the prior year. A variance analysis should accompany this statement that explains briefly the reason for any material variance (e.g., ±10 percent).

BALANCE SHEET. This summary-level balance sheet shows key line items within current assets and current liabilities as well as long-term assets and liabilities. The executive summary should discuss briefly the changes in A/R and WIP as well as current liabilities.

CASH FLOW STATEMENT. The cash flow statement reconciles the change in cash balance and details the major sources and uses of cash. Executives should pay particular attention to the first major subtotal that quantifies cash flows from operations because, over time, this is a key indicator of the firm's viability.

MONTHLY FORECAST. This forecast juxtaposes actual results for each month in the current year with projections for each of the remaining months of the year that, on a consolidated basis, will result in a forecast of the current fiscal year. This is arguably the most important report in the executive briefing package as it provides the best estimate as to the firm's performance for the year and it is from that forecast that key strategic decisions must be made.

ACCOUNTS RECEIVABLE AGING. This summary-level report of the aging of A/R by client shows total balances by each 30-day aging period. Firm management should be particularly concerned with any balance outstanding more than 30 days and should take personal action on balances more than 60 days past due.

METRICS. The firm's performance relative to others in its industry should be monitored and studied by senior management. To do that, certain ratios or metrics can be used as key barometers of the firm's financial health. Chapter 2 details metrics appropriate for professional services.

PROJECT/CLIENT COST ACCOUNTING. To hold individual project or client managers accountable for the resources they use, cost accounting reports should be reviewed and used to form the foundation for subsequent executive level project or client reviews.

TIMESHEET SUMMARIES. Executive management should review statistics on the performance of its most valuable and limited resource, its staff, and the number of hours available to charge to clients. Two reports are key to effective utilization of the firm's staff:

1. *Staff utilization:* These reports summarize the number and percentage of hours charged directly to clients and to nonchargeable administrative efforts. Staff utilization targets should be established during the annual planning process and measured each month (e.g., staff should have at least 90 percent of their time charged to clients; managers, 75 percent; senior managers, 65 percent; and partners, 50 percent).

2. *Missing timesheets:* Cost accounting in a professional services firm is meaningless unless all timesheets have been completed and incorporated into the cost accounting reports. If not well monitored by senior management, staff can fall behind in completing their timesheets as they focus their efforts on urgent client demands. If staff know that management receives a written report on who is late in completing their timesheets and follows up with firm support for their completion, the delinquency rate will be much lower than if such statistics were not publicized.

SUMMARY OF WRITE-OFFS/UNBILLABLE EXPENSES. This report provides executive management with a summary report of all amounts that the firm had to write off in the process of servicing each client, with a brief description of major items, to provide executive visibility with respect to mistakes and waste.

SUMMARY OF CAPITAL PROJECTS. This report summarizes the status of capital spending by listing each of the firm's approved capital projects, the amount approved, the amount spent or committed thus far, an estimate of additional funds required to complete the project, the new projected total (actual plus the estimate to complete), and the resulting variance from the original plan.

DAILY CASH RECEIPTS REPORT. Although not necessarily part of the monthly reporting package, it may be helpful to circulate a summary of cash receipts by client in order to keep executive management informed of each client's payment status, particularly if the executive will be meeting with the client. This procedure helps to avoid situations where a senior member of the firm might be in a meeting with a client and inquires about the status of its unpaid bills. If the bills have already been paid, the executive can avoid the embarrassment of having to apologize for referring to outdated information.

GRAPHING RESULTS.   Many executives in large and small firms alike prefer to review graphical renditions of their financial data to facilitate their review and understand results quickly in context of historical and relative trends. Key items that work well in graphical form include:

- *Revenue and expense graphs:* These combined line and bar charts show the firm's actual results as a bar and prior year, budget, and forecast data as lines for all key accounts including revenue, salaries, and other material overhead accounts.
- *Accounts receivable aging graphs:* To track the effectiveness of the A/R collection process, it is useful to graph the aggregate balance of amounts in each of the past due categories (e.g., all amounts over 60 days past due graphed over a two-year period).
- *Staff utilization:* Total hours charged, average rates, and utilization percentages over time can also be graphed.

Finance

There is a fine line between finance and accounting with many interdependencies and tasks being performed by the same personnel, particularly in smaller firms. A well-managed firm is one that has sufficient capital resources to weather storms, negotiate mutually beneficial deals with its clients, plan ahead, both in the short and long term, and invest in its future. In this section, we distinguish those aspects of financial management that pertain to financing, planning, forecasting, and managing a professional services firm.

Capital Structure

Privately owned professional services firms typically rely on a relatively simple capital structure consisting of owner's equity in the form of owner's capital and retained earnings, leasing of facilities and major capital equipment, and limited bank financing, typically used to help fund working capital requirements. To manage its limited capital resources well, the firm must work carefully with its vendors and clients to negotiate payment terms that minimize the firm's reliance on outside financing. Briefly, smart ways to reduce working capital requirements and improve the firm's cash flows include:

- *Invoice clients weekly or biweekly.* Although this may conflict with the client's normal accounts payable process, if you can negotiate this type of billing arrangement, you should be able to accelerate your cash flow significantly while reducing total credit exposure.

- *Collect A/R in a timely manner.* Dedicate resources, including senior management attention, to collect all receivables within 30 days of the invoice date, with significant managerial attention on any item over 60 days past due. Inclusion of late payment charges (e.g., interest) in contracts and invoices also may be helpful in accelerating payment.

- *Prebill.* As described earlier, in certain situations you may be able to negotiate terms with your clients to bill them based on an estimate of the actual costs incurred, particularly when the project is large or you will be procuring a significant amount of goods or services on their behalf.

- *Negotiate 45- to 60-day payment terms with vendors.* When establishing a relationship with a vendor, particularly if it is one that will be long term, try to negotiate terms that provide for payment within 60 days, but no less than 45 days, unless the vendor is willing to grant discounts for prompt payment. Most vendors will be delighted to work with customers who always pay their bills within 45 days without falling behind. Although the negotiations upfront are difficult, once the vendor agrees to it and you always make your payments on time, it will be a win/win situation for both parties. However, if you negotiate delayed payment terms and then fail to make payment within that period, your firm's credibility will be damaged and your ability to negotiate similar deals in the future will be impaired significantly. When asking for this concession, you must follow through and live up to your word.

Budgeting/Financial Planning

If you don't know where you are going, any road can take you there.

—Lewis Carroll, *Alice in Wonderland*

Financial planning is an art that combines historical facts with subjective assessments of future events to project the firm's financial performance in both the current fiscal year and in succeeding years. These future events could include winning new business, growing existing accounts, losing accounts/clients/projects, adjusting for staff compensation changes, as well as changes to all other cost components. The key in developing a forecast is to understand all assumptions, assess their probability of occurring, and quantify them in the form of both a high level long-range plan as well as a detailed annual operating budget. The remainder of this section addresses key planning process methodologies and issues.

LONG-RANGE PLANNING. Long-range planning is the process of setting forth certain goals and objectives for the firm to achieve over a specific period of time. Having a written plan enables management to unite behind a single set of objectives and provides a benchmark against which their performance can be measured. Every firm should have a long-range plan, regardless of size that meets the strategic or personal objectives of the owners. Managers of professional services firms are often so preoccupied with the state of their relationship with their current client base that they believe any sort of planning beyond the current quarter is meaningless and a waste of time. Often it is. However, smart managers acknowledge this paradox but still press forward in establishing goals for the firm.

Long-range plans (LRPs) may be developed for any period of time, normally for a minimum of 3 years, often 5, and sometimes 10 years. Obviously, the longer the term, the less reliable the plan will be, but any of these terms is useful in quantifying the goals of the senior leadership team. The key to the development of any plan is to quantify and document realistic targets for the firm, as well as the strategies the firm will employ to achieve its goals. By quantifying these goals and strategies in the form of projected financial statements, the firm will also quantify the order of magnitude of its cash requirements for working capital in future periods and thus can take action to secure that funding with as much lead time as possible with the best terms available. Once developed, the LRP should be updated each year as the initial step in the development of the annual budget. At a minimum, a well-developed LRP will include:

- Executive summary (outlining in narrative form the major issues facing the firm and its prospects for the future, the firm's goals, and its strategies for achieving those goals)
- Projected income statements (The LRP should be formatted in a way that maps exactly to the financial statements of the firm to facilitate reporting against the plan as well as provide a consistent foundation for historical trend analysis.)
- Projected balance sheets and cash flow statements
- Key metrics, such as:
  —Gross margins percentage
  —Revenue per employee
  —Operating margin percentage
  —Net income as a percentage of revenue
  —Staff cost as a percentage of revenue
  —Compound annual growth rate (CAGR) of revenue
  —CAGR for operating expenses, operating margin, and net income
  —Revenue conversion rate (change in revenue/change in operating margin) for each year
  —Current ratio
  —Debt to equity ratio

—Return on equity

—Return on assets

- Capital plan (outlining key capital needs required to support the plan, including the type and quantity of equipment needed and cost for new initiatives, as well as the long-range replacement plan for existing equipment)

ANNUAL PLANNING/BUDGETING. Once the LRP has been developed and approved, targets for the upcoming year's budget will result and, most importantly, they will have been developed in the context of long-range targets for the firm. Without achievement of the LRP's first-year targets, it is unlikely the firm will be able to achieve its long-term goals. But once those goals have been established at a high level, the firm can then prepare its detailed annual budget for the upcoming fiscal year.

Some firms prefer to avoid using the word *budget* because many managers assume that they can, and should, spend everything in their budget even though it may not be necessary, thus leading to higher expenses than absolutely needed. Instead, words such as *annual plan, forecast, outlook, first update,* or *latest update* may be used interchangeably to describe the firm's financial plan or budget for the upcoming or current fiscal year. Which term to use is a matter of management's personal preference, but they should recognize that most nonfinancial managers still will refer to the annual plan as their "budget," no matter what the firm calls it officially. The remainder of this chapter refers to the detailed annual plan as the "budget."

When establishing budgets to which line managers will be held responsible, it is critical that those managers participate actively in the development of their departments' detailed plans. If they do not actively participate in the process, the numbers they are given may be referred to as "the CFO's numbers," and it is less likely that the manager will buy into the numbers and ensure that his or her costs are managed accordingly. Situations where budget numbers are given to managers as their plan are often referred to as "top-down" budgeting. The best attribute of top-down budgeting is that the numbers for each department will add up to be consistent with the LRP for the firm. However, line managers are unlikely to buy into numbers they did not create, and, in many cases, those top-down plans will not reflect the line manager's knowledge of exactly what it will take to run his or her team—erring on the low side could endanger client relationships and the quality of work produced, while erring on the high side will result in unnecessarily high expenses.

"Bottoms up" budgeting is just the opposite of top-down budgeting. Line managers prepare budgets that they believe they need in order to achieve their objectives and then submit them to the finance department to consolidate. Without guidance from above, it is unlikely this first set of budgets will aggregate to numbers anywhere close to the LRP requirement for the firm. Once those initial drafts are submitted, it then may require an extraordinary amount of work to tailor them back to a level that the firm can afford, wasting valuable management time in the process as well as creating unnecessary ill will among stressed managers.

A practical solution for this situation is to take the best of both methods by providing managers with order of magnitude target numbers for their department that are based on the parameters set forth in the LRP and then let them develop their own detailed budgets using those targets as a guideline as to where their final numbers should come in. Targets can be as simple as two or three key numbers, including revenues from the clients for which they are responsible, total compensation costs, and other out-of-pocket costs. Having department heads or team leaders prepare their detailed budgets within those targets can provide them with a sense that their input is valued by senior management and, in the end, the firm normally ends up with a more feasible plan that will be supported by its key managers.

While setting targets, revenue should be broken down into its major components, including a revenue plan by client, average billing rates for each level of staff working on each client, total hours to be charged to each client, and overall staff utilization rate targets by staff level. When finalizing revenue targets, in general, it is better to develop realistic revenue estimates that are achievable except for certain major catastrophic events and not "push" them in the target setting process. By doing so, the firm is more likely to build its expense plan at a level that will be sustainable if relatively conservative revenue estimates hold true. When revenue projections are "pushed" to higher levels to motivate managers to improve overall performance, expenses are likely to be planned at a higher level and the firm will suffer if those more aggressive revenues fail to materialize.

In summary, a well-organized budgeting process will include many, if not all, of the following steps:

- Establish the firm's objectives first in the LRP process.
- Quantify the annual budget for the firm as a whole based on the numbers set forth in the LRP—for both revenue and expenses. The LRP and budget should be formatted in a way that maps exactly to the financial statements of the firm to facilitate monthly reporting against the plan as well as provide a consistent foundation for historical trend analysis.
- Break that budget down into departmental level targets that each manager can use to develop his or her own detailed budget. While setting those initial targets, be sure to allow sufficient funding at the "corporate" level to cover overruns from individual departments that may be necessary to finalize all budgets at the end of the process.
- Consolidate initial budget submissions from all departments to determine variances from original targets given as well as the overall plan for the firm in total. Determine, at a high level, how much needs to be cut from expenses (or added to revenue) to achieve LRP targets.
- CFO/senior financial management should conduct reviews of the first draft of the detailed departmental budgets to understand key issues and

reasons they might not be able to live within the target they were given. Finance then should provide department heads with specific guidance as to how much needs to be cut and offer suggestions as to the source of such changes (but be careful not to order certain cuts because that will undermine the main objective of this bottoms-up part of the overall process).

- Department heads will then revisit their plans and revise them if necessary.
- Department heads then make their budget presentation to the CEO/CFO for their review of final plan. To the extent necessary, it is at this point that the department head may negotiate resolutions to any significant variances with the CEO to ensure overall strategic goals of the firm are met.
- Once finalized with the CEO's approval, the CFO and CEO should present the budget to the board of directors for final approval. Final numbers then should be distributed to each responsible line manager to ensure that they are fully aware of the final numbers to which they will be held accountable. In an ideal world, all of the steps described would be completed before the commencement of the new fiscal year. However, in practice it is not unusual for final approval to slip into the first quarter of the new fiscal year. In those situations, it is important to ensure that line managers know how to operate while waiting for the budget to be approved, particularly the procedures required to procure "emergency" items.

MONTHLY FORECASTING—UPDATING THE ANNUAL BUDGET. Periodically, the annual budget should be updated to reflect changes in the firm's revenues and expenses that occur over time—both the actuals that have been booked year to date and the outlook for the remaining months of the year. Whether this occurs each month or each quarter is somewhat dependent on the volatility of the business, its capital reserves, and management's preference. Updating the budget/forecast monthly, although arguably more labor intensive, provides management with an economic outlook for the firm based on the most current information available. Further, by incorporating the forecasting process into the monthly managerial routine, it becomes more efficient and less of a "big project" that tends to paralyze finance and management staff when it is left to a quarterly update. For the remainder of this section, we presume that the outlook for the firm is prepared on a monthly basis and is referred to as the "forecast."

Development of the monthly forecast is much more of a bottoms-up exercise than is preparation of the annual budget because targets for the year already have been established and the validity of the forecast is highly dependent on line management's current assessment of their capacity to achieve their targets given actual performance year to date. When preparing the monthly forecast, consider the following:

- Set up a spreadsheet in a financial statement format that shows all major accounts listed in the same order shown in the firm's financial statements going down the page, with a separate column for each month going across the page. Array "actuals" for each month in the appropriate columns and budget (the first time the forecast is prepared) or the latest forecast for each line in the remaining months of the year. Adjustments then will be made to each of the future months based on the latest outlook for each account.

- Revenue forecasts must be made by client and must reflect input from each responsible client manager. When the compensation agreement with a particular client is complex, a supporting spreadsheet should be prepared and reviewed with the client manager. In some cases, particularly those where client managers are loathe to take responsibility for the forecast, it may be worthwhile for a senior financial person to sit down with the manager, review the calculations and, in particular, the underlying assumptions, and have the manager physically sign off that the projections are his or her best estimate based on knowledge at that point in time. Physical signatures, when managed properly, can dramatically improve the accuracy of the firm's forecast.

- Expenses can be forecasted based on direct input from line managers as well as a top-down analysis of the historical run rates for routine expenses (e.g., electricity costs vary from $10,000 to $20,000 per month, depending on the month—simply estimate future months based on historical expenses by month, with a subjective adjustment to reflect any percentage increase in rates or expected usage). In addition to a high-level review by account, financial managers may find it valuable to review the spreadsheet of expenses by vendor for each account to adjust for one-time anomalies past and future.

- Balance sheet and cash flow forecasts can be developed based on certain high-level assumptions. Most line items can be computed as a function of revenues or expenses, and the resulting impact on the firm's cash flows can thereby be estimated (e.g., A/R balance can be computed based on assumption for days sales outstanding). A financial model that integrates those assumptions into the workbook used to project the P&L forecast should be used so that whenever one assumption changes, its impact on all three financial statements will be computed automatically.

CAPITAL BUDGETING. The annual capital budget is a list of approved capital projects and approved dollar amounts. A capital project may consist of either a single item or a group of related purchases that have an expected life in excess of one year and exceed the firm's minimum dollar value threshold for capital treatment. For reporting purposes, capital is utilized when an irrevocable commitment is made—not when cash is paid or an invoice is prepared by a vendor or received by the firm.

In general, a capital budget for a given year covers that fiscal year only. For most firms, there is no automatic carryover of unused budget appropriations. If a project runs into a new fiscal year, the remaining spending requirement should be separately approved as part of the new fiscal year's budget.

When developing the capital budget, the same principles discussed earlier for long-range planning and annual budgeting apply, that is, set macrolevel targets within the context of the long-range plan and then have line managers develop the detailed plan within those parameters from the bottom up. In determining the actual level of capital spending for each department, the following metrics may be helpful in rationing scarce capital resources:

- Capital spending as a percent of projected revenue
- Capital spending per projected headcount

Approval of capital project requests should be based on an analysis of the project's economic rate of return as measured by an assessment of its net present value (NPV), internal rate of return (IRR), return on investment (ROI), and payback period. Since most capital expenditures in a professional services firm are related to information technology, many justifications for replacement of basic personal computing equipment will not yield a meaningful rate of return analysis. However, larger system development projects should be scrutinized carefully to understand fully not only the initial capital costs involved in developing the system, but also the ongoing operating and maintenance costs related thereto (i.e., the total cost of ownership).

Once a capital project is completed, a postanalysis should be prepared on all material projects to ensure assumptions that supported the original approval of the project in fact yielded benefits set forth in its economic justification analysis. In practice, completion of this important analysis often falls to the bottom of the priority list in favor of more urgent operational matters. By not insisting on an accounting for each significant project's actual returns, management bypasses an excellent opportunity to learn from actual experience that may be applied productively to future capital request analyses.

Cost Estimates: Prebilling Authorizations to Spend Your Client's Money

Prebilling your clients based on an estimate of future expenses can dramatically improve the firm's cash flows. Doing so for profit on the interest earned during the float period is not advised because it may significantly impair the relationship with your client. Rather, such billing arrangements should be utilized when the firm is asked to undertake projects for which significant out-of-pocket expenses are required on the client's behalf. In many cases, the firm may need to move quickly on behalf of the client, often before the client can physically forward the funds needed to cover the expenses. In these cases, the firm should establish and enforce a policy that requires written authorization from the client that a certain dollar level of funding has been approved for a specific purpose and that the client will pay that amount *before* any commitments are made on the client's behalf. If the firm fails to secure that written approval from the client and the client subsequently changes its mind about the project, the firm may be liable for all such expenses. Thus, it is critical that these authorizations, also referred to as "estimates," be signed before making any commitments. Finally, the firm should ensure that its written agreement with its client include clear language as to what types of expenses will be reimbursed to minimize any ambiguity that may occur as the assignment unfolds.

Project Cost Accounting

One of the most important factors executive management can monitor and control is the marginal cost of servicing its clients. The value of staff time is the most critical variable factor in determining the total cost of a project and thus must be rationed in accordance with expected revenues. In its simplest form, cost accounting in a professional services environment compares revenue from a client or project against the cost of providing labor, overhead, and nonreimbursed out-of-pocket expenses to the client. Each of those components is allocated as follows:

- *Revenue:* Revenues specifically related to the client and/or project are separately identified in the accounting system.
- *Direct labor:* In general, direct labor costs reflect the value of time spent on the client or project. Direct labor costs are computed by taking the number of hours recorded on each person's timesheet for each client and multiplying it by his or her per hour salary cost. In some cases, the salary cost may include a factor to cover related benefit costs as well. Further, some firms choose to use a standard hour factor other than 2,080 (52 weeks x 40 hours per week) as the denominator for the total number of hours in a year because not all of those hours will be chargeable due to vacations, sick time, and administrative time. The actual denominator used is subject to management discretion based on actual experience and may fall as low as 1,500.
- *Direct expenses:* Direct expenses include all out-of-pocket expenses incurred by the firm in conjunction with the client's assignment that are not reimbursable by the client.
- *Indirect labor overhead:* Rarely is every hour of every employee in a firm chargeable to clients. The value of the time not charged out to clients is normally assigned to an indirect labor overhead account. In simple form, it represents the salary cost of staff time spent on

administrative functions, including vacations and sick time. The total cost to the firm may be allocated among all of the firm's clients for cost accounting purposes in a number of different ways, the most popular of which is as a percentage of total direct labor or revenue.

- *Overhead:* All other costs not listed in the preceding category are grouped into an overhead category and are allocated among all the firm's clients in a manner similar to that described for indirect labor. Costs in this category include rent, taxes, insurance, office supplies, administrative travel and entertainment costs, utilities, IT expenses, and depreciation and amortization.

Once all costs have been allocated among the firm's clients and their respective projects, management can then evaluate historical performance in terms of each project's relative profitability. Doing so for the past is helpful, but using that information to evaluate and price future projects properly is vital to the firm's long-term existence. When evaluating the results of a cost accounting analysis, management must be conscious of the difference between marginal and fully loaded costs when determining if a project was good for, or well managed by, the firm.

Projects that show a loss on a fully loaded basis (i.e., with all labor, direct, and overhead costs included) may contribute positively to the firm's profit if revenue exceeded the marginal costs of performing the work. In the long run, a firm cannot remain profitable if all its projects are priced to cover only its variable or marginal costs, but in the short term, squeezing in a project that covers only its marginal labor and direct out-of-pocket costs may help increase the firm's overall profitability. In the very short term, even projects that do not cover their direct labor costs may still be profitable for the firm if it could not have avoided those labor costs otherwise because the staff that worked on the project was able to squeeze it into their normal schedule.

Client Compensation Contract Negotiations

Compensation contract negotiations with the firm's clients are one of the most critical factors in determining the firm's profitability. At the outset of a relationship, these negotiations form the foundation from which the firm will live, possibly for many years to come. Because of the long-term precedent-setting nature of these discussions, it is important that the firm negotiate the best terms possible. Often this may mean taking several months to negotiate in the case of a long-term relationship, but that upfront investment of time will, if done well, pay dividends for many years to come.

Most contracts include two main types of issues: financial and nonfinancial terms and conditions, including the scope of work. Getting the most favorable financial terms may not be best for the firm if it does not negotiate reasonable nonfinancial terms and conditions as well.

SETTING THE PRICE. Establishing the rate of compensation and the methodology to be used is the most basic and yet critical point in the negotiations. Regardless of compensation methodology used, the firm would be well advised to understand its projected costs by estimating the total number of hours by each type of staff required to complete the project. This analysis allows management to determine, a priori, the break point at which the firm will walk away from the negotiations. Compensation methodologies can take many forms and include:

- *Time and materials:* Under this type of agreement, the client agrees to pay the firm for its actual time and all out-of-pocket expenses. Normally, this type of arrangement is applicable to situations where the client recognizes that the scope of work is difficult to determine and thus it would not be fair to force the firm to commit to performance of a project that cannot be well defined. Sometimes the firm is able to negotiate prices to be at its "standard" hourly rates. Alternatively, rates for each level of staff may be negotiated separately. In some instances, the rate may be a simple flat rate irrespective of the level of staff (e.g., $250 per hour no matter who works on the project).

- *Fixed price:* In situations where the scope of work can be fairly well defined, it may be appropriate to negotiate a fixed price arrangement. This gives the client the comfort to know that the firm cannot exceed its budget without prior approval (assuming such a provision is negotiated), and it gives the firm a virtual guarantee of revenue. To negotiate this type of deal, the firm should first confirm the scope of work; then it can estimate the total number of hours required to complete the project and multiply those hours by standard hourly rates for each person or class of staff to participate in the project. It is important for the firm to recognize that it will be obligated to deliver the project in its totality even if it takes more time to complete than estimated originally, so it should ensure that it can in fact deliver within the time allotted; otherwise, it could face a significant financial liability.

- *Commissions:* Depending on the nature of the services to be rendered, it may be appropriate for the client to pay the firm as a percentage of the project's total costs. This method has been used for decades in the construction management and advertising industries. Depending on the volatility of a client's spending level, this method may provide potential for significantly increased or decreased revenues as compared to a labor-related cost-based approach.

- *Hybrids:* Depending on the specific circumstances of the client and the work assigned to the firm, some combination of the basic compensation plans mentioned earlier may be appropriate. For example, a time and materials contract may include a provision that the fees will not exceed a certain dollar level. A commission arrangement may guarantee the firm a certain minimum compensation level to ensure that it can provide the staff necessary to support the client's assignment. Also, the client may agree to add in a bonus component to the base compensation structure to incent the firm to achieve certain performance standards. In some cases, these standards may be objective and quantifiable whereas in other situations, criteria for payment may be more subjective.

- *When to reject a client's "best offer" for compensation:* In many cases, a client's budget will not be sufficient to cover the firm's initial cost estimate and the two sides must then negotiate a mutually beneficial fee. At some point, the firm must walk away from the assignment if the financial terms and conditions are not sufficient to meet its requirements to properly service the account. Determining that point is very difficult and involves both objective and subjective factors. Short-term projects that can be squeezed into the firm's normal schedule with its existing staff can, and probably should, be accepted if the revenue is anywhere near its direct labor cost, irrespective of its overhead component. Longer term or large-scale projects should be accepted as long as all of its direct and indirect costs, including overhead and a minimally acceptable profit margin, are covered. In some circumstances, there may be valid strategic reasons to accept an assignment that does not provide sufficient net income to the owners and may not even cover all fixed overhead allocations. Senior management should sign off on any client contract that is below the firm's guidelines for profitability. Acceptable profit margins vary by industry, but it is not unusual for professional services firm targets to exceed 15 percent to 20 percent of gross revenue.

NONFINANCIAL TERMS AND CONDITIONS.   As noted earlier, financial terms are only part of the equation in negotiating a mutually beneficial contract. Certain clients demand that the firm adhere to its "standard vendor agreement," ignoring the fact that most of those agreements are written to cover the procurement of materials, not services. Accordingly, the firm that recognizes that everything is negotiable will insist on the negotiation of a contract that is applicable to the type of work being performed. In many situations, the client's procurement team will try to accommodate that request, generally to a lesser rather than a greater extent. Whenever these types of contracts are being negotiated, the firm should employ legal counsel to ensure all terms and conditions are acceptable and understood. At a minimum, the firm's negotiations should address the following issues:

- *Liability and indemnification:* Terms of the contract should identify the circumstances under which each party will indemnify and defend the other party in the event a claim is made against it, often in the form of a lawsuit. The firm should be careful to insist that, in cases where the client will indemnify the firm, it will also defend it against any claim as well as indemnify a judgment or settlement. The difference here is that, without such a provision, legal costs to defend the firm against the claim remain with the firm and only the judgment, or settlement, is paid by the client. In many cases, legal costs to defend may be significant and may even exceed the amount being sought by the plaintiffs. By including the words "and defend" in the terms of the agreement, the firm can minimize its exposure against potential claims.

- *Timing of payment and billing frequency:* As noted earlier, the timing of payment from the client should be actively negotiated. Payment of fees ideally should coincide with the firm's payroll cycle (e.g., two times per month) and, when appropriate, include a provision that allows the firm to prebill certain types of approved estimated costs.

- *Notice period:* Every contract, by definition, has a termination date. The extent that the firm can negotiate a longer termination period while fees continue to accrue can provide a significant contribution to the firm's profits. For example, if the client is willing to initially offer the firm only 30 days' notice (which should always be required to be in writing) and the firm is able to extend that termination period to 90 days, it may have been able to improve its revenue and profit position by simply asking for and justifying a longer termination period. Many professionals are reluctant to ask for such terms, but many clients are willing to agree to them in exchange for other contract provisions.

- *Scope creep—getting paid for everything you do:* One of the most vulnerable areas of professional firm management is the definition of scope. Invariably, clients expect the firm to produce much more than the firm ever envisioned when originally accepting the assignment. Professionals, always eager to please their clients, may be reluctant to ask for additional funding if their actual work borders on a gray area not well defined in the original agreement. The key here is to ensure that the original agreement defines fully, and in objective terms to the extent possible, all the work that will (and in some cases won't) be performed. If well conceptualized and well written, it will be reasonably clear when the client has asked for something that is out of scope and thus entitles the firm to additional remuneration.

Administrative Efficiency

Administrative functions in professional services firms normally are not the focal point of executive management attention, nor should they be. Finance, accounting, human resources, IT, and facility management, the so-called "back office" functions when well managed, require little executive management attention. However, when back office functions receive little oversight, they may become suspect if their accomplishments are not well publicized. To ensure that such functions are productive and their results easily understood by executive management, tasks should be quantifiable and results measurable. If every staff person's position were organized in such a way that at least one major function is quantifiable, workload and results could be charted and graphed to portray an accurate picture of the relative efficiency of each department over time. Examples of quantifiable functions include:

- *Accounts receivable:* Total dollars past due by month
- *Billing:* Number of bills issued each month and on-time payment statistics
- *Cash collection:* Total cash collected
- *Accounts payable:* Number of invoices processed (also percentage processed without error); cash discounts achieved
- *Financial planning:* Percentage variance of actuals versus forecasts by quarter
- *Human resources:* Number of candidates interviewed versus positions accepted; number of separations processed; annual staff turnover rate
- *IT:* Number of help desk calls taken; average time to resolve a call
- *Facilities management:* Electricity consumption per headcount; maintenance costs per square foot and per headcount

By monitoring these key activities and rewarding excellent results with spot bonuses or other types of recognition, the firm can secure better than average productivity. However, in spite of these measures, as the firm grows, at some point additional administrative staff will be required. When to add that staff is a key question.

As a rule of thumb, a new position should be added once existing staff routinely is required to work more than 50 hours per week. With respect to financial staff, they normally may work 50-hour weeks during the monthly close and fall back to an average at or just slightly above 40 hours in other weeks. However, if existing staff are unable to close the books in five or fewer working days, either are understaffed or their procedures are insufficient. If it is determined that their procedures are adequate (which the graphs noted earlier may help illustrate), additional staff may in fact be needed.

Mergers and Acquisition: Time to Revisit Policies and Procedures

When a firm acquires another firm or it is acquired itself, this action provides management with an excellent opportunity to take a fresh look at policies and procedures at both firms and, when appropriate, take the best from each or simply upgrade them to meet identified needs. For example, if cash flow is insufficient to meet the combined firm's objectives, it may use the announcement of the merger as an opportunity to implement a semimonthly billing process. Similarly, treasury functions can be merged, including the implementation of credit limits for each client. Human resource functions can be consolidated and redundancies eliminated. Merger transition plans should also set forth the goals for the IT team and plans for integrating networks and eliminate unnecessary redundancies. As difficult as it may be to integrate two firms, if done well, clients from both firms may benefit from reduced administrative costs and improved systems.

Summary

In this chapter, we have discussed a wide range of issues that professional firm executives need to understand in order to provide their firm with sound fiscal leadership. HR functions are an integral component of the firm's financial management as the majority of costs are tied to compensation and related perquisites. Because so many of those HR issues involve interpretation of complex legal issues, HR professionals should be capable of recognizing when to utilize competent legal counsel and have the budgetary support to tap those resources as needed throughout the year. Employee performance should be evaluated in writing at least once per year and excellent results rewarded within an equitable market-based compensation system.

Executive management of the firm must ensure that GAAP are enforced, particularly by being conservative in its revenue and expense recognition policies. Long-range planning should be well documented and form the foundation for the annual budgeting process. Annual revenue, expense, and capital budgets that are developed from the bottom up by line managers within a set of high-level targets established in the long-range planning process are more likely to be effective than those set from the top down. Monthly updating of all budgets and forecasts helps to keep executive management well informed as to the fiscal health of the firm. A monthly briefing book, or executive reporting package, that includes historical financial statements, forecasts, and trend reports can expedite the review process and highlight key managerial issues. Finally, contract negotiations with both clients and vendors should focus on key terms and conditions as well as pricing. The masterful execution of these component principles is critical to a well-managed professional services organization.

16

Purchasing, Procurement, Vendor, and Asset Management

JOHN BASCHAB AND JON PIOT

People who work together will win, whether it be against complex football defenses or the problems of modern society.

—Vince Lombardi[1]

If, after the first twenty minutes, you don't know who the sucker at the table is, it's you.

—Unknown

This chapter outlines management practices for ensuring that the professional services firm selects and manages outside vendors in a manner that delivers the most value to the company in exchange for consideration paid to the vendors, all the while working in a partnership with the vendor to further the aims of both the company and the vendor.

In this chapter, we emphasize the importance of properly managing vendors and provide techniques for monitoring and assessing vendor performance. We cover the typical vendor types found in a professional services organization, how to set thresholds for prioritizing vendors that need scrutiny, and how to establish and assign the vendor management role within the firm. We also discuss how to take control of vendor relationships, particularly inherited ones, how and when to recompete vendor contracts, and provide guidance to the vendor manager on working with vendors in turmoil or financial trouble. The topics of vendor management, purchasing and procurement practices, and asset management are linked in most firms, and are covered here as well.

Why This Topic Is Important

Almost without exception, services firms must rely on a variety of vendors to accomplish their objectives. Outside vendors provide many of the functions outlined in this book, including legal, banking, information technology, telecommunications, marketing, public relations, and real estate services, as well as more mundane items such as office supplies, catering, and facilities. Because professional services providers such as lawyers, consultants, real estate agents, or doctors get little training in managing outside partners, including experience measuring service levels, selecting service providers, and negotiating pricing and terms, many professional services firms fall short in vendor management. This can be highly damaging to the firm, not only because of the reliance on vendors for such a wide variety of functions, but also because of the high expenditures on outside vendors. In aggregate, outside providers generally comprise the largest expenditure of a professional services firm besides labor costs. Failure to manage these expenditures and relationships suitably can be devastating to the firm.

A cooperative and amicable relationship is necessary to extract the most value out of vendor relationships, while applying regular management practices to ensure that the vendor is performing up to expectation and committed service levels. This can be challenging because of the periodic incongruent incentives of the firm and the vendor sales and delivery teams, and the wide variety of vendors that must be managed. Often, firms cover shortfalls in vendor performance by adding staff or other expenditures rather than confronting nonperforming vendors and instituting standard vendor management processes and procedures. Firm managers and staff must work to be taken seriously by vendors and to hold nonperformers accountable.

Vendors, like most businesses, pay the most attention to the customers who provide their largest revenue stream or the customers who are most vocal. Thus, smaller companies must learn to aggressively communicate their needs, requirements, and timelines to vendors and, for extremely critical vendors, to work together with other small customers to influence vendor policies and priorities. In addition, larger companies with significant vendor spending should ensure that the vendor is reflecting their needs appropriately in product or service development priorities, rather than submitting to a vocal minority. While influencing vendor priorities is important for professional services firms, vendor managers should prioritize their vendor influence efforts based on their individual situations. Paying attention to finding the best labor lawyers available and ensuring their proper performance is much more critical to a staffing services firm than, for example, ensuring that the office supplies are always delivered on time. Most professional services firms with sizable spending on vendors should assign an individual (or group of individuals) to take responsibility for managing the vendor relationships, a role that we refer to throughout this chapter as the *vendor manager.*

Topics discussed in this chapter include:

- How to work effectively with vendors to ensure that the full value of investments in products and services of outside providers can be achieved
- How to build a mutually beneficial partnership with a vendor
- The importance of establishing the vendor management function
- How to take control of vendor relationships
- How to set thresholds for determining which vendors to focus on
- The distinction between types of vendor contracts
- Important steps in establishing new vendor relationships
- Methods for establishing and managing vendor performance and service levels
- Gaining value and leverage by working with the vendor's other customers
- When and how to recompete vendor contracts
- Approaches for managing vendors experiencing business difficulties
- How and when to select vendors, including requests for proposal (RFPs) and contract negotiation

We have devoted specific chapters elsewhere in this book to the selection and management of particularly critical vendors for professional services firms, including providers of legal, information technology, real estate, and finance/accounting services.

Vendors as Partners

The most effective vendor relationships are the ones in which the vendor and customer build a close partnership. However, this relationship can be difficult to achieve. Vendors have a different set of incentives and priorities than the vendor manager, and finding ways to work to mutual benefit takes effort and willingness on both sides to accomplish. Most often, the proper tenor for the relationship is set during the selection or bidding process, which is covered at the end of this chapter. Exhibit 16.1 shows the typical vendor types engaged to provide products or services to professional services firms.

Legal Services
Banking and financial services
Tax and audit services
Information technology hardware/software and services
Real estate
Marketing and public relations
Telecommunications
Office supplies
Printing
Staffing/recruiting
Cleaning services
Catering/food service

**Exhibit 16.1   Categories of Vendors for
Professional Services Firms**

There are a number of ways for professional services firms and vendors to work in partnership to mutual benefit. Working with clients closely, the vendor can provide a wide range of benefits to the customer, including:

- New services or product features customized for the customer
- Free product updates in advance of official product release
- Free off-the-record consultation or advice on minor matters
- Telegraphing major company announcements in advance of official notification, where appropriate
- Concessions on pricing for future product or service purchases
- Discounts on maintenance, training, or other ancillary services
- After-hours or emergency support or availability
- Information on undocumented product features or provision of special services reserved for best customers
- Access to vendor internal resources for consultation
- Introductions to other clients with similar requirements or needs for brainstorming or consultation on specific problems

In return, the customer might provide:

- Breaks on minor delivery shortfalls by the vendor
- Continued business without any unnecessary or onerous recompetes
- Detailed feedback for improving the service or product
- Press releases and references for vendor's sales prospects
- Specific letters of recommendation for vendor's sales calls
- Potential sales leads for vendor with companies in same industry or contacts from other professional relationships

Typically, these items are provided to the opposite party on a best-efforts basis. The items proffered in a partnership are of relatively low cost to the partner providing them but can be of tremendous value to the other party. This type of relationship will significantly increase the value of the contract without requiring arm's length contract addendums whose cost and difficulty of enforcement often destroys much of the potential value and usefulness.

The longer the relationship exists, the higher the potential benefits for both parties. For the vendor, sales costs are virtually eliminated, and over time, the cost to serve generally declines due to experience effects, resulting in long-term gross margin improvement. For the customer, the vendor's cost reductions are typically shared with the customer via pricing discounts, additional no-charge services, and higher service levels or speed. The customer's cost to manage the vendor also declines, and "learning curve" costs from new vendor entrants are eliminated. Finally, the customer benefits from a vendor whose staff understands the business in intimate detail and can provide customer-specific solutions.

An important benefit of participating in a close relationship with a vendor is the opportunity to influence the vendor's product or service development process. This is particularly true for vendors that provide a critical product to a professional services firm, such as a software application for tracking projects and time provided to a business consulting firm or a candidate background screening process for a staffing services firm. Successful vendors invest immense resources in developing their current and future products and services. Many product vendors have an income stream emanating from maintenance contracts to devote to product enhancements and new features. By partnering closely with vendors and providing input to the prioritization process for new feature or capability development, the client firm can leverage vendor research and development (R&D) investment amounts far in excess of the amounts it could dedicate to internal development. The client then steers the product direction to its ultimate benefit.

One software application vendor we worked with invited 25 key customers to their corporate headquarters twice a year for product development and demonstration sessions. The vendor product manager would create an inventory of all enhancement requests, interface suggestions, and functionality recommendations from the biannual two-day affair, and work with the internal development staff to incorporate as many of the ideas as were possible and appropriate. Although the software vendor had thousands of clients and an annual users' conference, these 25 clients drove a disproportionate amount of software enhancements and greatly benefited from partnering with the vendor.

An important fact to consider in building a partnership is that some vendors may wish to partner initially; however, the partnership can rapidly turn negative if problems arise. A variety of events affecting the vendor or the client can cause the partnership to go awry, including turnover of key personnel, a merger/acquisition, a change in strategic focus, financial difficulties, high growth, new requirements, or even the acquisition of another customer who is providing much greater benefits and monopolizing the vendor's attention and resources. In these cases, it is best to reevaluate the value of the partnership to ensure that the client organization continues to receive the expected partnership benefits. It is also important to periodically reevaluate each vendor to ensure that the relationship is satisfactory for both parties. This process is described later in the chapter.

In the end, the customer is paying for the product and/or services. This should naturally put the customer in the position of most influence and provide final control of the terms of the relationship. When money has changed hands, vendors have a business obligation to discharge their contractual responsibilities. Often, vendors try to take advantage of the relationship if the customer is unaware, too busy, or inexperienced in dealing with vendors. Savvy customers know that they are, ultimately, the boss in any vendor relationship. Given a choice between a partnership and an adversarial relationship, all parties prefer the former. However, if a partnership is difficult to achieve, the vendor manager should be certain that his or her company's needs are met by the vendor even if aggressive, confrontational action is required.

Vendor Management Role

The vendor management function is vital to capture the benefits of vendor partnerships as discussed in the chapter. The vendor manager, as well as the firm professionals who directly use the vendor services, should be involved in the selection and ongoing management of key vendors. Other functions of the vendor management role should be delegated to an administrative resource. Tasks performed by the vendor manager include:

- Negotiate, execute, file, and maintain all contracts
- Assist firm managers in processing new contracts

- Provide reports on vendor performance and contract status to senior management
- Coordinate activities between internal teams and vendors
- Define and enforce processes and procedures for vendor management
- Assist with RFP and vendor selection administrative process
- Develop a standard approach to deal with each type of vendor used by the firm
- Establish and monitor service levels required, by individual vendor
- Execute internal vendor quality and satisfaction surveys
- Track and report upcoming vendor milestone dates
- Take appropriate action based on the results of vendor scorecards and surveys
- Maintain records related to the successful delivery of products or services
- Report progress on fixed bid contracts for services, for example, qualitative progress, percent complete versus percent billed
- Analyze vendor pricing compared to industry averages
- Collect and distribute service level reports from vendors

The tendency in most professional services firms is to ignore the vendor management function and by default decentralize all vendor activities. In fact, often the vendor management role goes to the individual who misses the meeting where the responsibility was assigned. However, the organization benefits through reduced costs, reduced risk, and more effective communication between the company and its vendors by centralizing the function. The vendor management role helps ensure that the company drives the relationship versus being driven.

Assigning a Vendor Manager

The first task is to assign the vendor management role. This person (or committee) will be responsible for the tasks previously described. The vendor manager will also be integral to the audit/cleanup process. In larger firms where a specific manager exists for internal functions such as IT or office management, the vendors used by that department should also be managed by that department. In these cases, the overall firm vendor manager function should help keep track of the department-specific vendors. This work includes ensuring that the department heads are following the guidelines in this chapter and that vendor contracts and pricing are being reviewed by senior management. The vendor manager in many ways functions as the company purchasing agent. A variety of seminars, classes, and organizations are available to provide training and expertise on purchasing and vendor management. The U.S. Bureau of Labor Statistics has this to say about training, certification, and continuing education for purchasing and vendor managers:

> Regardless of industry, continuing education is essential for advancement. Many purchasers participate in seminars offered by professional societies and take college courses in supply management. Professional certification is becoming increasingly important, especially for those just entering the occupation.
>
> In private industry, recognized marks of experience and professional competence are the Accredited Purchasing Practitioner (APP) and Certified Purchasing Manager (CPM) designations, conferred by the Institute for Supply Management, and the Certified Purchasing Professional (CPP) and Certified Professional Purchasing Manager (CPPM) designations, conferred by the American Purchasing Society. In Federal, State, and local government, the indications of professional competence are Certified Professional Public Buyer (CPPB) and Certified Public Purchasing Officer (CPPO), conferred by the National Institute of Governmental Purchasing. Most of these certifications are awarded only after work-related experience and education requirements are met, and written or oral exams are successfully completed.[2]

The National Association of Purchasing Management (now known as the Institute for Supply-chain Management; NAPM/ISM) has information on certifications available. The APP certification requires passing two exams as well as two years of experience (or one year of experience and an associate's degree). The CPM certification requires four exams and five years of experience (or three years and a four-year degree from an accredited institution). The details on certifications available can be found at the NAPM/ISM and American Purchasing Society web sites. A full list of related resources is found at the end of this chapter.

Taking Control of Vendor Management

There is a well-defined process for taking control of vendor management. This process is appropriate for companies with a track record of failed vendor relationships, a variety of unruly vendors managed by disparate groups or individuals across the firm, or simply a new vendor management process. Most professional services firm managers or partners at some point inherit a variety of disparate vendor relationships in various stages of health and efficacy. Without gaining control of these relationships, service and spending problems can quickly arise from malicious vendors in poor partnerships who are looking to take advantage of the chaos or changes at customer organizations or from benign vendors who are simply paying attention to the customers that work the hardest to manage the relationship. Inattentive vendors can wreak havoc on a firm relying on their services; a period of business change or ongoing weak management of the function can cause vendor and client agendas to diverge, and the relationships deserve special attention and tight performance management during these times. Exhibit 16.2 depicts the vendor audit/cleanup process.

The first task is to assign a vendor manager, or vendor management committee, as described in the previous section. Once this has been completed, the second task is to identify all current vendor relationships. These may exist in various departments, business units, functional units, and geographies. For every vendor relationship identified, all related legal, financial, and operational documents should be collected in a single repository. The vendor manager should review each contract and make particular notes about service level commitments, prices, maintenance agreements, evaluation/reporting procedures, and start and end dates of the agreement.

It is often difficult to locate the contracts for all service vendors in a professional services firm. The contracts may have been signed by a manager who has since departed and the original documentation lost, particularly for long-standing arrangements. A contract may be filed in the purchasing department, legal department, or human resources department; in larger organizations, the purchasing manager should keep a copy of the contract, as well as the manager of the functional area directly involved with the vendor (e.g., IT department, human resources department). Failing the location of an internal copy, the vendor manager can request a contract copy from the vendor. As a last resort, the vendor manager and vendor can renegotiate a contract to govern the ongoing relationship without necessarily changing the

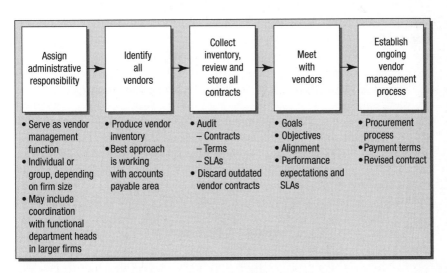

Exhibit 16.2 Vendor Audit/Clean-Up Process

original terms. Often, long-standing contracts will have expired without re-newal, while the firm continues to use the service or product. These situations create an ideal opportunity for the vendor manager to renegotiate the terms of the agreement.

As a next step, the vendor manager should meet individually with each vendor (if possible depending on the number of vendors; otherwise, select a vendor audit team to assist) to gain a deeper understanding about the vendor, its organization, products and services, history of the vendor-client relationship, contractual obligations, recent events, and to resolve any outstanding issues. This vendor checkup provides a clear view on which vendors are true partners with the firm and which vendors simply have arm's length relationships for specified products or services.

Finally, the vendor manager should rapidly implement vendor performance management processes to manage the vendor relationships based on the self-reporting and audit cycles described in this chapter. This rapidly drives out underperforming vendors and ensures that fees paid to vendors are providing the company the maximum possible return.

Beginning New Vendor Relationships

Getting off to a positive start with new vendors is critical to the success of projects and to the overall productivity of the firm. The vendor manager should develop an on-boarding checklist and one-page information document for new vendors. This document includes information about invoicing, addresses, key personnel, and so on that will ensure that the vendor and organization are ready to work together smoothly. One process we have seen work well is a "readiness" check performed by the vendor manager one week before the vendor comes onsite. This checklist, which is signed off by all involved internal parties, ensures that the internal team is freed and ready to begin work with the vendor on the agreed-to start date, the dependent products and staff are ready to go, the work space is ready, the contract is signed and filed, and the vendor has reconfirmed the start date. If any of the items are not checked, the date is postponed. A process such as this ensures that no vendor shows up before the company is ready. This process saves critical downtime for both internal teams and vendor teams. It helps to keep vendor costs down—in the spirit of the partnership and, ideally, benefiting the company in the long term.

Vendor Contracts

A solid legal agreement should always form the foundation of any vendor relationship. While contract negotiations can be painful, contracts often outlive the tenure of the individuals negotiating the terms on either side. We have seen many contract negotiations fall short of the proper due diligence because the individuals involved had personal relationships or ample reason to trust one another. After these individuals have left their respective firms, their successors are left to interpret what may have been agreed on but not documented, producing contention and sometimes resulting in a termination of the agreement entirely. Therefore, it is in both companies' best interests to clearly document their agreement for working together.

In every case, the contract should explicitly set forth the terms that govern the relationship and define each party's responsibilities to the other in unambiguous detail. Further, the contracts for many vendor relationships, such as IT services or software, are most often turgid, impenetrable, and complex. For purchases of any material significance, we recommend engaging attorneys or company legal counsel with experience negotiating contractual terms for large purchases or long-term, complex agreements. These professionals have seen the outcomes from poorly negotiated contracts and know which contract terms are of material interest, and they can identify the sometimes hidden, but significant, clauses in a contract. Chapter 19 contains information on entering into contractual agreements, as well as obtaining legal counsel.

We have seen that the outcome of poor contract negotiations is often detrimental to the client company, who is generally the loser in interpreting ambiguities in the contract. In one case, a product vendor found enough room for interpretation to ensure that the new features in its product be considered a "new product" and required new product use licenses to be purchased by the end client. The new features to be added should have most likely been included in a typical upgrade to the product and, therefore, provided free to all clients paying maintenance fees.

Negotiating the best terms for a vendor contract requires understanding the potential organization requirements not only today, but also in the future. In two other examples, clients have made smart decisions on possible future business actions and protected their rights contractually. In the first case, we assisted a mid-size firm in the spinoff of a subsidiary unit. Fortunately, some forward-thinking negotiator had crafted terms that allowed the licenses for the application system used to run the business to be split between entities and reassigned in the case of such a transaction. This point was at variance to the standard contract from the application vendor and would have likely resulted in significant new license fees payable to the vendor had it not been contracted in advance.

In another case, a firm decided to outsource a portion of its operations to a third party. The vendor that supplied IT systems to the firm was also in the business of outsourcing. The vendor protested vigorously against a third party operating its system, arguing an invasion of its intellectual capital rights and asserting that its licenses could not be reassigned to third parties.

Again, a prescient negotiator for the firm had included the irrevocable and perpetual right to assign the application license to any third-party vendor chosen as an outsourcing partner. Certainly, there was no consideration of outsourcing the technology department at the time of the contract signing, but the negotiation team made sure that all options were covered.

Several important contract terms for vendor services and products are described in the following list. Because of the broad number and types of vendors used by a typical professional services firm, the specific terms will vary from contract to contract; therefore, this list should be treated as merely a starter set for any vendor negotiation conversations:

- *Insurance:* In many cases, clients taking on significant business risk require the vendor to maintain malpractice insurance (often called *errors and omissions* [E&O] coverage). In any case, critical vendors should be required to provide proof of general and professional liability coverage. Additionally, the firm may choose to be specifically named as an additional insured under the vendor policy.

- *Completion sign-off:* Acceptance of services or delivery of the services, particularly for large projects or implementations of critical products, is an important negotiating point. Typically, the vendor chooses the first possible logical point in a project or service implementation to require payment. The risk to the firm is that the product may not perform as promised or the services are not completed as agreed. To reduce the risk that the company will be obligated to pay regardless of performance, specific acceptance criteria should be constructed. For services, detail the specific deliverables required for satisfactory performance of the contract, the requirements for the deliverable, quality metrics for acceptance, and required delivery dates and milestones.

- *Assignment rights:* Product vendors generally prefer to restrict the assignment privileges of the customer. However, this practice is not in the customer's best interest. To allow for company reorganizations and potential merger and acquisition activity, the customer should include a provision to assign rights and transfer the contract in the event of ownership changes, reorganizations, and to subsidiaries and minority interest affiliates.

- *Product license and maintenance fees:* The best case in purchasing product licenses is to obtain a perpetual, fully paid-up license that requires no annual license or maintenance fee. However, many product companies charge maintenance fees and aren't willing to support or provide upgrades unless an annual maintenance fee is paid. Set the future maintenance fees before the contract is signed; otherwise, the vendor will gain tremendous leverage during future fee negotiations. Maintenance fees should begin only when the product or service passes the acceptance criteria, not when actually delivered.

- *Nonsolicitation clauses:* It is in the interest of both the client and the vendor to specify that neither party may solicit to hire each other's employees or customers, both during the contract and for some period (usually 24 months) after the termination of the contract. This is generally not an issue for professional services firms, which employ delivery staff who would not be likely to join a vendor supplying a service outside their expertise.

- *Description of products or services:* Ensure that the description of the product or service to be provided is unambiguous and complete. Often, disputes arise postsigning on what specific service or product was agreed on. With product vendors, this is generally an easy exercise, but it can be particularly difficult to define for business consulting or other professional services vendors.

- *Right to withhold payment:* Ensure the right to withhold fees if vendor services are not properly delivered or product upgrades are not delivered as promised. The end customer or a clear and unambiguous deliverable or result should be the arbiter of what constitutes proper delivery.

- *Dispute resolution:* Consider mediation and arbitration alternatives, which can reduce the cost of disputes and require negotiation prior to legal action.

- *Future pricing:* The vendor will obtain significant leverage in the future if future pricing for products and services is not detailed in the contract. At a minimum, specify that future product or service pricing will be no more than the then-current list less the current customer discount percentage. Ideally, the prices are specifically fixed.

- *Liability:* Vendors will attempt to limit liability to the total sum of fees paid. Clients should attempt to achieve higher, but reasonable, liability limits.

- *Outsourcing clauses:* Provide the right for the customer to transfer license for a product to an outsourcing partner without the licensor's consent and without fees. This enables the company to outsource a function without approval from the vendor.

- *Payment terms:* Payment terms specify the cash payments to be paid. Net 30 days is typical for service vendors. Allow for suspension of payments if vendor or product is not performing as agreed.

- *Warranty:* Require the vendor to warrant that the vendor has the right to license the software or provide the services.

- *Training:* Negotiate free training with software products and specify it in the contract.

- *Volume/service-level discounts:* Prearrange volume or service-level discounts and specify it in the pricing section of the contract.
- *Vendor certifications:* For some vendors, special third-party certifications, such as SAS-70, CMM, ISO-9000, or other qualifications may be required.

The number of high-profile lawsuits involving the delivery of products and services to firms of all types confirms that contract negotiation and tight management of the vendor relationship is crucial to avoid business disruption and litigation, which can follow. This has been especially true in the IT field. In a study of technology vendor litigation, Cutter Consortium found that the top three causes for litigation include missing functionality or performance in the product, missed delivery or promise dates, and defects in the product, yielding it unusable.[3] Exhibit 16.3 shows percentage of grounds claimed in the technology lawsuits researched by Cutter. A solid contract will help build a strong relationship by clearly articulating key provisions and avoiding ambiguous statements that lead to future disputes.

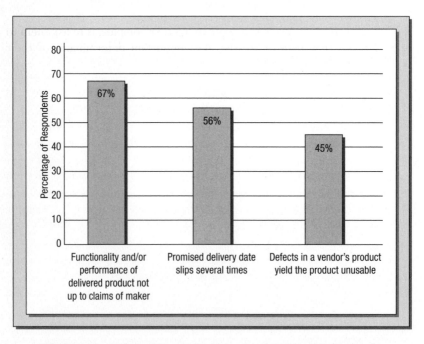

Exhibit 16.3   Primary Causes for Litigation in Technology Lawsuits

Managing Vendor Performance

A key piece of managing vendor relationships is building a mutual understanding of partnership expectations and ensuring that the vendor fulfills those expectations. Often, the success or failure of the vendor hinges on clearly setting performance metrics to be achieved and following through on those metrics. Ineffective vendor managers rarely get past the first step of setting the metrics, and when they do, they do not follow up with periodic measurement of the vendor's performance.

The process is basic. For each vendor, define expected performance, which may or may not be explicit in the contract; then track and monitor the performance, periodically report performance, take action to improve performance, or remove poor-performing vendors. The vendor manager should manage this process, with input from professional and administrative staff in the firm who have direct experience with the vendor providing the service or product.

Because of the large number of vendors that may be found in even small professional services firms, determining measures and monitoring them can be a resource-intensive and, therefore, cost-prohibitive process. The most effective way to determine how to measure and evaluate vendors when the contract does not have specific deliverables (e.g., vendors selling a specific product on a one-time basis, such as an office supplies provider or a caterer), or when the product or services is sophisticated or complex, is to ask them to provide metrics they believe are the most important determinants of their success with clients. Vendors know the most about their particular services and should be able to quickly articulate the top three to five metrics on which they should be judged. If they cannot identify how they should be evaluated, they are most likely not a vendor that the firm should be working with. The best vendors most often have internal benchmarks by which they measure their own performance, and they are usually happy to share those with customers who ask. In fact, the very best vendors drive the process by voluntarily scoring their performance on a monthly or quarterly basis for the benefit of the client.

By having some vendors design their own performance metrics, incorporating them into contractual guarantees, and then having vendors self-monitor, the bulk of the effort to monitor and measure performance is absorbed by the vendor. This process should not change the pricing materially because a quality vendor will have these reporting disciplines built into its processes to start. To ensure that vendors are behaving honestly, the vendor manager should periodically and randomly audit one or two of the vendor-supplied, vendor-reported measures. If the vendor falls short, the potential of a random audit, coupled with contractual penalties, is generally enough to eliminate or at least minimize any dishonesty or lack of diligence.

For the most mission-critical vendors, in addition to the vendor-driven approach outlined previously, the vendor manager should generate his or her own set of two to three key measures and perform the vendor assessments on a regular schedule. The vendor manager cannot afford to find out that a key vendor is falling short of agreed-on goals too late to mitigate the failure. The vendor manager should combine the key measures provided by the vendor with any other desired performance metrics to create a performance report card. This should be regularly completed and reviewed with the vendor to monitor ongoing performance and adherence to contractually established SLAs. If any SLAs have been violated, the customer can demand remediation in accordance with the contract specifications. Alternatively, in the spirit of partnership, the customer could make concessions in exchange for other benefits that could be provided without a monetary exchange, as illustrated previously. In every case, the client should be rigorous in establishing and adhering to the regular reviews. Without these reviews, vendor relationships can go unmonitored for long periods, and significant problems can often go unnoticed and unresolved.

In addition to vendor performance reviews, the vendor manager should periodically review all vendor contracts. This ensures that all service levels promised in the contract are being enforced or at least that goodwill is being built and acknowledged by not enforcing an agreed-on standard. Further, a review of the contract will ensure that any changes to terms or conditions based on changing business imperatives can be managed early on. We recommend reexamining every vendor contract annually at a minimum. For vendors on which the company relies significantly, these reviews should be done on a quarterly basis.

This periodic contract review is neglected surprisingly often in companies of all types. For example, a Cutter Consortium survey estimates that 7 percent of IT product and service provider contracts are never reviewed, and fewer than half of contracts are reviewed at greater than annual intervals.[4] Exhibit 16.4 shows Cutter's research results in this area.

In all cases, the client should ensure that it can withhold any fees (maintenance or otherwise) due the vendor in the case of contract breaches on the part of the vendor. One of the most rapid methods for getting the attention of a vendor experiencing performance problems is to withhold approval on accounts payable. We have seen countless client situations with poorly performing vendors who do not return phone calls or repeated appeals to fix problems.

The speed with which vendors respond from the highest levels once a steady flow of receivables dries up can be remarkable. While this approach should be a last resort, it is generally successful. When it is not successful, the firm has at least avoided continuing to fund a vendor that will not be part of the long-term picture and has saved money to invest in a relationship with a replacement vendor.

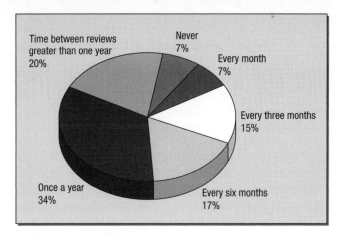

Exhibit 16.4   Contract Review Frequency in Surveyed IT Departments

Because typical professional services firms engage a wide variety of vendor types and sizes, vendor managers should be sure to allocate their time and attention according to vendor importance. The most critical vendors or those who receive the largest fees should be the focus of any measurement program. The vendor manager should set spending or criticality thresholds in advance, to be approved by firm senior management, to determine which vendors will be closely managed.

Automated and Online Purchasing

For many commodity products used by the professional services firm, purchasing is best completed using online services or brick-and-mortar enterprises with an online component. For example, office supplies, coffee service, magazine subscriptions, or related vendors can be easily managed online:

> Computers continue to have a major effect on the jobs of purchasing managers, buyers, and purchasing agents. In manufacturing and service industries, computers handle most of the routine tasks, enabling purchasing workers to concentrate mainly on the analytical and qualitative aspects of the job. Computers are used to obtain instant and accurate product and price listings, to track inventory levels, to process orders, and to help determine when to make purchases. Computers also maintain lists of bids and offers, record the history of supplier performance, and issue purchase orders.
> Computerized systems have dramatically simplified many of the acquisition functions and improved . . . efficiency of determining which products are selling. . . . Firms are linked with manufacturers and wholesalers by electronic

purchasing systems, the Internet, or Extranets. These systems permit faster selection, customization, and ordering of products, and they allow buyers to concentrate better on selecting goods and suppliers.[5]

The vendor manager should establish a single account or point-of-interaction with the chosen commodity vendor and ensure that all approved purchasers throughout the organization have access to the account login information. Many professional services firms fail to aggregate their purchasing, losing potential volume discounts and causing undue work for their accounts payable team and vendor manager.

Often for recurring purchase items, vendors perform automated replenishment by gauging usage and automatically delivering the appropriate items and quantities. Again, office supplies or other perishables such as snacks and soda can be set for delivery with minimal intervention or effort on the part of the internal resources.

Working with Vendors' Other Customers

An important resource in managing critical vendors, particularly larger vendors, is information sharing with their other customers. There are usually well-established user groups for almost every product or service on the market that has a reasonable-size client base. These groups typically communicate in online forums and web sites. For some of the major products, regional or national user group meetings or conferences can help facilitate communication among users. These groups provide a wealth of information, such as:

- Latest news about the vendors and their affiliated service or product provider partner networks
- Features, functions, and enhancements planned for future products or releases
- Best practices for using current products or services
- Workarounds for common (or obscure) problems
- Assistance with common contract terms and SLAs
- Useful third-party services or products
- Informal answers to common questions
- Direct response and ideas for addressing specific problems
- General pricing and contract terms information
- Shared metrics for vendor performance measurement

While most vendor managers usually pay attention to the "official" vendor-sponsored special interest groups, an often-overlooked and powerful tool for influencing vendors and driving pricing discounts is informal work with other customers in the same geographic region or industry. More direct interaction with other customers can provide deeper and more candid insights than are likely to be shared in a vendor-sponsored, public forum. Coordination with other vendor customers may reveal specific pricing information, specific SLAs or vendor metrics, legal problems or issues with the vendor, and other information useful in negotiating with and managing the vendor. The best customer partners are those using the same vendor, located in the same locale, but in a different industry. While working with other vendor customers in the same industry can provide highly valuable information on specific applications of the vendor's products or services, the competitive dynamic usually minimizes the information that each party is willing to share. The vendor manager may want to consider coordinating informal periodic meetings between managers and directors to get together and exchange information as a small group. The information exchanged, particularly on pricing or input to product or service development, can be used to win some concessions from a vendor or to significantly influence the research and development process for products. This is particularly true for smaller customers of a given vendor. As noted in the opening to this chapter, small customers often find it difficult to manipulate vendor agendas. By working together with several other small customers, they multiply their leverage considerably. Small customers should take the advice of Ben Franklin in working with other small customers: "Yes, we must, indeed, all hang together, or most assuredly we shall all hang separately."[6]

Other sources of information can include analysts, consultants, publications, and even the vendor's competitors. A detailed list of these information sources is included in a later section of this chapter, which covers information gathering as part of the initial vendor selection process. These information sources (research analysts, Internet sites, consultants, and others) continue to be highly valuable sources of information on the vendor, postselection.

A frequently underused source of information for vendor managers is industry analysts working in investment banks or money management firms. These professionals are typically charged with having a complete understanding of how a given vendor is expected to perform in the future. One of the most important ingredients for their research is the current opinions and experiences of customers. For this reason, analysts are usually enormously interested in talking with a vendor's customers about their experiences, and they may even collect informal surveys to quantify user opinions. These analysts can become a nerve center of information about particular vendors, providing insight into the health of the vendor, marketplace changes, and competitive outlook. In exchange for customer viewpoints and opinions, they are usually willing to share not only their objective third-party opinions concerning vendor direction and performance, but also their published periodic research reports. Further, the analysts are often willing to facilitate the introduction of the vendor manager to other customers for the formation of the informal information-sharing groups discussed previously. While this is a highly effective strategy, the vendor in question must be of a size and type to attract the attention of an industry analyst, which limits the number of vendors for which it is relevant.

In summary, the wide variety of information available on vendors with a minimum of research and effort should not be overlooked as a critical component of managing vendors, setting metrics, and ensuring best pricing.

Vendor Recompetes

If the vendor selection process is done correctly and the vendor relationship is properly managed as a mutually beneficial partnership, the need to recompete business should be infrequent. However, it is important to periodically test the market for enhanced products, services, and pricing. A recompete may not result in a new vendor choice, but it can be the springboard to introducing new thinking to an existing vendor relationship or to a firm. As a long-term client once remarked to a services provider, "We like your services and value the partnership; you just don't necessarily have the market cornered on good ideas."

Times to consider a recompete include:

- The end of a lengthy (5+ years) contract because products and services will have evolved considerably, so retesting the market for pricing, product, and service changes is appropriate.
- Major changes in the marketplace in terms of pricing or service quality because newer products or services in rapidly changing markets often improve in reliability and diminish in cost rapidly as the marketplace matures.
- Emergence of additional service providers offering better and/or more cost-effective products and services.
- Step-change evolution in technology, necessitating a new product or service.
- Discontinuation of a product or service, necessitating a new provider.
- Any severe performance problems with the vendor resulting in damage or potential damage to the customer's business.
- Significant structural changes at the vendor or client (e.g., merger, acquisition, divestiture).
- Material financial problems at the vendor or client.
- Mandate from firm senior management to investigate additional vendor options.
- Overreliance on a single vendor, resulting in business continuity exposure.

When any of these events occur, a recompete should be considered, but a full vendor selection as outlined later in this chapter should not necessarily be completed. Exhibit 16.5 shows a decision tree for deciding whether to recompete. The first step should be an economic analysis to determine the expected value to be created by recompeting the contract.

The benefits of recompeting should include:

- The difference between the present value of all the expected expenditures from a new vendor and the present value of all the expected expenditures from the current vendor
- Other decreased internal costs (e.g., maintenance, management, training)
- Increased revenue
- Improved control over the business (reduced risk)

In many cases, there are significant switching costs associated with changing a vendor. The costs should include all costs involved with switching between the original vendor and a new vendor. Examples of these costs include, but are not limited to:

- Time and resources to be expended in a new vendor selection process
- Any mandatory close-out costs dictated in the current contract

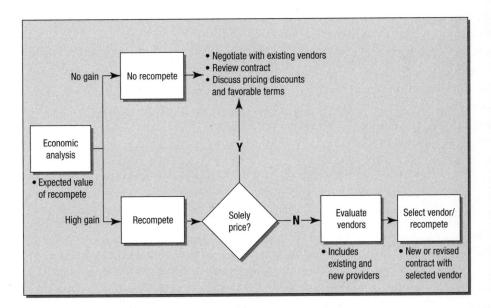

Exhibit 16.5   Vendor Recompete Decision Tree

- Initial upfront costs that must be incurred with the new vendor
- Internal resources lost to managing and implementing the transition
- Any probable business disruption during the transition
- Additional internal costs that must be incurred to achieve effectiveness with the vendor's service or product (e.g., management time, training)

Even with significant gains from switching vendors, the costs can often heavily outweigh the benefits. Vendors are very aware of these switching costs, and these costs are precisely the reason they are often able to increase prices for current customers while offering "great deals" to new customers. This switching cost only further emphasizes the importance of properly establishing contractual obligations and measuring vendors, covered previously in this chapter. The vendor manager should understand vendor relationships that entail high switching costs and those relatively easy to switch and aggressively manage the inclusion of tight performance metrics and severability in the contracts of the vendors with the highest switching costs.

If the economic analysis shows that the benefits still greatly outweigh the costs, a recompete should proceed to the next step. If the reason for the recompete is based purely on pricing advantages, a simplified form of the analysis shown to the vendor usually results in a price concession. If the reason for the recompete is more than price or the current vendor will not budge on price, the recompete should proceed using the standard vendor selection process detailed later in this chapter.

The length of the contract up for recompete should be based on the potential discounts available from vendors in exchange for a guaranteed term. For products or services that are rapidly changing and are rapidly coming down the cost curve (e.g., telecommunications services), the contracts should be no longer than a year. The savings of a new contract usually more than compensate for the lost term discounts on the original contract. For vendors that are difficult or unlikely to change, longer term contracts with heavy discounting are more appropriate.

Managing Troubled Vendors

Because of the wide variety of vendors used by a given professional services firm, inevitably, one or more of the vendors will experience financial or execution difficulties. The forward-looking vendor manager usually has ample warning of these troubles, particularly if he or she is participating in the informal forums, alternative information gathering, and vendor measurement activities discussed in this chapter. In these cases, it is crucial for the vendor manager to aggressively protect the firm's interests by ensuring that adequate coverage for the vendor product or service is available and that the company's financial exposure to the vendor is minimized or eliminated.

For well-established, competitive vendor marketplaces, ensuring adequate coverage in the case of vendor failure should be a relatively straightforward process of assessing competitive offerings and estimating the associated switching costs. For vendors providing highly specialized niche products or services, the vendor manager may have to conduct additional research to find alternative products, approaches, or workarounds. Often, the effort of conducting this research can be shared among several customers who coordinate through the informal information-sharing groups.

The financial exposure to a vendor can come from a variety of sources. Prepaid or partially paid orders for equipment or products, prepaid or currently due maintenance fees, or other contractually obligated sums are common instances. We have seen many companies victimized by vendors that file bankruptcy while significant receivables have been paid by customers in advance of product or service delivery. Not only is delivery of the product delayed, but the monies spent to acquire the product are usually lost forever. The vendor manager should work with the CFO, finance department, or firm senior management to minimize the risks of lost capital and work with the vendor to ensure that contractually obligated amounts due result in actual services received by the client. In extreme cases, the company must halt payment to the vendor and file a lawsuit to line up for restitution when the vendor refuses to refund for services not performed. Many times, the filing of the lawsuit will provide leverage—the vendor often cannot raise money or proceed with any restructuring until the suit is settled, which provides motivation for the vendor to step to the negotiating table.

In one client situation, a worried vendor manager consulted us about the quarterly maintenance fee due to a product vendor. While not concerned with the stability of the product, which was operating properly, the manager was worried that additional money invested in maintenance fees would be lost if the vendor continued to struggle. Careful research indicated that the vendor was indeed in serious trouble, and the client delayed the $100,000 maintenance payment based on various vendor contract breaches. One month later, the vendor filed bankruptcy, leaving no hope of additional product development or support. The impact of $100,000 spent for services that would never be delivered would have been devastating for the financial position of this particular client.

In every case, the vendor manager should ensure that the firm senior managers are fully informed of the company's operational risk and financial exposure because of troubled vendors. The senior management team can be instrumental in helping reduce the risk and can help the vendor manager manage the advance planning and alternative brainstorming needed to minimize the potential risks.

Vendor Selection

This section outlines the process for selection of major outside service and product providers and the subsequent management of the vendors. The list of external vendors used by even a small firm is often lengthy. Vendors provide products and services across a wide variety of categories, as outlined in Exhibit 16.1. Within a category, multiple vendors may be used by a larger professional services firm.

The selection approach defined here is an abbreviated version of a full-fledged, comprehensive methodology and should be adequate for most professional services firm vendor selection processes. For an overview of the exhaustive selection process for a large-scale vendor, particularly for IT, we suggest reading *The Executive's Guide to Information Technology* (Wiley, 2003). Chapter 10 covers the selection process topic in detail. As with all other frameworks described in this book, common sense should prevail, and the applicable portions of the approach should be applied to the specific situation at hand.

The successful selection of vendors plays a critical part in determining the overall success of the professional services firm and, as important, the ease with which the firm achieves success. Successful vendor selections can be complex and lengthy processes that require the collection and analysis of significant amounts of information, particularly for telecommunications and systems vendors. Well-thought-out vendor choices and solid vendors who behave as partners can ease the work of the vendor manager and the firm internal and professional staff considerably. Conversely, poor vendor selection can hamstring the organization with constant firefighting, failed initiatives, and angry staff and customers. Because outside vendors are generally a large source of expenditure for the professional services firm, the vendor manager cannot afford to ignore their proper selection and management.

Vendor interests and incentives, unfortunately, are not always precisely aligned with those of the vendor manager. While client satisfaction is a part of the equation for vendors, so are other factors such as product advancement, profitability, sales commission, quarterly revenue, and market penetration. A vendor salesperson's natural role is that of an advocate for his or her product or service. This means that to be most productive for the firm, the vendor manager must supervise and actively manage the delivery of services and products on an ongoing basis to ensure that vendor delivery and execution are consistent with the expectations and goals of the organization. Picking the vendors on which to rely can be a risky proposition. The selection process can go awry, wasting significant dollars, disrupting the business, and ending careers for vendor managers.

In spite of the criticality and risk associated with vendor selection, experience has shown that vendor managers are at a significant disadvantage in the vendor process, particularly vendor selection. A vendor manager may manage a selection process for a specific service or product a handful of times in his or her career, whereas his or her counterparts on the vendor side are generally senior-level sales professionals who close multiple deals each year. This puts the vendor manager at a distinct disadvantage to the vendor, from an experience standpoint alone.

Compounding the issue is the fact that once a vendor selection is complete, it is generally difficult to undo. If it turns out that better, more appropriate vendors are available, often the sunk cost and previously committed contractual obligations prevent their being engaged. Thus, the opportunity to replace a vendor may appear only once every few years, at best. This means that vendor selection can be a one-way street with very few turning off points and that vendor selection and management are a critical part of the successful vendor manager's toolkit.

Vendor managers should have a good plan for the activities associated with vendor selection, including:

- How to plan and execute a reasonably rigorous vendor selection process
- An approach for generating target vendor lists for a given product or service
- How to issue an effective request for proposal (RFP)
- An understanding of the work required to complete due diligence on vendors and their products and services
- How to produce meaningful feedback from vendor reference checks
- Vendor negotiation techniques that ensure best pricing and service

Overview of Methodology

Exhibit 16.6 shows an overview of the vendor selection methodology covered in this section. The methodology is intended to provide a reasonably detailed approach to the vendor selection process that will be applicable to most vendors required for a small-to-medium size professional services firm.

The process begins with the definition of scope for the product (or service) being acquired and proceeds through the identification of a team to support the selection process, the identification of potential vendors, the issuance of an RFP, the selection of vendor finalists, due diligence on the finalists, and final vendor pricing negotiations. Each of these steps is further detailed in the following section with a diagram highlighting the subtasks, required information, and outcome for each subtask.

Of critical importance throughout the selection process is to ensure that at all times the effort is being managed, organized, and driven by the vendor manager in charge. Top vendor sales professionals did not reach that status through passivity. Vendors are well practiced at the art of seducing the hapless vendor manager and will take on as much of the work and own or drive

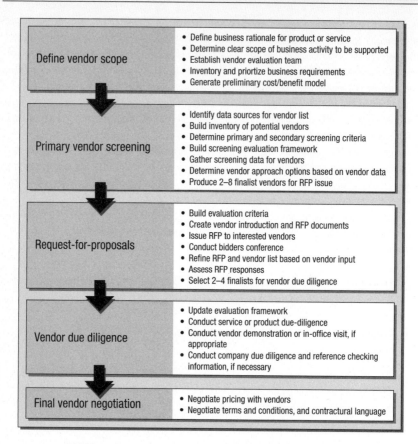

Exhibit 16.6 Vendor Selection Methodology Overview

as much of the effort as the manager lets them to remain in control of the process. A good way to ensure that the vendor manager remains in charge is the implementation of a code of ethics for purchasing. The topic is covered at the end of this chapter.

Second, the selection team is responsible for organizing a large amount of information being gathered from a variety of disparate sources. Keeping clear documentation on the raw data, analysis, and outcome of each step covered in this chapter helps explain to outside observers how the decision was reached, serves as organizational memory, and, most importantly, ensures that no steps are skipped and that the analysis is completed in a reasonably thorough fashion.

The third key to success is the analysis done by the team in preparation for the vendor sales call. This step should be completed before the first vendor is contacted. Vendors long ago perfected the courtship required to manage clients through the sales process, and if vendor managers have not done their homework in the form of the upfront analysis and scope work, they will be at the mercy of a sales process they neither control nor fully understand. The necessary objective analysis becomes lost in the feel-good haze of endless vendor dinner outings, rounds of golf, and vendor-led conference calls and visits. The result is, at best, a distorted, suboptimal outcome. We have observed dozens of vendor selections and have rarely seen success emerge from a vendor-driven process.

Define Vendor Scope

The vendor manager should first seek to clearly understand the full range of business activities to be supported by the service or product in question. The process for the vendor selection flows entirely from this scope, making this a critical step in the overall analysis. The efforts during this step provide dividends later as the vendor due diligence is executed. The evaluation team will be able to ask clear, concise questions of the vendors and communicate the priorities for the firm appropriately.

The scope definition can also be achieved by defining what is not in scope. For example, the scope might be defined as "all purchasing activities, not including receiving, payables, and forecasting" or "all purchasing of products, not including office supplies." The scope definition should also draw clear distinctions between business processes or systems that are replaced or supported and affected but not changed as part of the selected vendor service or product.

In every case, a detailed document that defines the specific scope under consideration is the first step in the vendor selection process. The document should define the scope in as detailed a manner as necessary, with appropriate illustrative charts and diagrams.

The final scoping step is to get sign-off from firm senior management. Any final ambiguities or inconsistencies in the scoping will be clarified under their scrutiny. Getting final scope sign-off may take several iterations of presentations and questions and answers.

Establish Evaluation Team

After the scope has been defined, the next task is to establish an evaluation team to provide expertise and effort to complete the selection process. The scope definition helps identify the individuals required for a successful assessment.

The team should include members from functions or departments who will use the vendor product or service. This ensures that the expertise and the business unit- or business function-specific knowledge is incorporated into the evaluation process from the start. Further, early participation from end users of the product or service facilitates the most rapid acceptance of the vendor selection outcome. Finally, these participants tend to catch potential issues that may be missed by the vendor manager or that the vendor manager is unaware of.

The overall team size varies by company size, scope of business functions under consideration, and the importance of the decision being made. A small vendor selection team might consist of the vendor manager and a representative from the business unit or function affected, along with ad-hoc participation from other firm staff and professionals. A large-scale selection team assessing, for example, a new system implementation for a large organization might contain 5 to 10 full-time team members and as many as a dozen part-time members.

The most effective way of building team membership is through nominations from firm senior management. The list of potential team members should be interviewed by the vendor manager to determine if they have the requisite skills, knowledge, interest, and ability. Achieving the right skill mix, participation level, and environment for the team will have a strong impact on the overall effectiveness and results of the selection process. Even small-scope vendor selection efforts are large undertakings and require considerable sustained effort on the part of the team.

Inventory and Prioritize Business Requirements

One of the toughest realities of vendor selection is that the only way to truly understand whether the vendor product or service is a good match (and where its weak points are) is to first understand the in-scope business requirements at a painstaking level of detail. Unfortunately, the work of documenting scope and business requirements is difficult and tedious. However, it is an absolute prerequisite of a successful vendor selection, and it forms the bedrock foundation of a successful process. Without understanding the scope of services to be provided or required product functions, the team cannot possibly judge the level of vendor fit, what the shortcomings are, how they are dealt with, or the costs and benefits of the selection. A superficial, weak understanding of business requirements and scope is a primary reason for the failure of vendor selection initiatives.

Because starting the "courtship" process with vendors is infinitely more enjoyable than nonstop internal team meetings where requirements are white-boarded at excruciating levels of detail, this step is also the most commonly skipped. The smart vendor manager waits until the proper amount of homework has been done before making the first vendor contact.

Preliminary Vendor Screening

The goal of the vendor-screening step is to rapidly build a comprehensive list of potential vendors. These vendors form the pool from which the final choice is selected. A successful preliminary screening lets the team cursorily review a comprehensive set of vendors to ensure all options have been considered but then rapidly narrow the list down to a handful of vendors for further due diligence. Exhibit 16.7 shows an overview of this process, from data gathering through due-diligence vendor selection.

The first step of the vendor screening is to identify a full set of potential vendors. The approach for this step is to conduct a sweep of the marketplace for vendors whose service or product offering fits in the scope defined in the previous step. If the scoping step was completed well, the vendor marketplace should be relatively easy to identify.

The team should employ a variety of sources for its vendor search:

- *Consultants:* Large-scale consulting firms often have entire practice areas specializing in the selection of the service or product in question; in these cases, they are often willing to provide free, upfront advice in exchange for an opportunity to be involved in the bidding for later work.

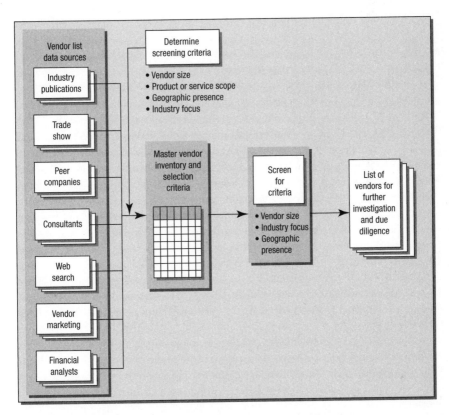

Exhibit 16.7   Vendor Screening Process Overview

- *Industry publications:* There are usually several credible, independent publications focused on the marketplace that can provide vendor lists.

- *Industry trade shows:* Many of the larger players in a particular field have a presence at professional services firm industry-specific trade shows.

- *Peer companies:* Managers from firms in the same industry are an often-overlooked source of information, and they can be particularly valuable for their objectivity. Developing peer relationships with similar professional services firms can provide insight into their decision-making processes and rationale as well as give a jump-start on vendor data gathering. Peer managers who have recently been through a similar vendor selection exercise can be particularly helpful.

- *Focused web search:* A web search can turn up candidate vendors as well.

- *Vendors:* Although obtaining facts from the marketing obfuscation found in many vendor brochures and web sites can be difficult, vendor-supplied information can be useful once a specific set of vendors has been identified.

- *Financial analysts:* As outlined earlier in this chapter, most large investment banks or money management firms have one or more full-time analysts covering the market in which a given large-scale vendor competes.

The evaluation team should manage its search using each of these sources to ensure that a reasonably comprehensive list is built. As the team reviews a variety of sources of data, the right list of vendors should fairly easily emerge. Except for the most unique searches, the team should avoid feeling that it needs to "scour the earth" to identify the suite of potential vendors—vendors that are difficult to find after multiple searches across a variety of sources are not likely to be viable vendors. Good vendors should not be needles in a haystack—the location of an obscure vendor is not necessarily the harbinger of success. Indeed, the best vendor names emerge repeatedly from the research.

The result of this step should be a list of vendors ranging from as few as four to as many as a dozen entries. Although vendors may be added as additional information is uncovered, this is probably the vendor list from which the winning candidate is drawn.

As vendors are added to the list, screening data should be gathered in a template to facilitate analysis. The specific information gathered depends on the vendor selection being completed, but it generally falls into a few categories. These categories are outlined, along with potential information to gather in each category and how much weighting each category might be given, in the following lists.

VENDOR SIZE. Vendors should be of adequate size to continue to invest in the product or service and continue to attract additional customers. Exceptions may be niche-product vendors providing highly specific products or services.

Potential Information to Gather
- Vendor revenues
- Vendor profitability
- Acquisition history
- Number of employees, staff, product specialists
- Number of customers
- Number of end users

GEOGRAPHIC PRESENCE. Does the vendor have the appropriate geographic focus and availability? Is the vendor sufficiently focused on the geographies that matter for the company (U.S. versus Europe versus Asia versus other geographies that impact how the product works or support is delivered)?

Potential Information to Gather
- Corporate headquarters location
- Nearest branch office
- Number of branch offices
- Proximity of branch offices to company branch offices
- Primary location of development team

INDUSTRY FOCUS. Does the vendor have sufficient expertise in the specific industry to ensure development of the best solution? Does the vendor have a product or service line dedicated to the company industry? Is industry-specific expertise relevant for this evaluation?

Potential Information to Gather
- Industry-specific additions/modifications to product or service
- Industry implementations of product or service (number of implementations/users)
- Presence of leading industry customers

This type of information is relatively easy to gather and can be used to narrow the vendor list down rapidly. As the information is gathered, the team should begin building a spreadsheet to capture the information.

This process is the most rapid, least-effort method to review the largest number of vendors and rapidly screen out the vendors that are not viable contenders for carrying through to due diligence. The preliminary screening forces out undercapitalized, unfocused, or otherwise inappropriate vendors, as well as allows the remaining vendors to be preliminarily ranked. The team should constantly ask the common-sense question: "Can you envision a scenario in which we would actually choose and rely on this vendor?" The result is a quality list of vendors participating in the marketplace, along with a clear, consistent rationale for the inclusion or discharge of each one.

Occasionally, at the end of a preliminary vendor screening process, no viable vendor or combination of vendors emerges. In these cases, the team should go back through the analysis and look for these common missteps in the process described previously:

- *Business scope set incorrectly:* Too narrow or too broad for a vendor solution to emerge
- *Scope indistinct:* Difficult to assess vendor capabilities due to lack of clarity on business scope, product or service requirements
- *Not enough vendors identified:* Not enough data sources searched to yield proper number of vendors; search of data sources too superficial
- *Vendor data incorrect or missing:* Team did not gather enough vendor data, or vendor data is incorrect leading to vendors screened out improperly
- *Primary or secondary screening criteria set too tight:* Criteria for vendor screen set too tight, forcing out viable vendors
- *Additional criteria needed:* Team adds additional relevant criteria with higher weighting, allowing viable vendors to pass primary and secondary screening

The team should analyze the process for these common mistakes, as well as other holes in the overall analysis. If the team concludes that the analysis has been completed correctly, the marketplace for the scope in question has no vendor participation, and the business needs will have to be filled with internally developed products or services.

Request for Proposal Process Management

An RFP is a time-honored method for choosing vendors in which the company gives a group of vendors the opportunity to show their capabilities by responding to a specific set of business requirements and information requests. RFPs typically request a broad swath of information—product or service data, vendor financial and structure data, customer references, qualifications with similar work, and more.

Requiring interested vendors to respond to a well-thought-out RFP can be a highly effective approach for both gathering additional data without imposing incremental workload on the team and screening vendors for ability to produce quality work. There are a variety of good reasons to conduct an RFP:

- It distributes data gathering effort to multiple vendors instead of an internal team.
- It allows vendors to withdraw if the RFP focus indicates they are not a good match.
- It introduces an element of natural selection to the process—vendors that cannot manage their way through an RFP process are not likely to be viable long-term partners.
- It gives a view of the vendor's capability for producing a "finished product" early on with little risk; if vendors cannot produce quality RFP responses (typos, clarity, answering the questions asked, organization), there may be similar issues with their products or service.
- It allows vendors to "self-team," working and proposing in concert on areas where a multivendor solution makes sense.
- It creates a level playing field for the vendors; all vendors see the same RFP request and provide the same response information; this has the double benefit of encouraging vendors to participate if they perceive a fair selection process and of forcing the internal evaluation team to consider each vendor equally, mitigating any potential biases.
- Multiple analyses of the requirements and information in the RFP by highly skilled vendor sales and delivery staff may point out shortcomings or inconsistencies in the previous analysis by the internal team and vendor manager.

Not every vendor selection is a good candidate for a full RFP. The team may elect to not conduct a full RFP for a variety of reasons. In these cases, the team may proceed straight to the vendor investigation and due-diligence process. Some examples include:

- The number of vendors identified during the previous screening is small enough to justify proceeding directly to due diligence.
- In a seller's market, the RFP may be considered too onerous by target vendors and discourage participation; they will opt to go after easier-to-win business.
- The preliminary vendor selection conducted in the previous step unearths enough information to satisfy the selection team.
- The final decision needs to be made rapidly, and not enough additional time is available for a full RFP-response-analysis cycle.
- The vendor(s) being selected is minor, or the level of investment is minor enough and does not justify the effort of a full RFP.

- There is a large separation between first- and second-place vendor, so first-place vendor takes the decision by default.

Creation of a high-quality RFP requires the team to have a clear command of the business scope of services or product requirements. If creating a good RFP is difficult for the team, it is likely that these elements were not clearly defined in the previous task. A good RFP not only reduces the effort for the team but also ensures enthusiastic and full participation by target vendors.

Exhibit 16.8 provides an overview of the RFP process. The steps are described in the following subsections.

CREATE REQUEST FOR PROPOSAL. A well-constructed RFP contains two primary sections: an overview of the company, which gives the responding vendor information on the company and required service or product to help in its response, and a section for vendors to provide a detailed response to specific questions on company, capabilities, functionality, and other relevant considerations. The first section may include the following company information:

- History of company
- Size of business: three- to five-year revenue history, number of employees
- Geographies covered: headquarters, branch offices, plant locations
- Service line overview
- Key points that differentiate the company business operations
- Single point-of-contact e-mail address for all questions and responses

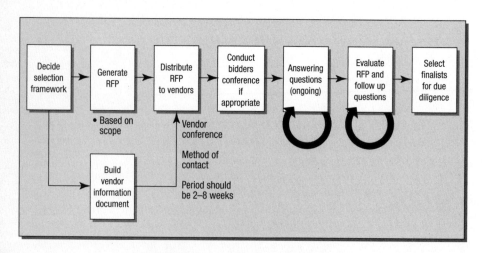

Exhibit 16.8   RFP Process Overview

The section should also include RFP process information such as:

- RFP distribution method
- Response required (number of copies, format)
- Names of decision makers on the evaluation team
- Vendors invited to participate
- Time line for response and review of RFP
- Criteria for selection and relative weighting

The focus of the document should be on providing information helpful to the vendors, as well as answering the qualifying questions that most smart vendors ask before pursuing a lead:

- Is the scope under consideration a good match with my product or service?
- Is the playing field level?
- Is there a budget approved?
- Who will make the decision?
- How long will the evaluation take?
- Which of my competitors will take part?
- Does the client have a clear understanding of what they are doing and a good process for getting there?

Although the buyer of products or services is in the driver's seat during an evaluation, going to the trouble of providing the right kind of information to the candidate vendors in this section ensures that the opportunity is attractive to successful, smart vendors—the exact kind that will be ideal partners.

Because the vendor orientation section of the RFP often contains company proprietary information, the team may want to consider having the vendor recipients sign nondisclosure agreements (NDAs). The firm's legal team or retained counsel can put together a simple NDA to be completed by all participants.

The second major section of the RFP should be focused on gathering the detailed data from the vendors; this helps determine which vendors should be carried forward through vendor due diligence. This information is similar to the data gathered for the preliminary vendor screening but goes into additional depth. Achieving this level of detail is possible because the individual vendors alone have the expertise to fully answer the questions and because the work is distributed across multiple vendors instead of the selection team.

The typical categories of information to be gathered in this section include:

- *Vendor:* Information concerning the vendor company—size, stability, and resources.
- *Contact information for this RFP:* Account manager, delivery sales representative, senior manager in charge.
- *Financials:* Three- to five-year revenue and profitability history for vendor.
- *Financials:* Three- to five-year revenue and profitability history for the product or service in question.
- *Company size:* Total company employees or other reasonable proxy for understanding overall company resources.
- *Service or product definition:* Details about the service or product under consideration.
- *Overview of vendor product or service lines:* Include revenue distribution among product lines.
- *Customer qualifications:* Positive references from existing customers with similar requirements.
- *Customer input method:* How it works and frequency.
- *Service levels:* How does the vendor measure its delivery or product or services—measures might be quality, user satisfaction, support calls, or other; how does the information get reported internally, and how often; how does information get reported to the customer?
- *Economics:* Vendor list pricing schedules; drivers for pricing.

To facilitate later comparison and analysis, the RFP should provide a clear format and organization for responding to questions. The RFP should also specify the number of hard copies that the vendor must provide, as well as desired electronic formats. The responses should be standardized as much as possible; reading through a large number of responses inconsistent in format and organization adds considerable work to an already labor-intensive process.

REQUEST FOR PROPOSAL ISSUE. After the RFP has been created, it should be distributed to the target vendors. The best way to manage the issuance process is to send paper and electronic copies to the sales professionals who have been identified at each vendor. A team member should be designated to make a follow-up call to each vendor to ensure that the package has been received.

To gauge interest in the RFP and provide an equal-footing forum for vendor questions and answers, the evaluation team should consider conducting a bidders' preconference one to two weeks after the RFP is issued. This timing ensures that the vendors have had enough time to review the information and show up with good questions. The invitation should limit the number of attendees per vendor to three or fewer. Otherwise, vendors sometimes send a small army of salespeople, particularly for large proposals. More than one bidders' conference we have attended has been so oversubscribed that it had to be postponed or moved to a new location. The conference is also an ideal time to distribute additional information to interested vendors in electronic or paper form.

The agenda for the conference should be simple. The vendor manager should introduce the selection team members and give a brief overview of the material in the vendor orientation portion of the RFP, with a particular focus on expected business benefits and evaluation process. A brief explanation of how the vendor invite list was created may be appropriate here as well. The bulk of the conference should be an open-end question-and-answer session for the vendor representatives. A scribe should document the questions asked (and answers given). If vendors ask questions for which the team does not have a ready answer, the question should be documented and a response sent later. In some cases, the team may simply choose not to answer the question. The entire process should take between 60 and 90 minutes, depending on the RFP complexity and the number of vendors in attendance.

After the conference, the team will have some new information to process. First, the vendor attendance should indicate the level of overall interest that the RFP has generated. If a number of vendors do not attend, there may be several reasons, including a mismatch between the RFP scope and vendors' capabilities, a misread of the RFP by the vendor, or even a simple mistake. In any case, the team should contact the vendors who have opted out to solicit their feedback and possibly revise the scope, RFP, or process based on the information.

Second, based on the questions asked by the vendors, the team may find holes in the RFP process. In this case, the team should decide whether any of the previous work should be revisited or refined and what corrective action, if any, to take. Unless the fault is particularly egregious, there should not be any disappointment in a few mistakes. Vendors are highly experienced in scouring and picking apart RFPs.

Within a few days of the conference, the full transcript of questions answered during the session, as well as follow-up questions, should be e-mailed to all vendor representatives. As incremental questions are asked by vendors, they should be documented and the questions and answers should be sent to all vendors.

During the RFP analysis process and the following vendor due diligence, the team should resist the urge to hold information too closely. While some information should not be revealed (e.g., targeted pricing), most information should be shared as widely as possible. A common misconception is that keeping information concealed or responses ambiguous and nonspecific somehow improves the team's negotiating position or negatively impacts the selection process. Quite the opposite is true—most vendors want to put their best foot forward and win a deal by having the superior product or service for the client's needs. Sharing as much information as possible with the vendors facilitates the process and ensures a quality selection. Often, a selection team's hesitance to share information with the vendor is indicative of a lack of confidence on the part of the team.

REQUEST FOR PROPOSAL RESPONSE ASSESSMENT. The process should allow between one and four weeks for the vendors to formulate a response, depending on the complexity of product or service, the level of investment in question, and depth of the RFP questions. Vendors should provide the requested hard copies and electronic versions of their responses by the date and time established in the RFP.

Vendors should also be asked to refrain from additional contact with the evaluation team during the evaluation period, with disqualification as a possible penalty. Without this threat, the most resourceful (or aggressive) vendors will pester the team (and anyone else in the company that may have influence) endlessly with follow-up questions, status checks, and offers to "provide additional information." By communicating clearly the evaluation process and setting hard deadlines for the decision, the team can satisfy the vendors' need for understanding the timing of the next steps.

In some cases, the team may have determined additional questions or data points to gather during the RFP response period or after reading the responses. In these cases, supplemental questions should be aggregated and distributed to all participating vendors via e-mail with a reasonable, but rapid, time frame for response.

The actual evaluation process should have the team reading each RFP in no particular order and scoring the vendor response based on the requirements and weighting determined before the RFP distribution. If possible, the team members should conduct individual reviews of the RFP responses to avoid biasing one another. Team members can debate the merits of each RFP after all the individual scoring is complete.

After the RFP reviews are complete, the scores should be summarized, with a final score by vendor created from the mean of the team scores.

SELECT FINALISTS. After the vendors have been scored by the selection team, it is a straightforward exercise to force-rank the vendor options by total score.

The team should conduct a final round of debates to ensure that the outcome passes a "sanity check" and that everyone agrees with the results of the analysis. After any alterations to the score have been made and a final force-rank vendor list is complete, the team should decide which vendors to carry through to the due-diligence process. The team should make the cut at the first point in the force-ranking where there is a significant drop-off in score. This point should usually be between two and three vendors, although a thorough due diligence on more than two vendors can be a challenging effort and can consume more value than it creates.

After the results have been finalized, the team should inform each of the vendor participants of the outcome in writing. The notification should thank them for their participation and provide a contact if the vendor would like follow-up information. It is not necessary to inform the losing vendors of the scoring or disclose which vendors will be carried forward through due diligence. A courteous, professional notification ensures the future participation of the vendors and provides a backup set of vendors if the due-diligence process produces unsatisfactory results. If time permits, the team should provide feedback to the losing parties. Most good sales professionals are interested in understanding how they can compete successfully in the future; they appreciate the feedback and will incorporate it into their next sales pursuit.

Vendor Due Diligence

The focus of this piece of the work is to prove to the satisfaction of the team the assertions made by the vendors in their RFP responses. The particular focus is on understanding the details of how the product or service will fit the firm's requirements. The team should also begin conversations with the vendors' customers to understand how well the vendors have served them, as well as beginning to build relationships with them for future information exchange. The team accomplishes this primarily by working with the vendor sales teams and taking the actual product through its paces.

As the team proceeds through the due-diligence exercise, it should focus the majority of its attention on points of differentiation among the vendors because it is on those points that the ultimate vendor decision is made. For example, if vendor locations are a consideration and both vendors have the same geographic coverage, the team should not spend time attempting to differentiate the vendors based on this criterion. Because vendors are often at competitive parity on many aspects, this approach dramatically cuts down the breadth of analysis required for due diligence, as well as ensures that the ultimate selection is based on the factors that provide real differentiation among the competing alternatives.

In vendor selections where investment is low, the product or service well understood, or a single vendor is the clear winner, the team may elect to deemphasize certain portions of the due diligence. In these cases, minimum research by the team should include a set of good reference checks.

CONDUCT PRODUCT OR SERVICE DUE DILIGENCE. Because the product or service provided is likely to vary widely by vendor type, we do not attempt to address the specifics that should be covered for all possible vendors. The previous business scoping and vendor scoring effort should provide a more-than-adequate baseline of requirements for ensuring that the competing products or services can be evaluated against one another.

CONDUCT COMPANY DUE DILIGENCE. The focus of the company due diligence is the verification of the RFP data provided by the vendor. Because most of this information is factual, this portion of the due diligence should be a fairly rapid "check the box" exercise. Information verifying the vendor's locations, revenue history, and relevant product or service lines should be readily available from a variety of sources on the Internet or from business research services such as Hoovers.

CHECK VENDOR REFERENCES. Vendor reference checking provides two important benefits. First, it provides independent verification and validation of a vendor's claims. Although the odds of discovering adverse information about the vendor are low, the effort expended is moderate, and the value of any adverse information is very high. The search, therefore, must focus on uncovering adverse or disconfirming evidence—any good management scientist knows that "the value of information is inversely proportional to its probability." The evaluation team would appear foolish and shortsighted indeed if a few phone calls would have turned up such critical information. Our consulting practice was helping a client salvage a particularly poor vendor relationship, where a few reference checks might have changed the outcome of the vendor selection. The client CEO remarked to the evaluation team: "So, this was important enough to spend two million of my dollars on, but not important enough to call a couple of people on the phone?"

Second, calling vendor references establishes a relationship with other customers, which can later facilitate best practices sharing, vendor information sharing, and other mutually beneficial exchanges. Over the long haul, having a relationship with other customers increases the company's ability to influence the vendor as well as provides additional information for negotiations.

There are usually two sources of customer references for a given vendor. First, as part of the RFP process, the vendor should have provided a list of clients according to similarity. The client references should be ranked according to similarity to the company, size, geographic footprint, or other relevant factors. The evaluation team should call on the references that have the most similarities to their situation.

The second reference source is customers identified by the evaluation team without assistance from the vendor. This is an important step because by going off the preplanned program devised by the vendor, the team improves considerably the odds of unearthing any adverse information. There are a variety of ways of identifying vendor clients. Although vendor web sites and trade-focused magazines can be helpful, we have found other methods to be the most effective, including scanning Internet job board resumes to determine which clients an employee of the vendor may have specifically worked with. If the firm does not have access to these boards, for a small charge most staffing services companies will be glad to complete a brief search for the team.

The vendor-supplied list and the team-constructed list form a master list of references to call. Depending on the size of investment being considered and the depth of the due-diligence effort required, the team should plan to call between two and four vendors from each of the lists. The vendor-supplied list provides contact information, and the vendor will likely prepare its customer contact for the call. In the case of the team-generated list, the team should identify the relevant purchasing decision maker at each potential reference and send a letter in advance of the call, outlining the reason for the call and providing a list of questions in advance. The team should then follow up with a phone call to perform the interview or determine whom the contact would designate from his or her team to take the call. If possible, the team should conduct the interviews in person and make a site visit as part of the interview.

The list of questions that the team asks varies from selection to selection. The team should have a specific list of questions prepared in advance but should also leave time for open-end responses from the reference. Many of the most interesting findings come from the unscripted portion of the interview. The focus is on determining how the vendor has performed for the client both before and after the sale, as well as getting a preview of any key lessons learned during the implementation.

Questions that we have found effective in a reference interview include:

- What products or services did you consider as part of your evaluation?
- What were your key decision criteria when making this decision?
- How did you weight the criteria (what was important to you)?
- What period did (will) it take to achieve a payback?
- When did you make your decision?
- How long did you take to complete your vendor evaluation?
- How was the vendor service after the sale?
- What were the surprises (good and bad)?
- What are the key lessons learned from the selection process?
- Would you do it again?

Final Vendor Selection

Once the due-diligence is completed, a front-running vendor will emerge. The final selection of the vendor should be confirmed with firm senior management. Following vendor selection, the final steps of contract negotiation and product or service commencement can begin.

Vendor Negotiation

After firm senior management has approved the project and vendor selection, the final vendor pricing negotiations can commence. It is important to wait until this point to maximize negotiating influence with the vendors. If vendors know the selection has been approved by firm senior management, they will know that the deal is imminent and will be prepared to rapidly get to their best pricing.

Vendor negotiation is a complex topic; vendor managers generally find themselves at a disadvantage in negotiations. Vendor sales professionals participate in pricing negotiations every single week. The vendor manager does not have the advantage of either practice or complete information. Thus, vendors often bring in consultants who are experienced in conducting vendor pricing negotiations. The best consultants are objective and not associated with a firm that uses or resells any vendor's products. They will also have conducted a negotiation with the specific vendor in question during the prior 12 months. The high cost of a large-scale vendor investment allows the client to recoup the negotiation specialist's consulting fees many times over.

Often, vendor managers have an inherent hesitance to ask for discounting before closing a deal with a vendor. There are a variety of reasons for this, including inexperience in negotiating pricing, not understanding vendor pricing drivers, or unwillingness to push back on the vendor sales representatives. This phenomenon can be costly for the company and earn the vendor manager a reputation for being a patsy. Vendor managers lose nothing by at least asking the question of vendors. We were asked to review a ready-to-be-signed contract for a new client as a "formality." We called the sales manager and asked whether this was the best pricing available. The sales manager remarked that no one had asked for a discount but that he would provide a 10 percent discount for an immediate execution of the contract. One phone call, five minutes, and $20,000 in savings was generated.

Because of the variety of factors involved in a large purchase, the vendor manager must proceed cautiously. Often, vendors will turn a loss on one portion of the negotiation into a major win on another piece. Therefore, the vendor manager must understand and negotiate each variable with a specific strategy and lock down agreed-on items in the process. Just as in buying a car, where savvy buyers negotiate a trade-in on a used car, the price of the new car, and the financing separately, the vendor manager is much more likely to receive the best possible deal by identifying and negotiating each point separately. Negotiations can be lengthy, often to the point of annoyance, but time is on the side of the buyer. The vendor manager should tightly control both the agenda and the pace of the negotiation. This allows the manager to keep the upper hand and achieve the best pricing and terms.

We have collected a few practices from participating in the vendor negotiations for a variety of large-scale service and product purchases. Key points are provided in the following listing. However, we highly recommend the engagement of a negotiation expert for large-expenditure items or, at a minimum, self-study with the negotiation texts mentioned in the bibliography for this chapter:

- *Negotiate each point separately.* Vendors are experienced in achieving a higher total price by bundling and shifting prices of individual components throughout the negotiation process. The opportunity for vendors to obfuscate the true pricing is high if a dozen separate items are negotiated simultaneously. Instead, the vendor manager should carefully identify and separately negotiate each point, starting with the points that drive the largest amount of cost first. Often, the vendors will give up ground on this piece, hoping to regain lost ground on the subsequent pieces.

- *Keep at least two vendors in the mix.* Keep a second option open until there is ink on the final contract; if the vendor senses that it is the only option, the manager's negotiating power declines significantly. As soon as a vendor thinks a final selection has been made—whether the winner or not—the vendor's negotiating stance will become more rigid. Further, it is possible that the negotiations would produce pricing concessions from the second-place vendor that would move it into first place.

- *Don't single-source the negotiation.* Because many product vendors offer a full suite of services in addition to their product, they often have a natural advantage in proposing consulting or training portions of a project. The team should still consider competing service providers to ascertain which vendor can deliver a better price or better service. The outcome of the negotiations may very well be a single-source approach for implementation, but driving to this solution early lowers the client's negotiating power.

- *Timing is everything.* Like most companies, product and services vendors are under pressure to achieve monthly, quarterly, and annual goals. A little research should reveal the fiscal calendar for the vendor in question. The maximum negotiating power is at a quarter or fiscal year end, as the vendor works to achieve its financial targets.

- *Keep talking to current and prospective customers.* Current data from other prospective customers as well as the installed base can give you insight into areas where the vendor might be more willing to offer concessions. With the right relationship built, vendor managers from peer companies will be willing to share costing and negotiation information about a specific vendor.

- *Don't compare apples to oranges.* Because of the large number of pieces involved in a complex negotiation, it can often be difficult to compare individual elements of the pricing to adequately compare vendors. The team should continue to ask questions and deconstruct vendor-pricing proposals until they can be compared side-by-side on an element-by-element basis.

- *Nominate a "bad cop" for your team in advance.* The team may occasionally need someone to take a tough line with the vendor. If a "bad cop" is needed during the negotiations, the firm CFO, corporate counsel, or other senior manager is often happy to fill that role.

- *Ensure that the vendor must close the deal.* Ensure that throughout the process, the vendor invests considerable amount of time in the deal; the vendor sales team then often engages in "sunk cost fallacy" and believes that it must complete the deal because of the high level of investment so far. This has the effect of swinging the balance of power considerably.

- *Employ "bogeys" to force reciprocal concessions.* This is a common negotiating tactic to put forward points that are not material considerations (bogeys); then quickly capitulate on the point to force reciprocal concessions from the vendor on other points. This can be an effective strategy, but it should be used with caution; it can quickly produce the reverse effect if the vendor agrees to the nonmaterial concession early.

- *Check the contract for liability limitations.* Vendors generally try to contractually limit their liabilities to the total of their fees or to the limits of their insurance coverage. These liability limits can sometimes be far lower than the actual damages experienced by a business if there is trouble. The team should push for liability limitations that acknowledge the risk for the customer, not the vendor. For high-profile, large-investment projects, the vendor should also carry malpractice or E&O insurance from a reputable insurance carrier.

- *Never prepay.* Occasionally, vendors offer discounts for prepaid services or products. The vendor manager gives up significant future influence over the vendor's behavior by prepaying these charges. We have seen clients with significant prepaid fees that are worthless because the vendor has gone out of business. However sharp the discount, the risk associated with prepaying is too high.

- *Know when to disappear.* If the sides are at an impasse, the vendor manager can "go dark" and avoid responding to vendor e-mail and voice mail; time is on the side of the buyer, and the dearth of information will put increased pressure on the vendor if the vendor's sales team believes that the deal is slipping away.

- *Know when to say when.* When the negotiation is close to complete on all pricing, terms, and conditions, the manager should have at least one final desired concession at the ready; the vendor usually gives this concession on the promise that the client will sign the contract immediately.

Vendor negotiations can be daunting, difficult, and exhausting experiences. However, they are an unavoidable part of the selection process and have to be managed carefully to ensure the best pricing and terms. As a senior management acquaintance of ours once remarked, "Every customer gets the vendors that they deserve."

Ethics in Purchasing and Vendor Management

Because purchasing often involves large transactions and the vendor selection process involves often arbitrary-seeming judgment calls, it is critical that those involved in purchasing adhere to the highest standards of ethics. This ensures the avoidance of both impropriety and the appearance of impropriety, as well as ensuring that the professional services firm receives the best value for its investment in outside spending.

Each firm should establish and publish policies for transactions with outside entities. To avoid any later confusion, these policies should be acknowledged and signed by all individuals involved in the purchasing decision-making process. While each individual firm may set its own specific principles or standards, the NAPM/ISM has created a good baseline from which to begin (see Exhibit 16.9).

An additional resource is the Illinois Institute of Technology's Center for the Study of Ethics in the Professions (CSEP), which has aggregated a tremendous number of codes of ethics—more than 850 at current count—available on its public web site (see the resources section at the end of the chapter). The CSEP library also includes guidelines and processes for establishing codes of ethics, resources links throughout the Web, and information on permissions. This searchable and comprehensive web site is the first stop on the Internet for those interested in establishing a code of purchasing ethics or for a broader, firm-wide code of ethical behavior.

Summary

Well-executed vendor selection and management is one of the keys to success for the firm overall. Because of high expense outlays and critical reliance on vendor-supplied products and services, professional services firms cannot afford to ignore the topic. The most experienced vendor managers find ways to share the burden of vendor management by instituting self-monitoring programs, which force vendors to report their own metrics and results and agree to be subject to periodic random audits of the scoring and performance. Further, they carefully allocate their attention in proportion to the vendor's overall importance to the business. These vendor managers approach vendor relationships with a keen appreciation of the value

1. Avoid the intent and appearance of unethical or compromising practice in relationships, actions, and communications.
2. Demonstrate loyalty, to the employer by diligently following the lawful instructions of the employer, using reasonable care and only authority granted.
3. Refrain from any private business or professional activity that would create a conflict between personal interests and the interests of the employer
4. Refrain from soliciting or accepting money, loans, credits, or prejudicial discounts, and the acceptance of gifts, entertainment, favors, or services from present or potential suppliers which might influence, or appear to influence purchasing decisions.
5. Handle information on a confidential or proprietary nature to employers and/or suppliers with due care and proper consideration of ethical and legal ramifications and governmental regulations.
6. Promote positive supplier relationships through courtesy and impartiality in all phases of the purchasing cycle.
7. Refrain from reciprocal agreements which restrain competition.
8. Know and obey the letter and spirit of laws governing the purchasing function and remain alert to the legal ramifications of purchasing decisions.
9. Encourage that all segments of society have the opportunity to participate by demonstrating support for small, disadvantaged and minority-owned businesses.
10. Discourage purchasing's involvement in employer sponsored programs of personal purchases which are not business related.
11. Enhance the proficiency and stature of the purchasing profession by acquiring and maintaining current technical knowledge and the highest standards of ethical behavior.

Exhibit 16.9   National Association of Purchasing Management Code of Ethics

of a partnership but also ensure that the vendors are delivering the value promised. Finally, they ensure that they receive a steady supply of information concerning critical vendors from objective third-party sources, including other customers and industry research analysts.

RESOURCES

Many of the resources and courses for purchasing are geared to manufacturing companies, which purchase raw materials and finished goods from outside suppliers in large quantities, or for federal, state, or local governmental agencies that must adhere to strict policies in purchasing process. However, the same vendor management principles apply to the lower volume purchasing experienced by professional services firms. Some resources are provided here:

http://www.napm.org
National Association of Purchasing Managers (NAPM)—recently renamed the Institute for Supply Chain Management (www.ism.org)—offers a wide variety of resources for purchasing managers, including seminars, books, negotiation advice, an online knowledge center, and self-paced classes. The NAPM (ISM) confers two certifications for purchasing professionals, the Accredited Purchasing Practitioner (APP) and the Certified Purchasing Manager (CPM).

http://www.cips.org
Chartered Institute of Purchasing and Supply (CIPS) is an international organization serving the purchasing and supply profession. CIPS is based in the United Kingdom and offers a variety of best-practice information, seminars, and other services to the purchasing manager.

http://www.amanet.org
American Management Association provides seminars, best practices, and information on a wide array of management topics, including purchasing management.

http://www.cmcamai.org
The Canadian Management Centre, an affiliate of the American Management Association, provides information on purchasing management and procurement best practices.

http://www.american-purchasing.com
The American Purchasing Society (APS) is a professional association of buyers and purchasing agents. It requires membership and provides subscription to *Professional Purchasing* monthly magazine. The APS confers two certifications for purchasing professionals: the Certified Purchasing Professional (CPP) and the Certified Professional Purchasing Manager (CPPM).

http://www.pmac.ca
Purchasing Management Association of Canada is an organization providing resources and information for purchasing and procurement managers.

http://www.nigp.org/index.htm
National Association of Governmental Purchasing provides public sector purchasing agents with training, education, research, and technical assistance.

Illinois Institute of Technology's Center for the Study of Ethics in the Professions (CSEP) http://www.iit.edu/departments/csep.

Training and Certification

Many universities, colleges, and other educational institutions offer courses and certifications in procurement or purchasing management. The University of Alabama—Huntsville is one: http://www.coned.uah.edu/procman.cfm, as well at the California Institute of Technology: http://www.irc.caltech.edu/courses/Strategic_Supplier_Management.htm.

Templates and Processes

Many government purchasing agencies (federal, state, and municipal) post online their purchasing policies and processes. These can be valuable sources of information for the new purchasing manager or purchasing group. They are easily identifiable using keywords such as *purchasing, procurement, agency,* or *office* in any Internet search engine.

Vendor Negotiation

There are a variety of good books and courses on this topic. A few of our favorites include:

Max H. Bazerman and Margaret A. Neale, *Negotiating Rationally* (New York: Free Press, 1992).

Robert B. Cialdini, *Influence: The Psychology of Persuasion* (Quill, 1993).

Roger Fisher and William Ury, *Getting to Yes* (New York: Penguin Books, 1991).

J. Edward Russo and Paul J. H. Schoemaker, *Decision Traps* (New York: Fireside, 1989).

Richard H. Thaler, *The Winner's Curse* (Princeton, NJ: Princeton University Press, 1994).

Vendor Selection

For an in-depth coverage of the vendor selection process see Chapter 10 of The Executives Guide to Information Technology: John Baschab and Jon Piot, *The Executives Guide to Information Technology* (Hoboken, NJ: John Wiley & Sons, 2003).

NOTES

1. Vince Lombardi, "Vince Lombardi's Quotes about Teamwork," available from http://www.vincelombardi.com/quotes/teamwork.html (December 19, 2002).
2. Bureau of Labor Statistics, U.S. Department of Labor, *Occupational Outlook Handbook*, 2004/2005 edition, Purchasing Managers, Buyers, and Purchasing Agents, available from http://www.bls.gov/oco/ocos023.htm.
3. Cutter Consortium, "78% of IT Organizations Have Litigated," *The Cutter Edge* (April 9, 2002).
4. See note 3.
5. See note 3.
6. Benjamin Franklin, at the signing of the Declaration of Independence (July 4, 1776).

17

Information Technology

JOHN BASCHAB, CRAIG E. COURTER, AND JON PIOT

We used to have a lot of questions to which there were no answers. Now with the computer we have lots of answers to which we haven't thought up the questions.

—Peter Ustinov[1]

Love it or hate it—you cannot escape technology. Clients expect even the most luddite professional to communicate by e-mail. Clients expect their professional advisors to be conversant in technology related to their business. Clients demand efficient operations and balk at excessive invoices where time spent on their work surpasses their expectations. One of their expectations includes the efficient use of technology by professional advisors. Clients are not the only ones demanding technology. New employees and mid level professionals expect current technology tools to assist their practice. The level of service required of IT by professional service firm employees is extremely high as professionals do not tolerate downtime and technical difficulties. If technology hinders the professional from completing their work, costs and revenue loss begin to accrue and rapidly escalate with the passage of time. There is tremendous pressure on IT to provide highly reliable systems that increase the productivity of the professional and decision-making capabilities of management. The cost of downtime is exorbitant. In most cases, management will demand a high level of reliable technology for efficient operations.

Managing technology presents special challenges for nontechnical managers, especially senior firm managers. It has a language all its own, often used by wily technical staff as a shield against critical review. It is also difficult to determine the right level of investment. New possibilities arise constantly, making it difficult to prioritize the new against the old. Partners read magazine article hype about the latest technical fad and conclude that the firm lags the competition. There is a danger, however, that much of this technology is still immature and risky to install. Technology systems crash at the most inopportune time. Technology projects are complicated and often overrun both time and costs. True value is difficult to measure and even more difficult to predict. Security breaches, viruses, and malware pose constant threats. Good IT managers and directors with relevant industry experience and well-rounded management and technical expertise are hard to find and expensive. How can this environment possibly be managed?

This chapter discusses how to manage IT in the professional services firm covering the key topics of IT strategy, architecture, organization, standards, operations, projects, budgets, and governance (steering committee / relationship building). Each of these is important for the success of the IT department within a professional services company.

Why This Topic Is Important

Managing IT in the professional service firm is critical to the core business of providing service whether the firm is a law, accounting, consulting, or other firm. If the firm cannot receive e-mails, then it is likely that critical communications are not being received, and one of the main mechanisms for exchanging documents and other work products is hindering the firm's ability to produce revenue. Not only can IT be a hindrance to produce revenue, but it can also greatly increase productivity. Firms that use technology wisely can obtain competitive advantage in the market place by servicing customers more efficiently and effectively. From a financial perspective, IT drives the most significant capital expenditures in a services organization and is one of the largest overhead costs for a firm. It is important to carefully manage IT to ensure the highest returns on this invested capital. From a management perspective, IT is generally not a core competency of any of the principals of the firm, and thus it can confiscate billable time when they have to spend significant time managing or dealing with unfamiliar issues and investment decisions. While the principals in the firm are not good managers of IT, it is also difficult to find reasonably priced and qualified IT directors. For example one firm we worked with hired three IT directors in 36 months. Two of the IT Directors were overcompensated for their market value while the third, a victim of the predecessors' failures, was significantly underpaid. Undermarket pay drove the third IT director to depart on her own volition to pursue a more lucrative contract after six short months. Finally, managing strategy, budgets, personnel, human resources issues, and varied systems are all activities that must be performed by the CIO; however, rarely is one person trained well enough to handle the wide-ranging duties. This chapter will address the foregoing subjects and discuss how the professional services firm can manage this function on an ongoing basis.

In many cases, IT personnel will grow up in the department. They can ascend through one of two routes. In some cases they will be heavily application and software focused and in other cases they will have significant experience in the infrastructure areas of networking, e-mail administration, or desktop support. Rarely has an individual been given the proper training while on this ascension to properly manage an entire IT department. To exacerbate the issue, the manager will be given decision-making authority for large budget items with little practical experience or formal training in making such decisions. When a large investment in technology goes bad, the senior firm managers finally take notice and begin making management changes. It is imperative for both firm managers and IT managers to learn the basics of good IT management. This chapter provides some insights into proper management practices. We have also borrowed heavily from our previous book, *The Executives Guide to Information Technology* (John Baschab and Jon Piot, New York: John Wiley & Sons, 2003). After reading this chapter, if you find that you need more detailed information on a technology subject, you will find the *Executives Guide* very comprehensive.

Strategy

We are all in the gutter, but some of us are looking at the stars.
—Oscar Wilde (1854–1900), *Lady Windermere's Fan*, 1892

Everyone talks about strategy, but we often mean different things. Gartner provides a simple definition: "A strategy takes a vision or an objective and bounds the options for attaining it."[2] A technology strategy provides the bounds to guide what the firm is trying to accomplish from a technology perspective. It is not as detailed as a road map, but it is sufficiently detailed to describe what major roads can be used to meet the objective. It is used for budget planning and to control project selection and implementation. It must be aligned with the firm's strategy as described in the firm's strategic plan.

Dividing an enterprise into domains for purposes of organizing and aligning strategies can be helpful. A *domain* consists of a group of related business processes that share a common, identifiable goal. Keep the number of domains addressed to a minimum to avoid complexity and redundancy. Different domains can and do trigger different strategies.

Examples of domains are production, financial, risk management, marketing, and infrastructure. The production domain includes systems that the professional uses to serve clients and conduct substantive work. The financial domain includes all financial systems from time and billing through reporting. The risk management domain includes conflict checking systems and business continuity. The marketing domain includes the intranet site and, potentially, client relationship management systems. The infrastructure domain includes the "pure" technology that underlies all other domains.

Different domains can and should have different strategies. For example, the strategy behind the financial domain and the infrastructure domain could be to reduce and control costs through consolidation and process improvement. At the same time, the strategy behind the production domain could be to innovate by introducing new systems aimed at better service.

The technology strategy should be cross-referenced to the firm's business strategy and core competencies. What are core competencies?

A *core competence* is "a root system that provides nourishment, sustenance, and stability."[3] It is not a product; it is experience, knowledge, and developed leadership. It is the organization of work and the delivery of value. It is something unique that distinguishes one firm from another. Many firms call their core competencies *service lines.*

Exploiting core competencies allows a firm to deliver end products. In the legal field, for example, end products are the specific legal services. Given the diversity of practices, most firms sell various end products. Each lawyer likely provides several different end products, oftentimes "reinventing" the end product for the particular client. For example, an attorney who has intellectual property litigation experience (end product 1) may consult with a client on how to minimize the risk of copyright litigation (end product 2). The attorney may also accept an engagement to register a copyright (end product 3).

Between core competencies and end products are a firm's *core products.* "Core products are the components or subassemblies that actually contribute to the value of the end products."[4] Law firm core products may include complex litigation, high-volume personal injury, medical malpractice, cross-border mergers and acquisitions—the list is virtually endless. In a properly aligned organization, core competencies are used to create core products. Core products are the building blocks to end products.

Identifying core competencies is critical. As budget pressure and technology costs increase, the number of noncore competencies must be minimized through standardization. For example, in a multioffice firm, what is the benefit of having one office run Microsoft Word and the other run Corel WordPerfect? While efficiently creating documents may be a core competency, doing it on a particular system is not. Setting aside religious preferences and absent a compelling client- or locale-driven requirement, the firm should standardize on one package. Standards provide economies of scale and resulting leverage to better negotiate license and maintenance costs. They allow development of expertise and training in fewer packages. They allow the ability to share work product. Whether or not standards make sense to the attorneys who have to shift to the new standard, unless the diversity serves a core competence or core product, standardization should be forced. Technology strategy should reflect and allow development of core competencies. Taking this approach allows a focused strategy and minimizes the watered-down effect of a shotgun approach.

Most corporate strategic plans will describe key goals that the company is striving to achieve as well as key metrics targets (e.g., backlog, pipeline, revenue, headcount, utilization rate). In general some of the following will likely be included in a strategy document:

- Core values
- Targets (three- to five-year financial and business target metrics)
- Key Threats
- Key Opportunities
- Key Initiatives (goals)

It is then the responsibility of the CIO to interpret the firms overall strategy and determine how IT can support the company in executing the strategy. This would entail matching current initiatives to each key goal as well as recommending or evaluating new technology requests against each key goal to ensure alignment. The ultimate arbiter of alignment will be the IT steering committee, which we will discuss later in the chapter.

The CIO should annually create an IT strategy document that shows key initiatives in IT and their relationship to business key initiatives. In general, the IT strategy should consider all pieces of the business strategy and core competencies. For example, if one of the goals of the firm is to increase utilization rates from 76 to 83 percent, do any current IT projects get us there? Do any prospective projects help? Perhaps by implementing a real-time-hours reporting system we expect consultants to manage their time more closely and to gain 2 to 3 percent increase in utilization with time management. If another corporate goal is to reduce days sales outstanding from 60 to 55, perhaps a better collections system can help the company achieve this goal. Similar to corporate strategy, the IT strategy document should include the following information:

- IT Department mission statement
- Near-term goals/initiatives (and how they map to corporate strategy)
- Long-term goals/initiatives
- Challenges/risks
- Actions required for each quarter and for the year

Architecture

Form follows function.

—Louis Henri Sullivan (1856–1924), *The Tallest Office Building Artistically Considered*

Technology architecture is a set of guidelines and standards used to direct IT decision making and planning. It is the part of the firm's technology strategy that says how we will accomplish our objectives. Architecture:

- Is broader than technology but usually handled within technology because no one else gives it much thought—but everyone must be involved.
- Flows from strategy.
- The Zachman Framework provides an example (see later discussion).
- Can increase or decrease maintenance costs by 25 percent.

Technology architecture normally dictates how systems will be designed and implemented. It must be consistent with the enterprise architecture, which is a broader concept. An enterprise architecture describes in various levels of details how the business is designed and functions. One common approach to enterprise architecture is the Zachman Framework. Zachman divides this description into five different views, which include an ever-increasing level of detail. The *scope view* identifies what will be included in the architecture. The *owners' view* describes the enterprise from how the owners understand it, without technical detail. The *designer's view* provides detail on the relationships required for the owners' view to be implemented. The *builder's view* describes how the systems are built and implemented. Finally, the detailed *subcontractor's view* shows the very detailed relationships.

The idea behind describing the architecture is to ensure there is one way to do each process, and each time you approach a new need, you do not create a stand-alone point solution. Rather, you leverage your existing investment. This simplifies your environment—both technology and nontechnology—and controls cost. Exhibit 17.1 shows an application architecture for a generic professional service firm. Key applications include time entry and tracking, project management, billing, financial reporting, document management, sales tracking and bid management, staffing, and intellectual capital management. Technical architecture illustrates the technical platforms that the company operates, the interfaces between these platforms, and the connections to external communication networks. Exhibit 17.2 shows all the categories of technology in an organization that will eventually make their way into the company's application and technical architecture.

Organization

The trouble with teams is that only the lead dog gets a change in scenery.

—Donald Walker, Sergeant Preston of the Yukon,
from *Never Try to Teach a Pig to Sing*

An IT organization must reflect the business. Typically, an organizational chart starts with the chief information officer or IT director and cascades from there. An example is shown in Exhibit 17.3. This is a traditional approach and would certainly allow someone to determine whose reporting structure

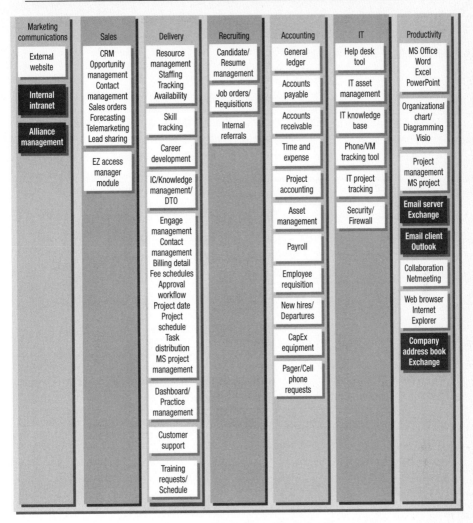

Marketing communications	Sales	Delivery	Recruiting	Accounting	IT	Productivity
External website	CRM Opportunity management	Resource management	Candidate/ Resume management	General ledger	Help desk tool	MS Office Word Excel PowerPoint
Internal intranet	Contact management Sales orders	Staffing Tracking Availability	Job orders/ Requisitions	Accounts payable	IT asset management	
Alliance management	Forecasting Telemarketing Lead sharing	Skill tracking	Internal referrals	Accounts receivable	IT knowledge base	Organizational chart/ Diagramming Visio
	EZ access manager module	Career development		Time and expense	Phone/VM tracking tool	Project management MS project
		IC/Knowledge management/ DTO		Project accounting	IT project tracking	
				Asset management	Security/ Firewall	Email server Exchange
		Engage management Contact management Billing detail Fee schedules Approval workflow Project date Project schedule Task distribution MS project management		Payroll		Email client Outlook
				Employee requisition		Collaboration Netmeeting
				New hires/ Departures		Web browser Internet Explorer
		Dashboard/ Practice management		CapEx equipment		Company address book Exchange
		Customer support		Pager/Cell phone requests		
		Training requests/ Schedule				

Reprinted with permission, *Executives Guide to Information Technology.*

Exhibit 17.1   Application Architecture for a Generic Professional Service Firm

any IT person fell within. Typically the organization is bifurcated by applications and the infrastructure (i.e., operations) groups. The applications management group is responsible for the performance of all the teams in the application development and support group. The application manager must have a complete understanding of the business systems used in each area of the business. The operations manager is responsible for the performance of all the teams in the IT operations group. The operations manager must have a basic understanding of the technologies used in each of the areas managed.

CATEGORY	TECHNOLOGIES
Computing hardware servers	Desktops Laptops PDAs Network attached storage (SAN)
Appliation software	Pachage software (EAP, CRM, other point-solutions) Custom developed software Application integratin/middleware e-mail
Systems software	Operating systems Virus detection/elimination System monitoring System performance management Configuration management Web services
Development	Development languages Databases Database design standards (normalization rules) Coding converions
Intrastructure and facilities	Cabling Equipment storage (racks/shelves) Environmental controls
Network	Routers Hubs Firewall Peripherals
Peripherals	UPS Network printers Desktop printers Tape backup Media burner (CDRWXXXX)
Outside services	Consulting (by application/technology area) LAN/WAN cabling

Exhibit 17.2 Sample Technology Inventory

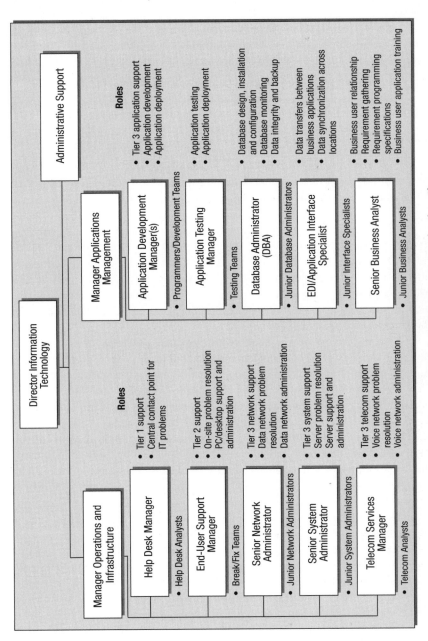

Director Information Technology

Administrative Support

Manager Operations and Infrastructure

Manager Applications Management

Help Desk Manager
- Help Desk Analysts

End-User Support Manager
- Break/Fix Teams

Senior Network Administrator
- Junior Network Administrators

Senior System Administrator
- Junior System Administrators

Telecom Services Manager
- Telecom Analysts

Roles
- Tier 1 support
- Central contact point for IT problems

- Tier 2 support
- On-site problem resolution
- PC/desktop support and administration

- Tier 3 network support
- Data network problem resolution
- Data network administration

- Tier 3 system support
- Server problem resolution
- Server support and administration

- Tier 3 telecom support
- Voice network problem resolution
- Voice network administration

Application Development Manager(s)
- Programmers/Development Teams

Application Testing Manager
- Testing Teams

Database Administrator (DBA)
- Junior Database Administrators

EDI/Application Interface Specialist
- Junior Interface Specialists

Senior Business Analyst
- Junior Business Analysts

Roles
- Tier 3 application support
- Application development
- Application deployment

- Application testing
- Application deployment

- Database design, installation and configuration
- Database monitoring
- Data integrity and backup

- Data transfers between business applications
- Data synchronization across locations

- Business user relationship
- Requirement gathering
- Requirement programming specifications
- Business user application training

Exhibit 17.3   Standard IT Department Organization Chart

439

When organizing a department we follow some general rules of thumb that we will share with you:

- Separate application and operations.
- When possible, hire good managers to oversee each group.
- Do not allow individuals to float around the organization in odd roles that don't report up through the two main lines (i.e., no floating boxes). When the organization chart must start reflecting personnel with floating boxes, chances are there is something dysfunctional occurring.
- Develop growth ratios for each position so that senior leadership can determine the proper headcount to assign to the group over time.
- Develop consistent titles and roles/responsibilities. Each person/ position should have a concise and clear one-page role description with quarterly or annual management objectives.

Another approach is to create a chart that indicates how the IT organization is structured to address user needs. While this type of chart is not as intuitive to read, a very brief textual description can accompany it and will provide users a better understanding of how the organizational structure is designed to support them. Describing the organization in this way can also help ensure efficient operations. A functional view of the organization will show where redundancies exist.

For multioffice professional services firms, IT department organization can become somewhat challenging. Should each office have a dedicated IT support person? Can local IT support purchase hardware or must that be accomplished at the headquarters? If the local office needs call for the addition of a server, must that server match the corporate standard? In general, most firms will want centralized management and control of IT support and purchasing decisions to ensure economies of scale and standardization of the environment to minimize support cost. Additionally, any office with more than 30 employees will typically need a dedicated IT support person. Offices under this size can manage via a local part-time or contract support resource. Most duties today can also be managed remotely by the corporate support team. Exhibit 17.4 shows how the staffing of the IT organization might change over time with the growth of the firm.

Another issue for multioffice firms is the collaboration between geographically dispersed IT employees. Many times the relationship between IT professionals in two markets may be acrimonious because of communication issues. Many firms have been successful at minimizing this behavior by organizing field personnel into virtual teams. For example, the virtual team responsible for IT process documentation may actually be composed of members from many different cities. This allows geographically separated employees to work together on IT projects and allows them to build a relationship while working

RESOURCE	COMPANY SIZE (NUMBER OF EMPLOYEES)				
	0–25	25–50	50–100	100–200	00–400
CIO/IT director	—	0.25	0.50	0.75	1.00
Network/systems engineer	—	0.50	0.75	1.00	1.50
Network/systems administrator	0.25	0.50	0.75	1.00	2.00
Help desk supervisor	—	—	0.50	1.00	1.00
Jr. network/systems administrator	0.50	1.00	1.50	2.00	3.00
Help desk/desktop support	1.00	2.00	3.00	4.00	5.00

Exhibit 17.4   Typical IT Operations Resources Required for Small- and Mid-Sized IT Departments (single location)

on a common cause. To fully build these teams, however, it is important for them to meet regularly. Consider having these teams meet at least once a month by conference call. Team members should be assigned action items and expected to move those action items to resolution and report on them regularly. Key members of the team should meet at least annually, in person, to discuss the more critical issues, plan for future development of the team, and build stronger interpersonal relationships. The relatively minor cost of these in-person gatherings is well offset by the benefits gained in system stability and overall technology expenditure.

One challenge with professional services companies is that sometimes offices are small. Even a small office, however, may need on-site support staff. This situation can cause the number of support staff compared to billable professional to increase, which, in turn, increases costs. This situation, however, can be mitigated with proper planning. First, the firm could simply decide that proper service to professional staff requires the extra cost. Even if a firm decides that in the first instance, it's likely that the firm will put extreme cost of pressures in other areas of technology. Therefore, technology leadership must find a way to get the most benefit out of the local asset.

One way to accomplish this is to recognize that a local office IT person will be doing things other than support. Certain support aspects must be provided locally. It is not possible for a remote call center to change a hard drive or a monitor. Rather, it takes hands on, feet on the street in the local office. The local office IT person, however, may not spend 100 percent of his or her time conducting the support. Rather, he or she may also spend some time monitoring the servers, planning and executing upgrades, testing software, and performing various other projects. Significant cost savings can be obtained by focusing on these ancillary tasks. Each IT person likely has strengths and weaknesses. If you can organize the tasks such that a local IT person is responsible for all of a region's efforts in a particular area, or potentially even the global firm's effort in a particular area, then that person can take his or her nonsupport time and spend it in that area. By using other local IT support to fill in the other areas that are needed in that local office, all aspects of technology can be covered. The benefit of proceeding this way is that you are minimizing redundant tasks, such as each office creating its own intranet system, or setting its own standards.

For example, if left to fill its own needs, each local office would likely create a document repository. This system would have features unique to that office and would likely have a unique platform. Electronic document sharing between the offices would be more difficult because the disparate systems would be difficult to integrate. Minimizing redundant tasks is likely the single biggest way that a large organization with multiple offices, especially smaller offices, can control costs and improve services.

Standards

The nicest thing about standards is that there are so many of them to choose from.

—Ken Olsen, founder of Digital Equipment Corp., 1977

Everything in life that's easy is made easy because of standards. Standards and difficulty are inversely proportional. Plugging in your notebook computer is easy because we have a standard voltage and connector. Visit a different country and your life might be a bit more difficult. Your connector might not fit in the receptacle on the wall, so you would need an adaptor. Luckily, there is a standard adaptor to bridge between two conflicting standards. Even then, the power supplied may be a different voltage, requiring you to use a transformer. If you did not have the adaptor or the transformer, you would not be able to connect. Your life would have been made more difficult as a result of lack of standardization. You should pay close attention to this simple concept throughout your technology enterprise.

That is not to say that everything should be standardized on a global basis. Many standards simply do not lend themselves to global application, perhaps because they address local or regional issues or because they themselves depend on other standards that conflict between geographic locations.

With standards comes a loss of control. For example, a program that deals specifically with U.S. taxes may not need to be a global standard, but rather a U.S.-based standard. Also, when rolling out a system globally, standards between locations may differ based on particular building codes or power configurations.

How do you determine where to set a standard? Exhibit 17.5 illustrates a process to use for determining and setting standards by area. Standards should be set at the highest level in the organizational structure at which they make sense. A wide area-networking standard, designed to connect all offices together, should be set at a global level. An accounting standard designed to ensure that data from all offices is compatible should also be set at a global level. Likewise, an application that has only local utility should be set at a local level.

The real difficulty or a special difficulty comes when setting a standard at a regional level. Many times the regional distinction is more a matter of convenience than logical necessity. Support regions are often set up to provide local time zone and local language technology support. There is not necessarily a user difference or a system difference between the regions.

Some distinctions may exist, however, where regional business management is attempting to meet different strategic objectives. Because technology should align to the business strategies, and not vice versa, differences between regional standards may result.

Another reason for differing standards, the reason that should be sparingly applied, is the difference in the maturity of a region in a particular matter or in a particular area. For example, if one region is significantly mature in its support structure, that region may require a standard call center software and approach. That same approach may not be practical in the other regions based on maturity. In such a case, that standard may not be set for the other regions. The standard could be set once the regions are ready to adopt call center technology.

Standards don't have to be perfect. A cubit is an ancient unit of linear measure. It was equal to the length of the forearm from the tip of the middle finger to the elbow. While this was a handy unit of measurement as people always had their arms with them, it was not particularly precise. Depending on who applied the measuring, the cubit would be of different lengths. Yet, it provided an important way to measure. With modern need for extreme precision, distances are much more precisely defined. For example, a *meter* is defined as "the international standard unit of length, approximately equivalent to 39.37 inches. It was redefined in 1983 as the distance traveled by light in a vacuum in 1/299,792,458 of a second."[6]

When setting a standard, you must determine the reason that the standard is needed. Standards for standards' sake do not advance the enterprise. In fact, they can do the opposite by limiting creativity. Also, you should communicate broadly when setting a standard. Every person in an enterprise who may be interested in considering the standard or to whom the standard would be applied should have the opportunity, at least indirectly, to comment.

This opportunity can be provided by an e-mail setting forth the projected standard or, better yet, an e-mail identifying the fact that a standard would

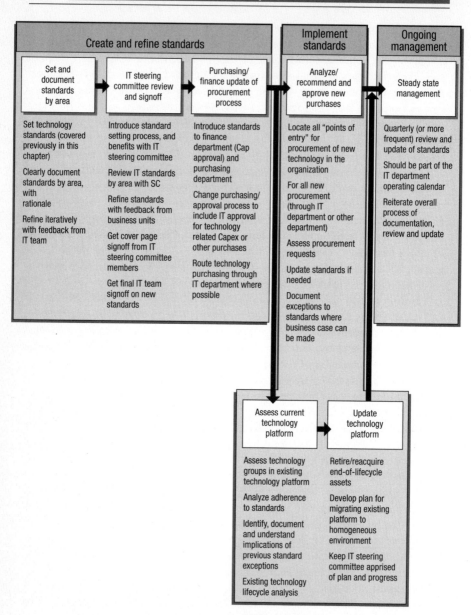

Exhibit 17.5   Process for Determining and Setting Standards by Area

be set and soliciting input. Then, send an e-mail identifying the particular standard with a discussion addressing the point raised in the first round of discussions. People like to be asked their opinions but oftentimes become jaded when it appears that their opinions were totally ignored. If the standard does not incorporate the opinion, a discussion attached to the standard should raise the issue and identify why it was not adopted.

Standards limit creativity and, as such, technical people often abhor standards. Perhaps even the same person who wrote the original standard, when faced with a different situation, might opt to ignore the standard. But the standard cannot be ignored. It must either be applied or modified.

For example, you are attempting to create an integrated document management system (DMS) throughout your enterprise. Assume you set a standard for your system, DMS-A. All of your offices except one purchased DMS-A, and you begin to integrate the solutions. One office, however, purchased DMS-B because they believed DMS-B was a better solution. It provided some additional functionality and fit better into their environment. This refusal to follow standards is sure to cause problems. First, even if DMS-A and DMS-B will integrate, that integration will be harder than simply integrating the same system worldwide. Second, your central project team, and any centralized support that may be required, must now learn two systems, DMS-A and DMS-B. Third, any future developments that you may consider must now also consider and test against each of the two DMSs. You have increased the complexity of your network, increased the cost of maintaining your systems, and increased the cost and complexity of future projects by failing to enforce the standard.

Operations

The road to good intentions is paved with hell.

—Donald E. Walker, *Never Try to Teach a Pig to Sing*

IT operations refers to the *utility* services provided by the IT department. IT operations generally covers management of hardware, network, network security, enterprise security, communications, user administration, and e-mail systems.

Approaches for effectively managing the operations area by implementing standard operating procedures (SOPs) for the most common, repetitive tasks are provided. This section also covers techniques for improving quality through process improvement and root cause analysis for diagnosing system problems. Additionally, it covers methods for calculating appropriate staffing levels for the operations areas.

The operations unit most often receives only negative attention when service outages occur, and rarely receives positive recognition. The techniques discussed in this section can help raise the visibility, service level, and positive feedback in the organization.

Scope of Operations

Operations incorporates the following processes and areas as shown in Exhibit 17.6:

- Problem management (help desk)
- LAN/WAN infrastructure and services management
- Systems and network security management
- Systems administration (patches, upgrades, tuning)
- E-mail administration
- User login and profile management.

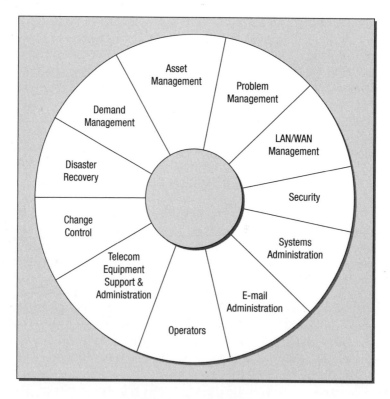

Exhibit 17.6   IT Operations

- Operators—daily systems operations (cost recovery, facilities, job scheduling, output management performance, production control, and quality assurance)
- Telecom equipment support and administration
- Change control (change requests, analysis of impact of changes, and test plans)
- Disaster recovery (business continuity and contingency planning, backup and restore procedures, and test plans)
- Demand management (service level management, service request management, and workload monitoring)
- Asset management (configuration management, contract and software distribution management, and inventory)
- Systems and infrastructure uptime monitoring
- Systems and network capacity measurement and management
- Vendor management (infrastructure, hardware, and systems software)

It all comes down to how well you do operations. You can implement the best systems, but if they don't work consistently, they have little value. You can develop processes, and if they are not followed, they might as well not have been developed. If your operations are not smooth, if your downtime is not kept under control, and if you don't do a good job supporting your users, your technology will be seen as a failure.

As with projects, operations' needs a framework, a set of standard processes. A good example can be found from Microsoft or the ITIL. Microsoft has developed its Microsoft Solutions Framework (MSF) to guide technology operation projects such as an Exchange deployment project or an infrastructure upgrade project. The Information Technology Infrastructure Library (ITIL) on the other hand is a set of books developed by the United Kingdom's Office Of Government Commerce (OGC). The books describe an integrated, process based, best practice framework for managing IT services. To date, these books are the only comprehensive, non-proprietary guidance for IT service management.

Change management. *Change management* is a process that controls changes in the technology environment. Its goal is to minimize downtime and surprises by proper planning, analysis, and communication.

Change management may slow down implementation in some instances, but this should be supported by firm management, not resisted. It's far better to fully plan a change than to implement it on short notice and wreak havoc on a production environment. The latter approach all too often results in more downtime. For this reason, firm management should not only support change management but also insist on it.

Another important aspect of operations is performance management. Performance management of the operations area is important because of the business critical to the nature of the services provided. Most companies have a high reliance on operations infrastructures that they have created. Outage of telephones, e-mail, and file and print capabilities can cripple a company. This heavy reliance means that extremely high reliability is required of the assets managed by the operations group. To ensure that the services provided by the operations group are being properly met, the group must quantify metrics for measuring their performance. The process for establishing these metrics begins with setting objectives based on business requirements, determining targets, creating a service level agreement, and specifying the targets. Once each service level has been defined and quantified each area in operations, the CIO, and the business should sign-off on the agreed terms. After the service levels have been defined and approved, the operations team will track and analyze their performance and make adjustments in each area depending on the analysis.

Each operations area should be managed on an ongoing basis according to the performance criteria summarized in the service level agreement (SLA). The SLA documents the expected tolerance levels that a particular process should operate within. For example, it may state that the Help Desk must respond to user requests within four hours of receiving a request. Another example is the Wide Area Network must be available and operating 99.8 percent of the time.

The SLA spells out processes, procedures, policies, and targets for each area. It dictates the metrics the IT groups will track. The SLA is essentially the document that defines the acceptable ranges for each performance metric dictated by the business. Often IT managers will implement a "dashboard" as a mechanism of reporting the actual performance results against those metrics in a simplified manner. The dashboard is created by selecting one to two key metrics from the SLA for each IT process. The IT director can also effectively manage each area by giving them a one-page dashboard with appropriate SLA metrics.

For the SLA to be effective is must be created in cooperation between the IT department and the business units. Operations departments that do not have an SLA established with their business users are missing a critical component to providing good service.

The IT Operations area typically receives less attention than the applications portion of the IT department. Yet, it often accounts for more than half of the spending in the department and provides the tools and infrastructure that users see most often. The help desk is the only interaction and communication with the IT department for many corporate users. Therefore, an effective operations department is critical to good customer service, the perception of a well-run IT department, and a high level of customer satisfaction. By implementing standard operating procedures, service level agreements, process control, root cause analysis, and infrastructure investment assessment methodologies, you can greatly improve the performance of the operation team and the infrastructure they manage.

Projects

Weiler's Law: Nothing is impossible for the man who doesn't have to do it himself.

—Anonymous.

Professional services technology staff must consistently deliver systems, services, process improvements, and capabilities to meet the firm's needs and support its strategic objectives. These must be done fast, right, and cheap, with success as the only benchmark. To achieve this success, a firm cannot allow project teams to continuously reinvent the wheel. A firm should have a preset project framework to guide project teams from inception of an idea to the closing celebration. It should work to follow project management best practices. It should provide form project documents with standard processes to follow. It should divide its projects into "quick wins" (described later in the chapter) to deliver consistent and incremental improvements in manageable chunks.

Project management is not as interesting as knowledge management. Project management is not as sexy as portal technology. Project management is not as fascinating as a new operating system. Yet, project management is necessary for any of these systems to be delivered successfully.

BASF Corporation, a major chemical company, had a well-advertised motto: "We don't make the products you buy, we make the products you buy better." The same can be said of project management. Most often, project management does not make the products you use at your firm, but properly run projects make your use successful. So, project management is about properly implementing knowledge management technology. It is about creating valuable portal technology. It is about implementing new operating systems. In fact, project management is about any incremental change made.

Accomplishing this requires a project framework. This is a process that helps project managers evaluate and execute their projects and ensures certain rigor along the way. A good starting point for developing a framework is Microsoft's web site, where it offers significant information on its recommended MSF. While the complete MSF is likely too extensively documented and too rigorous a process for most professional team projects, it is an ideal starting point for developing a more streamlined process to fit a particular firm's culture and needs.

A framework formalizes a project management process and jargon. MSF includes five phases: (1) envisioning, (2) planning, (3) developing, (4) stabilizing, and (5) deploying. Being told that a project is in the envisioning stage tells you a lot as long as the definition of *envisioning* and the processes in that stage do not change from project to project. MSF has predefined "roles" that project team members fill and that have predefined responsibilities. This helps to ensure that team members know what they are to do, and it ensures that all needed responsibilities are covered in each project.

For example, an IT department may be tasked with rolling out an accounts payable system. If it just considers the technology aspects of that rollout, it could easily overlook usability-related issues. A framework, however, should require assignment of a *product management* role. This person is responsible to ensure that the project satisfies its customers. The role could include a focus on marketing, developing, and measuring business value, and prioritizing requirements. A framework might provide that the project manager should never be the product manager, as the roles oftentimes are at odds with one another. The project manager is oftentimes motivated by schedule, whereas delivering features motivates the product manager.

A firm should define not only a framework and standard process but also standard documentation. When drafting an agreement, a lawyer seldom starts from a blank Word file. Most lawyers use prepared precedents, or past agreements, as a starting point. These provide structure and key terms. They keep the lawyer from reinventing the wheel at the client's expense. The same should be true for project managers.

Especially on smaller projects, it may be the first time a person has acted as a project manager. The person may be a skilled technician, but not a skilled writer. A standard document template can speed up the planning process. Even for skilled project managers who write well, a standard document template can ensure best practices are followed and keep them on the essential points, shortening the documents delivered.

Documents should be well focused. They should be written for their intended audience. A document that describes the project's objectives, scope, business justification, and budget, and is intended for steering groups and partners to read before the project is approved should be jargon free. A detailed design specification may be jargon rich.

Documents should be short. The goal is to communicate. If you e-mail a document to someone, who sees that it is 67 pages long, it is likely he or she will either simply scan it or put it aside for later. If, however, it is 5 pages long, it is much more likely to be read. If your documents never exceed 5 pages, reviewers will become accustomed to this, and you will receive better feedback. Break longer documents apart to focus on issues for particular audiences if need be, but always keep them short.

Speed of implementation can be critical in a competitive market (e.g., whether to meet a client's standard billing requirements, to provide an extranet, or to make an existing process more efficient), but it can be difficult to balance speed against the need to select the right system and establish clear user requirements and buy-in around the firm.

A firm should phase and structure projects to deliver substantial value quickly and then follow up by providing the remaining requirements in a later phase. This approach is referred to as "quick wins." Phasing and structuring allows projects and baseline efforts to deliver key requirements quickly to meet the stated business demand. Requirements that are less critical or simply harder to deliver will be scheduled for later phases of the project to allow progress on the immediate requirements. The quick win strategy, as a part of your project methodology, can increase customer satisfaction and reduce the project's exposure to risk.

A project framework, form documents, and a quick win philosophy provide certain economies. They keep project teams from reinventing the wheel. They allow you to identify, coordinate, and control project interdependencies. They help you move quickly to deliver value. But, perhaps most importantly, they allow the project teams to focus on the real issue, delivering the project, and improve the chances that the project will be on time, within budget, and deliver the expected value.

Project teams want to succeed. A project, however, is a minefield where ignoring principals of change management or working to the wrong requirements or underestimating the effort can make even a project that delivers what it promised look to its customers like a failure. A project framework rigorously applied can help avoid these mines. It also provides the project team comfort that it is proceeding properly and, as a result, instills an attitude of success.

A valid business justification should support every project undertaken at a law firm. This concept is easy to understand but oftentimes is hard to put into practice. Since projects cost money, it is best to justify them with money arguments. That approach is not, however, always feasible. A project might be justified because the firm's biggest client demands it. A project might be justified because it fits the firm's strategy. A project might be justified in that it makes life easier for the firm's attorneys, even if there is no direct financial gain. In short, there is no one-size-fits-all solution to determining business justification. There are, however, some accepted and customary approaches that should be considered.

For projects that will provide a direct and readily measurable income stream or cost savings, a financial analysis may be appropriate. This analysis can take many forms, but usually it includes a spreadsheet of project and ongoing operating costs set against income and cost savings over time. The project may be justified from a business perspective if this analysis shows the project breaks even or shows gain within a reasonable time period. This does not mean, however, that other nonfinancial issues should be ignored; this financial analysis is one justification, not necessarily the whole story.

For example, assume a mid-size office is considering whether to implement an automated fax solution for an office. The solution has a project cost (hardware, software, personnel resource cost) and an ongoing cost (software and hardware maintenance and support). The solution also provides financial benefits. It replaces a mail room employee. It provides an income stream through cost recovery (net of what was previously charged, if any). Comparing the costs involved with the costs saved and potential income and factoring in the potential that e-mail is replacing faxing (this requires an assumption as to the replacement rate), the firm can calculate whether this project will make or cost them money. This is a financial analysis.

Some businesses apply various financial measures. Some apply a *payback period* analysis where there is a set time frame within which a project must show a net positive for project approval. Some businesses apply a net present value approach, which requires a calculation of potential income stream in the future and potential costs in the future. If the project has a net positive present value, it is more likely to be approved by the firm. While this distinction is interesting from a theoretical point of view and may be a good way to set thresholds in other industries, a professional service firm likely uses a simpler calculation by just determining whether the project has a net positive or negative cash flow.

While a financial analysis should be conducted where appropriate, nonfinancial considerations normally play a major role in justifying projects. For example, the payback on a knowledge management application is typically long and would likely have a net negative value. In this case, these types of projects would never be approved if qualitative improvements were to be made. One argument for a knowledge management system is that it will reduce the time to prepare work product and improve the quality of that work product. Since law firms sell time, billable hours, adopting such a system would reduce the number of billable hours sold while keeping the same number of production use (the producers) lawyers. Therefore, from both a net present value and a payback rule perspective, a knowledge management system would not be appropriate.

Another issue with financial analyses is making valid assumptions. If you include cost of funds or a discount rate, how do you select them? A small change in that rate can change the financial viability of the project. In our previous fax example, if you assume a rate that e-mail is replacing faxing, how do you determine the correct rate to apply? If you have a way to measure this historically, for example, using manually recorded historical data available in your accounting system (if you billed clients for your manual faxes), you likely have some valid basis for such an assumption. Otherwise, consider ignoring the variable in your actual financial analysis and noting it textually as part of the overall justification. This avoids being seen as selecting values to make the analysis work. (Remember the adage: "Figures don't lie, but liars figure.")

In short, use financial analyses when there is good solid financial data, but don't stretch to make such an analysis. When you do, present the numbers you are confident with, and note the other factors in your textual discussion.

We refer to a third method for valuing projects as the "obscenity" method after the U.S. Supreme Court's Associate Justice Potter Stewart said, "I can't define obscenity but I know it when I see it."[7] Many partners look at projects and have an intuitive belief as to whether the project is justified. The problem here is that partners' intuition may not validly reflect the true value of the potential benefits. Since there is no escaping this approach, however, it is incumbent on the IT staff to provide sufficient persuasive information to help the partner make an "informed" intuitive decision.

An intuitive belief coupled with other methods for analysis is probably a valid way of valuing projects. It should not, however, be the only way. Intuition only goes so far. It ignores nuances that the person appointing intuition might not be aware. It is not a rigorous analysis.

Another method that is often argued, but should seldom be persuasive, is "loss of productivity." The argument goes something like this: It takes a typical lawyer six minutes each day clearing the spam from his or her inbox. We have 1,000 lawyers. Therefore, we are spending 6,000 minutes (100 hours) each day clearing spam. Our average billable rate is $300 per hour. Therefore, we are spending $30,000 each day clearing spam. With 250 business days each year, we would make $7.5 million each year by implementing an effective spam protection. Nuts.

The problem with this analysis is that while apparently logical, it ignores real life. To make this type of claim, a firm must analyze objectively actual patterns. The presumption in this argument is that if you get rid of spam completely from the environment, each attorney will bill six minutes more each day and the firm will make $30,000 additional revenue for each day. If an IT staff argues this position, it should be graded on its ability to increase the firm's bottom line by that amount.

We have seen the same arguments used to support redundancy and high availability systems. "If the network is down for a day, we would lose a zillion dollars." Is that a fact? There are, unfortunately, ways to accurately measure these claims. Every enterprise has suffered a major casualty where systems are unavailable for long periods of time, perhaps even a full day. Find one of these days and analyze the effect on the hours worked on client billable matters, compared with that normally worked on an average day. Compare not only the day of the casualty but also the week starting with the casualty. Were any hours missed on the first day made up on later days? Only after conducting this type of analysis can a true loss of productively claim comprise a business justification.

Perhaps the best way to approach return on investment is by deploying a real option strategy. The best way to describe real options is to think of a poker game. You sit down at the table and ante one dollar for the option of receiving your first cards. For that dollar you receive two "hole" cards and one card face up. You are in the game, but you're not required to stay in the game. If based on what you know (i.e., on your cards as compared to the other cards showing), you decide that you are in a favorable position, you can participate in the betting for that round and buy an option to proceed to the next round. If, however, you conclude that you are not favorably situated, you have the option to drop out. You've lost your one dollar, but you have not obligated yourself to the bitter end on what now appears to be a losing proposition. The game progresses with a series of options until you either opt to drop out, you win, or you lose.

The lesson here is to approve and analyze the business justification of projects in pieces. Put the riskier pieces upfront. When each piece is done, analyze your business justification based on what you know then.

Each time we roll out a new system, we should set benchmarks for its expected use, and we should ensure we have a way to measure our actual usage against those benchmarks. This should be included in and delivered by each project. For example, if we decide that an online employee evaluation system is valuable in that it would be used to create all evaluations, we should periodically check to make sure that it is being used. This can be done by counting the number of evaluations created or by comparing the people for whom evaluations were created against the employee list. To the extent that the system is not being used, we should contact management and develop management reports to provide the required emphasis. Or, management may decide to abandon the system.

As part of every project, we should establish metrics to ensure that the return on investment we anticipate is being attained.

As IT professionals, we should pride ourselves on undertaking projects that provide good business value. We should not use business value to justify our pet projects. To avoid this, we should implement best practices in arguing this justification. Then, we should provide a way to objectively measure and report on the system's actual results against those justification arguments.

A project is a temporary effort to create a product or service. It is to be distinguished from operations, which are regular and systematic efforts to continue to provide products or services on an ongoing basis. While both projects and operations need to be systematized, the way they are systematized differs. Operations are routine and often repetitive tasks. While projects have repetitive steps, how these steps are completed differs from project to project and is not subject to formula. Nevertheless, there are best practices to consider in managing projects.

Budget

I don't care too much for money—for money can't buy me love.

—the Beatles.

This topic presents a practical overview of IT budgeting and cost containment practices for the IT director. In creating the department budget, the IT director must analyze a large number of variables and balance multiple competing priorities, while devising the most cost-effective approach for delivering mission critical services. Because of the impact the budget has on the IT managers ability to run an effective department, budget creation is one of the most important jobs an IT manager has. Exhibit 17.7 displays the amount of IT spending as a percentage of revenue by industry. As you can see, professional services is high. Exhibit 17.8 illustrates IT spending per employee. And finally Exhibit 17.9 shows the ratio of IT personnel to the total company population. The previous three charts can help you determine the approximate dollars you should be spending on IT.

To prepare for budgeting, collect in advance the following types of information to help streamline and improve accuracy of the budget:

- Actual operating, capital, and budget variance figures from the previous year
- Initial statistics on employment growth or decline at the company
- Initial statistics on profit and sales expectations for the company for the coming fiscal year
- Any changes to company operating policies

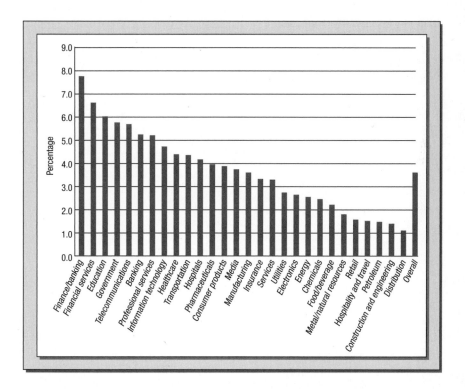

Exhibit 17.7   IT Spending as a Percentage of Revenue by Industry

	IT SPENDING PER END USER ($)
Financial services	137,538
Insurance	34,721
Energy	25,365
Utilities	24,509
Telecommunications	20,002
Information technology	17,489
Banking	16,612
Healthcare	14,187
Manufacturing	13,652
Consumer products	13,510
Pharmaceuticals	13,270
Hospitality and travel	11,406
Chemicals	10,822
Media	10,006
Transportation	9,887
Retail	8,846
Food/beverage	6,884
Electronics	5,998
Metals/natural resources	5,846
Professional services	5,098
Construction and engineering	4,003
Overall	13,968

Exhibit 17.8   Sample Technology Inventory

	IT EMPLOYEE PERCENTAGE OF TOTAL
Financial services	19.90
Insurance	11.88
Information technology	7.56
Banking	7.35
Telecommunications	7.34
Media	6.58
Hospitality and travel	5.91
Utilities	5.47
Healthcare	4.53
Pharmaceuticals	4.37
Energy	4.23
Consumer products	3.61
Electronics	3.28
Chemicals	2.84
Retail	2.54
Professional services	2.39
Manufacturing	2.37
Construction and engineering	2.31
Food/beverage	2.16
Metals/natural resources	2.08
Transportation	1.90
Overall	4.63

Exhibit 17.9   Employees in an Organization as a Percentage of Total Employee Population

- Any changes to major applications in the past 12 months affecting support or development
- Current approved IT project inventory and prioritization
- Estimation of current peer spending (see Chapter 3)
- Payroll statistics for the IT department

Following is an overview of the process:

- The budgeting effort is typically kicked off by the finance department in preparation for the next fiscal year.
- Most often the IT manager will be given the following information to get started:
  —Detailed accounting reports of the prior 12-month IT spending.
  —Template spreadsheet with budget categories already included and calculation complete.
  —Estimation of overhead line items to be allocated to the IT department.
- Complete a first draft—there are two different approaches to build the budget:
  —Zero-based budget (recommended, but more difficult).
  —Run-rate budgeting.
  —These methods are outlined later in this chapter.
  —The first draft should incorporate all known information on service level agreements and anticipated projects (see Chapters 7 and 15).
- Review the draft with CFO or other direct reporting relationship.
- Produce and present the second draft.
- Incorporate input and produce final draft.
- Final draft goes through approval with IT steering committee and senior management.
- Once approved, the final draft is sent to the accounting department as the "final new fiscal year" budget for IT.
- All actions for the subsequent 12 months will be judged against this final budget.
- At times there will be a quarterly and/or mid-year budget review sessions to adjust the budget to account for new known information.

Timing

The budget cycle usually kicks off between September and November, or one to four months before the end of company fiscal year. The budget, in most cases, needs to be finalized in the last month of the fiscal year.

Managing to the Budget

The company, its officers, its employees, and its shareholders are relying on the IT manager to meet his or her budget. If the department overspends the budget, both the company and its employees may be adversely affected. The corporate budgeting process and its subsequent success is dependent on all budget managers managing their share of the overall corporate budget and performing according to plan.

There are a variety of approaches the IT manager can take to help manage the budget on an ongoing basis:

- Schedule a regular monthly meeting with the CFO, controller, or finance analyst to review actual versus budget numbers. During this session, variances should be investigated, and the IT director should develop a list of key actions to improve any negative variance. After the meeting, the director should delegate the action items and get them completed quickly, to experience the benefits in the subsequent month's numbers.
- Give senior direct reports (usually operations and applications managers) budget responsibility for their areas and hold them accountable to hitting the numbers.
- When large variances occur, take fast action, as it takes time for changes to be reflected in the numbers. For example, if a vendor agreement is modified, it may take 30 days to finalize the agreement and another 30 days for the charges to take effect.
- Dithering and delaying decisions and ignoring high variances is a recipe for disaster. The IT director has a fiduciary responsibility for the department and must make the necessary corrections to perform as promised to the rest of the management team. Delay may lead to senior management or the IT steering committee making unilateral decisions without the involvement of IT.
- If you are anticipating a large negative variance in the budget, enlist the CFO as soon as possible to work with you to help correct the situation and explain it to senior management and the IT steering committee.

Handling Out-of-Budget
Business-Unit Requests

After the operating budget is set, business-unit requests that might impact the operating budget need to be discussed in the face of other investment decisions the company is trying to make. While, as noted above, meeting the committed budget is important, over the course of the year budget assumptions may change and some common sense and flexibility can be necessary.

Business units will often request projects that were not on their agendas when the budget was completed. As outlined in Chapter 15, projects should be evaluated on a business case basis and, if approved, executed. Large projects will likely hit the capital budget if approved and not affect the operating budget. Business-unit project requests should be documented, along with a business case, and sent to the IT steering committee for review and approval. Every new request must be considered in relation to the current operating budget and the capital budget. Possible outcomes include:

- Project is covered by the current capital budget and approved.
- Project is not covered by the current capital budget but is higher priority than another project. Downgrade the priority of the second project on the list of backlog projects and replace with the newly approved project.
- Project is not covered by the current capital budget. It is a high priority. There are no other projects to displace. New funding for the IT group is needed. The business case is sound, so additional funds are approved to complete the project, and the ongoing negative capital budget variance is approved (i.e., the capital budget is increased or some other nontechnology investment is displaced).
- Project is not a priority and has a substandard business case; therefore, it is not funded and further consideration is not necessary.

IT budgeting and cost containment practices are critical skills for the IT manager to master. Developing a sound budget, which provides a road map for managing the department and can withstand business changes and economic changes, is a challenge. Additionally, anticipating, understanding, and forecasting the known variables about the business distinguish an average IT director from a star performer. The average performer is reactive to the environment while the top performer has assessed the reliability of key assumptions and the associated risks and planned contingencies accordingly.

Concepts presented in the chapter, such as prioritizing discretionary spending areas and keeping this prioritized list handy, encourage the IT manager to act quickly and decisively to negative budget variances. Finally, ensuring that IT assets are deployed against revenue generating and customer-facing activities help ensure that budget dollars are flowing to the highest value activities. Companies whose IT managers routinely ensure this, as well as the business value of IT investments, see much higher productivity and profitability from IT investments.

IT Steering Committee Concept

The IT steering committee is composed of senior IT management and senior business leaders who meet on a regular schedule to review, discuss, prioritize, and resolve IT projects, issues, and strategy. Used properly, the IT steering committee is one of the most effective tools for creating the high-performance IT department. The steering committee conveys business priorities to IT so that IT management can direct resources to the highest priority business functions in real time. The committee provides approval, oversight, and high-level steering of projects, as well as finalizes project priorities based on IT demand management analyses. It also reviews proposed operating and capital budgets, IT operations service levels, and IT performance metrics. The committee has the membership and authority to facilitate the resolution of any organizational roadblocks to IT effectiveness. Perhaps the most important responsibility of the committee is to improve communication and business relationships between key line personnel and IT managers, facilitating better informal communication between groups outside of the committee. This chapter outlines the typical charter, responsibilities, membership, and ongoing operations of a properly functioning IT steering committee.

Exhibit 17.10 illustrates the communication flow and outcomes of the committee. Exhibit 17.11 displays the demand management process. The IT Steering Committee meeting is on Tuesday's.

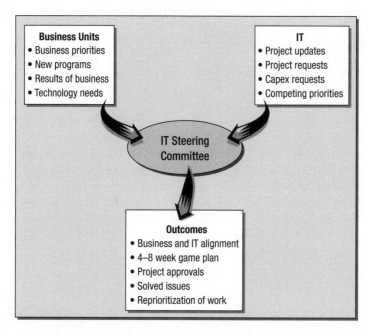

Exhibit 17.10   IT Steering Committee Communication Flows

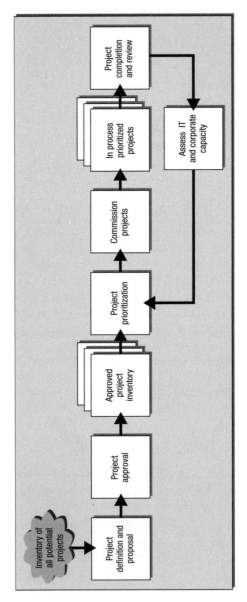

Exhibit 17.11 IT Demand Management Overview

Summary

IT is difficult to manage for most companies and even more difficult in professional service firms because of high expectations of management, staff, and clients. Here is a checklist of specific steps across five broad areas that can be taken in dysfunctional IT departments to improve performance:

1. Improve IT management:
   - Implement an IT steering committee as a "virtual CIO" to provide advice and leadership to the IT director and help speedily resolve issues between business and IT.
   - The committee should be composed of the top five to ten senior managers in the business; they should be required to attend every meeting.
   - Upgrade management talent in the IT department by hiring the right director.
   - The IT steering committee should source the candidates and hire the new director as a senior manager instead of a senior programmer.
   - Clean up the IT organization chart. This means no "floating boxes" and clean, clear lines of responsibility between applications management and operations without gaps or overlaps in coverage.
   - Every staff member should have a shorter-than-one-page roles and responsibilities document posted at his or her desk.

2. Add basic project management disciplines:
   - Establish a single, well-documented master inventory of projects.
   - Determine the ROI or business benefits for each project.
   - Projects that do not improve revenues, reduce costs, or improve control over the business should be ignored.
   - Prioritize projects by their benefits, difficulty, and adequacy of the current systems, generating a force-ranked list.
   - Determine the intrinsic project capacity of the IT department.
   - Limit the number of open projects to that capacity.
   - Expect this number to be shockingly small and disconcerting, but be comforted by the notion that the projects will actually be accomplished.
   - Assign a specific person from the IT department to be responsible for the management and execution of the project, and have them report progress in a five-minute update to the IT steering committee on a weekly basis.

- Each team lead must develop a clear work plan for accomplishing the assigned project, with work tasks, time lines, deliverables, dependencies, and required resources clearly defined.

3. Manage vendors:
   - Determine which vendors are good, productive partners and which are sapping the IT budget with overbloated fees and unproductive products, services, or billable hours.
   - Migrate business to the former and dismiss the latter.
   - Insist on favorable contracts and pricing in return for vendor exclusivity.
   - Migrate the technology platform in the department to homogeneity to facilitate ease of management and project execution.
   - Negotiate hard with vendors for best pricing, and aggressively manage them after the sale.
   - Ask vendors how they measure their own client-satisfaction performance internally, and require them to produce a report card on themselves at reasonable intervals.
   - If they don't know how to measure themselves internally, get them out.
   - If they do, hold them to the periodic reporting and help them improve their services with clear feedback.

4. Fiscal management/budgeting:
   - Recognize that most companies must generate $10 in revenues to cover every $1 spent in IT.
   - Build a reputation for saving the company money by "making do" and reserve capital expenditure requests for must-have items. Although more difficult, IT directors must become a business resource for the senior management team by suggesting ways to lower the company's overall operational costs through use of IT.
   - If budget variances appear, proactively explain them to senior management and provide fair warning for surprise capital or operating expenditures.
   - Build trust with the CFO by avoiding typical agency issues that accompany the budgeting process that give IT teams a bad reputation for being focused on the constant acquisition of new toys.

5. Improve relationship with the business:
   - Reduce finger pointing between IT and business users by initiating a "seat rotation" that has key IT staff members sitting with the businesses they support one to two days per week.
   - IT director should have a quota of two lunches per week with business-unit managers, functional managers, or members of the IT steering committee.

- Add effective business user relationship management to the appraisal process for all IT team members.

With the right leadership in place, and enthusiastic engagement from the senior management team, the IT department can lead the company in management excellence.

NOTES

1. Peter Ustinov, *Quotable Ustinov* (Amherst, NY: Prometheus Books, 1995).

2. R. Mack, *Creating an IT Strategy: An Alternative Approach* (New York: Gartner, 2002).

3. Gary Hamel and C. K. Prahalad, "The Core Competence of the Corporation," in *Harvard Business Review, Business Classics, Keys for Managerial Success* (Boston, MA: Harvard Business Press, 1990), p. 64.

4. See note 3, p. 68.

5. Louis Henri Sullivan, *The Tall Office Building Artistically Considered* (Philadelphia: JB Lippincott and Co., 1896).

6. www.dictionary.com (October 16, 2002).

7. Potter Stewart, Associate Supreme Court Justice, *Jacobellis v. Ohio,* 1964.

18

Real Estate and Facilities

K. TODD PHILLIPS

Always bear in mind that your own resolution to succeed is more important than any other.
—Abraham Lincoln[1]

This chapter addresses the various issues and questions that the professional services firm should consider when leasing commercial office space. Topics include: (1) preliminary questions that the professional services firm should address prior to looking for office space, (2) how to work with leasing agents and the value that they bring to the process, (3) developing a list of potential properties on paper, (4) conducting property inspections and the most important things to look for and consider, and (5) the lease negotiation process.

The chapter then focuses on the office design of the professional services firm, including a basic discussion of space planning issues and the options to consider in laying out the office, from reception and other common areas, to the professional and nonprofessional offices and work stations. Last, this chapter touches on some of the larger nontechnical capital expenses that you should expect to incur in setting up a professional firm, including items such as furniture and filing systems.

Why This Topic Is Important

Selecting the right office for the professional services firm is every bit as important as it is for other businesses. The cost of leasing office space is typically one of the largest fixed, non-labor monthly expenses that any professional services firm incurs; thus, from a strictly financial perspective, it is important to carefully consider the various leasing options that the firm will face in light of the firm's budgetary constraints. Not only is choosing the right office space important from an economic standpoint, but there are a host of subissues that are important for the firm to consider before entering a lease. For example, clients invariably have certain expectations about both the location and quality of their professionals' offices, and often use such things as a proxy for judging the quality of the services provided. To meet such expectations and maintain a happy and satisfied client base, which is critical to the success of any professional services firm, it is important to consider client concerns when deciding whether to enter a particular lease. In addition, commercial office leases and subleases are often complicated, long-term contracts that include various complex and unfamiliar provisions. Before the professional services firm enters into contractual negotiations over a lease, it should have a basic understanding of the more familiar and negotiable terms that are found in the standard commercial office lease. This chapter addresses each of the foregoing subjects, among others, and offers insights as to how the professional services firm might best arm itself to address these issues. Chapter 19, on legal counsel, also discusses some of the issues to be considered by the firm before entering into legally binding agreements such as leases.

Once a lease has been executed, there are still a host of issues that the professional services firm must address. If, for example, the office space in question has not been finished out, the firm must develop an office design and layout that is consistent with the image the firm hopes to project, and which promotes both productivity and cohesion among the professionals and staff. If, on the other hand, the office space has already been finished out by the landlord or sublessor, the firm must assess whether the current design meets its requirements and, if not, whether and to what extent additional construction must be undertaken. Finally, assuming that the office is not furnished, the firm must make arrangements to furnish the office space, which will include an assessment of the furniture and work-space needs of both the professionals and staff employed by the firm, as well as the common areas and back office of the firm.

Leasing Commercial Office Space

The most common arrangement for professional services firms to acquire office space is through a lease arrangement. This section covers the process for determining leasing needs and identifying appropriate space.

Preliminary Considerations

Before the professional services firm begins to search for office space, it should undertake a preliminary analysis of various factors that will help narrow the focus of the office search and ensure that the firm makes an educated and fully informed decision about its office lease alternatives. Such an analysis can be as formal as the firm decides it needs to be and can range from a rigorous written evaluation prepared by the management of the firm, to a simple checklist. While the form of the preliminary assessment will vary from firm to firm, it is important that the firm fully understand its needs and limitations before conducting a search for office space.

SPACE REQUIREMENTS. One of the most important things that the firm should assess upfront is its space requirements. This can be accomplished by simply counting the number of professionals and staff who are presently employed at the firm (or at least will be on-site on a consistent basis with some accounting for traveling staff) and allocating a predetermined number of square feet for each such individual. Partner offices in professional firms typically range from 250 to 300 square feet; associate offices, 120 to 150 square feet; and staff workstations, 35 to 50 square feet. Once the firm has established its office and workstation requirements, it should consider its needs with respect to common areas, including reception, conference rooms, filing rooms, restrooms, copy/facsimile rooms, and kitchen areas.

In determining its current space requirements, the firm must be careful not to overlook the projected rate of growth. Not only are leases typically long-term contractual commitments, but also searching for office space, negotiating a lease, and relocating the firm are all very time-consuming and expensive undertakings, and are difficult and disruptive to do frequently. Multiple locations within the same city can cause unnecessary travel and communication disconnects. Accordingly, the firm should do its best to determine what its long-term space requirements will be before it enters an office lease.

LOCATION. Another factor that the firm should initially consider is where the office should be located. Often, professional services firms are located in the central business district (CBD) of a city (generally defined as the downtown retail trade and commercial area of a city or an area of very high land valuation, traffic flow, and concentration of retail business offices, theaters, hotels, and services[2]); however, this need not be the case for all firms. Consideration should be given to locating the firm outside the CBD, such as in the suburbs or smaller business centers, where rental rates are often more affordable than in the CBD. Depending on firm priorities, an office location that is nearest to the largest number of on-site professional and administrative staff may be important.

Additionally, the firm should consider where it wants to office vis-à-vis other important locations in the city. For example, for law firms that are composed largely of lawyers who practice civil or criminal litigation, it is probably important for the firm to be located close to the criminal and civil courthouses. On the other hand, for law firms that are predominantly composed of transactional attorneys, it might not be as important to locate the office close to the courthouse, particularly if the firm can achieve material cost savings by locating the office elsewhere.

Last, the firm should undertake an analysis of how important it is to be in close proximity to the firm's clients and potential clients. The firm should consider how often client meetings are held in the office and the clients' expectations (if any) with respect to where they expect their professionals' offices to be located. While it is, of course, impossible to please every client, the firm should at least be sensitive to and consider where its clients' offices are located and whether a decision to office in a particular part of town would impose upon or inconvenience the client base.

BUILDING CLASSIFICATION.   There are different classes of office buildings that will be available to the firm. While many firms choose to be in Class A space, there are certainly other alternatives (Class B and C office buildings) that could be less expensive and might fit the firm's needs. The Building Owners and Manager's Association (BOMA) classifies buildings based on an alphabetic ordering. According to the Urban Land Institute:

- Class A space is characterized by buildings that have excellent location and access, attract high-quality tenants, and are managed professionally. Building materials are high quality and rents are competitive with other new buildings.
- Class B buildings have good locations, management, and construction, and tenant standards are high. Class B buildings have very little functional obsolescence and deterioration.
- Class C buildings are typically 15 to 25 years old but are maintaining steady occupancy.[3]

BUDGET.   The other major preliminary consideration that the firm should assess upfront is its budgetary restrictions with respect to rent, finish-out, and furnishings. As discussed more fully later, rent is typically calculated based on a per square foot basis; however, there are a number of additional expenses that, as a tenant, the firm should expect to be responsible for paying on a monthly basis. Moreover, the firm should anticipate being responsible for substantial upfront costs, such as a security deposit, and depending on the condition of the potential office space, the firm may also have to pay for all or a portion of the improvements and furniture necessary to bring the office space into satisfactory condition.

Accordingly, the firm should prepare a preliminary budget that sets forth an acceptable expense range for both the recurring monthly costs associated with a lease (rent plus expenses) and upfront costs that the firm might be expected to pay (security deposit, finish-out, furniture). As with any start-up, cash flow in the first few months and years of the life of the firm is critical; thus the firm should have a basic understanding of its budgetary constraints before it begins to search for office space.

SUBLEASING. Subleasing office space is often an attractive option for many professional services firms that are just getting started. Most landlords require future tenants to post a significant security deposit on a lease, particularly for new, start-up firms or companies without a proven track record. By subletting office space, the firm can avoid all or a portion of the financial burden associated with such a security deposit, because the sublessor is still contractually liable to the landlord for all rent due and owing under the primary lease. Thus, while the firm may be required to post a security deposit with the sublessor, the amount of such a security deposit may be significantly less than under a traditional lease.

Not only might the firm be able to obtain significant savings by avoiding or at least decreasing the amount of security required on a sublease, but it might also realize additional savings in rent by considering a sublease. Whether the potential sublessor has already moved out of the office space or is simply trying to sublease a portion of its current office space, one of the sublessor's primary objectives in subleasing office space is to offset the amount of rents due under the primary lease. Thus, for example, if the sublessor is contractually obligated to pay the landlord rent at $25 per square foot, the sublessee might be able to negotiate a sublease that calls for rent to be paid at $20 per square foot. In such a case, the sublessor will have offset the amount it is liable to the landlord by 80 percent. While the amount of rent savings that might be achieved depends in large part on the strength of the overall commercial real estate market in the area, the sublessor rarely expects to find a sublessee who is willing to pay the same rent as the sublessor is required to pay under the primary lease.

An additional area of potential cost savings that the firm can obtain by opting for a sublease relates to the design and finish-out of the office space. In many cases, office space that is being marketed as a potential sublease will have already been designed and finished out by the sublessor. In offering to sublease all or a portion of its leased space, the sublandlord rarely, if ever, tries to recoup from the sublessee the money it spent in initially designing and finishing out the office space, which can be costly. Although the overall design of the office, the size of the offices within the space, and the finish-out (e.g., carpeting, wall covering) may not be exactly how the firm would have designed the office space on its own, the firm must balance this concern with the savings in avoiding paying for the office design and finish-out. Under a traditional lease, landlords often provide the tenant with a finish-out "allowance," which is a negotiated amount that may or may not be sufficient to design and finish out the office space to the tenant's satisfaction.

Last, the sublessor may allow a sublessee to use some or all of the furniture and equipment currently in the office space at little or no cost to the sublessee. As discussed more fully later, furniture, fixtures, and equipment can account for a large portion of the start-up costs of any business, including the professional services firm. However, as with office design and finish-out, the sublessor will have already incurred the cost of furnishing and equipping the office space that it intends to sublease and, as a result, may be willing to allow the sublessee to use its furniture and equipment during the term of the sublease. The cost of using the furniture and equipment presently in the office space can simply be rolled into the amount per square foot that the sublessee agrees to pay under the sublease. Alternatively, the sublessee can offer to purchase all or a portion of the sublessor's furniture, which, as discussed more fully later, would still save the firm significant money over buying new furniture and paying for delivery. The subject of furniture and equipment is one of many potential points of negotiation between the sublessor and sublessee and may not even be an option if the sublessor is moving its entire business operation to another location. Nonetheless, in negotiating a sublease, the firm should consider these options.

Subleasing office space can be accomplished in different ways. The sublessee can assume a portion of an existing lease and share common areas and facilities with the primary tenant. On the one hand, such an alternative provides the firm with an opportunity to get to know the primary tenant and possibly obtain business and business referrals from the primary tenant. On the other hand, if the primary tenant is a competitor of the sublessee or there are other compatibility problems that cannot be resolved, sharing common space with the primary tenant may not make sense. One way to assume only a portion of the existing lease and avoid or minimize sharing common areas with the primary tenant is to construct a wall dividing the sublessor's office space from the sublessee and construct a separate entrance. Such construction adds to the upfront costs associated with the sublease, and the sublessee and sublessor must determine who will pay for the construction. How much these considerations impact the agreement will depend on the individual firms need for privacy, security and a separate identity within the office space.

An alternative to assuming only a portion of an existing lease is to take over the entire lease. This type of situation often arises when the sublessor already has or is considering relocating its entire office to another location.

In sum, there are various ways in which the professional services firm can go about subleasing office space. Subleasing office space provides the firm with an opportunity to save significant upfront capital on a variety of fronts, including security deposits, rent, finish-out, and furniture. On the negative side, however, subleases are often shorter in term than regular leases, and the sublessee may be forced to cooperate and coordinate with the sublessor on common areas, reception management, signage in the space, security and privacy issues.

Leasing Agents

Once the firm has established its basic needs and requirements, it should consider retaining a leasing agent. There are numerous benefits to retaining a leasing agent. First, leasing agents usually possess a greater degree of familiarity with the landlords and properties in the area and the real estate agents representing such landlords. The real estate community in many cities is close knit, and leasing agents can provide the professional services firm with their valuable impressions about the quality and reputation of the landlords who are offering office space, as well as the history and quality of the properties in question.

Second, leasing agents almost certainly possess greater knowledge of the commercial office space that is available than the professional services firm. Commercial leasing agents are in the business of familiarizing themselves with many, if not all, of the various office buildings in a particular city. Thus, while the professional services firm might possess a limited amount of knowledge about certain office buildings in town, leasing agents should bring to the table deeper historical insights about many office buildings.

Third, leasing agents can provide valuable counseling and insight into various office needs and requirements that the professional services firm may have overlooked. Leasing agents are not only professionals who help the professional services firm navigate the office search and lease negotiation process but also counselors who will have a great deal of experience in working with tenants and understanding their needs. The professional services firm should take the time to explain the firm's business model and goals to the leasing agent, who can then provide the firm with informed advice about the best leasing alternatives.

Last, as discussed more fully later, leasing agents often possess significant expertise in negotiating commercial office leases. The leasing agent may be able to help the firm obtain concessions from the landlord in the lease negotiations that the firm would not have considered or even requested. In almost all cases, the landlord is more sophisticated and experienced than the professional services firm in negotiating leases. However, the leasing agent can help level the playing field and explain any confusing or frustrating lease provisions.

When selecting a leasing agent, issues to consider and questions to ask include:

1. Who pays the leasing agent's fees, and how are they calculated? Leasing agent's fees are almost always paid by the landlord and range from 3 percent to 5 percent of the total value of any lease that is ultimately executed. The total value of the lease is calculated by multiplying the total square footage of the lease by the price per square foot by the term of the lease. Thus, if a five-year lease is executed for 5,000 square feet and

the price per square foot is $20, the leasing agent's fee would be somewhere between $15,000 and $25,000.

2. What experience does the potential broker have in placing professional services firms? Agents with experience representing tenants in the retail and/or industrial context may or may not bring adequate experience and knowledge to the table in assisting with a commercial lease. Thus, it is important to ask whether the broker has experience in the commercial realm and, in particular, whether he or she has prior experience representing professional services firms. Within the professional services firm arena, some brokers may have more expertise with specific firm types, such as financial services providers, lawyers, consultants or medical specialists.

   Similarly, it is important to determine whether the potential broker has experience assisting tenants with office space in the same size range as the professional services firm is considering. If the agent is used to dealing with larger clients and is actively representing a number of other larger clients, the firm might not warrant an adequate portion of the agent's attention or obtain the full benefit of the services.

3. Is the broker licensed by or affiliated with any professional leasing organizations? Two of the more familiar and reputable leasing organizations are the Society of Industrial and Office Realtors (SIOR) and Certified Commercial Investment Members (CCIM).

Although in many cases it makes sense to retain the services of a leasing agent to assist in leasing office space, it is not mandatory.

Develop a List of Potential Office Buildings

Either with the assistance of a leasing agent or without, at some point the professional services firm should identify several properties that, at least on paper, appear to fit its needs and are in line with its budgetary constraints.

In developing a list of potential office properties, the firm should consider certain issues to narrow the list of properties to inspect. The leasing agent can prove invaluable in preparing a professional market survey that includes much of the following information and that, at least preliminarily, appears to meet the firm's needs. Regardless of whether the firm retains a leasing agent to prepare a formal presentation, however, it can and should consider the following issues before it begins to conduct property inspections.

LOCATION.   Based on the information gathered during the preliminary assessment, it should be relatively simple for the firm to determine which of the potential office buildings meet its location needs. One way to accomplish this is to ask the leasing agent to prepare a map of potential office buildings, which can be as simple as a street map with flags denoting available properties. Such a map provides the decision makers within the firm a basic but helpful tool to assess the location of the buildings in relation to one another, as well as location of the buildings in the city. While most professionals are generally familiar with the more prominent buildings in a particular city, many of which are found within the CBD, if the firm is considering office space outside the CBD, a map can help clear up any confusion about building locations.

SURROUNDING AREA/FACILITIES.   The condition of the area immediately surrounding the office building is also important. The professional services firm would not want to office in an upscale, Class A building in a rough or unsafe neighborhood. Although the firm can and should consult a map to better understand where the available office buildings are located, the decision makers in the firm should be familiar with the areas surrounding the potential office buildings. If the firm is not familiar with the surroundings of any potential office buildings, the decision makers in the firm should, at a minimum, take the time to drive by the buildings and perhaps walk through the neighborhood.

Additionally, the professional services firm should have a general idea about the retail facilities and restaurants in the area immediately surrounding the office building. While office buildings located in the CBD of many cities provide professional services firms with a wide variety of retail services and restaurant alternatives, this is not true of all cities and locations. Moreover, office buildings located in smaller business centers or office parks may not provide the firm with sufficient retail options. Such options are important not only for the benefit of the professionals and staff who are employed at the firm but also for the clients and potential clients who will visit the firm's office.

OFFICE DESIGN AND LAYOUT.   When offering to lease or sublease office space, landlords or their agents will prepare floor plans that depict the layout of the space. If the office space is not finished out, the floor plan will reflect little more than where the office space is located on the floor, whether it is less than the whole floor, and where the demising walls are located. However, if the space has been finished out, as is often the case with subleases, the firm can get a good idea of the office design and layout simply by reviewing the floor plan. While it may be difficult to rule out potential office space simply by reviewing the layout, the firm can get a good idea of whether the current layout would be acceptable or whether a significant amount of construction would be required to bring the office space in line with the firm's needs.

In some cases, the landlord includes in its marketing materials photographs of the office building and the space for lease. Although photographs do not obviate the need for a thorough property inspection, they can provide the firm with a decent superficial look at the quality of the building and potential office space.

BUILDING HISTORY. In addition to reviewing any available office floor plans and photographs, the professional services firm should seek basic background on each potential office building, including the year the building was constructed, the building classification (A, B, or C), and the percentage of office space that is currently vacant. Moreover, the firm should ask whether and to what extent there have been environmental, zoning, or other major issues with a particular building, and if so, whether such problems have been satisfactorily remediated.

LANDLORD AND PROPERTY MANAGER. The professional services firm will encounter a number of different types of landlords when searching for office space. Landlords can range from very sophisticated real estate investment trusts (REITs) to less sophisticated individual owners. While landlords who have the same organizational structure do not always act in the same manner, in general, the more sophisticated the landlord is, the longer it will take to negotiate and agree to a lease. Often, larger institutional owners have very lengthy and complicated standard lease forms that contain a multitude of provisions, some superfluous and some relevant, that the professional services firm will need to carefully review, comment on, and negotiate with the landlord. This very time-consuming and costly process is only exacerbated if the organizational bureaucracy within the building owner includes the usual complement of real estate professionals, property managers, and lawyers.

On the other hand, if the landlord is an individual owner, he or she may not be inclined to a particularly sophisticated form of lease and may elect to save time and money by involving fewer people in the leasing process than the more sophisticated landlord. Moreover, in most cases, the individual owner will not have the financial resources and backing that larger institutional owners enjoy and, thus, may be more motivated to negotiate with and procure tenants in an effort to ensure steady cash flow in order to meet mortgage obligations on the property.

In addition to doing basic research on the size and sophistication of the landlords who are offering commercial office space, the firm should inquire about the reputation of the landlords. As is true with residential landlords, commercial landlords can vary dramatically in the manner in which they deal with tenant concerns and questions. The real estate community in most areas is fairly close knit, and, with little effort, the firm should be able to ascertain a particular landlord's reputation and determine whether the landlord is known for responsiveness (or lack thereof), flexibility and willingness to meet unanticipated tenant needs, which will invariably arise over the term of any lease.

The firm should inquire not only about the ownership at each of the available office buildings but also about the property management company that the landlord has selected to manage the building. The building manager is often a tenant's main point of contact in an office building and the individual to whom the landlord has entrusted responsibility for the maintenance and upkeep of the building. Thus, it is critically important that the property manager have a good working relationship with the current tenants in the building and that the building manager has demonstrated the ability to promptly resolve the various kinds of issues that arise in all office buildings, which can range from minor janitorial issues (e.g., keeping restrooms cleaned and stocked) to more significant engineering problems (e.g., flooding or mid-summer HVAC outages).

There are a wide variety of property management companies, from very small building management companies who are responsible for only a handful of buildings, to larger nationwide companies that manage buildings in many different cities. While the latter may provide the professional services firm with a higher degree of comfort, at least on a superficial level, the firm should nonetheless seek the input of other tenants about the building management company, as even the largest property management companies can experience varying levels of service between different cities and even between different buildings in the same city.

TENANTS. Before the firm narrows down the list of office buildings to those that it will visit and inspect, the firm should informally assess the other major tenants in the available office buildings. It is important that the firm determine whether any competitors are already tenants in the building and, if so, whether their presence would be an impediment to servicing existing clients or attracting new clients. For example, if an accounting firm (50 to 100 professionals) is considering office space in a number of buildings and one of those buildings is generally referred to by the name of one of its larger competitors (e.g., the KPMG Building), the firm should assess whether and to what extent its business would be impacted by the presence of that competitor. Additionally, the professional services firm should try to determine whether there are any unsavory or objectionable tenants in the building who might reflect poorly on the firm.

PARKING. Parking is one of the hidden costs that can add to the overall expense of a lease; thus, the firm should ask whether parking spaces are included in the rent and, if so, how many spaces. The number of parking spaces that a landlord is willing to provide a tenant free of charge is usually determined by a predetermined ratio of parking spaces per square feet of leased office space. Thus, for example, if the total lease size is 10,000 square feet and the landlord is willing to provide one parking space per every 1,000 square feet of leased space, the tenant will be provided 10 parking spaces at no charge. (The term "no charge" is a misnomer because the landlord will have built the cost of parking into the rental rate.) In this example, any additional parking that the tenant needs would be paid for by the tenant, whose costs are often passed through to the professionals and employees employed at the firm. The cost of parking and the allocation of parking spaces per tenant are often subject to negotiation between the landlord and tenant, but can wind up being a significant additional rent expenditure.

The firm should consider not only the cost and allocation of parking spaces but also the location of the reserved parking and whether there is sufficient visitor parking either in (or under) the building or nearby.

SECURITY.   Because of the sensitive nature of the work that professional services firms perform for their clients, the buildings in which they office must be secure. Building security can differ dramatically from one building to another; however, the firm should ascertain whether the office buildings under consideration provide protection, such as security guards, video cameras that monitor the common areas of the building and the parking garage, and access cards or keypad entry systems for the building's tenants. Additionally, the firm should ask whether access to the building, both externally and internally, is restricted during nonbusiness hours. Often, during nonbusiness hours, tenants in a building are granted access to only the floor or floors on which they office.

RENTAL RATE AND EXPENSES.   Of all the foregoing issues that the firm should assess on paper, perhaps the most important consideration is the price per square foot that the landlord is asking and what expenses the firm will be expected to pay. In almost all cases, commercial office space is quoted based on the price per square foot. However, this number can vary rather dramatically depending on the market. For example, in 2003 the average asking rent for a mix of Class A and B buildings in New York City was $47.02 per square. On the other hand, the average asking price for similar office space in Dallas was $20.35 per foot. Exhibit 18.1 shows the 2003 average price per square foot of Class A and Class B office space for 29 of the largest U.S. markets. The exhibit also reflects the 2003 vacancy rates in each market. The vacancy rate can have a dramatic impact on both rental rates (an inverse relationship exists between rental rates and vacancy rates), as well as the landlord's willingness to negotiate and give on certain terms of a lease. Although the asking price per square foot is negotiable and depends a great deal on the real estate market, it should be relatively simple for the firm to rule out alternatives that clearly fall outside the firm's preliminary budget.

In addition to the price per square foot, the landlord will also seek to recover from the tenant a portion of the operating expenses associated with the leased premises. What is included in the definition of *operating expenses* depends on how that term is defined in the lease; however, in

MARKET	VACANT SPACE		Y-T-D	QUOTED RENTAL RATES	
	VACANT SF	VAC %	NET ABSORP	CLASS A ($)	CLASS B ($)
1 Atlanta	38,212,470	17.4	488,847	20.96	16.19
2 Austin	11,003,756	18.7	467,487	19.56	17.12
3 Baltimore	12,265,346	14.6	511,516	21.44	17.83
4 Boston	41,914,373	14.9	(1,713,211)	25.52	18.84
5 Charlotte	8,316,639	14.3	115,031	19.54	16.01
6 Chicago	60,274,643	17.5	(2,084,261)	27.92	21.09
7 Cincinnati	9,568,033	15.0	(422,197)	18.57	15.15
8 Cleveland	14,599,859	16.7	(1,206,311)	20.96	18.03
9 Columbus	10,675,469	15.3	(224,831)	18.29	15.91
10 Dallas/Fort Worth	54,393,363	21.2	(1,321,402)	20.35	16.12
11 Denver	26,627,391	17.5	(333170)	19.56	15.84
12 Detroit	23,022,862	16.5	252,904	24.09	19.75
13 Houston	36,379,858	16.8	(1,562,424)	20.57	16.09
14 Jacksonville (Florida)	4,656,598	12.8	214,714	19.16	17.07
15 Los Angeles	47,088,090	12.8	3,627,294	25.67	22.11
16 Minneapolis*	11,995,159	23.1	(698,268)	19.48	17.75
17 New York City	49,894,973	10.3	809,767	47.02	32.53
18 Northern New Jersey	41,461,052	14.8	1,540,882	26.71	20.82
19 Orange County (CA)	15,261,193	12.2	3,872,769	24.56	22.31
20 Orlando	8,589,690	13.8	336,810	20.33	17.79
21 Philadelphia	40,568,678	15.9	(3,559,273)	23.47	18.52
22 Phoenix	17,166,985	15.9	3,250,136	22.15	19.35
23 Raleigh/Durham	7,805,438	17.5	595,488	18.76	15.89
24 San Diego	9,581,579	11.7	1,456,488	29.57	25.27
25 San Francisco Bay Area	55,327,833	17.4	491,690	26.54	22.97
26 Seattle/Puget Sound	16,936,507	13.3	1,190,471	24.53	19.65
27 South Florida	20,395,707	12.7	2,537,962	26.71	21.13
28 Tama/St. Petersburg	10,102,167	12.6	471,460	20.68	16.98
29 Washington	43,624,113	12.0	6,426,232	30.01	26.87
	Class A, B, C			Class A	Class B

U.S. OFFICE: YEAR-END 2003

Exhibit 18.1 Recent Square-Foot Lease Rates in Major U.S. Metro Areas. *Source:* CoStar Group. Inc. *NAIOP

general, operating expenses refer to the actual costs associated with operating an office building, including maintenance, repairs, management, utilities, taxes, and insurance.

Operating expenses are dealt with by one of two different types of commercial leases, the *gross lease* and the *net lease*. According to one author, the difference between the gross lease and net lease can be explained as follows:

> The primary difference between these fundamental lease types is the variation in responsibility of the payment of operating expenses. At one end of the spectrum, the gross lease generally requires the landlord to pay all of the operating expenses. At the other end of the spectrum, a net lease generally provides that the tenant will pay a pro rata share, as defined in the lease, of all operating expense items.[4]

GROSS LEASES. Under a traditional gross lease, the tenant's monthly rent will be higher than under a net lease because the landlord has assumed responsibility for all of the operating expenses. However, under a traditional gross lease, the landlord also assumes all of the risk that such operating expenses will increase during the term of the lease. Thus, it should come as no surprise that landlords today are rarely willing to enter into a traditional gross lease. Rather, landlords most often attempt to limit their exposure under a gross lease by inserting provisions in the lease that allow the landlord to offset the cost of any future increases in operating expenses. One way landlords might try to limit their exposure under a gross lease is to insert a provision that ties future increases in monthly rent to the Consumer Price Index (CPI). However, because market indices such as the CPI are large scale in nature, they rarely reflect the operating expense changes felt by the landlord at a particular building. As a result, while tying rent increases to the CPI is, from the landlord's perspective, an improvement over the traditional gross lease, landlords prefer to make any escalation under the lease relate more directly to operating expenses as opposed to the base rental rate.

One way that landlords can accomplish this is to insert an expense stop into the lease. An expense stop puts a dollar limit on the total operating expense that the landlord is obligated to pay. Expense stops are usually calculated on a dollar per square foot basis, which serves as the benchmark against which future increases in operating expenses will be measured. If, for example, the landlord agrees to pay $1.00 per square foot in operating expenses and such operating expenses increase to $1.10 per square foot in the second year of the lease, the tenant would be responsible for its pro rata portion of the additional 10 cents in operating expenses. The expense stop need not reflect the actual amount of operating expenses that the landlord is paying at the time the lease is negotiated. Rather, the expense stop is a negotiable amount that depends in large part on the strength of the commercial lease market. Thus, the higher expense stop that the tenant can negotiate, the better off the tenant will be if there are future increases in operating expenses.

Another way landlords try to limit their exposure to future increases in operating expenses is to insert a base year provision into the lease. Similar to the expense stop, a base year clause provides that the landlord will be responsible for paying the operating expenses incurred during whatever "base" year that the parties agree on, and the tenant will be responsible for paying for any increases in operating expenses that occur after the base year. Again, because operating expenses are almost always on the rise, it is in the tenant's best interest to try to negotiate a lease with a base year provision that is either the year the lease is executed or the following year, whereas the landlord will try to incorporate a base year provision that relates to the year prior to the lease commencement.

NET LEASES. As opposed to the modified gross lease that establishes a floor above which the tenant is responsible for paying operating expenses, under a net lease, the tenant pays its pro rata portion of the operating expenses. Net leases come in one of three different varieties: net leases, net-net leases, and triple-net leases. According to the Urban Land Institute, the difference between these versions of net leases can be explained as follows:

> In the net lease, the tenant is usually required to pay its pro-rata share of all utilities, ad valorem taxes, and any other special assessments associated directly with the leased premises. In the net-net lease, the tenant pays its pro-rata share all of the above costs of a net lease plus its pro-rata share of the cost of the ordinary repairs and maintenance of the common areas and building systems. The triple net lease usually requires that the tenant pay its pro-rata share of all of the above costs of the net-net lease plus the cost of certain capital improvements.[5]

Given the foregoing description of the various types of net leases, it should come as no surprise that landlords favor the triple-net lease.

GROSS UP. *Grossing up* is a mechanism that is often employed in an effort to account for increases in operating expenses when, in the base year, the building occupancy rate is less than 100 percent. If, for example, in a building that is 50 percent occupied, a tenant negotiates a lease with an expense stop or base year provision of $10 per square foot, then without a gross-up provision, the tenant will be liable for not only the annual increases in operating expenses that are contemplated when negotiating the lease but also any increases in operating expenses that are attributable to increased occupancy. Thus, in the foregoing hypothetical, if the building goes from 50 percent occupancy in year one to 100 percent occupancy in year two, the operating expenses for which the tenant is liable will increase dramatically, from the negotiated amount of $10 per square foot to, for example, $13 per foot.

Although occupancy rates have effectively doubled in this example, because a significant portion of operating expenses are fixed regardless of occupancy rates, operating expenses will increase by only a fraction of the increase in occupancy. Examples of fixed expenses include security, garage expenses, landscaping, and insurance, whereas variable expenses include items such as repairs and maintenance. If, in calculating the expense stop or base year, the landlord had grossed up expenses as if the building were fully occupied, the tenant might have been able to negotiate a higher expense stop or base year.

Thus, in considering the rental rate and expenses that are within the professional services firm's budget, the firm should confirm that any expense stop or base year provision is based on a grossed-up operating expense figure. Further, regardless of the manner in which the gross-up calculation is performed, the tenant should insist that the landlord be precluded from recovering more than 100 percent of its actual operating expenses in any given year.

Property Inspection/Walk-Through

Once a list of potential office buildings has been narrowed down, the next step is to arrange meetings with the appropriate leasing agents and landlords to conduct building inspections. Many of the things that the firm considers when conducting the physical property inspections are similar to the topics that the firm should have reviewed on paper. Nevertheless, to confirm or dispel any conclusions that the firm reached based on preliminary due diligence, it is important that the firm take into account each of the following considerations when touring potential office space.

FUNDAMENTAL ASPECTS OF THE BUILDING.   Are the building and proposed office space consistent with the image the firm is trying to project? While the design, finish-out, and furnishings can have a dramatic impact on the overall ambience and feel of the office, there are certain immutable things that the potential tenant cannot modify or which can be changed only at great cost. The façade of the building, natural lighting, landscaping, and access to parking (both tenant and visitor) are all factors that should be considered when conducting the physical inspection.

COMMON AREAS.   Bear in mind that the first thing a client or potential client is going to see when entering an office building is the foyer. Pay attention to the quality of the finish-out in the foyer and other common areas in the building. Additionally, note whether there is a tenant directory in the foyer, as well as an information/security desk.

PROPERTY MANAGEMENT/MAINTENANCE.   During the property inspection, note the general appearance of the interior of the building and the level of upkeep/maintenance. Although this should not be a problem in most Class A buildings, different property management companies have different styles and provide different levels of service. If the other tenants in the building have had problems with the building manager or it appears that management is not maintaining the building sufficiently, this alone might be a reason to rule out a particular building. On the other hand, if there have been problems with the building management, but the owner is committed to rectifying the situation by, for example, switching management companies, it might be a nonissue.

CURRENT OFFICE DESIGN. Although a cursory review of the office layout can be undertaken on paper, pay attention to the location of the interior walls, size of the offices, and whether significant improvements will need to be made before taking possession.

ELEVATORS. When touring an office building, note where the available office space is located in relation to the elevator bank. If the firm is not going to lease an entire floor of an office building, it may be important for the firm to be located close to the elevator bank so that it is one of the first offices that clients and potential clients see. Although the floor plan should depict where the office space is located vis-à-vis the elevator bank, the tour should give a sense of the exact location and whether the exposure is optimal.

TAKE NOTES. Whoever participates in the property tour on behalf of the firm should bring along a notepad or a form to complete during the property inspection because it is often difficult to remember details about each particular building as the tour proceeds. Notes will prove valuable when discussing the options with members of the firm who may not have participated in the property inspection.

MAKING A DECISION. Once the property inspection has been completed, the firm is ready to decide which building or buildings best suit the firm's needs. This decision is typically made by the management of the firm; however, management should consider getting the input of all, or at least a portion of, the professionals and employees at the firm. While the firm cannot please everyone with its selection of office space and location, conducting a survey or poll of the firm's employees will, at a minimum, make employees feel as though they had a hand in the decision and are part of a firm that considers their opinions when making a major decision such as office location.

Negotiating the Lease

Once the firm has decided which building meets its needs and requirements, it is time to initiate lease negotiations with the landlord. The process of negotiating a lease typically begins with the potential tenant sending a request for proposal (RFP) to the landlord, spelling out the firm's business needs.

The landlord will counter with a response to the RFP, and, assuming that the parties can come to an agreement on the business terms of the deal, the parties will enter more formal lease negotiations.

THE REQUEST FOR PROPOSAL PROCESS. The RFP is the first opportunity for the professional services firm to more formally convey to the potential landlord its business needs and requirements. Many, if not all, of the conditions contained in the RFP will be derived from the preliminary assessment and building inspection that the firm undertook. Depending on the level of sophistication and detail of the preliminary analysis, the firm should try to include in the RFP as many of its key business requirements as possible. Thus, for example, the firm should include in the RFP, at a minimum, its initial rental rate offer, the manner in which the firm is willing to pay for operating expenses, the firm's parking needs, the term or length of lease that the firm is willing to enter, and the size of the office space required.

In many cases, the RFP will also include additional requirements or specifications that the firm may not have considered preliminarily, but which will most assuredly be picked up in the lease. Examples of such provisions include options to extend or terminate the lease, assignment/subletting provisions, security deposit and prepaid rent provisions, and insurance requirements.

It is important to include in the RFP as many important lease provisions that the firm can identify because the RFP forms the basis of all future lease negotiations. Thus, for example, if the firm does not include in the RFP a right of early termination, it will be very difficult to try to go back and add such a provision to the proposed lease. In such a situation, the landlord would almost certainly feel that the firm was trying to retrade the deal by incorporating provisions that the firm had not contemplated or deemed important enough to include in the original RFP. As would be true with any other type of contract, in this situation you would expect the landlord to be very reluctant to add or delete important business terms in the 11th hour of the lease negotiations.

Although the professional services firm may have never submitted an RFP for commercial office space previously and is unfamiliar with all of the terms that it should include in the RFP, the firm can and should rely on the real estate agent to help inform (and possibly draft) the RFP. The real estate agent will be more experienced than the firm in initiating lease negotiations and submitting RFPs. In many cases, the real estate agent will have exhaustive form RFPs that can be modified by the firm (or the real estate agent) to reflect its needs and requirements. Indeed, it is entirely possible that the real estate agent will have recently negotiated a different lease with the landlord and will know what tenant requirements the landlord is willing to consider.

To some extent, the RFP will be reflective of and responsive to any initial marketing materials that have been provided by the landlord. For example, if the landlord has advertised 10,000 square feet of office space at $20 per square foot for a 10-year lease term, the RFP may include an initial offer of

8,000 square feet at $18 per square foot over a seven-year term. In addition, the RFP should include whatever key business terms that the professional services firm, in consultation with its real estate agent, deems important and necessary to any commercial office lease.

Depending on its level of motivation, which is often a product of the strength of the market, the landlord will respond to the RFP with its own counteroffer. In many cases, the landlord will respond to each of the items set forth in the RFP in turn; however, this does not always happen, and the firm should make sure that it keeps track of any terms that were not included in the landlord's response to the RFP. It is common for landlords to demonstrate their agreement to terms contained in the original RFP by simply not responding to or countering such terms; however, the firm should confirm that any terms not responded to by the landlord are agreeable and will be picked up in the lease. Assuming that the parties can come to an agreement on a majority of the business terms set forth in the RFP, they will proceed with more formal lease negotiations.

IMPORTANT LEASE PROVISIONS. Although the scope of this chapter does not permit a detailed analysis of all the different provisions contained in the typical commercial lease, the professional services firm should bear in mind that nearly everything in the lease is negotiable. The following are several of the more important, common lease provisions that the professional services firm and its real estate agent should look out for when negotiating a lease. The CD-ROM that accompanies this book contains a sample of a standard commercial office lease, which can be referred to when considering each of the following lease provisions:

1. The premises—usable versus rentable space: *Rentable space* is the amount of square feet that the tenant is actually paying for and includes common areas in the building such as hallways, restrooms, lobbies, elevator shafts, and stairwells. *Usable space* is the amount of square feet that can actually be used by the firm. In almost all commercial leases, the tenant will be required to pay for its pro-rata portion of the rentable space in the building, and the rental rate will be based on price per square foot of rentable space, not usable space. Thus, if the firm is considering entering a 10,000 square foot lease, at $20 per square foot (a total lease cost of $200,000 per year), the firm should ask what portion of the 10,000 square feet is usable to determine what it will be paying for the space that it can actually use. In this case, if the usable square feet totals 9,500, as opposed to 10,000 rentable square feet, the effective price per square foot will have increased from $20 to $21. Again, while it is not uncommon for rental rates to be quoted in this manner, before entering the lease, the firm should understand what it is paying for and make sure that the landlord isn't making a hidden profit by overallocating rentable square feet to the various tenants in the building.

2. The lease term and renewal rights: Most leases provide that the term of the lease begins on the "commencement date" and ends on the "termination date." As with many terms contained in the lease, however, these are defined terms contained elsewhere in the lease that the firm should understand and agree to before it executes the lease. For example, if the lease provides that the commencement date is the *earlier* of a date or the date on which the landlord completes tenant improvements, then, conceivably, the tenant could be responsible for paying rent *before* the premises are ready to be occupied. Obviously, the firm would want to avoid paying rent unless and until the premises are tenantable and, thus, might simply change the foregoing language to the *later* of a date certain or the date on which tenant improvements are completed.

In addition to the dates on which the lease begins and ends, the firm should make sure that the lease protects the firm in the event that the firm's office needs change over time, which is almost sure to happen. Most leases contain a renewal option that gives the tenant the right to extend the lease upon proper notice. The firm should try to negotiate a renewal option that can be exercised closer to the end of the term of the lease, which will allow the firm to continue paying rent in the premises at the prevailing fair market rate. Recognize, however, that the landlord will try to negotiate a renewal provision that obligates the tenant to exercise the option well before the end of the lease (to provide the landlord with sufficient time to re-let the premises, if necessary) and may try to secure a premium above fair market rates.

3. Landlord's work and obligations: The landlord is customarily responsible for, among other things, providing utilities for the building, maintaining both the interior and exterior of the building, and making any necessary repairs at the office building. However, the firm should be aware of exactly what the obligations of the landlord are and when the landlord is obligated to provide such services. For example, most leases provide that the landlord will be required to provide HVAC services during normal business hours, but not during off-hours or on holidays. Before entering the lease, the firm should make sure that the hours in which the landlord is going to provide HVAC services are compatible with the firm's business and that there is a mechanism for obtaining HVAC services, at a reasonable rate, during off-hours or on holidays. Similarly, if the landlord cannot provide such services, whether through its fault or that of a third party, such as a utility company, the firm should make sure that it is protected from any business interruption by a rent abatement clause and/or business interruption insurance.

4. Assignment and subletting: Assignment and subletting provisions are common in commercial leases and generally spell out the manner in which the tenant can pass off all or a portion of the leased premises to another tenant. In much the same way that the renewal option discussed earlier gives the tenant the right to protect itself in the event that future business needs change, so do assignment/subletting provisions. In reviewing the assignment/subletting

provision(s) in the lease, the firm should ensure that, although landlord approval is required prior to any assignment or sublease, such approval will not be unreasonably withheld or delayed.

5. Nondisturbance agreements: In the event that the landlord's mortgage on the office building is foreclosed, in many states, junior leasehold interests are wiped out. This effectively means that any buyer at a foreclosure sale is under no obligation to honor the existing leases in the building. To protect itself from exposure if there is a foreclosure on the building, the tenant should insist on a nondisturbance clause, which essentially provides that any buyer at a foreclosure must honor the terms of the existing lease and the tenant's rights thereunder.

ATTORNEYS. In addition to the real estate agent, the professional services firm should consider retaining legal counsel to assist in negotiating the lease. Although it may not be necessary to retain counsel while the office search is being conducted, once a choice has been made, the firm should retain counsel to help ensure that the business terms of the deal, as reflected in the RFP and the landlord's response(s) thereto, are accurately reflected in the lease. While there is a certain degree of overlap between the services being provided by the real estate broker and the real estate attorney, on average, the real estate attorney should possess a greater familiarity and understanding of *all* of the terms of the lease than the real estate broker. Retaining real estate counsel will invariably add to the cost the professional services firm incurs in leasing commercial office space; however, such costs are nearly always outweighed by the value that the real estate attorney adds to the lease negotiation process. Chapter 19, Legal Counsel covers the process of selecting an attorney by the professional services firm in detail.

Finalizing and Executing the Lease

Negotiating and finalizing a commercial office lease can take a significant amount of time, and the firm should be prepared to spend several weeks reviewing and negotiating the draft lease. It is important that the firm leave itself sufficient time to fully negotiate the lease and, if necessary, break off such negotiations and look elsewhere for office space. If the landlord is aware that the firm has to move out of its present office by a particular date or that the firm has few or no other options, the landlord will have a real advantage in bringing the lease negotiations to a close.

Nonetheless, once an agreement has been reached on the final terms of the lease, the firm and the landlord will execute the lease. If the firm has agreed to make prepaid rental and security payments, such payments are often due at the time the lease is executed. Thereafter, and depending on any finish-out that needs to be conducted in the premises, the firm should be in a position to take possession of the premises and begin its tenancy.

Office Design, Finish-Out, and Furniture

In addition to selecting an office and negotiating a lease, the firm should spend significant time in planning the office design, finish-out, and furnishings. Each of these components, among others, is of critical importance in both obtaining and maintaining client relationships. As one recent article noted with regard to law firms:

> Clients, particularly corporate entities, are conflicted in their perception of law firms. They want the legal practice they hire to be at the forefront of their profession, yet they expect the markers that signify solidity and stability.
>
> In response, some law firms have chosen to look more like their customer base. In San Francisco, for example, those [firms] targeting dot-com companies abandoned wood paneling and private offices for light, open, airy spaces. This approach furthered a perception of niche expertise, but the risks became painfully apparent in the technology downturn.
>
> What a law firm's offices look like is an issue because clients regularly visit. In contrast to management and technology consultants, which often do the bulk of their work at the client's site, law firms host their customers.
>
> To be most effective, the appearance of a firm's offices must match the image, or brand, clients receive in advertising, personal meetings, and other encounters with the firm. That appearance should reflect a firm's expertise without being so closely aligned to a market segment that it loses other business.[6]

Office design, finish-out, and furnishings not only are important from an external, client-related perspective but also play a crucial role in helping to form and foster the internal culture within a firm. Employee moral, motivation, health, and productivity can all be impacted by the foregoing factors, and as a result, the firm should pay careful consideration to each of these topics when planning for and setting up the professional services firm office.

Although the firm can and should analyze these and other factors on its own, the firm should also consider hiring a space planner/interior designer to assist in this very important phase of relocating to new office space. In much the same way that the real estate agent and attorney can provide valuable assistance and insight into the search for office space and the negotiation of the lease, the space planner can save the firm time and money by coming up with innovative ideas and solutions to the firm's office design and furniture needs.

Office Design

There are generally two types of office plans that the professional services firm can adopt: the *closed office plan* and the *open office plan.* A balance can be difficult to achieve, as noted by Gregg Hlavaty of Benson Hlavaty Architects: "The most prevailing dichotomy in office space design—and the one most difficult to achieve—is to provide work spaces which are both open and interactive, but also allow for privacy and contemplation." Examples of these two types of floor plans are shown in Exhibit 18.2.

CLOSED FLOOR PLAN. Traditionally, professional services firms have opted for the closed office plan, which generally provides more privacy for professionals. This type of office plan is predominated by exterior and interior offices of various sizes and internal walls that separate different groups or sections within the firm. Although the closed office plan affords the firm a greater degree of privacy, it is also more expensive than alternative floor plans.

OPEN FLOOR PLAN. The open plan is usually a more cost-efficient layout that promotes a more social work environment. An open office plan is most often predominated by a large open area that is divided up into individual or

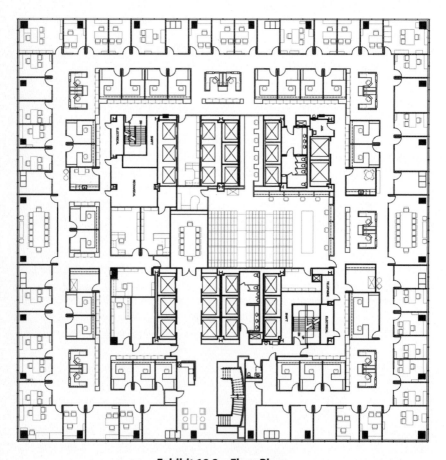

Exhibit 18.2   Floor Plans

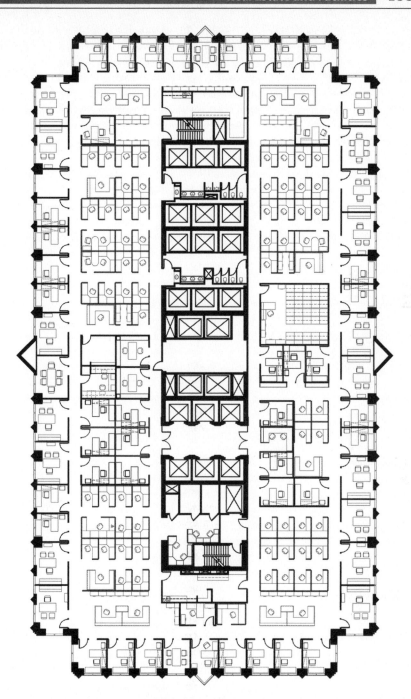

Exhibit 18.2 *Continued*

shared workstations by a series of partitions of varying heights. Although privacy is sacrificed in an open environment (and thus is probably not an option for some professional services firms, such as law firms, that put a high premium on privacy), open offices are effective in fostering interaction because professional and administrative are not isolated in individual private offices. Additionally, open floor plans often force people in the office to interact with one another more often than they might in the closed office environment. Indeed, some open office plans incorporate common walkways that force professionals in the firm to go out of their way to reach a destination (e.g., the restroom or kitchen), which can also be beneficial in encouraging spontaneous interactions. While these informal interactions may be deemed by the firm as more of a distraction than a benefit, such brief discussions can be healthy and help promote a greater sense of cohesion among the professionals and staff at the firm. Because the open plan has few boundaries and high visual access, however, the office can be very busy and may be distractive to some employees.

HOTELING.   One of the more recent developments in office design, which can be employed in either a closed or open office environment, is a concept known as *hoteling*. Hoteling most often occurs in firms where the professionals spend a good deal of time traveling, such as analysts or consultants who are often staffed on long-term engagements out of town. In such an environment, all of the offices and workstations are configured the same and are wired to be compatible with any computers or related equipment that the firm has issued to the professional. When a professional plans to be in town and requires office space, he or she calls ahead to reserve an office or workstation and any equipment needed.

Hoteling can help the professional services firm save significant money by avoiding paying rent for office space that goes largely unused. However, hoteling does not provide the professionals in a firm with their "own" office, which is something that many professionals have come to expect. Thus, if the firm is contemplating a hoteling office system, or some hybrid thereof, it should do so in consultation with the professionals in the firm to eliminate any discontent.

Finish-Out

The finish-out construction that needs to be completed before taking possession of the leased premises—often referred to as *leasehold* or *tenant improvements*—is the nonremovable installations such as walls that must be built in order to meet the firm's needs. New office space, which may consist of only exterior walls and flooring, often requires substantial finish-out before occupancy by the tenant; on the other hand, existing office space, or space that is going to be subleased, may include certain fixtures that the firm can take advantage of and use. In many cases, the landlord will be willing to pay for all or a portion of the finish-out that is required to bring the office space into tenantable condition by the firm.

The issue of finish-out is often raised during the lease negotiations; however, in the final analysis, it is important for the firm to have an understanding of what the landlord is paying for and whether and under what circumstances the firm will be responsible for completing any aspect of the finish-out. One way to accomplish this is to attach an exhibit to the lease that includes detailed descriptions, drawings, and specifications of exactly what improvements each party is responsible for making. Depending on the amount of work that is required, the finish-out of the premises could be accomplished relatively quickly or could take several months.

There are a number of different parts of the office that the firm should consider when it is assessing its needs and whether and to what extent finish-out is required. Most professional services firms include at least the following types of space within the office: professionals' offices, staff workstations and/or cubicles, reception area, filing areas and copy rooms, common areas and conference rooms, restrooms, and a kitchen or cafeteria. Again, the firm may be able to find existing office space that meets its requirements; however, it is much more likely that at least some finish-out will be required before the firm takes possession of the premises.

Furniture

In selecting furnishings for the professional services firm, there are various issues to consider.

DESIGN AND STYLE. The design and style of the furniture selected by the professional services firm is important for a number of reasons. As with many of the other issues that must be considered in opening a professional office, clients and potential clients have very real expectations about the style of furniture that they expect to see in a professional's office. Traditional furniture styles that incorporate dark woods, leather, and brass predominate many professional offices; however, it is not mandatory that all professional offices be furnished in this manner. Indeed, there is a wide range of contemporary furniture styles that should be considered in light of the image that the firm is trying to project and the business that the firm is trying to attract.

For example, if the firm's client base is largely high-tech companies whose executives and employees are accustomed to more modern office design and furnishings, they might not feel comfortable meeting in an office furnished with dark woods and leather chairs. In much the same way that wearing formal business attire in the wrong setting can have a chilling effect on client interaction, clients might perceive more conservative furniture as being dark and too formal and inconsistent with the image the client is trying to project.

On the other hand, many clients expect their professionals' offices to be designed and furnished in a more formal manner that conveys a greater sense of seriousness and tradition.

One furniture option that many professional services firms have selected, at least with respect to employees, is modular furniture. Modular furniture includes desks, credenzas, and work stations that are constructed based on standardized units or dimensions, which can be configured in a variety of ways depending on a particular employee's or professional's needs. Modular furniture provides a firm with a relatively inexpensive and easy way to adapt the office configuration and organization as the business ebbs and flows and as the employee base shrinks and swells. Rather than undertaking major office furniture purchases only when absolutely necessary, which can prove costly, time consuming, and disruptive, modular furniture provides the professional services firm with the opportunity to more closely tie office renovations and furniture purchases to business demands.

Although modular furniture is an attractive option for employees of the professional services firm, in many cases, the more senior members of the firm, such as partners, prefer to furnish their offices with unique furniture that they have personally selected. Furnishing their offices is one of the few ways that individual partners can personalize their offices, and it is considered one of the perks of achieving a more senior position in the firm. Unfortunately, high-end office furniture can be very expensive, and as a result, many professional services firms require partners to pay for all or a portion of the furniture that they select. Moreover, there has been a recent trend toward standardizing the furniture in partner offices in an effort to afford the firm greater flexibility as partners come and go and to help reduce conflicts among partners over status within the firm.

While there are myriad furniture designs and options available to the professional services firm, as a general rule, trendy, stylish furniture should be avoided. Furniture is often one of the largest upfront expenses that the professional services firm will incur when moving into new office space. To avoid having to replace furniture before it is necessary, the firm should avoid trendy furniture that can quickly go out of vogue and opt for more neutral furniture that reflects a professional tone. While it is true that the firm should consider its furniture options in light of client expectations, a balance must be struck between the cost of the furniture and client expectations. In striking this balance, the firm should err on the side of selecting furniture that will endure any passing trends.

EMPLOYEE PRODUCTIVITY AND SATISFACTION. Selection of office furniture can have a dramatic impact on employee performance and job satisfaction. The right office furniture should make it easy for both the professionals and nonprofessionals in a firm to perform their respective job functions efficiently and comfortably. Modular furniture that can be adjusted to meet individual needs is important to retaining happy, productive employees. According to one report, "Furniture systems that adjust to individual needs are key to keeping employees. . . . We really have to provide solutions that allow people to feel ownership with their workspace, to identify with the place that they spend a significant period of their lives."[7]

Purchasing comfortable and user-friendly furniture makes sense from an efficiency perspective, and ergonomically designed furniture can help save the firm the expense and downtime associated with cumulative trauma disorders and repetitive strain injuries. Disorders such as carpal tunnel syndrome and lower back pain account for a significant number of workers' compensation claims annually. Ergonomically designed chairs, keyboards, and workstations can help minimize these health risks and cut down on employee downtime.

PURCHASING AND/OR FINANCING FURNITURE.   When weighing its options with respect to furniture, the firm should consider whether to purchase new or used furniture. New furniture offers the firm a greater degree of flexibility in terms of selection and variety, whereas the options in the used furniture market are often much more limited. Thus, for example, if the firm were to choose to purchase used furniture, it is likely that there would be several different styles of furniture throughout the office, which, depending on the image the firm is trying to project, might not be an unattractive option.

While the options may be less plentiful in the used furniture market, the firm will pay considerably more for new furniture than used furniture. Depreciation of used office furniture occurs rapidly, and the firm may be able to find excellent quality used office furniture at a deep discount under what it would pay for new furniture. Moreover, in many instances, the firm may be able to meet all or a portion of its furniture requirements by purchasing or leasing furniture from the landlord or former tenant, particularly in a sublease situation where the former tenant has not relocated and does not want to incur the cost of moving its office furniture.

In most cases, the firm can defray some of the cost of furnishing its new office space by financing the purchase of office furniture, both new and used. Indeed, if the firm decides that it does not want to purchase office furniture, the firm could simply lease furniture. However, under both the financing and leasing scenarios, the firm would pay a premium in finance charges and interest, and as a result, despite the relatively high cost, simply buying the furniture upfront might be in the best long-term interests of the firm.

FILING SYSTEMS.   Although professional services firms rely on computers and electronic media more than ever before, they still generate a significant amount of paper. As a result, in addition to furniture, the firm will need filing cabinets, which, depending on the volume of paper being produced by the firm, can be expensive. Shelf files are a more efficient alternative to traditional drawer file cabinets. Additionally, the firm should consider cabinets that can be stacked five to seven drawers high to minimize the price per square foot that the firm is paying to simply store hard copies of documents.

Summary

Locating the right office space can be an incredibly important development in the life of a professional services firm. To make the right decision, the firm should critically assess its needs upfront and arm itself with as much information on the market as it can find. Leasing agents can prove to be valuable allies who possess a great deal of information and expertise. Once the firm has identified the office that best suits its needs, it should take care in negotiating with the landlord and, with the assistance of legal counsel, carefully review all of the various terms of the lease before execution. Last, the firm needs to decide what office design and furniture best suit its needs. Although the firm need not wait until a lease is executed to undertake this assessment, because office finish-out and furnishings can be such large expenses for the firm, it is important that, with or without the assistance of a space planner or interior designer, the firm properly budget for these expenses as early as possible in the office search process.

NOTES

1. Attributed to Abraham Lincoln in multiple sources including http://www.quotationspage.com/subjects/success.
2. American Public Transportation Association (APTA) online glossary available from http://www.apta.com/info/online/glossary.html.
3. The Urban Land Institute is available from http://www.uli.org.
4. Candace S. Baggett, *Desperately Seeking Space,* State Bar of Texas 22nd Annual Advanced Real Estate Law Course (July 12 to 14, 2000).
5. The Urban Land Institute, *Office Development Handbook* (2nd ed., 1998), available from http://www.uli.org.
6. *Workplace Trends in Law Firms,* white paper from Herman Miller, Inc. (2003).
7. Gail Repsher Emery, *Changes in Modern Office Mirror the Past* (Washington Technology, 2001).

19

Legal Counsel

Scott M. McElhaney and Michael W. Malakoff

A person who represents himself has a fool for a client.

—Anonymous

This chapter covers the selection and retention of legal advisors for professional services firms. As with most businesses, professional services firms require good legal advice—whether for client disputes, incorporation, mergers and acquisitions, or simple contract advice.

Why This Topic Is Important

Professional services firms cover a variety of industries, from real estate to medical practices to management consulting. While such firms may not need counsel on a day-to-day basis, inevitably the time comes when legal advice is required, or at least helpful. Using the right lawyer for the right situation in

---

Disclaimer: The material in this chapter has been prepared for informational purposes only. The chapter is not offered as legal advice on any matter and should not be used as a substitute for seeking professional advice from a competent attorney in your jurisdiction for your particular problem. Although we have attempted to be accurate, we do not guarantee that the information in this chapter is correct, complete, or up to date. The laws of different jurisdictions may be entirely different from what is described in this chapter. The authors will not be responsible for any action or failure to act in reliance on the information in this chapter. In addition, this information is not intended to create, and receipt of it does not constitute, an attorney-client relationship.

the right way can help professional services providers run their businesses more effectively and see legal services as a benefit to their businesses rather than a painful, distracting cost. Thus, we explain in this chapter: (1) the most common times (but not all the times) that the firm should solicit legal advice, (2) how to select, and organize legal service providers, and (3) how to manage the relationship with your legal service providers.

When the Firm Needs a Lawyer

An important aspect of managing a professional services firm is successfully navigating your way through the legal environment. When used properly, a qualified lawyer can help you take advantage of the opportunities the legal system provides, thereby helping you run your firm more effectively, as well as minimizing the difficulties that present themselves from time to time. In this section, we examine some of the situations in which the firm may want to consult a lawyer. This is, of course, not a comprehensive list. Rather, we intend to point out some of the more frequent situations in which a lawyer can be useful. Naturally, a given firm may have many other major needs, depending on the nature of the business and the specifics of the organization, size, geography and other factors.

Organizing Your Firm

Organizing your business is a challenging task for which a lawyer can be very valuable. The considerations when establishing and organizing your legal entity are complex. As discussed in Chapter 3, the firm's management will be presented with a variety of entity selections to evaluate—corporations, partnerships, limited liability companies, and so on—each with advantages and disadvantages that must be considered. The choices you make during the formation of your entity will have an impact on firm and partner tax liabilities, personal liability, and other important issues. The specifics of taxes, liability limits, and other relevant issues, however, are complex and vary by legal jurisdiction. Working with a lawyer can help you choose the best entity for your specific set of circumstances.

Once you have chosen your entity type, you will need to work through a variety of additional requirements associated with the set up of your entity. These diverse requirements range from bylaws to shareholder agreements to setting up the company checking account to a host of other checklist items. Again, working with a lawyer who helps establish new businesses frequently can help a new firm through the many complex issues associated with getting set up. The lawyers will likely have checklists and standard operating practices that may help avoid large omissions during the process and promote the efficient use of your time and money.

Employment Law Matters

In addition to seeking assistance in organizing your business, it is usually useful and, in the long run, extremely cost effective, to consult a lawyer who can guide you through the typical maze of rules and regulations that govern the relationship between your business and the people who work for it. This part of the chapter surveys some of the major topics and considerations you may want to discuss with a lawyer.

INDEPENDENT CONTRACTORS VERSUS EMPLOYEES.   If you need other people to help you in your business, one of the first questions you should address is whether it is more appropriate for you to hire employees or independent contractors.

There are several advantages and disadvantages to hiring employees. It can be easier to foster a sense of commitment, culture, loyalty, and teamwork in employees than in independent contractors. Hiring full-time employees also gives the employer a greater amount of control over the way employees do their work and allocate their time. On the other hand, hiring employees obligates the firm to pay payroll and other taxes and makes your business subject to numerous federal and state laws that must be navigated. Several of these laws are discussed later in this Chapter.

Hiring independent contractors presents a different set of issues. Independent contractors are typically hired to complete a particular project in a particular amount of time or to provide a specific skill-set. As such, contractors are generally entitled to determine how and even when and where to complete their assigned project. However, a business owner does not have to pay taxes or withhold income tax on money paid to an independent contractor. Depending on the needs of your business, hiring an independent contractor may or may not be a possibility. Typically independent contractors may be hired for specific engagements, but will generally not constitute the backbone or bulk of the firm's professional staff.

Even if a firm agrees to hire a person as an independent contractor, the firm's characterization of the relationship is not binding on others, such as the IRS. Depending on several factors, such as the amount of control over where, when, or how a person does his or her job and the permanency of the relationship, a person whom you initially hire as an independent contractor could later be deemed to be an employee, and your business, or you, may be liable to pay back payroll taxes or other benefits. Also, you may be liable for the conduct of the worker if he or she is later found to be your agent or employee; this is particularly troubling because your insurance company may exclude the lawsuit from coverage because the act was committed by someone you told the insurance company was an independent contractor. If you are considering hiring independent contractors, having a lawyer help you determine whether, given the type of help you need, the people you hire can be classified as independent contractors as opposed to employees can be well worth the money you spend in legal fees. You should also check with your insurance broker to make sure that any persons working for your business are covered by your general liability or automobile insurance, particularly if the workers are on the road for your business. Alternatively, you should demand proof of insurance from anyone working for you as an independent contractor. IRS publication 1779 provides an overview of IRS policies regarding this relationship. Exhibit 19.1 shows a summary of the characteristics of employment versus contractor relationships established by the IRS, often known as the "20-factor" test.[1] The IRS will make a determination for firms regarding the employment status of individuals. Firms can submit an IRS form SS-8 for this process. As noted at the end of this chapter, this is provided for informational purposes only and firms should consult an attorney regarding their specific situation.

Exhibit 19.2, summarizes a few of the related forms and publications available from the IRS regarding employment relationships.[2]

LAWS GOVERNING THE EMPLOYER-EMPLOYEE RELATIONSHIP. Once you make the decision to hire employees, a wide range of federal and state laws apply.

Minimum Wage and Maximum Hours—the Fair Labor Standards Act (FLSA) and State Law Requirements.   One of the most basic laws that applies to employees is the FLSA, the federal law that requires payment of a minimum wage and one and one-half an employee's pay rate for overtime worked. The FLSA distinguishes between what the law calls "exempt" and "nonexempt" employees. Exempt employees are excluded from the FLSA's coverage. Exempt employees include certain executive, administrative, and professional employees. Each of these categories has its own specific definitions and requirements, including minimum salary requirements, so it is useful to consult with a lawyer to ensure that someone who you believe may be exempt from the FLSA's requirements actually is exempt. Job titles alone are not determinative. In recent years, an increasing number of lawsuits have alleged that employees who should be classified as nonexempt have been misclassified as exempt and, thus, not given overtime pay. In such cases, the employer can be liable for a substantial amount of unpaid overtime and, in some cases, penalties for willful misconduct.

Employees who are nonexempt must be paid the federal minimum wage, which is currently $5.15 per hour. There are a number of U.S. states which have established higher minimum wages. Exhibit 19.3 has a summary of current minimum wages in states that exceed the Federal minimum.[3] As with any labor laws, these will change from time to time at the federal and state level and the firm should ensure that they are in compliance with the most recent applicable laws.

There are other exceptions to this rule as well. For example, food servers who earn tips can be paid a lower base wage rate as long as the tips they

EMPLOYEE OR INDEPENDENT CONTRACTOR?

Whether someone who works for you is an employee or an independent contractor is an important question. The answer determines your liability to pay and withhold Federal income tax, social security and Medicare taxes, and Federal unemployment tax.

In general, someone who performs services for you is your employee if you can control what will be done and how it will be done.

The courts have considered many facts in deciding whether a worker is an independent contractor or an employee. These facts fall into three main categories:

1. *Behavioral control:* Facts that show whether the business has a right to direct and control. These include:
   a. *Instructions:* An employee is generally told:
      i. when, where, and how to work
      ii. what tools or equipment to use
      iii. what workers to hire or to assist with the work
      iv. where to purchase supplies and services
      v. what work must be performed by a specified individual
      vi. what order or sequence to follow
   b. Training–an employee may be trained to perform services in a particular manner.

2. *Financial control:* Facts that show whether the business has a right to control the business aspects of the worker's job include:
   a. The extent to which the worker has unreimbursed expenses
   b. The extent of the worker's investment
   c. The extent to which the worker makes services available to the relevant market
   d. How the business pays the worker
   e. The extent to which the worker can realize a profit or loss

3. *Type of relationship:* Facts that show the type of relationship include:
   a. Written contracts describing the relationship the parties intended to create
   b. Whether the worker is provided with employee-type benefits
   c. The permanency of the relationship
   d. How integral the services are to the principal activity

For a worker who is considered your employee, you are responsible for:
- Withholding Federal income tax,
- Withholding and paying the employer social security and Medicare tax,
- Paying Federal unemployment tax (FUTA)
- Issuing Form W-2, Wage and Tax Statement, annually,
- Reporting wages on Form 941, Employer's Quarterly Federal Tax Return.

Exhibit 19.1   IRS Guidelines for Establishing Employee and Contactor Relationships

Tax Topic 762 Basic Information: To determine whether a worker is an independent contractor or an employee, you must examine the relationship between the worker and the business. All evidence of control and independence in this relationship should be considered. The facts that provide this evidence fall into three categories Behavioral Control, Financial Control, and the Type of Relationship itself.
Publication 1976, Section 530 Employment Tax Relief Requirements (PDF): Section 530 provides businesses with relief from Federal employment tax obligations if certain requirements are met.
IRS Internal Training: Employee/Independent Contractor (PDF): This manual provides you with the tools to make correct determinations of worker classifications. It discusses facts that may indicate the existence of an independent contractor or an employer-employee relationship. This training manual is a guide and is not legally binding. If you would like the IRS to make the determination of worker status, please file IRS Form SS-8.
Form SS-8 (PDF): Determination of Worker Status for Purposes of Federal Employment Taxes and Income Tax Withholding
Publication 15-A: The Employer's Supplemental Tax Guide has detailed guidance including information for specific industries.
Publication 15-B: The Employer's Tax Guide to Fringe Benefits supplements Circular E (Pub. 15), Employer's Tax Guide, and Publication 15-A, Employer's Supplemental Tax Guide. It contains specialized and detailed information on the employment tax treatment of fringe benefits.

Exhibit 19.2

receive reach a high enough level. Generally, if a nonexempt employee works more than 40 hours in a workweek, that employee must be paid overtime pay at a rate of not less than one and one-half times the regular rate of pay.

Discrimination and Related Legal Issues. Federal and state laws broadly prohibit discrimination on a variety of grounds in all aspects of the employment relationship, including the hiring, training, paying, promoting, disciplining, and terminating of employees. A lawyer can help you navigate these important laws.

Under Title VII of the Civil Rights Act of 1964, it is illegal to discriminate against a person in the terms and conditions of his or her employment because of race, color, religion, sex, or national origin. The Age Discrimination in Employment Act (ADEA) makes it illegal to discriminate against a person because of age if he or she is over 40. The Equal Pay Act generally mandates that men and women be paid the same for the same work. The Americans with Disabilities Act (ADA) prohibits discrimination against a qualified

STATE	MINIMUM WAGE ($)
Oregon	7.05
California	6.75
Alaska	7.15
Illinois	5.50
Rhode Island	6.75
Massachusetts	6.75
Maine	6.25
Vermont	6.75
Washington	7.16
Hawaii	6.25
Delaware	6.15
Connecticut	7.10

**Exhibit 19.3   Mimimum Wage
Standards by U.S. State**

person with a disability and imposes on covered employers the duty to provide a "reasonable accommodation" to an employee's or prospective employee's disability. Under the Family and Medical Leave Act (FMLA), larger companies—that is, those with more than 50 employees—must honor the need of employees to take leave from work to care for a newborn or to care for a family member's, or the employee's own, serious health condition.

Still other perhaps less well-known but important federal laws exist. These laws include provisions of the Civil Rights Act of 1866, which prohibits racial discrimination in the making and enforcement of contracts (and thus applies to independent contractors); the Employee Retirement Income Security Act (ERISA), which regulates employee benefit plans and pension plans; the Occupational Health and Safety Act (OSHA), which imposes various health and safety standards on employers; and the Comprehensive Omnibus Budget Reconciliation Act of 1986 (COBRA), which requires employees to be notified of their right to continue health insurance coverage for up to 18 months after termination. Finally, if you intend to do business with the federal government or with someone who does business with the federal government, you should consider whether you will be required to adopt an affirmative action plan and otherwise comply with the federal government's requirements concerning obligations to minorities, women, persons with disabilities, and veterans.

Although some of these federal laws do not apply to the smallest employers (e.g., Title VII generally applies only to employers with 15 or more employees), state laws that mirror or are broader than these federal laws might still apply. These state laws can be equally as important as their federal counterparts. For example, many states (and some local authorities, such as city or county governments) prohibit discrimination in employment on the basis of a person's sexual orientation, and practically all states prohibit retaliating against employees for filing a workers' compensation claim. States also have a wide variety of court-made rules that prohibit discharging employees for violating what courts declare to be the state's fundamental public policy. Although many of these "public policy" cases involve situations in which an employee claims that he or she was fired for refusing to break a law, the law in some states is broader.

The list of laws that provide protection to employees goes on. Retaining a lawyer to review your business's employment practices can help you avoid the legal pitfalls that can trap the unwary.

POLICIES, PAPERWORK, EMPLOYEE HANDBOOKS, AND OTHER EMPLOYMENT ADVICE. Another reason to consult with a lawyer is to create and improve your business's written policies and record keeping practices. Having detailed company rules and policies on, among other things, work hours, absenteeism, telephone and Internet usage, confidentiality, smoking, drug use, dress, equal employment opportunity, and harassment is essential. For example, one way to defend against many sexual harassment claims is to show that your business has an enforced, written policy that forbids harassing conduct and provides avenues through which employees can complain about actions they may feel to be harassing. Employees who claim to be victims of harassment but who fail to avail themselves of such a policy have a more difficult time succeeding in court. A lawyer who has an opportunity to learn the needs of your business can help you draft a full set of policies specifically tailored to your needs and can help you create or review an entire employee handbook, if appropriate. A sample of the topics which an employee handbook may address is included on the CD which accompanies this book.

Similarly, although lists of job qualifications and job duties are not specifically required by any law, they are useful and should be reviewed by a lawyer prior to implementation. Having a list of the "essential functions" for each position in your business can clarify your duty to reasonably accommodate an employee's disability. Additionally, creating a list of job qualifications can help you analyze what skill sets you need for your business's employees. However, some job qualification requirements can lead to claims that a requirement is discriminatory. In one case, courts found that a company's requirement that applicants for certain low-level, unskilled positions have a high school diploma and pass a test was liable for unlawfully discriminating against minorities. The requirements disproportionately affected racial minorities, and there was no legitimate business reason to have those requirements for those unskilled positions. A lawyer can help ensure that the job qualifications that you identify for the positions you create for your business are not similarly discriminatory. Sample role and responsibility documents are on the CD which accompanies this book.

Lawyers can also help guide you through the hiring and, if necessary, the termination process. It is important to know what types of inquiries to job applicants are lawful and about whether the decision to discharge an employee is likely to expose you to a lawsuit. A lawyer can also give you guidance about the types of records that you should keep on your business's employees and about the best way to maintain those records. Lawyers can help ensure that you follow the rules regarding posting the required legal notices and reporting new employees to appropriate government agencies. Lawyers can also guide you through the workers' compensation and unemployment insurance laws that apply to your business.

EMPLOYMENT CONTRACTS.   Most employees do not have written contracts with their employers, but professional services firms should consider several issues that may lead to the conclusion that an agreement with some or all employees regarding aspects of their employment is appropriate.

One consideration for employment agreements is the employee's length of service. Although most employment relationships are "at will"—that is, they can be terminated at the will of either the employee or the employer at any time and for any reason—written contacts can specify a time period of employment. However, a new business should carefully consider whether the need to commit to employ a person for a period of time outweighs the need to retain the flexibility to end his or her employment if conditions change. Written contracts are also often used to specify compensation packages that are more complicated than a set hourly wage rate or annual salary. Written employment contracts can be used to specifically delineate the employee's job duties and responsibilities as well.

Whether you have written contracts covering other aspects of employment or not, it is important to consider having explicit agreements with employees (or independent contractors) that cover any inventions or other intellectual property rights that may be created in the course of a person's work for your business. Such agreements should clearly assign those rights to the business. Entering into such agreements at the beginning of a person's work for your company can prevent later disagreements about inventions.

If you wish to enter into employment contracts with your employees, it is essential that you have a lawyer review the contracts to ensure that your business does not enter into agreements it cannot live with, especially if the employment relationship later sours.

NONDISCLOSURE AND NONCOMPETITION AGREEMENTS. Apart from formal employment agreements, it may be worthwhile to draft and require your employees to sign confidentiality or nondisclosure agreements. If an employee, or any service provider such as a Web site designer, is going to have access to information that you do not disclose to the public and you would not want shared with your competitors—such as customer lists, pricing information, business plans, or proprietary business methods—a nondisclosure agreement can give you an added level of security. Such agreements should make it explicit that the employee is prohibited from using or disclosing any confidential information that he or she learns from your business except as authorized by the business.

You may also want to consider having certain employees sign noncompetition agreements. In those agreements, employees agree not to compete against your firm for a given time period and sometimes in a specific area or with specific clients. If a person subject to a noncompetition agreement leaves your company and starts competing against you, it may be possible to go to court and get an injunction prohibiting the person from violating the agreement. However, it is essential to consult with a lawyer about entering into such contracts. The laws of different states differ widely. In some states, such agreements are not enforceable at all, and even in the states in which noncompetition agreements are enforceable, there are often specific requirements that must be met before such an agreement will stand up in court.

Intellectual Property Issues

Intellectual property issues also present a number of difficulties to the professional services firm. Often, intellectual property developed by the firm is one of the firm's most important assets, particularly for consulting firms. This part of this chapter outlines some major considerations with trademarks, copyrights, patents, and trade secrets.

TRADEMARKS. A trademark is a word, name, or symbol (or even a color, sound, or smell) that is used to identify products or services of a company and to distinguish them from another company's products or services. To have rights in a trademark, you must initially pick a mark that is protectable. Courts have found terms such as "Discount Muffler" or "Lite" beer to be too generic to be protectable trademarks. On the other hand, arbitrary or fanciful associations between a mark and a product—such as "Apple" computers—are protectable.

If you are the first one to use a protectable mark, you automatically obtain some rights in it by displaying it in connection with the sale or advertising of your service. However, to ensure that you will have rights in a trademark that you may spend money promoting, you should be sure that you are not using a trademark in which someone else already has rights. Although commercial trademark search firms exist, a lawyer often better can help you decide how thorough a search you need to undertake given your needs.

Trademarks do not automatically offer protection to your mark across the country. They typically apply only in the area in which you use the mark. Thus, it is possible for two businesses in the same line of work to have the same name, as long as they operate in different areas. You can receive "priority" in your mark nationwide if you register it with the United States Patent and Trademark Office. If you do not intend to operate nationwide, registration with your state's government may be sufficient. (Note that you do not obtain trademark rights in the name of your company simply by incorporating or by registering an assumed name under which to do business.) Seeking legal advice to guide you through the various questions you may have about how best to protect your trademarks can help ensure that the investment you make in the identity of your business does not go to waste.

COPYRIGHTS. Copyright gives legal protection against others who copy anything original that you write or record. You automatically have copyright rights in any book, article, advertisement, software, movie, or music recording that you create. Copyright protects the particular expression that you write or record; it does not, however, protect the underlying idea that you have expressed. Your copyright rights generally give you the exclusive right to reproduce, distribute, display, or create derivative works from your copyrighted material.

There is no requirement that a copyright owner put a copyright notice on a protected work, but printing the copyright symbol—©—along with the copyright owner and the date of publication on a copyrighted work alerts others to the fact that the material is copyrighted and perhaps reduces the chance of unauthorized copying in the first place. Attaching this notice can entitle the owner to enhanced damages in a copyright lawsuit as well.

Apart from attaching the copyright notice, it can be worthwhile to register copyrighted works with the Copyright Office of the Library of Congress. It is necessary to register a copyrighted work in order to recover statutory damages and attorney's fees from an infringer.

PATENTS. A patent is basically a government-issued monopoly over an invention. Many people think that patents apply only to machines, but patents are available for business processes and methods. You can protect a new hybrid of a plant with a patent, and you can obtain a design patent to protect the aesthetic look of a product. Patent protection is also available for improvements to preexisting inventions.

If you invent a new process or business method, you can obtain a patent to protect your invention, if you can show that your invention is useful, new, and nonobvious. For example, Amazon.com, Inc. obtained a patent on its "one click" Internet ordering process.

Obtaining a patent simply gives you the right to prevent others from using your invention by suing others who make, use, sell, or import a product produced by the process. Other people can be liable to you for patent infringement even if they did not know about your patent. There are a variety of reasons to consider seeking patent protection for your invention. Obtaining a patent can discourage others from copying your know-how, increase the recognition of your products or services, provide a potential source of licensing revenue, serve as a marketing tool, and attract investors and venture capital.

To obtain a patent, you have to apply for one within one year of the date you first used the invention publicly or commercially, although the safest course is to apply for a patent before you begin commercial use of your invention. A patent issued by the federal government is valid only in the United States. If you plan to do business in other countries, you will have to seek patent protection from those other countries. Finally, a patent is valid only for a certain number of years. Most U.S. patents are good for 20 years from the date you first seek patent protection.

The process of obtaining a patent can be complex, and it is usually worth the expense to hire a patent attorney to assist you in seeking patent protection for your invention.

TRADE SECRETS.   Finally, the professional services business should make special efforts to protect its trade secrets. Trade secrets can be anything that a business knows or does that gives it an advantage over competitors. Trade secrets can be customer lists, pricing information, marketing plans, and other processes. To be a trade secret, information need not be novel enough to be patentable, but it must be, and remain, secret. It can thus be useful to have a lawyer perform a "trade secret" audit for your business to ensure that you are doing all that you can to ensure that your protectable secret information remains secret. Such an audit can review your business's confidentiality notices, confidentiality agreements, and procedures to ensure that access to sensitive information is appropriately restricted.

Contract Review

Consulting a lawyer to review contracts that you enter into can also be a wise use of your resources. Particularly with major agreements, it is essential that the firm understands all of the terms of the contract it is are going to execute. Your lawyer should be able to explain the provisions of a proposed contract to your satisfaction; you should not rely on an interpretation of a proposed agreement made by the other party to the transaction. It is also a good idea to discuss with your lawyer the nature of the deal involved. Through a discussion of the matter, you and your attorney may identify areas of uncertainty that need to be clarified.

There is an advantage to having and using your own form contracts. Once you learn and become at ease with the terms of your own form, you will not have to analyze new proposed contracts from others with whom you do business to the extent your form is used. In addition, by using your own form contract as a starting point, you will often have a greater degree of control over the contents of the final agreement.

Selecting a Lawyer

The process of selecting a lawyer can be difficult. When a firm decides to hire a lawyer, either because it suddenly has a need or, preferably, because it is planning ahead, it is faced with a variety of choices. For some reason, it can be difficult to find a good lawyer who fits your needs. While there are many different contexts in which a professional services firm can benefit from the services of a lawyer (including those most typical circumstances discussed earlier), it can sometimes be difficult to expend the time and effort the firm would like to spend to make a good choice. Also, legal matters can be complex, and it can be a chore to dig in and understand what your firm needs. Nevertheless, a good attorney can significantly benefit your firm. Lawyers can be valuable advisors for overall company business in addition to driving resolution of strictly legal matters.

Ultimately, the choice of a legal advisor can rest on any number of factors, depending on the needs and preferences of the firm. In this section, we survey some of the major points you may want to consider in choosing legal services.

Establishing Selection Criteria

The first step in selecting a lawyer is to determine what characteristics in a lawyer are important to the firm. In this part of the chapter, we discuss some of the issues you may want to consider in determining what factors you will use in the selection process.

LAWYER VERSUS LAW FIRM AND THE PRIMARY LEGAL CONTACT. One issue that should be considered is whether to choose a large law firm or a smaller firm or sole practitioner. Often it is a good idea to focus, at least initially, on finding a good lawyer rather than a good law firm because in large law firms, as in other types of service businesses, the quality of the individual service provider varies, regardless of the quality of the overall firm. Additionally, it is useful to establish a relationship with a primary legal contact to help you work through issues. Even if the firm is outstanding, if your relationship with your primary contact is poor, you will most likely be dissatisfied. Accordingly, it is important to find a lawyer who is a good fit from a variety of standpoints, including among other things, skill-set, experience, knowledge, and personality.

GENERALIST VERSUS SPECIALIST.   Another issue to consider is whether to select a generalist or a specialist. Often an attorney with extensive specialized knowledge in a particular area can seem to be an attractive choice. In the course of business, however, a professional services provider is likely to encounter a wide range of legal issues. Thus, if you attempt to select a specialist for each issue that arises, you may end up with a large number of lawyers working on narrow, discrete items. In many cases, it may instead be preferable to select as your primary legal contact a strong generalist with good business sense. If you choose the path of the generalist, it is important to determine that he or she understands his or her weaknesses and "blind-spots" and understands when and how to call in an expert (or, put another way, a specialist). Further, the generalist should have an advantage if he or she has a broad range of quality legal contacts with specialized expertise.

ASSESSING FIT.   You will also be well served to consider whether a lawyer is a good fit for your particular firm. First, in assessing your candidates, it is imperative that you are comfortable that the lawyer has sufficient legal knowledge in the relevant areas. If a lawyer is not knowledgeable enough to complete (or appropriately delegate) the given set of tasks at hand at a high-quality level, that lawyer should not be doing the work.

Additionally, determine whether the lawyer has the desired general skills. For example, some lawyers (like some people) may be most skilled at negotiating, while others may be most comfortable doing research. Similarly, some may have stronger business skills than others. You should try to find a lawyer whose strengths meet your needs.

Another useful determinant of fit is how well the attorney understands your business. This measure is useful for two reasons. First, a lawyer who understands your business is more likely to recommend decisions in a manner supporting your business objectives. Second, the level of understanding a lawyer presents regarding your business can potentially serve as a measure for the level of client service you will receive. You may want to try to determine whether the lawyer has taken the time and made the effort to understand your firm. The answer to this question may yield a clue about the kind of service you can expect from that lawyer.

Yet another factor to consider is cultural fit. As most professional services providers know, cultural fit can be an important element of a successful relationship. This is especially so when selecting an important, sensitive position such as a lawyer. If the attorney moves too slowly for you or, on the other side, does not seem detailed enough for you, or seems to focus too much or not enough on business matters (as opposed to technical legal matters), you may become dissatisfied. This may not indicate a weakness on the part of either the lawyer (or law firm) or you as much as a different cultural orientation.

You also should consider what size law firm you want to work with. You will have to determine how much big firm bureaucracy you can tolerate and balance that against how complete a solution you would like to have in one place. Larger law firms are, by their nature, more bureaucratic and, therefore, potentially less responsive than smaller firms. For example, it may be more difficult to persuade a larger firm to show flexibility on fees because the lawyer may have more procedures to go through before he or she can agree to a billing approach that is outside standard firm guidelines. This is not necessarily a negative characteristic of large firms, but rather an observation on organization size. And this principle may apply to firms of any type, not just law firms. On the other hand, a larger firm may be more likely to be able to provide a more comprehensive solution to your legal issues. You may decide the reduced complexity and increased consistency provided by a larger firm outweighs the disadvantages.

It is also worth noting that these needs may vary over time. As a firm grows and its business and staff change, its legal needs and requirements change as well. As with any service provider or vendor, the legal relationship should be reviewed from time to time to ensure that it has remained productive and appropriate.

Conducting the Selection Process

Once you have determined what criteria matter to your firm, you will have to go through the actual process of engaging an attorney. The lawyer you hire will probably play an important role for your company, so the process you use should reflect that. This section provides a few suggestions you may find useful when conducting your selection process.

TREAT THE PROCESS AS IF HIRING AN EMPLOYEE. The process of hiring a lawyer should share many of the steps most firms use to hire senior employees. Ideas you may find helpful include:

- *Review each candidate's resume and track record.*
- *Check references.* Good sources of references may include current or former employers and clients.
- *Conduct a diligent interview process.* Too often lawyers get off easy in an interview process with prospective clients because of their unique (and sometimes intimidating) knowledge; do not hesitate to ask lawyers the tough questions.
- *Do independent research of the lawyer or firm.* Two places to start are the firm's web site and the legal resource site Martindale-Hubbell (www.martindale.com).

GATHER CANDIDATES FROM A VARIETY OF SOURCES. As you consider which lawyer or firm to engage, try to take the time to consider a variety of candidates. Candidates may come from many sources. One good way to identify quality candidates is by asking for referrals from people you know and trust. Another potential source of candidates is industry sources. Some useful industry sources may include, for example, other firms in your industry, lawyers you heard of in the context of doing good work on an industry-related matter, or attorneys who publish relevant articles or speak at industry events. Yet another source of potential candidates is the recommendation of other lawyers. Other lawyers can be especially helpful if they have worked with you in the past or know your business well.

CONSIDER AN IN-HOUSE COUNSEL. One act that can make a tremendous difference is hiring in-house legal counsel (or general counsel). An in-house lawyer can address a significant amount of your legal-related activities, thereby providing you with extra time to focus on other things. Further, if you have a high enough quantity of work, having legal work done in-house can save money. The benefits an in-house lawyer provides should include, among other things, improved ability to:

- Select outside attorneys when necessary.
- Evaluate fees.
- Distinguish among different firms based on skill sets (when selecting outside counsel for discrete projects).
- Identify legal issues that need to be addressed.

Additionally, you may improve your firm by having an in-house attorney execute some projects you might find are impractical to execute with an outside firm. These projects might include, for example, completing a whole set of form documents (reviewed by outside counsel) or developing a firm negotiating strategy for engagement contracts.

Your in-house general counsel should be a strong generalist with an extensive set of contacts in the legal community and good general business sense. You should not expect an in-house lawyer to handle everything. For example, if the firm confronts some very large, customized agreement or transaction (e.g., a complex licensing agreement), the in-house lawyer will probably need to bring in an outside attorney who specializes in that area. The in-house attorney, however, should be proficient in identifying and retaining specialists as needed. Finally, if a general counsel is effective, it is likely that over time he or she will become more involved in firm business activities, especially administrative matters and general firm strategic decision making.

The disadvantage to hiring an in-house counsel may be cost. Ultimately, to decide whether to hire an in-house counsel, the firm must do the math. Look at the firm operating history, and try to adjust for what has traditionally been missed that would be caught going forward. Bear in mind, however, that this analysis is complex. On one hand, the firm will probably get better advice on a more rapid and flexible basis. The in-house lawyer should be able to catch and address more legally related issues early. For example, he or she may be of assistance in identifying and resolving disgruntled employee issues, dealing with auditors, preparing for fund-raising, and so on. Also, you may end up having fewer issues that warrant legal attention, but previously had not received it, due to simple luck. For example, bringing in an in-house counsel may result in fewer contracts being signed without adequate legal review. All these matters, and whatever else is relevant to you, should be included in your analysis. The Risk Management chapter (Chapter 14) of this book discusses the process of analyzing the trade-offs around such business risks.

Managing the Relationship with Your Lawyer

Managing the relationship with your lawyer is an area where clients often fall short. In this section of the chapter, we look at some ideas for managing the relationship with your lawyer more effectively.

Defining the Relationship

Once you have selected your lawyer, you should spend some time clarifying the nature of the relationship. This part of the chapter provides some ideas for defining your relationship with your lawyer.

ENGAGEMENT LETTERS. Many law firms require their clients to sign an engagement letter before starting work. Frequently, however, the engagement letter is focused on issues that are of primary importance to the lawyer. For example, the engagement letter is likely to discuss what the lawyer will and will not be responsible for rather than the guidelines for how the lawyer will perform. You can use the engagement letter to cover items that are of primary importance to you. It may be useful to look at the engagement letter as a master services agreement. Different professional services firms care about different things, so we are not suggesting there is a specific way for you to structure your engagement letter. We note, however, a few areas that you may want to cover.

Generally, your engagement letter should cover how the ongoing operation and communication between your lawyer's firm and your firm works. Ultimately, to determine what is covered, you will have to cover what is important to your firm. One useful approach may be to start by looking at the master services agreement your firm uses with other professional services providers.

One thing every professional services firm cares about is the fees it will incur for legal advice. Thus, you will probably want to include detailed information about your lawyer's (and his or her law firm's) billing rates and practices in your engagement letter. Most engagement letters contain some information about fees, but you may want to check to see whether the information covers what you want it to cover. One important issue to consider is how the billing is structured. Depending on the nature of the work, you may prefer to opt for a flat fee or retainer structure instead of being billed on an hourly basis. For example, if the lawyer performs certain activities on an ongoing or recurring basis, a flat fee or retainer may be a desirable option. If, on the other hand, the activity appears to be a one-time event, you or your attorney may prefer to use an hourly billing approach. Additionally, there are billing questions to be covered in the area of procedure and extras. For example, how often will your lawyer bill you? What will the bill contain? And what are your lawyer's policies regarding extra expenses? Will the firm charge for long distance? Copies? Document delivery? There may be other concerns, depending on your situation.

Another item your engagement letter should include is the explicit identification of your primary contact. If the primary contact works at a firm, he or she should be the person who is responsible for ensuring that the work done for you is effective and efficient.

There is no special formula for covering everything. You may have any number of specific needs or concerns that you want to set out in the engagement letter. The important point is to understand the situation and cover what is important for you.

WORK ORDER MODEL. To take the professional services model to its logical conclusion, a client could implement a work order model with its lawyers. Under this approach, you and your lawyer would complete an engagement letter that served as a master services agreement. Each subsequent piece of work would be set forth in a statement of work containing information typically found in a statement of work, but tailored to address your specific situation. This approach would help promote a common understanding of the relationship between you and your lawyer as well as the lawyer's specific assignments.

Scope of Assignments

In addition to defining the nature of the relationship in the engagement letter, it will probably be useful to implement some measures to control the scope of each assignment. Having clarity about project scope before work starts is important to a successful completion of the project. In this section, we discuss several ideas you may want to consider as part of an effort to define each assignment's scope.

ESTABLISH A PRIMARY CONTACT FOR EACH MATTER. In addition to having your lawyer serve as the primary contact for the relationship as a whole, it should be useful to maintain a primary contact for each individual matter. While your primary contact should be able to help resolve issues for you on any particular matter, a primary matter contact will be more familiar with the nature and status of the particular piece of relevant work. Thus, a primary matter contact can provide updates more frequently and in greater detail. And the primary contact for a particular matter can also serve as a contact for your lawyer.

BE CAREFUL WHAT YOU ASK FOR.   In making requests to your lawyer, you will probably want to consider the surrounding business context of your request as it relates to what you ask the attorney to do. For example, what if you receive a lengthy contract from a large telecom provider for a small, inexpensive service, and you understand that the contract is essentially a form agreement that, given its size, is unlikely to be amended (or even seriously discussed) by the provider? And what if you have serious concerns about a single, stand-alone provision in the agreement? If you ask an attorney to review the agreement, without even providing context, you are placing the attorney in a situation where he or she, without understanding the business context, may spend many hours thoroughly and thoughtfully reviewing the document, perhaps providing extensive comments. And the accompanying fees are likely to be significant given the size of the agreement. While this may frustrate you, resulting perhaps in a negative experience with your lawyer, it would not necessarily be the lawyer's fault. By providing the attorney with the business context of the situation and educating the attorney about what issues are of particular concern to you, you will provide guidance and business context, leading to a more efficient result.

EXPLAIN THE ASSIGNMENT CLEARLY.   When you give an assignment to your lawyer, try to explain the assignment clearly and in detail. Complaints about lawyers who seem to float around sometimes center on the lawyer's inability to understand and act on what the client wants. It is unfair to the attorney, however, to expect him or her to have either a thorough understanding of a given matter or clear direction about the deliverable if the client has not provided adequate preparatory information. This explanation really falls into two areas: the background of the assignment and the assignment itself.

First, you should try to help your lawyer understand the background of the assignment. Remember, your lawyer does not shadow you all day every day, so he or she will not know all the background facts to the matter you are assigning. Additionally, the lawyer may not know what you are trying to achieve. You may be glad in the long run if you take the time and make the effort to provide your lawyer with a greater understanding of what is going on from a business perspective.

Second, ensure that the lawyer understands what you want delivered. Everyone has heard cautionary tales on this front: The client requests an answer to a seemingly simple question and 10 days later receives a 10-page memo on some esoteric choice of law issue. Lawyers are in the client service business, and most attorneys want to provide good client service just like any other professional services provider would, so when there is a major disconnect and failure in delivery, the client should recognize that the deliverables may not be clearly defined. Clients who take the time to clearly explain what they expect the lawyer to deliver will have a better chance of receiving the deliverable they want, even if the answer to a question is not the answer they hoped to receive, and receive fewer surprises.

Ask Questions. It sounds obvious, but it is nevertheless worth mentioning because it often emerges as a source of dissatisfaction with legal services providers. Legal matters can sometimes be difficult to deal with, especially for busy professionals who have other important matters on their mind. For example, you may not be sure how the lawyer expects the relationship and process to function. Or you may not understand the nature of the matter being addressed. Additionally, sometimes clients are hesitant to display what they may fear is a lack of sophistication about legal matters. Thus, they avoid questions they think may be perceived as dumb, perhaps assuming things are covered, and instead move their attention to something else.

If you do not understand what is happening, ask questions. You should take the time to understand the details of the legal relationship. Again, the majority of lawyers, like most other professional services providers, want to provide quality service. And most lawyers understand that it is valuable for his or her client to ask questions up front instead of learning about things at a later date. Thus, you may be well served to ask any questions you may have concerning issues ranging from operational matters such as billing, which lawyers will be working on the matter, and any number of other issues, many of which are covered in this chapter, to legal matters, such as, for example, what the client's options are on a given matter or the benefits and risks of a particular course of action.

Provide Clear Expectations about Cost. A final suggestion to help promote a solid understanding between you and your lawyer is in the area of cost. Too often we hear stories of people who are surprised (and disappointed) by the amount they are being billed by their lawyers. Most service clients would not allow another professional services provider, for example an IT consulting firm working on a software development project, to begin without first establishing some understanding about cost. The same principle should apply to legal services. Thus, before your lawyer begins work, establish an understanding about cost. Specifically, no work should be started before it is clearly defined and you have a clear cost estimate. One of two things should happen: The attorney will agree and you will have a mutual understanding that benefits both you and the attorney, or the attorney will inform you that your expectation is too low, in which case you will need to rethink your estimate, persuade the attorney to work at a lower rate, or consider other options. Regardless of the path you ultimately pursue, both you and the lawyer will likely be glad you recognized this disconnect up front instead of discovering an unwelcome surprise once the work was finished.

Monitoring the Work

Your relationship management activities should not end when your lawyer begins work. Even if you have done well in selecting a lawyer and defining the scope of the lawyer's work, you should benefit from diligently monitoring the work. In this section, we touch on a few ideas you may want to consider to help keep your legal matters on the right track.

First, try to understand your lawyer's knowledge and capabilities. Different lawyers have different strengths and areas for improvement. To know how to advance a given relationship and how to assign legal projects, you will be well served to understand what your lawyer is capable of.

Second, try to understand what your lawyer is doing. This may sound obvious, but it is not as easy as it seems without diligent monitoring. Some legal projects are large and complex, and often may involve issues unfamiliar to the firm management. You may want to spend some time understanding what your lawyer is doing to complete a project. It is inevitable that from time to time a lawyer or law firm may begin to drift off course (hence, the "choice of law" example earlier). If you understand what your lawyer is doing, you will probably be more capable of providing value-added suggestions or steering a drifting lawyer back onto the right track.

Another issue that can arise, especially when working with a large law firm, is that you may not know who is doing the work until you receive a memo or phone call from someone you do not know or, probably worse, see an unfamiliar name on your bill. There are at least two situations where this seems to come up: (1) matters requiring an attorney with expertise in a highly specialized area (e.g., an ERISA attorney) and (2) matters where junior attorneys are working on a less complex matter—something that can be concerning if you perceive that the junior lawyer is "learning on your dime." You can avoid this sort of thing by requesting to be notified as to who will be working on a given matter and what he or she will be doing.

Finally, review each bill carefully. By doing so, you improve the chance of catching any problematic trends early. You should be comfortable speaking with your attorney if the work description is insufficient to provide you with an acceptable understanding of what is going on.

Summary

Good legal advice is a must have for the professional services firm. From firm inception to daily operations, legal requirements affect the organization, employees, clients, and management of the professional services firm.

The identification and retention of an attorney for the firm is one of the first orders of business and should be done prior to an emergency need. The ongoing relationship of the firm with its legal advisor(s) requires effort from both parties but will yield results in the form of reduced risks, exposure to lawsuits, and positive outcomes for the firm, its employees and clients.

RESOURCES

IRS publication 1779 about contractor and employee relationships is available from http://www.irs.gov/pub/irs-pdf/p1779.pdf.

The HR Esquire web site has information on employment law and a specific section on Federal and State minimum wage information and is available from http://www.hresquire.com.

The U.S. Patent and Trademark office provides a variety of online resources, including search capabilities available from http://www.uspto.gov.

The copyright office of the Library of Congress provides information and frequently asked questions about registration for copyrighted works and is available from http://www.copyright.gov.

Martindale-Hubbell provides extensive search capabilities on individual attorneys and firms and is available from http://www.martindale.com.

NOTES

1. U.S. Internal Revenue Services (IRS) available from http://www.irs.gov/govt/fslg/article/0,id=110344,00.html.

2. US Internal Revenue Services (IRS) available from http://www.irs.gov/businesses/small/article/0,id=99921,00.html.

3. HR Esquire available from http://www.hresquire.com/minimum-wage-laws.htm.

20

Office Management

JOHN BASCHAB AND JON PIOT

There is no substitute for the comfort supplied by the utterly taken-for-granted relationship.
—Iris Murdoch, British novelist

This chapter discusses the key attributes of running an efficient and organized office. Your office(s) first and foremost needs to be a productive work environment for your staff. When hiring a new employee is the space, phone extension, and computer ready for them on the day he or she arrives—or are you scrambling to get these things set up during their first couple of weeks on the job?

Further, the professional services firm office is your face to clients and prospective and existing staff. It reflects either organization or disorganization, confidentiality, or lack thereof or it reflects simplicity or complexity. What catches your client's attention when entering your office space? What first impression does your office and staff leave?

Office management includes support services such as managing and maintaining the facility; organizing and managing the administrative staff; ensuring proper services are provided such as phones, offices, and document reproduction centers. Office management may also include some of the softer aspects of running the firm including fostering the firm's culture and capturing and maintaining the history of the firm. For smaller firms, office management duties are typically combined with other functions (e.g., book-keeping) that can be carried out by one person. In larger firms, office management may actually be the function of a dedicated full-time employee or a department of employees. In this chapter, we discuss many of the basic services provided by the office management function and the growth points in the life of the firm when transitioning from part-time staff to full-time staff and other organizational actions are appropriate.

517

Why Is This Topic Important?

This topic doesn't receive the attention it deserves because it is a *support* function. The bulk of professional services firm management attention, investment and discussions will appropriately focus on billable activity and business development. However, business development will suffer if one walks into a poorly run professional services office and notices immediately that no one is attending to the reception area, the phones are not answered consistently, and the space looks cluttered and unorganized. A disorganized office begs the question: If the firm is willing to treat its own offices this poorly, how well can it possibly service client accounts? Conventional thinking would suggest that running a simple function such as answering the phone or maintaining an impressive reception area should be an easy act for a professional services firm. Doing the work of the firm, selling, and working with clients is complicated; managing the office is not. Or is it?

Rarely does the "plant" run as smoothly as one wishes. Many important duties can get complicated due to inattention, time demands or office politics, for example:

- Assigning offices
- Optimizing administrative staff assignments
- Prioritizing duplication services
- Executing common tasks, such as new employee onboarding or recruiting events
- Filing confidential client or employee information

What can appear to be a simple office change for one attorney or consultant can cascade into a mess of negotiations and disgruntled workers who don't want to be moved or don't like their office assignment.

A well-run office management function is important for four key reasons:

1. It helps keep your billable staff from focusing on unproductive office and administrative matters.
2. The reception area and workspace are transparent to the client and reflect on the firm.
3. The organization of the workspace can increase staff productivity or hinder it.
4. The function can be (and most often is) a central force in promoting a culture.

A professional service firm maximizes profits by ensuring the professionals are as billable as possible. Their time is not well spent on office or facility issues. So the a critical objective for the office manager is to keep the professionals from having to spend precious time on nonbillable office management issues. Additionally, the office manager's goal is to provide services that make the job easier, or to facilitate doing components the job using a less expensive resource (i.e., graphics specialist, research analyst, typist).

This chapter provides an overview of the office management function. We discuss the typical support services provided, facility management best practices, and the hiring of office managers.

What Is Office Management?

Office management consists of three primary functions. First, office managers typically provide support services to the rest of the employees. These services include administrative support, scheduling, print and document reproduction services, design/graphics support, telecom, mail, and so on. Second, the office manager maintains the physical facility and manages the landlord and building services. Maintaining the facility encompasses space planning, maintenance, office moves, security, storage, vending and coffee service, break rooms, and so on. Finally, the office manager in some cases may be responsible for other duties such as coordinating local office social activities, celebrating major firm events, publishing firm newsletters, maintaining a history of the firm, and providing meeting space outside the building, to name just a few of the other miscellaneous duties.

Support Services

Support services are those common services that can be leveraged across all the staff. They are typically items that can be centralized relatively easily and they use standard processes to control scheduling and quality.

Support services are also activities that need to be routinely performed to support the professional staff in the normal course of their work (e.g., document duplication and filing). Support services sometimes require the acquisition of capital equipment (e.g., copying machines, graphics workstations, postal equipment). Plotters, high-end printing, paralegal services are just a few examples of support services.

When deciding which activities to support at a centralized office level, consider those which:

- Are required by all staff.
- Exhibit economies of scale.
- Can be effectively executed by lower-cost administrative staff than by professional staff.
- Are experiencing labor pool scarcity.

In most cases, any service that is required by all staff should be supported if not managed centrally. If most client work requires some kind of graphics production for reports, in most cases, it will be appropriate to have a graphics production group managed centrally. This ensures a unified look to graphics and that best practices can be easily adopted and adhered to, as well as achievement of scale economies in production. If this function is not centralized, then each professional staff group or project team would need to hire their own graphics production resource wasting valuable time and increasing costs.

Support services typically have some economies of scale, for example, copy machines. You wouldn't want each principal in the firm purchasing his own copy machine (with the resulting disparity of machine types, speeds, service plans, etc.). The benefits of centralizing purchasing and management where there are economies of scale is well-explored territory. Obviously, by grouping the purchase better pricing can be negotiated and volume discounts will apply lowering overall purchasing costs. Additionally, the expensive equipment can be located optimally so that appropriate staff can access and use it easily. Finally, this keeps your expensive professional staff billing clients for services, and not negotiating equipment leases.

Support activities also experience economies of scale in labor. For example, rather than hiring three half-time personnel to do estimating, you can centralize the function and do the same amount of work with one full-time person thus saving the fractional utilization of a half person. These activities are labor intensive and the firm can reduce costs by managing a centralized highly leveragable unit. These services include postal mail management, graphic production, paralegal services, administrative services, and so on.

Finally, you need to consider availability (or scarcity) of resources when analyzing centralization. For example, if most professional staff need a small but critical function for each client engagement, for example a project financial controller, and the labor pool for this function is small, the firm will be better off hiring one full-time equivalent and leveraging that resource across the business rather than having each principal try to procure the resource individually. Decentralization in this case would lead to low utilization of a full-time resource or the procurement of many high-cost part-time contractors neither of which is desirable. If each client proposal or project needs some specialized research for a short period of time, the firm is likely to create a centralized support group that provides research rather than having each principal hire their own research associate.

The most common support services include:

- Administrative staff management
- Document reproduction

- Travel booking and trip management
- Mail rooms
- Record keeping and document management

Administrative Staff Management

It is almost always more efficient to centrally manage the administrative staff. The job function of the entire administrative staff is usually similar, the pool of staff can share responsibilities, they typically have standard duties, and they keep the professionals billable and efficient. Professionals are notoriously poor managers of administrative staff, and will benefit from the improved attention to administrative staff management, careers and development accompanying a centralized management approach.

Developing standard administrative roles across the company is a best practice. The office manager can do this relatively easily. First, define the work requirements of each type of administrative staff. Next figure out the duties needed to support each level of professional staff and the required hours per week needed to support each professional staff type. For example, an associate may only receive filing and travel support thus requiring only four hours a week. A senior associate may require calendar scheduling assistance and expense management assistance thus requiring about eight hours a week of an assistant. A principal requires all of the above plus dictation, presentation support, marketing campaign support, and so on, thereby consuming at least 20 hours per week. Given this load, a single assistant could handle only one principal, two senior associates, and one associate. Alternatively an assistant could handle one principal, one senior associate, and three associates. The ratio that works for a given will depend on the specific type of work, number of professional staff and administrative burden for each.

Typically junior professional staff only receive basic administrative services (mail delivery, photocopying), while senior staff receive the full suite of services from the administrative team.

Document Reproduction

Document reproduction, copier centers, and scanning stations are provided through similar products and service models, and are well suited for central office management. Some firms charge out these services while others factor the cost into their services. Regardless, the most critical aspect of running one of these services is the process for requests, the turnaround time, the delivery of finished product, and billing for the services. Most firms will determine that the tradeoff of a $10 to $20 per hour resource doing this work is well worth saving the high cost of a professional doing the same.

Travel Booking and Management

Travel planning, scheduling and management is another service worthy of centralizing. Travel agents and administrative staff know the travel market and keep traveler preferences, and so on. Firm-wide travel policies can be implemented routinely. Travel agents are much better at locating low cost airfares, car rentals and accommodations than the typical layman thus lowering overall travel costs. Depending on the size of the firms annual travel budget, travel agencies may provide this service for free because they will be paid a commission by the airline, hotel, and rental car companies. In any case, having someone who can check flights and make rapid changes for professional staff on the fly (e.g. while they are en-route to the airport) can be an enormous time-saver and benefit.

Mail Room

The mail room is a basic and familiar centralized resource in most companies. This function is important to an efficient operation. The scale and scope of this function will depend on the type of firm and the volume of outbound and inbound mail received. For most small to mid-size firms, assigning this task as one part of administrative persons duties will suffice. Many third-party delivery services (UPS, Federal Express, DHL, et. al.) will provide high-quality outsourced services for outbound mail management on-site and can keep the mail-room effort to a minimum.

Record Keeping and Document Management

Record keeping is critical for most firms, particularly medical practices, law offices, architects and other document-dependent services. Record keeping is typically a subset of administrative duties. In many cases, record keeping can be mandated by the law. A good filing system is critical. Storage and retrieval of files should be a core competency of the administrative staff. The office manager is responsible for ensuring an efficient system. Today many firms are going paperless which consists of scanning paper documents, particularly original signed documents, and storing them on a computer system for easy indexing, search, and retrieval. Today's office manager should be well aware of these systems and be able to implement one with outside help if requested. A variety of cost-effective, feature-filled systems such as Microsoft SharePoint are available and can be economical even for the small office.

Other Services

Depending on the type of professional service organization, other services may be candidates for centralized support. These services should be looked at individually and using some of the criteria discussed earlier determines whether any should be centralized in your firm. Other services may include:

- Local technology support
- Appraisal and professional staff career track support
- Paralegal support
- Graphics support
- Telecommunications support
- Tele- and video-conferencing support
- Research services

Whenever deciding to centralize a support function, consider several additional infrastructure issues. Ensure that whatever you are centralizing can be done as or more efficiently than what the typical professional could do on their own. If the professional can complete a job faster without use of the support function, then they will not use a centralized support function. Therefore it is incumbent on the office manager to maintain efficiency and fairness when operating the function. Professionals will not want to:

- Wait an inordinate amount of time before receiving the support.
- Be overcharged for the services (over market rates).
- Have onerous administrative burden to receive the service (complex forms to fill out, approvals, complicated phone menus).
- Get substandard quality (must be equal or better).

Additionally the administrative staff will need to design a streamlined efficient process. Make sure you have developed a system to efficiently do the following:

- *Handle service requests quickly and efficiently.* Determine how requests will be prioritized—by title, by client, by urgency, and so on.
- *Schedule the work.* Can reservations be made? How early can requests be submitted (a week or a month in advance)? Labor must be scheduled to address peaks and valleys in demand.
- *Deliver the finished product in the format needed.* How will graphics be delivered (i.e., Adobe Acrobat or Powerpoint format?).
- *Ensure that service is high quality.* The office manager must periodically solicit feedback from professional staff on the quality of the services provided. Annual surveys, staff feedback, random sampling, and service level reporting are all tools that can be used to measure quality.

Managing Facilities

Facilities management is the other major function of office management. These activities comprise the following:

- *Space planning:* Managing physical office space including the reception area and ergonomics of workspaces. This topic is covered in depth in Chapter 18, Real Estate and Facilities.
- *Space maintenance and repairs:* The office manager should be the primary liaison with the office building management and maintenance. The goal is to ensure that maintenance is routinely provided by the building for all plant items that are in need of repair (e.g., HVAC, lighting, restrooms, electric power, elevators and building security).
- *Meeting space and scheduling:* The office manager will manage or assign an administrative assistant to manage central scheduling for meeting spaces and the policies governing such. The goal is to promote easy accessibility and fairness. Additionally the responsible party should ensure that the meeting spaces are stocked with all required items such as dry-erase markers, erasers, easels, conference phones, food service items, and so on.
- *Storage:* Items that only need to be accessed in the event of an emergency, less than once a year, or confidential stored records may be stored off-site in less expensive real estate. The office manager is responsible to procure the storage space, ensure its security, and coordinate the storage and retrieval of items.
- *Furniture:* The office manager is responsible for the maintenance and procurement of office furniture.
- *New hires, office moves, and employee departures:* The office manager support human resource policies and procedures regarding the onboarding and off-boarding of employees. The office managers responsibilities typically include preparing office space and equipment for new hires, managing office moves, and ensuring equipment and security access is returned when an employee leaves.

Other Duties

In many cases, the office manager is dubbed the firm's culture keeper and firm historian. There are other support personnel who might assume some of these responsibilities, but generally the office manager has the tenure and visibility into cross-firm activities that make them the ideal choice.

Culture

Culture is a critical component of any professional service firm. Staff morale is an important driver of overall effectiveness, and a positive, strong firm culture is an enormous contributor to staff morale, as well as work ethic, quality focus and client service attitude. On the other hand, a demoralized staff can lead to a death spiral in which lower and lower productivity reduces client satisfaction which reduces revenue and profits which causes cutbacks in staff which leads to negative culture and the repetition of a vicious cycle. Building and maintaining a good culture is important and must be proactively managed whether it is the responsibility of the office manager or another individual. In fact, culture is clearly a shared responsibility. Many activities can lead to a positive culture. There are four types of events commonly found in a professional service firm:

1. *Reward events:* The firm acknowledges individuals for outstanding service.
2. *Social events:* The firm promotes activities outside the office so that team members can bond outside the office.
3. *Team-building events:* The firm sponsors activities that promote team building.
4. *Information sharing:* These events allow specific units in the company to find out the latest information on the firm.

The most important aspect of this role is for the office manager to work with the firm's principals to determine a schedule of events on an annual basis.

These typically include business update meetings, annual meetings, semi-annual "state of the firm" meetings. Whatever the appropriate slate of meetings, the office manager must develop a schedule of the monthly, quarterly and annual activities that will help define firm culture and execute them on a routine basis. Additionally there are quarterly and annual activities that are important both for the business and for the history/culture. Many companies also have annual retreats or company meetings that typically have the following agenda:

- Introduction of key people
- Update on business performance
- Recognition of top clients and team performance
- Discussion on one to two year strategic plan
- Breakout sessions for practice areas

Finally, the a host of less significant, but equally important activities such as birthday celebrations, office decorations, holiday parties, charitable support activities, and pro bono work all contribute to the culture of the company. These activities are typically managed or coordinated by the same person.

Historian

The responsibility of maintaining the history of the firm is most often assigned to the office manager as well. This role is very important as it defines and promotes culture and draws employees to the legend of the firm. Critical components include assigning responsibility and agreeing to proper storage, retrieval, and use of firm history. Additionally, a written background of the company should be maintained and approved periodically for inclusion in proposals, recruiting materials and so on. The background should include information on key events in firm history, founders, and firm values statements. The administrative team should take pictures at company events and save these in albums, online storage, and frames for the reception area.

Hiring an Office Manager

Not all firms can afford to hire an office manager. However, at some point during the growth of the business, having a full-time dedicated office manager may actually increase the profitability of the business by reducing the burden of billable staff of these functions, and by coordinating all the activities mentioned in this chapter. Additionally, a good office manager can improve overall productivity by streamlining and efficiently running the office. A typical job description follows:

> **Office Manager Job Description:** The role of an office manager is to organize and supervise all of the administrative activities that facilitate smooth running of an office. The office manager may report to the CFO, managing partner, director of human resources, or Chief Administrative Officer, depending on the organization. If the organization has multiple offices with enough scale, the office manager in each location will have similar job functions and report to the same person. Exhibit 20.1 demonstrates the typical firm-size to office-manager requirements.

The office manager is expected to carry out a wide range of administrative and facility-related tasks. The office manager is ultimately responsible for ensuring the office runs smoothly:

Typical Responsibilities
- Manage and organize administrative staff (include hiring and firing).
- Manage meeting space and scheduling.

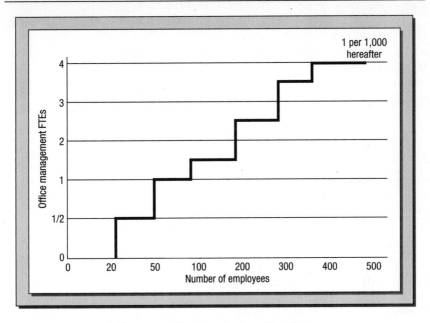

Exhibit 20.1   When to Hire an Office Manager

- Manage copy services.
- Manage travel.
- Managing "office" budget.
- Conduct administrative appraisals.
- Manage building maintenance.
- Meet with senior professionals on office projects and prioritization.
- Manage work space.
- Others (mentioned previously in chapter).

Characteristics
- Salary: office managers. Depending on firm size salary will range from $40,000 to $90,000 per year. For most firms hiring their first office manager, the salary will be in the $40,000 to $55,000 per year range.
- Work hours are typically 50 to 55 hours per week.
- Dress is appropriate to professional staff.
- Career path can include promotion to full-time position, promotion to management of entire function for firm, and graduation in Human Resources or Finance.

- Candidates will have at least a bachelors degree in business administration.

Personality
- Candidate will show evidence of loyalty, reliability, initiative, problem solving skills, and organizational capabilities.

There are a variety of higher-learning institutions with a curriculum focused on office-management. Candidates graduating from these programs are ideal for hiring in to such a position.

Summary

Managing the office efficiently and effectively will give the firm the best opportunity to be as productive as possible thereby leading to increased profits, as well as professional staff morale and a culture which inculcates the values important to the firm. Whether the firm begins with a part-time office manager or a full-time person, creating the position, monitoring performance, and putting structure into place will enable efficiency and is critical to promoting culture and impressing clients.

Determining the appropriate services to centralize at the office level will also enable the firm to capture economies of scale and leverage scarce resources. It will also reduce the amount of time professionals worry about managing such resources.

Maintaining the facility is equally important. The office manager is well positioned to manage this function. Providing an ergonomic and well-maintained office space that enables efficiency and productivity for the professional is critical.

Successful firms also find a systematic way to build culture and capture firm history. The office management is well suited for this responsibility.

Finally, hiring the right office manager is important because they lead these functions and set the tone of the office.

RESOURCES

The Association of Professional Office Managers (APOM). APOM promotes excellence in office administration and management.

APOM supports the performance and professional careers of office managers by providing central resources and services designed to functionally assist members with their responsibilities. The APOM has web-based resources available to members including reading lists, white papers, and policy and procedure recommendations. APOM can be found at http://www.apom.us.

Information on Microsoft's SharePoint document management and collaboration tool is available from http://www.microsoft.com/sharepoint.

Office-aide, an office management software productivity suite is available from http://www.office-aide.com.

The Professional Association of Health Care Office Management specializes in information and resources for physician practice management professionals is available from http://www.pahcom.com.

LOMA is an association of insurance and financial services professional services companies. LOMA was founded in 1924 and has over 1,250 affiliated firms in 70 countries. LOMA is focused on research and education to member firms interested in improving company operations is available from http://www.loma.org.

The Institute of Management and Administration is available from online at http://www.ioma.com.

About the CD-ROM

This appendix provides you with information about the CD that accompanies this book. For the latest updates, please refer to the ReadMe file located on the CD.

System Requirements

- A computer with a processor running at 120 Mhz or faster.
- At least 32 MB of total RAM installed on your computer; for best performance, we recommend at least 64 MB.
- A computer capable of running Microsoft Office.
- A CD-ROM drive

NOTE: Microsoft Office Suites is capable of reading Microsoft Office files. However, users should be aware that a slight amount of formatting might be lost when using a program other than Microsoft Office.

Using the CD with Windows

To install the items from the CD to your hard drive, follow these steps:

1. Insert the CD into your computer's CD-ROM drive.
2. The CD-ROM interface will appear. The interface provides a simple point-and-click way to explore the contents of the CD.

If the opening screen of the CD-ROM does not appear automatically, follow these steps to access the CD:

1. Click the Start button on the left end of the taskbar and then choose Run from the menu that pops up.
2. In the dialog box that appears, type *d:\setup.exe.* (If your CD-ROM drive is not drive d, fill in the appropriate letter in place of *d.*) This brings up the CD Interface described in the preceding set of steps.

What's on the CD

The following sections provide a summary of the software and other materials you'll find on the CD.

Content

As part of this comprehensive guide to professional services firm management, we have built an electronic library of relevant planning and operational documents. The documents, checklists, tools and spreadsheets will be helpful to the professional services firm in executing the approaches and methodologies covered in this book. We hope they are as useful to you as they have been for us.

The templates, links and files provided are intended as a guide to provide a head start and to help drive critical thinking on the subjects. As with any tool, they must be refined for usage within any organization, and the specific circumstances being addressed.

The files are included on the accompanying CD-ROM, and are organized by chapter.

Any material from the book, including forms, slides, and lesson plans if available, are in the folder named "Content."

Applications

The following applications are on the CD:

Adobe Reader
Adobe Reader is a freeware application for viewing files in the Adobe Portable Document format.

Word Viewer
Microsoft Word Viewer is a freeware viewer that allows you to view, but not edit, most Microsoft Word files. Certain features of Microsoft Word documents may not display as expected from within Word Viewer.

Excel Viewer
Excel Viewer is a freeware viewer that allows you to view, but not edit, most Microsoft Excel spreadsheets. Certain features of Microsoft Excel documents may not work as expected from within Excel Viewer.

PowerPoint Viewer
Microsoft PowerPoint Viewer is a freeware viewer that allows you to view, but not edit, Microsoft PowerPoint files. Certain features of Microsoft PowerPoint presentations may not work as expected from within Power-Point Viewer.

OpenOffice.org

OpenOffice.org is a free multi-platform office productivity suite. It is similar to Microsoft Office or Lotus SmartSuite, but OpenOffice.org is absolutely free. It includes word processing, spreadsheet, presentation, and drawing applications that enable you to create professional documents, newsletters, reports, and presentations. It supports most file formats of other office software. You should be able to edit and view any files created with other office solutions.

Shareware programs are fully functional, trial versions of copyrighted programs. If you like particular programs, register with their authors for a nominal fee and receive licenses, enhanced versions, and technical support.

Freeware programs are copyrighted games, applications, and utilities that are free for personal use. Unlike shareware, these programs do not require a fee or provide technical support.

GNU software is governed by its own license, which is included inside the folder of the GNU product. See the GNU license for more details.

Trial, demo, or evaluation versions are usually limited either by time or functionality (such as being unable to save projects). Some trial versions are very sensitive to system date changes. If you alter your computer's date, the programs will "time out" and no longer be functional.

User Assistance

If you have trouble with the CD-ROM, please call the Wiley Product Technical Support phone number at (800) 762-2974. Outside the United States, call 1 (317) 572-3994. You can also contact Wiley Product Technical Support at **http://www.wiley.com/techsupport.** John Wiley & Sons will provide technical support only for installation and other general quality control items. For technical support on the applications themselves, consult the program's vendor or author.

To place additional orders or to request information about other Wiley products, please call (800) 225-5945.

Index

For more information about the CD-ROM, see the **About the CD-Rom** section on pages 531–533.